INDIA

Government and Politics in a Developing Nation

FIFTH EDITION

INDIA

Government and Politics in a Developing Nation

FIFTH EDITION

Robert L. Hardgrave, Jr.
The University of Texas at Austin

Stanley A. Kochanek
Pennsylvania State University

Harcourt Brace Jovanovich College Publishers
Fort Worth Philadelphia San Diego New York Orlando Austin San Antonio
Toronto Montreal London Sydney Tokyo

Publisher: Ted Buchholz
Acquisitions Editor: David Tatom
Project Editor: Mike Hinshaw
Production Manager: Erin Gregg
Book Designer: Pat Bracken

Cover image: is from a cushion cover: mordant-resist-dyed and painted cotton. Genre scenes, floral foliage and animal motives.
35 × 24 1/2 inches. 28.159.2
The Metropolitan Museum of Art, Rogers Fund, 1928.

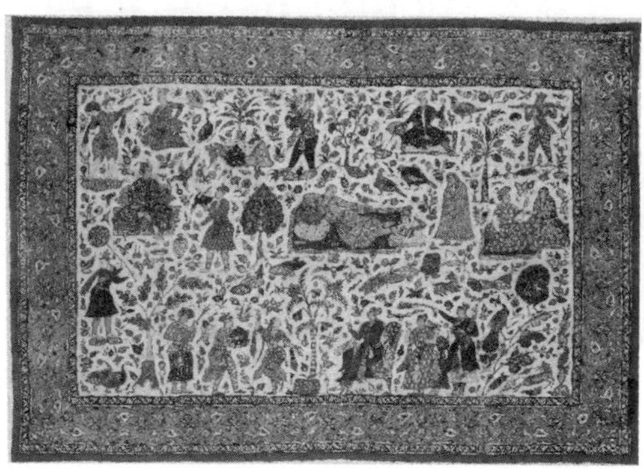

Maps by Carol Zuber-Mallison

ISBN: 0-15-500384-4

Library of Congress Number: 92-073194

Address editorial correspondence to:
301 Commerce Street, Suite 3700, Fort Worth, TX 76102

Address orders to:
6277 Sea Harbor Drive, Orlando, FL 32887
1-800-782-4479 outside Florida, 1-800-433-0001 inside Florida

PRINTED IN THE UNITED STATES OF AMERICA

3 4 5 6 7 8 9 0 1 2 016 9 8 7 6 5 4 3 2 1

Preface

The assassination of Rajiv Gandhi in May 1991 brought an end to the dynasty that had dominated the politics of "the world's largest democracy" for nearly half a century. This remarkable family produced three prime ministers, Jawaharlal Nehru, his daughter Indira Gandhi,* and her son Rajiv Gandhi, who served India for all but about four years since India's independence in 1947.

In the years since the fourth edition of *India: Government and Politics in a Developing Nation* was published in 1986, India has witnessed dramatic change. There have been two elections; the nation's first minority and coalition government; four prime ministers; and the end of a dynasty. In the Punjab, with a mounting death toll, Sikh militants continued their struggle for an independent state, and Kashmir erupted in secessionist violence. Caste conflict sharpened over the issue of reservations of government jobs for the "backward" classes, and Hindu–Muslim antagonism deepened as Hindu militants sought to rebuild the temple to Lord Ram at Ayodhya where a mosque now stands. In economic policy, India rejected its long commitment to regulation and central planning in favor of a liberalized, market-oriented approach, and in foreign policy, it sought to adjust its international relations to the collapse of the Soviet Union and the end of the Cold War.

Update Ayodhya

The controversy over the site at Ayodhya claimed by Hindus to be the birthplace of the god Rama and upon which a mosque was con-

*Indira Gandhi, India's first prime minister, was in no way related to the Mahatma, Mohandas Gandhi. To avoid possible confusion, she will be identified either as Indira Gandhi or as Mrs. Gandhi (following Indian usage), rather than simply as Gandhi. Again, to avoid confusion and to follow Indian usage, Indira Gandhi's two sons are frequently identified solely by their given names, Sanjay and Rajiv.

structed in the sixteenth century is discussed in Chapter 5, pp. 182–83. As this book goes to press, Ayodhya returned dramatically to capture headlines around the world. On December 6, 1992, some 200,000 Hindu militants converged on Ayodhya, stormed through the police barricades, and demolished the Muslim shrine. The police and paramilitary guarding the mosque offered no resistance.

The Vishwa Hindu Parishad (VHP), the organization leading the Ayodhya movement, and the Hindu nationalist Bharatlya Janata Party (BJP), the largest opposition party in Parliament, had vowed that on December 6, they would begin construction of the temple to Lord Ram at the sacred site. The Indian government thus had sufficient warning, but it deployed only 15,000 paramilitary troops to the area rather than the more reliable Indian Army forces. Prime Minister Narasimha Rao took the Hindu leaders at their word that they would not defy the Supreme Court order protecting the mosque and would offer only "symbolic" temple construction. The leaders, however, could not control the fervor of the devotees they had aroused, and at the hour Hindu holy men deemed propitious, Hindu militants surged forward with picks and iron rods to destroy the mosque and offer their worship to Lord Ram.

The Prime Minister denounced the action as "a betrayal of the nation" and attacked the BJP for exacerbating Hindu-Muslim tensions in a bid to "grab power, whipping up communal frenzy to undermine the secular fabric of the nation." In neighboring Pakistan and Bangladesh, Muslim mobs attacked and burned Hindu temples, and in Jiddah, Saudi Arabia, the 50-nation Organization of the Islamic Conference expressed outrage at the Indian government's failure to protect the mosque from Hindu extremists. As reports of the destruction of the mosque spread, Indian Muslims responded with attacks on Hindus and Hindu temples, and rioting erupted across India. In the following six days of violence, despite curfews, more than 1200 persons were killed in rioting and police-firings—the vast majority Muslims. In Bombay, the riots were the worst since India became independent in 1947.

The BJP Chief Minister of Uttar Pradesh, the state where Ayodhya is located, submitted his resignation, and the President dismissed the legislative assembly and imposed President's Rule, thus bringing India's largest state under the direct control of the central government. The BJP's L. K. Advani resigned as leader of the opposition in Parliament, but other Hindu leaders remained defiant. Ashok Singhal, head of the Vishwa Hindu Parishad, declared that any government efforts to impede construction of the Ram temple would result in "a confrontation of unimaginable magnitude."

Singhal, Advani, and BJP President Joshi were among the hundreds arrested, charged with inciting the militants, and the government banned for two years three Hindu communal organizations—the powerful Rashtriya Swayamsevek Sangh (RSS), the Vishwa Hindu Parishad, and the Bajrang Dal—and two Muslim fundamentalist groups—the Jamaat-i-Islami and the Islamic Sevak Sangh. At Ayodhya, troops cleared the site of Hindu devotees, leaving behind a temporary shrine to Rama. But the government seemed largely paralized; Parliament was unable to convene, as members screamed at each other in raging pandemonium; and Prime Minister Narasimha Rao, promising that the mosque would be rebuilt, was clearly shaken by the events and was reported to have virtually ceded control to the powerful Cabinet minister Arjun Singh, long an advocate for a hard line against the BJP and the Hindu militants.

The implications of the events at Ayodhya will be far-reaching for India in its relations with the Muslim world and for the government and the Congress party in dealing with India's own vast Muslim minority. And attacked from the Hindu right and the secular left, the Narasimha Rao government is itself under siege. The most profound impact, however, will be on India as a secular state and its capacity to secure democracy, justice, and equality in a multicultural society.[1]

India: Government and Politics in a Developing Nation, Fifth Edition, introduces the reader to the problems of political development as shown through the experience of one nation. India, one of the first new states to emerge from colonial rule after World War II, has confronted a wide range of problems, and dramatizes—perhaps more than any other developing nation—the crisis imposed by the limited capacity of institutions to respond to expanding participation and rapidly increasing demands. The book examines India's struggle for independence and national unity, its experience with democratic political institutions, and its efforts to establish itself as a power in South Asia and the world.

Although the book reflects a particular theoretical perspective, it is not essentially theoretical in either content or purpose. It is designed to provide a sense of the cultural and historical milieu in which political development takes place and to give a balanced treatment of structure and process, of institutions and behavior, and of policy and performance in Indian politics. India provides the framework, then, in which problems of political development common to a major por-

[1]This account draws largely from reports in *India Abroad* and *The New York Times,* December 7–13, 1992.

tion of the world are explored and, in addition, reflects the growing global importance of nonwestern nations.

The first three editions of this book were written by Robert L. Hardgrave, Jr. Fifteen years after the book first appeared, he was joined by Stanley A. Kochanek in the revision for the Fourth Edition, and the Fifth Edition is again co-authored. Over the life of the book many people have assisted with suggestions for revision. Their number now precludes individual acknowledgment, but our appreciation and gratitude are in no way diminished. We would, however, like to give special thanks to those who helped us with their suggestions and criticism for this new edition: Granville Austin, Upendra Baxi, Sumit Ganguly, R. B. Jain, S. R. Maheshwari, James Manor, Jagat Mehta, Thomas Thornton, and Douglas Verney.

Robert L. Hardgrave, Jr.

Stanley A. Kochanek

Contents

Preface v

Tables and Figures xii

Chapter 1
The Globalization of the Development Challenge 1
- The Crisis of Political Development 1
- The Context of Political Development in India 4
- The Development Challenge in India 14
- The Current Dilemma: The Revolution of Rising Frustrations 23

Chapter 2
The Legacies of National History 26
- The British Rise to Power 27
- Awakening Indian Nationalism 31
- The Achievement of Swaraj 50

Chapter 3
The Framework: Institutions of Governance 59
- The Constituent Assembly 60
- Fundamental Rights and Directive Principles Established in the Constitution 63
- The President and the Vice President 64
- Parliament 76
- The Prime Minister and the Council of Ministers 83
- The Public Services 91
- The Supreme Court and the Judicial System 100
- State Government 105
- Union Territories 110
- Local Government 110
- The Military 116
- The Responsive Capacity of India's Governmental Framework 119

Chapter 4
The Challenge of Federalism 125
The Origins and Nature of Federalism in India 126
States Reorganization 136
The Politics of Language 145
Regionalism in Indian Politics 147

Chapter 5
Arenas of Conflict: Groups in Indian Politics 167
India's Political Culture 168
The Role of Interest Groups in Indian Political Development 170
Arenas of Conflict 174
Law and Order 205
The Prospects for Political Stability 212

Chapter 6
Parties and Politics 216
Parties and Political Tendencies 217
The Congress Party 225
The Non-Congress Parties: The Struggle for Unity 272
The Bharatiya Party 290
The Communist Parties 294
Regional Parties in India 300

Chapter 7
Elections and Political Behavior 309
The 1991 Elections 311
Elections 318
The Indian Electorate 343
Political Mobilization and India's Future 349

Chapter 8
Policy and Performance: The Politics of Development 354
Economic Policy 355
The Politics of Agriculture 374
Planning Priorities and Contradictions 378
Performance 380
The Politics of Economic Management 385

Chapter 9
Policy and Performance: The International Context 392
Indian Foreign Policy: Nonalignment 393
Foreign Relations 395
The Quest for Security 420

Research Guide 426

Index 441

Tables and Figures

Table 1–1 Religion in India: 1971/1991 6
Table 1–2 Major Language Groups in India by Population 11
Table 3–1 Presidents and Vice Presidents of India 66
Table 3–2 Prime Ministers of India 84
Table 4–1 States and Territories of the Indian Union and their Principal Languages 143
Table 6–1 Indian Political Tendencies, 1952–1991 218
Table 6–2 The Growth of the BJP, 1984–1991 Lok Sabha Elections 293
Table 7–1 1991 Lok Sabha Elections 314
Table 7–2 1991 Lok Sabha Elections by State and Territory 315
Table 7–3 The Distribution of Candidates, Seats, and Votes in Lok Sabha Elections, 1952–1989 319
Table 7–4 The Index of Opposition Unity and Congress Vote and Seats 329
Table 7–5 How Indians Vote: Exit Polls, 1989 and 1991 340
Table 7–6 Election Data, Indian Parliamentary Elections, 1952–1991 347

Figure 2–1 India under the British 29
Figure 4–1 India 1951 137
Figure 4–2 India 142
Figure 6–1 The National Decision-Making Structure of the Congress 231
Figure 6–2 The Janata Party and BJP Since 1977 283
Figure 7–1 Symbols of the Major Political Parties, 1991 Elections 333
Figure 8–1 Index of Industrial Production: 1951–1990 381
Figure 8–2 Index of Agricultural Production: 1949–1950 to 1990–1991 382
Figure 8–3 Real National Income at 1980–1981 Prices 383

INDIA

Government and Politics in a Developing Nation

FIFTH EDITION

Chapter 1

The Globalization of the Development Challenge

INDIA, THE WORLD'S LARGEST DEMOCRACY, SUSTAINS A fragile stability and confronts an indeterminate political future—a future dominated by scarcity and by what Adlai Stevenson once called "the revolution of rising expectations." Politically conscious, increasingly participant, India's masses are an awakening force that has yet to find coherence and direction. The image of spiritual, Gandhian India pales before continuous agitation, intermittent rioting, and a rising level of violence. The turbulence of modern India brings into focus processes of change experienced throughout the world.

The Crisis of Political Development

In the aftermath of decolonization following World War II, theorists and statesmen saw the problems of poverty, economic stagnation, accelerated socioeconomic change, ethnic upheaval, and the need to create and sustain political order and legitimacy as a unique set of challenges that confronted the new states of Asia and Africa on their way to modernization and development. By the early 1970s, however, the advanced industrial societies of Europe, North America, and Japan were themselves convulsed by similar challenges as rapid technological change, global energy crises, raw material shortages, and a deteriorating environment found governments straining to satisfy rising expectations in a world of diminishing resources. It became increasingly evident that the problems of change and institutional adaptation were not the product of some isolated process of transformation from traditional to modern, agrarian to industrial, or developing to developed, but a continuous process of social, political, economic, and psychological adjustment to persistent pressures and challenges generated by alterations in the internal and external environments.[1] There was no final social or political order that somehow would be reached by a magical process of "development" or "modernization," but a constant set of challenges that would continue to test human ingenuity in adapting to changing political, social, economic, and institutional imperatives.[2]

The globalization of the development challenge became most dramatically illustrated at first in the case of Great Britain, a longtime model of continuity and change. From World War II to the mid 1960s, Britain was seen as an almost ideal type or model of orderly sequential development, secular democracy, and stability. Britain had led the way in the rise of self-government, industrialization, and political civility. Early development theory drew heavily on the British historical experience in an effort to outline the path that newly independent states and even older states might take in their march toward modernity. "In those early postwar years," wrote one perceptive commentator, "it might have seemed that as Britain had led the way out of the age of absolutism, creating classic protections for the rights of individuals and extending the power of the people toward a democratic standard, so now it was setting an example to advanced industrial societies in its managed economy and welfare state."[3]

From the mid 1960s onward, however, the image of Britain as the ideal model of a modernized, secular, stable democratic order began to change. Economic stagnation, ethnic upheaval, and a paralysis of public choice led increasingly to a characterization of Britain as the sick man of Europe, "a country on its knees."[4] Britain seemed unable to cope with its changing global and domestic environment. As time

[1] Samuel P. Huntington, "The Change to Change: Modernization, Development, and Politics," *Comparative Politics*, 3 (April 1971): 283–322.

[2] David E. Apter, "The Passing of Development Studies—Over the Shoulder with a Backward Glance," *Government and Opposition*, 15 (Summer/Autumn 1980): 263–75; and Dudley Seers, "The Birth, Life and Death of Development Economics," *Development and Change*, 10 (1979): 707–19.

[3] Samuel H. Beer, *Britain Against Itself: The Political Contradictions of Collectivism* (New York: W. W. Norton, 1982), p. xii.

[4] Ibid., p. xi.

passed, however, the paralysis of political development that had been seen as unique to Britain began to spread to other major advanced industrial societies of the West.[5] The developed world became increasingly preoccupied with its own problems and much less sympathetic to the development needs of the Third World.

In the late 1980s and early 1990s there came an even more dramatic change marked by the collapse of the Communist model of development and the attempt by the states of the old Soviet Union and Eastern Europe to move toward Western-style democracy, and market economies, and to integrate into the global economic system. Mainstream development models suddenly became increasingly universal in scope and objective. The Cold War had come to an end and talk of a new world order dominated the debate. The death of Communism was accompanied by the rise of nationalism in all its diverse forms as ethnic upheaval, religious fundamentalism, and new tensions came to dominate the development debate. Increasingly, the significance of political organization and administrative competence of governments emerged as the key variables in the development process.

The crisis of political development that has come to confront the entire world has made it clear that all states were part of a continuous process of change in which public choice played a key role in shaping, directing, and managing the adaptation and transformation of the political order. The process of political, economic, and social change was not a transitory phenomenon confronting traditional agrarian societies on their march toward industrialization, secularization, and modernity, but part of a continuous process of global transformation brought about by accelerated technological advance and rising expectations in a world of finite resources. In short, all countries are developing countries in one way or another, and the study of the process of development must be incorporated into the mainstream of comparative political analysis.

For analytical purposes a political system can be thought of as a pattern of interacting elements, each changing at a different rate. The four key components are: the political culture, elites and groups, structures of decision making, and political performances.[6] Political culture involves the values, attitudes, orientations, and myths rele-

[5]Ibid., p. xiv.

[6]Samuel P. Huntington and Jorge I. Dominguez, "Political Development," eds. Fred I. Greenstein and Nelson Polsby, *Macropolitical Theory, Handbook of Political Science*, vol. 3 (Reading, Mass.: Addison-Wesley, 1975), pp. 1–114.

vant to politics and the social structures that help shape those beliefs. The study of elites and groups involves a delineation of the major social and economic formations and how they participate in politics by controlling or making demands on political structures. Structures of decision making include not only the formal organization through which societies make authoritative decisions, but also the role of groups and individuals who play a dominant leadership role within these structures and help shape the behavior and legitimacy of political systems. Finally, a focus on policy and political performance reveals not only the outcome of governmental decisions but also the distribution of benefits and penalties in the society. These four key components function in an environment shaped by history, socioeconomic circumstances, and divergent forces affecting the timing, rate, and scope of change.

The Context of Political Development in India

India, among the first of the colonies to emerge from the yoke of imperial rule, gained independence from Great Britain in 1947. Today it epitomizes both the problems of, and the prospects for, political development in the non-Western world. With 850 million people, India is the world's largest democracy. Its leadership is confronted by an almost overwhelming cultural diversity, by often intransigent traditions rooted in the village and in religious values, and by poverty bred by scarcity of known resources, ignorance, and staggering population growth.

Jawaharlal Nehru spoke of the "essential unity" of India, of a civilization that was "a world in itself" and gave shape to all things: "Some kind of a dream of unity has occupied the mind of India since the dawn of civilization," he wrote.[7] But the unity of India was more a quest than a reality. The diversity of India has given richness and variety to its traditions, but diversity has been accompanied by patterns of social and cultural fragmentation historically rooted in, and sanctioned by, religion. Almost every known societal division can be found in India: The Indian people are divided by religion, sect, language, caste, dress, and even by the food they eat. These divisions are compounded by the chasm between the

[7]Jawaharlal Nehru, *The Discovery of India* (Garden City, N.Y.: Doubleday, 1959), p. 31.

rich and poor, between the English-speaking elite and the vernacular mass, between the city and the village.

Indian Social Structure

In India, as in most Third World countries, the nation shares loyalties with a variety of other sociocultural identities. These identities play a major mediating role between politics and society and represent a natural and potential source of political mobilization by competing elites who attempt to translate group loyalties into focal points of political solidarity, behavior, and group advantage. In its diversity and continental size, India shares more of the characteristics of the European community than the more integrated, multiethnic, and unified politics of the United States.

India contains all of the major world religions; it is subdivided into a myriad of castes; and it has 15 major languages whose speakers number in the millions, as well as 47 other languages, dialects, and tribal tongues, each spoken by over 100,000 people, and another 720 languages and dialects spoken by less than 100,000 people. These diverse groups are organized into 25 states and 7 union territories.

Political mobilization and the accelerated process of social change have heightened the sense of awareness and identity of these sociocultural groups and have resulted in increased competition, tension, and social conflict. Identities based on religion, caste, and language have strong appeal and have challenged the ability of the political elite to manage them effectively. In general, however, India's political leadership has proven to be much more successful in managing these sources of diversity than have most leadership elites in the Third World.

Religion

All the major religions of the world are represented in India (see Table 1–1). However, the vast majority of the population—almost 83 percent—are Hindus. It is the sheer size of the Hindu community that has raised fears among India's religious minorities of being overwhelmed or absorbed in a Hindu sea.

Hinduism is a religion unique to India, and, like other religions of the subcontinent, it is undergoing a revival. Hindus believe that each person is born into a particular station in life, with its own privileges and obligations, and must fulfill an individual *dharma* (sacred law or duty). According to the sacred Hindu text, the Bhagavad Gita, it is better to do one's own duty badly than another's well. The sufferings

Table 1–1
Religion in India: 1971/1991

	1971 (millions)	*Percentage*	*1991* (millions)*
Hindu	453.2	82.7	702.95
Muslim	61.4	11.2	95.20
Christian	14.2	2.6	22.10
Sikh	10.3	1.9	16.15
Buddhist	3.8	0.7	5.95
Jain	2.6	0.5	4.25
Other	2.2	0.4	3.40
	547.7		850.0

*Based on the 1971 percentages of a 1991 population estimate of 850 million. The rates of growth for the various religions, however, are not equal, and the 1971 census indicated a rate of growth approximately one-third higher than the national average for non-Hindus. If those growth rates remained constant over the past 20 years, the relative proportion of Hindus to non-Hindus is lower than the conservative estimates above. The Muslim population could be as high as 100 million and the Sikh population as high as 20 million.

of people's existence can be explained by their conduct in past lives, and only by fulfilling the dharma peculiar to their position in life can they hope to gain a more favorable rebirth and ultimate salvation. There is a quality of resignation, of passiveness and fatalism, in this religious belief that has manifested itself in the political attitude of the many Indians who simply accept the government they have as the one they deserve. Expanding communications and political competition have, however, increasingly challenged the traditional order. The vote has brought a new sense of efficacy and power and a willingness to question what was previously accepted simply as written by the gods.

Hinduism, while uniting India in the embrace of the great Sanskritic tradition, also divides the subcontinent. Each cultural–linguistic area has its own "little" tradition and local gods, and it is within the little tradition, rather than in the realm of Brahminical Hinduism, that most villagers live their religious life. The two levels of tradition penetrate each other, however, as the elastic pantheon of Hinduism absorbs the local tradition and is modified by it. Religion at the "higher" level need not be in conflict with the goals of modernization, Gunnar Myrdal argues, but the inertia of popular belief, giving religious sanction to the social and economic status quo, remains a major obstacle to social transformation. "Religion has, then, become the emotional container of this whole way of life and work and by its sanction has rendered it rigid and resistant to change."[8]

Despite the creation of Pakistan, partition did not solve India's communal problem. India still has one of the largest Muslim populations in the world, and Muslims constitute over 11 percent of the population. Having lost the bulk of its leadership at the time of partition, the Muslim community in India has only recently begun to develop new leaders and a greater sense of its position in Indian society. As Indian Muslims have begun to gain self-confidence, education, and identity, they have become increasingly assertive. Because this assertiveness has been accompanied by a similar movement toward Hindu revival among the majority community, there has been a sharp rise in tension between the two and a substantial increase in the intensity and scope of communal conflict.

In addition to Muslims, a smaller but more militant religious minority with a strong sense of group identity can be found in India's 16–20 million Sikhs. Although Sikhs comprise only 2 percent of the population, they are prominent in Indian life, with a highly visible presence in construction and transport and in the military, where they number some 12 percent of the enlisted men and 20 percent of the officer corps. The Sikhs are concentrated in their home state of Punjab, the granary of India, where they are predominantly agriculturalists and form a slight majority of 55–60 percent of the population. The Sikhs, who have long feared the loss of their separate identity, are increasingly apprehensive over an ethnic balance within the state that is shifting against them, because of both the out-migration of Sikhs and the immigration of Hindus. These anxieties fueled a political movement that by 1984 had taken an increasingly violent turn, precipitating a series of events that led to the army's siege of the Golden Temple, the citadel of Sikhism, and the assassination of Prime Minister Indira Gandhi.

Communal strife in India has tended to be initiated or exacerbated by groups seeking political advantage in a society of scarcity. Each seeks to define its identity as a mechanism for gaining benefits for the group as a whole. There is nothing inevitable about translating these group identities into political action.[9] It depends largely upon the

[8]Gunnar Myrdal, *Asian Drama: An Inquiry into the Poverty of Nations*, 3 vols. (New York: Pantheon, 1968), 1:112.

[9]Marguerite Ross Barnett, *The Politics of Cultural Nationalism in South India* (Princeton, N.J.: Princeton University Press, 1976), pp. 3–10; 314–28.

character of the leadership that emerges in the process and on how effective government is in dealing with the demands and actions of such groups. India, with all its diversity, has been more successful than most in accommodating, managing, and containing these conflicts by a process of political and institutional adjustment.

The Caste System

Despite its numerical size, the Hindu community of India does not represent a unified religious bloc. Hindus are divided into a myriad of castes, and the appeal of militant Hindus for the creation of a state committed to the defense of the Hindu religion is limited accordingly. There are more than two thousand castes, or *jati*, in India. Most are confined to relatively small geographical areas within a linguistic region. Marrying only among themselves, the members of each caste share, by tradition, a common lot and occupy a defined status and role within village society by virtue of their birth. Each caste is hierarchically ranked according to the ritual purity of its traditional occupation–whether or not the occupation is still followed. Castes can be distinguished from one another even in the same village by the manner of behavior and speech, the style of dress and ornaments, the food eaten, and the general life-style. The behavior of each caste is restricted. Deviation may bring action from the caste itself through the *panchayat*, the council of caste elders, or it may incur the wrath of the higher castes and bring punitive measures against the aberrant individual or the caste group as a whole.

Although traditionally conflict between castes certainly occurred, caste as a system ideally presupposes the interdependent relationship of occupational groups, each functioning according to prescribed patterns of behavior, with the system providing both economic security and a defined status and role. The caste system is what Alan Beals calls "being together separately." "To survive," he says, "one requires the cooperation of only a few jati; to enjoy life and do things in the proper manner requires the cooperation of many."[10] Kathleen Gough, however, characterizes the system as one of "relationships of servitude."[11] A typical village might have from half a dozen to 20 castes within it. Traditionally each by its ascriptive status occupied a par-

[10] Alan Beals, *Gopalpur: A South Indian Village* (New York: Holt, Rinehart and Winston, 1963), p. 41.

[11] Kathleen Gough, "Criteria of Caste Ranking in South India," *Man in India*, 39 (1959): 15–17.

ticular position in relation to the land. In a system of reciprocity and redistribution, each caste provided the landlord with its services, agricultural or artisan, and received in return a portion of the harvest. The relationship of the lower castes to the high-caste landlord was hereditary, but their dependent status carried certain rights. All behavior within the system, however, served to emphasize superordination and subordination, congruent inequalities of power, wealth, and status. Control over land was the critical lever of social control, and today land remains the fundamental resource of political power.

The ascriptive identity of caste cannot be escaped, even by abandoning the traditional occupation. Although an individual cannot move from one caste to another, within the middle range of castes between the Brahmins and the untouchables, there is considerable movement in the local hierarchy, as castes adjust their ritual position to accord with shifting economic status and political power. Such shifts, usually with a lag of several generations, are accompanied by changes in life-style, such as the adoption of vegetarianism in "sanskritized" emulation of higher castes. This movement occurs within the framework of the *varna* system. Classically castes have been divided into five divisions, the four varna and those beyond the pale of a caste. The varna represented the classes of ancient Aryan society. Ranked hierarchically, the first three varnas included the Brahmins, who acted as the priests; the Kshatriyas, who were the rulers and the warriors; and the Vaisyas, who were the mercantile classes. The Sudras, the lowest varna, were the common people, the agriculturalists and artisans. Beyond the embrace of the varna were the outcastes, or untouchables, polluted by their traditional life as scavengers and sweepers and therefore relegated to the lowest rungs of society. Untouchables, who number more than 135 million, make up about 15.8 percent of India's population, or some 18 percent of the Hindu fold.

The heterogeneity of India and the divisions of caste and sect within Hinduism itself have sustained the secular state and weakened the aspirations of the few who have sought a Hindu polity. Although a heightened Hindu consciousness has nurtured increased militancy, support for a Hindu state remains largely confined to a minority among the higher castes of the Hindi-speaking areas of North India. Indeed, setting religion aside, adding to the 17 percent of the population that is non-Hindu, the 25 percent of the population from the lower, "backward castes" and the 24 percent who make up the "scheduled castes (untouchables) and tribes," India's population has little stake in the creation of a Hindu state.[12]

Tribals

India's tribals, numbering 7.8 percent of the population, live largely in areas they regard as their "homeland." Many of these are designated as reserved or "scheduled areas," where tribal lands and rights are protected by the central government. Although tribals are scattered in pockets throughout India, they are concentrated in three main regions—the Northeast (where they make up the majority populations in Nagaland, Meghalaya, and Arunachal Pradesh), the hill areas of central India, and western India. Overall, they remain socially and economically depressed, but some among them have begun to advance, and tribal consciousness is growing.[13]

Language

Next to religion, the most explosive issue faced by India's post-independence leadership has been the problem of language. India has over a dozen major language groups, each with its own distinctive history. Many are very highly developed, with their own distinguished literary traditions. Subnational loyalties based on language developed almost simultaneously with the nationalist movement, and one of the persistent demands of the Congress had been for redrawing the map of British India along linguistic lines. The Congress itself was organized on the basis of regional languages as early as 1920. The administrative map of India was not redrawn until 1956, and since then the Indian states have been reorganized on the basis of the unilingual principle. The creation of unilingual states reinforced the federal character of the Indian system, but at the same time it created a variety of problems for linguistic minorities, interstate migrants, and interstate communications.

As seen in Table 1–2, Indian languages can be divided into two distinct groups: the Indo-Aryan languages of the North and the Dravidian languages of the South. The largest single language in India is Hindi, which, along with English, is recognized as the official lan-

[12] Susanne H. Rudolph and Lloyd I. Rudolph, "The Centrist Future of Indian Politics," *Asian Survey*, 20 (June 1980): 579–80.

[13] Myron Weiner, "India's Minorities: Who Are They, What Do They Want?" in James R. Roach, ed., *India 2000: The Next Fifteen Years* (Riverdale, Md.: Riverdale, 1986), pp. 111–13. Also see Christoph von Furer-Haimendorf, *Tribes of India: The Struggle for Survival* (Berkeley: University of California, 1982).

Table 1–2
Major Language Groups in India by Population

	Percentage	*1991** *(millions)*
Indo-Aryan Languages		
Hindi	30.4	258.4
Bengali	7.7	65.5
Marathi	7.6	64.6
Gujarati	4.6	39.1
Oriya	3.6	30.6
Punjabi	2.5	21.3
Assamese	1.6	13.6
Dravidian Languages		
Telegu	8.6	73.1
Tamil	7.0	59.5
Kannada	4.0	34.0
Malayalam	3.9	33.2
Other		
English	2.5	21.3
Urdu	5.3	45.0

*Estimated.

guage of India. Although the languages of North India have a common Sanskritic base, Hindi is distinctive, as are each of the Romance languages of Europe. Moreover, Hindi is very different from the Dravidian languages of the South, which have a totally different root.

It is this linguistic particularism that has served as a base for many of the regional parties that have arisen in India. Although most of these language-based regional parties have been single-issue, grievance-oriented, and transient, some have persisted for an extended period of time. The most durable have been the Dravida Munnetra Kazhagam (DMK) and its offshoot, the All-India Anna DMK (AIADMK), reflecting Tamil particularism. The newest manifestation of regionalism is the Telegu Desam of T.N. Rama Rao in Andhra. Language has also reinforced the religious base of the Akali Dal, the Sikh party in the Punjab, and the National Conference of the Kashmiri Muslims.

In a developing society like India, the principal sources of cleavage continue to center around status groups and cultural communities, as leaders seek to use these identities for political advantage. Conflicts based on religion, caste, and language have increased as ascriptive loyalties have intensified, and competition has been sharpened by the "revolution of rising expectations" in a society of scarcity.

Social Class

In addition to the existence of powerful status groups based on religion, caste, and language, India has also begun to develop a class system. India's class structure, however, remains tenuous. The slow pace of industrialization and urbanization has led to a highly uneven pattern of class growth, and status groups continue to cut across class lines. As a result, the development of class identities and political mobilization based on class appeals has been severely inhibited.

India's urban-based class structure is small and embryonic.[14] In 1981 the 23 million industrial workers in the organized sector of the economy made up only 10 percent of the total workforce of 230 million. Of these, only 3 percent work in large, modern factories. The industrial workforce, moreover, is not only small but its portion of the total labor force has also remained remarkably stable over the past several decades. Until very recently the Communist movement in India focused most of its attention on the mobilization and organization of this small urban, industrial sector with mixed success. The largest trade union in India remains Congress-dominated.

Organizing the rural sector on the basis of class presents even greater problems. In 1981 rural India contained 77 percent of the population, and some 67 percent of the labor force was engaged in agriculture. The land reforms introduced by the Nehru government shortly after independence essentially eliminated the old feudal, landed class. In their place there emerged a powerful new rural force composed of a mixed status–class group of middle peasant cultivators. These middle peasants, whom the Communists call India's "kulaks," own between 2.5 and 15 acres of land, control 51 percent of the land, and constitute 35 percent of the rural households and 25 percent of the total population of India. They have emerged as a powerful political force in rural India and have come to challenge the formally dominant position of the older traditional notables and large landowners who own more than 15 acres of land, control 39 percent of the total land, but make up only 6 percent of the rural households.[15]

Although the landless and the small landowners constitute almost

[14] Lloyd I. Rudolph and Susanne H. Rudolph, *In Pursuit of Lakshmi: The Political Economy of the Indian State* (Chicago: University of Chicago Press, 1987), pp. 20–59.

[15] Ibid., pp. 50–59.

60 percent of the rural households, they have low levels of political consciousness, lack a sense of solidarity, have proven to be difficult to mobilize and organize, and are unevenly distributed throughout the subcontinent. These tenants, small landholders, and landless are still largely under the influence of the traditional notables and large landowners. Mobilization of the rural poor represents a long-term prospect, and it will take some time before they are reached by modern forms of political organization. Moreover, the landless and small landowners do not share a common interest. The small landowners holding less than 2.5 acres of land and controlling 10 percent of the total land do not identify with the needs and aspirations of the bottom 27 percent of the rural landless population. Finally, the distribution of the landless population is very uneven. Landless laborers tend to comprise a higher proportion of the rural sector in the southern states of Kerala, Tamil Nadu, and Andhra and in the northeast province of West Bengal, where they constitute 34–37 percent of the rural population. In contrast landless labor in the North Indian Hindi belt states of Uttar Pradesh, Madhya Pradesh, Rajasthan, and Punjab and in the western state of Gujarat represent only 12–23 percent of the rural sector. But throughout India, their numbers are growing, both in absolute numbers and relative to landholders.

The existing class structure of India poses a serious challenge to economic growth with social justice. Fundamentally, as Baldev Raj Nayar writes,[16]

> the levers of political and state power have rested in the hands of what may broadly be termed the "middle sectors" of economic and social life in both urban and rural areas—the educated and professional groups, town merchants and small businessmen in the urban areas; and the middle peasantry or kulaks in the villages.

They command a position of relative privilege in a nation of poverty and economic backwardness:

> [T]he source of their power lies in the strategic combination of considerable population size with extensive economic resources and significant social status, as against the greater economic power but small numbers of the upper business and land owning classes and the large numbers but economic destitution of the lower classes. Socialism to

[16]Baldev Raj Nayar, "Political Mobilization in a Market Polity: Goals, Capabilities and Performance In India," in Robert I. Crane, ed., *Aspects of Political Mobilization in South Asia* (Syracuse, N.Y.: Maxwell School, Syracuse University, 1976), pp. 148–49.

> the middle sectors has meant, apart from what may fairly be described as tokenism toward the scheduled castes, the bringing down of the upper classes to their own level, but no redistribution or levelling down below that level. Democracy has served these classes well in this regard by facilitating the conversion of economic privilege and numerical strength into political power while at the same time giving it an aura of genuine legitimacy.

But in an environment of political and economic uncertainty, the middle sectors "have been the major block to redistribution in behalf of the underprivileged classes."[17] In competition for the scarce resources, the middle sectors are now challenged from below by newly politicized classes, but it is less in terms of "class" than of localized and particularistic groups that their protests are voiced.

In short, India is a highly pluralistic and segmented society in which social conditions lack uniformity. Each of India's 25 states and 7 union territories has its own distinctive cultural, linguistic, and social mosaic that makes it a distinct political unit requiring its own strategy and tactics. Moreover, this very segmented character of Indian society has tended to focus political competition among social groups and cultural communities based on language, region, caste, and religion and not on class. These status groups cut across class lines and inhibit the development of class identities and mobilization based on class appeals.

The Development Challenge in India

Among the states of the Third World, India, like China, represents one of the great intellectual and practical development challenges of the century. India is significant not only in its own right, but also because its size, population, and geostrategic location make it one of several competing models for the states of Asia and Africa that are at similar stages of development. As the jewel in the crown of the British empire, it set the tone for national and political reform that had a significant imitation effect elsewhere, and as a major developing state in Asia, it is a testing ground for theories and models of development and change. The development challenge in India involves the trans-

[17] Ibid., p. 150.

formation of one of the oldest, most complex, continuous civilizations in the world into a modern nation state. Its success or failure will have significant regional and global consequences.

The pattern of Indian development over the past four and one-half decades has confounded existing theories of modernization, development, and dependency and has required substantial re-evaluation of these notions. Quantitatively, in terms of levels of urbanization, industrialization, secularization, education, media consumption, and welfare, India appears to be almost a stereotype of a less-developed country (LDC) and has few of the alleged socioeconomic requisites of democracy. Yet, qualitatively, India has a comparatively high level of institutional development and has one of the few surviving democratic polities in the Third World. Indian development, moreover, does not appear to be progressing neatly through a series of predetermined stages nor through a set sequence from traditional to transitional to modern. It has political structures that are modern, competitive, and institutionalized and yet a political style that is highly traditional, consensual, and personalized.[18] Moreover, India's governing elites can in no way be characterized as *comprador* (i.e., foreign-controlled), as dependency theory would have it, and its poverty and inequality are no more a result of the international economic order than is its ethnic heterogeneity.[19] India, it seems, fails to conform to existing explanations and, for that reason, an understanding of the Indian experience is both of interest in its own right as well as in providing a better understanding of the development process itself.

The Indian Experience

The decline of Mughal power, the rise and fall of British colonial rule, and some 45 years of independence have resulted in a rapidly accelerating process of social, economic, and political change that is fundamentally altering one of the oldest civilizations in the world. This process of transformation, in beginning to reorder Indian society, has upset traditional status relationships among major social groups and has begun to create new identities and demands. This process of transformation has accelerated in scope, rate, and impact

[18] Samuel J. Eldersveld and Bashiruddin Ahmed, *Citizens and Politics: Mass Political Behavior in India* (Chicago: University of Chicago Press, 1978), pp. 3–18.

[19] Baldev Raj Nayar, *India's Quest for Technological Independence*, 2 vols. (New Delhi: Lancers, 1983), 1:85–132.

in recent decades. Thus, any attempt to analyze these changes is like slowing down a motion picture and stopping it in order to examine tentatively a single frame, knowing full well that each succeeding frame will be different.

At the macro level the process of transformation taking place in India can be measured quantitatively by examining key socioeconomic indicators that tend to reflect underlying changes taking place in the society. These statistical indicators outline the broad context within which political development is taking place and the major problems that confront political decision makers. By almost any measure India has made considerable progress since 1947, and yet in many ways the data yield ambiguous results. This is especially the case when evaluating India's economic performance. The Indian economy is like the proverbial half-filled vessel: Is it half empty or half full?

The fundamental challenge facing India's governing elites is to integrate a continental-size country, as large and diverse as all of Europe minus the former Soviet Union. India is a mosaic society composed of diverse regional, ethnic, and religious communities spread over a land area of 1.3 million square miles. It has a large and rapidly expanding population; it is predominantly rural; it has one of the lowest per-capita incomes in the world; and it has limited resources and low levels of urbanization, literacy, and life expectancy. At the same time it has a large and increasingly prosperous middle class, the third largest pool of scientific and professional talent in the world, and the most extensive industrial infrastructures in the Third World.

Population

Perhaps the most potent social change of all in India is its rapidly expanding population. This "population bomb," as it has been described, has a devastating impact on limited resources, political management, and planned development. The control of disease in the past 70 years has brought a rapid decline in the death rate, the Malthusian equalizer. From 251 million in 1921, India's population more than doubled by 1971, reaching 548 million. By the census of 1981, the population reached 684 million. Preliminary results of the 1991 census show a population of 850 million. The annual rate of population growth has increased from 1.1 percent between 1921 and 1931 and 2.2 percent between 1961 and 1981. At the present growth rate of 2.1 percent, India's population will exceed one billion by the year 2000.

To reduce birth rates, the Government of India has undertaken one of the most extensive family-planning programs in the world. To overcome the fatalistic belief in "God's will," propaganda posters are omnipresent. Billboards, radio, and films proclaim: "A small family is a happy family." The campaigns have yielded mixed results. Although millions of women have had intrauterine devices (IUDs), or "loops," inserted, the initial success of the IUD has succumbed to side effects. The condom (or Nirodh, "prevention") is being heavily promoted, and research is now underway to develop an antifertility vaccine that will bring temporary sterility.

The major thrust of India's family-planning program involves vasectomies. From 1952 until mid-1976, more than 19 million men had undergone voluntary sterilization. Mobile vasectomy camps were organized, and incentives—even transistor radios—were offered to volunteers. But during the Emergency (1975–77), incentives were displaced by coercion as overzealous officials sought to fill quotas. The campaign surpassed its target of 7.5 million vasectomies, but allegations of compulsory sterilization became a major issue in Indira Gandhi's 1977 electoral defeat. The fear generated by the vasectomy campaign—and the Janata Party's successful exploitation of the issue—posed a serious setback for birth control in India, a setback symbolized by the responsible ministry's change in name from "Family Planning" to "Health and Family Welfare." Since 1977 no political party has called for control of population nor has any election manifesto mentioned it.

For all the government's efforts, many people, particularly among the poor, simply do not feel a compelling need for family planning. Aside from the fact that a male heir has ritual importance and additional future wage earners will augment family income, "those babies who are a planner's worry are also a parent's hope and joy."[20] They are social security for old age in a society untouched by the welfare state. Beyond this, the calculations of democratic politics have led many groups to consciously endorse population growth among their own so as to translate greater numbers into more power and influence. Critics, moreover, charge that government claims of success in family planning tend to be highly exaggerated.

[20] David G. Mandelbaum, "Social Components of Indian Fertility," *Economic and Political Weekly*, 8 (February 1973): 171.

As a result of its pattern of population growth, the age structure of India's population is like a great pyramid, and half of the nation's population is below the age of 16. Thus, even with the most successful birth-control program, there would be little immediate impact on population growth. Moreover, as the young mature, the demands of this expanding population for education, housing, government services, jobs, and, above all, food will place an increasingly heavy burden on India's limited capacity.

Urbanization

Only a small proportion of India's population lives in urban areas, but urbanization, which has been relatively slow in the past, is beginning to accelerate. India's urban population has increased from 11 percent in 1901 to 26 percent in 1991—some 221 million people. This population is undergoing a massive change in life-style, as women enter the urban work force in larger numbers and as consumption habits change in the growing appetite for consumer goods once considered a luxury. In 1965–66, only 500 people owned a TV set. By 1980 1.1 million people owned TV sets, and the figure reached 16.9 million by the late 1980s, with more than 100 million viewers. By the year 2000, estimates project more than 60 million sets and a viewing audience of nearly 380 million.[21] Similar increases are expected in the case of motor scooters, refrigerators, radios, and home appliances.[22] The size of the urban population represents a consumer market larger than the entire European Economic Community.

Incredibly crowded, lacking in adequate housing, transportation, and sewerage, however, Indian cities have become almost ungovernable and, for some, unlivable. But because they offer new economic opportunities, rich and varied cultural experiences, and intellectual stimulation, cities are preferable to rural areas for most urban dwellers. And in terms of relative deprivation, even the burdens of the poor in Calcutta, the problem city of the world, may represent an improvement over the marginal subsistence of the village. Nevertheless, with rapid social change, high levels of communication, and a frustrated middle class squeezed by rising prices and a deteriorating standard of living, India's cities suffer a deepening malaise. It is within the cities—where the government finds itself least able

[21] See Arvind Singhal and Everett Rogers, *India's Information Revolution* (New Delhi: Sage, 1989).

[22] "The Consumer Boom," *India Today* (New Delhi), 15 February 1984, pp. 48–56. See also *India Today*, October 31, 1988, pp. 38–47.

to respond to accelerating demands—that political unrest is most sharply evident.

Rural Society

India, like most of the developing world, is overwhelmingly rural and agricultural. About 74 percent of India's population lives in some 600,000 villages, most with less than a thousand people. Village life was traditionally narrowly circumscribed, and even today the world of the average villager extends only a few miles beyond the place of birth. Although the villages have now been penetrated by radio, film, and increasing contact with government officials and aspiring politicians, they remain the font of traditional values and orientations. If they are often eulogized as an ideal of harmony and spirituality, even by those who have chosen to leave, traditional villages are nevertheless bastions of parochialism and inequality.

Ownership of land has been the traditional means of both wealth and power in India. Land ceilings and tenancy reforms have been more symbolic than substantive. Unimplemented by state governments politically dependent on the landed peasantry or evaded, often with the connivance of officials, reforms in most states have little affected the radically unequal distribution of land ownership.[23] In the early 1970s, over 95 percent of India's rural households owned less than 20 acres of land; 43 percent owned less than 5 acres; and 24 percent owned no land at all, with the percentage of landless labor increasing. The disparities in land ownership are revealed in the fact that 30 percent of the rural families held 70 percent of the arable land.[24]

Rural India has increasingly become divided into two broad categories based on the percentage of wage labor in agriculture, the percentage of product marketed, and the degree of penetration of rural society by communications. One set of districts is predominantly based on subsistence agriculture and covers the areas of eastern Uttar Pradesh, northern Bihar, eastern and southern Rajasthan, and the nonindustrial regions of Orissa and Madhya Pradesh in central India. The second set of districts is now commercialized, more prosper-

[23]For an account of the failure of land reform in one state, see F. Tomasson Jannuzi, *Agrarian Crisis in India: The Case of Bihar* (Austin: University of Texas Press, 1974).

[24]Francine R. Frankel, *India's Green Revolution: Economic Gains and Political Costs* (Princeton, N.J.: Princeton University Press, 1971), p. 204; and Wolf Ladejinsky, "How Green Is the Indian Green Revolution?" *Economic and Political Weekly*, 8 (December 29, 1972): A–137.

ous, and increasingly urbanized. This includes much of the Punjab and Haryana, Gujarat, western Uttar Pradesh, the irrigated areas of Rajasthan, Maharashtra, Andhra, Karnataka, and Tamil Nadu, and the rural hinterland of the metropolitan cities. These are the areas of the green revolution that have transformed Indian agriculture and rural life.

Resources

A major portion of India's national income is from the land, but there is little beyond the 425 million acres now under cultivation that can be redeemed for agriculture. The soil, though capable of being rejuvenated by rotation and fertilization, has been depleted by centuries of harvest. Rain is irregular, and the monsoon, which determines the difference between prosperity and subsistence, is uncertain. The uses of irrigation, pesticides, fertilizers, improved seed grain, and modern agricultural techniques have increased India's agricultural output enormously without expanding present acreage, but most of India's peasants, with little access to credit and a tenuous hold on the land they till, cannot afford to assume the risks involved in innovation. Moreover, regional disparities are stark. Against the booming agricultural prosperity of the Punjab stands Bihar—backward, caste-ridden, and desperately poor.

After a decade of massive grain imports, India by the mid-1970s was self-sufficient in food production. As a result of modern agricultural technology, hailed as "the green revolution," production of wheat and rice—the principal food crops—expanded to record levels. By 1991 India produced 170 million tons of foodgrains, compared to 63 million tons in 1951–55. But Indian agriculture remains hostage to the vagaries of the monsoon. Whether the breakthrough in irrigation and agricultural technology can sustain production through a series of bad years is doubtful. The periodic failure of the monsoons and resulting widespread drought underscore India's dependency on rainfall.

In raw materials India possesses the resources for substantial industrial growth. In the Bengal-Bihar-Orissa triangle, coal, iron ore, and transport facilities provide the base for a major steel industry. Oil reserves have been opened in Assam and off the western coast (the "Bombay High"); but despite rapidly expanding production over the past decade, India still imports roughly half of its petroleum requirements—a heavy cost on economic development efforts. India is pursuing an active nuclear-energy program, though thus far with modest success, and its rivers offer great hydroelectric potential that has only been touched. Production of electricity has expanded enormously since 1947, but India's generating capacity is hindered by inefficiency and strained by rapidly increasing demands. The inadequate power supply remains a serious bottleneck to both agricultural and industrial development. Overall, India's resources are bounteous, but remain underutilized.

The Economy

Although India is still a predominantly agricultural country with 67 percent of its population dependent upon agriculture for a livelihood, the Indian economy has changed considerably. At the time of independence India had a small industrial base and one of the largest rail systems in the world, but the business and industrial sectors contributed only 5 percent of the nation's income. By the late 1980s, industry contributed 29 percent of the Indian GNP. India is the 17th most industrialized nation in the world[25] and is self-sufficient in consumer goods and in such basic commodities as steel and cement. India manufactures ships, locomotives, trucks, machine tools, and sophisticated electronic equipment. Manufactured goods constitute a growing portion of India's export trade and, despite protectionist barriers, India is aggressively expanding its markets throughout the world. Although India still imports more than it exports, its unfavorable balance of trade has been bridged by remittances from Indians working abroad—especially in the Middle East.

India entered independence determined to raise the standard of living of its people and protect its newly won freedom. These objectives were to be accomplished by a process of rapid economic growth and industrialization. During the first half of the 20th century, from 1900 to 1946, Indian national income under colonial rule rose by 0.7 percent annually, while its population grew at the rate of 0.8 percent, resulting in a stagnant per-capita income.[26] From 1950–51 to 1990–91 India has achieved an average annual growth rate of 3.9 percent—considerably higher than under British rule. During the 1980s India's growth rate was 5.2 percent per year. With a population growth of

[25] Although in 1960 India stood 10th in the World Bank's industrial ranking (excluding Eastern European countries), it had fallen to 17th in gross industrial product by 1981, and perhaps 22nd or 23rd if Eastern Europe were included. See Jay Dubashi, "Industrialization: Descent into Mediocrity," *India Today* (New Delhi), January 31, 1984, pp. 70–71.

[26] Nayar, *India's Quest*, 1:109.

2.2 percent, however, the net increase in per-capita income has been a modest 1.7 percent. Thus, India's growth rate, while well above pre-independence levels, has fallen far below expectation and is considerably below the 8 to 10 percent of the high-growth Asian states like Japan, South Korea, Taiwan, Hong Kong, and Singapore, and lags substantially behind China.

Although the Indian growth rate has eliminated the mass starvation of the past, it has failed both to meet the rising expectations of its population and to reduce major disparities. Slow growth has failed to transform the basic economic structure of Indian society. Approximately 35 to 40 percent of the Indian population lives below the poverty line, officially defined as the estimated minimum per-capita monthly expenditure necessary to maintain good health. The poverty line is calculated for rural and urban households.

Over the past two decades the percentage of Indians below the poverty line has declined, and there are a variety of indicators which imply that India is not as poor as standard statistical data would have us believe. A Physical Quality of Life Index (PQLI) calculated by Morris D. Morris, based on the three criteria of infant mortality, longevity, and literacy, shows India ahead of several states with much higher per-capita incomes. From 1970–75, for example, India had a PQLI as high as that of Iran, even though Iran's per-capita income was 10 times higher than India's. India had a PQLI higher than Algeria, Ghana, Kenya, and Pakistan, even though these countries had higher per-capita incomes.[27]

Health, Education, and Welfare

There has been a dramatic decline in mortality in India as a result of advances in medical technology, but even with the control of epidemic and endemic diseases, sanitation and elementary hygiene have improved little. Despite expanding agricultural production, nutritional standards remain low, and the diet of the poor is both monotonous and inadequate in terms of the minimum caloric intake required to maintain health. Life expectancy has risen from 32 years in 1947 to 58 years today, but even this figure suggests a continuing high rate of infant mortality. The number of medical colleges has increased from 30 to 128, yet India has only one physician for every 4850 people (compared to 1 per 419 in the United States). Despite efforts to establish a system of rural health centers, most doctors practice in the major urban areas, and many leave India as part of the "brain drain."

[27] Ibid., 2:533.

Education in India has expanded rapidly, from 23 million children in school in 1951 to more than 130 million today, but as many as half of India's children between 6 and 14 are not in school. Many instead work—often in dangerous occupations—to help their families in the struggle for survival.[28] In 1951 the rate of literacy (inclusive for all ages from birth) was about 16 percent. By 1991 it was 52 percent (64 percent for men, 39 percent for women). Despite this progress, some 324 million people in India are illiterate, and India is the largest producer of illiterates in the world. Literacy is overwhelmingly in the mother tongue alone, but increasingly Indians outside the Hindi heartland of northern India have some knowledge of Hindi. (About 2 percent of the adult population is literate in English.) Education, in its strictly instrumental aspects of attitude change and dissemination of practical knowledge, is vital for progress and development. But education has also raised the sights of the Indian people and has stimulated their aspirations toward a better life. The possibilities of satisfying these demands depend on both the will of the government to respond and its capacity to mobilize resources in a context of scarcity.

The Current Dilemma: "The Revolution of Rising Frustrations"

The challenge of population growth demands radical change in the form of a fundamental transformation of society. The inertia of tradition can be broken only by creating "felt needs," by stimulating discontent and aspiration toward a better life. The leadership of India, committed to economic development and a more equitable distribution of income, has sought to induce social change, and has succeeded to a considerable degree. Through the universal franchise it sought to expand political participation in order to foster national integration, political legitimacy, and enhanced institutional capacity. But its period of grace was short. The "revolution of rising expectations" has become a "revolution of rising frustrations" as the gap between aspiration and achievement has widened. As demands have increased, as new groups have entered the political system in the expanding participation, the capacity of the government to respond

[28] Myron Weiner provides a devastating indictment of India's failure in primary education in *The Child and the State in India: Child Labor and Education Policy in Perspective* (Princeton, N.J.: Princeton University Press, 1991).

effectively has not kept pace. But beyond capacity, India has often lacked the will to initiate and respond to rapid change. Under pressure from sectors of society with a vested interest in preserving the inequalities of the status quo, the Indian leadership has been undermined by the paradoxical position in which it finds itself:[29]

> On a general and noncommittal level they freely and almost passionately proclaim the need for radical social and economic change, whereas in planning their policies they tread most warily in order not to disrupt the traditional social order. And when they do legislate radical institutional reforms—for instance in taxation or in regard to property rights in the villages—they permit the laws to contain loopholes of all sorts and even let them remain unenforced.

India's leaders must have the capacity and the will to respond to increasing demands if they are to fulfill the hope for the transformation of society and the achievement of both growth and equity. In a process of social mobilization, with the breakdown of traditional society, the expansion of communications and transportation facilities, and heightened political competition, more and more people have become political participants and, at the same time, more highly sensitive to the poverty in which they live. Yet distributive response to demands can dissipate the capacity for growth. The distributive requirements of equity must go hand in hand with increased production. Striking the balance will not be easy. How the Government of India responds to this situation is of more than academic interest: It is among the most critical questions in the world.

Recommended Reading

*Bill, James A., and Robert L. Hardgrave, Jr., "Modernization and Political Development," Chapter 2 of *Comparative Politics: The Quest for Theory*. Washington, D.C.: University Press of America, 1981. A critical analysis of concepts and theory in the study of political development.

*Cassen, R. H., *India: Population, Economy, Society*. London: Macmillan, 1978. A study of the relations between population growth and economic and social development in India.

[29]Myrdal, *Asian Drama*, 1:117.

*Available in a paperback edition.

*Cohn, Bernard S., *India: The Social Anthropology of a Civilization*. Englewood Cliffs, N.J.: Prentice-Hall, 1971. A succinct and thoughtful portrait of Indian civilization.

*Farmer, B. H., *An Introduction to South Asia*. London and New York, Methuen, 1983. A general introduction to the countries of the region by a distinguished British geographer.

*Huntington, Samuel P., *Political Order in Changing Societies*. New Haven, Conn.: Yale University Press, 1968. Explores the problems of political development in terms of the relationship between institutionalization and political participation, emphasizing the creation of stability and order.

*Kolenda, Pauline, *Caste in Contemporary India*. Menlo Park, Calif.: Benjamin/Cummings, 1978. An excellent analysis of the caste system and its role in modern Indian society.

*Mandelbaum, David G., *Society in India*, 2 vols. Berkeley: University of California Press, 1970. A comprehensive survey of modern research on Indian society.

*Moore, Barrington, Jr., *Social Origins of Dictatorship and Democracy*. Boston: Beacon Press, 1966. The section on India examines the history of underdevelopment in South Asia.

*Myrdal, Gunnar, *Asian Drama: An Inquiry into the Poverty of Nations*, 3 vols. New York: Pantheon, 1968. Abridged one-volume edition, New York: Vintage, 1972. A vast study of the problems of economic development in South Asia by one of the world's most astute economists, encyclopedic in its breadth, depressing in its conclusions. See in particular the specific sections on India.

Roach, James R. (ed.), *India 2000: The Next Fifteen Years*. Riverdale, Md.: Riverdale, 1986. A broad-ranging examination of India in change.

*Weiner, Myron, *The Child and the State in India*. Princeton: Princeton University Press, 1991. An excellent study of Indian policy and elite attitudes toward child labor and compulsory education and its impact on development.

*Weiner, Myron, and Samuel P. Huntington (Eds.), *Understanding Political Development*. Boston: Little, Brown and Company, 1987. An excellent collection of essays that attempt to assess the state of contemporary scholarly thinking on the study of political development.

Chapter 2

The Legacies of National History

ON AUGUST 15, 1947, INDIA GAINED INDEPENDENCE FROM Great Britain and emerged as one of the first new states of the post-colonial era. Its leaders were determined to create a new political order that would be capable of transforming Indian society and developing the economy. The character of the new system was shaped by the legacies of Indian history. Three factors played an especially critical role: the pluralist character of the traditional Hindu social order; the timing, scope, and duration of the colonial experience; and the nature of India's nationalist struggle for independence. These forces combined to produce an Indian political elite committed to the creation of a liberal democratic order and a political authority strong enough to subordinate the military and bureaucratic structures inherited from the vice regal system of the British Raj.

The society of the vast subcontinent, varied and complex in its rich heritage, is among the oldest in the world. Five thousand years of history have nourished the growth of a great civilization, vitalized through cross-cultural contact and characterized by diversities of culture and race, caste, religion, and language. In India there are examples of virtually every known type of societal division: six major religions—Hinduism, Islam, Sikhism, Christianity, Buddhism, and Zoroastrianism; two major language families, Aryan and Dravidian, with eighteen official languages and innumerable dialects and tribal tongues; three racial strains, Aryan, Dravidian, and proto-Australoid; and over two thousand castes, hierarchically ranked, endogamous, and occupational.

The great tradition of Hinduism unites the diverse cultural regions, but within its elastic framework are a myriad of sects and local traditions. Perhaps by more than anything else, traditional India has been characterized by localism, a fragmentation not simply of cultural-linguistic regions but of villages themselves. By no means completely isolated, the cultural world of the villages nevertheless remains narrowly circumscribed.

In the past the villages were little affected by the changes of governmental authority. For the villager, "it did not matter much who ruled in Delhi—Mughal, Maratha, or Englishman. His concern was with his crops, with the next monsoon, and with the annual visitation of the collecting officer."[1]

Even the most sophisticated administrative system, like that of the Mughals, penetrated the village for almost wholly extractive purposes. Neither the Mughals, the Muslim rulers who came to power in 1526 and reigned for over three hundred years, nor the great Hindu emperors before them extended their sway over the whole of India. India was a concept, not a political entity. Pockets remained beyond the reach of even Asoka, whose empire in the third century B.C. extended from the Hindu Kush to the Bay of Bengal. Islamic authority never established itself in the extreme South; and even as the Mughals attained the height of their power, they were faced by revolts among the Jats, Rajputs, and Sikhs in the North and challenged by the rising power of the Marathas in the West. These internal conflicts were both exploited and exacerbated by the appearance of the European powers in India in the 15th century.

The British Rise to Power

The British entered the struggle for a commercial foothold in India through the British East India Company, founded in London in 1600 during the reign of Akbar. Within a few years the company had secured limited trading privileges from the Mughals, and by the end of the century it had established commercial enclaves at Bombay, Madras, and Calcutta. As Mughal power declined in the 18th century, the British pushed for more extensive privileges and wider territories. The inability of the Mughals to control increasing disorder led the company, as early as 1687, to instruct its Madras representative "to

[1]Percival Spear, *A History of India*, vol. 2 (Baltimore: Penguin, 1965), p. 43.

establish such a politie of civil and military power, and create and secure such a large revenue to secure both . . . as may be the foundation of a large, well grounded, secure English dominion in India for all time to come."

In expanding their hold, the British played one ruler against another, annexing a widening range of territory. The princely states led a precarious and vulnerable existence. The price of preservation from Indian conquest was the acceptance of British suzerainty. Security of trade ultimately demanded that the powers opposed to the company be brought under control and that Pax Britannica be extended over the whole subcontinent. By the middle of the 19th century the company had assumed direct control over three-fifths of India, and the remaining areas were held by more than 500 princely states subject to British control and intervention.

Westernization

As successors to the Mughal empire, the British sought to restore order, reorganize the revenue system, and create a strong central political authority. Conditions were chaotic, and the opportunities for trade were restricted by inland transit duties, a wholly inadequate road system, and the constant dangers of *dacoity*, or gang robbery, which rendered safe travel almost impossible. In the course of pacification, however, the British began the construction of transport facilities—roads, canals, and railroads—opening the interior for the extraction of raw materials and the development of trade.

The British wanted to establish an equitable land and revenue system. In Bengal revenues had previously been collected by hereditary *zamindars*, who as agents of the government also held police and magisterial powers. The British mistook the zamindars for landlords and under the Permanent Settlement confirmed them in their jurisdictions, thus creating a new class of wealthy landlords at the expense of the peasants. The mistake was soon evident, and subsequently in Madras the settlement was made directly with the peasant cultivators under the *ryotwari* system.

The British, content in the early years of company rule to let most things continue very much as before, had taken a position of neutrality with regard to the religious and social affairs of their subjects. In the early 19th century, however, demands for reform, voiced in England by the Utilitarians and the Evangelicals, were soon felt in India. The Utilitarians, committed to the rule of reason, sought to secure social harmony and justice through the free development of

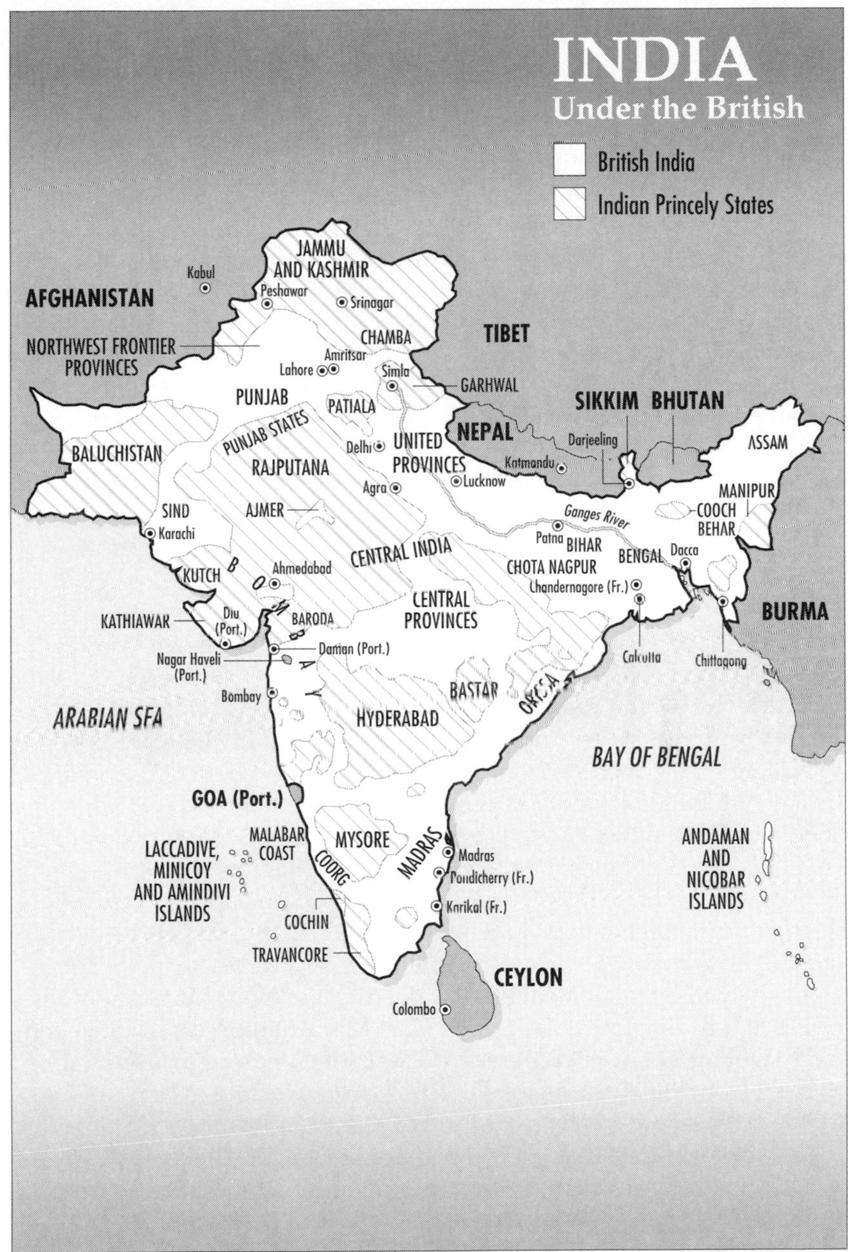
INDIA
Under the British
British India
Indian Princely States
JAMMU AND KASHMIR
Kabul
AFGHANISTAN
Peshawar
Srinagar
NORTHWEST FRONTIER PROVINCES
CHAMBA
TIBET
Amritsar
Lahore
Simla
GARHWAL
PUNJAB
PATIALA
SIKKIM
BHUTAN
PUNJAB STATES
NEPAL
Darjeeling
ASSAM
BALUCHISTAN
Delhi
UNITED PROVINCES
RAJPUTANA
Katmandu
Agra
Lucknow
MANIPUR
SIND
AJMER
Ganges River
COOCH BEHAR
Karachi
Patna
BIHAR
CENTRAL INDIA
BENGAL
Dacca
CHOTA NAGPUR
KUTCH
Ahmedabad
Chandernagore (Fr.)
BOMBAY
CENTRAL PROVINCES
BURMA
KATHIAWAR
Diu (Port.)
BARODA
Daman (Port.)
Calcutta
Chittagong
Nagar Haveli (Port.)
Bombay
BASTAR
ARABIAN SEA
HYDERABAD
BAY OF BENGAL
GOA (Port.)
MALABAR COAST
MYSORE
MADRAS
ANDAMAN AND NICOBAR ISLANDS
LACCADIVE, MINICOY AND AMINDIVI ISLANDS
COORG
Madras
Pondicherry (Fr.)
Karikal (Fr.)
COCHIN
TRAVANCORE
CEYLON
Colombo

Figure 2–1

human virtue and common sense, unfettered by superstition and tradition. The Evangelicals, driven by a personal pietism and public humanitarianism, expressed horror at the abominations of the benighted heathen. Both Utilitarians and Evangelicals found little in India that they liked; both were ready to condemn and eager to change.

Under pressure from the English reformers, the government took action against those Hindu customs offensive to Western sensibilities. The reforms brought outcries of protest from the orthodox, particularly against the outlawing of *sati*, the self-immolation of a widow on the pyre of her husband. But the measures won the support of many reform-minded Hindus, notably Ram Mohan Roy (1772–1833), "the father of modern India." In general, however, the British sought to interfere as little as possible, and reform was largely negative.

The Sepoy Mutiny

The changes introduced by the British, both by accident and by design, threatened the old order, and religion particularly was thought to be in danger. Brahmins, who served in large numbers as *sepoys*, or soldiers, were alarmed by rumors of Christian conversion in their ranks. They feared that they would have to serve overseas and thus break the religious prohibition against leaving India. Muslim resentments were stirred by the annexation of the state of Oudh for alleged misgovernment in 1856. In this atmosphere of fear, mutiny broke out in 1857 when soldiers discovered that the cartridges for their new Enfield rifles were greased with the animal fat of both the cow and the pig, pollutants to Hindus and Muslims, respectively. "A consciousness of power," wrote one British official, "had grown up in the army which could only be exorcized by mutiny, and the cry of the cartridge brought the latent spirit of revolt into action."

In revivalist reaction Muslims rallied to the aged Mughal emperor of Delhi, Hindus to the heir of the last Maratha *peshwa*, or head minister. Discontent was centered in Oudh, but among those in revolt there was no unity of purpose. The Maratha princes were not eager to see a resurgent peshwa and remained aloof from the mutiny. The Sikhs, though defeated only 10 years before by the British, by no means wanted to resurrect Mughal power and thus gave active support to the British in crushing the revolt. The South remained virtually untouched by and uninvolved in the whole affair. Western education brought the Indian middle classes prospects for the enjoyment of status and privilege in a new order, and they pledged their loyalty and active support to the British. "So far from being the first war for independence or a national revolt in the modern sense, the Mutiny was a final convulsion of the old order goaded to desperation by the incessant pricks of modernity."[2]

The mutiny was, as Nehru later wrote, "essentially a feudal rising," and although it had directly affected only a limited area, "it had shaken up the whole of India."[3] The East India Company was abolished, and in 1858 the Crown assumed direct control over British India. The revolt, with all its savagery, marked a fundamental change in British attitude and in the relationship between the Indians and the English. The English became deeply distrustful of their native wards, particularly of the Muslims, who were believed to have been strongly committed to the mutiny. The manner of the British response to the mutiny reflected changes of conditions and attitudes that by 1857 were already well underway. The rise of popular imperial sentiments in England would soon have brought continued company rule into jeopardy had not the mutiny brought matters to a head.[4]

Awakening Indian Nationalism

The British were now determined to be in closer touch with established classes of traditional authority who could keep the masses under control. They rewarded princes for their loyalty during the revolt and guaranteed their territories. They secured landlords in their tenure on conditions of "loyalty and good service." Thus the relics of the past, the vested interests of conservatism, were tied to the British presence in India. At the same time the British exercised new caution in Westernization. Their new policy reflected both a desire to placate the conservative upper classes and a certain disappointment and pessimism over the Indians' inability to change. "Public works rather than public morals or western values was the guiding star of the post-Mutiny reformer."[5] India was assumed to be changeless, perhaps irredeemable, and it was to be the "white man's burden" to bring enlightened rule to those incapable of governing themselves.

[2]Percival Spear, *India, Pakistan, and the West*, 4th ed. (New York: Oxford University Press, 1957), p. 116.

[3]Jawaharlal Nehru, *The Discovery of India* (Garden City, N.Y.: Doubleday, 1959), pp. 239–40.

[4]Francis G. Hutchins, *The Illusion of Permanence* (Princeton, N.J.: Princeton University Press, 1967), p. 86.

[5]Spear, *History*, p. 144.

The British sought to reinforce traditional institutions, to minimize social change, and to soften the impact of the West. Their policy "went hand in hand with a new and avowedly imperial sentiment which glorified the British Raj and consigned the Indian people to a position of permanent racial inferiority."[6] While the British looked for support to the moribund traditional ruling classes, the rajas and zamindars, they virtually ignored the rising westernized middle class—the clerks and subordinate officials, the teachers and lawyers. "The fissure between the British and the new India began at this point."[7]

British colonial rule was to have both direct and indirect consequences. The indirect consequences were largely the result of the British presence and had their major impact in the social and economic spheres. As colonial rulers the British lacked both the capacity and the will to reorder Indian society.

The direct impact of British colonial rule resulted from British colonial policy and had its major effects on law, administration, and education. Of all the changes brought about by the British colonial policy, the most profound was the new concern for education introduced in the 19th century under pressure from the Utilitarians and Evangelicals.

The Utilitarians advocated "useful knowledge"; the Evangelicals, "moral improvement." The English language was, in the words of Governor General Bentinck, "the key to all improvements." The whole of Hindu literature was seen as less valuable than any shelf of English books. Indeed, Lord Macaulay envisaged in his famous Minute of 1835, "a class of persons, Indian in blood and colour, but English in taste, in opinion, in morals, and in intellect."[8]

In 1835 English replaced Persian as the official language of government and thereby became the vehicle of advancement and progress. In establishing schools and, later, universities the British focused on the English education of the middle classes. The aristocrats for the most part held aloof; the masses, except for missionary concern, were largely ignored. The aspiring Hindu middle classes—particularly those castes with a literary tradition, like the Brahmins—were quick

[6]Thomas R. Metcalf, *The Aftermath of Revolt* (Princeton, N.J.: Princeton University Press, 1964), p. 324.

[7]Spear, *History*, p. 153.

[8]John Clive and Thomas Pinney, eds., *Thomas Babington Macaulay: Selected Writings* (Chicago: University of Chicago Press, 1972), pp. 237–51. For a discussion of the Education Minute, see John Clive, *Macaulay: The Shaping of the Historian* (New York: Knopf, 1973), pp. 342–426.

to respond to the advantages of English education. There were those of the *babu* stereotype who sought only a sinecure in the new bureaucracy, but others were eager for the knowledge of the West—science, medicine, and the values of political liberalism.

The rise of the new middle class, which Percival Spear has called "the most significant creation of the British in India,"[9] shifted the balance in the relationship of the various classes in Indian society. The old aristocratic landowning classes were rapidly losing their position of status and power.

This new Indian class was characterized by a unity of sentiment, but at the same time this unity was undercut by the growth of regional identity and of self-awareness and assertiveness among different communities, particularly in religion. The West had a double impact on India: It introduced Western liberal thought, but it also prompted the recovery of what was valuable in tradition. The Indian response to the West came in the forms of reform and revivalism. The movement for reform sought to reconcile tradition with modernity, to eliminate those elements of tradition repugnant to reason and liberal values and to reaffirm those that were compatible with them. Revivalism, in contrast, sought to regain the past through a traditionalistic reaction against the West, and, although often involving radical reform, it was nurtured by the nostalgia for an idealized "golden age."

Reform and revival represented a quest for national self-respect and drew deeply on both those who damned and those who praised Indian tradition and society. While often acutely self-critical, reformers and revivalists reacted sharply to the criticism of the Evangelicals, who saw only benighted heathen and a society of superstition and dark ignorance. They were unwilling to accept the latent, and often manifest, racism that relegated the Indian to a position of inferiority and described him, in Rudyard Kipling's words, as "half devil and half child." In defense of Indian civilization, both reformers and revivalists drew on the Orientalists, the European scholars who, like Sir William Jones and Max Müller, revealed the richness of Indian antiquity and the wisdom of the Sanskritic tradition.

Ram Mohan Roy paved the way for a century of social reform, and in 1843 his philosophy was institutionalized in the establishment of the *Brahmo Samaj*, or Divine Society.[10] The society, directed

[9]Spear, *India, Pakistan, and the West*, p. 110.

[10]See David Kopf, *The Brahmo Samaj and the Shaping of the Modern Indian Mind* (Princeton, N.J.: Princeton University Press, 1979).

toward the literate middle classes, gained a small intellectual following, but under renewed leadership in the 1860s it became increasingly vigorous in its advocacy of monotheism and social reform. Branches were established throughout India, but only in Bengal and Maharashtra, where it sparked the Prarthana Samaj, did it meet with significant success. The Prarthana Samaj had become the center of social reform in western India under the leadership of M. G. Ranade.[11] Believing revival impossible, Ranade sought to preserve tradition through reform. The Arya Samaj, founded in Bombay in 1875 by a Gujarati Brahmin, Swami Dayananda, took a more aggressive and revivalist stance. The Arya Samaj sought to lead India "back to Vedas," the earliest Hindu scriptures, in an effort to recover and restore the Aryan past. Like Roy and Ranade, Dayananda believed in one god and denounced the evils of post-Vedic Hinduism—idolatry, child marriage, and the restrictions of caste—but he also rejected Western knowledge, claiming that the scientific truths of modern thought were all to be found in the Vedas, if seen with enlightened eyes. The Arya Samaj reacted strongly to the influences of Islam and Christianity, and its proselytic fundamentalism contributed to the rise of enmity toward the Muslim community, particularly in the Punjab and in the United Provinces, where the society found its greatest success.[12]

The conflict between Hindus and Muslims engendered by the activities of the Arya Samaj served only to underscore the alienation of the Muslim community in India. The collapse of Mughal rule brought confusion and doubt to the Muslims. The Muslim reaction to British rule was by no means uniform, but, clinging to traditions of the past and to memories of their former glory, many Muslims remained unresponsive to the changes around them. Because they regarded English as "the highway to infidelity," they failed to take advantage of English education and were soon displaced in the civil services by the rising Hindu middle class. As the resentment of the Muslim community turned suspicion and hostility upon them, the Muslim reformer and educator Sayyid Ahmed Khan sought to convince the British of Muslim loyalty and to bring the community into cooperation with

[11] Richard Tucker, *Ranade and the Rise of Indian Nationalism* (Chicago: University of Chicago Press, 1972).

[12] See Kenneth W. Jones, *Arya Dharm: Hindu Consciousness in 19th Century Punjab* (Berkeley: University of California Press, 1977). For a comprehensive discussion of important movements, see Kenneth W. Jones, *Socio-Religious Reform Movements in British India* (Cambridge: Cambridge University Press, 1989).

British authorities. At the same time, he warned of the dangers of Hindu domination under democratic rule. Hindu rule would fall more heavily upon Muslims than the neutral authority of the British Raj.[13]

Growing Political Consciousness

The rise of the new Indian middle class and the movements for reform, while regionally based and accentuating divisions within Indian society, nevertheless served as a catalyst for the development of a national self-consciousness. Upon Bengali and Marathi regionalism, the new class grafted an all-India nationalism. "Mother India had become a necessity and so she was created."[14] The obstacles to the growth of Indian nationalism were many and difficult to overcome—the divisions between British India and the various princely states, the divisions between the linguistic regions, and the divisions of religion and caste within the society. The new middle class transcended these divisions, in part, through its unity of mind and speech. Its members' knowledge of English, commitment to liberal values, and pride in Indian civilization were the foundation for a common all-India view. Reforms served to offer the promise of a better future, and increasing opportunities were opening in the government services for educated Indians. At the same time, however, the British in India often acted without regard to Indian opinion. Indians were virtually excluded from the higher offices of the civil service, and the arrogant stance of imperialist responsibility cut deeply into Indian self-respect. That the behavior of the British in India contrasted so starkly with the values of English liberalism in which the Indian middle class had been steeped served to deepen their national consciousness.

In 1876 Surendranath Banerjea, dismissed—on insufficient grounds—from the Indian Civil Service, founded the Indian Association of Calcutta, which provided the groundwork for an all-India movement for the redress of wrongs and the protection of rights. "Indianization" of the Indian Civil Service (ICS) was a central issue. The ICS had become the "steel frame" of British administration, and member-

[13]For an analysis of the early growth of communalism in India, see Sandria B. Freitag, *Collective Action and Community: Public Arenas in North India* (Berkeley: University of California Press, 1989) and Gyanendra Pandey, *The Construction of Communalism in Colonial North India* (Delhi: Oxford University Press, 1990).

[14]Spear, *History*, p. 166. See also Charles H. Heimsath, *Indian Nationalism and Hindu Social Reform* (Princeton, N.J.: Princeton University Press, 1964), pp. 135–36.

ship carried prestige and status. The Charter Act of 1833, introducing a system of competitive examinations for the service, provided that no Indian "shall by reason only of his religion, place of birth, descent, colour or any of them be disabled from holding any office or employment under the Company." This was reaffirmed in the Queen's Proclamation and in the Indian Civil Service Act of 1861.

There was, however, an obvious reluctance to admit Indians. The examinations were held only in London, and the examination itself virtually required study in England. As an increasing number of Indians successfully surmounted these barriers, admission to the Indian Civil Service was rendered more difficult when, in 1878, the maximum age for application was reduced from 22 to 19.[15] The occasion served as an opportunity for Banerjea to organize a national protest. "The underlying conception, and the true aim and purpose of the Civil Service Agitation," he wrote, "was the awakening of a spirit of unity and solidarity among the people of India." The agitation demonstrated that "whatever might be our differences in respect of race and language, or social and religious institutions, the people of India could combine and unite for the attainment of their common political ends."

It was the Ilbert bill, however, which provided the catalyst for the development of an all-India organization. The bill, introduced in 1883, was intended to remove distinctions between Indian and European judges, thus revoking the exemption of the English in India from trial by native judges. The nonofficial English community in Calcutta exploded in an outburst of racial feeling. They formed a defense association and collected funds to support their agitation against the legislation.[16] The furor led the government to withdraw the bill. The success of the agitation against the bill left the new Indian middle class with a sense of humiliation, but the effectiveness of organization as a political instrument had been impressed upon them.

The Creation of the Congress

In response, Banerjea founded the Indian National Conference in 1883. In that same year a retired English civil servant, A. O. Hume,

[15] The Indianization of the ICS was negligible in the early years. In 1913, 80 years after the Charter Act, the proportion of Indians in the services was only 5 percent. By 1921 it was 13 percent, but by the time of independence, 48 percent were Indian. Naresh Chandra Roy, *The Civil Service in India* (Calcutta: Mukhopadhyay, 1958), p. 154. See also B. B. Misra, *The Bureaucracy in India* (New York: Oxford University Press, 1977).

[16] See Metcalf, *The Aftermath*, p. 309.

addressed an open letter to the graduates of Calcutta University, urging the organization of an association for the political regeneration of India—what, as he later said, might form "the germ of a Native Parliament." The first meeting of the Indian National Congress, attended by 72 delegates, was held in Bombay in 1885. Soon thereafter Banerjea merged his own association with the Congress.

The Congress movement passed through three stages of development from 1885 to 1947: the period of the moderates (1885–1905); the period of the extremists (1905–1920); and the Gandhian era (1920–1947). Each stage was marked by increasing differentiation and broadening of the Congress elite and by an ever more clearly articulated set of nationalist demands.

The Period of the Moderates: 1885–1905

The Indian liberals who dominated the Congress from 1885 to 1905 had an almost unlimited faith in British democracy.[17] "England is our political guide," Banerjea declared. "It is not severance that we look forward to—but unification, permanent embodiment as an integral part of that great Empire that has given the rest of the world the models of free institutions." Even Dadabhai Naoroji, who formulated the "drain theory" of India's exploitation by British economic imperialism, remained "loyal to the backbone" and was the first Indian elected to the British House of Commons.

The Congress affirmed its loyalty to the Queen, and, with the dignity and moderation of a debating society, it sought by resolutions made at its annual meetings to rouse the British conscience to certain inequities of British rule and to the justice of Indian claims for greater representation in the civil services and in the legislative councils at the Center and in the provinces.

In these early years the government regarded the Congress favorably as a "safety valve" for revolutionary discontent, but remained unresponsive to its polite resolutions and humble petitions. Indeed, Hume was led to remark that "the National Congress had endeavored to instruct the Government, but the Government had refused to be instructed." As Congress liberals sought to bring somewhat greater pressure on the Government, the Raj expressed its official disapproval of the policy and methods of the association. The Viceroy denounced the Congress as reflecting only the interests of the educated

[17] The first 20 years of the Congress and its relations with the larger Indian society are examined in John R. McLane, *Indian Nationalism and the Early Congress* (Princeton, N.J.: Princeton University Press, 1977).

middle class, who constituted but a rootless, "microscopic minority" that could hardly be taken as representative of Indian opinion. The British conceived themselves to be the servants of truly representative Indian interests. The "real" India was not to be found among the effete babus of the city, but in the timeless villages, citadels of rugged peasant virtue.[18]

With growing disillusionment, the Congress assumed a stance of constitutional opposition to the government, but such leaders as G. K. Gokhale retained faith in the "integrity and beneficence of that which was best in the British tradition."[19] Gokhale, friend and disciple of Ranade, was deeply committed to liberal reform and, toward that end, had founded the Servants of India Society in 1905. In that same year, as its dominant leader, Gokhale was elected president of the Indian National Congress.

The Period of the Extremists: 1905–1920

Within Congress ranks, however, a militant Extremist wing grew impatient with the gradualism of the Moderates. The demand for administrative reform was replaced by the call for *swaraj*, or self-rule. Extremist support was centered in the Punjab, Bengal, and Maharashtra, where the militants drew inspiration not from the ideals of English liberalism but from India's past. Reform appealed to the cultivated intellects of the English-educated middle classes, but only the passion of revivalism could capture the imagination of the masses and provide the foundation for wider participation. Aurobindo Ghose in Bengal infused the movement with a "neo-Vedantic" mysticism, and in western India, Bal Gangadhar Tilak evoked the memory of Shivaji, founder of the Maratha kingdom, and of his struggle against the Muslim invaders. Tilak recalled the days of Maratha and Hindu glory and, not without concern among Muslims, sought to stir a revival of Hindu religious consciousness to serve his political ends. Tilak castigated the Moderates for what he regarded as their cultural capitulation to the West. Struggle, not reform, was the keynote of his message: "Swaraj is my birthright and I will have it." In examining the role of Tilak, "the Father of Indian Unrest," Stanley Wolpert writes,[20]

[18]See Hutchins, *Illusion*, pp. 156–57.

[19]Stanley Wolpert, *Tilak and Gokhale* (Berkeley: University of California Press, 1962), p. 299. Also see B. R. Nanda, *Gokhale: The Indian Moderates and the British Raj* (Princeton, N.J.: Princeton University Press, 1977).

[20]Wolpert, *Tilak and Gokhale*, p. 304.

> His dream was not an India made in its foreign master's image, but one restored to the glory of its own true self. The quicker the British left, the happier he and his land would be. There could be no salvation for India in the self-deception of constitutional cooperation. Better to rely on the yoga of boycott.

In 1905 Bengal was divided into two provinces; East Bengal comprised what is today Bangladesh. The partition gave impetus to the boycott of British goods and advanced the *swadeshi* movement for the use of indigenous products. The partition, designed solely with regard for administrative efficiency, completely ignored the renascent Bengali consciousness. A storm of protest, under the leadership of Surendranath Banerjea and such eminent Bengalis as Rabindranath Tagore, brought widespread popular opposition to the British Raj. Boycott offered the possibility of mass participation. The emotion vented in agitation was accompanied by terrorism and, in the name of the demonic goddess Kali, assassination.

The Bengal partition brought a new urgency to the aspirations of Indian nationalists, and at their meeting in 1906 the Congress resolved to support the demand for swaraj. Gokhale and the Moderates envisioned responsible government within the British Empire—a position wholly unacceptable to the Extremists. The following year the Congress meeting at Surat broke up in an uproar as the Extremists walked out, leaving the Moderates in control of the organization. Tilak, now in a political wilderness, was drawn increasingly toward the advocacy of violence in "political warfare" against the British. The government enacted increasingly repressive measures to bring the wave of terrorism under control, and Tilak was arrested. Released after six years, he pledged his support and loyalty to the Congress. It was Tilak, however, given the title *Lokamanya*, or Honored by the People, who more than any of the early Congress leaders had sought to reach the masses, to transform the nationalist cause into a popular movement.

The Moderate position within the Congress was strengthened by the Morley–Minto Reforms of 1909 and the rescission of the Bengal partition. From shortly after the assumption of direct rule by the Crown, there had been some degree of Indian representation in government, but as Morris-Jones argues, "whether or not the British Empire was won in a fit of absent-mindedness, such a mood seems to have had a good deal to do with the establishment of parliamentary institutions in India. . . ."[21] Under the Indian Councils Act of 1861,

[21] W. H. Morris-Jones, *Parliament in India* (London: Longmans, Green, 1957), p. 73.

three Indians were appointed to the advisory Legislative Council at the Center as nonofficial members. Not until 1891, however, partly to placate the Congress, did the government increase the number of members in the Central and provincial legislative councils and concede the principle of election, at least indirectly. The Morley–Minto Reforms, drafted in consultation with Gokhale and other Indian leaders, expanded the legislative councils, thereby increasing Indian representation; introduced direct election of nonofficials under limited property franchise; and in the provinces provided for nonofficial majorities. Recommendations of the councils, however, could be disallowed at the discretion of the Viceroy or of the provincial governor; thus, the councils were to a degree representative, but not responsible. In fact, Morley declared that "if it could be said that this chapter of reforms led directly or indirectly to the establishment of a parliamentary system, I, for one, would have nothing to do with it."

The reforms provided limited institutional access to the new Indian middle class and sought to accommodate a range of moderate demands for representation. The Congress carried little weight, however, in the face of the highly institutionalized structures of the British Raj. The repressive powers of the bureaucracy and the army could at any time be used against the few politically active Indians. The Congress had not yet gained the political capital of widespread popular support, of mass participation, that would allow it to challenge the British presence seriously. The Moderates were ready to work within the framework of imperial rule, making limited, though increasing, demands for greater access; the Extremists, lacking broad support and harassed by the government, had been driven underground. The British lack of more genuine responsiveness to even the limited aspirations of Indian leaders and their readiness to use the power of repressive order to suppress opposition served, however, to awaken the political consciousness of the growing middle class.

The Morley–Minto Reforms, by their acceptance of Muslim demands for separate electorates, introduced the principle of communal representation. In presenting their case before the government, the Muslim notables argued that without separate electorates the Muslim community would be submerged in the Hindu majority, which was becoming increasingly participant and vocal in its demands for representation.

To advance their position, these notables organized the Muslim League in 1906 at Dacca. The League was the first real attempt by Indian Muslims to utilize an organization to secure a more favorable position. Its membership was middle class and concerned primarily with more jobs, better educational opportunities, and higher social and economic status. More a clique than a movement, it nevertheless reflected the awakening of Muslim political consciousness.[22]

The award of communal representation to the Muslims was attacked by Congress nationalists as an attempt to weaken national unity with the strategy of divide and rule. The British had found in the Muslim community a useful counterpoise to the growing force of the Congress. Within the League, however, the position of the loyalist Muslims was soon challenged by the Young Muhammadans, who sought political confrontation, rather than accommodation, with the Raj. By 1916 the Congress seemed prepared to accept separate electorates in exchange for the support of the Muslims, who had been roused to anti-British feeling because of the war between Great Britain and Turkey. The Lucknow Pact, concluded in that year at a joint session of the Congress and the Muslim League, called for the achievement of self-government.

The Lucknow Congress, held a year after Gokhale's death, marked the re-emergence of Tilak as Congress leader. In that same year Tilak founded the Home Rule League, and he was followed soon after by the English theosophist Annie Besant, who organized a Home Rule League in Madras. In alliance, Tilak and Besant reasserted the Extremist faction within the Congress, and in 1917, while interned by the British government, Besant was elected president of the Indian National Congress. Moderate leaders soon withdrew to found the Indian Liberal Federation.

The Morley–Minto Reforms, while gradually moving India closer to responsible government, did not fulfill the rising expectations of Indian nationalists. India's involvement in the world war had brought a commitment of loyalty that soon turned to frustration and a diminished awe of imperial power, as the British called for sacrifice in exchange for vague promises of reform "after the war." Indian agitation for change was strengthened by Woodrow Wilson's declaration of the right of all nations to self-determination. As the demands for swaraj intensified with the home rule movement, Edwin Montagu, who had succeeded Morley as Secretary of State for India, announced in 1917 the government policy "of increasing association of Indians in every branch of the administration and the gradual development of self-governing institutions with a view to the progressive realization of

[22] Wayne A. Wilcox, *Pakistan: The Consolidation of a Nation* (New York: Columbia University Press, 1963), p. 20. See also Khalid B. Sayeed, *Pakistan: The Formative Phase, 1857–1948*, 2nd ed. (New York: Oxford University Press, 1968).

responsible government in India as an integral part of the British Empire."

The first step toward implementing this policy was the enactment of the Montague–Chelmsford Reforms in 1919. Under the act, authority was decentralized, with a division of functions between the Center and the provincial governments. At the Center there was little substantive change. Bicameralism was introduced, with an elected nonofficial majority in the lower house, but the Governor General, responsible to London, retained the overriding powers of certification and veto. In the provinces, however, the reforms introduced *dyarchy*, or dual government, under which the governor retained authority over certain "reserved" subjects—largely in the areas of revenue and law and order—while "transferred" subjects, such as local self-government, education, health, public works, agriculture, and industry, came under the control of ministers responsible to popularly elected legislatures. Council memberships were enlarged, and the principle of communal representation was extended both at the Center and in the provinces.

For many Congress leaders the reforms were just a sop. This seemed confirmed by the enactment of the Rowlatt Bills in 1919, extending the emergency powers assumed during the war to permit imprisonment without trial in political cases. In protest against the repressive "black bills," demonstrations and strikes were held throughout the country. Feelings were most intense in those more politically self-conscious regions where revivalism, and later Extremism, had gained a foothold among the masses. In the Punjab, where the situation was particularly tense, the arrest of two Congress leaders sparked a riot. Martial law was proclaimed and a ban on all public meetings was imposed. Defying the ban, an estimated 20,000 people gathered at the central park of Amritsar, Jallianwalla Bagh. Under the command of General Dyer, 150 troops suddenly appeared at the entrance and ordered the crowd to disperse. With the military blocking the only entrance, Dyer then gave the order to fire point-blank into the unarmed masses. When the ammunition was exhausted, 379 Indians were dead and some 1200 more wounded. Dyer intended the massacre "to teach the natives a lesson."

At the end of the year the Indian National Congress met at Amritsar in a mood of outrage and shock. The Montagu-Chelmsford Reforms were denounced as "inadequate, unsatisfactory and disappointing," but Tilak, who was to live less than a year, had mellowed, and he urged a policy of "responsive co-operation" with the government. Indian restraint, however, was pushed beyond the limit of its endurance when in 1920 the House of Lords gave a vote of appreciation to General Dyer for his services. Mohandas Gandhi, the new Congress leader, proclaimed that "cooperation in any shape or form with this satanic government is sinful."

The Gandhian Era: 1920–1947

Gandhi was born into a Gujarati Vaishya family in Kathiawar, where his father was the *diwan*, or head minister, of a petty princely state. After completing university studies in Bombay, Gandhi read for the bar at the Inner Temple in London. After two years, still very much an Indian, he returned to India for legal practice. But the young barrister was soon invited to South Africa to plead the case of the Indian community against discriminatory legislation. He planned to stay one year; he remained for twenty.

In South Africa, with the Gita as his "infallible guide of conduct," he began his experiments with *satyagraha*, or nonviolent resistance, which he translated as "soul force."[23] It was satyagraha that was "to revolutionize Indian politics and to galvanize millions into action against the British Raj."[24] Already known for his South African victory, Gandhi was greeted with the title *Mahatma*, or Great Soul, upon his return to India in 1915. For the next three years, however, he remained a silent observer of the political scene, taking the advice of his political mentor Gokhale to keep "his ears open and his mouth shut" for a time.

During this period Gandhi became increasingly sensitive to the gap between the predominantly urban middle-class Congress and the Indian masses, and shifted his attentions to the villages and the peasants. In 1918, while introducing satyagraha in India, Gandhi courted arrest in support of the indigo plantation workers of Bihar. A year later, when the repressive Rowlatt Bills were introduced, Gandhi organized the Satyagraha Society, pledged to disobey the unjust law as a symbol of passive resistance. To mobilize mass support he called for a day of fasting and *hartal*, or general strike, in protest against the legislation.[25] The violence that marred the demonstrations led Gandhi

[23] Mohandas Gandhi, *An Autobiography, or The Story of My Experiments with Truth* (Ahmedabad, India: Navajivan Publishing House, 1927), p. 195. See also Joan V. Bondurant, *Conquest of Violence* (Berkeley: University of California Press, 1965).

[24] Michael Brecher, *Nehru: A Political Biography* (New York: Oxford University Press, 1959), p. 59.

[25] Explaining this political tactic in the cultural context of India, Spear notes, "In theory, the soul is too shocked by some abuse to be able to attend to practical affairs for a time." Spear, *History*, p. 191.

to regard satyagraha as premature, as a "Himalayan miscalculation." For others, however, it marked the turning point of the struggle for swaraj.

Gandhi regarded his participation in the 1919 Amritsar meeting as his "real entrance" into Congress politics. Thereafter, he became its guiding force. In seeking to mobilize mass resistance to the government, Gandhi gained Muslim support through his appeal on the emotionally charged Khilafat issue, denouncing the dismemberment of the Ottoman Empire and the deposition of the Caliph, the religious head of all Muslims.[26] The noncooperation movement was launched with the call for a boycott of the impending elections and the law courts, and for withdrawal from all government schools and colleges. Middle-class Indians, institutionally co-opted by the British Raj, were now drawn into new patterns of political participation. Congress members were asked to resign from government office and to renounce all titles. More than 30 thousand Congressmen, including Motilal Nehru and his son Jawaharlal, courted arrest in defiance of "lawless laws" and gained honor through imprisonment. The civil disobedience was accompanied by the outbreak of sporadic strikes, by the rebellion of Muslims in Malabar on the southwestern coast, by no-tax campaigns, and, on the visit of the Prince of Wales, by a nationwide hartal. In February 1922, to the dismay of Congress leaders, Gandhi abruptly called an end to the movement, as he had done before, when mob violence in a small town in Uttar Pradesh left 22 policemen dead. Gandhi declared that he would not purchase independence at the price of bloodshed. Within days he was arrested and tried for sedition.

During the two years that Gandhi was imprisoned, Hindu–Muslim unity was broken by the outbreak of communal rioting. Upon his release in 1924 Gandhi began a 21-day fast for Hindu–Muslim solidarity, but to no avail. Thereafter, the Muslim League, claiming to represent the Muslim community, took an increasingly separate path from that of the Congress. The breach seemed irrevocable when the Congress refused in 1928 to accept separate communal electorates as part of the proposed constitutional change.[27]

Within the Congress the solidarity forged during the noncooperation movement gave way to division on the issue of council entry. The

[26]See Gail Minault, *The Khilafat Movement: Religious Symbolism and Political Mobilization in India* (New York: Columbia University Press, 1982).

[27]See Mushirul Hasan, *Nationalism and Communal Politics in India, 1885–1930* (New Delhi: Manohar, 1991).

legislative councils, boycotted by the Congress, were growing in importance and prestige under the provincial non-Congress ministries. While Gandhi was still in prison C. R. Das and Motilal Nehru led the Congress in the formation of the Swaraja Party to contest the next council elections with the purpose of destroying the reforms from within by "uniform, consistent and continuous obstruction." The very entry of the Congress into the councils, however, increased their prestige and made them all the more difficult to subvert. Many Swarajists were led increasingly to favor a position of "responsive cooperation" with the government for the achievement of swaraj. The Gandhians, or "no-changers," opposed the Swarajist strategy and, losing their dominance in the Congress for the time, retired to engage in "constructive work." From his *ashram*, a retreat near Ahmedabad, Gandhi worked for the uplift of the untouchables, whom he called *harijans*, or "children of God," and with his own hands performed their "defiling" tasks. While the Swarajists debated in the councils, Gandhi led his swadeshi campaign for the use of *khadi*, a homespun cloth. Clothed simply in a loincloth and shawl, he would spin for a half-hour or more each day and urged all Congressmen to do likewise. The spinning wheel, emblazoned in the center of the Congress flag, became the symbol of the society Gandhi sought to achieve—a peasant society, self-governing and self-sufficient. Purity of the soul was requisite to the attainment of swaraj; only through self-discipline could India prepare itself and make itself worthy of freedom.

In accordance with the provision of the Montagu-Chelmsford Reforms for a parliamentary review after 10 years, the Simon Commission was appointed for the recommendation of constitutional changes. The Congress regarded the commission's all-British membership as not in accord with the principle of self-determination and resolved to boycott its proceedings. In 1928 the Congress, the Muslim League, and the Liberal Federation came together in an All-Parties Convention to frame a constitution for an independent India. The report, drafted by Motilal Nehru, called for responsible government and dominion status. The young radicals Jawaharlal Nehru and Subhas Chandra Bose opposed the recommendation for dominion status. With the intervention of Gandhi, the Congress agreed to accept the Nehru Report, but only if the proposed constitution were accepted in its entirety by Parliament before the end of 1929. Failing this, the Congress would launch nonviolent noncooperation in pursuit of independence.

The Governor General, Lord Irwin, announced that "the natural issue of India's Constitutional progress . . . is the attainment of Dominion status" and that toward that end a round-table conference would be held in London to discuss the recommendations of the Simon Commission. In accordance with its pledge, the Congress met in December 1929 at Lahore and their declared complete independence as its goal. It was resolved to boycott the legislative councils and the Round Table Conference and, under the direction of Gandhi, to begin a program of civil disobedience and nonpayment of taxes. At Lahore, the elder Nehru, with little more than a year to live, passed the chair of the Congress presidency to his son. On December 29, Jawaharlal Nehru hoisted the national flag of India.

The Civil Disobedience Campaign[28] In launching the campaign of civil disobedience, Gandhi announced his intention to violate the salt tax, a burden on even the poorest peasant and a source of bitter resentment against the Raj. He would march from his ashram to the sea, a distance of 241 miles, and there, by taking salt from the sea, would disobey the law. The dramatic march lasted 24 days, and with this act of defiance, mass demonstrations, hartals, and civil disobedience began throughout India. The government quickly responded with repressive measures. More than 100 people were killed in police firings, and indiscriminate beatings of men and women were widespread. In less than a year some 60,000 people were imprisoned.

During the Congress campaign, non-Congress representatives attended the Round Table Conference, but the Viceroy realized that any decisions would be hollow without Congress participation. In 1931 he released Gandhi and began a series of conversations that concluded in the Gandhi-Irwin pact. The government agreed to withdraw its repressive measures and to release all political prisoners except those guilty of violence. Gandhi called off the civil disobedience campaign and agreed to attend the next round-table conference as a representative of the Congress. The London conference deadlocked on the question of communal electorates, and Gandhi returned "empty-handed" to India. With the renewal of government repression, the Congress reopened the civil disobedience campaign and called for the boycott of British goods. By March 1933 more than 120,000 people had been imprisoned.

At this inopportune moment, the government announced its constitutional proposals, which included a provision for separate electorates for the untouchables. Believing the untouchables to be an inte-

[28] See Judith M. Brown, *Gandhi and Civil Disobedience: The Mahatma in Indian Politics, 1928–34* (Cambridge: Cambridge University Press, 1977).

gral part of the Hindu community, Gandhi, in jail, vowed to "fast unto death" against the provision. Gandhi began the fast despite the pleas of all. On the fifth day, as Gandhi's life was believed to hang in the balance, Dr. Ambedkar, leader of the untouchables, gave way and agreed to abandon separate communal electorates, but, to safeguard the interests of the untouchables, he demanded that a number of seats be reserved for them within the allotment of seats to the Hindu community.

The fast, while stirring concern for the untouchables, diverted attention from the issue of independence and brought the collapse of the civil disobedience campaign. Radicals within the Congress declared that Gandhi had failed as a political leader and called for a new leadership. In the radical view the nationalist movement under Gandhi had become what was later described as "a peculiar blend of bold advances followed by sudden and capricious halts, challenges succeeded by unwarranted compromises. . . ."[29]

British Accommodation: The Government of India Act of 1935 The British sought to respond to widening political participation and increasingly vocal demands with the Government of India Act of 1935, which adapted the high levels of institutional capability to a changing environment. Abandoning its policy of repression, the government sought to buy stability through accommodation; stability was the *raison d'état*. The Act abolished dyarchy and provided for provincial autonomy with responsible government, accountable to a greatly expanded electorate. The franchise continued to carry a property qualification, but by the Act the electorate was expanded from 6 million to 30 million, one-sixth of the adult population. The federal arrangement—never actually brought into operation—provided for the integration of princely states with British India. The all-India federation, which provided the model for the federal structure of independent India, was to consist of governor's provinces, chief commissioner's provinces, and those acceding princely states. Legislative power was divided according to detailed lists, distinguishing Central, provincial, and concurrent jurisdiction. Representation in the federal legislature was heavily weighted in favor of the princes, giving a conservative cast to the Central government. At the Center, a dyarchical arrangement was introduced by which the Governor General, responsible only to the British Parliament, was invested with a number

[29] A. R. Desai, *Social Background of Indian Nationalism* (Bombay: Popular Book Depot, 1959), pp. 343–44.

of discretionary powers and enjoyed "reserved power" over such departments as defense and external affairs. A. B. Keith, in his study of the constitutional history of India, argues that these provisions rendered "the alleged concession of responsibility all but meaningless."[30] Nehru termed the reform act a "slave" constitution—yet many features of the 1935 Act were later incorporated into the Constitution of the Republic of India.

In a very real sense the provincial autonomy granted under the Act was a substantive move toward meeting Congress demands for swaraj. Once again, as in 1922, the Congress resolved to work within the new reforms, and in 1937 it swept the provincial elections for Hindu seats and formed ministries in 7 of the 11 provinces. The Muslim League fared poorly among the Muslim electorate and failed to secure majorities in any of the 4 predominantly Muslim provinces. Mohammed Ali Jinnah, the westernized leader of the League, offered to form coalition ministries with the Congress in each province, but the Congress refused to recognize the League as representative of India's 90 million Muslims. "There are," Nehru remarked, "only two forces in India today, British imperialism and Indian nationalism as represented by the Congress." History, however, bore out Jinnah's response: "No, there is a third party, the Mussulmans." The Congress was to pay dearly for its imperious attitude: "The opening shots had been fired in the calamitous Congress-League war which was to envelop north India in flames and ultimately result in partition."[31] In 1940, Jinnah declared that the Hindus and Muslims formed two separate nations. The Muslim League now adopted as its goal the creation of a separate and independent Islamic state, Pakistan.

During their term of office the Congress ministries demonstrated considerable administrative ability and produced a distinguished record of achievements in social reform.[32] Inevitably, with their assumption of office, questions arose as to the relationship between the ministries and the party. Participation in provincial government was only one aspect of the Congress struggle, and Nehru emphasized the primary responsibility of the ministries to the Congress high command from whom they would take their directive. The high command itself was by no means united. In 1939, however, with the resignation of

[30] A. B. Keith, *A Constitutional History of India: 1600–1935*, a reprint of the 2nd, 1926 edition (New York: Barnes & Noble, 1969), p. 474.

[31] Brecher, *Nehru*, p. 231.

[32] For a discussion of the Congress ministries, see Reginald Coupland, *The Constitutional Problem in India* (New York: Oxford University Press, 1944).

Bose after his confrontation with Gandhi, the two main factions—the old guard (Rajendra Prasad and Sardar Vallabhbhai Patel) and the socialists (Nehru)—united behind Gandhi's leadership.

Bose formed a new party, the Forward Bloc and, in 1941, appeared in Germany and later in Japan to secure support for the Government of Free India, which he proclaimed in Japanese-occupied Singapore. There Bose, now called *Netaji*, or Leader, organized the Indian National Army.[33]

Renewed Demands for Independence The tide of war imposed a new strain on the nationalist cause. In 1939 the Viceroy proclaimed India's involvement in the war without consulting Indian leaders. The Congress condemned fascist aggression but declared that India could not associate itself with the war effort unless it was given immediate independence and equality as a free nation. When this demand was ignored, the Congress directed the provincial ministries to resign in protest. In August 1940, Congress again offered complete cooperation in the war in exchange for at least a provisional national government. The Viceroy made vague allusions to independence "after the war," but went on to promise the Muslims and other minorities that Britain would not accept any constitutional modification to which they were opposed.

The Muslim League refused to cooperate with the Congress, and after the resignation of the Congress ministries, it proclaimed a "Day of Deliverance" from the "tyranny, oppression and injustice" of Congress rule. The departure of the Congress from provincial government at that critical time left the League in an advantageous position, one that by the end of the war would be virtually irresistible.

With the failure of the Congress offer, Gandhi again assumed leadership and opened a campaign of individual civil disobedience designed to symbolize Congress protest without disrupting the British war effort. Congress moderation was met by severe government reaction. In 1942, however, as the Japanese advanced through Burma, Sir Stafford Cripps, on mission from London, promised the establishment of a constituent assembly and full dominion status after the war. Nehru and perhaps the majority of the Congress high command were responsive to the offer, but Gandhi, firmly opposed, held the balance. Nehru held out until the last, but finally submitted to Gandhi's persuasion. In August 1942, Gandhi demanded that Great Britain "quit

[33]See Leonard A. Gordon, *Brothers against the Raj: A Biography of Indian Nationalists Sarat and Subhas Chandra Bose* (New York: Columbia University Press, 1990).

India" or confront mass civil disobedience. The government declared Congress illegal, and within hours Gandhi and the Congress leadership were taken into custody. They spent the rest of the war in prison. (C. Rajagopalachari, unable to support the resolution, resigned from the Congress.) The arrests set off a political explosion. Violence erupted throughout India, and, by the end of the year, about 100 thousand people had been arrested and more than a thousand killed in police firings.

The Quit India movement represented the apogee of the independence struggle in terms of mass involvement, but in a nation of nearly 400 million people the relative numbers of participants must have been small indeed. The various noncooperation movements beginning in the 1920s under Gandhi fundamentally changed the character of the Congress, transforming it from an urban middle-class coterie into a movement with an extensive social base reaching into the villages. If by 1942 Congress had enlisted 4 to 5 million members and widespread support, other millions, for various reasons of self-interest, remained loyal to British rule, and even greater numbers remained uninvolved or wholly unaware of the dramatic events transpiring around them. The nationalist movement, even in penetrating the villages, had limited impact. Those who were mobilized in the rural areas were far more likely to be the fairly prosperous peasants than the landless laborers. The mobilization of the still largely inert Indian masses to political consciousness and participation would remain the developmental task of India's leaders in the years after independence.

The Achievement of Swaraj

With the release of Gandhi in 1944, negotiations began again, as the Governor General proposed the formation of a national government. Discussions broke down when the Congress refused to recognize the League as the sole representative of the Muslim community. The war years had consolidated Jinnah's strength in the Muslim areas, however, and in the elections held at the beginning of 1946, the League swept the Muslim seats, as did the Congress the general seats. "The two-nations theory of Mr. Jinnah had found political expression."[34]

[34]Spear, *History*, p. 231. See also Ayesha Jalal, *Sole Spokesman: Jinnah, the Muslim League and the Demand for Pakistan* (Cambridge: Cambridge University Press, 1985). For a biography, Stanley Wolpert, *Jinnah of Pakistan* (New York: Oxford University Press, 1984).

Prime Minister Attlee now announced the appointment of a Cabinet mission to India "to promote, in conjunction with the leaders of Indian opinion, the early realization of full self-government in India." Confronted with the widening gap between the Congress and the League, the mission sought to preserve a united India and to allay Muslim fears of Hindu domination through the proposal of a loose federation. Although dissatisfied, both sides accepted the plan, but the Congress rejected the proposals for an interim government, again over the issue of allotment of seats; the Congress, representing all India, was unwilling to accord the Muslim League its claim to represent all Muslims and therefore to have the right to fill all seats reserved for Muslims in the Cabinet. The Congress announced that it would, nevertheless, participate in the Constituent Assembly to frame the constitution. Jinnah countered by declaring a day of "direct action," unleashing a wave of communal rioting.

In September 1946, Nehru took office as *de facto* Prime Minister of the interim government. Fearing isolation, Jinnah brought the League into the government, but only to demonstrate that the Hindu and Muslim communities could not work in harmony and that the formation of Pakistan was the only solution. The obstructionist stance of the League brought negotiations to an impasse. At this point, on February 20, 1947, the British government declared that it intended to quit India no later than June 1948 and that Lord Mountbatten had been appointed Viceroy to arrange for the transfer of power to Indian hands—however prepared they might be to accept it.

Communal rioting again broke out, and the Punjab approached civil war. Gandhi was prepared to see the whole of India burn rather than concede Pakistan. Congress power, however, lay with Nehru and the more traditional Sardar Vallabhbhai Patel,[35] both of whom by this time had come to accept the inevitability of partition. With their agreement Mountbatten laid out the plan for the transfer of power. The predominantly Muslim provinces would be allowed to form a separate Islamic state and to draw up their own constitution. Bengal and the Punjab, where the two communities were almost equal in numbers, would be divided as defined by a boundary commission. In the Northwest Frontier Province, where a pro-Congress Muslim government had a precarious majority, a referendum would be held. The princely states, released from British paramountcy, would be given the freedom to accede to either India or Pakistan—or, presumably, to

[35]For a definitive biography, see Rajmohan Gandhi, *Patel: A Life* (Ahmedabad: Navajivan Publishing House, 1990).

declare their independence. Moving with incredible speed, Mountbatten, who was to stay on as the first Governor General of the new India, moved up the calendar of British withdrawal. On August 15, 1947, India became an independent nation. "Long years ago," Nehru declared, "we made a tryst with destiny, and now the time comes when we shall redeem our pledge. . . ."

The Partition and Gandhi's Assassination

The achievement of swaraj was dimmed by the tragedy of partition and the assassination of Mohandas Gandhi. The partition, in dividing Hindus and Muslims, had shattered Gandhi's dream of a free and united India, but the territorial division left millions of each community on both sides of the border. In the Punjab the boundary award, as anticipated, divided the cohesive and militant Sikh community almost equally between the two states. Here, in mounting hysteria, violence, and atrocity, Muslims fell upon Sikhs and Hindus in the West, and Sikhs and Hindus upon Muslims in the East. Before the end of the year half a million people had been killed. In the movement of refugees 4½ million Hindus and Sikhs left West Pakistan for India; 6 million Muslims moved in the other direction. Rioting broke out in Bengal, but massacre was avoided, in part because of a Bengali consciousness that transcended religious division, but also because of the presence of Gandhi in Calcutta, "a one man boundary force." The costs of human suffering were, nevertheless, enormous: More than one million persons crossed the Bengal border from East Pakistan into India, leaving behind most of their possessions and bringing with them a bitterness that was to infect the communal life of Calcutta for years to come.

The Punjab was brought under control, but as hundreds of thousands of refugees poured into Delhi, the Muslims who either had chosen to remain or else could not leave, now faced a bloodbath of revenge. Gandhi sought to reconcile the two communities by his presence, to protect the Muslims and urge them to stay, and to calm the troubled city. On January 13, 1948, Gandhi began a fast, to death if necessary, to stir "the conscience of all"—Hindu, Muslim, and Sikh. The fast, which lasted five days and brought the Mahatma near death, ended only with the Indian government's agreement to release Pakistan's share of the assets of British India and with the agreement by representatives of all communities, led by Nehru, Prasad, and Azad, to "protect the life, property, and faith" of the Muslims.

Some within the Congress, such as Sardar Patel, did not approve of Gandhi's intervention on behalf of the Muslims. Others, the Hindu militants of the Mahasabha party and the Rashtriya Swayamsevak Sangh (RSS), openly denounced Gandhi for allegedly helping the Muslims against the Hindus. A bomb attempt was made on Gandhi's life, and then on January 30, 12 days after he had broken his fast, as he proceeded to his prayer meeting on the lawn of the palatial Birla House, Gandhi was shot by a young Hindu fanatic who had once belonged to the RSS. That evening, Nehru announced to the world, "The light has gone out of our lives and there is darkness everywhere. . . ."

Gandhi had served to mobilize widespread support for the Congress struggle for independence, and if he did not hasten its arrival, he nevertheless imbued the movement with moral concern and stirred the conscience of the world. By making the Congress a more representative organization, Gandhi fundamentally changed the character of the nationalist struggle for independence. He broadened the base of the party in his appeal to the masses, but at the same time served to "Indianize" the middle class. His vision of society, however, had turned him from the path of the modernists and their commitment to industrialization and Western parliamentary government, and with independence, he urged Congressmen to leave politics for "constructive work." Gandhi argued that the Congress "as a propaganda vehicle and parliamentary machine [had] outlived its use" and that "it must be kept out of unhealthy competition with political parties." Gandhi's death, mourned by all, brought a national reaction against the Mahasabha and Hindu extremism. It also served to free Nehru from the constraints of Gandhi's vision—but Gandhism had entered the political culture, more a charismatic memory than a revolutionary force, espoused by every shade of opinion and utilized for every purpose.

Formation of the Indian Union

In the wake of partition and Gandhi's death, India faced the problems of consolidation: the integration of the princely states and the framing of a constitution. Approximately two-fifths of the area under the Raj had been made up of these 562 principalities, ranging in size from a few square miles to an area as large as Hyderabad, with 17 million people. With persuasion and pressure, Sardar Vallabhbhai Patel succeeded by Independence Day, August 15, 1947, in securing the accession of all states with the exception of three—Junagadh, Hyderabad, and Jammu and Kashmir.

Junagadh was a tiny state in Kathiawar with a Hindu population and a Muslim ruler, surrounded by Indian territory. When the state acceded to Pakistan, it was occupied by Indian troops, and after a plebiscite, Junagadh joined the Indian Union. Hyderabad, with a Muslim ruler, the Nizam, and a Hindu majority, presented a similar but more complicated situation. The largest of the princely states, Hyderabad, though landlocked in the heart of India, sought independence as a sovereign state and entered a one-year standstill agreement with India while negotiations proceeded. With increasing disorder in Hyderabad and the rising influence of paramilitary Muslim extremists, the Indian government moved troops into the state in a "police action" to restore law and order. Hyderabad then acceded to the Indian Union.

The state of Jammu and Kashmir, contiguous to both India and Pakistan and acceding to neither, had a Hindu ruler and a predominantly Muslim population. The Muslims were centered in the central valley, the Vale of Kashmir, with the Hindu minority concentrated in the region of Jammu to the south. As invading Pathan tribesmen from Pakistan pushed toward the capital of Srinagar, the Maharaja called upon India for military assistance. India, on the recommendation of Mountbatten, refused to send troops unless Kashmir agreed to accede formally to India. With accession India announced its intention, once peace was restored, to hold a referendum on the choice of India or Pakistan. Because of armed conflict between the two states over Kashmir in 1948 and the subsequent demarcation of a United Nations cease-fire line, the plebiscite was never held. Since then India, over the protest of Pakistan, has come to regard Kashmir as an integral part of its own territory, arguing that Kashmir legally acceded to India and that the large Muslim population of Kashmir serves as a force for secularity in India and as a protection for the millions of Muslims left in Indian territory after partition.

Once the princely states had acceded to India, the process of integration began. Smaller states were merged with the neighboring provinces. Others were consolidated as centrally administered areas. States of another class, because of their affinity, were consolidated as new federal units; these included Rajasthan, Saurashtra, and Travancore-Cochin. Mysore, Hyderabad, and, in a separate class, the state of Jammu and Kashmir retained their integrity as separate states of the Indian Union. Each new unit developed from the former princely states was to have as its head a *rajpramukh*, elected by the Council of Rulers, which was made up of the former princes. Some princes, such as the Maharaja of Mysore, distinguished themselves in government service, and others entered political life, but most of them, provided for a time with special privileges and privy purse allowances, became relics of the past in a democratic state.[36]

The man who guided the integration of states never captured the imagination of the Indian people or the attention of the world, as did both Gandhi and Nehru, but for the period of transition, 1947 to 1950, Sardar Vallabhbhai Patel shared power with Nehru in an uneasy alliance that Brecher has termed the "duumvirate."[37] Temperamentally and ideologically the two men could hardly have been more unalike. Nehru, reflective and sometimes considered indecisive, was a man of international vision, a committed socialist, secular in approach, of aristocratic Brahmin background and European manner. Patel, of Gujarati peasant stock, plebeian and orthodox, "was a man of iron will, clear about his objectives and resolute in his actions."[38] He was the realist, the machine politician, the defender of capitalism, of Hindu primacy, and of traditionalism. In the duumvirate, created by Gandhi to hold the Congress together and sustained by his memory, Patel, the Deputy Prime Minster, held the critical domestic portfolios, which along with the party organization gave him effective control over domestic affairs. Nehru was responsible for foreign affairs. "In the broadest sense they were equals, with one striking difference. Patel controlled a greater aggregate of power in the short-run, through the party and the key ministries of government, but Nehru commanded the country at large."[39] With the death of Patel in 1950, Nehru assumed full leadership within the Congress, the government, and the nation.

One of the most important achievements of this period of transition was the Constitution. This document, symbol of India's new freedom, embodied the basic principles for which the Congress had long struggled and provided the institutional framework for the political life of modern India. Before the leaders of India lay the tasks of po-

[36] Bejeweled maharajahs will always be a part of the romantic image of India, but they were an expensive anachronism in modern India. In 1971, after a long legal battle, the Twenty-sixth Amendment to the Constitution abolished purse and privilege. The princes were no more. See D. R. Manikekar, *Accession to Extinction: The Story of Indian Princes* (Delhi: Vikas, 1974). The broader historical context is examined in Barbara N. Ramusack, *The Princes of India in the Twilight of Empire: Dissolution of a Patron–Client System*. (Columbus: Ohio State University Press, 1978), and Robin Jeffrey, ed., *People, Princes and Paramount Power: Society and Politics in the Indian Princely States* (Delhi: Oxford University Press, 1978).

[37] See Brecher, *Nehru*, pp. 389–425.

[38] Ibid., p. 392.

[39] Ibid., p. 400.

litical development, of creating and sustaining an institutional structure designed not simply to maintain order, but to stimulate expanded participation, to provide access to increased demands, to secure social justice for all, and to effect a fundamental transformation of society.

Recommended Reading

*Bayly, Christopher A., *Indian Society and the Making of the British Empire*. Cambridge: Cambridge University Press, 1988. In the superb New Cambridge History of India series, this rich volume covers the period 1700 to 1858.

*Brecher, Michael, *Nehru: A Political Biography*. New York: Oxford University Press, 1959. Completed before Nehru's death, the book brilliantly utilizes the leader's life as the thread that weaves together the dramatic events of the nationalist movement and the first critical years of independence.

*Brown, Judith M., *Gandhi: Prisoner of Hope*. New Haven: Yale University Press, 1989. Widely acclaimed as the best of the many biographies of Gandhi.

*———, *Modern India: The Origins of an Asian Democracy*. New York: Oxford University Press, 1984. A text by the author of major works on Gandhi.

*Charlesworth, Neil, *British Rule and the Indian Economy, 1800–1914*. London: Macmillan, 1982. A survey of the major issues and interpretations of the economic aspects of British colonial rule in India.

*Collins, Larry, and Dominique Lapierre, *Freedom at Midnight*. New York: Avon, 1976. A dramatic, sometimes sensationalized, account of the struggle for Indian independence, taken largely from Lord Mountbatten's perspective.

Embree, Ainslie T., ed., *Encyclopedia of Asian History*, 4 vols. New York: Charles Scribner's Sons, 1988. Contains excellent entries for major subjects treated in this chapter.

*Gandhi, Mohandas, *An Autobiography, or The Story of My Experiments with Truth*. Ahmedabad: Navajivan Publishing House, 1927. Although dealing only with his early life, the autobiography is a deeply revealing portrait of this highly complex and charismatic leader.

*Available in a paperback edition.

Gopal, Sarvepalli, *Jawaharlal Nehru: A Biography*. Cambridge, Mass.: Harvard University Press, vol. 1, 1976; vol. 2, 1979; vol. 3, 1984. The official biography by a distinguished Indian historian.

Guha, Ranajit, ed., *Subaltern Studies: Writing on South Asian History and Society*, vols. 1–6. Delhi: Oxford University Press, 1982–89. On the histories of the "voiceless" and oppressed, particularly questioning historiography of "colonialist," "capitalist," and "national bourgeois" orientations.

Hardy, P., *The Muslims of British India*. Cambridge: Cambridge University Press, 1972. Surveys Muslim-Indian history under the British, emphasizing the role of religion in the growth of political separatism.

Hodson, H. V., *The Great Divide*. London: Hutchinson, 1969. One of the best studies yet written of the events surrounding partition.

Hutchins, Francis G., *The Illusion of Permanence*. Princeton, N.J.: Princeton University Press, 1967. An exploration of the changing self-image of the British presence in India and of the development of a fragile imperial confidence.

*McLane, John R., *Indian Nationalism and the Early Congress*. Princeton, N.J.: Princeton University Press, 1977. A superb portrait of the Congress in its first two decades, from 1885 to 1905.

Menon, V. P., *The Transfer of Power*. Princeton, N.J.: Princeton University Press, 1957. A detailed and dispassionate account by the man who served as constitutional adviser to the Governor General from 1942 to 1947.

Metcalf, Thomas R., *The Aftermath of Revolt: India, 1857–1870*. Princeton, N.J.: Princeton University Press, 1964. An analysis of the impact of the mutiny on British imperial policy and on the people of India.

Moore, R. J., *Escape from Empire: The Attlee Government and the Indian Problem*. Oxford: Clarendon Press, 1983. The most recent major scholarly examination of the transfer of power.

*Nehru, Jawaharlal, *The Discovery of India*. Garden City, N.J.: Doubleday, 1959. Written during the time of his imprisonment, this history of India reveals Nehru's understanding of its heritage and his perspective on the nationalist struggle.

*Sarker, Sumit, *Modern India, 1885–1947*. London: Macmillan, 1983. A basic text reflecting recent research in an attempt to write Indian history from the bottom up.

Seal, Anil, *The Emergence of Indian Nationalism: Competition and Collaboration in the Later Nineteenth Century*. Cambridge: Cambridge University Press, 1968. Examines the social roots of the Indian nationalist movement.

Sisson, Richard, and Stanley Wolpert, eds., *Congress and Indian Nationalism: The Pre-Independence Phase*. Berkeley: University of California Press, 1988. Essays on the development of the Congress party.

*Wolpert, Stanley, *A New History of India*, 3rd ed. New York: Oxford University Press, 1989. A useful, if somewhat Anglo-centric, history of modern India.

* Available in a paperback edition.

Chapter 3

The Framework: Institutions of Governance

WITH THE END OF COLONIAL RULE, LEADERS IN THE THIRD World were concerned with the consolidation of central control and a development program that would enhance their position, the welfare of the people, and the security of the state. Most believed that they could accomplish these objectives best by limiting rather than expanding popular participation. India was a major exception. Social pluralism, education in liberal democratic values, and the experience of the nationalist struggle shaped a leadership that favored the creation of a secular state and a parliamentary system of government based on adult suffrage.

The framework of the new system was determined by a constituent assembly that met for $2\frac{1}{2}$ years, from 1947 to 1950. During this transition period the new nation, with the unrelenting burden of mass poverty, faced a succession of crises—the violence and dislocation of partition; the assassination of Mohandas Gandhi; the integration of princely states; and war with Pakistan. India's leaders were undaunted in their commitment to parliamentary democracy and deepened in their resolve that it should be both centralized and federal in character. The great challenges India faced demanded a strong Center; recognition and accommodation of Indian diversity required a federal structure. Against the backdrop of partition and in the face of the continuing pressures of regionalism, the nation's leaders were determined that India remain secular and united.

The Constitution of India, adopted in 1950, is among the longest in the world, with 395 articles, 9 schedules, and, as of 1992 has been amended 74 times. It continued the constitutional development that took place under the British, retaining the basic precepts of the Government of India Act of 1935 and taking from it approximately 250 articles, verbatim or with minor changes. The constitution created a democratic republic with a parliamentary form of government. The key institutions of governance at the Center are the executive, composed of the President, the Council of Ministers (headed by the Prime Minister), and the bureaucracy; Parliament; and the Supreme Court at the peak of a national judicial system. In both theory and practice, power is concentrated in the hands of the Prime Minster.

The Constituent Assembly

The task of the Constituent Assembly was to draft a constitution that would provide a framework for democratic government and an institutional structure capable of both sustaining and accelerating change. It was to provide the instrument for stimulating increased participation and for securing the higher levels of institutionalization necessary to accommodate expanding demands.

Under the Cabinet mission's provisions for the transfer of power, the Constituent Assembly was indirectly elected in 1946 by the provincial assemblies. Reflecting the Congress victories in the provincial elections the year before, the Congress commanded an overwhelming majority in the assembly, and Rajendra Prasad was elected president at its opening session. The boycott of the assembly by the Muslim League clouded the first sessions, however, and anticipated the settlement that was to divide India and provide a separate constituent assembly for Pakistan.

When India gained independence, the assembly, functioning under a modified Government of India Act of 1935, became the Provisional Parliament. Its fundamental task, however, remained that of framing the constitution. Dr. Ambedkar chaired the drafting committee and steered the document through nearly a year of debate over its various provisions. Four leaders—Nehru, Patel, Prasad, and the Congress Muslim leader Maulana Abul Kalam Azad—through their commanding grip on the Congress Assembly Party and the assembly's eight committees, constituted a virtual oligarchy within the assembly. Issues were openly debated, but the influence of the Congress leaders was nearly irresistible.[1] Although they themselves were by no means always of one mind, they sought to promote consensus, and in the end the constitution was adopted by acclamation. On January 26, 1950, Republic Day, the new constitution went into effect.

The preamble of the Constitution embodies the substance of Nehru's Resolution on Aims and Objectives and reflects the aspirations of the nationalist movement.

> WE, THE PEOPLE OF INDIA, having solemnly resolved to constitute India into a SOVEREIGN SOCIALIST SECULAR DEMOCRATIC REPUBLIC[2] and to secure to all its citizens:
>
> JUSTICE, social, economic and political;
>
> LIBERTY of thought, expression, belief, faith and worship;
>
> EQUALITY of status and opportunity; and to promote among them all
>
> FRATERNITY, assuring the dignity of the individual and the unity of the Nation;
>
> IN OUR CONSTITUENT ASSEMBLY . . . DO HEREBY ADOPT, ENACT AND GIVE TO OURSELVES THIS CONSTITUTION.

The new India was to be a parliamentary democracy, federal, republican, and secular. There were some members of the assembly who pushed for a Gandhian constitution, one that would provide for a decentralized state with the village panchayat as its nucleus. The vast majority, however, were committed from the beginning to a centralized parliamentary government. India had had a lengthy experience with representative institutions, and its leadership had been tutored in the liberal democratic tradition. The foremost task of the new government would be to restore order and unity to the nation. Only through the centralized authority of a modern state, they believed, could India achieve the stability requisite for economic progress. Only through democratic institutions could India begin to fulfill its aspirations for social revolution. The assembly, "with an abundant faith in the common man and the ultimate success of democratic rule,"[3] sought to break down the parochialism of local loyalties through the provision for direct election by adult suffrage.

[1] Granville Austin, *The Indian Constitution* (New York: Oxford University Press, 1966), p. 22.

[2] The words SOCIALIST SECULAR were not in the preamble as originally enacted, but were added through the 42nd Amendment in 1976.

[3] Alladi Krishnaswami Ayyar in the Constituent Assembly debates, quoted in Austin, *Indian Constitution*, p. 46.

Changes in the structure of India's government—the establishment of the dyarchy in 1919 and of a federal system in 1935—brought about a devolution of authority, but power remained centralized. To achieve the goals of social change and to overcome the "fissiparous tendencies" of communalism, the pattern of centralized authority was retained in the new constitution. The quest for unity was tempered, however, by demands to accommodate India's diversity. Provincial politicians, substantially represented in the Constituent Assembly, had had a taste of power and were, therefore, unlikely to yield to a purely unitary constitution. Moreover, there was a fundamental suspicion of the concentration of power that had enabled a handful of Englishmen to hold down a nation of 400 million people. Most critical was the problem of integrating the princely states under a single constitution. With these considerations, the assembly concluded, "The soundest framework for our constitution is a federation with a strong Centre."[4]

The assembly determined also that India would be a republic, free and independent of the British Crown. After the transfer of power in 1947, India had become a dominion in the British Commonwealth of Nations. The head of state was the Governor General, appointed by the King on advice of the Indian Prime Minister. Lord Mountbatten, the last Viceroy, was asked to remain as the first Governor General, and he was succeeded by C. Rajagopalachari, who served until the promulgation of the Constitution and the accession of Prasad to the Presidency. As India was to be a republic, the government sought to retain full membership in the Commonwealth without allegiance to the Crown. The formula was expressed in India's willingness to accept the King as the *symbol* of the free association of the member nations and as such the head of the Commonwealth. The first former British colony to request republic status within the Commonwealth, India served as the example to others seeking a continued relationship with Britain that was compatible with nationalist integrity.

The Constitution of India provides for a secular state. Nehru, the architect of Indian secularism, rejected the demand for a restoration of Hindu raj as he had rejected, but without success, the notion that India was two nations, one Hindu, one Muslim. The creation of a Hindu nation, *Bharat*, as demanded by the Hindu communalists, would have vindicated the Muslim League and recognized the legiti-

[4]Second Report of the Union Power Committee, July 5, 1947, quoted in R. L. Watts, *New Federations: Experiments in the Commonwealth* (New York: Oxford University Press, 1966), p. 18.

macy of Pakistan as an Islamic nation. It would, as well, have placed India's religious minorities, particularly the 40 million Muslims left after partition, in an unenviable, if not disastrous, position. Under the Constituent Assembly, communal tension had reached a peak, and war with Pakistan was imminent. Hindu nationalists, including Sardar Patel, demanded, on the one hand, retaliatory action against Indian Muslims for expulsion of Hindus from Pakistan and, on the other, a favored position for Hindus in India. The assembly did not succumb to fanaticism, however, and adopted instead impressive guarantees of religious freedom and equal protection of all faiths. But the pressures of Hindu communalism have not subsided, and they remain today a potent force in Indian political life.

The formal institutions of government established by the Constitution provide a framework for political behavior. These institutions, often familiar in form, are frequently unfamiliar in operation. Traditional forms of behavior merge with the modern and adapt with resiliency to a changing environment. "Nothing in India is identifiable," E. M. Forster wrote in *A Passage to India*; "the mere asking of a question causes it to disappear or to merge in something else." If modern political institutions in India are often not what they appear, however, they are not mere facade to cloak a resurgent traditionalism. The structure of a political system is not simply passive and dependent. It not only responds to the environment, it also shapes the environment. In the process of development, the political system through its institutions will determine whether the nation has the capacity to meet the challenges of economic growth and social justice.

Fundamental Rights and Directive Principles Established in the Constitution

The Indian Constitution, as Granville Austin states, is "first and foremost a social document."[5] The core of its commitment to a fundamental change in the social order lies in the sections on Fundamental Rights and the Directive Principles of State Policy, "the conscience of the Constitution."[6]

The Fundamental Rights, embodied in Part III of the Constitution, guarantee to each citizen basic substantive and procedural protec-

[5] Austin, *Indian Constitution*, p. 50.

[6] Ibid.

tions against the state. These rights, which apply to both the Center and the states, fall into seven categories: (1) the right of equality, (2) the right to freedom, (3) the right against exploitation, (4) the right to freedom of religion, (5) cultural and educational rights, (6) the right to property, and (7) the right to constitutional remedies. The right of equality guarantees equal protection before the law. It provides for equal opportunities in public employment, abolishes untouchability, and prohibits discrimination in the use of public places on the ground of religion, race, caste, sex, or place of birth. The rights of minorities are specifically protected in the provisions for freedom of religion and for the right of minorities to establish and administer their own educational institutions and to conserve a distinct language, script, and culture.

The Directive Principles of State Policy delineate the obligations of the state toward its citizens. Almost a platform of the Congress party, the Directive Principles instruct the state "to promote the welfare of the people by securing and promoting as effectively as it may a social order in which justice, social, economic and political, shall inform all the institutions of the national life."[7]

The precepts of the Directive Principles are not justiciable—that is, they are not enforceable by a court, as are the Fundamental Rights. They are designed, rather, to serve as a guide for the Union Parliament and the state assemblies in framing new legislation. Although T. T. Krishnamachari, later Union Finance Minister, dismissed them as "a veritable dustbin of sentiment,"[8] the Directive Principles incorporated into the Constitution the aspirations of a new nation and are, according to Article 37, "fundamental in the governance of the country." In evaluating the impact of the Fundamental Rights and Directive Principles, Austin doubts "if in any other constitution the expression of positive and negative rights has provided so much impetus towards changing and rebuilding society for the common good."[9]

The President and the Vice President

Under the Indian Constitution, executive power is formally vested in the President, the head of state and symbol of the nation. The Presi-

[7] Constitution of India, Article 38.

[8] Constituent Assembly debates, quoted in Austin, *Indian Constitution*, p. 75.

[9] Austin, *Indian Constitution*, p. 115.

dent exercises these powers on the advice of the Council of Ministers, with the Prime Minister at its head. Both theory and practice have concentrated power in the hands of the Prime Minister.

The President serves a five-year term, may be re-elected, and is subject to impeachment by Parliament for violation of the Constitution. The Constitution specifies a complicated procedure for electing the President that is designed to insure uniformity among the states as well as parity between the states as a whole and the Union. The electoral college is composed of all elected members of the legislative assemblies in the states and of Parliament. The value of the assembly votes is in proportion to the population of the states; the value of the parliamentary votes is equal to the total allotment for the assembly.[10]

Members indicate on their ballots their first and second preferences. If an absolute majority is not obtained by any candidate on the tabulation of first preferences, the second preferences indicated on the ballots of the candidate with the fewest number of votes are then transferred to the remaining candidates. The procedure is repeated until the sufficient majority is obtained. A candidate could conceivably win even with fewer first-preference votes than the major opponent.

Rajendra Prasad, who had presided over the Constituent Assembly, was elected by that body as the first President of the Republic. Under the provisions of the new Constitution, he was re-elected in 1952 and again in 1957. Prasad was succeeded by the distinguished Oxford philosopher, Dr. Sarvapalli Radhakrishnan.

The 1967 presidential election was the first to be seriously contested, but the Congress candidate, Zakir Hussain, a Muslim, was returned by a substantial majority. In May 1969, President Hussain died, and the Vice President, V. V. Giri, took over as Acting President until elections could be held. The events that followed divided the Congress and underscored the potentially decisive position of the Indian President. The 1969 contest was between the official Congress candidate, Neelam Sanjiva Reddy, V. V. Giri, running as an independent with the silent support of the Prime Minister, and C. D. Deshmukh, candidate of the right-wing opposition parties. On the first count no candidate received a majority, but on the tabulation of the second preference votes, Giri went over the number of votes needed to win.

The drama of the 1969 election was not repeated in 1974. Congress candidate Fakhruddin Ali Ahmed won an easy victory over a single,

[10]The procedure is specified in Articles 54 and 55 of the Constitution.

Table 3–1
Presidents and Vice Presidents of India

Election	*President*	*Vice President*
1950	Rajendra Prasad	
1952	Rajendra Prasad	Dr. S. Radhakrishnan
1957	Rajendra Prasad	Dr. S. Radhakrishnan
1962	Dr. S. Radhakrishnan	Dr. Zakir Hussain
1967	Dr. Zakir Hussain (died 1969)	V. V. Giri
1969	V. V. Giri	G. S. Pathak
1974	Fakhruddin Ali Ahmed (died 1977)	B. D. Jatti
1977	Neelam Sanjiva Reddy	
1979		Mohammed Hidayatullah
1982	Zail Singh	
1984		R. Venkataraman
1987	R. Venkataraman	Shankar Dayal Sharma
1992	Shankar Dayal Sharma	K. R. Narayanan

weak opponent. In 1977, only a month before the parliamentary elections that ended 30 years of Congress rule, President Ahmed died. The Janata Party sought a consensus candidate and won the support of all parties, including the Congress, for Neelam Sanjiva Reddy. Reddy, a Janata leader from South India, had been the Congress nominee in 1969—only to lose the presidency when Indira Gandhi withdrew her support. Following Indira Gandhi's return to power, Reddy submitted his resignation, and the Congress candidate Zail Singh, a Sikh, was elected President in 1982.

Zail Singh's election, behavior, and performance in office have made him the most controversial President of India since independence. Given his limited formal education, background, and stature, many felt that his sole qualification was his loyalty to Indira Gandhi and the Nehru dynasty. These suspicions were reinforced by the way the President handled the succession following Indira Gandhi's assassination. The transition may have been orderly, but it was handled more like a dynastic succession and coronation than a democratic selection process. There were no meetings of the Cabinet, the Working Committee (the executive committee of the Congress), or the Congress party in Parliament as had been the case in past successions. Nor did Singh bother to appoint a caretaker Prime Minister. Instead the entire process was initiated and managed by a small group of retainers close to Rajiv Gandhi and Mrs. Gandhi's household, in co-operation with a handful of bureaucrats in the Prime Minister's Secretariat.[11] Rajiv Gandhi, son of the Prime Minister, one of the eight General Secretaries of the Congress party and a Member of Parliament, was immediately sworn in as Prime Minister after Zail Singh, President of India, received a letter from the Congress Parliamentary Board, an eight-person subcommittee of the Congress Working Committee, conveying its choice of Rajiv as leader. Only after the swearing in had taken place was this decision endorsed by the Working Committee and the Congress party in Parliament. The selection process, in the words of one opposition political leader, disregarded both "propriety as well as precedent." The procedure, he added, "goes contrary to parliamentary principles and practice and only betrays the ruling party's dynastic rule."[12] The process itself reflected the institutional decay that had become a major legacy of the Indira Gandhi era.

Shortly after Zail Singh selected Rajiv to be Prime Minister, however, friction developed between the two leaders. The exact source of the estrangement was unclear, but appeared to involve the Punjab issue and Singh's relations with Sanjay Gandhi, Rajiv's deceased brother. As Prime Minister, Rajiv stopped calling on the President, did not consult him, refused to brief him on foreign trips, and discouraged foreign and domestic presidential travel. The Prime Minister ignored all of Singh's efforts to patch things up and even kept silent when his own party members openly criticized the President.[13]

Initially Zail Singh suffered in silence. By late 1986 and early 1987, however, he began to counterattack. Singh, an old-time Congress politician, cleverly used the prestige of his office to question government assaults on such important institutions as the judiciary, the media, and the opposition parties. As President he demanded to know why the government did not have a clear policy on the appointment of judges, and objected to the government's failure to follow proper procedures in making judicial appointments. He refused to sign the Indian Post Office (Amend) Bill, which authorized the government to censor personal mail.[14] He questioned the government's television coverage policy, demanded an explanation from the Chief

[11] See *Economic and Political Weekly*, November 3, 1984, p. 1857, and November 24, 1984, p. 1970.

[12] *Overseas Hindustan Times* (New Delhi), November 17, 1984, p. 16.

[13] See "Mother's Boy: A Survey of India," *The Economist* (London), May 9–15, 1987.

[14] While the Indian President possesses no veto power over acts of Parliament, Singh's action provides the basis for what some Indian jurists see as the emergence of a *de facto* power.

Election Commissioner on the reasons for delaying the Haryana elections, and he warned the Congress(I)-appointed Governor of Andhra about getting involved in state politics. He also began to freely meet with members of the opposition and, even worse, with Congress(I) dissidents.[15]

The President's counterattack forced the Prime Minister to play down the rift. By early 1987, Rajiv began regularly to telephone the President and sent emissaries to seek his approval of proposed legislation. He dismissed charges of an alleged rift with the President as being fostered by his opponents. The conflict escalated into a major crisis in early March, however, when the Prime Minister, pressed by repeated rumors of a rift, publicly assured both houses of the Indian Parliament that the President had been kept informed and briefed on all important matters. Rajiv's assurances were expected to end the matter.

By late March, however, the rift mushroomed into a major political and constitutional crisis. In a letter to the Prime Minister which was leaked to the *Indian Express*, the President asserted that the facts were "at variance with" what Rajiv had told Parliament and listed a whole series of major issues about which he had received no briefing.[16] The revelations touched off a political storm. Matters were made worse when the Central Bureau of Investigation (CBI) raided the New Delhi residence of Ram Nath Goenka, chairman of the *Express* group of newspapers, searched the offices of S. Gurumurthy, an advisor to Goenka, and later arrested him.

His credibility severely damaged, Rajiv rushed to heal the break. Zail Singh's term of office was rapidly drawing to a close and a new presidential election was scheduled for July 1987. Rajiv and his advisors feared that Zail Singh might use the controversy to run for reelection, split the Congress(I) and topple Rajiv's government. Senior Congress members quickly arranged a meeting between Rajiv and Singh in early April and urged the two to sort out any misunderstandings. The effort succeeded in temporarily calming the atmosphere. Rajiv and Singh met for two hours at the President's house for a frank exchange of views.

Congress paranoia, however, reached a fever pitch as the presidential elections approached in the midst of a series of corruption scandals involving kickbacks on defense contracts, most notably involving the Swedish company Bofors. Congress panicked when the President

[15] *India Today*, February 28, 1987, pp. 16–23.

[16] *The Overseas Hindustan Times* (New Delhi), March 28, 1987.

demanded to see the entire Bofors file, and they almost went into convulsions following the Congress defeat in the Haryana elections. Opposition parties and Congress dissidents contributed to the atmosphere of crisis when they began to hold private talks with the President. Wild rumors spread that a "presidential coup" was in the making to topple the Rajiv government. Fears eased somewhat in early May when Singh issued a public statement asserting that all "reports and comments" that he intended to dismiss the Prime Minister were "utterly devoid of any basis." Even leaders of the opposition dissociated themselves from any idea of a presidential coup. Despite all of the denials and assurances, however, the fear that Rajiv might be toppled persisted. By late May, Rajiv began warning about destabilizers and asserted that his government was answerable only to the people.[17]

The immediate crisis came to an end with the Presidential elections on July 13, 1987. Because of strong objections from India's Communists, the opposition was unable to persuade Singh to seek reelection. Under Communist pressure the opposition was forced to accept V. R. Krishna Iyer, a retired Supreme Court justice, as their candidate. The Bharatiya Janata Party (BJP), however, refused to endorse Iyer, and opposition unity collapsed.[18] As a result the Congress candidate R. Venkataraman was able to sweep the polls and was sworn in as President on July 25, 1987. The first major threat to Rajiv's tenure as Prime Minister had come to an end. The conflict had, however, substantially eroded the Prime Minister's credibility.

In 1992, the Congress party nominated Vice President Shankar Dayal Sharma as its presidential candidate. The opposition parties split. The Communists and their Left Front allies supported Sharma. The Janata Dal, joined by the BJP, supported George G. Swell, a Christian tribal from the northeastern state of Meghalaya. The Janata Dal raised the issue of caste, arguing that Sharma was a high caste Brahmin and that it was time for the President to be selected from among the "depressed classes." The BJP, for its part, wanted to broaden its almost exclusively Hindu base into the Christian community. In the July balloting, Sharma secured 65 percent of the electoral college vote and was sworn in as India's ninth President.

The Vice President is elected for a five-year term by members of both houses of Parliament sitting in joint session. Votes are tallied according to the same system of simple majority and alternative pref-

[17] *India Today*, May 15, 1987, pp. 24–29.

[18] *The Far Eastern Economic Review*, July 9, 1987, p. 25.

erence. In 1992, Congress nominee K. R. Narayanan, a distinguished member of India's Foreign Service, was elected without opposition. The selection of Narayanan, an "untouchable" from the southern state of Kerala, served to balance the presidential choice of Sharma, a North Indian Brahmin. The Vice President is the ex officio chairman of the upper house of Parliament, the Rajya Sabha, and acts for the President when the chief executive is unable to carry out functions due to absence or illness. In the event of the death, resignation, or removal of the President, the Vice President assumes the responsibility of the office as Acting President until a new President is elected. Under these circumstances a presidential election must be held within six months.

Powers of the President

By oath of office the President must act "to preserve, protect and defend the Constitution." The Constitution confers an impressive list of powers on the President, but the Constituent Assembly determined that these powers should be exercised in accordance with the advice of the Council of Ministers. "Under the Draft Constitution the President occupies the same position as the King under the English Constitution," Dr. Ambedkar stated. "He is head of the State but not of the Executive. He represents the nation but does not rule the nation."[19] This view reflected a distrust of executive power nurtured by the colonial experience, but the constitutional conventions regulating the relationship between the King and Cabinet in Great Britain were not easily translated into written form. Although there were no specific provisions in the Constitution, Prasad expressed the hope in the Constituent Assembly debates that "the convention under which in England the King acts always on the advice of his Ministers will be established in this country also. . . ."[20] It was Prasad, however, who sought as President to challenge this convention. Within two months after the preliminary draft constitution was published and subsequently throughout his tenure as President, Prasad argued that "there is no provision in the Constitution which in so many words lays down that the President shall be bound to act in accordance with the advice of his ministers."[21] He frequently spoke out on policy matters and would have assumed discretionary powers, but he was per-

[19] Quoted in M. V. Pylee, *Constitutional Government in India*, 4th ed. (New Delhi: S. Chand, 1984), p. 265.

[20] Ibid.

[21] See Austin, *Indian Constitution*, pp. 135, 142.

suaded to accept a more limited role and exercise his power in accordance with convention.

Any doubt as to whether the President is bound by the advice of the Council of Ministers was eliminated in 1976 with the passage of the Forty-second Amendment, specifying that "the President *shall*, in the exercise of his functions, act in accordance with such advice."[22] In practice this means that the President acts only on the advice of the Prime Minister. The President's discretion *is* limited, but in a situation of political instability, a range of opportunities opens for decisive Presidential action. "In the ultimate analysis," M. V. Pylee states, "it is the political climate that must dictate the use of his power."[23]

There are two circumstances in which presidential discretion can come into play during periods of political instability. The first involves the power of the President to appoint the Prime Minister, and the second the power of the President to dissolve the Parliament. The first was amply demonstrated in the government crisis of July 1979. Following Prime Minister Morarji Desai's resignation, President Reddy could have dissolved Parliament and called for elections. Instead, he turned to the opposition to see whether a cohesive government could be formed. He did so with parliamentary propriety and political skill. But the new government under Charan Singh lasted only 24 days. Faced with a government crisis, President Reddy dissolved Parliament and called for fresh elections. His actions provoked a storm of controversy and denunciation from those who believed that Janata leader Jagjivan Ram should have had a chance to form another government.

A more delicate problem arose in March 1991 when the minority government of Chandra Shekhar resigned even though unchallenged by a vote of no confidence in Parliament. Although President R. Venkataraman accepted the resignation and requested the Prime Minister to continue until alternate arrangements were made, he reserved the decision on holding fresh elections. Following six anxious days of wild speculation and accusations of partisan behavior, the President announced his decision to dissolve Parliament and hold new elections. In announcing the decision, the President insisted that the delay was due solely to enable Parliament to dispose of pending financial business that would avoid a financial crisis and allow time for passage of

[22] Emphasis added. The amended constitutional article 74(1) is discussed in Durga Das Basu, *Constitutional Law of India*, 3rd ed. (New Delhi: Prentice-Hall of India, 1983), pp. 125–28.

[23] Pylee, *Constitutional Government*, p. 277.

the legislation that would extend President's Rule in the Punjab.[24]

The President appoints the Prime Minister, who then advises the President on the remaining appointments to the Council of Ministers. Under ordinary conditions the President has no discretion; the choice for Prime Minister is the leader of the majority party in the Lok Sabha, for the Prime Minister is responsible to the lower house and remains in office only as long as he or she commands its confidence. But if no party holds a clear majority, or if the majority party is torn by factional disputes, the President may play a critical role in determining who among the conflicting claimants might form a stable ministry. The Prime Minister holds office at the pleasure of the President. If the Council of Ministers has lost the support of Parliament by defeat on a major issue or by vote of no confidence, the Prime Minister must resign but may advise the President to dissolve the Lok Sabha and call for new elections. Although the President may accept such advice, parliamentary convention would suggest doing so only after surveying the possibilities for the formation of a new government by the opposition. If formation of a new government seems doubtful, the President would then dissolve the lower house and call for elections. The defeated ministry would then be invited to continue as a caretaker government until a new ministry could be formed.

On November 7, 1990, V. P. Singh's government became the first to be voted out of office by a vote of no confidence. As mentioned before, in 1979, Prime Minister Desai had resigned before the vote was taken, and Charan Singh who succeeded him lasted only 24 days and never had a chance to even face Parliament. In the 1990 crisis, instead of disbanding Parliament, the President appointed Chandra Shekhar as the new Prime Minister. Chandra Shekhar had the support of 60 MPs but was also backed by the 211 Congress (I) members led by Rajiv Gandhi.

As intended by the Constituent Assembly, the convention that presidential power be exercised on the advice of the Council of Ministers has become well established. On the advice of the Prime Minister, the President appoints the governors of the states, the justices of the Supreme Court and the state high courts, as well as members of various special commissions, including the Attorney General, who serves as legal advisor to the President, and the Comptroller and Auditor General of India, who, as guardian of the public purse, sees that both Union and state expenditures are in accord with legislative ap-

[24] *The Hindu* (Madras), March 23, 1991, and *India Today*, March 15, 1991, p. 26.

propriations. The President: serves as the commander-in-chief of the armed forces; has the power of pardon; calls Parliament into session; and has the power to dissolve the lower house. Every bill passed by Parliament must be presented to the President, who may, except in the case of a money bill, withhold assent or return the bill for reconsideration. Parliament can override presidential veto simply by passing the bill again in both houses.

Under Article 123 of the Constitution the President, on the advice of the Prime Minister, may promulgate ordinances when Parliament is not in session if satisfied that existing circumstances demand immediate action. It was through such ordinances that India was largely ruled during the 1975–77 emergency. A presidential ordinance has the same force and effect as an Act of Parliament, but the ordinance must be laid before Parliament within six weeks after it reconvenes. More extraordinary powers are given to the President in provision for three types of emergency: a threat to security by war or external aggression or by internal disturbance, a breakdown in the constitutional government of a state, and a threat to financial stability.

Under the Emergency Provisions of the Constitution (Part XVIII), the President may suspend the right to freedom and the right to constitutional remedies in situations of national emergency. In its original form, Article 352 reads:

> If the President is satisfied that a grave emergency exists whereby the security of India or of any part of the territory thereof is threatened, whether by war or external aggression or internal disturbance, he may, by Proclamation, make a declaration to that effect.

The proclamation automatically lapses if not approved by Parliament within two months.

The emergency proclaimed on June 26, 1975, by President Fakhruddin Ali Ahmed on advice of the Prime Minister, Indira Gandhi, was imposed in response to an alleged threat to internal security by the political opposition. A national emergency had been declared on two previous occasions—both in response to the threat of external aggression: the 1962 Chinese invasion and the Indo-Pakistani War in 1971 for the liberation of Bangladesh. The 1971 emergency proclamation was still in effect when the new emergency was imposed in 1975. The powers assumed by the government under this "double emergency" were unprecedented in their scope and severity.

The proclamation of the emergency in 1962 was followed by the enactment of the Defence of India Act, which provided for the detention of any person

> whom the authority suspects on grounds appearing to that authority to be reasonable, of being of hostile origin, of having acted, acting, being about to act or being likely to act in a manner prejudicial to the defence of India and civil defence, the security of the State, the public safety or interest, the maintenance of public order, India's relations with foreign states, the maintenance of peaceful conditions in any part of India or the efficient conduct of military operations.

The emergency was revoked only in 1968, long after the immediate threat of invasion, and the Defence of India Rules (DIR) were used by the government to justify preventive detention (a legacy of British days) for various offenses unrelated to national security. When the emergency was finally lifted in 1968, the rules were suspended, but in 1971, during the Bangladesh war, the DIR were again imposed. Though the actual emergency had passed, the rules remained in force and were used for unintended and miscellaneous purposes, such as the arrest of striking railway workers in 1974. The majority of those arrested during the emergency of 1975–77 were detained under the Defence of India Rules. Others—including leaders of the opposition—were arrested under the provisions of the Maintenance of Internal Security Act (MISA) of 1971. Both the DIR and MISA provided for detention without trial, and during the emergency, by Presidential ordinance, MISA was amended to enable the government to arrest persons without specifying charges—either to the detainee or to a court.

Before stepping down as Prime Minister in March 1977, Mrs. Gandhi lifted the internal emergency she had imposed 21 months before. Among the first acts of the new Janata government was to end the external emergency proclaimed in 1971. Soon afterward, Parliament repealed the DIR and MISA. In response to the abuses of the emergency, the Janata government enacted the 44th Amendment, substituting the words "armed rebellion" for the more general "internal disturbance" in the emergency provisions of Article 352. After the emergency was lifted, several states enacted their own preventive detention laws, and in mid-1979 Prime Minister Desai called for the enactment of preventive detention legislation at the Center in order to contain growing lawlessness. But the Constitution itself provides for preventive detention, sanctioning the confinement of individuals in order to prevent them from engaging in acts considered injurious to society. It was generally agreed in the Constituent Assembly that the times demanded extraordinary measures, but that detention procedures should be strictly controlled.[25] The experience of the 1975 emergency exposed its potential for abuse, as have, critics charge, the emergency measures imposed against terrorism in the Punjab.[26]

Under proclamation of a war emergency, such as that invoked in 1962 and in 1971, the federal provisions of the Constitution may be suspended and the area affected brought under direct Central control. Such proclamations must be laid before Parliament for approval within two months.

The President may also declare a constitutional emergency in a state if, on receipt of a report from the Governor, a situation has arisen in which the government of the state cannot be carried on in accordance with the Constitution. The President may then (1) assume any or all of the state functions or may vest these functions in the Governor, (2) declare that the powers of the state assembly shall be exercised by Parliament, and (3) make other provisions necessary to fulfill the objectives of the proclamation, including the suspension in part or whole of any constitutional body or authority in the state except the judiciary. The proclamation must be approved by Parliament; ordinarily it expires after six months, but it may be extended by Parliament for a maximum overall period of one year. In the years of Congress dominance, President's Rule was invoked sparingly. Its most dramatic use came in the 1959 supersession of the Communist government in Kerala, when the Center intervened in what it called a breakdown of law and order. In the months immediately following the 1967 elections, however, unstable coalitions in the North toppled one state government after the other, and within two years the Center had intervened in six states, initiating tremendous controversy over the specific events of each case and the wider problem of the Center–state relationship.

Under Prime Ministers Nehru and Shastri, from 1950 to 1966, President's Rule was imposed a total of eight times. During Mrs. Gandhi's two periods of tenure as Prime Minister, it was imposed 42 times, often with clearly partisan motivation. The dismissals of the opposition governments in Gujarat and Tamil Nadu during the 1975–77 emergency provide especially dramatic examples. This trend contin-

[25] Austin, *Indian Constitution*, p. 111.

[26] See Pannalal Dhar, *Preventive Detention under Indian Constitution* (New Delhi: Deep & Deep, 1986).

ued under Rajiv Gandhi and even the minority governments of V. P. Singh and Chandra Shekhar from 1989 to 1991.[27]

In January 1991, Prime Minister Chandra Shekhar directed the President to dismiss Tamil Nadu's Dravida Munnetra Kazhagam (DMK) government, a National Front ally of Chandra Shekhar's adversary, V. P. Singh. Opposition parties branded the action "shocking" and demanded the resignation of the two-month old Chandra Shekhar government. The Prime Minister justified dismissal of the DMK government for failure to control activities of Sri Lankan Tamil militants in the state, but the Governor had reported no breakdown of law and order and, indeed, had exonerated the state government of the allegations. The imposition of President's Rule was taken solely at Center initiative, and, in protest, the Governor resigned.

Controversy over the use of President's Rule was sharpened by action taken by the Janata government soon after it took office in 1977. To consolidate its position, the Janata Party sought fresh elections for the assemblies in those states where Congress retained power but had suffered defeat in parliamentary polling. Congress denounced the effort to dislodge "duly constituted" state governments. Averting a confrontation with the Janata government that threatened to become a constitutional crisis, Acting President Jatti dissolved the assemblies and imposed President's Rule in nine states, pending new elections. On its return to power in 1980, Congress followed the Janata precedent. The Center imposed President's Rule and called new assembly elections in those opposition-controlled states where Congress had swept the parliamentary polls. This pattern appears to have now become an established part of the system.

Parliament

The Parliament of India, as defined by the Constitution, consists of the President and the two houses, the Lok Sabha, the lower house, and the Rajya Sabha, the upper house. The fact that the President is

[27]See Sarkaria Commission, *Commission on Centre–State Relations Report*, Pt. 1 (Nasik: Government of India Press, 1988), pp. 161–89; B. L. Fadia and R. K. Menaria, *Sarkaria Commission Report and Centre–State Relations* (Agra: Sahitya Bhawan, 1990), pp. 77–105; Bhagwan D. Dua, *Presidential Rule in India, 1950–1974: A Study in Crisis Politics* (New Delhi: S. Chand, 1979); J. R. Siwach, *Politics of President's Rule in India* (Simla: Indian Institute of Advanced Study, 1979); Rajiv Dhavan, *President's Rule in the States* (Bombay: N. M. Tripathi, 1979); and S.R. Maheshwari, *President's Rule in India* (Delhi: Macmillan, 1977).

a part of Parliament stresses the interdependence, rather than the separation, of the Executive and Legislative in the parliamentary system.

The Lok Sabha

The Lok Sabha, or House of the People, consists today of 545 members. Of these, 543 are directly elected on the basis of adult suffrage—530 from the 25 states and 13 from the 7 Union Territories. In addition, the President may nominate not more than two representatives of the Anglo-Indian community, if none have been elected to the house. Seats in the Lok Sabha are allocated among the states on the basis of population, and each state is divided into territorial constituencies that are roughly equal in population. In 1976 the Forty second Amendment froze the allocation of seats, as based on the 1971 census, until the year 2001. The action was taken so that no state would be penalized through loss of seats for effective implementation of family planning programs.

The term of the Lok Sabha is five years from the date of its first meeting, but, as in Great Britain, the Prime Minister may choose the most advantageous time to go to the polls and may thus advise the President to dissolve the house and call new elections. Under a proclamation of emergency the President may extend the life of the house for one year at a time, but not beyond six months after the suspension of the emergency rules. The Constitution specifies that the house must meet at least twice a year, with no more than six months between sessions. In practice it has held an average of three sessions each year. The business of Parliament is transacted primarily in English or Hindi, but provision is made for the use of other Indian languages when necessary. Although most members have been able to speak either English or Hindi, some have been determined to speak in their mother tongues. A few have had no other choice.

Elected by the house from among its own members, the Speaker presides over the Lok Sabha, is expected to stand above partisan conflict, and is entitled to vote only in a tie. The Speaker's powers are extensive, however, and the office's influence may be considerable. The Speaker is responsible for the maintenance of order and the conduct of business in the house. Eighteen standing committees carry the burden of most of the routine business in the Lok Sabha. Some are primarily concerned with organization and parliamentary procedure. Others, notably the three finance committees, act as watchdogs over the Executive. Specific committees scrutinize the budget and governmental economy, governmental appropriations and expenditures, the exercise of delegated power, and the implementation of ministerial assurances and promises.

The Lok Sabha may conduct business only with a quorum of one-tenth of the membership, and normally questions are decided by a majority of members present and voting. The first hour of the parliamentary day is devoted to questions that bring the government to the dock of public scrutiny. At this time a minister responds to the questions that have been submitted in advance by members and faces supplementary questions from the floor that demand skill and quick judgment in answering. As in Britain, the question hour supplies information to Parliament, but more significantly it is designed as an instrument of control over the Prime Minister and the Cabinet. The questions may highlight government activity in a variety of areas, but they can also serve to insure that the Cabinet will remain responsive to the opinion of the legislative majority and sensitive to the criticism of the opposition. In the hands of the opposition, questions may seriously embarrass the government, revealing inefficiency, incompetence, or scandal. The ultimate control of the Lok Sabha over the Executive lies in its power of censure, the motion of no confidence that can bring down the government.

For a group or party to be considered an "official" party, it must have at least 50 members in the house. In the first two decades after independence, opposition at the Center was weak and heterogeneous, and it was not until the Congress party split and the breakaway Congress (O) emerged in 1969 that any party other than Congress attained sufficient strength to meet the requirements for official recognition. But whatever their strength in Parliament, members of the opposition have been consulted on the arrangement of business in the house, represented on various committees, and recognized by the Speaker in the course of debate.

The Rajya Sabha

The Rajya Sabha, or Council of States, consists of a maximum of 250 members, of whom 12 are nominated by the President for their "special knowledge or practical experience" in literature, science, art, and social service. The allocation of the remaining seats among the states corresponds to their population, except that small states are given a somewhat larger share than their numbers alone would command. The representatives of each state are elected by the members of the state legislative assembly for a term of six years. The Rajya

Sabha meets in continuous session and is not subject to dissolution. The terms are staggered, as in the United States Senate, so that one-third of the members stand for election every two years.

In the debates of the Constituent Assembly, some argued that second chambers were undemocratic bastions of vested interest and acted as "clogs in the wheels of progress." Others upheld the chamber as "an essential element of federal constitutions," declaring that it introduced "an element of sobriety and second thought" into the democratic process. In any case, as Morris-Jones wrote in his study of the Indian Parliament, "Whatever uncertainty there may have been on the purpose of an Upper House, there was at no stage any doubt that the House of the People would be the more powerful."[28] The government rests on the confidence of the popular assembly. The Council of Ministers is responsible only to the Lok Sabha, and although the Rajya Sabha has the right to be fully informed of the Government's activities, it is not empowered to raise a motion of censure and has failed to evolve a distinct role for itself.

The Legislative Process

Decision making on public policy in India is concentrated at the highest levels of authority—with the Prime Minister, the Cabinet, and the top echelons of the bureaucracy. It is the primary responsibility of the government to draft legislation and introduce bills into Parliament, although private members' bills are considered in an allotted period once a week. Any bill other than money bills may be introduced in either house. Most bills originate in the Lok Sabha, however, and proceed through three readings, as in the British Parliament. The bill is introduced in the first reading, usually by title only and without debate. It may then be referred to a select committee of the house, appointed specifically for consideration of the bill, or in the case of bills of particular importance or complexity, to a joint committee of both houses. After the bill has been reported from the committee and accepted for consideration by the house, the second reading takes place; each clause is debated and voted on. Amendments may be moved at this stage. The third and final reading of the bill is the motion that the bill be passed. After passage, the bill is transmitted to the Rajya Sabha, where it follows the same procedure.

Differences between the bill as passed by the two houses may be

[28] W. H. Morris-Jones, *Parliament in India* (London: Longmans, Greene, 1957), p. 90.

resolved by sending the bill back and forth for reconsideration. If agreement is not reached, the President calls for a joint sitting of Parliament, and the disputed provision is decided on by a simple majority vote. When the bill has passed both houses, it is sent to the President for his assent. He may return the bill to Parliament for reconsideration, but if it is passed again, the President may not withhold assent.

Bills for taxing and spending—money bills—may be introduced only in the Lok Sabha. If amended or rejected by the Rajya Sabha, such a bill need merely be repassed by the lower house and sent to the President. There are certain powers relating to the position of the states, however, that are conferred upon the Rajya Sabha alone. It may, for example, declare by a two-thirds vote that Parliament should for a period up to one year make laws on the matters reserved by the Constitution to the states. In most legislative matters, including constitutional amendments, the Rajya Sabha exercises the same power as the Lok Sabha.

Although the Supreme Court may hold an Act of Parliament unconstitutional, the Parliament may amend the Constitution with relative ease. The Indian Constitution combines both rigidity and flexibility in its amending process. The provisions may be amended in three ways: The greater portion of the Constitution may be amended by a majority of the total membership of each house and by at least two-thirds of those present and voting. Some parts, however, may be amended by a simple majority of each house, the vote required to pass ordinary legislation. For example, the Parliament may by ordinary legislative procedure, create, reorganize, or abolish the constituent states and territories of the Union if the President, after consultation with the state assemblies, so recommends. Other provisions, such as those dealing with the legislative powers of the Union and the states, may be amended only with a two-thirds majority in Parliament and ratification by not less than one-half of the states. As of 1992, there have been 74 amendments to the Constitution.

During the Nehru era, the Lok Sabha was often criticized as the Prime Minister's *durbar*, or princely court; but even though the Congress dominance was overwhelming, the opposition was respected, and Parliament was often the arena of significant debate that the Cabinet could not ignore. Although not genuinely a deliberative, policy-making body, Parliament occasionally played an important role in modifying legislation submitted to it for ratification. Although policy was initiated primarily from within the Executive, there existed a fairly regularized policy process, providing an open hearing and wide consultation on major domestic issues. The process began, as one author describes it,[29]

> with the appointment of a commission of inquiry, composed of distinguished citizens, to investigate the problem. The commission takes public testimony from various groups and individuals and produces a report which includes a set of specific policy recommendations. The ministry concerned and the cabinet study the report, consider its recommendations, and note public reactions before drawing up a draft bill, which usually includes most of the recommendations of the commission. The draft bill is next submitted to Parliament. . . .

The 1975–77 emergency reduced Parliament to a rubber stamp. Members were jailed; others simply chose not to attend; and press censorship helped silence the few critics who remained. In March 1977, parliamentary elections brought down the government of Indira Gandhi and ended the 21-month emergency. The Janata victory restored Parliament to a body of consequence, but with Indira Gandhi's return to power Parliament was again brought under the Prime Minister's shadow.

During the 1980s the role and status of the Indian Parliament declined substantially due to the attitude of Prime Ministers and the character and behavior of the Members of Parliament. Even after her return to power in 1980, Indira Gandhi totally subordinated the Parliament to executive domination. She showed scant respect for the institution, spent less and less time in the house, and used her majority to dominate the legislative process. Rajiv exhibited even less attention and respect for Parliament and spent very little time in the house. Although he worked in his office in the Parliament building, he was absent from the floor even during major debates.

The erosion of the role of Parliament brought on by increased centralization of power in the hands of the Prime Minister has been reinforced by the lack of knowledge, interest, training, competence, discipline, and decorum of its members. Most Members of Parliament have no knowledge or training in the legislative process, fail to do their homework, and lack technical competence. Absenteeism has increased as members cultivate their home constituencies or pursue varied extra-parliamentary interests. They are indifferent to executive abuse of the system, ignore poor drafting of legislation, and provide minimal scrutiny of the budget. As a result, complex bills are rushed

[29] Stanley Kochanek, *Business and Politics in India* (Berkeley: University of California Press, 1974), p. 57.

through in mere minutes, perfunctory replies to questions are provided without challenge, and grants for an increasing number of ministries and departments are passed without discussion. The decorum of Parliament has often been disrupted by rowdy confrontations between the majority party and opposition MPs.

Still, the government must remain attentive to Parliament. Although the more illustrious debaters once fielded by the opposition parties are sorely missed, Lok Sabha debates are closely followed in the daily press, and through the pressure of this publicity, Parliament keeps the Prime Minister sensitive and responsive to its opinion.

Members of Parliament

Many of the individuals who served during the 1950s and 1960s as members of Parliament, in the opposition parties as well as in the Congress, were prominent leaders of the nationalist movement and had served in the legislative bodies both in the states and at the Center. Even in the first Lok Sabha, however, returned by the 1951–52 elections, more than half the members had never before served in a legislative body. Recent turmoil in the party system has produced a considerable degree of the elite circulation in the Indian Parliament.

A profile of Lok Sabha members from 1952 to 1991 shows significant changes in education and social background over the past four decades. Contrary to expectation, however, the number of women in Parliament has not dramatically increased from the 22 (4.4 percent) in the first Lok Sabha, elected in 1952. Their number has varied over the years, with a high of 44 (8.1 percent) elected in 1984. The 1991 elections returned 36 women to the Lok Sabha (7 percent of the contested seats).

Educational standards in the Lok Sabha have been high, with 58 percent of the first Lok Sabha's MPs holding college degrees, with an upward trend to 74 percent graduates in the tenth Lok Sabha, elected in 1991. A significant trend in representation has been the change in occupational background for its members. The proportion of urban professionals—lawyers, social and political workers, teachers, journalists, and doctors—has declined steadily. The number of lawyers—the largest group in the first Lok Sabha—dropped from 37 percent in 1952 to 7 percent in 1991. These urban groups have been replaced by representatives increasingly drawn from the rural sector. The proportion of those who report agricultural backgrounds has risen steadily from 22.5 percent in 1952 to 40 percent in 1991.[30] The authors of a

[30] *India Today*, April 15, 1991, p. 72.

study of Parliament conclude that their most important finding is this "basic transfer of political power from the urban middle class as represented by the legal profession, to the rural agricultural class."[31]

The Indian Parliament, while becoming more representative and reflective of Indian society, has seen its role decline in influence, status, and effectiveness. On the whole, Parliament continues to draw members of considerable ability, although in recent years, as the states have become increasingly important political arenas, many of the more able and ambitious have been attracted to the state assemblies rather than to the Lok Sabha. As a result, many MPs find themselves in a dependent position. Unlike members of the legislative assemblies, they often lack a base of local power from which to bargain and are, therefore, likely to owe their seats to the party leadership.

The Prime Minister and the Council of Ministers

From the time of independence, India has had nine Prime Ministers, the most recent being P. V. Narasimha Rao, who assumed leadership of the Congress (I) following the assassination of Rajiv Gandhi and led the party to victory in the May–June 1991 parliamentary elections.

The Constitution provides for the appointment of the Prime Minister by the President, but by parliamentary convention, and because the ministers are responsible to the Lok Sabha, the President will choose the leader of the majority party in that house or, if there is no clear majority, a member who can command the confidence of a sufficient coalition.

The Prime Minister selects ministers, who are then appointed by the President. They are not only responsible to Parliament, but are also part of it. A minister must be a member of either the Lok Sabha or the Rajya Sabha. To draw on ministerial talent outside Parliament, however, the Constitution permits the appointment of a nonmember if, within a maximum of six months, that person becomes a member of Parliament, either by nomination or through a by-election for an open seat. Although a minister is entitled to vote only in the house to which he or she belongs, the minister may participate in the proceedings of both the Lok Sabha and the Rajya Sabha to answer questions or pilot a bill through passage.

The connecting link between the Ministry and the President as well

[31] V. A. Pai Panandiker and Arun Sud, *Emerging Pattern of Representation in the Indian Parliament* (New Delhi: Centre for Policy Research, 1981), p. 101.

Table 3–2
Prime Ministers of India

Jawaharlal Nehru*	Congress	1947–1964
Lal Bahadur Shastri**	Congress	1964–1966
Indira Gandhi	Congress	1966–1977
Morarji Desai	Janata	1977–1979
Charan Singh	Janata	1979–1980
Indira Gandhi	Congress	1980–1984
Rajiv Gandhi	Congress	1984–1989
V. P. Singh	Janata Dal	1989–1990
Chandra Shekhar	Samajvadi Janata Party	1990–1991
P. V. Narasimha Rao	Congress	1991–

*When Nehru died, Gulzari Lal Nanda became Acting Prime Minister (May 27 to June 9, 1964).
**When Shastri died, Nanda was once again Acting Prime Minister (January 11 to 24, 1966).

as between the Ministry and Parliament, the Prime Minister is, in Nehru's words, "the linchpin of Government." The extensive powers vested in the President are in fact exercised by the Prime Minister, who, with the ministers, controls and coordinates the departments of government and determines policy through the submission of a program for parliamentary action. While commanding the majority in the Lok Sabha, the Prime Minister's government is secure, but if defeated on any major issue, or if a no-confidence motion is passed, it must, by the conventions of Cabinet government, resign. Custom in Great Britain has established that the Prime Minister shall be a member of the popularly elected lower house. It was presumed that the convention would be retained in India, and the selection of Indira Gandhi, a member of the Rajya Sabha, as Prime Minister was criticized as an unhealthy precedent. She subsequently was returned from a Lok Sabha constituency. P. V. Narasimha Rao was not a member of either house of Parliament when he was appointed Prime Minister on June 21, 1991. He succeeded, however, in winning a stunning victory in a by-election in November 1991 by one of the largest margins in the electoral history.[32]

The Council of Ministers is made up of Cabinet ministers, ministers of state and deputy ministers. In accommodating various party factions with office, as well as providing representation to different

[32]For an overview, see R. N. Pal, *The Office of the Prime Minister in India* (New Delhi: Ghanshyam, 1983).

regions and groups, the Council has grown to the unwieldy number of 50 or more ministers. In the allocation of portfolios (administrative assignments), each minister is charged with responsibility for one or more ministries of Government. Typically the Prime Minister may retain certain key portfolios, such as foreign affairs. In theory, the ministers are collectively responsible for all decisions of the government, and no minister may publicly dissent from its policy. In fact, however, the Council of Ministers does not meet as a body, and although every minister is expected to accept collective responsibility, the principle has not served to protect ministers from bearing individual responsibility for policy decisions. When heavy criticism has been leveled against a particular minister, that person has frequently been dropped—as was Krishna Menon in the wake of the 1962 Chinese invasion—and the Ministry has thereby been vindicated.

The ministries and departments organized within the Central Secretariat have expanded since independence in both number and scope. Each is responsible for the execution of government policy in a particular area and is headed by a minister accountable for all that passes within the office's sphere of administration. A minister may be in charge of one or more ministries, some of which are then divided into departments. The ministry or department has as its permanent head a senior civil servant, the secretary, who acts as the principal adviser to the minister in matters of policy and administration and who is responsible to the minister for efficient and economical administration.

The Cabinet

The Cabinet is not mentioned in the Constitution, but usage has equated its functions with those assigned to the Council of Ministers under the Constitution. The Cabinet, the inner body of the council, is composed of the principal ministers who, while holding important portfolios, are responsible generally for government administration and policy. The Cabinet has four major functions: to approve all proposals for the legislative enactment of government policy, to recommend all major appointments, to settle interdepartmental disputes, and to coordinate the various activities of the government and oversee the execution of its policies.[33]

The Cabinet must be small enough not to become unwieldy, but its size, about 15 to 20, has more often been the result of political considerations than of decision-making efficiency. The composition of the

[33] Pylee, *Constitutional Government*, p. 284.

Cabinet reflects a concern for a degree of regional balance and for the representation of important communities—Muslims, Sikhs, and untouchables. The Prime Minister's choice of Cabinet members may be further constrained by the necessity to include those members of Parliament, across the political spectrum, who command a position of factional strength, although Indira and Rajiv Gandhi, to ensure that they had no rivals, appointed ministers who were both personally loyal and without independent political bases. In the Cabinet, as in the larger Council of Ministers, the distribution of the major portfolios and ranking is determined largely by the political weight of each claimant. Each member of the Cabinet is formally ranked. "Ranking of members of the Cabinet," Michael Brecher notes, "appears to be based on a composite of the incumbent's political importance in the party and seniority, as intuitively perceived by the Prime Minister. . . . Yet formal status is not a measure of influence or involvement in the decision process."[34]

Only members are entitled to attend the weekly meetings of the Cabinet, but ministers of state, chief ministers, and technical experts may be invited to attend discussions of subjects with which they have special concern. Votes are rarely taken in the Cabinet; decisions usually are reached after discussion by a sense of the meeting. Only major issues are referred to the Cabinet, and frequently even these, such as the preparation of the budget, are decided by the appropriate minister in consultation with the Prime Minister. Most matters are resolved within the separate ministries and departments, and the work of the Cabinet itself is handled largely by committee.

The Cabinet committees, organized by the Prime Minister to coordinate the functions of the various ministries, have been largely dominated by the same few ministers. As Prime Minister, Nehru himself was chairman of 9 of the 10 committees, and the Home Minister was a member of all committees and was chairman of the tenth. The Finance Minister was a member of 7. "Appointments to these committees have been made more on personal considerations than on considerations of bringing only the ministers concerned together in relevant committees."[35] In Nehru's last years the Emergency Committee of the Cabinet, set up in 1962 and composed of six senior ministers including the Prime Minister, came to assume the role of an inner cabinet and took over many of the decision-making responsibilities of

[34] Michael Brecher, *Nehru's Mantle: The Politics of Succession in India* (New York: Praeger, 1966), pp. 112–13.

[35] Asok Chanda, *Indian Administration* (London: George Allen & Unwin, 1958), p. 91.

the whole Cabinet. As Prime Minister, Nehru exercised a pre-eminent role; his dominance of the Cabinet was overwhelming.

Under Shastri the Emergency Committee declined in relative importance. The Cabinet's primacy was restored in domestic affairs, as each minister was given a greater role of initiative and discretion. If under Nehru decisions had frequently been imposed from above, decisions under Shastri reflected more of a genuine consensus. The quest for consensus reflected the new balance of power between the Union and the states as well. What Brecher termed the "Grand Council of the Republic" was an informal body that came into being during the Shastri succession, made up of those who commanded decisive influence within the Congress—in the party and in the government, at the Center and in the states. It was "the collective substitute for Nehru's charisma."[36]

The charisma of Nehru as a personality, however, has come to reside, in part, in the office of the Prime Minister, giving added strength and legitimacy to the most critical position in the Indian political system. With the authority of the office itself and her own charisma, augmented by considerable political skill, Indira Gandhi, daughter of Nehru, came to exercise enormous power, bringing the Cabinet into virtual eclipse as a source of policy influence. Through constant change and the reshuffling of portfolios, Mrs. Gandhi deftly preempted the power of her lieutenants. Although by no means ever wholly free of constraints, she commanded such unprecedented personal power in that brief period following the mandate of the 1971 parliamentary elections and the subsequent euphoria of the victory over Pakistan and the creation of Bangladesh that there were those who proclaimed her "Empress of India."

In consolidating her power, Mrs. Gandhi created the Political Affairs Committee, composed of a small group of senior Cabinet ministers under her chairmanship. Responsible for the coordination of major Cabinet concerns in domestic and international affairs and in defense, the committee became the "most important decision-making body in India after the Prime Minister herself."[37] After 1972 Mrs. Gandhi made increasing use of an informal inner circle of trusted advisers, but even their tenuous position rested on personal favor.

The Cabinet and its committees are assisted by the Cabinet Secretariat. Headed by the Cabinet Secretary, a senior member of the administrative service, it has a wide range of functions in coordinating

[36] Brecher, *Nehru's Mantle*, pp. 123–24.

[37] Kochanek, *Business and Politics*, p. 57.

the business of the Cabinet. In 1964, to ease the burdens of transition, Shastri set up the Prime Minister's Secretariat, analogous to the White House staff. Although the formal functions of the Secretariat involved the preparation "of important speeches, statements and letters," the office carried "the seed of influence," and recalling the days of the "steel frame" under the British Raj, demonstrated "the reemergence of the Civil Service as a powerful pressure group on policy."[38] The Prime Minister's Secretariat was augmented in technical expertise and strengthened under Indira Gandhi, and became the "nerve centre of political and administrative power" in India.[39] The Secretariat guards access to the Prime Minister and is composed of senior advisers, headed by the Principal Secretary, together with a staff of some 200. It is the responsibility of the Secretariat to keep the Prime Minister informed on policy issues and to shape the options for decision by the Prime Minister. Virtually every matter of importance passes through the Prime Minister's Secretariat, and under a succession of able Principal Secretaries the office has come to be the locus of decision making within the Indian government.

Within the Cabinet Secretariat is the Research and Analysis Wing (RAW), India's CIA. Established in 1968, with responsibility for external intelligence, RAW performed with a high level of accuracy during the liberation of Bangladesh in 1971, but few people even knew of its existence. Under Mrs. Gandhi, RAW reported directly to the Prime Minister, and during the 1975–77 emergency it assumed domestic political surveillance operations. RAW has now been reorganized, and its internal surveillance activities have been restricted.[40]

As power was centralized in the hands of the Prime Minister, it became more personal. The decision in 1975 to impose the emergency was taken within the "household"—Mrs. Gandhi's inner circle. No member of the Cabinet was consulted. During the emergency the circle closed to a half-dozen persons, of whom Sanjay Gandhi, the Prime Minister's 29-year-old son, was dominant. For many decisions—perhaps even her call for elections in 1977—Mrs. Gandhi kept her own counsel.

Under Morarji Desai the Cabinet acquired new importance. With few exceptions its members had independent bases of political power

[38] Brecher, *Nehru's Mantle*, pp. 115–20.

[39] C. P. Bhambhri, "A Study of Relationship between Prime Minister and Bureaucracy in India," *The Indian Journal of Public Administration*, 17 (1971): 369.

[40] See Asoka Raina, *Inside RAW: The Story of India's Secret Service* (New Delhi: Vikas, 1981).

and were leaders of the Janata Party's major factions. Finance Minister Charan Singh (who served also as Deputy Prime Minister) and Defense Minister Jagjivan Ram were the Prime Minister's major rivals. Indeed, in the clash of personalities, the Cabinet was less a decision-making body than an arena for the Janata's factional conflict.

Despite his talk about the need for decentralization, Rajiv Gandhi not only continued his mother's tendency toward the centralization of power but took a variety of steps to concentrate even more power in the hands of the Prime Minister. This was done by strengthening the role of the Prime Minister's Secretariat, further eroding the authority of Cabinet ministers and the collective responsibility of the Cabinet, and selecting for key government positions young, inexperienced members of Congress with little base of support in the party in the name of management efficiency.

Rajiv Gandhi's system concentrated power in the Prime Minister's Secretariat rather than in the Cabinet. The Secretariat was used as a mechanism to monitor almost all activities of government and to be Rajiv's private think tank. Initially the Secretariat was staffed by members of Rajiv's personal coterie, who came to exercise enormous power. In a major reorganization of his government in September 1985, however, Rajiv reverted to his mother's system of appointing top-level civil servants to all key posts in his Secretariat, while at the same time moving his former close advisers into official positions in the party and the government. The result of this reshuffle was to reduce the enormous informal power wielded by some of Rajiv's immediate political coterie, while strengthening the hand of the more controllable bureaucrats who replaced them.

The strengthening of the role of the Prime Minister's Secretariat was accompanied by a reduction in the authority of Cabinet ministers and the collective responsibility of the Cabinet. In the early years of Rajiv's system, although senior members of Congress held most key Cabinet-level portfolios, they had little independent power or control of their ministry. Cabinet ministers lost the right to allocate work among their junior ministers, and in several cases junior ministers controlled all the key functions of the ministry. Perhaps the most glaring example of this new phenomenon was revealed in the reorganization of the Home Ministry in 1986, traditionally one of the most important ministries in the government of India. The appointment of a variety of young Ministers of State assigned direct responsibility for a vast variety of specific subjects clearly reduced the power and importance of senior Cabinet members. This was true not only in the case of Home Affairs but also in several other ministries. The decrease in power of senior ministers and the increase in power of the Prime Minister's Secretariat run by bureaucrats placed Rajiv in a dominant position, and substantially reduced the collective responsibility of his Cabinet.

In a series of major Cabinet reshuffles, Arun Nehru, Arun Singh, and V. P. Singh were dropped or transferred as Rajiv's manipulative style of management was repeatedly applied to the Council of Ministers and Cabinet. In his first three years, the Indian Cabinet was reshuffled at least a dozen times and each change was accompanied by a promise that additional adjustments would follow. Every Cabinet minister had been transferred at least once, and some ministers had changed jobs four times.[41] No one was in office long enough to learn the job or take any meaningful action. The pattern continued throughout Rajiv's term in office, and by 1989, he had made changes in the Cabinet 36 times—an average of once every seven weeks.

The game of musical chairs that plagued the party, the Council of Ministers, and Cabinet also affected the higher echelons of the civil service. During the first half of Rajiv's term alone, an estimated two-thirds of India's top civil servants were reposted. This mad search for talent, however, appeared to have totally unclear objectives. The criteria for selection remained a mystery. People with backgrounds in agriculture were posted to culture; those with an expertise in finance were sent to education. People who become inconvenient were simply sent back to their home states. The demoralization caused by frequent transfers was reinforced by alteration of promotion lists, disregard for seniority, and a considerable amount of lateral entry at the top.

As Prime Minister, therefore, Rajiv Gandhi centralized power to an even greater extent than did his mother. Almost all files had to go up to the Prime Minister, and power was concentrated in the hands of a very small, narrowly based group of inexperienced personal advisors in the Prime Minister's Secretariat. This pattern of decision making enfeebled his administration and further weakened India's political institutions.

Neither V. P. Singh nor Chandra Shekhar was in a position to replicate or sustain the Indira–Rajiv Gandhi style of leadership and decision making. Both Prime Ministers headed minority governments and did not enjoy the overwhelming political authority of their immediate predecessors. V. P. Singh attempted to manage conflict and

[41] See Myron Weiner, "Rajiv Gandhi: A Mid-Term Assessment" and Francine Frankel, "Politics: The Failure to Rebuild Consensus," in Marshall M. Bouton, ed., *India Briefing, 1987* (Boulder: Westview Press, 1987), pp. 1–23 and 25–48.

maintain his authority by playing off competing interests in the party, the government, and among his opposition party supporters. During his brief tenure in office, Chandra Shekhar sought to retain control by a deft combination of the illusion of consultation and a process of vague compromises. With only 60 supporters in Parliament, Chandra Shekhar was subject to the dictates of Rajiv Gandhi and the Congress (I), which provided the essential votes to keep him in office.[42]

The election of P. V. Narasimha Rao as Prime Minister following the assassination of Rajiv Gandhi in May 1991, and the formation of a minority Congress (I) government after the national elections in June marked another major change in the role of the Prime Minister in the Indian system. Rao was born June 28, 1921, and had joined the Congress in 1938 at the age of 17. After independence he became a member of the Andhra state legislature and became Chief Minister in 1971. After 20 years in the state legislature he was elected to the Lok Sabha and became an influential member of Indira Gandhi's brain trust and a loyal supporter of the Gandhi dynasty. Despite diabetes and heart bypass surgery, he was elected leader of the Congress (I) at the age of 69. Rao was the seniormost member of the party leadership and was a compromise candidate.

Rao was a Congress member of the old school who believed in consensus politics. Initially he was haunted by the Sonia factor—the attempt by Rajiv's supporters to maintain their influence by pressing the widowed Sonia Gandhi to become the leader of the Congress (I). Sonia's refusal to enter politics and Rao's massive by-election victory in November 1991 helped the new Prime Minister to emerge gradually from the shadow of the Gandhi family. He has attempted to restore democracy to the Congress (I) by holding the first party elections in 20 years, has delegated greater power to his ministers in selecting their top civil-servant staff, has introduced a major economic reform package, and has gradually attempted to assert his authority. Still, Rao enjoyed a tenuous hold on the party, and was seen as a transition leader who could hold the party together as the Congress attempts to rebuild itself following decades of dynastic rule.

The Public Services

During the struggle for swaraj, the Indian Civil Service (ICS) was condemned as an instrument of imperialism and exploitation, its Indian

[42]Dipankar Sinha, "V. P. Singh, Chandra Shekhar, and No-Where Politics in India," *Asian Survey*, 31 (July 1991), p. 598.

members as traitorous agents of a "satanic government." At the time of independence Sardar Patel rose to defend the service. "Remove them," he said, "and I see nothing but a picture of chaos all over the country." Nehru, who had once denounced the ICS for its "spirit of authoritarianism," declared, "the old distinctions and differences are gone. . . . In the difficult days ahead our Service and experts have a vital role to play and we invite them to do so as comrades in the service of India."[43] Those who had once governed were to become servants. The instrument for law and order was to become the agent of change and development.

The structure of the public services, the "steel frame" of the British Raj, was left largely intact. The services are characterized by "open entry based on academic achievement; elaborate training arrangements; permanency of tenure; responsible, generalist posts at central, provincial, and district levels reserved for members of the elite cadre alone; a regular, graduated scale of pay with pension and other benefits; and a system of promotion and frequent transfers based predominantly on seniority and partly on merit."[44] The services are divided into three categories: state services, central services, and all-India services. Each state has its own administrative service, headed in most cases by the chief secretary to the government, and a variety of technical, secretariat, and local government services. The central government services, now 53 in number, include the Indian Foreign Service, the Central Secretariat Service, the Postal Service, and the Indian Revenue Service. Each has its own recruitment procedure, rules, and pay scales. There are also separate technical and specialist services.

The Constitution specifies two all-India services, the Indian Administrative Service and the Indian Police Service, but additional all-India services can be created by Parliament, provided there is approval by two-thirds of the Rajya Sabha. Thus far, only one, the Indian Forest Service, has been constituted. The states have opposed the creation of additional all-India services. They have argued that the higher pay for all-India officers would impose a financial strain, but in fact the states resist sharing control over the services with the central government. They also fear that local candidates

[43] Jawaharlal Nehru, *Independence and After* (New York: John Day, 1950), p. 9.

[44] David C. Potter, "Bureaucratic Change in India," in Ralph Braibanti, ed., *Asian Bureaucratic Systems Emergent from the British Imperial Tradition* (Durham, N.C.: Duke University Press, 1966), p. 142. See also David C. Potter, *India's Political Administrators, 1919–1983* (Oxford: Clarendon Press, 1986), and Hugh Tinker, "Structure of the British Imperial Heritage," in Braibanti, *Asian Bureaucratic Systems*, pp. 23–86.

may fail in an all-India competition and that the posts will be filled by candidates from outside the state.[45]

The Indian Administrative Service

At the time of independence the Indian Civil Service was 52 percent British in membership, but few chose to continue their service under the new government. With the departure of the British and the loss of Muslim officers at partition, the ICS cadre was reduced from 932 to 422. These officers retained their prestigious ICS designation and were integrated into the new Indian Administrative Service (IAS). Most of the initial appointments to the IAS were made on an emergency basis without the usual examination, but the entrance examination was soon resumed. Out of a total of more than 17 million government employees in India, the IAS has a strength of less than 5 thousand officers, representing the elite cadre of the bureaucracy.

The IAS is composed of separate cadres for each state, and recruits are permanently allocated to a particular state by the Center. To promote national integration and to secure freedom from local influence, one-half of the IAS cadre in each state should come from other states. This provision has long been under pressure, for with the reorganization of states on a linguistic basis, the vernacular became the language of administration within each state, displacing English and imposing serious hardships on those civil servants with less than perfect command of the local language. Moreover, the states have exerted increasing pressure for a policy of local recruitment. Seventy percent of the IAS officers serve the state governments and are under their administrative jurisdiction. There is no Central cadre for the IAS; senior posts are filled by officers on deputation from the states who rotate, at least theoretically, between their states and the Center. IAS officers tend to stay longer at the Center, and in practice the Center and the states are engaged in a "tug-of-war" to keep the best people. At both levels IAS officers occupy the highest positions in the bureaucracy. In recent years, however, the states have drawn more heavily upon the state services to fill top administrative posts.

The Union Public Service Commission, an independent advisory body appointed by the President, is responsible for all matters relating to recruitment.[46] The commission also concerns itself with disciplinary

[45] Chanda, *Indian Administration*, pp. 102–104.

[46] See M. A. Muttalib, *Union Public Service Commission* (New Delhi: Indian Institute of Public Administration, 1967).

matters affecting members of the services and functions to protect the services and the merit system from political interference. Its relations with the government are coordinated by the Ministry of Home Affairs, but in its day-to-day work the commission deals directly with the various ministries and departments through its own secretariat.

Despite the pervasive corruption, political interference, and comparatively low pay that has weakened the Indian bureaucracy over the past two decades, the public services continue to attract men and women of impressive ability, and at the highest levels India is well served. But senior officers earn a fraction of the salaries of their private-sector counterparts, and the result has been an unprecedented hemorrhaging of the IAS. Some of India's most competent government servants retire early or simply resign to make a lateral shift to high-level management positions in business and industry.

Recruitment to the elite all-India services is by competitive examination. Until 1978 the exams were conducted in English only, but the UPSC now permits candidates the option of writing in one of the regional languages. Recruitment can still be highly selective: In 1988, the most recent year for which figures are available, some 85,000 applicants took the examination, and about 800 were recommended for appointment. Of these, fewer than 150 went to the IAS. Competition is limited to college graduates between the ages of 21 and 28. (The age limit is 31 for members of Scheduled Castes and Tribes, those who, because of their backward or depressed status, are listed in government schedules for special protection or benefits.) Although once the highest position to which one might aspire, the IAS has lost much of its attractiveness for India's brightest youth, who may now find business offering both greater prestige and financial reward. The service continues to be dominated by the urban, westernized, and wealthy classes, but the social background of recruits has begun to change. By the 1980s approximately 20 percent of recruits to the IAS were women. Some 25–30 percent of new entrants came from the Scheduled Castes and Tribes and from the depressed classes, and an increasingly large portion was drawn from more backward states, such as Bihar and Orissa. The result is that the services are no longer as socially homogeneous as they once were, nor are recruits as westernized and "sophisticated" as their predecessors. The services are being "Indianized," but if often less polished by European standards, they are not necessarily less competent.[47]

[47] Robert L. Hardgrave, Jr., *India under Pressure: Prospects for Political Stability* (Boulder, Colo.: Westview Press, 1984), pp. 104–105.

The IAS examination reflects the generalist orientation of the service; English and general knowledge examinations and an essay that tests logic and expression are required. In addition candidates may be tested on a wide range of nonadministrative subjects. Scores are considered in combination with a screening interview, but a candidate can no longer fail on "personality" alone. Recruits, on probation, receive a year of training at the service academy at Mussoori, where they take a foundation course that provides a basic background on the constitutional, economic, and social framework of modern India, broad principles of public administration, and the ethics of the profession. On completion of the course, recruits must pass a written examination and qualifying tests in Hindi and the language of the state to which they will be allotted. A riding test, a relic of the past, lingered until the mid-1970s.

After completing their training period the recruits are assigned to one of the state cadres for one or two years to receive training in the field. The state program is organized to provide on-the-job training at every administrative level in a wide range of practical problems.[48] In the British "tradition of the amateur" the IAS officer is a jack-of-all-trades, rotated between the district and the state secretariats, between the state and the Center. At each level the demand for specialized training is far greater than in the days of the British Raj. The chief task of administration is no longer simply the maintenance of order, but development.[49]

Bureaucracy

The mistrust of the bureaucracy that characterized the period of the nationalist movement has been perpetuated in the public mind by the rigidities of the system, impersonal treatment, the preoccupation with form and procedures, and the unwillingness of lower officials to accept responsibility. This image of the officialdom has opened "a chasm between the administration and the general public."[50] The achievement of development goals, however, depends on the growth of mutual attitudes of support and responsiveness between citizens

[48] See S. P. Jagota, "Training of Public Servants in India," in Braibanti, *Asian Bureaucratic Systems*, pp. 83–84.

[49] For an examination of the All-India Services, their recruitment and training, see S. R. Maheshwari, *Problems and Issues in Administrative Federalism* (New Delhi: Allied Publishers, 1992).

[50] Rajni Kothari, "Administrative Institutions of Government," *Economic Weekly*, 27 May 1961, p. 825. The tensions between the use and abuse of bureaucratic power are examined in O. P. Dwivedi and R. B. Jain, *India's Administrative State* (New Delhi: Gitanjali Publishing House, 1985).

and administrators. The results of various surveys, although inconclusive, suggest that increasing contact between a citizen and an official tends to mobilize the citizen's support *if* that person believes the official responsive. If the official is unresponsive, as is often the case, increased contact can serve to widen the gap between aspiration and achievement, causing criticism, cynicism, and hostility.[51] Expanding participation has brought larger numbers of people into contact with the bureaucracy. If it is to cope successfully with the increasing demands made upon it, the bureaucracy must be more open, flexible, and less centralized in its decision-making responsibility. An increased specialization of function, with structural differentiation; a decline of the tradition of the amateur; and an opening of the ranks of the services to a broader social base have all served to enhance the capacity of the bureaucracy to meet the problems posed by expanded participation, but the bureaucracy remains essentially an instrument of order rather than of democratic responsiveness. It has not yet successfully adapted to the new political environment, and because it has lost much of its prestige and once-legendary efficiency, some have argued that the "steel frame" has become a cheap alloy.

The structure of an administration is an important determinant of its capabilities. At the lower rungs of the bureaucracy, formalism has served to stifle bureaucratic initiative and imagination. Procedure involves "the hierarchical movement of paper."[52] Unwilling to accept responsibility even for minor decisions, petty bureaucrats refer the files, neatly tied in red tape, to a higher level. In India, it is said, "the British introduced red tape, but *we* have perfected it." Responsibility is diluted in delay and inaction. "Red tape becomes a technique of self-preservation," writes Kothari, "and reverence for traditional forms is matched only by attachment to strict routine and an unwholesome preoccupation with questions of accountability."[53] Paul Appleby argues that it is not a question of too much hierarchy, but rather that there is an irregular hierarchy, disjointed and impeding effective com-

[51] See Samuel J. Eldersveld et al., *The Citizen and the Administrator in a Developing Democracy* (Chicago: Scott, Foresman, 1968), pp. 133–34. John O. Field finds that

> those who are most inclined to make demands on government in the sense of believing it to be relevant to the solution of various problems and in the sense of actually participating in politics beyond mere discussion or voting . . . are the people who are most likely to credit government with good intentions and satisfactory performance.

"Partisanship in India: A Survey Analysis," unpublished doctoral dissertation, Stanford University, 1973, p. 427.

[52] Paul Appleby, *Public Administration in India: Report of a Survey* (New Delhi: Government of India, Cabinet Secretariat, 1953), p. 18.

[53] Kothari, "Administrative Institutions," p. 824.

munication.[54] Administrative structure is not truly pyramidal, for authority is overly concentrated at the top. The permanent secretary to a state or central government department or ministry is accountable to a minister who holds that portfolio. The permanent secretary may exercise considerable influence over the formation of policy through advice, but more frequently the minister intervenes in the administrative process to make particular decisions rather than general policy and, when criticized, shifts responsibility to the civil servants, a situation hardly calculated to sustain morale. In an atmosphere of distrust the civil servant may seek to separate policy and administration, sabotaging the former for the protection of the latter.[55]

A relationship characterized by mutual respect between the politician and the bureaucrat is critical. The civil servant must be neither arrogant nor slavish, but in a democratic system subject ultimately to nonbureaucratic control. Over the past 20 years the bureaucracy has been increasingly penetrated, as politicians—ministers and legislators—have interfered in day-to-day administration. The moral dilemma of the public servant was dramatized in 1981 when a senior IAS officer in Bihar refused to accept promotion to a higher post because of his "disillusionment over the utterly subservient role and the insignificant authority to which the public servants in the state have been reduced."[56] In later writing of his experience, the officer, A. K. Chatterjee, identified the root of the problem as the departure from norms and a weakening of the rule of law by politicians seeking favor for their relatives and friends—friends who often consist of criminal elements, "mafia-kings and smugglers, bribe-takers and underhand-dealers." "The choice before the public servant in such a state is awkward." If yielding to political pressure in violation of law, the civil servant may not only get a share of the "grease-money," but also enter the politician's circle of friends. "That enables him to wield greater effective power through the counter-system and to 'get things done' for his own friends in contravention of rules, regulations and norms. . . . Or else, he may try to resist the privileged deal." By doing so, however, the civil servant earns the politician's wrath and "is branded as tactless and obstructive, becomes unacceptable to the political executive, and is fated to face continuous harassment and fre-

[54] Appleby, *Public Administration*, p. 28.

[55] Morris-Jones, *Government*, p. 133.

[56] Quoted in R. B. Jain, "Role Relevance and the Moral Dilemma of Public Services in India," in R. B. Jain, ed., *Public Services in a Democratic Context* (New Delhi: Indian Institute of Public Administration, 1983), p. 16. The essays in this volume were presented in a seminar organized by IIPA in 1982. Among the 60 participants were 20 senior civil servants from both Center and state levels.

quent transfers, leaving him no opportunity to show results and get any job satisfaction. Sooner or later, he feels demoralised, for in the eyes of the people too, he has been a 'failure' in service."[57]

Political interference is present to some degree in the administration of most states and at the Center. Politicians (mostly ministers) have gained leverage over bureaucrats by the threat of transfer to the *mofussil* (the "boondocks") and by control over the avenues of appointment and promotion. In Madhya Pradesh and Bihar, particularly dramatic cases, legislators as well as ministers have been able to transfer civil servants in order to bring in political cronies, to oblige relatives, or to extort favors. The result has been a decline in bureaucratic morale and efficiency. In the most extreme cases, such as Bihar, ministerial incompetence and venality have gutted effective administration.

At the same time that the bureaucracy in many states has been eroded by political interference, corruption, and low morale, its power at the Center (and in some states) has grown—so much so that it has been described as "civil service raj." Bureaucrats were subjected to enormous political pressures during the 1975–77 emergency; most acquiesced to whatever orders came down from above; some were overzealous in their exercise of newfound power. Following the change of political power to the Janata Party in 1977 and back to the Congress in 1980, punitive transfers took their toll on bureaucratic morale, but by 1982 Mrs. Gandhi—in part to restore morale, but primarily to further centralize executive authority—began to insulate senior civil servants at the Center from ministerial interference. Indeed she increasingly bypassed ministers to deal directly with the highest echelons of the bureaucracy. The secretaries of each ministry came to play increasingly important decision-making roles and were linked to the Prime Minister through the Prime Minister's Secretariat, which also opened channels to the state chief secretaries, strengthening the civil-service tie between the Center and the states.

During the transition from Congress to Janata and back again, the bureaucracy provided continuity in administration, as it did in 1947 with the transfer to power from the British to an independent India. During the last months of the Janata government and under the caretaker government of Charan Singh, the bureaucracy provided stability in a period of political crisis. Ministries and ministers may come and go, but the bureaucrats remain to provide "permanent government."[58]

Under Rajiv Gandhi the civil service again became increasingly de-

[57] A. K. Chatterjee, "Tinkering with the Rule of Law," in Jain, *Public Services*, pp. 23–26.
[58] Hardgrave, *India under Pressure*, pp. 106–107.

moralized by frequent transfers, alteration of promotion lists, disregard for seniority, and, even more devastating, Rajiv's petulant outbursts and public humiliation of high-level officials. The most dramatic incident occurred in February 1987 when Rajiv publicly announced the replacement of A. P. Venkateswaran, who had been Foreign Secretary for only 10 months, before a nationally televised press conference. Venkateswaran, who was at the press conference, was absolutely stunned. The incident touched off a public uproar and fueled the growing sense of resentment in the civil service, with the result that implementation of Rajiv's policies was adversely affected.

Although the highest levels of the Indian bureaucracy continue to command respect, that respect has diminished in recent years as cases of corruption have tarnished the image of the elite services. Corruption has long been endemic in the lower and middle levels of bureaucracy, but it has begun to reach higher, especially in those states in which there has been considerable political interference in administration. All generalizations about India are subject to qualification in terms of regional variation, and this is especially evident in judging the character of state governments. Within the Indian federal system, states range from the reasonably well administered to those that are in virtual collapse. Most states are served by senior officers of capability and integrity, but every state administration is under pressure. In some state ministries corruption is widespread and cynically accepted as a fact of life.[59]

While most people continue to see government service as prestigious, their confidence in it is low. Public servants are described as ineffectual, self-seeking, and dishonest. In a survey of residents of Delhi State, almost 60 percent felt that at least half the government officials were corrupt.[60] Corruption may be greatly exaggerated in India, because economically frustrated individuals seek a scapegoat in official misbehavior, but A. D. Gorwala argues that "the psychological atmosphere produced by the persistent and unfavourable comment is itself the cause of further moral deterioration, for people will begin to adapt their methods, even for securing a legitimate right, to what they believe to be the tendency of men in power and office."[61] Moreover, the public may decry corruption, but traditional attitudes often condone it, and fatalism may lead many to accept it as inevi-

[59] Ibid., p. 105.

[60] Eldersveld, *Citizen*, pp. 29–30.

[61] *Report on Public Administration* (New Delhi: Government of India, Planning Commission, 1953), p. 13.

table. Nepotism is officially condemned, but in traditional terms it may be viewed as loyalty to one's family, friends, and community.

In India, as in any country in which the power of a public servant far exceeds income, corruption is a major problem. The scope of corruption is greater at points where substantive decisions are made in such matters as tax assessment and collection, licensing, and contracts. "Speed money" to expedite papers and files, even when nothing unlawful is involved, is perhaps the most common form. And it probably takes its greatest toll from the poor, who can least afford it. The government has engaged in vigorous anticorruption drives, yielding numerous complaints of petty graft. Less easily substantiated are the reports of corruption at the highest levels of government. Stories circulate in the bazaars of ministers who grow rich in office and favor their family and caste fellows.

Corruption in itself constitutes an informal political system. It opens channels of influence, but access is limited to only those with the right connections and the sufficient wealth to bend political decisions to their favor. Corruption serves to augment, through illegal means, the advantages those of wealth already command through more institutionalized means of access: the press, elections, and pressure-group activity. Its consequence is fundamentally conservative.[62]

Since 1947 the central government has set up more than 20 committees and commissions to examine the bureaucracy and recommend administrative reform. Beyond *ad hoc* adjustments of nuts and bolts, however, few reforms have been implemented. Politicians are faced with more pressing demands, and bureaucrats resist any change that would weaken their power, prerogative, and privilege. As S. R. Maheshwari writes, "The bureaucracy is a cluster of vested interest which officials zealously protect and even promote."[63]

The Supreme Court and the Judicial System

The Supreme Court of India stands at the apex of a single, integrated judicial system. Although India is a federation, the centralized judi-

[62] See James C. Scott, *Comparative Political Corruption* (Englewood Cliffs, N.J.: Prentice-Hall, 1972), pp. 2–35; Stanley A. Kochanek, "The Politics of Regulation: Rajiv's New Mantras." *The Journal of Commonwealth and Comparative Politics*, 23 (November 1985): 189–211; and Stanley A. Kochanek, "Briefcase Politics in India: The Congress Party and the Business Elite," *Asian Survey*, 27 (December 1987): 1278–1301.

[63] S. R. Maheshwari, "Strengthening Administrative Capabilities in India," *Public Administration and Development*, 4 (1984): 62.

ciary is regarded as "essential to maintain the unity of the country."[64] The Court has original and exclusive jurisdiction in disputes between the Union government and one or more states and in disputes between two or more states. It has appellate jurisdiction in any case, civil or criminal, that involves, by its own certification, a substantial question of law in the meaning and intent of the Constitution. The Supreme Court is the interpreter and guardian of the Constitution, the supreme law of the land. Unlike Great Britain, where no court may hold an Act of Parliament invalid, all legislation passed in India by the Center or the states must be in conformity with the Constitution, and the constitutionality of any enactment is determined under the power of judicial review by the Supreme Court. A remarkable feature of judicial review in India is the power of the Supreme Court to rule a constitutional amendment invalid if it violates the "basic structure" of the Constitution, and it did so in 1975 in striking down provisions of the 39th Amendment.[65]

The scope of judicial review in India is not as wide as in the United States. The detail of the Constitution gives the Court less latitude in interpretation, and the emergency provisions severely reduce the Court's review powers in the area of personal liberty. The declaration of emergency itself is not justiciable, that is, it may not be challenged in the courts. Through its power of judicial review, however, the Court exercises control over both legislative and executive acts. The Court first invoked its power of supremacy in 1950 when it held a section of the Preventive Detention Act invalid and unconstitutional. The Court has since held more than 100 Center and state acts invalid, either in whole or in part, and most of its decisions have been unanimous.

The Supreme Court's decisions with regard to the protection of the Fundamental Rights, Articles 12 through 35, have been a source of particular controversy, leading Nehru to refer to the Court as the "third House of Parliament." When courts invalidated state laws to abolish zamindari estates on the basis of the equal protection clause of the Constitution, Parliament enacted the first constitutional amendment, denying courts the power to declare government acquisition of property invalid on the ground that it abridges any of the Fundamen-

[64] Dr. B. R. Ambedkar in the Constituent Assembly debates, quoted in Austin, *Indian Constitution*, p. 185.

[65] *Indira Nehru Gandhi v. Raj Narain, All India Reporter* 1975, *Supreme Court* 2299. On the "basic structure" doctrine, see Upendra Baxi, *Courage, Craft, and Contention: The Indian Supreme Court in the Eighties* (Bombay: Tripathi, 1985), pp. 64–110, and S. P. Sathe, *Constitutional Amendments, 1950–1988: Law and Politics* (Bombay: Tripathi, 1989), pp. 68–94.

tal Rights.[66] Two subsequent amendments, the Fourth and the Seventeenth, were required to free land-reform legislation from court jurisdiction. Then in 1967, in the historic *Golaknath* case, the Supreme Court ruled that the Fundamental Rights cannot be abrogated or abridged by Parliament—even by constitutional amendment.[67]

The continuing controversy between the Court and Parliament over the right to property was again confronted dramatically in 1970 when the Supreme Court struck down the bank nationalization law and the Presidential Order abolishing the privy purse and privileges of the princes. The measures had been among the most popular of Indira Gandhi's new policy proposals, and they provided the vehicle by which she could secure basic changes in the Constitution. To secure these changes, the Prime Minister sought a mandate in the 1971 parliamentary elections. With an overwhelming majority in Parliament, Mrs. Gandhi led the passage of the Twenty-fourth Amendment, effectively securing for Parliament the power to amend any provision of the Constitution, including the provisions of Part III relating to Fundamental Rights. In the landmark *Kesavananda*[68] decision, the Court upheld the Twenty-fourth Amendment, but declared any amendments passed by Parliament that attacked the "basic structure" of the Constitution would be invalid. The issue was again taken up under the 1975–77 emergency with the passage of the Forty-second Amendment (1976), which sought to bar the Supreme Court from reviewing any constitutional amendment. In the 1980 *Minerva Mills* case,[69] however, the Court struck down this portion of the Forty-second Amendment, reaffirming the doctrine set forth in *Kesavananda* that the basic structure of the Constitution cannot be altered.[70]

The Supreme Court consists of the Chief Justice and 25 associate justices. Each judge is appointed by the President after consultation with the judges of the Supreme Court and the high courts of the states, as deemed necessary. Consultation with the Chief Justice is obligatory. The judges hold office until retirement at age 65, as speci-

[66] H. C. L. Merillat, *Land and the Constitution in India* (New York: Columbia University Press, 1970), pp. 126–33.

[67] *Golaknath v. State of Punjab, All India Reporter*, 1967, *Supreme Court* 1643. See also G. C. V. Subba Rao, "Fundamental Rights in India Versus Power to Amend the Constitution," *Texas International Law Forum*, 4 (Summer 1968): 291–339.

[68] *Kesavananda Bharati v. State of Kerala, All India Reporter*, 1973, *Supreme Court* 1641.

[69] *Minerva Mills Ltd.* v. *Union of India, All India Reporter*, 1980, *Supreme Court* 1789.

[70] See Lloyd I. Rudolph and Susanne H. Rudolph, "Judicial Review *versus* Parliamentary Sovereignty: The Struggle over Stateness in India," *Journal of Commonwealth and Comparative Politics*, 19 (November 1981): 231–56.

fied in the Constitution, and may be removed only by Parliament on grounds of "proved misbehaviour or incapacity." Appointments to the Supreme Court are usually made from the benches of the high courts of the states. Although not constitutionally binding, the appointment of the Chief Justice has come to be automatic, with the elevation of the seniormost judge to that office on the retirement of the incumbent. Precedent was broken in 1973 when the President, acting on the advice of the Prime Minister, appointed A. N. Ray to succeed, superseding three senior judges, who then resigned in protest from the Court. The appointment provoked an outcry of "political motivation" from the legal profession. The Prime Minister defended the action—though hardly satisfying her critics—as in the interest of "social justice." Again in January 1977, Indira Gandhi bypassed the seniormost judge in appointing a new Chief Justice. In 1978 the Janata government returned to the principle of seniority in selecting Y. V. Chandrachud as Chief Justice, despite criticism that the justice had been less than vigorous in opposing the 1975–77 emergency.

Overall, the virtual capitulation of the Supreme Court to political pressures during the 1975–77 emergency eroded its credibility, and its prestige has not yet been recovered. In 1991, the Supreme Court was shaken by an unprecedented motion of impeachment filed by 108 Members of Parliament against a sitting justice. The motion was taken in response to charges in a government audit that Justice V. Ramaswami had, during his tenure as chief justice of the Punjab and Haryana High Court, misused state funds. Ramaswami received a temporary reprieve with the dissolution of the Lok Sabha and the 1991 elections, but, observed *India Today*, "the motion has clearly opened a new chapter in India's constitutional history."[71]

The Court is overburdened by cumbersome procedures and a staggering case load. Where the U.S. Supreme Court accepts less than 200 cases from the 4000 or more petitions it receives each year, the Indian Supreme Court accepts as many as 100,000 cases in a year, and those unresolved are added to the expanding backlog of cases. By 1990, the number of cases pending had increased to over 150,000.

If the Court is mired in judicial trivia, however, it has also taken important steps in social action (public interest) litigation and in supporting citizens' rights against arbitrary encroachment by the state. In recent years the Court has ruled on behalf of bonded laborers, tribals, women, the homeless, and "undertrials"—those jailed, some-

[71] *India Today*, March 31, 1991, pp. 44–45. Also see *India Today*, February 15, 1991, p. 41.

times for years, while awaiting trial.[72] Social action litigation in India has been an expression of judicial activism, as it has been primarily "judge-led and even judge-induced."[73] Justice V. R. Krishna Iyer took the lead toward judicial populism and from the late 1970s, with Justice P. N. Bhagwati, opened the Court to petitions from the downtrodden, expanding the protection of fundamental rights and personal liberty under the Indian Constitution.

The judges of the 18 state-level high courts are appointed by the President, usually from lower benches, after consultation with the Chief Justices of the Supreme Court and the state high court and with the Governor of the state. The selection process, however, has become increasingly politicized as state Chief Ministers have sought to place their political cronies on the bench. The number of high court judges varies from 60 in the Allahabad High Court (the high court for the state of Uttar Pradesh) to 2 for Sikkim.

In 1981, pursuant to the Center's desire that all High Court chief justices and at least a third of the judges should be from outside the state, the President transferred two chief justices to other states without their consent. This, together with the practice of transferring additional judges from one court to another, drew sharp criticism as an attempt by Mrs. Gandhi to "tame the judiciary" through intimidation. The Supreme Court, however, in a 1486-page judgment, confirmed the right of the President to transfer any judge without his or her consent—a decision by which the judiciary seemingly subordinated itself to the executive. Moreover, in the appointment of judges, the President—that is, the ruling party—was given a free hand. The constitutional provision that the Chief Justice of the Supreme Court be consulted did not mean that concurrence was required.[74]

The politicization of the judiciary has had a devastating impact on state courts. Judges feel that their recommendations are increasingly ignored, and critics argue that political considerations, caste, community, and nepotism have come to dominate the appointment process. As a result, there is a growing perception that the caliber of judicial appointments has declined and that faith in the judiciary is being undermined. In the 1980s, a series of major controversies came

[72] "The Supreme Court: The Conflicts Within," *India Today*, 15 November 1984, p. 96.

[73] Upendra Baxi, "Taking Suffering Seriously: Social Action Litigation in the Supreme Court of India," in Rajeev Dhavan, et al., eds., *Judges and the Judicial Power* (London: Sweet & Maxwell, 1985), p. 291, and, more generally, pp. 289–315.

[74] Bhagwan D. Dua, "A Study in Executive–Judicial Conflict: The Indian Case," *Asian Survey*, 18 (April 1983): 463–83. The *Judges' Transfer* case is cited as *S. P. Gupta and others* v. *Union of India, All India Reporter*, 1982, *Supreme Court* 149.

to threaten the credibility of the judiciary. For the first time since independence, the integrity of High Court judges has been called into question. Exemplary of the problem is the 125-year-old Bombay High Court, rocked by scandal in 1990 involving a property dispute that led the major bar association in Maharashtra to pass a resolution that expressed "complete lack of confidence" in four judges and asked them to step down or face a boycott.[75]

The jurisdiction of the high courts is not detailed in the Constitution, but it is provided that they retain their general appellate jurisdiction as established during British rule. In addition the high courts have original jurisdiction on revenue matters; superintend all courts within the state; and have the power to issue writs or orders for the enforcement of the Fundamental Rights guaranteed under the Constitution. Below the high courts are the district and subordinate courts, similar in structure throughout the country. At every level the case load is staggering. In 1990 there were two million cases pending in 18 high courts, and even more in the lower courts.

The modern judiciary, established by the British as a rule of law—universal, impersonal, and impartial—is today accepted as legitimate throughout India. Indeed Indians make ready use of the courts and have developed an almost unrivaled capacity for litigation. Although the modern legal system has largely displaced that of tradition, traditional groups have used the modern system for their own ends. Marc Galanter argues that "the new system is Indian: it is a unique system, peculiarly articulated to many of the interests and problems of modern India; and it is a new kind of unifying network through which various aspects of the civilization may find new expression."[76] Although the judiciary in India continues to be held in high esteem and judges enjoy a considerable degree of respect, by the early 1990s, the system has come under increasing public criticism for the first time since independence.

State Government

Each of India's 25 states reproduces in miniature the structure and organization of the Union government.

[75] See "The Judiciary: Crisis of Credibility," *India Today*, July 15, 1990, pp. 18–23.

[76] Marc Galanter, "Hindu Law and the Development of the Modern Indian Legal System," unpublished paper presented at the annual meeting of the American Political Science Association, Chicago, September 9–12, 1964, p. 86. See also Upendra Baxi, *The Crisis of the Indian Legal System* (New Delhi: Vikas, 1982), pp. 58–83.

The Governor

In his relationship to the Chief Minister and the state council of ministers and to the state legislative assembly, the *Governor* holds a constitutional position much like that of the President at the Center. The Governor is usually from another state, free from local political commitments and, presumably, able to view the problems of Union–state relations with detachment and objectivity.[77] Appointed by the President for a term of five years, the Governor may be dismissed before the expiration of the term. Until the 1970s it was the practice to consult the Chief Minister of the state as to a candidate's acceptability. In recent years, however, such consultation has lapsed as part of the larger erosion of Indian federalism. Under such circumstances, writes L. P. Singh, one of India's most distinguished civil servants and himself a former Governor, "the Governor is likely to be regarded as an imposition, and an agent of the Central Government, more so when the Centre and the State have Ministries of different political complexions. Instead of serving as a useful link between the Centre and the State, and contributing towards a smooth working of the federal system, he becomes an object of suspicion to the State Ministry."[78]

Like the President, the Governor holds the formal executive power. Although this power is, in fact, exercised by the council of ministers, the Governor has important discretionary powers to perform as the agent of the central government. It is the Governor's decision as to what lies within personal discretion. The Governor formally appoints the Chief Minister. If no clear majority is returned to the state assembly, the Governor may exercise discretion in the selection of a leader who can form a stable ministry, and although the confidence of the assembly is required, the Governor's role may be critical.

The 1967 elections highlighted this role and brought the position of the Governor into controversy. Five states were without clear majorities after the election, and in other states subsequent liquidity of support, with the defection of members to the opposition in floor-crossings, brought on so much instability that Governors had considerable room to act. In the states without clear majorities Governors

[77] M. V. Pylee, *Constitutional Government in India*, 4th ed. (New Delhi: S. Chand, 1984), p. 394.

[78] L. P. Singh, "Role of the Governor," unpublished manuscript, 1984, pp. 7–8. Also Douglas V. Verney, "The Role of the Governor in India's 'Administrative Federalism': A Comparative Perspective," *Indian Journal of Public Administration*, 31 (1985), pp. 1243–68, and "Federalism," *Seminar*, 357 (May 1989).

had to assess which of the competing coalitions could marshal majority support for a ministry; in the other states they had to determine whether the ministry retained the confidence of the assembly and, if not, whether a new ministry could be formed. If no government can be found, a state may then be brought under President's Rule. The Governor, as agent of the Union, then assumes the emergency powers of administration. Since the 1967 election the process has become a familiar one. What was once an extraordinary measure of central intervention is now almost a regular occurrence.

It was the intention of the framers of the Constitution that the Governor exercise authority independently of central control. In practice, however, the Governor has frequently functioned as "the eyes and ears" of New Delhi and has been so regarded in the states. The use of the Governor's discretionary power to dismiss a ministry has long been a subject of controversy, but the politicization of the office was no more evident than in 1984, when the Center intervened to bring down popularly elected governments in Sikkim, Jammu and Kashmir, and Andhra. The action in Andhra brought a national outcry of protest against "the murder of democracy." When the deposed Chief Minister, T. N. Rama Rao, successfully demonstrated that he retained his majority in the legislative assembly, he was reinstated—but not before the Governor submitted his resignation. Prime Minister Indira Gandhi claimed to have had no role in the affair, but the mark of central intervention was clearly evident.

In addition to emergency powers, the Governor also has certain legislative powers, including the power to promulgate ordinances. Every bill passed by the assembly goes to the Governor for assent. Most bills are government-sponsored, and refusal to assent would bring the Governor into conflict with the state ministry. However, the Governor is empowered to return any bill except a money bill to the assembly for its reconsideration. If, in the Governor's opinion, a bill threatens the position of the high court, it may be reserved for the assent of the President.

While many critics have demanded the abolition of the office of Governor, the Sarkaria Commission on Centre–State Relations concluded that the Governor served as "a vital link between the union government and the state government" and, therefore, the office must be retained.[79] It argued that most of the problems that have arisen could be solved by the development of proper traditions and

[79]Government of India, *Commission on Centre–State Relations Report*, Pt. I (Nasik: Government of India Press, 1988), p. 118.

conventions. Governors must not misuse their authority by acting as agents of the dominant party that controls the central government but must restrict their administrative role in the states to real emergencies. Similarly, the Governor must not act in ways that would thwart the popular mandate of state-level parties but should develop a responsible parliamentary role as titular leader of the state.

The Chief Minister

The Chief Minister occupies a position in the state comparable to that of the Prime Minister at the Center. Appointed by the Governor, the Chief Minister is responsible with the ministry to the popularly elected legislative assembly. Until 1967 the number of ministers in each state averaged about a dozen. In the process of ministry formation after the 1967 elections, however, the ministries were greatly expanded as additional posts were offered to counter opposition attempts to lure members into defection through the promise of ministerial positions in new governments. The Janata Dal government in Bihar, elected in 1989, had a record 76 ministers, 26 of Cabinet rank.

The Legislative Assembly and the Legislative Council

The Constitution provides that in each state there shall be a Legislative Assembly (Vidhan Sabha). Five states also have a second chamber, the Legislative Council (Vidhan Parishad). The assembly is directly elected for a 5-year-term, with a membership of not more than 500 or fewer than 60. In order to maintain uniformity in the population represented, the constituencies are reapportioned with each election in accordance with the census.

In those five states with a bicameral legislature the upper house, the Legislative Council, is selected by a combination of direct election, indirect election, and nomination, with a total membership not more than one-third of the number in the Legislative Assembly but not fewer than 40. The council is not subject to dissolution, and like the Rajya Sabha, it renews one-third of its membership every two years. Unlike the Rajya Sabha, however, the upper house of the states exercises what in fact is an advisory role alone. At most, it can delay the passage of a bill and has been attacked as a "costly ornamental luxury."

Members of the Legislative Assembly

Members of the state legislative assemblies (MLAs) command positions of increasing importance, for it is the assembly rather than

Parliament that is the legislative unit closest to the people. Likewise, assembly elections are viewed within the states as far more critical than parliamentary elections. The social character of the assembly differs considerably from that of Parliament in reflecting generally lower levels of education and westernization. The MLA is highly astute politically, however, and it is through this office that the masses make their most effective contact with the elite. Reflecting an increasing parochialization as local bosses, adept in the arenas of traditional village politics, rise to positions of state power, the legislative assemblies are the focal point of modern and traditional political styles. The successful MLA is likely to combine the styles in the role of political broker. What the voters want in an ideal MLA might well approximate the villagers' ideal described by F. G. Bailey in his study of Orissa[80]:

> Their MLA is not the representative of a party with a policy which commends itself to them, not even a representative who will watch over their interests when policies are being framed, but rather a man who will intervene in the implementation of policy, and in the ordinary day-to-day administration. He is there to divert the benefits in the direction of his constituents, to help individuals to get what they want out of the Administration, and to give them a hand when they get into trouble with officials. This is the meaning which the ordinary villager—and some of their MLAs—attach to the phrase "serving the people."

With each election the assemblies have become more nearly representative of the people, with members drawn from increasingly varied backgrounds. In Tamil Nadu, for example, the first assembly (1952–57) was dominated by a highly educated, westernized, English-speaking elite—middle class lawyers, landlords, and a variety of hereditary notables. Through the creation of a unilingual Tamil state, States Reorganization increased the number of opportunities for mobilization and participation and encouraged more traditional and less well-educated leaders to enter the government. Knowledge of English was no longer essential. Sufficient education to be an effective intermediary between the government and the people was necessary, but increasingly the MLAs lacked an adequate education for effective policy making and came to rely more heavily on the bureaucratic structure. The "legislative life" of the MLA is secondary to the role of political broker. "The average MLA comes into his own not on the floor of the Assembly but in helping his constituents to get places

[80] F. G. Bailey, *Politics and Social Change: Orissa in 1959* (Berkeley: University of California Press, 1963), p. 25.

in college, permits, licenses, and jobs. It is this kind of work that occupies most of his time, and this that pays the greatest electoral dividends."[81]

In several states, most notably Bihar and Uttar Pradesh, patronage networks and jobbery have been the conduit by which criminal elements—goondas, dacoits, and mafia-chiefs—have entered public life. In the Bihar Legislative Assembly, some 35 members are known to be criminals with offenses that range from robbery and extortion to kidnapping and murder.[82] And mafia dons—the term has become a part of Indian parlance—hold sway over extensive areas of the state. No political party has been immune from the infection, and the mix of crime and politics in Bihar and in other parts of northern India is both notorious and deeply rooted.

The states have become increasingly turbulent arenas of conflict, as new entrants—especially from the "weaker sections" of society—have sought political access. But few states, if any, have developed the institutional and resource capacity to accommodate expanded participation and new and varied demands.

Union Territories

In addition to the 25 states, there are 7 Union Territories administered by the central government through an appointed Lt. Governor or Chief Commissioner. The President makes the appointments on the advice of the Prime Minister. The territories have councils of ministers and legislative assemblies, or their equivalent, such as Delhi's Metropolitan Council, but although they may make laws with respect to matters in the state field insofar as they are applicable, Parliament may also legislate on such matters.

Local Government

The system of local government in India today retains a fundamental continuity with the past. Its hierarchical structure was built by the

[81] Duncan B. Forrester, "State Legislators in Madras," *Journal of Commonwealth Political Studies*, 7 (March 1969): 39.

[82] *Far Eastern Economic Review*, March 5, 1992, p. 22. Also see "Bihar: Domain of the Dons," *India Today*, January 31, 1992, pp. 37–41.

British on the foundations of Mughal administration and has been refined by independent India to suit the needs of a developing society.

The Local Administrative Hierarchy

The major unit of local administration is the district. There are 476 districts in India, varying in size and population from state to state and often within a state. The average area of a district, however, is about 2666 square miles, with a population of 1,785,000.

Under the British, a single district officer, commonly referred to as the collector, was charged with keeping the peace, collecting revenue, and administering justice in each district. With the combined roles of magistrate, collector, and judge, the collector represented the highest quality of the Indian Civil Service. For most Indian villagers the "Collector Sahib" was in fact *the* government. Subordinate to the collector were the district superintendent of police and the chief engineer. In the latter years of the 19th century, specialized departments for education, agriculture, and health were established, their district field representatives coordinated by the collector. Today, following the constitutional directive principle that "the state shall take steps to separate the Judiciary from the Executive in the public services,"[83] most states now have a district judge, in no way subordinate to the collector. The collector continues to be the most important government official in local administration, however. As the government has taken increased initiative in rural development and social welfare, responsibilities have been greatly enlarged, and the collector carries an almost overwhelming workload. At the same time, the role has become increasingly ill defined as both power and responsibility in local government have been decentralized, and the collector has become increasingly subject to political intervention from above.

The collector is appointed by the state government from the Indian Administrative Service or the State Civil Service. As an agent of the state, the collector is responsible for all government action in the district. The powers of office are extensive and, to some extent, discretionary. The Bombay Revenue Department Manual specifies, for example, that "nothing can or should pass in the District of which the Collector should not keep himself informed."[84] He must frequently

[83]Constitution of India, Article 50.

[84]Quoted in David C. Potter, *Government in Rural India* (London: London School of Economics and Political Science, 1964), p. 68.

be on tour, accessible to all villagers and responsive to their needs. Daily visitors may include wealthy businessmen, influential politicians, or a delegation of illiterate villagers. They come to seek favor, to register a complaint, or simply to make their presence known.[85]

In the structure of local administration, the district is divided into *taluqs* (or *tehsils.*) The taluq, usually comprising from 200 to 600 villages, is headed by a *taluqdar*, who is responsible for the supervision of land records and the collection of revenue. The government representative in the village is the *patwari*, "the eyes and ears of the Collector." Although no longer possessing the power today of the colonial period, the patwari, or "village accountant," is still "the general busybody of government."[86] Primarily concerned with land records, however, the patwari thus has a position of power with an opportunity for graft that is often difficult to resist. Traditionally the village is also served by a headman, whose position is hereditary, and by a police officer, really a watchman.

Village Government: Panchayati Raj

In the centuries before British rule, the village communities, although subject to periodic visitation by tax collectors, were left to govern themselves through a council of elders, the traditional *panchayat*, meaning literally "council of five." The panchayats declined under the British Raj, however, as a result of improved communications, increased mobility, and a centralized administration that emphasized the individual in society and not the elders of the village. By the mid-19th century the panchayats had ceased to be of real importance. At that point, however, the British sought to revitalize the institutions of local self-government. Lord Ripon declared that it was "our weakness and our calamity" that "we have not been able to give to India the benefits and blessings of free institutions." In pursuance of his Resolution of 1882, elected district boards were established to give representation and practical experience in self-government to the Indian people. The district boards (which were retained for a period after independence) were given responsibility for public works, health, and education. There were also some attempts to revive panchayats on a statutory basis as popularly elected bodies. In villages where the older, unofficial panchayats of elders still existed, these new bodies

[85] Ibid., p. 71.

[86] E. N. Mangat Rai, *Civil Administration in the Punjab*, Occasional Papers in International Affairs, No. 7 (Cambridge, Mass.: Harvard University Center for International Affairs, 1963), p. 13.

were frequently constituted as parallel panchayats, giving official recognition to matters that had been decided informally by the traditional leadership.

During the independence movement, the panchayats of ancient times were eulogized as democratic "little republics." Gandhi sought to recapture that ideal in a revitalization of village life, but for many, like Dr. B. R. Ambedkar, the village was "a sink of localism, a den of ignorance, narrow-mindedness, and communalism." According to Nehru, the Congress had "never considered" the Gandhian view of society, "much less adopted it."[87] At the Constituent Assembly a Gandhian constitution was offered, based on the principle of economic and political decentralization. The village panchayat was to be the basic unit in a hierarchy of indirectly elected bodies. A national panchayat at the top was to be responsible for such matters as currency and defense.[88] The assembly did not accept the Gandhian proposal. Stability, unity, and economic progress demanded a more centralized government, but the Constitution directed the states "to organize village panchayats and to endow them with such powers and authority as may be necessary to enable them to function as units of self-government."[89] The aim was to foster democratic participation, to involve villagers in the development effort, and to ease the administrative burden on the states. Institutions of local self-government were to be both instruments of economic development and social change and agents of community mobilization. They were intended to stimulate participation and provide channels for meaningful political expression.

In 1959 the government introduced a new system of *panchayati raj*, a three-tier model of local self government. The three tiers were linked by indirect elections. The popularly elected village panchayat was the basic unit. All elected chairs of the panchayats within a block area constituted the second tier, the *panchayati samiti*. The third tier, the *zila parashad*, congruent with the district, included all the samiti chairs in the district. In its operation, given India's size and diversity, unevenness in performance was inevitable. Structures and functions changed over the years, and it was pursued more vigorously in some states than in others. Resources available to elected bodies were meager, and MPs and MLAs generally perceived the emerging panchayati

[87]Jawaharlal Nehru, *A Bunch of Old Letters* (Bombay: Asia Publishing House, 1960), p. 509.

[88]Austin, *Indian Constitution*, p. 39.

[89]Constitution of India, Article 40.

raj leadership as a threat to their own political positions. After an initial phase of ascendancy, panchayati raj passed into stagnation and then decline by the mid-1960s.[90] Some critics have argued that the first efforts to decentralize in the 1950s and 1960s through community development and panchayati raj failed to take hold because they were unaccompanied by land reforms; given insufficient revenue or tax base; and had little real authority because state governments were unwilling to decentralize.

A second major effort at decentralization was begun in the late 1970s and 1980s by the Communist-controlled government of West Bengal and the Janata government in Karnataka. These reform schemes handed over major powers and resources to elected bodies at district, intermediate, and village levels. The West Bengal system added the important innovation of making the district collector chief executive of the Zila Parashad. In May 1989 Rajiv Gandhi attempted to pre-empt this popular reform initiated by the opposition in preparation for parliamentary elections. Rajiv introduced the Constitution 64th Amendment Bill, which would have created a nationwide program of decentralization. In the statement of objectives, the bill argued that a review of the existing system of panchayati raj had shown that the system had been unsuccessful in many states because of a failure to hold regular elections, prolonged supersessions, inadequate representation of vulnerable minorities, lack of financial resources, and inadequate devolution of power and responsibility. The new bill, argued the government, was designed to correct these defects. The bill would make it mandatory for all states to establish a three-tier system of village-, intermediate-, and district-level local bodies. Representatives would be directly elected to these bodies for five-year terms, and seats would be reserved for women, scheduled castes, and scheduled tribes. These local government bodies would be given power to prepare plans for local development and would receive financial grants from the state governments to help them carry out these plans. Elections to these local bodies would be supervised by

[90] For a review and evaluation of its operation, see *Report of the Committee on Panchayati Raj Institutions*, Asoka Mehta, Chairman (New Delhi: Government of India, Ministry of Agriculture and Irrigation, 1978). The phases are periodized on p. 4. The Communist Party (Marxist) Government in West Bengal was the first in India to allow political parties to compete in panchayat elections and used the panchayats as a basic element of its overall political and development strategy. The CPM has used these "red panchayats" to consolidate its base within rural West Bengal. Atul Kohli, "Communist Reformers in West Bengal: Origins, Features, and Relations with New Delhi," in John R. Wood, ed., *State Politics in Contemporary India: Crisis or Continuity?* (Boulder, Colo.: Westview Press, 1984), pp. 93–96.

the National Election Commission, and financial records would be reviewed by the Controller and Auditor General of India.

While the idea of greater decentralization was very popular in India, Rajiv's proposal came under attack from a variety of quarters. Critics charged that Rajiv's plan was a propaganda ploy designed to steal a popular reform introduced by opposition parties in the states. The proposal sought to legislate on a subject that was reserved to the states, and it bypassed the state governments by making local governments directly responsible to the Center. Rajiv's bill was seen by critics as a formula for greater centralization of power in the name of decentralization. The bill was defeated in the Rajya Sabha and was never implemented. The need for greater decentralization is seen by many Indians as essential to the very survival of the Indian union. Greater decentralization from the Center to the states, however, must precede any decentralization of power to local bodies.[91]

Urban Government

India is overwhelmingly rural, but according to the 1991 census, 26 percent of India's population lives in towns and cities of over 5000, and a sizable portion of these people are concentrated in the major metropolitan areas. The provisional 1991 census lists 36 cities with a population over 500,000 and, in a dramatic rise from 1951, when there were 5 metropolitan cities, 21 cities with a population of one million or more. Greater Bombay is the largest with an estimated population of 12.57 million, followed by Calcutta with 10.86 million, Delhi 8.38 million, and Madras 4.27 million. The larger cities are governed by municipal corporations, composed of a popularly elected council and a president or mayor, elected from within the council. A commissioner, appointed by the state government, is the chief executive, and the state may supersede the municipal corporation if it is deemed incapable of maintaining order and effective government. Smaller towns are governed by municipal committees or boards.[92] City government is responsible for the safety, health, and education of its citizens. It is charged with the maintenance of sanitation facilities, streets and bridges, parks and public facilities—responsibilities that it is increasingly unable to meet effectively.

The weakness of urban government in India is related in substan-

[91] See "The Panchayati Revival," *Seminar*, 360 (August 1989).

[92] The distinction between "larger" cities and "smaller" towns is not uniform but varies considerably from state to state.

tial part to the fact that the key to formal power is at the state level, external to the city. As Rodney Jones has argued, "The narrow scope of municipal government limits the service and patronage opportunities of municipal politicians to build durable political constituencies or to organize loyal clienteles. Governmental functions and services that impinge most continuously and vitally on the bulk of the urban population are not directly accessible to municipal politicians."[93] Over the past two decades, as Center–state relations have been increasingly distorted by the centralization and personalization of power in New Delhi, so the states have increasingly penetrated the autonomy of local government. At any one time, as many as half of all municipal bodies in India are in receivership, superseded by state authority, their elected assemblies dissolved in a state version of President's Rule over the cities.

It is within the city that tradition is most severely challenged by rapid change and a heterogeneity of values and behavior. The cities are the locus of new economic and cultural values, of new social roles and action patterns. The availability of mass communications and the density of urban populations have facilitated the mobilization of city-dwellers for political action. India's cities have been centers of opposition and political unrest. Demonstrations, strikes, and riots have become daily occurrences as demands rise beyond the government's capacity to respond. The city may offer rural migrants a chance for a better life, but for the middle classes it can nourish explosive frustrations. Municipal governments, stagnant and lacking adequate authority and finance, cannot begin to meet the problems before them. The state governments, responsive to the rural base of their support, have been unwilling to assume the burden of the deepening urban crisis. A high and accelerating level of political participation and a low and static level of institutionalization pose the problem of political development in stark form.

The Military

In a large part of the developing world the military has played a prominent role in political life. Coups, both bloodless and violent, have left few new nations free of military intervention. The Indian

[93] Rodney Jones, "Linkage Analysis of Indian Urban Politics," *Economic and Political Weekly*, 7 (June 17, 1972): 1198. See also Jones, *Urban Politics in India: Area, Power, and Policy in a Penetrated System* (Berkeley: University of California Press, 1974).

army has remained remarkably nonpolitical, however. The explanation does not lie in the character of the military, for with essentially the same traditions, organization, and social background, the army seized power in Pakistan. The most important causes of military intervention are political and are to be located in the availability of meaningful channels of political access and of institutions for mediating and resolving conflict. If the political system is unable to respond to increasing participation and escalating demands and at the same time maintain order, the military, cohesive and bureaucratized, may step in.

The Indian Army, numbering over one million volunteers—the fourth largest in the world—has a proud and romantic tradition, regimental color, and Sandhurst tastes. Morale, having suffered from the humiliation of the Chinese invasion, was bolstered by the heroism of Indian soldiers in the 22-day war with Pakistan in 1965 and by the stunning victory 6 years later in the liberation of Bangladesh. Indian defense expenditure declined from 1950 to 1961, then rose rapidly in response to the Chinese threat, and has since maintained an overall average of approximately 20 percent of total government expenditures, ranging from 3 to 4 percent of the Gross National Product · considerably below the world average of 7 percent.[94] Between 1972 and 1987 Indian strategic doctrine placed increasing emphasis on the use of force, and India became a major regional power. Indian troops intervened in the Sri Lankan civil war in 1987, reversed a mini-invasion of the Maldive Islands in 1988, and became involved in major confrontations with Pakistan over the Siachen glacier and Kashmir. Indian defense outlays accelerated in the second half of the 1980s to 4.2 percent of GNP in 1988–89 as India acquired a blue water navy, extended arms purchases with the West, and successfully test-fired its own short-range and intermediate-range ballistic missiles. Increased defense expenditures not only placed an increasing strain on India's domestic budget but also resulted in a series of defense scandals involving the purchase of German submarines and Swedish artillery pieces, which played a major role in the defeat of Rajiv Gandhi in the 1989 parliamentary elections. India's nuclear program has also begun to create increasing problems for Indian diplomacy with the United States and Russia.

In India, as elsewhere, however, defense expenditures are often hidden in a variety of budgetary allocations. Military expenditure

[94] See Ragu G. C. Thomas, *Indian Security Policy* (Princeton: Princeton University Press, 1986), pp. 211–15.

may thus be considerably larger than official figures indicate. In addition, India received considerable military assistance from the Soviet Union. The defense establishment has gained a powerful position in bidding for scarce resources within the public sector, but as yet the military has not sought greater leverage in political life.

The military plays an important domestic role in its "aid to the civil," that is, military intervention in civil disturbances to restore law and order. Such intervention has increased dramatically over the years, and the army has been called in to quell a series of police and paramilitary strikes; control ethnic unrest and Hindu–Muslim violence; belatedly, to put down the anti-Sikh riots in New Delhi and other cities in the wake of Mrs. Gandhi's assassination; and in countering terrorism and insurgency.[95] In Kashmir and in the ethnically unstable Northeast (especially Nagaland and Mizoram), the military has maintained a strong presence, and from the 1980s, as terrorism mounted in the Punjab, the military—armed with an impressive array of coercive legislation and ordinance—has played a major role in the troubled state's government, stepping in where civil authority had virtually collapsed.

In addition to the Army's continued role in internal security, police and paramilitary forces were expanded enormously during the period from 1969 to 1977. Between 1969 and 1971 alone, central government expenditures for police forces doubled. The units involved included the Border Security Force, the Central Reserve Police, and others organized along military lines, housed in barracks, and subject to military discipline.[96] Stephen P. Cohen, a close observer of the Indian military, writes: "It is certain that the expansion of the police apparatus was partly intended to lessen the need for regular Indian Army units to come to the aid of the civil, although it also gives the central government an enhanced capacity for coercion."[97]

[95]For an enumeration of these instances, see Stephen P. Cohen, "The Military and Indian Democracy," in Atul Kohli, ed., *India's Democracy: An Analysis of Changing State–Society Relations* (Princeton: Princeton University Press, 1988), pp. 123–28. Also see Sumit Ganguly, "From the Defense of the Nation to Aid to the Civil: The Army in Contemporary India," *Journal of Asian and African Studies*, 26 (1991): 11–26; and Fadia and Menaria, *Sarkaria Commission Report and Centre–State Relations*, pp. 106–16. The role of the military and paramilitary in controlling domestic unrest is examined more fully in Chapters Four and Five.

[96]See "The Police and Internal Security," in Chapter Five, pp. 206–09.

[97]Stephen P. Cohen, "The Military," in Henry C. Hart, ed., *Indira Gandhi's India: A Political System Reappraised* (Boulder: Colo.: Westview Press, 1976), p. 24. Also see Stephen P. Cohen, *The Indian Army: Its Contribution to the Development of a Nation*, rev. ed. (Delhi: Oxford University Press, 1990).

The military played no direct role in the 1975–77 emergency, and it was not called upon during the period of emergency rule to intervene in civil disturbances. At the time of Mrs. Gandhi's 1977 defeat, there were rumors that she might call upon the Army to secure her position as Prime Minister. She did not, nor is there any reason to believe that the Army would have acted to set aside the results of the election. The Army retains its apolitical stance,[98] but even if it were to overcome its tradition of restraint, a coup would require the concerted action of the five regional commands—no easy task. The military, nevertheless, is an important factor in Indian politics, if only in its potential. Despite the experience of the emergency, there are those within Indian society who remain enamored with authority, order, and discipline, and for whom military rule would be a welcome alternative to democratic politics.

The Responsive Capacity of India's Governmental Framework

The Constitution provided the formal framework of a political system for independent India. Once created, however, the new political institutions of the republic had to develop support and legitimacy; socialize the people into new modes of action and identity; develop linkages between the state and society, elite and mass, center and periphery; and generate policies and programs capable of meeting internal needs and external challenges.

At the time the Constitution was adopted in 1950, one of its prime architects, Dr. B. R. Ambedkar, warned that "democracy in India is only a top-dressing on an Indian soil which is essentially undemocratic." "Constitutional morality is not a natural sentiment. It has to be cultivated."[99] The Constitution was to be the agent of that cultivation. Democracy was to be achieved through its exercise.

Over the years since Indian independence, the institutions of government, established by the Constitution on the framework of the British Raj, have taken root in the Indian soil. Although transplanted, they are no longer regarded as foreign imports; they have gained le-

[98] Concern about political interference in the army was raised in 1983 when, for the second time, the seniority principle was violated in the selection of the chief of staff from among the senior generals. See Hardgrave, *India under Pressure*, pp. 108—109, and Cohen, "The Military and Indian Democracy," pp. 221–22.

[99] Constituent Assembly debates, quoted in Pylee, *Constitutional Government*, p. 7.

gitimacy and widespread acceptance by the people across the ideological spectrum and throughout India. Their meaning and operation have been adapted to the Indian environment, and they are still taking form.[100]

The great paradox is that just as the new democratic institutions were beginning to expand, deepen, and acquire support and legitimacy among the mass of society, they came into question and were repudiated by important segments of the post-independence ruling elite who wanted to impose greater order and a concentration and centralization of power upon Indian society. Led by Indira Gandhi, many of the sons and daughters of the nationalist elite who had reached maturity under the new system of competitive politics and mass franchise increasingly came to see these democratic institutions as unsuitable and incapable of coping with the problems of modern India. They saw India as politically weak, economically depressed, and lacking the international stature and recognition it deserved. They wanted a stronger, more centralized, presidential system, perhaps along Gaullist lines, that could impose order on a divided society. Mrs. Gandhi attempted to alter the system during the 1975–77 emergency, but despite her failure the dream of reshaping the system did not die. With Indira Gandhi's return to power in 1980, the debate over the future of the Indian political system was rekindled. The massive electoral victory achieved by Rajiv Gandhi in 1984 initially set the debate over a presidential system aside, but Rajiv's managerial and result-oriented style had great appeal to those who would reshape the polity in the name of stability and order. His technocratic approach brought a needed professionalism to administration, but "efficiency" is not a substitute for politics, for dialog, accommodation, and compromise.

By 1987, halfway through Rajiv's five-year term, the national mood of euphoria and renewal that had characterized his first two years deteriorated into one of despair and uncertainty, and India once again found itself in the midst of a major political crisis that threatened both the stability of the regime and the country. While some saw the crisis as resulting from the cumulative effects of Rajiv's leadership style and poor performance, many members of the Indian elite saw the problem as a crisis of the system and called for the creation of a new second

[100]For a discussion of how the institutions of Indian government took root and developed in the first phase after independence, see James Manor, "How and Why Liberal and Representative Politics Emerged in India," *Political Studies*, 38 (1990): 20–38. Also see Roger Louis and Ravinder Kumar, eds., *India: The First Ten Years of Independence* (Oxford: Clarendon Press, forthcoming.)

republic. These critics argued that India was too heterogeneous and complex to function under the Westminster model of parliamentary government, and they revived calls for the creation of a presidential system.[101] In the past, calls for a shift to a presidential system had come from the Congress (I), and many saw this demand as designed to preserve dynastic rule. By the late 1980s, however, even opposition leaders like R. K. Hedge, the Janata leader of Karnataka, and BJP President L. K. Advani began to advocate a change in the system. In the words of Romesh Thapar, "the hard fact is that our complex land cannot function under the Westminster model with any degree of coherence."[102]

Those who saw the problem as a crisis of leadership that had undermined the constitutional framework called for reform rather than replacement of the system in order to strengthen it. Among the reforms proposed were a term limit on the President and Prime Minister, electoral reform to reduce the number of parties, decentralization of power to the states and local bodies, state funding of political parties, strengthening of the judiciary, and the creation of a new development consensus.

The flexibility, adaptability, and resiliency of the Indian political system have proven to be unique among the developing nations of the Third World. Its primary strength rests in its ability to channel, manage, and reconcile conflict within a set of accepted political institutions. Its chief weakness lies in the threat of paralysis that might occur should the party system totally fragment and prove incapable of producing a stable and effective central government. One thing seems certain, however. A more centralized, brittle system is unlikely to perform more effectively in such a large, culturally diverse, pluralistic society as India without at the same time threatening to balkanize the country.

The political system has been resilient in the face of rapid change and increasing demands, but its increasing capacity is fragile, for India is only now beginning to feel the full impact of rapidly expanding political participation. The rising level of demands and their deepening intensity may strain the system beyond endurance. On gaining

[101] Among those who have argued for a presidential system is B.K. Nehru, a distinguished civil servant, former Ambassador to the U.S. and Governor of Jammu and Kashmir. See, for example, "A Fresh Look at the Constitution," *Mainstream*, January 25, 1992, pp. 9–18. Also see A. G. Noorani, *The Presidential System: An Indian Debate* (New Delhi: Sage, 1989).

[102] Statement of "The Problem" for the topic, "A Second Republic," *Seminar*, 336 (August 1987): 13.

independence, India inherited a highly institutionalized imperial regime. Relatively low levels of participation and demands provided India with a period of grace during which the institutions of order were adapted to new democratic functions. But India has, if not fallen from grace, at least outrun its institutional advantage. The revolution of rising expectations now places continuous challenge upon these institutions to respond. India's institutions are today weakened and under pressure. Indeed, in the words of Rajni Kothari, "This is the basic crisis facing India—institutional erosion in the face of massive change."[103]

Recommended Readings

Austin, Granville, *The Indian Constitution*. New York: Oxford University Press, 1966. An extremely well-written history of the Indian Constituent Assembly and an analysis of the Constitution it created.

Basu, Durga Das, *Shorter Constitution of India*, 10th ed. New Delhi: Prentice-Hall of India, 1988. A standard reference.

Baxi, Upendra, *The Supreme Court and Politics*. Lucknow: Eastern Book, 1980. A study of the Supreme Court as a political institution.

Braibanti, Ralph, ed. *Asian Bureaucratic Systems Emergent from the British Imperial Tradition*. Durham, N.C.: Duke University Press, 1966. A collection of essays dealing with various aspects of the history and structure of the government services in India.

Cohen, Stephen P., *The Indian Army*, rev. ed. Delhi: Oxford University Press, 1990. An analysis of the development of the Army, the doctrine of civilian control, and its role "in aid of the civil."

Das, B. C., *The President of India*. New Delhi: S. Chand, 1977. A detailed study of the evolution and role of the office.

Dhavan, Rajeev, *Justice on Trial: The Supreme Court Today*. Allahabad: Wheeler, 1980. A view of the Court under pressure and in need of radical reform.

Grover, Verinder, ed., *Political System in India*, 10 vols. New Delhi:

[103] Rajni Kothari, "The Crisis of the Moderate State and the Decline of Democracy," in Peter Lyon and James Manor, eds., *Transfer and Transformation: Political Institutions in the New Commonwealth* (Leicester: Leicester University Press, 1983), p. 42.

Deep & Deep, 1989. An anthology of 411 articles in 10 volumes and 7321 pages.

Jain, R. B., ed., *Public Services in a Democratic Context*. New Delhi: Indian Institute of Public Administration, 1983. An important collection of essays, examining the political penetration of the bureaucracy and the moral dilemma of the public servant.

Jones, Rodney W., *Urban Politics in India: Area, Power, and Policy in a Penetrated System*. Berkeley: University of California Press, 1974. An analysis of municipal government as affected by bureaucratic and political linkages to the state level.

Kukreja, Veena, *Civil Military Relations in South Asia: Pakistan, Bangladesh and India*. New Delhi: Sage, 1991. A study of the dynamics of civil–military relations.

Louis, Roger, and Ravinder Kumar, eds., *India: The First Ten Years of Independence*. Oxford: Clarendon Press, forthcoming. Essays exploring the Indian development in the formative Nehru early years.

Maheshwari, S. R. *Indian Administration*, 2nd ed., New Delhi: Orient Longman, 1974. A systematic and detailed description of Indian administrative structure, federal, state, and local.

———, *State Governments in India*, Delhi: Macmillan, 1979. An examination of state administration and Center–state relations.

———, *Local Government in India*. New Delhi: Orient Longman, 1971. Traces the history of local government and examines the structure and function of both rural and urban institutions.

Pal, R. N., *The Office of the Prime Minister of India*. New Delhi: Ghanshyam Publishers, 1983. A detailed study of the role and evolution of the office.

Potter, David C., *India's Political Administration, 1919–1983*. Oxford: Clarendon Press, 1986. On the durability of a bureaucratic tradition.

Pylee, M. V., *Constitutional Government in India*, 4th ed. New Delhi: S. Chand, 1984. A detailed analysis of the Constitution and the formal structures of Indian government. Highly recommended.

———, *India's Constitution*, 5th ed. New Delhi: S. Chand, 1992. A clear and concise examination of the principles and provisions of the Indian Constitution.

Seervai, H. M., *Constitutional Law of India: A Critical Commentary*, 4th ed., 2 vols. Bombay: Tripathi, 1990, 1991. The major treatise on Indian constitutional law. A valuable and authoritative source.

Shukla, J. D., *State and District Administration in India*. New Delhi: National, for the Indian Institute of Public Administration, 1976. A systematic description of the structure of administration.

Venkateswaran, R. J., *Cabinet Government in India*, London: George Allen & Unwin, 1967. An examination of Cabinet operations under Nehru and Shastri, and Indira Gandhi in the first year of her leadership.

Chapter 4

The Challenge of Federalism

ELITES IN DEVELOPING COUNTRIES ARE DETERMINED TO create strong centralized states in order to sustain national integration, ensure security, and direct development. Yet even in the West the history of state making has demonstrated that these efforts will always be resisted by antecedent social forces.[1] In India the nationalist elite, drawing on the colonial experience and faced by the chaos of partition, the integration of princely states, and demands for the creation of unilingual states, created a highly centralized federal system. Initially this decision faced only a minimum of opposition from existing constituent units. As the immediate post-independence crisis passed and the nationalist elite accepted the demand for redrawing the administrative map of India along linguistic lines, the politics of mass franchise gradually began to strengthen the federal base of the Indian polity. During the 1970s, however, Indira Gandhi sought to reverse this process of devolution of power to the states, thus bringing about increased tensions in center–state relations and a crisis in Indian federalism. As a result, of all the decisions made by the Constituent Assembly, the federal compact is under most severe pressure, with demands for greater state autonomy and secessionist movements in the Punjab, Kashmir, and the Northeast.

[1] See Charles Tilly, ed., *The Formation of National States in Western Europe* (Princeton, N.J.: Princeton University Press, 1975) and Raymond Grew, ed., *Crises of Political Development in Europe and the United States* (Princeton, N.J.: Princeton University Press, 1978).

The Origins and Nature of Federalism in India

The Indian Constitution provides for a federal system with certain unitary features and a formal bias in favor of the Center. A unitary system of government places all legal power in the central government. Lower units of government are created by the Center. They derive their power from the Center and exist for its administrative convenience. In contrast, a federal system is one in which powers are divided between a central government and certain units of local government, typically states. Each level of government exercises some powers independently of the other. Federations take many forms, and the division of powers between the Center and the states may be very unequal.

Because of its origins, traditions, and development, federalism in India has evolved a unique form. Federalism did not come about as a device to control power or as a result of a coming together of a group of independent states, but through a gradual process of the devolution of power from a highly centralized colonial regime. From the earliest Governmental Regulatory Acts of 1773 until independence, India was governed as a unitary and not as a federal state. Although provinces existed in British India, they were primarily administrative and not political units. They had no legal rights and acted solely as agents of the central government.

The idea of a federal solution for India's problems was first introduced after World War I. The debate did not become pronounced until the 1930s, when the principle was finally accepted. Federalism emerged as a possible political formula to solve two of the most intractable problems that existed in British India: the future of the semiautonomous princely states and the Muslim demands for greater autonomy.[2] Prior to independence the Indian subcontinent was divided into two separate entities—the provinces of British India and 562 princely states. The provinces of British India were under the direct control of the British Crown. The princely states were under the rule of local Indian princes who enjoyed a great deal of autonomy within their states, while at the same time accepting the paramountcy of the British Crown over their defense and foreign affairs. The Princes controlled about two-fifths of the Indian subcontinent and ruled over some 60 million people.

The Muslims represented one of the two major religious commu-

[2]S. P. Aiyar, "The Federal Idea in India," in S. P. Aiyar and Usha Mehta, eds., *Essays on Indian Federalism* (Bombay: Allied Publishers, 1965), pp. 1–33.

nities of India and totaled 24 percent of the Indian population prior to partition. Although most of the Muslims were concentrated in western and eastern India, large numbers were also located in the states of Hyderabad and Kashmir, with the remainder largely scattered across the great Gangetic Plain. As a minority, the Muslims feared being submerged in a Hindu sea, and demanded a variety of constitutional safeguards that the federal principle seemed to provide.

In an attempt to satisfy the demands of these two important constituencies, the British introduced a set of political reforms in 1935. The reforms were contained in the Government of India Act of 1935, and marked a sharp break with the former unitary tradition of British control. For the first time since the British conquest, there was to be created a federal union consisting of the autonomous provinces of British India and those Indian princely states that agreed to join it. Because the reforms of 1935 assumed continued British rule, however, the federal system envisioned was highly centralized and provided for a wide variety of special powers to be exercised by the Governor General, the representative of the British Crown in India. Although the full provisions of the Government of India Act of 1935 never came into force, the Act established the principle of federalism for the Indian subcontinent.

Despite the partition of the subcontinent into India and Pakistan and the integration of the princely states into these successor republics of British India, the idea of federalism seemed to be taken for granted by those who drafted a constitution for free India. However, the form of federalism that emerged from the Constituent Assembly was highly centralized. In theory, the system was so highly centralized that some critics have characterized it as quasi-federal[3] or even unitary.[4] Others have called it cooperative federalism.[5] Several factors contributed to the particular pattern of federalism that emerged in India after 1947. In the first place, the British colonial pattern of centralization had a substantial impact on the thinking of the Indian political leadership, and their immediate colonial experience tended to influence their decision. Second, states' rights never loomed large in the early debates on the future government for a free India and did not emerge until much later. Issues of states' rights were primarily subordinate to the larger issue of communal rights and communal

[3]K. C. Wheare, *Federal Government* (New York: Oxford University Press, 1951), p. 28.

[4]Asok Chanda, *Federalism in India* (London: George Allen and Unwin, 1965), p. 124.

[5]Granville Austin, *The Indian Constitution: Cornerstone of a Nation* (London: Oxford University Press, 1966), p. 187.

status between Hindus and Muslims. Once partition took place, the need for federalism seemed less urgent, whereas partition itself seemed to have demonstrated the inherent dangers of separatism. Third, the Indian provinces carved out by the British were primarily administrative units rather than linguistic, cultural, or ethnic units. Therefore they lacked the natural basis of identity that emerged later with the creation of unilingual states. Fourth, the series of crises that followed independence and occurred while the Constituent Assembly deliberated predisposed the political leadership toward centralization. The chaos of partition, communal frenzy, the India–Pakistan war, and the problem of integrating the princely states into the Indian Union all combined to create an atmosphere that favored a centralized form of federalism. Fifth, the goals of economic development and modernization seemed to require a strong central authority capable of directing the economy. Finally, the existence of a highly centralized, dominant, mass party and the absence of strong state and regional parties supported a centralized formula. In short, although no one seemed to seriously question the notion that India should be a federal republic, a variety of factors combined to ensure that the form of federalism would be highly centralized.[6]

Although there are numerous special features of the Indian Constitution that give it its highly centralized form,[7] the two most important are the distribution of powers between the central government and the states and the financial provisions affecting the distribution of revenues.

In India the states do not have their own separate constitutions.[8] The Constitution of India defines the powers of both the Center and the states and provides for the governmental structures of each. Under the Constitution the division of powers between the Center and the states is laid down in the Seventh Schedule of the Constitution in three lists exhausting "all the ordinary activities of government." The Union List gives the Center exclusive authority to act in matters of

[6] Austin, *Indian Constitution*, pp. 188–91.

[7] Other centralizing features of the Indian constitution include: a single integrated hierarchical judicial system; all-India administrative services that provide officers at the national, state, and district levels; a national police force; and a national Election Commission that supervises all national and state elections. The states play a role in the amending process with respect to only a few constitutional provisions, and certain state bills require presidential assent.

[8] Kashmir, with its own constitution, is the exception. The terms of accession in 1947 granted Kashmir special status in the Union of India, and Article 370 exempts Kashmir from various provisions of the Indian Constitution.

national importance and includes among its 97 items defense, foreign affairs, currency, banking duties, and income taxation. The State List, with 66 items, covers public order and police, welfare, health, education, local government, industry, agriculture, and land revenue. The Concurrent List contains 47 items over which the Center and the states share authority. The most important are civil and criminal law and social and economic planning. The residual power lies with the Union, and in any conflict between Union and state, Union law prevails. The paramount position of the Center is underscored by the power of Parliament to create new states, to alter the boundaries of existing states, and even to abolish a state by ordinary legislative procedure without recourse to constitutional amendment.

Not only does the central government have a wide range of powers in its own right under the Union List, but these powers are also enhanced by the fact that the central government is vested with a variety of powers which enable it, under certain circumstances, to invade the legislative and executive domain of the states. These special powers take three forms: the emergency powers under Articles 356, 352, and 360; the use of Union Executive powers under Articles 256, 257, and 365; and special legislative powers granted under Article 249.

The emergency powers contained in the Indian Constitution enable India, under certain circumstances, to transform itself into a unitary state. There are three types of constitutional emergency powers that combine to create a highly centralized pattern of federalism: (1) an emergency, under Article 356, arising out of a failure of the constitutional machinery in a state; (2) a national emergency, under Article 352, involving the security of India or of any part threatened by war, external aggression, or internal disturbances; and (3) a special emergency, under Article 360, involving a threat to financial security, stability, or credit. Under these emergency provisions, the Union Executive and the Parliament can direct a provincial government in the use of its powers or assume all of its powers, the Union Executive acting for the Provincial Executive and the Parliament enacting legislation as if it were the provincial legislature.

Under Articles 256, 257, and 365, the central government may take on Union Executive powers that give direction to state governments and invoke substantial penalties for noncompliance. Articles 256 and 257 state that the executive power of a province must be exercised so as to comply with Union laws and so as not to impede or prejudice the exercise of Union Executive authority. To ensure that both these stipulations are obeyed, the Union Executive may give direction to a state government as to the manner in which it should act, and if a state government does not comply with these directions, the Union government, under Article 365, may take over the running of the state.

Finally, under Article 249, the Rajya Sabha, the upper house of the Indian legislature, may give the Parliament special legislative powers over any matter included in the state legislative list. Thus, if legislation is called for on a national scale, the central legislature has the power to enact it, even if it is in the State List.

In addition to its constitutional right to modify the distribution of powers between the Center and the states under certain circumstances, the central government also has vast powers over the collection and distribution of revenues, which make the states heavily dependent on the central government for financial support.[9] Under the Indian Constitution, financial assistance flows from the central government to the states in two major ways. The first is through a system of divisible taxes and grants-in-aid under Article 275. In India the Union government acts as a banker and collecting agent for the state governments. With the exception of taxes concerned with land, sales taxes, and certain taxes levied by the Union but collected by the states, most taxes in India are levied and collected by the Union government. Part of the revenue collected is retained by the Union government, but substantial portions of the revenue collected by the Union are redistributed to the states, based on a formula determined every five years by a semijudicial adjudgment of the Finance Commission. Funds distributed yearly according to the Finance Commission's formula are used to finance normal state budget expenditures and account for a significant portion of the state's annual budget.

In many ways, however, the devolution of revenue under Article 275 has been superseded by Article 282, which gives the Union government the power to make grants for any public purpose, even though the purpose is one for which Parliament cannot normally legislate. Under this provision the central government allocates vast amounts of development funds to the states as part of the Indian Five Year Plans drawn up by the Planning Commission, an extra constitutional advisory body of the central Cabinet. The resources available under the plan are substantial because of the significant taxing power of the central government and its control over foreign aid and deficit financing, which represent an important part of plan investment.

[9]See P. K. Bhargava, "Transfers from the Center to the States in India," *Asian Survey*, 24 (June 1984):665–87.

Thus, the discretionary control of grants to the states far exceeds the amounts which are transferred through divisible taxes and grants-in-aid under Article 275, and the decisions of the Planning Commission have a far greater impact on what the states can do than do the recommendations of the constitutionally based Finance Commission.

In short, several things impart to Indian federalism a highly centralized form: the constitutional right of the central government to invade the legislative and executive domain of the states; the power of the Center to intervene in state affairs and exercise supervisory powers over the states; and the heavy dependence of the states on central financial assistance, both for their regular budgetary needs as well as for capital expenditures. Moreover, the existence of a dominant party that controlled both the central government and almost all of the state governments reinforced these constitutional provisions at the political level for some time.

Despite the unitary features of the Indian Constitution, the centralizing impact of planning, and the existence of a dominant party, however, the Indian political system evolved a distinctly federal style. Several factors combined to impart to the Indian political system an explicitly federal character that we might more accurately describe as cooperative federalism than as a quasi-federal or unitary system. These factors included the limited but significant constitutional powers enjoyed by the states under the State List, the critical administrative role performed by the states, and the political devolution of power that followed the introduction of a mass franchise and the creation of unilingual states.

Despite the constitutional powers of the central government, the states of India are not without significant constitutional powers of their own. In fact, they control some of the most important functions of the state, such as education, agriculture, and welfare. In addition, the central government depends heavily on the states to implement many of its policies. As Paul Appleby has observed, "No other large and important government . . . is so dependent as India on theoretically subordinate but actually rather distinct units responsible to a different political control, for so much of the administration of what are recognized as national programs of great importance to the nation."[10] Because state political leaders were sensitive to their own bases of political support, they were often independent and refused

[10] Paul Appleby, *Public Administration in India: Report of a Survey* (New Delhi: Government of India, Cabinet Secretariat, 1953), p. 21.

to carry out policies recommended by the central government that might undercut their political support. This reluctance was clearly reflected in the case of such major policy areas as land reforms and the taxation of agricultural incomes, both of which are within the constitutional jurisdiction of the states. The central government, in turn, exercised considerable restraint in attempting to impose its will on the states. Thus, the political and administrative dependence of the central government on the states in critical policy areas resulted in a cooperative federalism based on a bargaining process between the Center and the states.[11]

The essentially federal character of the Congress party, with its strong party bosses before the split in 1969, provided the political base for this bargaining process—a process that took place within the Congress "family" so long as the party retained power both at the Center and within the states. It was a politics of accommodation, but one weighted toward the Center.

The bargaining process between the Center and the states involved a complex balance based on political and functional interdependence. The states in India are not homogeneous entities but are themselves divided along social, religious, subregional, and ethnic lines that are a source of conflict. The factional and alliance styles of politics within each state enabled the central government to penetrate state political systems, and the states themselves were constantly forced to turn to the central government for assistance in containing the forces that threatened their political control. Thus, although state leaders were powerful, they were so vulnerable to factions that they needed the brokerage role of the Center to keep them in power or to restore stability. Moreover, collectively, state leaders were divided. They were noted for their lobbying efforts to secure benefits for their state, and they were too busy trying to stay in power to confront the national leadership on major questions.[12] Thus, though new state elites developed greater regional self-consciousness and self-assertiveness, they were not separatist.[13] They were primarily parochial and concerned with distributive politics in an effort to stay in power. Although state leaders were dependent on the central government to stay in power,

[11] Stanley A. Kochanek, *The Congress Party of India* (Princeton, N.J.: Princeton University Press, 1968), pp. 233–66, 407–47.

[12] Norman K. Nicholson, *Rural Development Policy in India* (De Kalb, Ill.: Center for Governmental Studies, Northern Illinois University, 1974), pp. 17–26.

[13] Selig S. Harrison, *India: The Most Dangerous Decades* (Princeton, N.J.: Princeton University Press, 1960), pp. 3–11.

the central government was dependent on the state leaders for policy implementation and the development of political support. The central government could not sustain unpopular governments in the states or maintain central rule indefinitely. Although it might intervene to assist in the restoration of stability, it could not create that stability by itself. Thus, political and functional interdependence was a critical part of Center–state relations in India.

Until 1967 the bargaining process of Center–state relations took place primarily within the framework of the dominant Congress party, supplemented at the governmental level by the constitutional and extraconstitutional devices that collectively resulted in cooperative federalism. As long as the Congress party controlled the central government and almost all of the state governments, differences over issues of policy or Center–state relations could be handled as a kind of family quarrel to be mediated by Congress elders.[14] With the loss of Congress hegemony, however, problems once dealt with quietly as intraparty affairs required more or less public negotiations by a process of Center–state bargaining through officially constituted governmental mechanisms such as the Conference of Chief Ministers and the National Development Council. The National Development Council dealt with all issues involving economic planning, whereas the Conference of Chief Ministers handled nonplanning political issues requiring national uniformity, coordination, and Center–state cooperation.

Even under the best of circumstances, Center–state relations generated a variety of tensions. These tensions were bound to increase as more and more states came under the control of opposition political parties, particularly when the opposition party was purely regional in its support, appeal, and program. It is not surprising, therefore, that among the most vocal of the states has been Tamil Nadu, governed since 1967 by a regional political party, the Dravida Munnetra Kazhagam (DMK) and its offshoot, the All-India Anna DMK (AIADMK). As early as 1967, C. N. Annadurai, founder of the DMK, called for the federal system to be restructured so that the central government would only have powers relating to defense, foreign affairs, interstate communication, and currency. All residual powers

[14]Kochanek, *Congress Party*, pp. 421–22. Myron Weiner explored this process in the context of five districts in *Party Building in a New Nation: The Indian National Congress* (Chicago: University of Chicago Press, 1967). Atul Kohli re-examined those districts more than 20 years later to reveal dramatic changes in *Democracy and Discontent: India's Growing Crisis of Governability* (Cambridge: Cambridge University Press, 1990).

would be in the hands of the states, and the federal and state governments would be completely independent of each other in their respective spheres.[15] Similar demands were voiced by leaders of the Communist government of West Bengal and, from time to time, from other states on the periphery of India's Hindi-speaking heartland.

Supporters of greater states' rights insisted that their demands were not designed to encourage secession or to jeopardize national integrity. However, the central political leadership, the bureaucracy, the military, urban intellectuals, and the Indian industrialist elites tended to see demands for greater state autonomy as a threat to national unity and integrity. These elites favored a strong central government. Three wars with Pakistan (1948, 1965, and 1971) and a major border war with China (1962) had created a fear of foreign incursions and a deep concern for national security. In addition, the increased level of caste, language, religious, and regional conflicts raised new fears of fissiparous tendencies and political separatism. These fears, combined with the slow and erratic pace of economic development, led these elites to demand a stronger and more forceful central government. Prime Minister Indira Gandhi capitalized on these fears.

Indira Gandhi was a centralizer. She believed in a strong central government and the concentration of power in party and government in her hands. Following the split of the Congress party in 1969 and her highly personal electoral victories in 1971 and 1972, she set about reversing the earlier tradition of cooperative federalism, and restructured the federal base of the Indian polity. All elected bodies within the Congress organization ceased to be elected and were appointed from New Delhi; party tickets were allocated by the central party headquarters under Indira Gandhi's supervision; and state chief ministers became the personal appointees of Mrs. Gandhi, regardless of their ability to build a local base of support. In fact, such efforts were discouraged, and those who attempted to build an independent base of support were quickly removed from office. No individual or organization was to be in a position to challenge Indira Gandhi's centralized control.[16]

The result of this pattern of centralization was the disintegration of

[15]Government of Tamil Nadu, *Report of the Center-State Relations Inquiry Committee* (Madras: Director of Stationery and Printing, 1971), p. 7.

[16]See Stanley A. Kochanek, "Mrs. Gandhi's Pyramid: The New Congress," in Henry C. Hart, ed., *Indira Gandhi's India: A Political System Reappraisal* (Boulder, Colo.: Westview, 1976), pp. 93–124, and Bhagwan D. Dua, "India: A Study in the Pathology of a Federal System," *Journal of Commonwealth and Comparative Politics*, 19 (November 1981): 257–75.

state Congress governments, the rise of mass protest, and an authoritarian response on the part of the central government when it appeared that the opposition might successfully challenge continued Congress rule. The emergency period from 1975 to 1977 accelerated the move toward the centralization and personalization of power in Indira Gandhi's hands. Mrs. Gandhi's defeat and the end of the emergency brought a temporary halt to this process, but following her return to power in 1980 the decay in Center–state relations became even more acute. "Mrs. Gandhi's style," W. H. Morris-Jones observed, "has transformed these relations from one of political bargaining to one akin to feudal tutelage."[17] Under Indira Gandhi the politics of manipulation displaced the politics of accommodation. The centralization of power centralized problems, nationalizing issues that were once locally resolved within the context of a state or in bargaining between the Center and the state. The inability of personally appointed retainers to cope with local problems created a range of new and increasingly dangerous headaches for the central government. At the same time, the Center's intransigence or insensitivity in handling these disputes resulted in a deepening crisis for the Congress party and the nation.

President N. Sanjiva Reddy warned in 1981 that the vastness and diversity of India "made it almost impossible for a Central authority in distant Delhi to deal with the multifarious problems in different parts of the country promptly and efficiently."[18] And in 1983, the non-Congress chief ministers of the four southern states met to voice their demands for greater state autonomy. At the same time, the movement for greater state autonomy in the Punjab took on an increasingly violent character. In response, Prime Minister Indira Gandhi named retired Supreme Court justice R. S. Sarkaria to head a commission to inquire into Center–state relations and to recommend appropriate changes consistent with the framework of the Constitution. The commission addressed such concerns as state financial dependence on the Center; the capacity of the President to withhold assent to bills passed by state legislatures; the assignment of all-India services to state administration; central appointment of state high court judges; and the role of the Governor. The Sarkaria Commission, in its 1988 report, emphasized the importance of a strong Center "to pre-

[17] W. H. Morris-Jones, "India—More Questions than Answers," *Asian Survey*, 14 (August 1984):811.

[18] *Hindustan Times* (New Delhi), November 1, 1981.

serve the unity and integrity of the country" and cautiously recommended an approach that would enhance "co-operative federalism."[19] Those who saw in the commission an opportunity to redress the balance between the Center and the states were sorely disappointed. The commission did urge that measures be taken both to provide a more equitable sharing of revenues and to prevent the arbitrary dismissal of state governments. Even in its measured proposals, however, the Sarkaria Commission report was largely ignored.

Rather than addressing the federal relationship in more comprehensive terms, the central government responded to the various demands for greater autonomy on an ad hoc basis, state by state, very much as it had in the process by which the states themselves were organized.

States Reorganization

With the accession of the princely states in 1947, the process of national integration began. The components of the new Union were divided into four categories, depending on their makeup and their relationship with the Center. Some—former Governor's provinces and princely states alike—retained their boundaries. Others, however, were formed from the union of various contiguous states. A number of the smaller territories remained under Central administration. (Fig. 4–1 shows India in 1951, after integration.)

The 27 states of the Indian Union were heterogeneous linguistically and, except for their common link with the past, culturally. From the 1920s, and as late as 1945, the Congress party had called for the formation of linguistic provinces. The provincial branches of the party itself had been reorganized in 1921 on a linguistic basis, with units established for what are today the states of Andhra, Kerala, and Maharashtra. With independence, the Dar Commission was appointed to advise the Constituent Assembly in its deliberations on demands for linguistic states. The commission's report, submitted at the end of 1948, warned that linguistically homogeneous provinces would have a "subnational bias," threatening national unity, and that, in any case, each state would have minorities. The report was received with general disappointment. The issue had become critical, and the Con-

[19] *Commission on Centre–State Relations Report*, 2 vols. (Nasik: Government of India Press, 1988). Also see B. L. Fadia and R. K. Menaria, *Sarkaria Commission Report and Centre–State Relations* (Agra: Sahitya Bhawan, 1990).

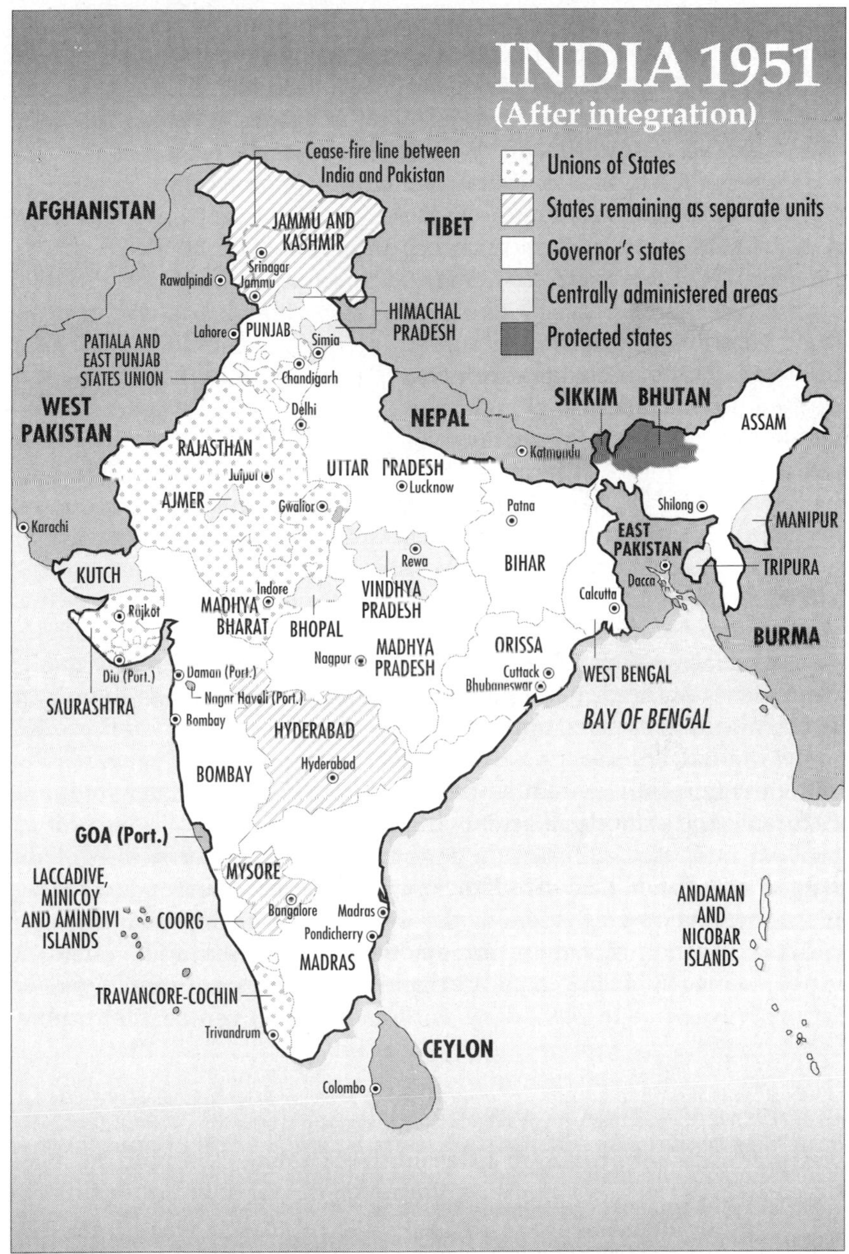
INDIA 1951
(After integration)
Unions of States
States remaining as separate units
Governor's states
Centrally administered areas
Protected states
Cease-fire line between India and Pakistan
AFGHANISTAN
JAMMU AND KASHMIR
TIBET
Srinagar
Rawalpindi
Jammu
HIMACHAL PRADESH
Lahore
PUNJAB
Simla
PATIALA AND EAST PUNJAB STATES UNION
Chandigarh
WEST PAKISTAN
Delhi
NEPAL
SIKKIM
BHUTAN
ASSAM
RAJASTHAN
Katmandu
UTTAR PRADESH
Jaipur
Lucknow
AJMER
Gwalior
Patna
Shilong
MANIPUR
Karachi
EAST PAKISTAN
Rewa
BIHAR
TRIPURA
KUTCH
Dacca
Indore
VINDHYA PRADESH
Calcutta
MADHYA BHARAT
Rajkot
BHOPAL
BURMA
MADHYA PRADESH
ORISSA
Nagpur
Cuttack
Bhubaneswar
WEST BENGAL
Diu (Port.)
Daman (Port.)
Nagar Haveli (Port.)
SAURASHTRA
BAY OF BENGAL
Bombay
HYDERABAD
Hyderabad
BOMBAY
GOA (Port.)
MYSORE
LACCADIVE, MINICOY AND AMINDIVI ISLANDS
ANDAMAN AND NICOBAR ISLANDS
Bangalore
Madras
COORG
Pondicherry
MADRAS
TRAVANCORE-COCHIN
Trivandrum
CEYLON
Colombo

Figure 4–1

gress appointed Jawaharlal Nehru, Vallabhbhai Patel, and the party president, Pattabhi Sitaramayya, "to examine the question in the light of the decisions taken by the Congress in the past and the requirements of the existing situation."[20] The "JVP" Committee, fundamentally concerned with the problem of national unity, reaffirmed the position of the Dar Commission. "It would unmistakably retard the process of consolidation [and] let loose, while we are still in a formative stage, forces of disruption and disintegration. . . ."[21] It conceded, however, that a strong case might be made for the formation of Andhra from the Telugu-speaking region of Madras, and that, if public sentiment was "insistent and overwhelming," this and other cases might be given further consideration. "This was the opening wedge for the bitter struggle over States Reorganization which was to dominate Indian politics from 1953 to 1956."[22]

The demand for a separate state of Andhra had deep roots among the Telugu people. It had won the agreement of the Madras government and obtained the support of the Tamilnad Congress Committee, but only after a fast-unto-death by one of the leaders of the Andhra movement did the Center finally respond. In 1953 the state of Andhra was created. Nehru argued against the "foolish and tribal attitudes" of provincialism. The states, he said, were only for administrative purposes—but the demand had been recognized, and other linguistic groups would now have nothing less.

The State Reorganization Commission, appointed by Nehru to examine the question, sought a "balanced approach" between regional sentiment and national interest. In its 1955 report, the commission rejected the theory of "one language one state," but recognized "linguistic homogeneity as an important factor conducive to administrative convenience and efficiency. . . ."[23] The commission recommended that the political divisions of the Union be redrawn generally in accordance with linguistic demands. The States Reorganization Act, as it was finally passed by Parliament in November 1956, pro-

[20] Quoted in Joan V. Bondurant, *Regionalism versus Provincialism: A Study in Problems of Indian National Unity*, Indian Press Digests—Monograph Series, no. 4 (Berkeley: University of California Press, 1958), p. 29.

[21] Ibid.

[22] Michael Brecher, *Nehru: A Political Biography* (New York: Oxford University Press, 1959), p. 481. For a broad view of that struggle, see Joseph E. Schwartzberg, "Factors in the Linguistic Reorganization of Indian States," in Paul Wallace, ed., *Region and Nation in India* (New Delhi: Oxford & IBH, 1985), pp. 155–82.

[23] *Report of the States Reorganization Commission* (New Delhi: Government of India, 1955), p. 46.

vided for 14 states and 6 territories. The boundaries of each state were to be drawn so that they would conform with the region of a dominant language. Following the recommendations of the commission, however, Bombay and the Punjab, two of the most sensitive areas, were not reorganized on a linguistic basis. The demands for separate tribal states, including Jharkhand and Nagaland, were also bypassed.

The commission opposed the division of Bombay into Marathi and Gujarati states largely because of the critical question of Bombay City. Marathi speakers constituted its largest language group, but the city was dominated by Gujarati wealth. Bombay politics was polarized linguistically, and only after widespread rioting and continued agitation did the Congress, in 1960, give way to the demand for reorganization. Gujarat and Maharashtra were constituted as separate linguistic states, with the city of Bombay included as part of Maharashtra.

In the Punjab the Akali Dal, the political party of Sikh nationalism, had long demanded a Sikh state within India, if not the independent Sikh nation it sought at the time of partition. The demand for a separate state of the Punjab (Punjabi Suba) was voiced not in communal but in linguistic terms. There was no real language problem in the Punjab, however; it was rather a problem of script and, fundamentally, of religion. Punjabi is the mother tongue of Sikhs and Hindus alike, but communal passions had led large sections of the Hindu community to renounce the Punjabi language by naming their mother tongue as Hindi for census tabulation. As spoken, the languages are very similar, but Punjabi is distinguished by the use of Gurmukhi, the script of the Sikh holy books. Hindus in the Punjab write in Urdu or in Devanagari script. "The only chance of survival of the Sikhs as a separate community," it was argued, "is to create a State in which they form a compact group, where the teaching of Gurmukhi and the Sikh religion is compulsory. . . ."[24]

The States Reorganization Commission contended that the formation of a separate Punjabi-speaking state would solve neither the language nor the communal problem, but "far from removing internal tension, which exists between communal and not linguistic and regional groups, it might further exacerbate the existing feelings."[25] In the 1956 reorganization, the states of PEPSU (Patiala and East Punjab States Union) and the Punjab were merged into a single state; the

[24] Khushwant Singh, *A History of the Sikhs*, vol. 2 (Princeton, N.J.: Princeton University Press, 1966), pp. 304–305. For an analysis of the issue, see Baldev Raj Nayar, *Minority Politics in the Punjab* (Princeton, N.J.: Princeton University Press, 1966).

[25] *Report of the States Reorganization Commission*, p. 146.

Sikhs, forming only about one-third of the population, were concentrated in the western districts. Punjabi and Hindi were both official languages. But the Akali Dal, encouraged by the bifurcation of Bombay in 1960, began agitating for Punjabi Suba. Akali volunteers courted arrest and filled the jails, while Sikh leaders Sant Fateh Singh and Master Tara Singh engaged in abortive fasts. Agitation continued, but without response from the government. Then, abruptly in 1966, supposedly as a concession to the valor and suffering of the Sikhs in the Indo-Pakistan war of 1965, but partly in response to the growing demand in the Hindi areas for a separate state of Haryana, the government announced that the Punjab would be divided into two units, Punjabi Suba and Haryana, corresponding to the regions of language dominance. The Sikhs at last constituted a majority in the Punjab—though barely more than 50 percent of the population. The hill districts of the old Punjab became part of Himachal Pradesh, stimulating a demand there for full statehood that was fulfilled in 1971. Chandigarh, the modern capital designed by the French architect Le Corbusier, was made a Union Territory and joint capital for the Punjab and Haryana. The Sikhs had their Punjabi Suba, but the failure of the Akalis to secure political power again brought the Punjab to crisis in the 1980s, confronting India, as we shall later see, with the greatest challenge to its national integrity since independence.

The demand for the creation of Jharkhand out of the Chota–Nagpur region of southern Bihar and the contiguous tribal districts of Orissa was a product of the increasing self-consciousness of the scheduled tribes in the area. The Jharkhand party, organized by a wealthy, Oxford-educated Munda tribesman, Jaipal Singh, secured various concessions from the Bihar government, but it did not succeed in its demand for a separate state.[26]

The demand for the creation of Nagaland posed a more serious problem. The Naga tribes in the hills along the Assam-Burma border had never been completely brought under control by the British, and they were eager to assert their independence from the new Indian government. The situation was further complicated by the conversion of many of the Nagas to Christianity by American Baptist missionaries. Their missionary tie gave the Nagas outside leverage. When the government sought to bring formerly unadministered areas of the Naga hills under its control, the Nagas appealed to the United Nations, protesting what they called an Indian invasion, and the

[26]For a discussion of tribal aspirations across India, see K. S. Singh, ed., *Tribal Movements in India*, 2 vols. (New Delhi: Manohar, 1982).

Naga National Council was organized to function as a parallel government with Assam. With money and arms secured by the Naga leader A. Z. Phizo, who later set up an exile government in London, the rebellion became increasingly serious. In 1956 the Indian government sent in troops to pacify the area. The Naga People's Convention, representing the more traditional leadership of the Naga tribes, opposed Phizo and proposed a settlement "within the Indian Union." The Nagas were finally released from Assamese administration, and in 1963 the state of Nagaland came into being.

Violence among the tribes continued, however, and Mizo rebels launched guerrilla action in a bid for secession. In 1972 the northeastern region was reorganized in an attempt to secure the support of moderate tribal leaders. The Union Territories of Manipur and Tripura and the Meghalaya section of Assam gained full statehood, the North East Frontier Agency (NEFA) was formed into the Union Territory of Arunachal Pradesh, and the Mizo district of Assam became the Union Territory of Mizoram. But in Mizoram armed clashes between the Indian Army and insurgents of the Mizo National Army took on new intensity in the late 1970s. The Mizo National Front—outlawed in 1979—called for an independent Mizoram. In 1984 renewed negotiations between the Front and the Government of India opened the way for a political settlement, and in February 1987, Mizoram gained statehood, with Laldenga, leader of the Mizo insurgency, its first chief minister. At the same time, Arunachal Pradesh was also raised from the status of Union Territory to that of a state, an action that drew protest from China, asserting its own claim to the disputed area.

In May 1987, Goa became India's 25th state, and the other former Portuguese colonies of Daman and Diu (with which Goa had been formerly administered) were made a separate Union Territory.

Today India is composed of 25 states and 7 Union Territories. (See Figure 4–2 and Table 4–1.) The political map has been modified over the years as boundaries have changed and new states formed. In 1975, however, India acquired new territory with the addition of Sikkim to the Indian Union.

Sikkim had been a protectorate of India. In effect, having inherited the status of paramount power from the British, India exercised control over Sikkim's foreign affairs and defense. Although the state formally retained "full autonomy in regard to its internal affairs," India, in fact, exerted extensive influence through Indian administrative officers and advisers to the *Chogyal*, Maharaja, of Sikkim. In addition, India provided an annual subsidy. In 1973–74, when the Nepali ma-

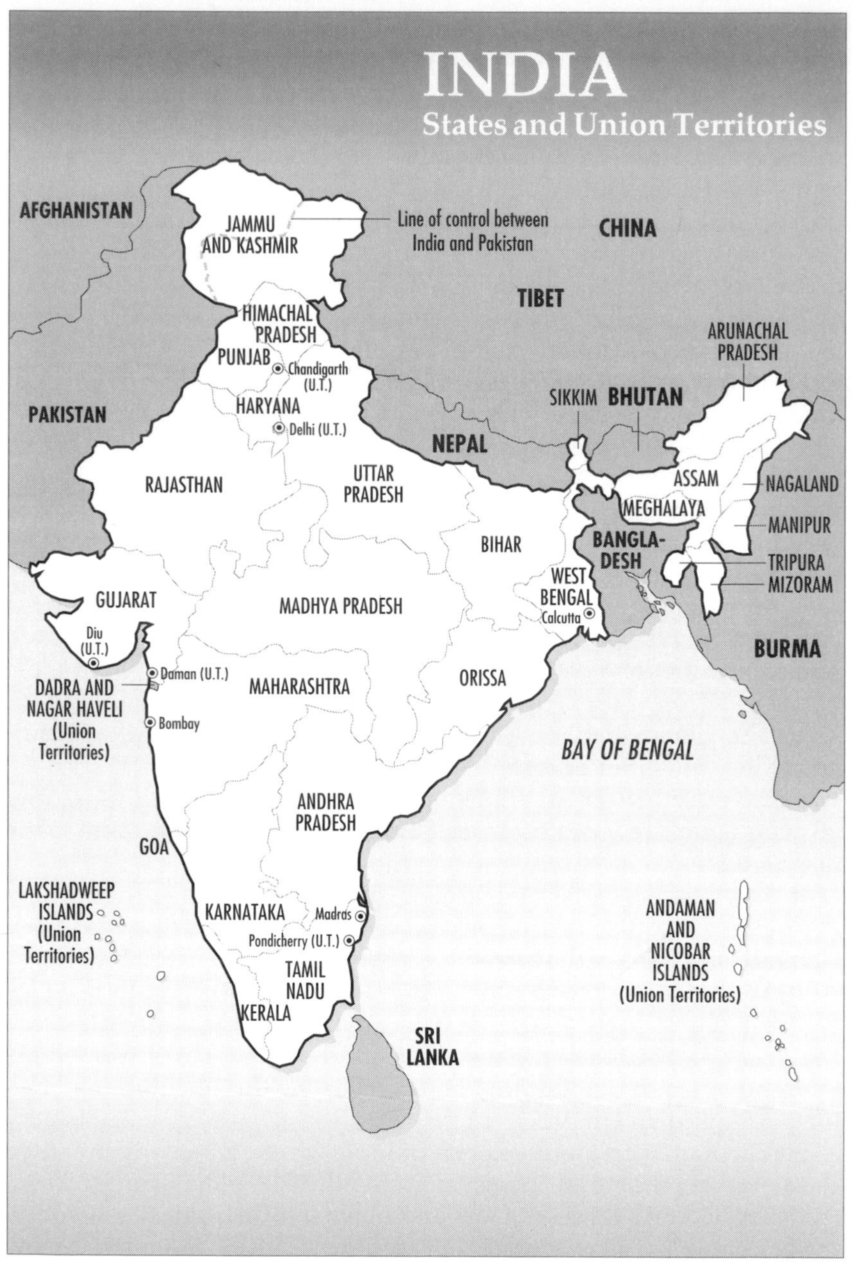
INDIA
States and Union Territories
AFGHANISTAN
JAMMU AND KASHMIR
Line of control between India and Pakistan
CHINA
TIBET
HIMACHAL PRADESH
PUNJAB
Chandigarth (U.T.)
HARYANA
Delhi (U.T.)
PAKISTAN
ARUNACHAL PRADESH
SIKKIM
BHUTAN
NEPAL
RAJASTHAN
UTTAR PRADESH
ASSAM
NAGALAND
MEGHALAYA
MANIPUR
BIHAR
BANGLA-DESH
TRIPURA
MIZORAM
WEST BENGAL
Calcutta
GUJARAT
MADHYA PRADESH
Diu (U.T.)
BURMA
Daman (U.T.)
DADRA AND NAGAR HAVELI (Union Territories)
MAHARASHTRA
ORISSA
Bombay
BAY OF BENGAL
ANDHRA PRADESH
GOA
LAKSHADWEEP ISLANDS (Union Territories)
KARNATAKA
Madras
Pondicherry (U.T.)
ANDAMAN AND NICOBAR ISLANDS (Union Territories)
TAMIL NADU
KERALA
SRI LANKA

Figure 4–2

Table 4–1
States and Territories of the Indian Union and Their Principal Languages

States	*Principal Languages*
Andhra Pradesh	Telugu and Urdu
Arunachal Pradesh	Monpa et al.
Assam	Assamese and Bengali
Bihar	Hindi
Goa	Konkani and Marathi
Gujarat	Gujarati
Haryana	Hindi
Himachal Pradesh	Hindi and Pahari
Jammu and Kashmir	Kashmiri, Dogri, and Urdu
Karnataka (formerly Mysore)	Kannada
Kerala	Malayalam
Madhya Pradesh	Hindi
Maharashtra	Marathi
Manipur	Manipuri
Meghalaya	Khasi, Garo, and English*
Mizoram	Mizo and English*
Nagaland	Naga dialects and English*
Orissa	Oriya
Punjab	Punjabi
Rajasthan	Rajasthani and Hindi
Sikkim	Bhutia, Nepali, Lepcha, and English
Tamil Nadu (formerly Madras)	Tamil
Tripura	Bengali, Kakbarak, and Manipuri
Uttar Pradesh	Hindi and Urdu
West Bengal	Bengali
Union Territories	
Andaman and Nicobar Islands	Delhi
Chandigarh	Lakshadweep Islands
Dadra and Nagar Haveli	Pondicherry
Daman and Diu	

*English is the language used for administrative purposes as a result of both practical necessity and missionary influence.

jority within the state began to agitate for political rights, India tightened its hold over Sikkim's internal affairs. The Chogyal, stripped of his power, had no choice but to yield. The position of the Indian government was that Sikkim was no different from those princely states that had acceded to India in 1947. In response to the request by the

Sikkim Assembly and a later plebiscite, India extended an ambiguous "associate" status to Sikkim, and in 1975, through the Thirty-sixth Amendment, full statehood.[27]

In order to counter divisive tendencies among the linguistic states, the States Reorganization Act established five zonal councils to promote cooperation and coordination of policies. An additional Northeastern Council was established in 1972. Each council consists of the Union Home Minister, acting as chairman, the chief ministers of the states within the zone, and other ministers from each state nominated by the Governor. The councils have only an advisory capacity, and the results have been less than impressive.

Interstate disputes are principally of two types. Border disputes are the inevitable product of the creation of linguistic states, when boundaries are unable to make precise divisions between ethnic groups, as in the conflict between Maharashtra and Karnataka over the ethnically mixed Belgaum District. Perhaps more serious are disputes over the allocation of river water—a major issue, for example, between the Punjab and the neighboring states of Haryana and Rajasthan. The Constitution empowers the Center to settle such disputes, and it does so through appointed tribunals, with the consequence that state frustrations and demands are often directed toward the Center, converting interstate conflicts into issues of Center–state relations.[28]

This was the pattern in the century-old dispute over the waters of the Cauvery River in South India. When, in December 1991, the tribunal handed down an interim award favorable to Tamil Nadu, the Karnataka government protested and called a general strike, precipitating a wave of arson and violence against the Tamil minority in the state. Tamil Nadu reacted with demands that the Center intervene to protect the Tamils, and the ruling party in each state threatened to withdraw support from the Congress government at the Center unless the Prime Minister came down on its side in the dispute. For each state it was a matter of pride.

Reorganization gave the states a political identity congruent with their culture and language.

> [It] brought State politics closer to the people, and made it easier for traditional leaders and influential regional groups to capture control,

[27] For a critical account, see Sunanda K. Datta-Ray, *Smash and Grab: Annexation of Sikkim* (New Delhi: Vikas, 1984).

[28] Fadia and Menaria, *Sarkaria Commission Report and Centre–State Relations*, p. 24.

> or, at least, exercise much influence over the use of power. . . . Thus, in a sense, reorganization made State politics more democratic, but less western in style. It meant, for one thing, that State politics would be increasingly conducted in the regional language rather than English; thus power was now open to others than the small English-speaking elite.[29]

States Reorganization provided the framework for expanded participation. It made the people more accessible to political mobilization and, at the same time, provided them with increased institutional access for the articulation of demands—but demands that have often reflected the parochialism of region and language.

The Politics of Language

The creation of linguistic states has reinforced regionalism and has stirred demands for increased state autonomy—expressed most stridently by the Communist Party of India (Marxist) in West Bengal; by the DMK and AIADMK in Tamil Nadu, evoking the earlier call for secession and the creation of an independent Dravidian state; the Telugu Desam in Andhra; and by the Akali Dal in the Punjab. Almost every state has spawned a militant nativist movement directed against outsiders. The fundamental issue has been employment for local people, and many state governments, either officially or unofficially, have supported the protection of jobs for the "sons of the soil."[30] Of the movements, one of the most virulent has been the Shiv Sena, founded in 1966 in Bombay. Exploiting Maharashtrian grievances and economic frustration, the Shiv Sena, under the banner "Maharashtra for the Maharashtrians," directed its attack, both verbal and physical, initially at South Indian immigrants and in recent years at Muslims.[31]

[29]Duncan B. Forrester, "Electoral Politics and Social Change," *Economic and Political Weekly*, special number (July 1968): 1083.

[30]See Myron Weiner, *Sons of the Soil: Migration and Ethnic Conflict in India* (Princeton, N.J.: Princeton University Press, 1978), and Myron Weiner and Mary Fainsod Katzenstein, *India's Preferential Policies: Migrants, the Middle Classes, and Ethnic Equality* (Chicago: University of Chicago Press, 1981).

[31]See Ram Joshi, "The Shiv Sena: A Movement in Search of Legitimacy," *Asian Survey*, 10 (November 1970): 967–78, and Mary F. Katzenstein, *Ethnicity and Equality: The Shiv Sena Party and Preferential Policies in Bombay* (Ithaca, N.Y.: Cornell University Press, 1979).

Language has been the subject of continued conflict in the states of the Indian Union. India has 1652 "mother tongues," and of these, the government has recognized 18 regional languages as "official" in the Eighth Schedule of the Constitution. The most recent additions to the list came in 1992, with the inclusion of Konkani, Manipuri, and Nepali in response to growing political pressure.

During the years of British rule, the language of administration and that of the educated elite was English. For Mahatma Gandhi and the Congress party, English had usurped the rightful place of the indigenous languages. Hindi, as the most widely spoken of the Indian languages, was to replace English with the achievement of independence. The Constitution embodied this aspiration in Article 343, which stipulated that "the official language of the Union shall be Hindi in the Devanagari script." The Constitution also provided that English should remain the language of administration for no longer than 15 years.[32]

The South, where English standards in school remained high and where there was little knowledge of Hindi, was uneasy. The changeover from English to Hindi would place those for whom Hindi was not a mother tongue at a severe disadvantage, especially in competition for coveted positions within the public services. In response to growing opposition—especially in Tamil Nadu—to the "imposition" of Hindi, Nehru assured the South that English would remain "as an alternative language as long as the people require it. . . ." In 1961 the National Integration Council recommended the adoption of the "three-language formula," which would require in all schools compulsory teaching in three languages: the regional language and English, with Hindi for the non-Hindi states and another Indian language for the Hindi-speaking states. The northern Hindi advocates demanded that the South make Hindi a compulsory part of its curriculum, but they themselves refused to adopt the three-language formula, feeling Hindi alone was sufficient.

Nehru's assurance had eased the fears of Tamil Nadu, but on Republic Day, January 26, 1965, in pursuance of the Constitution, Hindi became the official language of India. In the two months of anti-Hindi demonstrations and riots that followed in Tamil Nadu, more than 60 people were killed in police firings, and unofficial reports placed the number of deaths as high as 300. Two young men poured gasoline upon their bodies and immolated themselves in protest. Hindi books were burned, and Hindi signs in railway stations were defaced or ripped down. All colleges and high schools in the state were

[32]For a discussion of the language issue, see Paul R. Brass, *The Politics of India Since Independence* (Cambridge: Cambridge University Press, 1990), pp. 135–168.

closed, and student demonstrations gave way to mob violence. An uneasy peace was restored only with regiments of armed police and soldiers.[33]

The DMK, self-appointed voice for the Tamil cause, demanded that all major regional languages be the "official languages of the respective states with English as the link language between the States and the Centre." Despite pro-Hindi agitation in the North the government came forward with an amendment to the Official Languages Act, giving statutory form to Nehru's assurances. Although the three-language formula is today official policy, it is honored in breach. Tamil Nadu has specifically eliminated Hindi from the school curriculum, and the Hindi heartland of North India remains almost wholly monolingual. English remains, for the most part, the language of the central government, but as a "link" it is increasingly tenuous.

Regionalism in Indian Politics

From the time of India's independence in 1947, cultural politics—whether in the demands for linguistic states, in the controversy over Hindi as the national language, or in the nativism of the "sons of the soil"—has deepened regional identities. Episodic movements have been both the vehicle of politicization and its inevitable result. The government has typically met cultural demands with vacillation and indecision—sometimes by calculated neglect—only to be followed, in the face of prolonged agitation, by a combined response of force and accommodation.

Regionalism is rooted in India's cultural and linguistic diversity. Projected in geographic terms, it is, at the state level, both an ethnic and economic phenomenon. It is an expression of heightened political consciousness, expanding participation, and increasing competition for scarce resources. For the state, competition is for central financial allocation and Plan investment; for the individual, it involves access to education and jobs. Economic grievances—expressed in charges of unfairness, discrimination, or Center neglect—may be fused with cultural anxiety over language status and ethnic balance. It is this fusion that gives regionalism its potency. Language and culture, like religion, are at the core of an individual's identity and, when politicized, take a potentially virulent form.

[33]See Robert L. Hardgrave, Jr., "The Riots in Tamilnad: Problems and Prospects of India's Language Crisis," *Asian Survey*, 5 (August 1965):399–407.

As long as most states were under the Congress umbrella, conflict *between* states and Center, *among* states, and *within* states could be accommodated within the framework of the party. Today regionalism increasingly manifests itself through opposition to the Congress party—in regional parties like the AIADMK and DMK in Tamil Nadu, the Akali Dal in the Punjab, and the Telegu Desam in Andhra Pradesh and in demands by opposition parties across the ideological spectrum for greater autonomy for the states.

The demand for greater state autonomy—namely, increased financial resources, decentralization of planning, more independence in administrative areas for which states are constitutionally responsible—reflects, at least in part, an aspiration to bring government "closer to the people." The arguments are familiar in the American context, for federalism by its nature is "an invitation to struggle." That struggle in India, however, is aggravated by gross regional disparities, both in levels of development and in rates of growth, such that the gap between advanced and backward regions continues to widen.

Disparities mean that the struggle between the states and the Center necessarily involves a struggle among states. All states do not share the same interests. More prosperous states, such as the Punjab, may resist redistribution of income among states by the Center, claiming that they are being unfairly exploited or that they do not receive a fair share back for what they contribute to the national economy. Other states, like Assam, Bengal, and Kerala, claim to be victims of Center neglect or discrimination. The backward states, especially those of the Hindi heartland, look to the Center to redress disparities.

There are cross-cutting interests, and alliances among the states are likely to be ad hoc and temporary. Nevertheless, because regionalism, as it expresses itself culturally and in the demand for greater state autonomy, is almost wholly a phenomenon of the non-Hindi speaking periphery, it continues to arouse fears of national disintegration.

The federal relationship involves a permanent tug-of-war, and "rising regionalist tendencies" were a predictable response to increasing centralization in both government and the Congress party under Indira Gandhi. Regionalism will probably impose increasing stress on the federal system as state movements seek to restore greater balance, but it does not pose a threat to the integrity of the Union. While we may be witnessing a regionalization of politics in India, there are countervailing forces of national integration. The development of a national system of communications and the growth and extension of a national market economy have increasingly bound India together.

Greater interdependence sharpens consciousness of regional disparities, however, and intensifies the struggle among states to protect and advance their interests. Greater national integration, ironically, may deepen the stress on the federal system rather than alleviate it.

To say that India's national integrity is fundamentally secure is not to minimize the serious problems posed by disturbances in the Northeast, the Punjab, and Kashmir. These are strategically sensitive border areas, and prolonged agitation involves basic interests of national security. The Government of India will do whatever it takes to bring these areas under control. In both Assam and the Punjab, the government initially pursued a policy of purposeful neglect ("constructive inaction") in the hope that the movements would burn themselves out. Instead, they grew in intensity. In the Northeast, Assam erupted in violence as "sons of the soil" asserted their claims against "foreign" encroachment. In the Punjab, the movement for greater state autonomy gave way to a terrorist movement for an independent Sikh nation of Khalistan. And in Kashmir, insurgents raised the banner of liberation and secession, bringing the state under seige and India and Pakistan to the brink of war.

The Northeast

In the tribal regions of the Northeast, the government has faced periodic armed insurrection from the time of independence. The creation of Nagaland in 1963 and the reorganization of the Northeast in 1972, with the formation of Mizoram, were welcomed by most tribals. On the whole, insurgency has been contained, but guerrilla activity by various underground organizations has not been brought wholly under control. Tribal regions of the Northeast remain under a form of quasi-martial law, reflecting both the continuing danger of unrest and the strategically vulnerable nature of the region. The Chinese no longer provide arms and training to tribal insurgents, but the adjoining region of northern Burma lies effectively outside the control of Rangoon and is both a source of arms into the Northeast and a haven for guerrillas.

The oldest of the tribal insurgencies is led by the National Socialist Council of Nagaland. Although it lost much popular support with the formation of the Naga state in 1963, it remains an active guerrilla force and, like secessionist groups in neighboring Manipur, engages in periodic terrorist attacks against civil and military authorities. The Mizo insurgency, a response to years of economic neglect, began in 1966, and in the late 1970s and early 1980s, clashes between the Indian

Army and insurgents of the Mizo National Army grew in intensity. In 1986, Laldenga, the Mizo leader, signed an accord with the Government of India, ending the rebellion in exchange for amnesty for the Mizo insurgents, protection of tribal identity and traditions, and statehood for Mizoram. In 1988, Prime Minister Rajiv Gandhi reached a similar agreement with leaders of the tribal insurgency in Tripura, ending the 10-year struggle for an independent homeland. The terms of the Mizo and Tripura accords have not been wholly fulfilled by New Delhi, and tribal discontent could again spark secessionist movements, with the potential—as some groups have sought—for a united insurgency by tribal peoples for the creation of an independent federation of the Northeast.

The situation in the seven states and Union Territories of the Northeast is aggravated by the incursion of nontribals onto tribal lands. Tribals—economically, culturally, and politically threatened—have responded in violence. The problem, which goes back well into the British period, has been exacerbated over the past decade as a result of immigration from Bangladesh and, to a lesser degree, from Nepal. In Tripura the influx of Bengali refugees has shifted the ethnic balance and reduced tribals to a minority. Efforts to protect tribal lands and culture have not been successful, as the slaughter of 350 Bengalis in Tripura in 1980 bears tragic witness. In Manipur and Meghalaya student-led agitations against "foreigners"—Bengalis and Nepalese—have taken their lead from the movement in Assam.

The volatile situation in Assam is complicated by the unrest engendered by the occupation of tribal lands by both Assamese and Bengalis. Lalung tribals were responsible for the massacre of more than 1000 Bengali Muslims at Nellie during the 1983 election violence.[34] Tribal grievances are directed as much against the Assamese, however, as clashes between Bodo tribals and Assamese villagers clearly reveal. From the 1960s various Assam plains tribal groups have called for the formation of a separate state within India for the protection of tribal languages, cultures, and economy. Most important has been the All-Bodo Student Union agitation for "Bodoland," a tribal state that would divide Assam in half to create a homeland for the Bodo tribals.

It is not tribal demands, however, but the "foreigner" issue that has been the center of the political turmoil in Assam for the past decade. Immigration—primarily involving Bengalis from Bangladesh, most of whom are Muslim—has aroused Assamese fears that they

[34] *India Today* (New Delhi), 28 February 1983, pp. 12–21; 15 March 1983, pp. 8–23.

will be reduced to a minority in their own state, if this has not, in fact, already taken place. The issue is political power. The conflict, rooted in the old love–hate relationship between Assamese and Bengalis, has been fueled in this century by Assamese apprehension that their language and culture are threatened. Bengalis have long dominated Assam state administration, but the extension of their control over the economy since independence has stimulated demands—primarily by Assamese youth—for the protection of jobs for "the sons of the soil." Economic concerns have been compounded by grievances that the Center has neglected and exploited the state.

There is no way in this brief discussion, nor is it really necessary, to recapitulate the history of the Assam conflict.[35] Suffice to say that it was the discovery of "foreigners"—illegal aliens from Bangladesh—on the voter rolls in 1979 that acted as the catalyst for a movement that engulfed Assam and confronted the Center with a seemingly intractable problem. Led by the All-Assam Students' Union and joined by other political organizations, the agitation mounted in intensity and came to embrace virtually the whole of the Assamese-speaking population in its support.

The conflict is essentially ethnic, but it took an increasingly communal character as both Hindu and Muslim organizations exploited mutual anxieties. In the course of the agitation, the Jamaat-i-Islami and the Tabligh Jamaat became increasingly active among Muslims, and the Hindu nationalist Rashtriya Swayamsevak Sangh (RSS), warning that Assam is being overrun by Muslim infiltrators, dramatically expanded its activities in the state.

Center delay and Assamese intransigence made a "solution" more difficult, and in the course of the six-year-long agitation, more than 5000 people were killed in the ethnic conflict. In 1986 the Rajiv Gandhi government reached a settlement with leaders of the anti-immigrant movement. Under the terms of the accord, all immigrants who arrived after 1965 were to be disenfranchised. Those coming between 1966 and 1971 would become full citizens of India in 1995. Those who arrived after 1971 were to be deported—a decision to expel hundreds of thousands of Bengali aliens that raised a range of practical problems and exacerbated the potential for renewed vio-

[35]See Sanjib Barvah, "Immigration, Ethnic Conflict, and Political Turmoil—Assam, 1979–1985," *Asian Survey*, 26 (November 1986): 1184–1206; Weiner, *Sons of the Soil*, pp. 75–143; Weiner, "The Political Demography of Assam's Anti-Immigrant Movement," *Population Development Review*, 9 (June 1983): 279–92; Shekhar Gupta, *Assam: A Valley Divided* (New Delhi: Vikas, 1984); and A. K. Das, *Assam's Agony* (New Delhi: Lancers, 1982).

lence. The government did not act upon their decision, however. On other issues, the central government promised to intensify the economic development of the region and to provide "legislative and administrative safeguards to protect the cultural, social, and linguistic identity and heritage" of the Assamese people. Following the terms of the agreement, new state assembly elections were held, and the Asom Gana Parishad (AGP), the reincarnation of the student movement as a regional political party, took power in December 1985.

Assam's agony was by no means over. In 1979, the United Liberation Front of Asom (ULFA) formed as a militant wing of the anti-foreign movement. But, with the 1985 accord, as other groups turned to mainstream politics, the ULFA, in a blend of Assamese nationalism and Maoist ideology, embarked on a terrorist campaign for secession. Financed through extortion and with alleged links to elements within the AGP government, the ULFA secured effective control in many areas of Assam. In November 1990, the central government, at the direction of Prime Minister Chandra Shekhar, dismissed the Asom Gana Parishad government for failure to maintain law and order in the state and imposed President's Rule. In the June 1991 state assembly elections, the Congress returned to power in Assam, defeating the factionally divided and discredited AGP. Over the course of 1991, the Indian army launched major operations against the ULFA. In January 1992, ULFA leaders, following secret negotiations, signed an accord in New Delhi to end the rebellion, even as ULFA hardliners from their base in Bangladesh vowed to continue the struggle.

The Punjab[36]

No ethnic conflict has been more traumatic politically and emotionally than that of the Punjab. Following its fall from power in the Punjab in 1980, the Akali Dal—the Sikh political party—submitted a

[36] See Paul Wallace, "Religious and Ethnic Politics: Political Mobilization in the Punjab," in Francine R. Frankel and M. S. A. Rao, eds., *Dominance and State Power in Modern India*, Vol. II (Delhi: Oxford University Press, 1990), pp. 416–81; Wallace, "Sikh Minority Attitudes in India's Federal System," in Joseph T. O'Connell et al., eds., *Sikh History and Religion in the Twentieth Century* (Toronto: South Asian Studies, University of Toronto, 1988), pp. 256–73; Paul Wallace and Surendra Chopra, eds., *Political Dynamics and Crisis in Punjab* (Amritsar: Guru Nanak Dev University, 1988); Paul Brass, "The Punjab Crisis and the Unity of India," in Atul Kohli, ed., *India's Democracy* (Princeton, N.J.: Princeton University Press, 1988), pp. 169–213; Robin Jeffrey, *What's Happening to India?* (New York: Holmes & Meir, 1986); M. J. Akbar, *India: The Siege Within* (New York: Penguin, 1985), pp. 103–209; and Khushwant Singh, *A History of the Sikhs*, 1839–1988, Vol. 2, rev. ed. (Delhi: Oxford University Press, 1991), pp. 319–417. Developments in the Punjab have been especially well covered by *India Today*.

memorandum of demands and grievances to the Prime Minister, and in 1981 launched the agitation that was to bring increasing violence to India's most prosperous state. The agitation was, in part, a continuation of the earlier movement for a Sikh-majority state of Punjabi Suba and for the protection of Sikh culture, religion, and the Punjabi language.

In 1966 the Center yielded to Sikh demands for a separate state, but the creation of the Punjab and Haryana left the question of Chandigarh, the capital, unresolved. The decision, taken in 1970, to award the city to the Punjab, with two Punjab *tehsils* (subdivisions) going to Haryana in exchange, was never implemented, and this was one of the major issues of the renewed agitation. Another issue involved the allocation of river water for irrigation among the Punjab, Haryana, and Rajasthan. The Akalis demanded a greater share to meet the vastly greater needs of the Punjab, India's granary. Various religious demands, such as recognition of Amritsar (site of the Golden Temple) as a "holy city," relate to Akali concerns for Sikh identity. The Akali demands embodied in the 1973 Anandpur Sahib Resolution included virtually complete autonomy for the state, leaving to the Center only defense, external affairs, communications, currency, and railways. These demands—short of the call for an independent "Khalistan" sought by the outlawed Dal Khalsa—were more a talking point on Center–state relations than a serious aspiration for the moderate Sikh leaders who initiated the movement. These leaders, however, were increasingly pressed by extremists led by Sant Jarnail Singh Bhindranwale, a zealot who stirred Sikh revivalism and fueled Hindu anxieties.

Given the success of the Sikh community, its representation in the public services and in the military, and the wealth of the Punjab (with a per-capita income nearly twice that of India's overall average), little sympathy existed among Hindus for Sikh claims of discrimination. Moreover, much to the outrage of Sikh extremists, most Hindus do not regard Sikhism as a separate religion, but as part of the Hindu fold. This attitude deepened the widespread fear among Sikhs of merging back into Hinduism and of losing their separate identity.

The problem in the Punjab, as in Assam, is political power, and it is partly a question of ethnic balance. The Sikhs constitute 55–60 percent of the population in the Punjab, reflecting a relative decline due to their own success as a community. Entrepreneurial spirit has led to an out-migration of Sikhs, while agricultural prosperity in the Punjab drew Hindu laborers into the state.

The Akalis had struggled for Punjabi Suba, but after their goal was attained in 1966, they found themselves excluded from power except for brief interludes of coalition government. The Akalis themselves were factionally divided and engaged in continuous internecine struggle, but the Sikhs, divided by sect and by caste, were not wholly behind the Akali Dal. Non-Jat Sikhs (the Jats are the major agricultural caste of the region) joined hands with Hindus in support of the Congress party, and, given the ethnic balance in the state, the effect was to exclude the majority of Sikhs, represented by the Akali Dal, from power. A succession of Sikh Congress chief ministers ruled the state, but without the confidence of the larger number of their own community. During the period when the Akalis were in power, 1977–1980, it is commonly accepted that the Congress party sought to undermine Akali strength by clandestinely supporting the rise of the Sikh fundamentalist, Sant Bhindranwale.[37]

The possibility of an early compromise between the government and the Akalis was pre-empted by Congress efforts to split the Akalis, driving a wedge between the moderates and the extremists. But the continued agitation, while exposing divisions among the Sikhs, strengthened Sikh revivalism and heightened political consciousness, especially among unemployed, educated youth. Center delay, insensitivity, and ineptitude strengthened the hands of Bhindranwale and the Sikh extremists.

In the wake of increasing violence over the course of 1983, Hindu–Sikh antipathies deepened as Hindu chauvinists—the RSS, numerous Hindu "defense" organizations, and even some "secular" political parties—responded in kind to the increasing stridency of the Sikh extremists led by Bhindranwale. In October 1983, armed Sikh militants stopped a bus and shot its six male Hindu passengers. The same day another band of Sikh terrorists killed two officials on a train. None too soon, the central government, invoking emergency powers under the Constitution, dismissed Punjab's Congress (I) ministry and imposed President's Rule. Police and paramilitary forces, with sweeping powers, sought to restore order as the new Governor and his advisers settled in for a long and difficult period of negotiation. Government indecision and Akali intransigence, however, had transformed the Punjab into a cauldron of discontent. From his sanctuary within the Golden Temple, the citadel of the Sikh religion, Bhindranwale directed the campaign of terrorism in the Punjab.

[37]Ayesha Kagal, for example, in *The Times of India*, September 22, 1982, in writing of Bhindranwale's growing power, stated that "the irony, of course, is that the Sant was originally a product, nurtured and marketed by the Centre to cut into the Akali Dal's spheres of influence."

In March 1984 the government banned the radical All-India Sikh Students Federation and slapped a sedition charge on Akali President Harchand Singh Longowal, driving moderates closer to the extremists. Then, in response to a series of murders by Sikh assassins—believed to be under orders from Bhindranwale—the government declared the whole of the Punjab "deeply disturbed." Under an amendment to the National Security Act, the police in the Punjab were permitted to enter and search homes without warrant, to arrest and detain suspects for up to six months without giving a reason, and to imprison persons without trial for as long as two years.

Bhindranwale had transformed the Akal Takht, his headquarters within the Golden Temple, into an armory and a sanctuary for terrorists. He conducted his campaign with seeming impunity. In April and May the killings increased, bringing the total murdered in the Punjab from January 1 to June 3, 1984, to 298. In the five days before the Army entered the Golden Temple, 48 people were killed. By June, military action against the Golden Temple seemed inevitable, if not already too late, but "Operation Bluestar," as the action was code-named, proved far more costly than its planners had anticipated. The extremists were in greater numbers and far better armed than intelligence reports suggested, and they met the Army's initial call for surrender with machine-gun fire. Rather than a surgical commando raid, the operation turned into a bloody three-day siege. By official count, 576 people were killed, including 83 soldiers. Unofficial estimates put the number as high as 1000. Among the dead, found together in a basement of the Akal Takht, were Bhindranwale, the leader of the Sikh Students Federation, and a dismissed major-general of the Indian Army who reportedly had trained Sikh terrorists. Coordinated with the attack on the Golden Temple were raids against 44 places of worship in the Punjab where terrorists were believed to be based.[38] Throughout the state, police arrested Akali leaders, whose militancy had intensified in rivalry with Bhindranwale and the Khalistan extremists.

Four of the six generals in charge of Operation Bluestar were Sikhs,

[38]See Mark Tully and Satish Jacob, *Amritsar: Mrs. Gandhi's Last Battle* (London: Jonathan Cape, 1985); and the Hindu-Sikh collaboration by two of India's most able journalists, Kuldip Nayar and Khushwant Singh, *Tragedy of Punjab: Operation Bluestar & After* (New Delhi: Vision Books, 1984). For the official version of the operation and the events leading up to it, see Government of India, *White Paper on the Punjab Agitation* (New Delhi: July 10, 1984). An indictment of official policy and action is presented by Sachchidanand Sinha, et al., *Army Action in Punjab: Prelude & Aftermath* (New Delhi: Samata Era Publications, 1984).

but their involvement did little to assuage the deep sense of humiliation and anger among nearly all Sikhs. The Army's entry into the Golden Temple was seen as a sacrilege, and rumors spread rapidly that the most sacred shrine, the Harmandir Sahib, had been destroyed. In fact, though used by the terrorists for gun emplacements, it had been spared at considerable loss of life to the Indian Army. The Akal Takht, however, had suffered serious damage. Rumors triggered mutinies among Sikh troops—nearly all raw recruits—in eight separate rebellions. In Bihar some 1000 Sikh soldiers went on the rampage, killing their Hindu commander, then charging off in commandeered vehicles for New Delhi with the cry, "Death to Mrs. Gandhi." All told, more than 2500 Sikh deserters were detained; another 55 were killed in shootouts with loyal army units. The mutineers numbered a small fraction of the estimated 120,000 Sikhs in the armed forces, but the indiscipline—the most serious since independence—introduced an element of distrust within the military that was far-reaching.

Opposition party leaders generally stood behind the government's action in entering the Golden Temple as "inevitable," but they registered sharp criticism of Indira Gandhi's handling of the events leading up to Operation Bluestar—a seeming policy of drift, a weakening of the Akali moderates, and a cultivation of Hindu support by playing on communal animosities. Sikhs were almost unanimous in condemning the action, and two Congress (I) members of Parliament resigned from the party in protest. The Punjab was effectively under military rule, and the resentment and alienation of Sikhs were deepened by the continued Army occupation of the Golden Temple. In September, after more than three months, the government returned control of the temple to the five head priests, but there was little basis for reconciliation between Sikhs and the government. Khalistan, once dismissed as a fanciful aspiration of a handful of overseas Sikhs, was now winning adherents in the Punjab. Bhindranwale, who in death came to be revered by more than followed him in life, had bequeathed a spirit of bitterness and rage. The Akali leaders were in jail, discredited in public eyes either because they had acquiesced in the desecration of the Golden Temple as Bhindranwale turned it into a base for terrorism, or because they had "surrendered" in the siege. The government faced a political vacuum in the Punjab, with no credible representative of the Sikhs with whom it might negotiate.

On October 31, 1984, Prime Minister Indira Gandhi was assassinated by two Sikh members of her security guard. As word of the assassination spread, mobs surged through the streets of New Delhi in search of Sikhs upon whom they might vent their rage. In three days of arson, looting, and murder, the capital witnessed its greatest violence since partition. Sikhs were attacked, their hair and beards cut, and in some instances they were butchered or immolated before the eyes of their families. In the hysteria, the police simply stood by as rioters destroyed homes, shops, trucks, and taxis. Rajiv Gandhi, succeeding his mother as Prime Minister, issued a joint appeal with opposition party leaders "to restore sanity and harmony." "To subject Sikhs as a whole to violence and indignity for what a few misguided persons have done, however heinous the crime, is most irrational and unbecoming of our heritage and tolerance. This madness must stop." It did stop, but only with the belated entry of the army into New Delhi and eight other cities. While the body of Indira Gandhi lay in state, violence claimed more than 2700 lives, most in the capital area. The Punjab was mercifully quiet. The violence was not as spontaneous as it first appeared, but orchestrated. The mobs were made up largely of "lumpen elements"—mainly untouchables and Muslims from slums on the outskirts of Delhi—and some were reported to have been led by Congress (I) functionaries.[39] What was spontaneous was the protection given by Hindus to their Sikh friends and neighbors, but this was not enough to save the Sikhs from the deep trauma that widened the communal divide.

Rajiv Gandhi announced that his first priority as Prime Minister was the Punjab, and among his first acts was the appointment of a high-level Cabinet committee to review the options for a political solution to the crisis. But it was nearly three months before Rajiv made his first move, with the release of eight jailed Akali leaders, including Akali President Longowal. A month later, in concession to Sikh demands, Rajiv at long last ordered an independent judicial inquiry into the anti-Sikh riots that followed his mother's death. Against a backdrop of factional division and discord within the Akali Dal, Longowal entered into secret negotiations with the government toward a resolution of the Punjab crisis. Their efforts were given greater urgency by the midair explosion of an Air India 747 with 329 passengers aboard—the apparent result of a terrorist bomb.

In August 1985, Prime Minister Rajiv Gandhi and the Akali leader signed a "memorandum of settlement." With a sense of relief, shared by the vast majority of his fellow Sikhs, Longowal said, "The long period of confrontation is over and we are fully satisfied with the deal." The government had conceded to the major Akali demands. Under the terms of the accord, Chandigarh was to become the capital

[39]See *Who Are the Guilty? Report of a Joint Inquiry into the Causes and Impact of the Riots in Delhi from 31 October to 10 November* (New Delhi: People's Union for Democratic Rights and People's Union for Civil Liberties, 1984).

of the Punjab. A commission would be constituted to determine the specific Hindi-speaking areas of Punjab that would go to Haryana by way of compensation. The dispute on the allocation of river waters would be referred to a tribunal, and the decision would be binding on both Punjab and Haryana. Other provisions provided assurances against discrimination to Sikhs in the military; for regulation of Sikh temples "in consultation with the Akali Dal"; and for the promotion of the Punjabi language.

Although some moderate Sikh leaders initially objected to the accord as a "betrayal" of Sikh interests in falling short of the full demands, they acquiesced, and the Akali Dal formally approved the agreement. Militant Sikhs denounced the accord, and in Haryana and Rajasthan, Congress and opposition leaders protested what they viewed as government capitulation to the Sikhs.

To return Punjab to representative government, Rajiv Gandhi announced that state assembly and parliamentary elections would be held in late September 1985. Longowal and opposition party leaders, arguing that more time was necessary to calm the atmosphere, urged that polling be postponed. In Gandhi's view, however, to put off elections was to yield to terrorist intimidation. Isolated and increasingly desperate, Sikh terrorists struck, first with the murder of a Congress MP who was alleged to have played a role in the anti-Sikh rioting following Indira Gandhi's death, then by the assassination of Longowal as he addressed a meeting in a Sikh temple. Longowal's death, less than a month after he had signed the accord with the Prime Minister, heightened fears of greater violence to subvert the Punjab settlement and sabotage the elections. Despite the threat of violence and the militant call for a boycott, Punjabis repudiated extremism in an electoral turnout of 67 percent. For the first time on its own, the Akali Dal, led by Sikh moderates committed to the accord, won an absolute majority in the assembly. It was, Rajiv Gandhi declared, a victory for democracy and India—but hope for peace in the Punjab was short-lived.

The Akali government, headed by Surjit Singh Barnala, was virtually immobilized by factionalism, and the Akali party split. Extremists, with Khalistan as their goal, again seized the initiative, taking control of the state committee that managed Sikh temples and "excommunicating" Chief Minister Barnala. With rising violence, the Center mounted new military and paramilitary operations that further alienated the people from the government. In May 1987, declaring the state government unable to control terrorist activities, the Center imposed President's Rule.

The Barnala government, however, had been undermined by the

Center itself and by the failure of Rajiv Gandhi to implement the terms of the 1985 accord. The reason was basically political. Gandhi feared alienating Hindus, especially in Haryana, where elections scheduled for June threatened Congress power. The Center backed away from its commitment to transfer Chandigarh when the Chief Ministers of the Punjab and Haryana were unable to agree on land compensation. The Center failed as well, however, to move on adjudication of the water dispute between Punjab and Haryana, and it took no action to identify and prosecute those responsible for the 1984 anti-Sikh riots.

Force supplanted efforts to find a political solution in the Punjab. Terrorism and police excesses fed upon the other in escalating violence.[40] Sikh militants reoccupied the Golden Temple, and in May 1988, in what might have been a replay of Operation Bluestar, paramilitary forces surrounded the temple and, in a 10-day siege that left 50 dead, cleared the temple of extremists. Events in the Punjab sharpened international tensions as well, as India denounced Pakistan for alleged support—training and supply of arms—for Sikh terrorists.

New hope for the Punjab came with the formation of the National Front/Janata Dal government at the Center in December 1989. Gandhi and the Congress (I) were out of power, opening the possibility of negotiations into which Sikh militants might enter without loss of face. Expectations rose as Prime Minister V. P. Singh went to Amritsar to offer his prayers at the Golden Temple, but the minority government was itself hostage to Hindu sentiment and its dependency on the Hindu nationalist Bharatiya Janata Party. The subsequent Chandra Shekhar government, dependent on Gandhi's support, fared no better. A few Sikh militants were willing to enter into political dialogue, but for many terrorist gangs, political goals had been displaced by extortion, robbery, and murder as a way of life.

Every year the death toll increased, with 4768 people, including 2177 militants, killed in 1991. From the beginning of the agitation in 1981 through 1991, more than 16,000 people died in Punjab violence. From 1987, with President's Rule extended every six months, a succession of Governors directed state administration and counterterrorist operations. State assembly and Lok Sabha elections were to have returned the Punjab to the political process in 1991. The people, sickened by both terrorism and police repression, were ready. One day before balloting, however, the central Election Commission cancelled the elections, citing the violence that had taken the lives of 29 candi-

[40]For an assessment of human rights violations, see Asia Watch, *Punjab in Crisis* (New York: Human Rights Watch, 1991).

dates. The action was taken in all likelihood at the behest of the Congress (I), which had boycotted the elections and which, had elections been held, would have been closed out politically. Elections were rescheduled, only to be cancelled again, then set for February 19, 1992.

To ensure security during the elections, more than 300,000 troops and police were deployed. All but one of the Akali factions boycotted the elections, and Sikh militants threatened to kill the first person to vote at any polling station. The voter turnout was 21.6 percent (down from 67.6 percent in 1985). In rural Punjab, where Sikhs are concentrated, only 15.1 percent voted, and in hundreds of villages not a single person turned out at the polls. In urban areas, those who did vote were largely Hindu. The results gave the Congress (I) 12 of the 13 parliamentary seats, strengthening Narasimha Rao's position in the Lok Sabha. In the state legislative assembly, Congress won 87 of the 117 seats. After 56 months of direct rule from New Delhi, elections brought a new government to power in the Punjab. For most Sikhs, however, it was a Center puppet without legitimacy, and militants vowed to continue their struggle for Khalistan.[41]

Jammu and Kashmir[42]

Jammu and Kashmir, in the Himalayan ranges, is India's only Muslim majority state. From the time of partition, it has been the subject of dispute with Pakistan, and for this reason alone, any unrest in Kashmir has been viewed in New Delhi with particular alarm. Kashmir has a special status under Article 370 of the Constitution, with an autonomy that distinguishes it from all other states. This status, the result of the conditions on which Kashmir acceded to the Union in 1947, has been jealously guarded, and any action by the Center or by Kashmiri politicians perceived as diminishing that autonomy has heightened anti-Indian feeling among the strongly nationalist Muslims. Kashmiri Muslim leaders of the National Conference, the dominant regional party of the state, supported union with India. Many Kashmiris, however, do not regard themselves as Indian. From the time of partition, some have been avowedly pro-Pakistan and others,

[41] Paul Wallace, "India's 1991 and 1992 Elections: Regional Factors in Haryana & Punjab," in Harold A. Gould and Sumit Ganguly, eds., *India Votes: The Quest for Consensus, 1989 and 1991* (Boulder, Colo.: Westview Press, 1993).

[42] For an overview of the Kashmir dispute and the movement for secession, see Raju G. C. Thomas, ed., *Perspectives on Kashmir: The Roots of Conflict* (Boulder, Colo.: Westview Press, 1992), and M. J. Akbar, *Kashmir: Behind the Vale* (New Delhi: Viking Penguin, 1991).

no doubt, sympathetic, yet the larger number, had they the opportunity to express their preference by plebiscite, would likely have opted for an independent Kashmir.

The state of Jammu and Kashmir, forged by the Hindu Dogra maharajas in the 18th and 19th centuries, is ethnically and religiously divided. Kashmir proper, with the capital Srinigar and its valley, is overwhelmingly Muslim, with a small Hindu minority—largely Brahmin Pundit families—with whom historically the Muslims enjoyed good relations. To the south, Jammu is predominantly Hindu, with the Dogras the dominant ethnic group. There incipient Dogra "nationalism," fed by Hindu resentment against Kashmir's Muslim majority, has periodically raised the demand for a separate state of Jammu. To the west is the high arid region of Ladakh, sparsely populated by Tibetan Buddhists, who favor separate political status within India as a Union Territory.

India and Pakistan have fought two wars over Kashmir, at the time of partition and again in 1965, when Pakistan invaded Kashmir with the expectation that Muslims there would rise up in revolt. There was no uprising, but, over the years, more and more Kashmiri Muslims—increasingly alienated by fraudulent elections, widespread corruption, and failure of the Center to develop the state economically—responded to the nationalist call for the liberation of Kashmir from "Hindu India."

In 1988, the Jammu and Kashmir Liberation Front (JKLF) and an assortment of separatist and fundamentalist groups initiated a wave of strikes, bombings, and assassinations. The state National Conference–Congress (I) coalition government under Chief Minister Farooq Abdullah, inept, corrupt, and lacking credibility, had lost effective control of the Kashmir valley to the separatists. The National Front government had hardly taken office at the Center, when in December 1989 the JKLF abducted the daughter of the new home minister—the first Muslim to serve in that sensitive position—and held her hostage for the release of five jailed militants. When the exchange was made, jubilant crowds throughout the valley raised the banner of the Liberation Front and called for India to "Quit Kashmir." In the ensuing turmoil, the Center dismissed the Farooq government and imposed President's Rule, only to face widespread resistance and a mounting death toll. Targeted by militants, Hindus in the valley fled their homes for refuge in Jammu and Delhi.

Kashmiri insurgents launched attacks against police stations and government offices and engaged in assassination, summary executions, and terrorist bombings in public places. India responded with what was decried as an indiscriminate use of force, mass reprisal, and the alleged use of torture to extract information, deepening and extending the alienation of the people of Kashmir.[43] *India Today*, India's leading news magazine, portrayed the situation starkly:

> Kashmir is at war with India. It is a declared war with open moral, financial, and logistical support from Pakistan. . . . [T]he secessionists have virtually achieved the administrative and psychological severance of the [Kashmir] valley from India. . . . In Kashmir nobody, either out of fear or out of the total alienation that pervades the region, now talks for India or even a settlement with the Center.[44]

There are three principal groups involved in the Kashmir insurgency, each with a number of loosely allied organizations operating under its aegis.[45] The Jammu and Kashmir Liberation Front, founded in 1965, affirms a secular identity in pursuit of a separate and independent Jammu and Kashmir. The JKLF and its allies are believed to have the widest base of popular support, but they are increasingly challenged by the fundamentalist Hezb-ul-Mujahideen (HUM), closely linked to the Pakistani Jammiat-i-Islami party and the presumed recipient of Pakistani largess. The third, also fundamentalist, is the Jammu and Kashmir People's League, which explicitly seeks the merger of Kashmir with Pakistan.

The sources of the separatist movement are internal to Kashmir and owe their origins to years of "maladministration and political manipulation" by authorities in both New Delhi and Srinagar, but the agitation has been supported and exacerbated by elements within Pakistan.[46] "Incontrovertible evidence of direct Pakistani involvement in the training and arming of the insurgents is hard to establish," as Sumit Ganguly notes,[47] but it is clear that the insurgents find sanctuary in Pakistani-held Azad Kashmir and have ready access to the Pakistani arms bazaar.

[43] Sumit Ganguly, "The Kashmiri Insurgency As a Challenge to Indian Secularism," unpublished paper, presented at the conference on "Religion, Politics, and Identity," at the University of Hull, England, October 24–27, 1991. Both sides in the Kashmir conflict have been responsible for human rights abuses. See Asia Watch, *Kashmir under Siege* (New York: Human Rights Watch, 1991).

[44] *India Today*, "Kashmir: Perilous Turn," April 30, 1990, p. 10.

[45] Sumit Ganguly, "Avoiding War in Kashmir," *Foreign Affairs*, 69 (Winter 1990/91): 64–65.

[46] Jagat S. Mehta, "Resolving Kashmir in the International Context of the 1990s," in Thomas, *Perspectives on Kashmir*, pp. 388–409.

[47] Ganguly, "Avoiding War in Kashmir," p. 65.

India has the military power to hold Kashmir, but any solution is likely to come at a high cost. India–Pakistan relations have already fallen victim, as domestic politics in each nation inflated the rhetoric of mutual hostility and, in the spring 1990, brought the two countries close to war. The Indian government's options are limited. Kashmir is a potent symbol in India. No government can yield to demands for a plebiscite and politically survive, but the argument that Kashmir as a part of India is at once a denial of the "two nation" theory and a "guarantor" of Indian secularism hardly washes when Kashmir is held by a force of occupation. Indeed, such conditions deepen feelings of insecurity among India's 100 million Muslims, but to let Kashmir go might only compound the tragedy, with the potential for reprisals against Indian Muslims and an invigorated attack on secularism by the forces of Hindu nationalism.[48]

As an expression of that force, the Bharatiya Janata Party launched a 15,000-kilometer motor caravan, the Ekta Yatra, or Pilgrimage of Unity, on December 11, 1991, from Kanyakumari, at the southern tip of India, to Srinagar, where on Republic Day, January 26, 1992, the Indian tricolor would be unfurled. Led by BJP President Murli Manohar Joshi, with the demand that Article 370, giving special status to Kashmir, be rescinded, the yatra was to be both an affirmation of Indian unity and a challenge to Kashmiri separatists. As the caravan crossed the Punjab, Sikh assassins opened fire on buses carrying the Hindu militants, killing six. A day later, as the BJP leaders entered Jammu, Kashmiri rebels detonated a bomb destroying the police headquarters at Srinagar and vowed that Joshi's caravan would be stopped. Unable to protect even their highest officers, Indian security forces, despite the presence of some 200,000 troops, could not secure the entry of the caravan into the valley. With Srinagar under curfew, Joshi and his closest colleagues were flown in during the night, and at daybreak, on January 26, they raised the Indian flag.[49] But rather than evoking Indian unity, the Ekta Yatra dramatized the challenge of regionalism in a religiously and ethnically divided society and multinational state.

The Continuing Challenge

The regionalization of politics in India is an expression of the growth of mass politics—of heightened political consciousness, ex-

[48] Ashutosh Varshney, "India, Pakistan, and Kashmir: Antinomies of Nationalism," *Asian Survey*, 31 (November 1991): 1002–03.

[49] *The New York Times*, "Hindus Raise India's Flag in Kashmir," January 27, 1992, p. 4.

panding participation, and increasing competition for scarce resources. The coming years will likely witness new unrest in movements for the protection of language and culture; for greater state autonomy; for the formation of new states or autonomous regions; and for reservations in education and employment for "sons of the soil."

The cultural distinctiveness and economic and social disparities that nourish regionalism at the state level are found within a number of states. With heightened political consciousness and increased competition, demands for the creation of new states or for autonomous regions within states may be the catalyst for social unrest. Separate statehood movements, varying greatly in support and intensity, exist throughout India and frequently involve depressed regions, such as the tribal areas of Bihar, Orissa, and Madhya Pradesh; the hill districts of Bengal; the eastern districts of Uttar Pradesh; the Saurashtra region of Gujarat; the Vidarbha region of Maharashtra; and the Telengana region of Andhra. Of a somewhat different character is the demand by some in Haryana for adjacent districts of Rajasthan and Uttar Pradesh in order to create Vishal (greater) Haryana.

Such movements tend to be episodic, as seen, for example, in the mid-1980s, when the All Jharkhand Students Union revived the demand for the creation of a tribal Jharkhand state of the mineral-rich Chota–Nagpur region of southern Bihar and contiguous tribal districts in the neighboring states of Orissa, Madhya Pradesh, and West Bengal. In early 1992, the militant Jharkhand Mukti Morcha (JMM) flexed its muscles in a dramatic 10-day economic blockade that stopped the supply of coal to the nation's power and steel industry. Potentially more serious in the movement for Jharkhand is the organization of a JMM commando unit that could take the region along the path of Assam.

In the northern hill district of Darjeeling in West Bengal, the ethnically dominant Nepalis (Gurkhas) have periodically voiced demands for greater autonomy. In 1986, frustrated by economic exploitation and lack of political power, the Gurkha National Liberation Front (GNLF) launched a struggle for the creation of a separate state of Gurkhaland to be carved out of West Bengal. After two years of violence, in which more than 300 people were killed, the GNLF accepted the West Bengal government's proposal to form what would be, in effect, an autonomous region within the state of West Bengal. Its elected Darjeeling Gurkha Hill Council was granted wide powers in finance and control over such matters as education, health, agriculture, and economic development.

In the non-Hindi states the forces of nationalization and centralization have reinforced a consciousness of their distinct cultural identities. With it has come a plethora of chauvinistic movements, rivaled perhaps only by the chauvinism of the Hindi region itself. Such movements are nourished by heightened competition for resources aggravated by slow economic growth; by widening regional disparities; and by the sense of relative deprivation they inevitably engender.

Nativist "sons of the soil" movements have arisen in regions where culturally distinct migrants from outside the state are perceived as blocking opportunities for "locals" to advance. They are almost wholly urban and express the frustrated aspirations of an expanding, educated lower-middle-class. A number of states—Maharashtra, Karnataka, Tamil Nadu, and West Bengal—have enacted legislation providing educational and employment preferences for "sons of the soil." The most virulent movements have been the Shiv Sena in Bombay and the Kannada Chaluvaligars in Bangalore. Although now quiescent, they could again erupt in violence. Under the pressure of competition for jobs, similar movements could grow throughout India. As aspirations rise, social conflict is likely to deepen.

Recommended Reading

Bose, Tarum Chandra, ed., *Indian Federalism: Problems and Issues.* Calcutta: K. P. Bagchi, 1987. A useful collection of papers exploring a range of issues in Center–state relations.

*Brass, Paul R., *Ethnicity and Nationalism: Theory and Comparison.* New Delhi: Sage, 1991. An extension of his earlier *Language, Religion, and Politics in North India* (1974); with particular attention to the Punjab, it is a powerful and provocative study.

*———, *The Politics of India since Independence.* Cambridge: Cambridge University Press, 1990. An excellent study of the Indian state, society, and economy, especially good in treatment of the politics of language and ethnic conflict.

Datta, Abhijit, ed., *Union–State Relations.* New Delhi: Indian Institute of Public Administration, 1984. Penetrating analyses of a range of problems in the federal relationship.

Fadia, Babulal, *State Politics in India,* 2 vols. New Delhi: Radiant, 1984. An examination of the structures and processes of politics in the states in their historical and social contexts. Very useful.

*Available in a paperback edition.

Harrison, Selig S., *India: The Most Dangerous Decades*. Princeton, N.J.: Princeton University Press, 1960. Posing the problem of India's viability as a nation, this often-cited book examines the stresses imposed by the "fissiparous tendencies" of linguistic regionalism, caste, and political extremism.

*Jeffrey, Robin, *What's Happening to India? Punjab, Ethnic Conflict, Mrs. Gandhi's Death and the Test for Federalism*. New York: Holmes & Meir, 1986.

Menon, V. P., *The Story of the Integration of the Indian States*. Bombay: Orient Longman, 1956. An account of the merging of the princely states with the former provinces of British India into a single nation of India, written by one who played an instrumental part in the events, Sardar Patel's lieutenant, the ICS secretary to the newly created Ministry of States.

Pal, Chandra, *State Autonomy in Indian Federalism: Emerging Trends*, New Delhi: Deep & Deep, 1984. An analysis of the demands for greater state autonomy from a legal perspective.

Phadnis, Urmila, *Ethnicity and Nation-Building in South Asia*, New Delhi: Sage, 1989. A study of the dynamics of ethnic identities and movements.

Prasad, Anirudh, *Centre and State Powers Under Indian Federalism*, 2nd ed., New Delhi: Deep and Deep, 1984. A detailed constitutional-law perspective.

Wallace, Paul, ed., *Region and Nation in India*. New Delhi: Oxford University Press, 1985. A collection of essays in honor of the late Richard L. Park, an American political scientist who influenced a generation of young India specialists.

Weiner, Myron, *Sons of the Soil: Migration and Ethnic Conflict in India*. Princeton, N.J.: Princeton University Press, 1978. Examines the clash between the migrants' claims to equal access and the claims of local groups to protection by the state.

*Wood, John R., *State Politics in Contemporary India: Crisis or Continuity?* Boulder, Colo.: Westview Press, 1984. Perceptive essays on selected Indian states.

Chapter 5

Arenas of Conflict: Groups in Indian Politics

NO POLITICAL SYSTEM CAN SATISFY ALL THE DEMANDS OF all its members all the time. Its response to public pressure is calculated in accordance with the political capital that backs various demands—numbers, wealth, prestige, or violence. The legitimacy of a particular demand, that is, its congruence with basic values in the society, is a major factor in political response. More important still is the access afforded demands in general, which is of critical importance in the development of a stable and responsive political system. If resources are limited, demands may far outrun the capacity of the government to respond. Rational economic planning may conflict with the exigencies of democratic response, and decision makers may come to consider demands as such illegitimate and argue that the compulsions of a backward society require the restriction of political access and democratic competition. From this point of view competition serves only to stimulate the formation of demands, as parties bid for support and thus raise the level of frustration.

In India there is a basic distrust of politics as a struggle for power, reflecting the traditional view that those who seek power are suspect. "Each man must accept his own *dharma* (duty) and perform his duty well. . . . Authority is acceptable, but to struggle for a position of authority is not."[1] W. H. Morris-Jones has written of a "paradoxical or ambivalent attitude to authority. Authority in India appears to be

[1]Myron Weiner, "Struggle against Power: Notes on Indian Political Behavior," *World Politics*, 8 (April 1956): 395.

subject at once to much more abusive criticism and much more effusive adulation than one is accustomed to elsewhere."[2] Leaders, ideally, are to be above politics. Mahatma Gandhi, for example, was not a formal member of the Congress party. Socialist leader Jayaprakash Narayan renounced party politics altogether to follow in the steps of Vinoba Bhave, the "walking saint," whose *Bhoodan*, or land-gift, movement called for self-sacrifice and "polity without power." A fundamental tension exists, however, between modern democratic values and the nostalgia for consensus, whether it is in the name of tradition or rationality. The expectation that politicians are to wear a saintly mantle of self-sacrifice and the realization that they are all too often the victims of human foibles have bred a general cynicism about political life even as the political system itself has gained increasing legitimacy.

India's Political Culture

Political culture involves the values, attitudes, orientations, and myths relevant to politics and the social structures that help shape them.[3] The Indian nationalist elite superimposed the framework of a liberal democratic state on a highly traditional, diverse, stratified, and pluralistic social order. It was this contrast between a polity based on egalitarian values and a society that was rigidly hierarchical that led many observers to question the meaning, utility, and impact of democratic politics in India.

A variety of detailed studies conducted by both Indian and non-Indian scholars, however, demonstrate that colonial rule, the nationalist struggle, socioeconomic change, and more than four decades of competitive politics based on mass franchise have begun to alter pro-

[2] W. H. Morris-Jones, *Parliament in India* (London: Longmans, Green, 1957), p. 34. In an incisive essay on politics and society in India, Morris-Jones writes of the "three languages" of politics in which Indian politics is conducted: the modern, the traditional, and the saintly. *The Government and Politics of India*, 3rd ed. (London: Hutchinson, 1971), pp. 52–61.

[3] Ashis Nandy provides a penetrating analysis of aspects of India's political culture in *At the Edge of Psychology: Essays in Politics and Culture* (Delhi: Oxford University Press, 1980). In a symposium on the Nandy volume in *The Journal of Commonwealth and Comparative Politics*, 22 (November 1984), see especially Franklin A. Presler, "Studying India's Political Culture," pp. 224–34, and Ashis Nandy, "Cultures of Politics and Politics of Cultures," pp. 262–74. Also see Ram Avtar Sharma and Sushma Yadav, eds., *Political Culture in Post-Independent India* (New Delhi: Sharma Yadav, 1989).

foundly Indian social structure, values, and political behavior.[4] Thus, although this accelerated process of change has generated substantial tensions among India's antecedent social groups, the new political institutions created by the nationalist elite came to play a significant role in helping to channel, moderate, and manage these tensions, and have contributed to the integration of India's heterogeneous social structure and regional diversities. Competitive party politics and political pluralism have contributed substantially to the level of integration and legitimacy that the Indian political system has achieved.

From the time of independence, the mass franchise began to expand the size and scope of the political community and legitimized political participation as a mechanism for the achievement of group aspirations and goals. Just as the nationalist movement had socialized the upper and middle levels of Indian society into politics, so the new political order began to draw the bottom sectors of Indian society into public life as participants.[5] Politics acquired greater relevance to more and more groups who sought to achieve their objectives through the political process rather than from outside. This transformation, in turn, led to a gradual dispersion of political power in India.

The dispersion of political power was accompanied by the gradual extension of linkages from national to state to village levels. Thus a combined process of modern politics from above and societal pressure from below was linked through the process of mass franchise. As the system of recruitment, mobilization, and participation from above grew and spread, it resulted in a continuous exposure of formerly inert sections of Indian society to new political forms, and it socialized the polity into new modes of identity and action. Gradually the initial process of mobilization through traditional loyalties and dependencies was transformed into a process of mass politics. Traditional and modern modes of behavior were being fused as the system deepened and expanded its influence and penetrated the countryside. Participation increased in scope, intensity, and relevance.

By the early 1970s it became increasingly clear that democratic politics in India was beginning to take root as people became genuinely involved in the new institutions and processes of the system. They were acquiring a more sophisticated knowledge of the system and

[4]See Samuel J. Eldersveld and Bashiruddin Ahmed, *Citizens and Politics: Mass Political Behavior in India* (Chicago: University of Chicago Press, 1978); John Osgood Field, *Consolidating Democracy: Politicization and Partisanship in India* (New Delhi: Manohar, 1980); and David Elkins, *Electoral Participation in a South Indian Context* (New Delhi: Vikas, 1975).

[5]Bashiruddin Ahmed, "Trends and Options," *Seminar*, 248 (April 1980): 13.

were developing a sense of commitment to these institutions. The increase in the level of interest, knowledge, and efficacy, in turn, affected their political behavior. Those who were involved and participated tended to hold a positive image of the political system and its legitimacy.[6]

Ironically, at the very time when larger and larger segments of society had become increasingly socialized to believe in and participate in the political system, sectors of India's ruling elites began to have doubts about its continued efficacy. These doubts were due, at least in part, to the heightened social tensions and conflict that developed in the wake of increasing fragmentation and competition brought on by the accelerating process of social, economic, and political change.

Modern politics, economic development, and increased levels of participation have tended to Indianize the political process, politicize and intensify the sense of identity among antecedent groups in the society, and heighten social conflict at a time when the mechanisms of political management began to weaken. Sectors of the political elite began to see the assertion of religious and ethnic loyalties as threats to national unity, social change, and economic development rather than as indicators of the very nature of that change itself. Many saw a more centralized—perhaps presidential—system as a way of imposing unity from above and warding off the dangers of these divisive, balkanizing threats. Supporters of the existing system, however, felt that successful management of India's diverse religious, linguistic, caste, class, and regional diversities required the very type of open, pluralistic, participatory system created by India's 1950 Constitution. They feared that a centralized system would be less representative, less responsive, and more brittle, and that it would bring about the very balkanization that proponents of centralization sought to prevent.

The Role of Interest Groups in Indian Political Development

As wider sectors of Indian society have been politicized through the expansion, dispersion, and democratization of power, larger numbers of people have been drawn into the political system. Political life at state and local levels—and increasingly at the national level—is

[6]The study of Indian political behavior by Eldersveld and Ahmed—*Citizens and Politics*—documents the gradual increase in interest, knowledge, efficiency, and participation.

directed by a new leadership, with roots in the villages and sensitivity to factional and caste loyalties and to emerging class interests. The credentials of the new leadership are instrumental, not sacrificial; government and party are something to be used.[7]

Although the new entrants into politics may often operate in a traditional mode, the political issues are by no means traditional. "There is nothing traditional about demands for more schools, roads, wells, fertilizers, and jobs."[8] Traditional structures and patterns of behavior may be resilient and adaptive to new and changing environments, becoming, for example, channels of interest articulation and instruments of political pressure. The distinction between tradition and modernity blurs as, in dialectical relationship, they "infiltrate and transform each other."[9] In this process politics has become more meaningful to the mass electorate, potentially more responsive to its demands. As politics has become more vernacular, however, it has been decried by those suspicious of group pressure as pandering to narrow and special interests and the irrationalities of castism, communalism, and regionalism. Interest groups, as agents of political demands, are seen as disruptive of order and consensus.

In India interest groups have been slow to develop, but although they now number in the thousands, they are disparate and weak. They have been unable to accommodate and channel rapidly expanding participation and the emergence of new groups to political consciousness. Under the British those individuals and groups commanding traditional sources of power exerted pressure at the local administrative level. Those without power had little access to the administration, and from a position of powerlessness they regarded the government as an extractive force to be avoided whenever possible. Most mass organizations developed from the activities of the nationalist movement, and even in the years since independence, most interest groups have been connected with political parties, more agents of mobilization than of interest articulation.

Most Indians have a low sense of political efficacy. In their opinion, government officials are generally distant, unresponsive, and corrupt. Officials, on the other hand, regard interest-group activity with

[7]Myron Weiner, "India's Two Political Cultures," in Lucian Pye and Sidney Verba, eds., *Political Culture and Political Development* (Princeton, N.J.: Princeton University Press, 1965), p. 212.

[8]Weiner, "India's Two Cultures," p. 241.

[9]Lloyd I. Rudolph and Susanne H. Rudolph, *The Modernity of Tradition* (Chicago: University of Chicago Press, 1967), p. 3.

distrust. Rational policy formation, they argue, should be unaffected by their narrow demands. Consequently, group pressure in India has been directed toward influencing the administration and implementation of policy rather than its formation. Its greatest success has been achieved in forestalling certain government actions and in modifying policy rather than in initiating it. It is at the state and local administrative levels that officials have been particularly responsive to such pressure, and it has been the landed interests which have been most adept in applying it; land-reform legislation may be quietly forgotten as development funds are channeled into the hands most capable of utilizing them, the landed middle peasantry. Those who have nothing are unlikely to reap the benefits of government action, for they lack the resources of immediate political capital. In the long run, however, once mobilized, they pose a major challenge.

In the name of rationality and the public interest, decision makers have often turned deaf ears to the demands of interest groups. Because the government is unresponsive, groups resort to mass demonstrations, hartals, strikes, and civil disobedience to force government action. This, in turn, only confirms the official image that the groups are irresponsible and that such mass activity is against the national interest. The government does respond to such action, however; the political capital to which it has proved most sensitive is violence. Various legal measures, such as the Preventive Detention Act and the emergency provisions in the Constitution, have been enacted to restrain political activity that threatens public order. The line between activities that do threaten public order and those that do not may be thin, since group politics itself is regarded with suspicion. Disaffected groups have used Gandhian techniques of civil disobedience against the Indian government. Based on a tradition of direct action, such acts are nevertheless officially viewed as an unfair and perverted use of satyagraha. Mass political activity has often been violent, but disorder seems vindicated by success. "Only when public order is endangered by a mass movement is the government willing to make a concession," Myron Weiner writes, "not because they consider the demand legitimate, but because they then recognize the strength of the group making the demand and its capacity for destructiveness. Thus, the government often alternates between unresponsiveness to the demands of large but peaceful groups and total concession to groups that press their demands violently."[10] The ca-

[10]Myron Weiner, *The Politics of Scarcity* (Chicago: University of Chicago Press, 1962), p. 201.

pitulation of the government to the demands for states reorganization only in the wake of widespread rioting and the re-evaluation of official language policy only after prolonged agitation are classic examples of the efficacy of violence. That mass actions have succeeded so frequently has given them a certain legitimacy.

Protest in India takes many forms, and the various terms used to describe them are working their way into the English language, just as such words as "thug" and "goonda" did earlier.

Satyagraha, Gandhi's "truth force" of civil disobedience, is used by groups of every political hue, although it is officially viewed as unjustified in the context of an independent and democratic India.

Hartal, another Gandhian technique, is a general strike involving the cessation of all public activity.

Bandh, popularized by the left, is a strike in which confrontation is an integral part of the protest.

Dharna is a refusal to clear the area when ordered to do so. It is common to see protestors with flags, pickets, and placards in front of government offices as well as private companies. In a "sitting dharna," prominent persons—typically politicians—seat themselves before the building of the offending party. They sometimes dramatize their protest by a hunger strike. The threatened "fast unto death," used by Gandhi with such effectiveness, remains a potent weapon if the person is of sufficient prestige. In 1975 Indira Gandhi yielded to the demand for elections in Gujarat in the face of Morarji Desai's fast. Were he to have died, serious rioting would surely have posed a major threat to Mrs. Gandhi's government. As a form of political extortion, leading as it did to the Congress's electoral defeat, Desai's fast was one of the many ingredients in Mrs. Gandhi's decision months later to impose the emergency.

Gherao involves the physical encirclement of a managerial staff—usually that of a company or university—to secure "quick justice."

Jail boro involves mass violation of the law in order to inundate the jails and clog the courts.

Rasta roko, literally "block the road," involves the formation of a gridlock by protestors in order to disrupt traffic. Prosperous farmers demanding higher crop prices have blocked roads with their tractors, and striking university students have snarled traffic in Connaught Circus, the hub of New Delhi. A variation on the tactic is the *rail roko*, blocking the railways.

Morcha, a military term meaning battle formation, has been taken by the Akalis to describe their protest movement in the Punjab, and by V. P. Singh in his People's Movement, Jan Morcha.

On any given day there are hundreds of such protests (or *anandolan*) throughout India, most of which proceed peaceably, but each of which carries the potential for violence. The tempo of violence has increased yearly in India. Because the Indian government officially defines a riot as involving five or more people, the category, which includes brawls, gives little indication of the intensity or seriousness of the dispute, and obviously the statistics do not record "official violence"—for example, police repression, police firings, and lathi charges—attacks with the long sticks used by Indian police as enforcement weapons. Hundreds of riots are recorded each year, with the widening perception that there is a breakdown of law and order.[11]

The relationship between order and responsiveness lies at the heart of the development process. In India the solution has too often been a declamation of radical intent followed by conservative inaction, reflecting the power of interests upon which political support rests. The plea for a "bargaining culture" of pluralism only brings to the surface what is already a political reality: The government will be responsive to those groups with effective political resources. As increasingly larger numbers have sought access to the political system over the years of India's independence, social conflict has sharpened. Within the arenas of conflict, groups abound, but they remain localized, fragmented, and inchoate—tessera in the vast and complex mosaic of Indian society.

Arenas of Conflict

For all the pressures upon it, India's stability stands in sharp contrast to most nations of the Third World. Since independence in 1947, the regime has never been seriously threatened by uprisings, coups, or revolution, nor does such a prospect lie on the horizon. India's political order—parliamentary democracy—has a legitimacy paralleled in few nations of the Third World. On the death of three prime ministers, Nehru, Shastri, and Indira Gandhi, it witnessed orderly succession. Through free and competitive elections, India has undergone peaceful transitions of political power from one party to another. Indian national unity, though challenged by separatist movements, is

[11]Robert L. Hardgrave, Jr., *India under Pressure: Prospects for Political Stability* (Boulder, Colo.: Westview Press, 1984), pp. 14–16; Michael T. Kaufman provides a brief glossary in "In India, There's a Protester to Suit Any Given Occasion," *New York Times*, 23 April 1981.

bound by an increasingly national economy, a national system of communications, and (despite heightened regional sentiment) a growing national consciousness.

Popular images—terrorism in the Punjab, massacre in Assam, secessionist struggle in Kashmir, communal riots, atrocities against untouchables—belie India's fundamental political stability and national integrity. Having said this, the fact remains that social unrest is endemic in India, but it is—or, at least it has been—fundamentally manageable. It has been manageable for three principal reasons: the strength of India's institutions, particularly the Congress party; the nation's democratic political framework; and the sheer complexity of Indian society that with its multiplicity of social cleavages has tended to compartmentalize unrest.

It is ironic that the social complexity decried as the bane of national unity is one of the most important sources of India's stability. The cross-cutting divisions of caste, class, tribe, sect, religion, language, and region give India the character of a vast mosaic. Each social compartment is, to varying degrees, insulated from the other. This pattern is reinforced by the federal system in which state boundaries follow, for the most part, major divisions of language and regional identity. Structurally quarantined, social unrest that arises in one state rarely spreads to other states. Thus contained, it is more readily managed and controlled.

Whether this will continue to be true remains to be seen. The sources of national unity, particularly the increasingly integrated economy and communications systems, may provide the basis for an expression of all of India's discontent. What happens in one part of India increasingly has an impact throughout the nation and invokes a similar response. Whether it is a rise in the price of onions in Maharashtra, drought in Tamil Nadu, or strikes in the Bihar coalfields, few Indians are unaffected today. Throughout India, the media, multiplied in their effect by word of mouth, bring reports of the conversions of untouchables to Islam in a Tamil village, the farmers' movement in Maharashtra, and student protests in Delhi. Social unrest, once contained within state boundaries, may spill over into a movement of national dimension. From the vantage point of New Delhi, it is one thing to put out isolated brush fires as they occur, quite another to face many at the same time—especially as they may join in a national firestorm of social unrest. Social unrest, as it grows in intensity and, even more critically, as it arises simultaneously in a number of states, places an increasing strain on India's institutional capacity. The institutional strength of its party system (of which the Congress has been the nucleus), its bureaucracy, and its army is the bedrock of India's political stability. As those institutions are weakened, so too its capacity to accommodate and reconcile political demands, to cope with change, and to control social unrest is inevitably reduced.

The strength and responsiveness of India's democratic political institutions undergird its political stability. If the complexity of Indian society is at once a source of both conflict and stability, it is also the most compelling reason why some form of democracy is necessary to ensure that stability. There is in India a broad-based commitment to democratic politics that has been reinforced and extended with each successive election. Democracy in India provides the framework by which expanding participation can be absorbed and ordered, by which the nation's many interests can find meaningful expression, and by which conflicts can be reconciled. It does so imperfectly and incompletely—but the remedy is not less democracy. Censorship of the press, banning of political parties, postponement of elections, imprisonment of political opponents—in short, the closure of political access—may put a lid on the expression of discontent, but it does not enhance the capacity of the government to cope with change. Instead, it isolates those in authority, as it did during the 1975–77 emergency, and deepens alienation and discontent within society.

Change exacerbates inequalities and disparities because it is experienced differentially. Inevitably, some benefit as others are hurt. It is not in the most backward regions and among the most depressed classes that discontent is most likely to manifest itself. Rather, the sources of social unrest are most likely to be found in those regions and among those classes experiencing more rapid change. This change may involve improvement or decline (real or imagined), either in absolute or relative terms. As in the movement of the earth's tectonic plates, conflict occurs along social fault lines, between groups in competition for the scarce goods of prosperity and power. It occurs most sharply between those groups which are rising and those which feel themselves threatened.

Communalism

The specter of communalism has been omnipresent in Indian political life, threatening unity and the secular ideal of the Constitution.[12]

[12]The concept and role of secularism in India has come under serious debate. See T. N. Madan, "Secularism in Its Place," *The Journal of Asian Studies*, 46 (November 1987): pp. 747–59; Ashis Nandy, "The Politics of Secularism and the Recovery of Religious Tolerance," in Veena Das, ed., *Mirrors of Violence: Communities, Riots and Survivors in South Asia* (Delhi: Oxford University Press, 1990), pp. 69–93; and, in response to Ma-

While Hindu–Sikh enmities have arisen in the Punjab crisis, the term "communalism" remains associated principally with Hindu–Muslim conflict. With the memories of partition still bitterly nurtured, Hindu–Muslim tensions are sustained by jealousy and fear. Each year several hundred incidents of communal violence are officially reported.[13] Most begin as a minor incident—frequently a dispute arising over a Hindu procession near a mosque—but however minor in themselves, they have frequently turned into major riots. The pattern is familiar, from rumors to bloodshed, with police intervention and then accusations of police excesses. This is usually followed by more clashes, often over a fairly wide area. Then, like a plague of locusts, it passes and the situation returns to "normalcy."

Communal riots are fueled by change and by "the revolution of rising frustration," the product of the widening gap between expectation and achievement. Their sources are in the volatile mix of religion and economic insecurity, and although evidence exists of organized preparation among both Hindus and Muslims in recent riots, they are essentially anomic, cathartic releases of rage. Muslims have been the principal victims of communal rioting, both in numbers (with three times as many casualties as among Hindus) and in a deepened sense of insecurity.

Communal violence is primarily an urban phenomenon—perhaps because most rural Muslims are too weak to pose a threat or to offer resistance. In instances of rural violence, however, the results can be devastating, as in Bhagalpur district in Bihar, where in 1989 nearly 1000 people died in a month-long communal frenzy. Rioting tends to be ad hoc, intermittent, and normally limited to a single city or locality—and it is thus manageable with sufficient application of force. But in recent years, in the growing confrontation between Muslim fun-

---

dan and Nandy, Upendra Baxi, "The 'Struggle' for the Redefinition of Secularism in India: Some Preliminary Reflections," unpublished paper, 1991. Also see Subrata Kumar Mitra, "Desecularising the State: Religion and Politics in India," *Comparative Studies in Society and History*, 33 (October 1991): 755–77.

[13]See the analyses of the nature and origin of communal violence in Asghar Ali Engineer, ed., *Communal Riots in Post-Independence India* (Hyderabad: Sangam Books, 1984); Imtiaz Ahmed, "Political Economy of Communalism in Contemporary India," *Economic and Political Weekly*, 2 June 1984, pp. 903–907; Asghar Ali Engineer, *Communalism and Communal Violence in India: An Analytical Approach to Hindu–Muslim Conflict* (Delhi: Ajanta, 1989); Riyaz Punjabi, "Inter-Religious Conflicts and Rise of Fundamentalism in India," *Mainstream*, 5 January 1991, pp. 15–21; and M. J. Akbar, *Riot after Riot: Reports on Caste and Communal Violence in India*, rev. ed. (New Delhi: Penguin, 1991). For a broad perspective by some of India's most distinguished analysts, see Veena Das, ed., *Mirrors of Violence: Communities, Riots, and Survivors in South Asia* (New Delhi: Oxford University Press, 1990).

damentalism and Hindu revivalism, communal rioting has been widespread and sustained. Not a year has passed without its high toll of deaths in communal violence. In 1987, in one of a series of riots across North India, organized gangs from both Hindu and Muslim communities in Meerut, Uttar Pradesh, ignited two days of rioting, with the police joining Hindus in the rampage that left 100 dead. And in 1989 and 1990, the Ayodhya temple dispute precipitated a wave of rioting and communal violence unrivaled since the partition of India in 1947.

Hindu Communalism

Hindus, who make up 83 percent of India's population, embrace a multitude of sects and worship god in many forms. Thus there is no distinct Hindu community as such, but Hindu chauvinism poses a major threat to the secular state. Rooted in the 19th-century Hindu revivalism of the Arya Samaj and the extremism of Tilak, Hindu communalism today is nourished by the tradition of the Hindu Mahasabha and is most prominently represented by the Rashtriya Swayamsevak Sangh (RSS) and its Vishwa Hindu Parishad (VHP) affiliate.

The Hindu Mahasabha was founded in reaction to the Muslim League, but in its early years the organization was obscured by the Congress party, with which most of its members were associated. The Lucknow Pact of 1916 and the ascendancy of the Moderates within the Congress alienated many of the Hindu extremists, however, and under the leadership of V. D. Savarkar, an admirer of Tilak and, like him, a Chitpavan Brahmin from Maharashtra, the Mahasabha parted with the Congress in a call to "Hinduize all politics and militarize Hinduism." Reform fused with revivalism in opposition to untouchability and caste inequality. To overcome the fragmentation of sect, caste, and language, the Mahasabha launched a movement for the consolidation of Hindu *rashtra*, or the Hindu nation. The movement sought to reclaim those who had left the Hindu fold, and it denounced the creation of Pakistan as the "vivisection" of Mother India.[14] Since 1960 the Mahasabha has been in decline, and is today no longer a potent force.

The Rashtriya Swayamsevak Sangh[15] was founded as a paramili-

[14]Donald E. Smith, *India As a Secular State* (Princeton, N.J.: Princeton University Press, 1963), pp. 455–64.

[15]See Walter K. Andersen and Shridhar D. Damle, *The Brotherhood in Saffron: The Rashtriya Swayamsevak Sangh and Hindu Revivalism* (Boulder, Colo.: Westview Press, 1987), and K. Jayaprasad, *RSS and Hindu Nationalism* (New Delhi: Deep & Deep, 1991).

tary organization in 1925 by Dr. Keshav Hedgewar. On his death in 1940 he was succeeded by M. S. Golwalkar, under whom the RSS grew rapidly. The RSS claims to be a movement directed toward achieving the cultural and spiritual regeneration of the Hindu nation through a disciplined vanguard that represents the ideal model of Hindu society. In January 1948, Mahatma Gandhi was assassinated by a Hindu fanatic who had been associated with both the Mahasabha and the RSS. In the face of an explosive public reaction, the Hindu Mahasabha, under the leadership of Dr. S. P. Mookerjee, who had succeeded Savarkar as president in 1943, suspended political activity. The RSS was banned by the government. The ban was lifted more than one year later only after the RSS agreed to renounce political activity and to publish a constitution. It was again banned during the 1975–1977 emergency imposed by Indira Gandhi, and a major portion of those arrested during the emergency were RSS members.

From 1977, the RSS undertook a major effort to expand membership, and it met with resounding success. It is estimated that there are today more than 1,000,000 members who attend meetings of the *shakha*, or unit, every day of the year. Here, for about one hour at either dawn or dusk, RSS volunteers uniformed in khaki shorts engage in an intensive program of ideological discussion, physical exercise, and military discipline. There are some 25,000 shakhas throughout India, each having up to 100 active members, with a neighborhood base.

RSS support is predominantly urban and lower middle class. From its traditional geographic core in North India, the movement has spread into the Northeast and into South India. It has also begun to make inroads into the countryside and has won support among Harijans and tribals. The RSS places increasing emphasis on social work and has been active in flood relief and in literacy campaigns. Its power is expanded through a web of more than 50 affiliated groups. Among the most important are the Bharatiya Mazdoor Sangh, India's second largest trade union; the Akhil Bharatiya Vidyarthi Parishad, the largest student group in India; and the Vishwa Hindu Parishad (VHP). RSS trusts publish 8 daily newspapers and 40 weeklies, including the English-language *Organiser*. In addition, the various affiliated organizations publish their own periodicals.

In the "family" of RSS affiliates, the Vishwa Hindu Parishad, under the leadership of Ashok Singhal, has assumed particular prominence. The VHP was established in 1964 to give the RSS a direct link to the Hindu ecclesiastical community. The organization had three objectives: "(1) to consolidate and strengthen Hindu society; (2) to protect and spread Hindu values, ethical and spiritual, and to make them relevant in contemporary Hindu society; and (3) to establish and strengthen the links among Hindus living in different countries."[16] VHP leaders are almost all RSS members, but the majority of its members in some 3500 branch units are not RSS cadres. Sanctioned by the RSS, the VHP has shaped its own family of organizations directed to social welfare work among untouchables, tribals, and the rural poor—those most vulnerable to religious conversion. Through its affiliates, the VHP operates student hostels, orphanages, vocational schools, medical missions, and temples. VHP prominence has been gained primarily through its campaigns to strengthen Hindu identity and solidarity, symbolized most dramatically by its leadership in the Ayodhya temple movement, discussed below.

Distinct from both the RSS and the VHP, the militant Bajrang Dal has been closely associated with the VHP in the movement to "liberate" Hindu holy shrines at Ayodhya and other sites where mosques now stand. The Dal is one of many *senas*, the armed gangs that have been described as the face of Hindu fascism. Their symbol and weapon is the *trishul*, the god Shiva's trident. In the Punjab, the Hindu Shiv Sena formed to counter Sikh terrorism; the Hindu Manch was a response to attacks on Hindus in the Punjab and Kashmir; and Shiv Shakti Dal organized in the wake of the anti-Sikh riots in Delhi. Most powerful is the Shiv Sena in Maharashtra, which since 1984 has transformed its earlier Marathi nativism into a stridently anti-Muslim party of Hindu chauvinism.[17] Led by Bal Thackeray, its founder, the Shiv Sena controls the Bombay city government and is the second largest party in the Maharashtra legislative assembly. The Shiv Sena has no direct ties to the RSS, but in the 1989 and 1991 parliamentary elections, it entered into an alliance with the Bharatiya Janata Party (BJP), the political party most closely associated with the RSS.

The political voice of the RSS was the Jana Sangh until its merger into the Janata Party in 1977, but the relationship of the RSS to the new party was a source of bitter internal dispute. Even the Jana Sangh faction was divided on the proper role of the RSS. With the collapse of the Janata government and the breakup of the party in 1980, the old Jana Sangh re-emerged as the Bharatiya Janata Party (BJP). The RSS constituted its cadre core, but as the BJP sought to expand its social base, the relationship grew increasingly uneasy. In the 1983

[16] Andersen and Damle, p. 133.

[17] Surendra Jondhale, "Resurgence of Militant Hindu Nationalism," *Mainstream*, 8 August 1987, pp. 9–14.

assembly elections in Jammu and Kashmir, where Indira Gandhi made an openly Hindu appeal, the RSS extended support to the Congress party, and in the 1984 parliamentary elections a substantial portion of the RSS abandoned the BJP for the Congress party. Although the BJP has resecured its RSS ties, the RSS maintains contact and cooperation with the Congress (I), and some high RSS leaders are known to favor a BJP–Congress (I) coalition.

The rise of Islamic fundamentalism in Iran, Pakistan, and Bangladesh has heightened Hindu consciousness, and fear of resurgent Islam in India was deepened by the issue of religious conversion. In 1981, more than 1000 Harijans in the village of Meenakshipuram in Tamil Nadu converted *en masse* to Islam. Picked up by the press, reports of "mass conversions" stirred the fear that Hinduism was in danger. The RSS alleged that a "foreign hand" was behind the conversions and that the goal—political power—could be achieved by expanding the numerical strength of the Muslim community. Money from the Persian Gulf countries, in its view, had become today's Khyber Pass through which Muslims sought to gain domination over India. The RSS and the Arya Samaj responded by a call for a ban on conversions to Islam and Christianity, and the Vishwa Hindu Parishad set about to reconvert the Harijans at Meenakshipuram and, more broadly, to bring Indian Muslims back into the Hindu fold.

Hindu revivalists portrayed Hinduism under seige, and Hindus, in vast majority in India's population, responded as a threatened minority—a majority with a minority complex.[18] The rhetoric of Hindu nationalism took on increasing militance, and at every level of Indian society, from the *senas* of the back streets to the parlors of Delhi intellectuals, secularism came under heightened assault. Minorities, in their view, had been appeased and pampered long enough, and it was time for Hindus to restore *Ram-rajya*, the ideal rule of the mythic age of Lord Rama. The ideology of Hindu nationalism found expression in various forms—from crude anti-Muslim and anti-Sikh slogans and wall graffiti to considered critiques of the secular state. Its conceptual catalyst is *Hindutva*, "Hindu-ness," a term that has become synonymous with Hindu nationalism.[19] It embodies the notion that all Indians—including Muslims—are part of a Hindu *nation* and that Rama and the gods and heroes of Hindu mythology are part of their

[18] See *India Today*'s cover story, "Hindus: Militant Revivalism," 31 May 1986, pp. 30–39.

[19] The term was first used as the title of a book written in 1922 by V. D. Savarkar. See Sumanta Banerjee, "'Hindutva'—Ideology and Social Psychology," *Economic and Political Weekly*, 19 January 1991, pp. 97–101.

patrimony. Those unwilling to accept their "Hindu-ness" are thus not just apostates but traitors.

Lord Rama gave renewed fervor to Hindu revivalism through the modern medium of television. In January 1987, Doordarshan, India's state-owned television network, began an 18-month series of the epic *Ramayana* that drew 100 million devoted viewers. This was followed by the even more successful *Mahabharat*, the greatest of Hindu epics, in 91 weekly episodes.

Mythology entered the arena of conflict in dramatic form in the 1980s in the Ram Janmabhumi–Babri Masjid dispute.[20] In 1528, the first Mughal emperor, Babur, constructed a mosque at Ayodhya, in Uttar Pradesh, on the site where Hindus claim a temple stood that marked the birthplace of Rama. Against a backdrop of nearly a century of conflict over the shrine, the government in 1949 proclaimed the premises a disputed area and locked the gates. In 1984, the Vishwa Hindu Parishad took Ayodhya as its cause and called for the "liberation" of the Ram Janmabhumi temple. In 1986 a district judge ordered the gates opened to Hindu worshippers. Barred from entry, Muslims formed the Babri Masjid Action Committee and observed nationwide "mourning." As tensions sharpened between Hindus and Muslims, more than 300,000 Muslims gathered in Delhi in March 1987 to demand the return of the mosque, the Babri Masjid. It was the largest rally of Muslims held since independence, and was followed a month later by a massive Hindu rally organized by the VHP.

In 1989, the VHP with other revivalist groups launched the movement to demolish the Babri Masjid and "recapture injured Hindu pride" through the construction of a new Ram Janmabhumi temple on its site. As Hindu devotees from all over India, each bearing a brick for the new temple's construction, made their way to Ayodhya, India witnessed perhaps its most serious Hindu–Muslim communal rioting since partition in 1947. In one village, Bhagalpur in Bihar, estimates of the dead ranged from 200 to 1000.

In the wake of violence and as the 1989 elections approached, the VHP—probably at the behest of the BJP—called off its march on Ayodhya. The BJP, linked to the VHP through the RSS, now sought to make Ayodhya its own cause. To galvanize Hindu sentiment behind the BJP, party president L. K. Advani launched his *rath yatra*

[20] See Sarvepalli Gopal, ed., *Anatomy of a Confrontation: The Babri Masjid–Ram Janmabhumi Issue* (New Delhi: Viking, 1991); Asghar Ali Engineer, ed., *Babri Masjid–Ramjanmabhoomi Controversy* (Delhi: Ajanta, 1990); and A. G. Noorani, "The Babri Masjid–Ram Janmabhoomi Question," *Economic and Political Weekly*, 24 (4–11 November 1989): 2461–66.

(chariot pilgrimage), a 10,000-kilometer journey in a van fashioned to look like a mythological chariot across the heartland of North India to Ayodhya, where on October 30, 1990, construction of the new temple was to begin. As that date neared, in growing communal tension, tens of thousands of Hindu militants, led by Advani, converged on Ayodhya. Prime Minister V. P. Singh, invoking the principles of secularism, warned that the High Court's interim order to secure the status quo at the disputed site would be enforced and that the mosque at Ayodhya would be protected "at all costs." On October 23, as they were about to enter Uttar Pradesh in the drive to Ayodhya, Advani and other BJP leaders were arrested. The arrests and clashes at Ayodhya between paramilitary forces and Hindus intent on destroying the mosque sparked a wave of Hindu–Muslim violence that left more than 300 persons dead. Hindu militants withdrew from Ayodhya with the promise to return.

The incident had immediate political impact. Following Advani's arrest, the BJP withdrew its parliamentary support from V. P. Singh's National Front government, and on a vote of no-confidence, Singh submitted his resignation as Prime Minister.

Ayodhya is only one of a number of places where mosques stand on what Hindus believe to be the sites of earlier temples, and the VHP has vowed to liberate them all. Among its first acts, in 1991, the new Congress (I) government under Prime Minister Narasimha Rao secured passage of the Places of Worship Act. The act specifies that all religious places shall be maintained according to their status as of August 15, 1947—except the Ayodhya shrine, now before the courts. For Hindu nationalists, the act was the embodiment of the secular "appeasement" they are determined to resist.

See Preface for Ayodhya update.

Muslim Communalism

The Muslims of India, although a minority of only 11 percent, number almost 100 million—making India the fourth most populous Muslim nation in the world, after Indonesia, Bangladesh, and Pakistan. India's Muslims, however, are themselves heterogeneous. They are not only culturally varied (distinguished, for example, by language and custom among the Urdu-speaking Muslims of North India and Andhra Pradesh, the Malayalee-speaking Mappillas of Kerala, and the Tamil-speaking Labbais of Tamil Nadu), they are also divided on religion and politics. They range from Islamic fundamentalists to secular Communists.

In the years immediately following partition, India's remaining

Muslim population assumed a position of low visibility. The Muslim League, which had successfully challenged the secular Congress party in securing the partition of India and the creation of Pakistan, virtually disappeared in India, surviving with any strength only in Kerala. Like other minorities in India, Muslims have looked to government as their protector and have, with the notable exception of 1977, given their electoral support to the Congress party. Indeed, with a decisive vote in many closely contested constituencies, Muslims have been a crucial element in the Congress base of support. As the erosion of that support in the 1989 and 1991 elections revealed, however, it can no longer be taken for granted. Muslims today are more politically conscious and more assertive. Although the vast majority of Muslims remain backward and depressed in rural areas, there is a rising urban Muslim middle class, mainly small-business owners and entrepreneurs. New prosperity for many Muslim families has also come through remittances from the Persian Gulf. The money sent home by Indian Muslims working in the Gulf has provided capital for the rising entrepreneurs, but it has also gone into the purchase of land, new houses, and the construction and improvement of mosques and Muslim schools.

Not surprisingly, the Muslims' visible success has aroused jealousy among Hindus who have done less well or who now feel threatened by Muslims who expect their rightful share of the economic pie—a pie that is not growing fast enough to satisfy the expanding claimants pushing up from below. The communal riots of recent years have been fed by economic competition and resentment. Despite their new confidence, increased communal tension has deepened the Muslim sense of vulnerability and fueled Islamic revivalism.[21]

Indian Muslims today feel threatened, and fundamentalists have exploited these fears, as dramatically seen in the reaction of the Muslim community to the Supreme Court's judgment in the case of Shah Bano in 1985. The case involved a 73-year-old woman, Shah Bano, divorced after 43 years of marriage by her husband in the traditional Muslim manner. The judgment granted her a monthly maintenance from her husband, where Muslim personal law would have required none. Muslim clerics, with the cry of "Islam in danger," denounced the decision as interference in Shariat law and as a step toward a uniform civil code that would deny Muslims the right to follow the injunctions of the faith. In describing Muslim reaction, *India Today*

[21] See Iqbal A. Ansari, ed., *The Muslim Situation in India* (New Delhi: Sterling, 1989).

wrote, "Not since the pork and beef fat-smeared cartridges caused the great upheaval of 1857 has a single nonpolitical act caused so much trauma, fear and indignation among a community."[22]

In an attempt to stem the loss of Muslim support from the Congress (I) party, Prime Minister Rajiv Gandhi (initially favorable to the court's judgment) announced support for the Muslim Women (Protection of Rights on Divorce) Bill that would remove Muslim divorce from provisions of current law and, in effect, scuttle the Supreme Court decision.[23] Though welcomed by traditional Muslims, the bill came under immediate attack from more progressive Muslims, women, secularists, and Hindu chauvinists. The bill became law in May 1986, "even though," as Ainslie Embree writes, "perhaps no other piece of legislation since 1947 had aroused such widespread and impressive opposition."[24]

Muslim communalism has been represented, most notably, by the Jamaat-i-Islami. Along with the Jamiat-ul-Ulema, it is the representative of Muslim orthodoxy, and its demands embrace a wide range of measures for the protection of the Muslim community, such as the preservation of Muslim personal law; compulsory instruction in Islam for Muslim children; the censorship of publications, particularly school textbooks, in order to eradicate materials repugnant to Muslim belief; and the prohibition of alcoholic beverages.[25] The Jamaat-i-Islami was banned during the 1975–77 emergency, and again like the RSS, it has enjoyed a resurgence of activity since 1977.

As among Hindus, the conversion issue activated Muslim communal groups in the early 1980s, and along with the Jamaat-i-Islami, various proselytizing organizations were associated with untouchable conversions. In the mid-1980s, the Shah Bano case became the *cause célèbre*, mobilizing Muslim groups against what they feared as a threat to Islam and Muslim identity in India. And then in the late 1980s, in response to the Ayodhya dispute and the rise of the Vishwa Hindu

[22] *India Today*, 31 January 1986, p. 50. The cover story, "The Muslims: A Community in Turmoil," pp. 50–60, examines the Shah Bano case and the reaction to the court judgment. Also see *India Today*, 15 March 1986, pp. 18–21, and Asghar Ali Engineer, ed., *The Shah Bano Controversy* (Hyderabad: Orient Longman, 1987).

[23] See *India Today*, 31 March 1986, pp. 14–17, and V. R. Krishna Iyer, *The Muslim Women (Protection of Rights on Divorce) Act* (Delhi: Eastern Book Co., 1987).

[24] Ainslie T. Embree, *Utopias in Conflict: Religion and Nationalism in Modern India* (Berkeley: University of California Press, 1990), p. 110.

[25] Theodore P. Wright, Jr., "The Effectiveness of Muslim Representation in India," in Donald E. Smith, ed., *South Asian Politics and Religion* (Princeton, N.J.: Princeton University Press, 1966), pp. 105–106.

Parishad, the Babri Masjid Action Committee, with its powerful clerical leaders, shaped an Indian Muslim consensus unparalleled since the Khalifat movement of the 1920s.[26] As India entered the 1990s, Hindus and Muslims were polarized in communal confrontation, and the secular state itself was under siege.

Other Religious Communities

Among other religious minorities, Christians, although by no means united politically or religiously, are in certain areas sufficiently numerous to exercise a powerful political force. In Kerala, where they number about a quarter of the population, they have been the main support of the Congress party, and the pulpit has frequently served as a rostrum for political exhortation. Likewise, in the Punjab the *gurdwaras* (Sikh shrines) have served as bases for the political activity of the Akali Dal. Some 83 percent of India's people are Hindu, however, and through the RSS and VHP, Hindu communalism is a potent force in Indian politics. The nostalgia for Bharat, Hindu India, is a dynamic element of nationalist feeling readily exploited by the forces of Hindu revivalism.

Caste

The mantle of Indian civilization covers divisions and conflicts of region, language, caste, tribe, and religion. "Fissiparous tendencies" of regionalism and communalism have posed a serious threat to the creation of an Indian political community and a viable democratic system. In the process of economic change and social mobilization, India's increasingly participant communities[27] have grown more politically self-conscious, and this self-consciousness has deepened existing cleavages.

Though decried as a reversion to "tribalism," the increasingly prominent role played by community associations in political life, for all the problems it presents, reflects an extension of the particularistic and ascriptive ties of primordial sentiment to wider horizons of identity. The development of primordial sentiment into a cultural nationalism—at the level of the linguistic region or within a religious or caste community—may be regarded with horror by those who see it

[26] See Mushirul Hasan, "Competing Symbols and Shared Codes: Inter-Community Relations in Modern India," in Gopal, *Anatomy of a Confrontation: The Babri Masjid–Ramjanmabhumi Issue*, p. 101.

[27] In India, *community* usually refers to a racial, caste, linguistic, or religious group rather than to a locality, as in the United States.

as the seed of separation or destruction. It may in fact be, however, an effective vehicle for the transference of loyalty to the larger political community, a channel of linkage between the masses and the elite, between traditional behavior and modern democratic processes.

The caste association, representing the adaptive response of caste to modern social, economic, and political changes, reveals the potential "modernity of tradition." Combining the traditional and the modern, the caste association is a voluntary association with a formal membership of perhaps only a few thousand drawn from the ascriptive reservoir of the community as a whole. As various caste communities have sought social uplift and economic advancement, they have organized to secure more effective political access.[28] The caste association, Lloyd I. Rudolph and Susanne H. Rudolph have written, "provides the channels of communication and bases of leadership and organization which enable those still submerged in the traditional society and culture to transcend the technical political illiteracy which would otherwise handicap their ability to participate in democratic politics."[29] The meaning of caste itself has changed in the encounter between tradition and modernity. "By creating conditions in which a caste's significance and power is beginning to depend on its numbers rather than its ritual and social status, and by encouraging egalitarian aspirations among its members, the caste association is exerting a liberating influence.[30] In writing of Kerala, Marxist leader E. M. S. Namboodiripad argues that the caste association was "the first form in which the peasant masses rose in struggle against feudalism."[31] As he rightly suggests, however, such associations consolidate community separatism and must be transcended if the peasantry is to be organized as a class.

With secular aspirations after a "casteless" society, most Indian political leaders have viewed the demands of community associations as illegitimate. Although each of the major parties has spawned a variety of affiliated mass organizations—labor, agrarian, youth—to mobilize political support, they have for the most part sought to avoid the appearance of intimate association with any particular commu-

[28]Among the largest and most successful caste associations is that of the Nadar community. See Robert L. Hardgrave, Jr., *The Nadars of Tamilnad: The Political Culture of a Community in Change* (Berkeley: University of California Press, 1969).

[29]Lloyd I. Rudolph and Susanne H. Rudolph, "The Political Role of India's Caste Associations," *Pacific Affairs*, 33 (March 1960):5–6.

[30]Ibid., p. 9. See also Rudolph and Rudolph, *Modernity of Tradition*.

[31]E. M. S. Namboodiripad, *Kerala: Yesterday, Today and Tomorrow* (Calcutta: National Book Agency, 1967), p. 115.

nity. Close identification between the party and one caste, for example, might seriously affect the party's ability to aggregate wide support, for in few constituencies, much less an entire district or state, does one caste so predominate as to command a majority. In practice, however, the parties have been ready to secure support wherever and however available, and in each election have courted various communities. Politicians and political scientists alike speak of the "Ezhava vote" or the "Jat bloc," just as people in the United States often talk of the black, Irish, or Italian vote.

The process by which an atomized and divided community gains consciousness and unity, entering the political system as a major factor, is a familiar one in the broader process of political behavior. The unity of such blocs is situational and temporal, however, varying from constituency to constituency and from time to time. Community associations are themselves the agent of increasing internal differentiation. As the association secures its goals, the social and economic gaps within the community widen, at the same time dispersing political support. The association thus becomes the agent of its own destruction, for in the process of differentiation, individuals are subjected to the cross-cutting ties of a multiplicity of interests and associations.[32] Yet today, even in a more open stratification system, caste remains a potent factor in Indian political life. It functions often as a surrogate for class in a society in which class identity is weak.[33] Caste conflict cuts deeply in India's fragmented society.

The Untouchables

The Constitution of India abolishes untouchability and also specifies that no citizen shall on the grounds of religion, race, caste, sex, or place of birth be subjected to any disability or restriction with regard to places of public use or accommodations. There are more than 130 million "ex-untouchables," or Scheduled Castes, as they are officially termed.[34] Although the Constitution abolishes untouchability,

[32]For a discussion of the process of differentiation within caste and the emergence of class segments that form the basis for new interests and associations, see Robert L. Hardgrave, Jr., "Caste: Fission and Fusion," *Economic and Political Weekly*, 3, special number (July 1968): 1065–70; reprinted in Robert L. Hardgrave, Jr., *Essays in the Political Sociology of South India* (New Delhi: Usha, 1979), pp. 125–34.

[33]Harold A. Gould, in *The Hindu Caste System*, vol. 3, *Politics and Caste* (Delhi: Chanakya Publications, 1990) explores the dynamics of caste and class in Faizabad District, Uttar Pradesh.

[34]The term "Scheduled Caste" was adopted in 1935, when the lowest ranking Hindu castes were listed in a "schedule" appended to the Government of India Act for pur-

and the Untouchability (Offenses) Act tightened and extended the provision, the Scheduled Castes continue to suffer from discrimination. Many find protection in the anonymity of the city, but 90 percent of the untouchables live in villages, and here many disabilities remain enforced by custom. The position of Scheduled Caste members in society is characterized by two mutually reinforcing factors: the stigma of pollution and material deprivation.[35]

The government has sought to respond to this situation through a system of protective discrimination.[36] On the assumption that a one-to-one correlation exists between the ritual status of a caste and the material condition of its members, specific castes were designated to receive special favor in education, government employment, and political representation. These benefits were granted to the Scheduled Castes, the aboriginal Scheduled Tribes, and an open-ended category, "Other Backward Classes."[37] Eager to avail themselves of government favor, virtually every caste in India sought "Other Backward" classification, and in 1963 the Central government and many states began to impose economic conditions in addition to caste criteria as prerequisites for benefits.

In central government services, 22.5 percent of all positions are reserved for Scheduled Castes, although at the higher levels untouchables have been unable to reach the maximum allowed reservation. In the elite Indian Administrative Service (IAS), for example, Scheduled Castes fill 9.7 percent of the positions. What does not appear in the raw figures, however, is, as Eleanor Zelliott reminds us, that with even comparatively few positions at the highest levels, reservations

---

poses of special safeguards and benefits. For government purposes, untouchables who have converted to Christianity or, more recently, Buddhism, are not included within the Scheduled Castes. Lelah Dushkin, "Scheduled Caste Politics," in J. Michael Mahar, ed., *The Untouchables in Contemporary India* (Tucson: University of Arizona Press, 1972), p. 166. The term "Harijan," introduced by Mahatma Gandhi, is used mainly by those within the Congress party and is regarded by many untouchables as patronizing. Today politicized untouchables prefer *dalit* to any other name. The term, meaning "oppressed," suggests their low status is no fault of their own. Eleanor Zelliot, "Dalit: New Perspectives on India's Untouchables," in Philip Oldenburg, ed., *India Briefing, 1991* (Boulder, Colo.: Westview Press, 1991), pp. 97–98.

[35] Andre Beteille, "Pollution and Poverty," in Mahar, ed., *The Untouchables*, p. 414.

[36] Marc Galanter provides a comprehensive analysis of this Indian version of "affirmative action" in *Competing Equalities: Law and the Backward Classes in India* (Berkeley: University of California Press, 1984). Also see Galanter, *Law and Society in Modern India* (Delhi: Oxford University Press, 1989).

[37] See Marc Galanter, "Who Are the Other Backward Classes?" *Economic and Political Weekly*, 28 October 1978, pp. 1812–28.

have "created a huge mass of educated, often socially conscious men and a few women, with the capacity to operate within the system for the good of others."[38]

The system has been controversial.[39] Many caste Hindus, particularly Brahmins who have been denied government employment or entrance into universities, feel that they have been victims of reverse discrimination. The reservation of benefits for the Scheduled Castes has also given rise to the charge that it has built in a vested interest in backwardness and has served to perpetuate some of the very evils against which the government has fought. To receive benefits one must virtually wear a badge of untouchability. All untouchables have not benefited equally, however. There has emerged what Lelah Dushkin identifies as a "new class," those who have benefited from scholarships, reserved seats in higher education, and, above all, government jobs. "With the operation of the system over the years, the gap between those more fortunate ones and the rest of the Untouchables seems to have widened."[40] Another major criticism has been that the system is primarily a tool of those who control it, a means by which the government can dominate and control "a minority which might otherwise have proved troublesome."[41] Protective discrimination, particularly the arrangements for government jobs, is thus seen as "an efficient and inexpensive mechanism for social control."[42]

Of all the areas of government benefits to the Scheduled Castes and Tribes, one of the most important has been the reservation of seats in Parliament and the state assemblies in proportion to their population.[43] At present, of the 543 elected seats to the Lok Sabha, 119 are reserved—78 for Scheduled Castes and 41 for Scheduled Tribes. A similar proportion of seats are reserved for Scheduled Castes and Tribes among the some 4000 state assembly seats. As set forth in Article 330 of the Constitution, reservations were to end in

[38] Zelliott, "Dalit: New Perspectives on India's Untouchables," p. 111.

[39] See I. P. Desai et al., *Caste, Caste-Conflict and Reservation* (Delhi: Ajanta, 1985), and Haroobhai Mehta and Hasmukh Patel, eds., *Dynamics of Reservation Policy* (New Delhi: Patriot, 1985).

[40] Dushkin, "Scheduled Caste Politics," p. 212. See also Dushkin, "Backward Class Benefits and Social Class in India, 1920–1970," *Economic and Political Weekly*, 7 April 1979, pp. 661–67; and Barbara R. Joshi, *Democracy in Search of Equality: Untouchable Politics and Indian Social Change* (Delhi: Hindustan Publishing, 1982).

[41] Dushkin, "Scheduled Caste Politics," p. 165.

[42] Ibid., p. 217.

[43] Marc Galanter, "Compensatory Discrimination in Political Representation," *Economic and Political Weekly*, 14 (Annual Number 1979): 437–53.

1960, but by constitutional amendment they have been subsequently extended in 10-year intervals.

The reserved seats guarantee representation. Although members of the Scheduled Castes and Tribes may run for general seats, they do so infrequently, and victories are rare. In constituencies designated as "reserved," all voters make their selection among candidates from the Scheduled Castes. Because the untouchables are a minority in all but a very few constituencies, it is normally caste Hindus who decide the elections in reserved constituencies. Scheduled Caste candidates consequently have tended to assume a low political profile. Scheduled Caste MPs and MLAs tend to concentrate their efforts on matters relating to protective discrimination. Few have taken a strong position against the continuing disabilities that most of their fellows suffer.

Violence against untouchables, endemic over much of India, tends to be ad hoc, highly localized, and overwhelmingly rural. It is thus difficult to control and often passes publicly unnoticed. In recent years, there has been a marked increase in reported attacks upon untouchables. This may be due, in part, to more vigorous press coverage and to a greater willingness among untouchables to file complaints. But most observers believe that the reported increase is not a statistical artifact and that caste violence has, in fact, increased. In any case the 10,000 to 15,000 incidents officially reported are but a fraction of the acts of violence committed against untouchables each year.[44]

The sources of caste violence are fundamentally economic, and the attacks on untouchables are at once vengeance against those who have sought to assert their rights and better their condition, and a warning to others not to stray from their traditionally assigned roles. The increase in violence is a measure of economic and social change—of the rise of untouchables through education, greater political consciousness and participation, and increasing economic and political power.

Dr. Ambedkar, leader of the Scheduled Castes until his death in 1956, had sought to weld the untouchables into a separate organization for political action.[45] He led the conversion of more than 3,000,000 untouchables to Buddhism, but the Republican Party, which he founded in 1942 as the Scheduled Caste Federation, had minimal success. The Bahujan Samaj Party (BSP), led by Kanshi Ram, today

[44]For accounts of such incidents, see M. J. Akbar, *Riot after Riot: Reports on Caste and Communal Violence in India*, rev. ed. (New Delhi: Penguin, 1991).

[45]See Eleanor Zelliot, *From Untouchable to Dalit: Essays on the Ambedkar Movement* (New Delhi: Manohar, 1991).

claims the legacy of Dr. Ambedkar. More militant, however, are the Dalit Panthers.[46] The word *dalit* means "the oppressed" and is used in an explicitly caste context. The Panthers have come primarily from among urban youth, educated and unemployed. It is in the villages, however, that the greatest changes are underway. Traditional agrarian relationships have yielded to the uncertain wages of the market economy; religiously sanctioned inequalities are now challenged by education, mass communications, and the power of the vote; and a consciousness of poverty and deprivation nurtures increasing discontent and growing militance.

Other Backward Classes: The Mandal Commission Controversy

Above the untouchables in the Hindu caste hierarchy are those castes officially designated "Other Backward Classes" (OBCs) and defined by their low level of social and educational advancement. Predominantly rural, they account for 52 percent of India's population and in many states command significant political power. In response to that power, a number of states have extended reservations in university admissions and government employment to the "backward" castes. In Karnataka, for example, 50 percent of all state government jobs are reserved for OBCs. In central government employment, however, their numbers are comparatively few—12.6 percent of all classes of service. At the highest level, they constitute only 4.7 percent of Class I Officers, as against 89.3 percent for the upper castes and 5.7 percent for the Scheduled Castes and Tribes.[47]

In 1980, the Backward Classes Commission, chaired by former Bihar chief minister B. P. Mandal, issued its report, recommending the reservation of 27 percent of all central government jobs for the backward castes in addition to the 22.5 percent already reserved for Scheduled Castes and Tribes.[48] It classified 3743 castes and subcastes as OBC beneficiaries. The report gathered dust for a decade, but in August 1990, Prime Minister V. P. Singh announced that his government would implement the Mandal recommendations. The decision

[46] See Barbara R. Joshi, *Untouchable! Voices of the Dalit Liberation* (London: Zed Books, 1986).

[47] Government of India, *Report of the Backward Classes Commission*, Vol. 1 (New Delhi: 1980), pp. 63, 92.

[48] In addition to the report itself, cited above, see S. R. Maheshwari, *The Mandal Commission and Mandalisation* (New Delhi: Concept, 1991); Asghar Ali Engineer, ed., *Mandal Commission Controversy* (New Delhi: Ajanta, 1991); and Anirudh Prasad, *Reservation Policy and Practice in India* (New Delhi: Deep & Deep, 1991).

brought widespread criticism from the press and strong opposition from higher castes, especially students. In New Delhi and other urban areas in North India, violent protests, acts of self-immolation, and police firings raised the specter of "caste war." In his decision, V. P. Singh appealed directly to one of his major constituencies, the backward peasant castes who make up more than half of India's 850 million people. The National Front platform had supported the reservations in a commitment to equity and social justice, but the timing and haste with which Singh made the decision suggested the Prime Minister sought to undercut his rivals in the Janata Dal for support among the backward castes. The Bharatiya Janata Party and the Communists of the Left Front, upon whom Singh's minority government depended, expressed displeasure in not having been consulted and indicated, each for its own reasons, preference for education and income, rather than caste, as criteria for job reservation. The BJP also saw the reservation issue as dividing the Hindu community to which it appealed, and it was this above all that spurred BJP leader Advani to undertake his *rath yatra* to Ayodhya—the action that precipitated the series of events that brought down the National Front government. In his fall, V. P. Singh assumed the position of a martyr for secularism and social justice, and these were the themes of his campaign in the 1991 elections.

For all its political appeal to the backward castes, however, the Mandal reservations offered little substantive hope for improvement. Each year there are typically some 220,000 vacancies at all levels in central government employment. With a 27 percent reservation, this involves only 60,000 jobs for which hundreds of thousands of backward-caste applicants will compete. Critics argued that the reservations policy "threatens to pit Indian against Indian in a ferocious caste war for what are essentially a few crumbs."[49] Not only does it sharpen conflict between upper and backward castes, but rivalries among the backward castes may deepen, as the rewards of reservation go disproportionately to the more advanced of the designated Other Backward Classes.

In the streets the reservations proposal was met with protest and violence. In the courts, an avalanche of petitions challenged the legality of the Mandal recommendations, and in October 1990, the Supreme Court granted the petitioners a stay against implementation,

[49] *India Today*, 15 September 1990, p. 36. The cover story, "Mandal Commission: Dividing to Rule," pp. 34–39, reflected the general response of the Indian press. For a debate on the issue by leading observers, see *India Today*'s "Cross Fire" feature, "Reservations: Emerging Battle," 31 May 1991, pp. 33–41.

pending review of the constitutional issues.[50] With the court order still in effect, in October 1991, the new Congress (I) government of Narasimha Rao announced its intention to implement the Mandal reservation, with an additional 10 percent of all central government jobs reserved for the poor among the "forward" upper castes, as well as Muslims and Christians. With so great a portion of the population as beneficiary, no political party raised its opposition. In contrast to the turmoil a year before, protest demonstrations were weak and sporadic. Without political support, the anti-Mandal agitation lost steam—but the issue of the validity of the Mandal reservations remains before the Supreme Court.

Rural Unrest

Agrarian interests in India are today expressed primarily through the influence of the landowning middle peasant classes at local and state levels. The landless and poor peasants, lacking the effective resources of money and organization, have carried little weight in shaping legislation. Even when policy has been directed to their benefit, landed interests have often frustrated its implementation at the local level. Each of the major parties has adjunct peasant organizations, but they are designed more to mobilize support than to articulate interest. The All-India Kisan Sabha, founded in 1936 as a federation of state peasant movements, began as a Congress front but quickly came under Communist control. The Congress had its own peasant organizations, but the party proved ineffective in representing the interests of tenants and landless laborers, for at the local level the Congress was controlled by those who would be most hurt by land-reform legislation.

In recent years the most potent linkage between political parties and the peasantry has been through various incarnations of the non-Congress centrist parties in North India—today represented in factions of the Janata Dal. These centrist parties obtained their strength from middle and backward-caste farmers. Its purist form was embodied in Charan Singh, whose support was based among the 10 million Jats of northern India. In 1978, as Home Minister in the Janata government, Singh founded the All-India Kisan Sammelan as a broad-based peasant movement to enhance his own faction in the ruling party. To demonstrate his strength, he staged a massive kisan (peasant) rally in New Delhi. More than 800,000 peasants attended. They came by

[50] *India Today*, 31 October 1990, p. 17.

train, truck, and bullock cart, but the 10,000 tractors driven into the capital city served to symbolize their new prosperity and power.

In the first two decades after independence, the center of political power in India shifted from the landlords and upper peasants of the traditionally dominant castes to peasant cultivators of the middle castes. Once the high-caste absentee landlords were effectively eliminated in the early 1950s, the principal political struggle until the mid-1960s was between the upper peasantry and the middle peasantry. As the middle peasants consolidated their power, they formed an alliance with small peasants based on caste ties and reinforced by economic incentive. These middle peasant castes, numerically preponderant, have sought to resist the challenge from below by sharecroppers and landless laborers—especially more politically and socially advanced untouchables.

Land reform has been subverted in most states, and ceilings on land holdings frequently remain unenforced, for the state governments are unwilling to alienate their base of support among the middle peasants. Agitation by sharecroppers and landless laborers has been sporadic and uncoordinated, but in favoring the interests of the landowners, rhetoric aside, the Indian government may simply be laying the foundations for future agrarian unrest.

A number of peasant revolts have occurred in India. In this century the Telengana uprising in the state of Hyderabad was one of the most dramatic and ill fated. It began with sporadic outbreaks in 1946. By 1948, despite the Nizams' campaign of suppression, the movement, which was led by the Communist party, claimed to have "liberated" some 2500 villages by turning out landlords and their agents and establishing communes. Support came primarily from poor peasants and landless laborers. During the period of the movement's greatest strength, rents were suspended, debts were canceled, and land was redistributed among the landless in the area under Communist control. In September 1948 Indian troops took over the state and moved against the Communists in Telengana. The leadership of the movement was jailed, and the Communist party was outlawed in the state. The movement was officially called off by a Communist Party of India (CPI) directive in 1951, beginning a new phase in Communist strategy.[51]

[51] The 25th anniversary of the Telengana revolt stimulated a re-examination of the nature and significance of the struggle. See Mohan Ram, "The Telengana Peasant Armed Struggle, 1946–51," *Economic and Political Weekly*, 9 June 1973, pp. 1025–32; and P. Sundarayya, *Telengana People's Struggle and Its Lessons* (Calcutta: Communist Party of India [Marxist], 1972).

More widespread were the "Naxalite" rebellions, beginning in the late 1960s and continuing episodically to the present. In 1967 agricultural tenants of Naxalbari in the hill district of Darjeeling in West Bengal began to occupy forcibly the lands they tilled. As the handful of peasants in Naxalbari sought to secure their position against the landlords, Radio Beijing proclaimed the area a "red district" and lauded the heroic effort to create a "liberated base" from which to wage a protracted revolutionary struggle. The Indian government reacted with alarm to what it viewed as Chinese infiltration in the sensitive border region, and the rebellion was put down in short order. Naxalbari was to become the rallying cry for armed revolution, and from this uprising Indian Maoists took on the name "Naxalites."[52]

More substantial than Naxalbari was the 1968 peasant struggle in the Andhra hills of the Srikakulam district. Concentrated in the 800-square-mile Girijan tribal agency tract, Communist-led Girijan guerrilla bands—armed with spears, bows and arrows, axes, and captured guns—began to engage in clashes with landlords and police. The peasant struggle attracted college youth and a seasoned party cadre, but although Srikakulam was hailed by Beijing as a victory for Maoist tactics in India, the movement was suppressed by the end of the following year.[53]

Agitation by poor peasants and landless laborers has been sporadic and uncoordinated. Through the 1970s spasmodic outbreaks of violence occurred, and in 1980 an upsurge of Naxalite activity in various parts of rural India was brought quickly under control. The late 1980s witnessed a resurgence of Naxalite activity, most visibly in Bihar, northern Andhra Pradesh, and portions of Orissa and Madhya Pradesh, where support comes principally from tribals and landless untouchables. Naxalites today are scattered among as many as 40 rival groups, and operate through armed insurgency units, and front organizations. In Bihar, they have contested elections. Naxalite insurgents there also attack police stations and engage in battles with the

[52]See Rabindra Ray, *The Naxalites and Their Ideology* (Delhi: Oxford University Press, 1988); Sumanta, Banerjee, *India's Simmering Revolution: The Naxalite Uprising* (London: Zed Books, 1984); Biplap Dasgupta, *The Naxalite Movement* (Bombay: Allied Publishers, 1974); Asish Kumar Roy, *The Spring Thunder and After* (Calcutta: Minerva, 1975); Sankar Ghosh, *The Disinherited State: A Study of West Bengal, 1967–1970* (Calcutta: Orient Longman, 1971), pp. 97–114; and Marcus F. Franda, *Radical Politics in West Bengal* (Cambridge, MA: MIT Press, 1971), pp. 149–81.

[53]See Mohan Ram, *Maoism in India* (Delhi: Vikas, 1971), pp. 106–36; and Bhabani Sen Gupta, *Communism in Indian Politics* (New York: Columbia University Press, 1972), pp. 329–46.

"private armies" hired by landowners and rich peasants, but even small peasant landholders have been massacred in Naxalite raids on villages. In Andhra, Naxalite factions, most notably the People's War Group, engage in extortion, kidnapping, and assassination.

Rural unrest is not limited to the oppressed. Indeed, it is most pronounced in the protests and agitations staged by capitalist farmers. Constituting some 15 percent of all rural landholding households, they own 60 percent of the cultivatable land. These farmers of the green revolution are dependent on modern agricultural inputs—fertilizers, pesticides, electricity, and diesel for irrigation pumps and tractors—and are caught between rising input costs and low returns for cash crops.

In 1980, in the Nasik district of Maharashtra, Sharad Joshi—an international bureaucrat-economist turned cultivator—organized the Shetkari Sanghatana and launched what was to become "the farmers' movement."[54] The issue in Maharashtra was the price of onions, sugar, and cotton. In demands for higher agricultural support prices and lower input costs, Joshi's farmers blocked roads with tractors and gheraoed (encircled) public officials—and won basic concessions from the state government. Again, in 1988, Joshi's Shetkari Sanghatana extracted major concessions from the Maharashtra government, which wrote off outstanding farm loans and raised price supports to avert threatened agitation by cotton farmers. That same year, in Uttar Pradesh, Mahendra Singh Tikait (a rough-hewn peasant, in contrast to the suave Joshi) led the Bharatiya Kisan Union (BKU) in a protest that brought 100,000 farmers to Meerut for a three-week siege of government offices that virtually paralyzed the city. Their demands included higher prices for their products, higher subsidies for inputs such as power and fertilizer, write-offs for rural loans, and a bigger say in shaping agricultural policy. Although Tikait called off the agitation to avoid impending violence, the message of the protest was not lost on India's politicians. The BKU claims a following of 10 million in Uttar Pradesh, and similar movements in India's more advanced agricultural regions are a formidable force.[55] In 1991, when the new Congress (I) government of Narasimha Rao announced its decision to reduce the subsidy on fertilizers, an immediate protest by farmers forced the government to back down.

[54] See "The Angry Farmer," cover story in *India Today,* 16–31 January 1981, pp. 26–34.

[55] *India Today,* "Farmers' Movements: The Gathering Storm," 30 November 1987, pp. 50–52; and *Far Eastern Economic Review,* 24 March 1988, pp. 13–14, and 23 February 1989, pp. 20–22.

For all the power of the farmers' movement, its potential is weakened by lack of an overarching organization. Despite efforts for coordination at the national level, the various groups remain closely bound to the interests of particular districts or states and often to particular crops. And while their leaders, like Joshi and Tikait, proclaim rural solidarity, the movement is primarily that of the more affluent farmers—those who produce marketable surpluses. Moreover, it has not been able to bridge the conflicts of caste and class—between upper and backward castes, between landowning peasants and landless laborers. Nevertheless, agitations and mass rallies have demonstrated the farmers' capacity to bring enormous pressure on the government at both state and Center levels, and their numbers command a vote bank, or support base, with which every politician must reckon.

Urban Unrest

Cities have been the locus of unrest in various regional movements, in sons of the soil and linguistic agitations, in caste conflict over reservations, and in communal tension between Hindus and Muslims. Such unrest has been episodic and essentially a phenomenon of the vulnerable middle class. The urban poor, unorganized, without leadership and resources, have been less able to express their discontent. Theirs are lives of quiet desperation. Among the poor, however, especially in the slums that surround the major cities, are migrants from the countryside for whom the city represents opportunity and a chance for a better life.

Urban unrest is manifest most intensely among those who feel threatened by sharpened competition for jobs and among those who have suffered losses—real or imagined—relative to others. As educational opportunities widen the number of claimants for "middle-class" jobs and raise aspirations in a situation of scarcity, unrest is likely to increase. Urban unemployment continues to grow, and unemployment among the educated is growing at an even faster rate. The frustration of the educated unemployed and of students for whom job prospects are dismal is an especially volatile ingredient in the urban situation.

Students

Students have been at the forefront of protest movements and agitations from the time of independence. If the urban poor are politically inarticulate, students are loudly vocal. While organized, however, they often lack direction and coherence. "Student indiscipline" is endemic, and at any time a major portion of India's colleges and universities are closed because of campus disorder. "Indiscipline" embraces a wide range of disruptive activities, from demonstrations and strikes relating to university-specific demands to involvement in political movements of the larger community.

Students looking for a cause—as, for example, in protest over the firing of a menial employee—have paralyzed universities. Campus disorder has become increasingly violent, with gheraos and physical attacks on administrators and faculty, the murder of a Vice Chancellor, and terrorism of fellow students. Warring student factions are armed with automatic weapons on some campuses in North India, and hostels have been turned into virtual arsenals. By no means is everyone involved actually a student. Aligarh Muslim University, the scene of frequent turmoil, recently discovered that it had considerably more "students" living in the hostels than were formally enrolled in the university. Every campus has a sizable number of hangers-on, a lumpen element readily activated for protest.

The campus, however, has rarely been able to contain student politics or unrest. Activated by a mixture of idealism and frustration, students have sought a wider arena. Students were the major force in bringing down state governments in Orissa in 1964 and in Gujarat in 1974. They played a central role in the anti-Hindi agitation in Tamil Nadu in the mid-1960s, in the Telengana movement, and in the Naxalite violence in West Bengal and Andhra. The All-Assam Students' Union spearheaded the movement against "foreigners" in Assam. In 1985 students in Gujarat and in Madhya Pradesh engaged in agitations against state policy on reservations (quotas) for members of the Scheduled Castes and backward classes. In 1990, the Janata government's decision to implement the Mandal reservations for backward castes brought upper-caste students into the streets in protest. In Delhi, students went on a rampage smashing public buses, and across North India, in expression of anomic protest and their own sense of hopelessness, 163 students attempted suicide by self-immolation; 61 died.

More than 4 million students are registered in some 7000 colleges and universities in India. Most students are not politically involved, but the activists provide a reservoir from which political parties and protest movements can draw leadership and support. Campuses have long been centers of political opposition, and student government elections are usually fought out along party lines.

The RSS student movement, the Akhil Bharatiya Vidyarthi Parishad, is now the largest student organization in India. The Congress party, the Bharatiya Janata Party, and the Communist Party (Marxist) all have their campus affiliates. At Delhi University, for example, the RSS–BJP student organization has dominated campus politics, while across the city at Jawaharlal Nehru University, the Marxists struggle for control of the student union. Because of their concentration on the campus, their frustration, political consciousness, and availability, students are readily mobilized, and they can be expected to be a continuing factor in urban unrest.

Labor

Labor unions in India, as in most developing countries, have been highly political. Reflecting the central role of the state in labor relations, union demands for better working conditions and higher wages are directed less often toward management than toward the government. Government tribunals for binding arbitration as well as wide ministerial discretion have made the government the critical focus of pressure. With both labor and management dependent on government intervention, collective bargaining is virtually nonexistent, and the government has come to bear the brunt of all dissatisfaction. Government labor policy is guided, for the most part, by an effort to reduce the number of strikes and lockouts, and it handles labor disputes with a combination of the carrot and a stick.

No more than 10 million workers—roughly 3 percent of India's labor force—are even nominally unionized. Because they are organized and are situated in strategic sectors of the economy, however, they command considerable power, if not influence—at least to disrupt. There are some 25,000 unions in India, most tied directly to political parties and affiliated with one of the major trade union federations. The Indian National Trade Union Congress (INTUC), the largest federation, is associated with the Congress (I) party and has often served as an arm of government labor policy. The fastest growing union has been the Bharatiya Mazdoor Sangh (BMS), with ties to the Bharatiya Janata Party. Much of its growth has come at the expense of the two Communist party federations—the All-India Trade Union Congress (AITUC), associated with the Communist Party of India, and the Centre of Indian Trade Unions (CITV), associated with the Communist Party (Marxist). One of the more militant unions is the faction-ridden socialist Hind Mazdoor Sabha (HMS).

Indian law, which permits any seven persons the right to form a union and to raise any dispute, has contributed to the proliferation of unions and to the fragmentation of the trade union movement. Interunion rivalry has itself been a major factor in fermenting labor unrest, as is most evident in the activities of independent labor leader Dr. Datta Samant.

Samant, a former Congress (I) politician, came to the labor scene in Bombay in the mid-1970s and infused the trade union movement with new militancy. Through his aggressive tactics and by his early record of success in winning wage increases, Samant gained control of hundreds of unions, with membership in the early 1980s totaling at least 600,000, nearly all in the Bombay industrial region. The strikes led by Samant have often been both violent and prolonged. The Bombay textile strike—the longest major strike in India's history—dragged on for nearly two years. Involving 250,000 workers at its peak, the strike all but paralyzed the textile industry. Workers gradually began to return to the factories, and the final collapse of the strike in 1983 reduced Samant's influence and underscored the strength of industry and government in relation to labor unions.

Wages are the central issue in most industrial disputes. They vary greatly across industries and regions, but, on the whole, unionized workers are a "privileged class," commanding wages 10 to 15 times that of their rural counterparts. Their wages have barely kept up with inflation in recent years, however, and workers continue to press for increases. Yet for all the rhetoric, for all the strikes, and for all the millions of work hours lost, Indian industrial labor is basically conservative. Surrounded by poverty and unemployment, they at least have jobs, and few are prepared to risk losing them.

The government has the capacity to control labor unrest, as its suppression of the 1974 railway strike dramatically demonstrated. The strike by the 2,000,000 workers belonging to the All-India Railwaymen's Federation threatened to cripple the nation economically. The Prime Minister refused to negotiate the demands for a doubling of wages; the army was moved into many key rail installations; some 6000 labor leaders were immediately arrested; and in the course of the strike—the most serious India has confronted—more than 30,000 workers and union activists were jailed. After 20 days, the strike was abandoned, and from their cells the union leaders called upon workers to return to their jobs.

The draconian means by which the railway strike was broken anticipated the nature of governmental action against labor under the 1975–77 emergency. Strikes were banned and wages frozen in the imposition of an industrial peace. With the end of the emergency in 1977, strikes again brought unrest to the Indian urban economy. In 1981 the government enhanced its power through the Essential Services Maintenance Act (ESMA), which empowers it to ban strikes in such crucial sectors of the economy as defense, rail, coal, power, steel, fertilizer, and irrigation.

Industrial unrest has been contained, but both factory and office remain plagued by slowdowns, "pen down" strikes (where people come to work but do nothing), and "mass casual leave" (where people simply stay home). If these labor protests do not entail mass agitation and violence, they take their toll economically in reduced productivity and contribute to the daily chaos of urban life in India.

Gandhians and Public Interest Groups

Only hours before his death, Mahatma Gandhi drafted a resolution—often called his "last will and testament"—in which he called on the Congress party to renounce politics and to transform itself into a people's service society. Although they may have looked to Gandhi for guidance, few members of Congress were willing to follow his path. One man fully prepared to follow the footsteps of the Mahatma was Vinoba Bhave, who envisaged a society built upon the principles of *Sarvodaya*, "the welfare of all." Sarvodaya emphasized service, nonviolence, and a political and economic decentralization focused on the village. In 1954, Jayaprakash Narayan, socialist leader and the man many believed to be Nehru's political heir, renounced "party-and-power politics" and dedicated his life to Sarvodaya. To the conflict orientation of his own earlier Marxism, Narayan sought a Gandhian alternative.[56]

In 1974, as India's political and economic situation became increasingly serious, and as discontent in his home state of Bihar erupted into widespread agitation, Narayan—or J. P., as he was known—came out of his self-imposed political retirement. In Patna, the state capital, he led half a million people in procession to present the Governor with 2,000,000 signatures in support of the demand for dissolution of the Bihar legislative assembly. Narayan, supported by individual members of the opposition parties, called upon assembly members to resign, for students to boycott classes, and for the people to refuse to pay taxes: Narayan launched satyagraha against the state government.

[56]For the life and thought of Narayan, see Jayaprakash Narayan, *Towards Total Revolution*, 4 vols. (Bombay: Popular Prakashan, 1978); Ajit Bhattarcharjea, *Jayaprakash Narayan: A Political Biography*, rev. ed. (New Delhi: Vikas, 1975); and David Selbourne, ed., *In Theory and Practice: Essays on the Politics of Jayaprakash Narayan* (Delhi: Oxford University Press, 1985).

The J. P. Movement took on a national character, as we shall see in Chapter 6, in the crisis arising from the decision against Mrs. Gandhi by the Allahabad High Court. Narayan, joined by leaders of the opposition, called for the Prime Minister to step down. Instead, she imposed a state of emergency. J. P. was arrested even before the emergency was officially proclaimed. Suffering from a serious kidney disease, he was released from jail after five months, his health broken but his vision of a society based on the principles of the Mahatma intact.

In January 1977, with the announcement of parliamentary elections, Narayan successfully united the opposition and formed the Janata Party. J. P. held back from formal leadership, but he was its spiritual guide, and the Janata's factional leaders empowered him to select the new Prime Minister after the 1977 elections. The Janata Party manifesto offered the people of India "a Gandhian alternative," but once in power the party was beset by factionalism and petty squabbles. Instead of the "total revolution" for which he had called, Jayaprakash Narayan, disillusioned, saw only politics as usual. In 1979, his dream unfulfilled, Narayan died at the age of 77.

Today the Gandhian alternative is to be found principally in the increasing number of voluntary "grass-roots" organizations that have arisen outside the framework of government and political parties.[57] These nongovernmental organizations (NGOs in their popular acronym) represent a range of experiments, movements, and associations that are directed to the needs of India's poorest and most vulnerable citizens. They include women's rights groups, environmental groups, cooperatives and rural development schemes, and legal-aid societies and civil liberties organizations. Typically, they combine an emphasis on self-help and political struggle. Localized, highly fragmented, and viewed generally with suspicion by government, however, NGOs have yet to make national impact.

The 1980s witnessed the growth of heightened consciousness among women and the emergence of a "panoply of organizations"

[57]Lokayan ("Dialogue of the People"), pioneered by Rajani Kothari and sponsored by the Centre for the Study of Developing Societies in New Delhi, has sought to provide an informal secretariat to link the various voluntary organizations throughout India. For a discussion of its activities and of the voluntarist movement more generally, see Rajni Kothari, *Politics and the People: In Search of a Humane India*, Vol. II (Delhi: Ajanta, 1989); D. L. Sheth, "Grass-roots Initiatives in India," *Economic and Political Weekly*, 11 February 1984, pp. 259–62; and D. L. Sheth, "Grass-roots Stirrings and the Future of Politics," *Alternatives*, 9 (1983):1–24. For a Gandhian critique of Indian politics, see Rajni Kothari, *State against Democracy: In Search of Humane Governance* (Delhi: Ajanta, 1988).

from every level of society, with leadership drawn largely from the upper middle class.[58] Political parties have long had auxiliary groups, the oldest being the Congress party's All-India Women's Conference. Beginning in the late 1970s and inspired in part by the feminist magazine *Manushi* (English and Hindi),[59] started in 1979, however, autonomous groups formed to address a range of women's issues. Many urban-based groups, such as the Forum Against Oppression of Women, organized in Bombay in 1981, focused on violence against women—rape, battering, dowry-harassment, sati (the self-immolation of a widow on the funeral pyre of her husband).[60] Concerns, however, were directed to the status of women in Indian society more generally, including property rights, divorce laws, education, and economic exploitation. Among the most successful development organizations is the Self-Employed Women's Association (SEWA), founded by Ela Bhatt in Ahmedabad in 1972, enabling thousands of poor women to support themselves and their families. Various organizations, many sustained financially by international support, seek to involve rural women in social and economic uplift.[61] Women have also been at the forefront of "grass-roots" environmental movements, such as the Chipko ("tree-hugging") movement to protest deforestation in a Himalayan hill district.[62] Their strategy, which captured national attention, was one of Gandhian resistance: They would hug the trees and lie down in the roads to stop tree-cutting operations.

Environmental groups in India have increased in number over the past decade, but their influence is still limited.[63] Most are regional and specific in their concerns. Many form as protests against particular projects, such as the successful movement to stop construction of the

[58] Mary F. Katzenstein, "Organizing against Violence: Strategies of the Indian Women's Movement," *Pacific Affairs*, 62 (Spring 1989), pp. 53–71. See also Madhu Kishwar and Ruth Vanita, "Indian Women: A Decade of New Ferment," in Marshall M. Bouton and Philip Oldenburg, eds., *India Briefing, 1989* (Boulder, Colo.: Westview Press, 1989), pp. 131–52.

[59] For a selection of articles from the bi-monthly, see Madhu Kishwar and Ruth Vanita, eds., *In Search of Answers: Indian Women's Voices from Manushi* (London: Zed Books, 1984).

[60] Katzenstein, pp. 60–69.

[61] For a study of nongovernment organizations for the uplift of rural women in Karnataka, see Vanita Viswanath, *NGOs and Women's Development in Rural India: A Comparative Analysis* (Boulder, Colo.: Westview Press, 1991).

[62] Ramachandra Guha, *The Unquiet Woods* (Berkeley: University of California Press, 1990), and Thomas Weber, *Hugging the Trees: The Story of the Chipko Movement* (Delhi: Viking, 1988).

[63] See Renu Khator, *Environment, Development and Politics in India* (Lanham, Md.: University Press of America, 1991).

hydroelectric Silent Valley Project in Kerala, or the more recent action against the ambitious Narmada Valley Project in central India. Environmental concern has been directed to water and air pollution—although in a poor nation the costs of emission controls and cleanup impose a staggering burden—and chemical hazards have raised national alarm. In 1984, at Bhopal, a gas leak at the Union Carbide plant resulted in the death of at least 4,000 people and serious injury to some 200,000 others.[64] The most serious industrial accident anywhere in the world, the disaster spawned more than a dozen new groups, international protest, and continuing court cases involving unprecedented claims for recovery.

In the 1980s, new organizations formed to defend the rights of prisoners subjected to police abuse or forced to languish in jails for years while awaiting trials in courts that had forgotten their existence. Led by judges, most notably Supreme Court justices V. R. Krishna Iyer and P. N. Bhagwati, the movement sought to use judicial activism to expand the protection of fundamental rights through "social action litigation."[65] Attorneys established legal-aid societies for the poor, and civil-liberties groups—the People's Union for Democratic Rights, People's Union for Civil Liberties, Citizens for Democracy, and others—organized to investigate and expose the abuse of human rights. Civil-liberties groups have targeted the Punjab and Kashmir for special concern, reporting police and paramilitary excesses such as unjustified detention and torture. More broadly, they have protested various laws passed to strengthen the government's power to deal with terrorism as a threat to the liberty of all Indians.

Law and Order

For more than a decade, Indian newspaper articles and editorials have described an increasing breakdown of law and order. Press coverage of specific incidents of violence, however, tends to project a national image of widespread unrest that is not wholly true. Most of India's countryside and cities have a relatively low level of unrest and

[64] *India Today*, "Bhopal: City of the Dead," 31 December 1984, pp. 4–25. For a broad examination of Bhopal and its policy consequences, see Sheila Jasanoff, ed., *Learning from Disaster* (forthcoming).

[65] Upendra Baxi, "Taking Suffering Seriously: Social Action Litigation in the Supreme Court of India," in Rajeev Dhavan et al., eds., *Judges and the Judicial Power* (London: Sweet & Maxwell/Bombay: Tripathi, 1985), pp. 288–315.

violence, but over the past decade violence has markedly increased; although it remains localized, no region of the nation is wholly immune.

In much of the Hindi heartland—Bihar, major portions of Uttar Pradesh, and parts of Madhya Pradesh and Rajasthan—gang rule and *dacoity* (banditry) are on the rise. In this region of North India, handmade guns and automatic weapons are widespread, and the level of violence—official and nonofficial—marks a drift toward anarchy. Rival gangs of armed young toughs, typically with some education and a strong dose of Hindi film romance, operate with impunity in many districts, smaller towns, and industrial areas. Political parties use them to raise funds, to intimidate opponents, and to protect themselves against similar tactics by other groups. Often in connivance with police officials, they engage in various criminal activities and hold local areas under mafia-like control. In fact, the term *mafia* has come to be used in India most frequently in connection with the politically linked gangster domination of the Dhanbad coalfields in Bihar.

There has been a rise in reported dacoit activity in North India, particularly in Uttar Pradesh—not only in robbery, but also in its use against assertive untouchables and political rivals. For centuries dacoity has been endemic in districts of southwestern U. P., but today the gangs are extending their influence throughout the state and have established ties with police and politicians of all parties. Such ties among criminals, police, and politicians are not a wholly new phenomenon nor is it by any means distinctly Indian. As political scientist Rajni Kothari and others argue, however, criminals have now become politicians. Although it is surely an exaggeration to speak of the "criminalization of politics" in India, it is widely believed that many U. P. politicians, including ministers, have dacoit connections and that Bihar's mafia gangs are closely linked to state political leaders. In both states a number of legislative assembly members are reputed to have criminal records, and many have pending cases against them.[66]

The Police and Internal Security

The police in India are held in generally low esteem, and they, in turn, are demoralized, unreliable, and increasingly militant. In 1979 the report of the National Police Commission stated that "in the per-

[66] "The Underworld of Indian Politics," *Sunday* (Calcutta), 3–9 March 1985, pp. 14–31; *India Today*, "Bihar: Domain of the Dons," 31 January 1992, pp. 37–41; and *Far Eastern Economic Review*, 3 March 1992, p. 22.

ception of the people, the egregious features of the police are—politically-oriented partisan performance of duties, brutality, corruption and inefficiency."[67] The 1980 police blinding of prisoners in Bhagalpur, Bihar, and the jail deaths in Tamil Nadu were widely publicized cases of police brutality, but there is a widespread belief that the police are getting worse and that they can no longer maintain law and order. Indeed, they are often the perpetrators of violence. In communal riots in North India over the past decade, the police are alleged to have entered the fray with unprovoked attacks upon Muslims.

In a survey of "The Image of Police in India" conducted for the Home Ministry, 77 percent of the people interviewed blamed the police for "protecting or shielding *goondas* or criminal elements in the country" and for such malpractices as "putting up false cases, non-registration of complaints, use of third degree methods, highhandedness and illegal detentions at police stations." Survey respondents gave "political interference" as the principal cause of police malpractice.[68] Police officers are under constant pressure from politicians and bureaucrats, with the threat of transfer used to secure compliance. Transfers are also used to open positions for caste and familial favoritism. Other factors contributing to low police morale are low pay, long hours, poor living conditions, and a shortage of labor and logistical support, although there is considerable variation in conditions from state to state.[69]

These conditions have generated police demands for improved pay, better working conditions, and unions to represent their grievances. The depth of discontent was first made clear in the 1973 mutiny of the Provincial Armed Constabulary in Uttar Pradesh, in which nearly 100 police were shot to death by the Army. Over the years since, the military has been brought in on various occasions to control police or paramilitary unrest. In 1982, for example, the Maharashtra

[67] Government of India, *First Report of The National Police Commission* (New Delhi: 1979), p. 7.

[68] The survey by the Bureau of Police Research and Development covered both urban and rural areas, and the people interviewed included political leaders, professionals, educators, traders, members of panchayats, and trade union representatives. Reported by Kuldip Nayar, "Police Find That Their Image Is Poor," *Sunday* (Calcutta), 30 May–5 June 1982, p. 7.

[69] See David H. Bayley, "The Police and Political Order in India," *Asian Survey*, 23 (April 1983): 484–96. Also see David H. Bayley, *The Police and Political Development in India* (Princeton, N.J.: Princeton University Press, 1969); P. D. Sharma, *Police and Political Order in India* (New Delhi: Research, 1984); and N. S. Saksena, *Law and Order in India* (New Delhi: Abhinav, 1987).

government's ban on the police union and arrest of its top leaders led to a strike by the 23,000 members of the Bombay constabulary. The government crackdown ignited serious rioting that was brought under control only by the deployment of Indian Army units in the city.

In controlling domestic unrest, the government has four layers of force to which it can turn:

1. the civil police (armed only with *lathis*, long sticks)
2. the provincial armed constabulary
3. the paramilitary forces
4. the Indian Army.

Under various names, the provincial armed constabularies are organized and paid for by the states and are the first to be called in if the civil police are unable to control disturbances. Altogether, the police (civil and armed) number more than 900,000 men and women.

Sixteen paramilitary units exist, with a combined force of more than 450,000, housed in barracks and subject to military discipline. They fall under several ministries of the central government. The Central Reserve Police Force (CRPF), the major riot-control force, assists state police whenever necessary. The Border Security Force (BSF), the largest paramilitary unit with roughly 170,000 personnel; the Assam Rifles (the oldest paramilitary force); the Indo-Tibetan Border Police (ITBP); and the Ladakh Scouts have as their primary mission the patrol of India's borders. Other paramilitary units include: the Defense Security Corps (DSC), which protects defense installations; the Central Industries Security Force (CISF), which guards public-sector industrial facilities; and the Railway Protection Force (RPF), which does just what its name suggests. The newest paramilitary unit, the National Security Guards (NSG), formed in 1985, is intended to be an elite, antiterrorist force. The NSG also has responsibility for protecting leading political figures.

Since 1967 paramilitary forces have been greatly expanded, both to enhance the coercive capacity of the government and to reduce the necessity of calling in regular Army units in aid of the civil. With little regard to their primary mission, they have increasingly been called in to back up state police. The Border Security Force, for example, has been used to quell disturbances far from border areas—such as to control communal disturbances and to put down the police riots in Bombay. However, paramilitary forces themselves have not been immune from indiscipline and unrest. They are often poorly trained and, like the civil police and provincial armed constabulary, suffer from low pay and poor working conditions.

The increasing centralization of decision making with respect to law and order and the extensive use of central government paramilitary forces have tended to "nationalize" local problems. By identifying the central government with the problem and its resolution, Mrs. Gandhi, in particular, weakened the buffers of the federal system that formerly insulated local problems more fully and absorbed much of the blame.

The central government expanded paramilitary forces, in part, to insulate the Army from law-and-order functions. Given the unreliability of both the civil police and paramilitary forces, however, the Army has played an increasingly prominent role in controlling domestic unrest. The Army has long been involved in maintaining order in the Northeast, and more recently it has been deployed in combatting terrorism in the Punjab and rebellion in Kashmir. The Army has been drawn increasingly into riot control, most notably to quell communal disturbances. In 1991, the Army raised a new force, the Rashtriya (National) Rifles, eventually to comprise 10,000 troops, specifically charged to deal with terrorism, rioting, and communal violence.

Once the Army enters "in aid of the civil," it assumes command over the otherwise uncoordinated police and paramilitary forces already on the scene. Although it has performed well, the Army has never been at ease with its role in controlling domestic unrest. When facing not a foreign enemy but fellow Indians, Army morale is sure to suffer, but officers also fear that frequent use of the Army in aid of the civil may diminish the respect in which it is held.

The use of the Army in controlling domestic unrest could well have wider political implications. Military officers could become convinced that civil authorities—specifically the politicians, for whom they have no great respect in any case—are unable to maintain law and order and that the Army should step in to take control of the government. At present, there is nothing to suggest that the military is prepared to intervene or even that there is much sympathy among the officer corps for such a move, but growing domestic unrest and increasing reliance upon the military to control it could well invite greater military involvement in the governance of India.

Instruments of Law

The Government of India possesses a formidable array of laws for the control of domestic unrest.[70] Beyond the constitutional powers of

[70]See Kuldeep Mathur, "The State and the Use of Coercive Power in India," *Asian Survey*, 32 (April 1992), pp. 337–49.

the President to declare an emergency, discussed earlier, a number of ordinances are promulgated by the President under his emergency powers and subsequently enacted by Parliament into law. These instruments of law significantly enhance the power of the paramilitary forces and of the military in "aid to the civil."

The Armed Forces Special Powers Act (1956, subsequently amended) empowers the central government to declare a state or district a "disturbed area." In areas where the declaration comes into force, Army and paramilitary commanders have the authority to arrest suspects, conduct searches, and use lethal force.

The National Security Act (1980) authorizes security forces to arrest and detain without warrant people suspected of undermining national security, public order, and essential economic services. Detainees can be imprisoned without trial for three months, with as many as three subsequent three-month extensions. Provisions for judicial review exist in order to minimize abuse, but the intent of the legislation is to give the armed forces a relatively free hand in dealing with agitators, rioters, and terrorists. This was made clear in June 1984, in the wake of the Army's entry into the Golden Temple, with the National Security (Second Amendment) Ordinance, which, in effect, permits security forces to override judicial objection to detention so long as the detainee is not held for a total period of more than one year. Many provisions of the National Security Act are identical to those of the Maintenance of Internal Security Act (MISA), which served as the principal instrument of arrest and detention during the 1975–77 emergency. In 1981 the Supreme Court upheld the National Security Act as constitutional, but warned the government that "care must be taken to restrict (its) application to as few situations as possible."

The Essential Services Maintenance Act (1981) identifies 16 "essential supplies and services," such as oil and rails, whose disruption would threaten the economy. ESMA empowers the government to prohibit strikes and lockouts in the crucial sectors and to replace striking workers with Army troops. Strikers would be subject to arrest under provisions of the National Security Act.

The Unlawful Activities Prevention Act (1967) empowers the government to ban any subversive organization, such as those advocating secession. The Dal Khalsa and the National Council of Khalistan in the Punjab and various secessionist groups in the Northeast have been outlawed under the act.

The Terrorist Affected Areas (Special Courts) Ordinance, promulgated in 1984 with special reference to the Punjab, provides for secret tribunals to try suspected terrorists and confers unprecedented powers of arrest and detention upon security forces. The ordinance, together with the second amendment to the National Security Act, drew the editorial concern of India's major English-language newspapers, and the People's Union for Civil Liberties warned that their extraordinary powers can be used "against dissenters and for narrow political ends by the ruling party."[71]

In 1985, in the immediate wake of the terrorist bombings in New Delhi and its environs, Parliament passed the Terrorist and Disruptive Activities (Prevention) Act. The law, in addition to prescribing the death penalty for fatal terrorist actions, gives officials the power to tap telephones, censor mail, or raid any premises when authorities believe the people involved endanger the unity or sovereignty of the nation. As provided in the 1987 extension of the act, trials may be conducted by special courts *in camera,* and with the submission of certain kinds of evidence, the accused are assumed guilty unless they can prove themselves innocent. Incommunicado detention is permitted, and, specific to the Punjab, persons may be detained for up to two years without trial.[72]

In addition to these ordinances, subsidiary legislation enables the central government to impose censorship, regulate travel, and enforce curfews in areas that are "disturbed." This stunning array of legislation and ordinance has given the military and paramilitary forces enhanced power in many affected areas of Assam, Punjab, Kashmir, and other states. "For millions of Indians," Stephen Cohen writes, "the effective government is the local area or subarea commander."[73]

In 1988, as if the 18 special laws already passed in the previous four years to enhance the power of security forces in the Punjab and elsewhere were not enough, Parliament enacted the 59th Amendment to the Constitution. It provided for the declaration of an emergency for a period of two years under conditions of "internal disturbance"[74] and empowered the central government to suspend Article 21 of the Constitution—India's "due process" clause, guaranteeing the fundamental right to life and personal liberty. Opposition party leaders

[71] People's Union for Civil Liberties, *Black Laws 1984* (Delhi, 1984), p. 2. Also see A. G. Noorani, "The Terrorist Ordinance," *Economic and Political Weekly,* 28 July 1984, p. 1188.

[72] *India Today,* 30 September 1987, p. 107.

[73] Stephen P. Cohen, "The Military and Indian Democracy," in Atul Kohli, ed., *India's Democracy: An Analysis of Changing State–Society Relations* (Princeton, N.J.: Princeton University Press, 1988), p. 128.

[74] In 1979, in a response to the abuses of the 1975–77 emergency, the Janata government passed the 44th Amendment, substituting the words "armed rebellion" for the more general "internal disturbance" in the emergency provisions of Article 352.

have denounced each of these acts as a step toward reimposition of the 1975–77 emergency. Another national emergency is an unlikely prospect, but the government has armed itself with the legal instruments and police power to make so extreme an action unnecessary. Political stability cannot be purchased through repression, however, as the 1975–77 emergency itself bears witness.

The Prospects for Political Stability

Predictions of national disintegration, the collapse of democracy, social chaos, and revolutionary violence have accompanied the processes of change in India from the time of independence. In the face of illiteracy, poverty, and the "fissiparous tendencies" of caste, religion, language, and region, there are many who have seen democracy as a system that India can ill afford. Cassandras—both Indian and foreign—have greeted each parliamentary election as inevitably its last. The 1975–77 emergency was widely mourned as the death of democracy. Some viewed it, no doubt, as proof apparent that democracy cannot work in India. The "restoration" of democracy in 1977, with the squabbling Janata government, and the return of Indira Gandhi in 1980 witnessed heightened expectations, sharpened social conflict, and increasing political malaise. The assassinations of Indira Gandhi in 1984 and Rajiv Gandhi in 1991; turmoil in Assam, the Punjab, and Kashmir; and the political instability at the Center inherent in the minority governments formed since 1989 have brought new forecasts of doom for Indian democracy.

Dire predictions, if made often enough, may ultimately find fulfillment. Yet India has survived its "dangerous decades" reasonably well, and its political institutions, perhaps somewhat the worse for wear, have demonstrated remarkable resilience. Of the many nations that have emerged from colonial rule since World War II, India is one of the few that has retained free elections and democratic institutions. India does face enormous problems, however. It is a nation under pressure, and its stability is by no means assured.

The prospect for stability in India lies in the balance between the maintenance of order and the satisfaction of basic demands for economic improvement and social justice. It is imperative that India maintain a steady—and, if at all possible, heightened—rate of economic growth and that it expand agricultural production to ensure continued self-sufficiency in food. It is imperative that there be greater equity in the distribution of income and that the basic needs of India's poor be met. No government, however, can satisfy all of the people all of the time. Even in the best of times the satisfaction of the demands of any one group is likely to be opposed by another. All of this is made more difficult by the entry of new groups into the political arena, by heightened expectations, and by sharpened conflict in the competition for scarce resources.

India's political stability will be measured less by the challenges of social unrest than by the strength of its institutions. Weak political institutions are less the result than the cause of unrest. It is not the pace of change but rather the capacity of institutions to cope with change that is at issue.

Recommended Reading

Andersen, Walter K., and Shridhar D. Damle, *The Brotherhood in Saffron: The Rashtriya Swayamsevak Sangh and Hindu Revivalism*. Boulder, Colo.: Westview Press, 1987. A major study of religion and politics.

Basu, Amrita, *Two Faces of Protest: Contrasting Modes of Women's Activism in India*. Berkeley: University of California Press, 1992. Studies of the highly-organized CPM in West Bengal and the grass-roots Shamrik Sangathana in Maharashtra.

Björkman, James W., ed., *Fundamentalism, Revivalists, and Violence in South Asia*. New Delhi: Manohar, 1988. Studies of religious violence and communal politics.

*Bondurant, Joan V., *Conquest of Violence*. Berkeley: University of California Press, 1965. A sympathetic study of satyagraha and Gandhian political theory.

*Calman, Leslie, *Protest in Democratic India: Authority's Response to Challenge*. Boulder, Colo.: Westview Press, 1985. A study of the Srikakulam Naxalite movement in Andhra Pradesh and the Shramik Sanghatana and Bhoomi Sena movements in Maharashtra.

Das, Veena, ed., *Mirrors of Violence: Communities, Riots and Survivors in South Asia*. Delhi: Oxford University Press, 1990. Essays by distinguished social scientists on the nature of communal conflict and rioting.

*Available in a paperback edition.

Embree, Ainslie T., *Utopias in Conflict: Religion and Nationalism in Modern India*. Berkeley: University of California Press, 1990. A thoughtful study of competing visions for the just society.

Frankel, Francine R., and M. S. A. Rao, eds., *Dominance and State Power in Modern India: Decline of a Social Order*, 2 vols. Delhi: Oxford University Press, 1989, 1990. Studies in state–society relations, with special attention to class, caste, ethnicity, and dominance.

Galanter, Marc, *Competing Equalities: Law and the Backward Classes in India*. Berkeley: University of California Press, 1984. The major study of India's "affirmative action" programs for untouchables and Other Backward Classes.

*Gopal, Sarvepalli, ed., *Anatomy of a Confrontation: The Babri Masjid–Ramjamabhumi Issue*. New Delhi: Viking/Penguin, 1991. Important studies of Hindu–Muslim communalism.

*Hardgrave, Robert L., Jr., *India under Pressure: Prospects for Political Stability*. Boulder, Colo.: Westview Press, 1984. A study of Indian trends in social change, political stability, and international relations.

———, *The Nadars of Tamilnad: The Political Culture of a Community in Change*. Berkeley: University of California Press, 1969. An analysis of the relationship between social structure and political behavior within a changing caste community in South India.

Karnik, V. B., *Indian Trade Unions: A Survey*, 3d ed. Bombay: Popular, 1978. A study of the development of labor unions in India.

Kothari, Rajni, ed., *Caste in Indian Politics*. New Delhi: Orient Longmans, 1970. Nine case studies of the interaction between caste and politics within the context of social change.

Lynch, Owen M., *The Politics of Untouchability: Social Mobility and Social Change in a City of India*. New York: Columbia University Press, 1969. A study of the Jatav caste of Agra.

*Mahar, J. Michael, ed., *The Untouchables in Contemporary India*. Tucson: University of Arizona Press, 1972. A superb collection of papers focusing on social and political change among the Scheduled Castes.

Oommen, T. K., *Protest and Change: Studies in Social Movements*. New Delhi: Sage, 1990. An analysis of protest as a source of social change.

———, *Social Structure and Politics: Studies in Independent India*. Delhi: Hindustan Publishing, 1984. Essays by one of India's leading sociologists.

Rao, M. S. A., ed., *Social Movements in India*, 2 vols. New Delhi: Manohar, 1979. Important studies of peasant, backward classes, sectarian, tribal, and women's movements.

Roy, Ramashray, and Richard Sisson, eds., *Diversity and Dominance in Indian Politics*, Vol. 2: *Division, Deprivation, and the Congress*. New Delhi: Sage, 1990. Essays on social diversity and partisanship.

*Rudolph, Lloyd I., and Susanne H., *The Modernity of Tradition*. Chicago: University of Chicago Press, 1967. A study of the ways in which tradition and modernity penetrate one another in a dialectical relationship. The dynamics of tradition are explored in the context of caste associations, the personality of Mahatma Gandhi, and the Indian legal system.

Shah, Ghanshyam, *Social Movements in India: A Review of the Literature*. New Delhi: Sage, 1990. Valuable source, with chapters on peasant, tribal, untouchable, backward caste, women's, students', and labor and middle-class movements.

Srinivas, M. N., *Caste in Modern India and Other Essays*. Bombay: Asia Publishing House, 1962. A classic analysis of politics and social change in India.

Varshney, Ashutosh, *The Myth of Rural Powerlessness: Town–Country Struggles in India's Development*. Cambridge: Cambridge University Press, 1993. Argues that democracy has empowered the rural sector, but that its power may have peaked, as politics based on religion, caste, and region cuts across and splits rural India.

*Weiner, Myron, and Mary F. Katzenstein, *India's Preferential Policies: Migrants, the Middle Classes, and Ethnic Equality*. Chicago: University of Chicago Press, 1981. A study of "reservations" in pursuit of the goals of equality.

Chapter 6

Parties and Politics

INDIAN POLITICAL PARTIES AND THE PARTY SYSTEM HAVE been shaped by the pluralism and cultural diversity of the country, the traditions of the nationalist movement, the contrasting styles of party leadership, and clashing ideological perspectives. Despite the umbrella character of the nationalist movement, the pre-independence Indian National Congress was never completely successful in encompassing all of India's diversity within a single organization. Political forces based on ideology, caste, community, and region existed either as separately organized groups within the Congress or as independent political organizations. Although the Indian National Congress became the dominant party of post-independence India, these political forces emerged after 1947 as the core of a fragmented multiparty system. Gradually as social stratification was altered by economic and social change and mass politics activated more and more political groups, a process of alignment and realignment took place both between and within parties, and the powerful arithmetic of caste, community, language, and region lay behind party labels. As the power of the Congress began to decline, political parties in India became more regionalized, and coalition and alliance politics became increasingly important.

The fragmenting tendencies of the party system have been partially offset by systemic factors inherent in Indian political institutions. Among the most important systemic factors is the use of the single-member district plurality, or "first past the post," system of voting, in which victory goes to the candidate who gets the most votes. The system results in a vast representational gap between an electorally strong but highly fragmented opposition and the ability of a large, nationally organized party or coalition of parties to gain a sizable legislative majority with only a plurality of the votes. Under the Indian electoral system a plurality of 40 to 45 percent of the popular vote can produce legislative majorities of 60 to 75 percent in Parliament. In 1984, for example, the Congress (I) party gained 79 percent of the seats with only 48 percent of the vote. Although this anomaly has led to demands that India change its electoral laws from the present plurality-voting system to some form of proportional representation,[1] the existing system does compel parties and factions to combine into broad-based umbrella parties, coalitions, or united fronts if they are to have any chance of victory. The inherent tendency toward fragmentation both within and between parties, therefore, has been partially offset by the political necessity of coalition building that transcends party program, ideology, or class interests. As seen in Table 6–1, the overall level of opposition unity is measured by an Index of Opposition Unity (IOU) based on a scale of 0 to 100.[2] The higher the level of opposition unity, the better the chances of victory. The resulting pattern of factional alignment or coalition, however, always remains tenuous and subject to the threat of defection or realignment. The management of such fluid alignments, therefore, requires considerable leadership and organizational skills; yet all parties have become less and less institutionally capable and effective at this form of political management.

Parties and Political Tendencies

Although Indian parties have repeatedly split, combined, recombined, and changed their names, electoral behavior is often more stable than the fluidity of the parties would indicate. As seen in Table 6–1, a remarkable continuity in major political tendencies remains. The strength of these tendencies is reflected in the total party vote

[1]Election Commission of India, *Report on the General Elections to the House of the People and the Legislative Assemblies 1979–80 and Vice Presidential Election 1979*, 1 (Jaipur: Government Central Press, 1980):39–40.

[2]For a detailed analysis of this concept, see David Butler, Ashok Lahiri, and Prannoy Roy, *India Decides: Elections 1952–1991* (New Delhi: Living Media, 1991), pp. 30–41.

Table 6–1
Indian Political Tendencies, 1952–1991

	Percentage Vote for National Parties								
	Right	*Center*			*Left*		*Others*		
Year	*Jana Sangh, Swatantra, Bharatiya Janata Party*	*Janata Party*	*Congress Party*	*Janata(S) Lok Dal/DMKP, Janata Dal Parties*	*Socialist Party*	*Communist Parties*	*Regional & Other Parties*	*Independents*	*Index of Opposition Unity (IOU)*
1952	3	—	45	—	16	3	16	16	—
1957	6	—	48	—	11	9	8	19	—
1962	15	—	46	—	13	10	8	11	67
1967	19	—	41	—	11	9	6	14	67
1971	21	—	44	—	4	10	13	9	71
1977	—	45	35	—	—	7	7	6	90
1980	—	19	43	9	—	9	14	6	65
1984	7	7*	48	6	—	9	15	8	74

1989	11	—	40	18	—	9	17	5	77
1991	21	—	38	15	—	9	12	5	66

Congress = Dominant Congress party in each election, e.g., 1971 and 1977, Congress (R); 1980 to 1991, Congress (I)

Socialist Left = Kisan Mazdoor Praja Party, Praja Socialist Party, Socialist Party, Samyukta Socialist Party, Republican Party

Communist Left = Communist Party of India, Communist Party of India (Marxist)

Janata Dal (1989) = Janata Paty, Lok Dal (DMKP), Jan Morcha, Congress (S)

Janata Dal (1991) = Janata Dal and Samajvadi Janata Party

Right = Jana Sangh, Swatantra, Bharatiya Janata Party

Regional & Other = All other parties

Independents = All who contested as such

---

*Includes Congress (S)

SOURCE: The table draws upon a study by Richard Sisson and William Vanderbok, "Mapping the Indian Electorate: Trends in Party Support in Seven National Elections," *Asian Survey*, 13 (October 1983): 1142; Richard Sisson, "India in 1989: A Year of Elections in a Culture of Change," *Asian Survey*, 30 (February 1990): 111–125; Walter K. Andersen, "India's 1991 Elections: The Uncertain Verdict," *Asian Survey*, 31 (October 1991): 976–989; David Butler, "Predictability of Indian Election Results" in Subrata Kumar Mitra and James Chiriyankandath, eds., *Electoral Politics in India: A Changing Landscape* (New Delhi: Segment, 1992): 264–66; and Arun Kumar/Press Trust of India, *The Tenth Round: Study of Indian Elections 1991* (Calcutta: Rupo 1991): 131–32. Sources vary slightly on election returns, and figures are adjusted to correspond to Table7–3, pp. 219–21.

and in the decline of the number of successful independent candidates since 1952. Indian political parties can be grouped into two major categories, national and regional, and are so recognized by the Election Commission of India. In 1991, for example, 9 national parties and 38 state parties[3] were recognized. National parties can be grouped on the basis of ideological tendency along a right-to-left spectrum. This ideological classification is based primarily on the party's economic program, but also includes the party's position on what Indians call "the communal issue," that is, the relationship between religion and politics.

As seen in Table 6–1, the centrist Congress party dominated Indian politics from 1947 to 1977 when it was defeated by the Janata Party, a united front of non-Communist opposition parties. The breakup of the Janata experiment restored the Congress to power from 1980 to 1989. Congress dominance was successfully challenged once again in 1989 when the party was defeated by a second united front of opposition parties. Unlike 1977, however, the Congress defeat came at the hands of a loose electoral alliance of opposition parties in which no single party was able to win a majority, and new elections had to be held after only 18 months. Elections for the Tenth Lok Sabha took place in the summer of 1991 and produced another minority government, this time led by the Congress (I). Thus, for the first time in Indian history, two elections within a period of 18 months failed to produce a stable governing majority.

Despite the dominant role played by the Congress party since 1947, India has always had an electorally strong but divided group of non-Congress parties reflecting Indian ideological and cultural diversities. This fragmented multiparty system has evolved through four distinct periods. The first period from 1947 to 1977 can be separated into two phases coinciding with the pattern of change in the Congress itself. The second period from 1977 to 1980 was noted for the creation of the Janata Party, the first successful but short-lived effort at forging a national, centrist alternative to the Congress. The third period from 1980 to 1989 was characterized by renewed fragmentation of parties and a return to the pattern of shifting alliances, splits, and mergers. The fourth period, which began in 1989, was marked by a decline in

[3]Formal recognition is granted on a state-by-state basis to a party if it meets specified criteria as established by the Election Commission of India. A party recognized in four or more states is accorded the status of a national party. With less than four, it is designated as a state party.

Congress support, a second but unsuccessful effort to forge a national, centrist alternative to the Congress, a growing regionalization of parties, and the increased importance of coalition and alliance politics.

The first period of party development was characterized by the emergence of a number of political parties reflecting the basic ideological tendencies of Marxism, socialism, Gandhianism, communalism, and liberalism that had come to dominate the Indian political scene. These tendencies roughly paralleled the factional mosaic within the Congress itself that gave rise to what Rajni Kothari characterized as the "Congress system."[4]

On the left of the political spectrum, separate communist and socialist parties emerged. The Communist Party of India (CPI), founded in the 1920s, adopted a strategy of a united front with the Congress party, and its members entered the Congress Socialist Party (CSP) in hope of capturing the nationalist movement from within. They were expelled in 1939, but the Congress Socialist Party remained a distinct entity within the Congress organization. The CSP withdrew from Congress after independence, dropped the name Congress, and later joined with a group of Gandhian dissidents to form the Praja Socialist Party (PSP). In this and in various other incarnations, the socialists in the 1950s were substantially weakened when the Congress itself declared its objectives to be the creation of a socialist pattern of society. The parties of the left have been plagued by endemic factionalism and splits, but they remain a persistent, if declining, force on the Indian political scene.

On the right of the political spectrum, the forces of Indian conservatism became divided on the basis of communal versus noncommunal loyalties. The first major political party to develop to the right of the Congress was the Bharatiya Jana Sangh (or, more commonly, Jana Sangh), founded in 1951 and drawing inspiration from the Hindu communal orientation of the pre-independence Hindu Mahasabha and its organizational strength from the paramilitary Rashtriya Swayamsevak Sangh (RSS).

Indian conservatism did not attempt to organize on a noncom-

[4]The party system in India has been characterized in this way by Rajni Kothari, in "The Congress 'System' in India," *Party System and Election Studies*, Occasional Papers of the Centre for Developing Societies, No. 1 (Bombay: Allied Publishers, 1967), pp. 1–18; by W. H. Morris-Jones, in "Parliament and Dominant Party: Indian Experience," *Parliamentary Affairs*, 17 (Summer 1964):296–307; and by Gopal Krishna, in "One Party Dominance—Developments and Trends," *Party System and Election Studies*, pp. 19–98.

munal basis until 1959. Alarmed at the growing level of socialist rhetoric in the Congress, a combination of free-enterprise, liberal business people, former princes, and medium-sized landowners came together to form the Swatantra Party, the first party in India to openly challenge planning, government control, and the development consensus evolved by Nehru. The party survived until 1974, when it merged with the forerunner of the Bharatiya Lok Dal, a North Indian peasant party.

Although the Communist, Socialist, Jana Sangh, and Swatantra parties enjoyed limited electoral success until 1967, they served as key forces of pressure on their sympathizers within the Congress party during the period of one-party dominance. Strengthened by Congress defections from 1967 onward, the opposition parties came to serve as building blocks for the creation of a series of alliances, coalitions, and united fronts that were ultimately successful in challenging Congress hegemony.

The vulnerability of the Congress party to united fronts and to defection was not fully recognized until the late 1960s. Success for the long-frustrated and splintered opposition first came at the state level in 1967 with the formation of Samyukta Vidhayak Dals, broadly based multiparty coalition governments which ended Congress control over half the states in India. Loss of Congress hegemony in the states was followed by a wave of local-level defections in 1967; the historic split in the Congress in 1969; and a second round of defections that followed the lifting of the emergency in 1977. The defections of 1977 were the result of Indira Gandhi's oppressive policies followed during the period of emergency rule from 1975 to 1977. Congress defectors formed a number of new parties: the Bharatiya Lok Dal (BLD), the Congress (O), and the Congress for Democracy (CFD). These Congress fragments united with the Socialists and the Jana Sangh in 1977 to form the Janata Party, a national, centrist alternative to the Congress that raised the IOU to 90 and brought an end to 30 years of Congress rule.

The unity achieved in repudiation of the emergency and electoral challenge to the Congress in 1977 was soon undermined by internecine struggle. Having accomplished its primary objective of restoring democracy to India, the Janata Party disintegrated into its constituent elements. Although the party had united in theory, each of its constituent parties had retained its own organizational structure, and when differences arose over leadership, personality, economic policy, and political objectives, the Janata government collapsed in 1979.

The third period of party development from 1980 to 1989 brought a renewal of opposition fragmentation, unsuccessful efforts at realignment, and an increased regionalization of Indian politics. Significantly, most of the new parties, despite their new names, continued to reflect the basic tendencies of the past. The old Jana Sangh became the Bharatiya Janata Party, whereas the Congress (O) and the Socialists retained the Janata Party label. The most erratic was the Bharatiya Lok Dal, which changed names several times as it split and combined with the breakaway factions of other parties, emerging as the Dalit Mazdoor Kizan Party (DMKP), and then, in 1985, changing its name back to Lok Dal, which later split into two factions. As in the past, opposition ranks were also strengthened by the defection of Congress dissidents. In October 1987, a group of Congress dissidents joined V. P. Singh, a former Finance Minister in Rajiv Gandhi's Cabinet, to form the Jan Morcha (People's Movement) to carry out a program of social and political reform. The various opposition parties that have developed since 1947 have increasingly become "national" in name only, and their strength is concentrated in only a few states. Still, these parties have at least a pretense to national status. Beyond the national parties, however, a number of regional parties exist whose support is limited to a single state. The most significant are the DMK and AIADMK in Tamil Nadu, the Telugu Desam in Andhra Pradesh, the National Conference in Kashmir, the Akali Dal in the Punjab, and the Asom Gana Parishad in Assam.

In preparation for the 1989 parliamentary elections, India's disparate opposition made a new attempt at forging opposition unity. Unlike the Janata experiment of 1977 to 1979, the new coalition was designed to bring together a group of national and regional parties into a National Front. The core of the National Front was the newly formed Janata Dal, a centrist party based in northern India and led by V. P. Singh. The Janata Dal was composed of the rump of the old Janata Party led by Chandra Shekhar, the Lok Dal (A) led by Ajit Singh, the Lok Dal (B) led by Devi Lal, and the Jan Morcha. They were joined by the regionally based Asom Gana Parishad of Assam, the Telugu Desam of Andhra, the DMK of Tamil Nadu, and the Congress (S) led by S. C. Sinha. The National Front, in turn, entered into electoral agreements with the BJP on the right and the Communists on the left, raising the Index of Opposition Unity (IOU) to 77, its highest level since 1977.

Although the electorally unified alliance was able to defeat the Congress (I) in the 1989 elections, no single party was able to win a majority of the seats, and the result was a hung Parliament. The performance of the National Front fell far below expectations as its regional allies went down to defeat, and the Front was reduced to the Janata Dal. The Janata Dal was able to form a minority government with the support of the BJP and the Communists. Like the Janata Party in 1979, however, the Janata Dal government collapsed due to internal factionalism and the breakup of the alliance.

New elections for the Tenth Lok Sabha were held in the summer of 1991. Opposition unity broke down, and the first round of balloting indicated a continued swing away from the Congress. The elections, however, were interrupted by the assassination of Rajiv Gandhi on May 21, 1991, by a Sri Lankan Tamil militant. Due to the assassination, the second and third rounds of polling were delayed until mid-June. Despite a drop in its overall popular vote, a marked swing of sympathy votes in favor of the Congress (I) enabled the party to win enough seats to form a minority government with the support of the Janata Dal and the Communists. The most significant result of the elections, however, was the sharp increase in support for the BJP. As a result, traditional anti-Congress sentiments are gradually giving way to a stop-BJP movement.

As India enters the 1990s, the Indian party system is still in the process of evolution and development. Despite the end of the Nehru dynasty, the Congress remains the largest single party and the only genuinely all-India party. The left has been reduced to the Communists and their allies and has a static electoral support base of about 9 percent. Finally, while attempts to forge a national, centrist alternative to the Congress have failed, the BJP has begun to build a solid block on the right of the Indian political spectrum. Its electoral support increased from 7.4 percent in 1984 to 21 percent in 1991.

In the absence of some unifying event or shock, such as the 1975–77 emergency, each of the non-Congress parties of India will continue to pursue a pattern of coalition, alliance, and a united front, while simultaneously trying to expand its own base of support. Personality, ideology, program, and conflicting bases of support, however, continue to fragment the national opposition parties and frustrate their attempt to forge a united front. This fragmentation has been accompanied by their decline as national parties and by a strengthening of the regional base of Indian politics—through the rise of regional parties and the regionalization of parties that are national only in name.

Each of India's major opposition parties has its own history, organization, program, and base of support. Each faces its own set of problems that continue to threaten its internal unity and prevent realignment into a national political force—and yet each has demonstrated a remarkable degree of resilience.

The Congress Party

The largest, most successful, and most durable political party in India has been the centrist Congress party. Although the party as it exists today traces its history back to the Indian National Congress, which was founded in 1885 and led the fight for independence, repeated splits, fragmentation, organizational weakness, and personalization of power have made it a very different entity.[5] The post-independence development of the Congress can be divided into four periods. The first, from 1947 to 1967, was a period of one-party dominance based on the Congress "system." The second, from 1967 to 1977, witnessed the breakdown of the Congress system, a split in the party, a personalization of power, and the eclipse of Congress dominance. The third period, from 1977 to 1991, can best be characterized as the era of "Indira and Sons." It represented the high point of dynastic rule but ended in the assassinations of Indira Gandhi in 1984 and Rajiv Gandhi in 1991. The fourth phase began in May 1991 with the end of dynastic rule and a desperate search by the Congress for new leaders and a new identity.

One-Party Dominance, 1947–1967

The Indian National Congress, from its founding in 1885 until independence in 1947, was the major force of nationalism in South Asia. With swaraj, as the movement was transformed into a political party, the Congress organization reached from New Delhi throughout India into each state and district. For three decades the Congress was the only genuinely all-India party, not merely in terms of its geographic distribution but in terms of its capacity to appeal to virtually all sections of society. By almost any variable—social, eco-

[5]The Congress centenary, celebrated in 1985, was the occasion for the publication of a number of books. See, among others, Paul R. Brass and Francis Robinson, eds., *The Indian National Congress and Indian Society, 1885–1985: Ideology, Social Structure, and Political Dominance* (Delhi: Chanakya, 1987); Ram Joshi and R. K. Hebsur, eds., *Congress in Indian Politics: A Centenary Perspective* (Bombay: Popular Prakashan, 1987); and the official All-India Congress Committee (I), *A Centenary History of the Indian National Congress (1885–1985)*, 5 vols. (New Delhi: Vikas, 1985).

nomic, demographic—the base of Congress support was the most heterogeneous and differentiated of any political party in India.

From the time of independence until 1967, the critical arena of political competition was the Congress "system" of one-party dominance. This system, operating effectively in India until the mid-1960s, was a competitive one, but one in which the single party of consensus occupied a dominant, central position. In this system the dominant Congress party, itself factionally divided, was both sensitive and responsive to the margin of pressure; the opposition did not constitute an alternative to the ruling party but functioned from the periphery in the form of parties of pressure. In such a system the role of the opposition parties, writes Rajni Kothari,

> is to constantly pressurize, criticize, censure and influence it by influencing opinion and interests inside the margin and, above all, exert a latent threat that if the ruling group strays away too far from the balance of effective public opinion, and if the factional system within it is not mobilized to restore the balance, it will be displaced from power by the opposition groups.[6]

The one-party dominance system had two prominent characteristics. "There is plurality within the dominant party which makes it more representative, provides flexibility, and sustains internal competition. At the same time, it is prepared to absorb groups and movements from outside the party and thus prevent other parties from gaining strength."[7]

The breakdown of the Congress "system" was rooted in its own dynamics—the internal contradictions within the party.

The Factional Character of the Congress Within the Congress in the years of dominance, factions interacted in "a continuous process of pressure, adjustment and accommodation" to provide a built-in opposition.[8] The party retained the character of the nationalist movement in seeking to balance and accommodate social and ideological diversity within an all-embracing, representative structure. During the struggle for independence, the Congress party, as the vehicle of the nationalist movement, brought together an eclectic body of individuals and groups in united opposition to the British Raj. Claiming

[6] Kothari, "Congress 'System,'" p. 3.

[7] Ibid., p. 6.

[8] Rajni Kothari, "Party System," *Economic Weekly*, 3 June 1961, p. 849.

sole legitimacy as the nationalist party, the Congress sought to resolve or avoid internal conflict, balance interests, and blur ideological distinctions in its search for consensus. Within its ranks, however, in factions and internal parties, were the roots of opposition. Organized groups emerged from the Congress umbrella as distinct parties, but each left within the Congress an ideologically congruent and sympathetic faction. Thus each of the opposition parties—the Jana Sangh, Swatantra, the Socialists, and the Communists—retained access to the Congress that provided it with an influence disproportionate to its size.

The responsiveness of the Congress to these pressures was revealed in the flexibility and contradictions of its programs and practices. The Congress sustained itself by undermining the opposition, taking over their programs, conceding basic issues, and co-opting their leadership. At the national level, the Congress stole the thunder of the Praja Socialist Party through its 1955 resolution in support of a socialist pattern of society. In the states the Congress became the voice of regionalism in order to undercut the growth of separatism. At the local level, the party relaxed its policy of land reform to win support from the landlords and keep Swatantra at a distance. At the top, the Congress party repeatedly denounced casteism as a reversion to a tribal mentality, but, at the bottom, the Congress, like the Janata and even the Communists, anchored its organization among the dominant castes.

In consolidating its power after independence, the Congress sought to achieve a national consensus through the accommodation and absorption of dominant social elements that had kept aloof from the nationalist movement. Traditional caste and village leaders, landlords, and business people made their way into the Congress.

> In its effort to win, Congress adapts itself to the local power structure. It recruits from among those who have local power and influence. . . . The result is a political system with considerable tension between a government concerned with modernizing the society and economy and a party seeking to adapt itself to the local environment in order to win elections.[9]

With the resources of government power and patronage, the Congress attracted careerists, who sought to gain support by appealing

[9]Myron Weiner, *Party Building in a New Nation* (Chicago: University of Chicago Press, 1967), p. 15.

to the parochial loyalties of language, caste, and community. "The composite character of the party was preserved," writes Gopal Krishna, "indeed made more heterogeneous by promiscuous accommodation of divergent elements, whose commitments to the new consensus created around the objectives of economic development, socialism and democracy remained superficial."[10] Paul R. Brass concurs: The Congress party chose "to make adjustments and accommodations, to interact with rather than transform the traditional order. In India modernization is not a one-way process; political institutions modernize the society while the society traditionalizes institutions."[11]

As the party penetrated society, it was influenced by it. Political mobilization served to stimulate a new consciousness and solidarity. As a channel of communication and integration providing effective vertical linkage, the party drew increasing numbers into political participation. In a capillary effect, they infused the party with a new leadership, regional in the base of its support, more traditional in the idiom of its political behavior. Political consciousness was activated faster than the integrative process, however, and as a result group identity was often emphasized at the expense of the national community. As the new electorate, caste-conscious and parochial in orientation, was drawn into a more participant political life, the Congress and the opposition parties sought to win their support through the tactics of the American political machine—patronage, favors, promises, and bargains. As the electorate was politicized, the parties were traditionalized. The parties became "mediating agencies between the largely traditional and politically diffuse electorate and the modern state system with its emphasis on citizenship, purposive direction of public policy and political integration."[12]

Although all parties served to induct the new citizens into the political culture, the Congress, as the dominant party, was the critical channel of linkage between the elite and the masses. Mahatma Gandhi had attempted to bring the Congress directly to the masses, but it was the development of the party organization, with its roots in tradition, that consolidated the Congress and made politics both comprehensible and meaningful to Indian peasants. In the process,

[10] Krishna, "One Party Dominance," p. 29.

[11] Paul R. Brass, *Factional Politics in an Indian State: The Congress Party in Uttar Pradesh* (Berkeley: University of California Press, 1966), p. 2.

[12] Krishna, "One Party Dominance," p. 32.

however, the Congress became an advocate of much that it had opposed, encouraging both sectionalism and integration, preaching socialism, and sustaining the *status quo.*

Brass, in his study of the Congress in Uttar Pradesh, describes the internal life of the party during this period in terms of factional conflict. The conflict is not ideological but personal; it is characterized by shifting political coalitions: "Alliances develop and splits and defections occur wholly because of the mutual convenience and temporarily shared power-political interests of the group leaders." The groups are "loose coalitions of local, district faction leaders, tied together at the state level partly by personal bonds of friendship, partly by caste loyalties, and most of all by political interest."[13] Although there seem to be no persistent conflicts, Brass argues, there is in each faction a relatively solid inner core, bound together in personal loyalty to the leader and divided from other factions by deep personal enmities. Factional conflict is rooted at the district level, and factional systems are largely autonomous, arising out of conditions and personalities peculiar to the district. This served to compartmentalize conflict, to quarantine discontent, and to make discontent more manageable.

Factionalism in the party was closely related to factionalism in the villages, since traditional village factions increasingly sought to ally themselves with a party group. The factional character of the Congress served to accommodate local conflict and to internalize it. If the Congress were unable to tolerate factions, opposition parties would secure the support of one of the two factions in each village—as in certain regions they were already beginning to do. Highly institutionalized, the factional system within the Congress, until 1967, was able "to sustain popular support in the midst of intense intra-party conflict."[14]

Although factionalism often leads to paralysis at the level of local government, it may also perform certain integrative functions. The faction, as a vertical structure of power, cuts across caste and class divisions and is based on a combination of other traditional loyalties and individual interests. "All faction leaders seek cross-caste alliances, for it is political power they desire and not merely the advancement of the claims of their own communities."[15] Factional conflict

[13]Brass, *Factional Politics,* pp. 54–55.
[14]Weiner, *Party Building,* pp. 159–60.
[15]Brass, *Factional Politics,* p. 236.

also broadens the base of participation within the party as each faction competes for wider group support. By drawing in new caste and religious groups, for example, factions politicized them in secular terms.[16]

Factionalism, however, may also lead to a form of *immobilisme*, as each faction holds the other in check. The factional character of the Congress meant that the chief opposition to the government frequently came from within the Congress itself. Conflict between the governmental and organizational wings of the party virtually constituted a two-party system, but one hardly designed for coherent and effective policy. With minimum response to the problems of economic inequality and social injustice, the Congress system was governed by conflict avoidance and the politics of patronage.

Federalizing the Congress System In theory the Congress was a highly centralized party, but in the years of one-party dominance it became increasingly federalized in practice. During the struggle for independence, the Congress organization was structured as a parallel government, extending down to the village level. Except for the fact that Congress provincial units were organized along linguistic lines, this structure corresponded to administrative boundaries, such as that of the district, not to electoral constituencies. After independence the system was retained, with parallel party and government structure from top to bottom. In each state, the locus of Congress power was the Pradesh Congress Committee. At the apex of the national structure, shown in Figure 6–1, was the Working Committee and the party president.[17]

The first few years after independence were marked by conflict between the party and the government. The organization attempted to assert its supremacy, but the political center of gravity had shifted from party to government. In 1951 Nehru was elected Congress president, thus bringing the party and government under the control of a single leader. His emergence as undisputed leader of the Congress "confirmed the pre-eminent role of the Prime Minister. . . ."[18] Nehru held the position of party president for only three years, but he ensured thereafter the subordination of the organization.

Under Nehru, the Working Committee was brought under the

[16] Ibid., p. 242.

[17] For specifics of Congress organization, see Stanley A. Kochanek, *The Congress Party of India* (Princeton, N.J.: Princeton University Press, 1968).

[18] Ibid., p. 53.

Figure 6–1
The National Decision-Making Structure of the Congress.

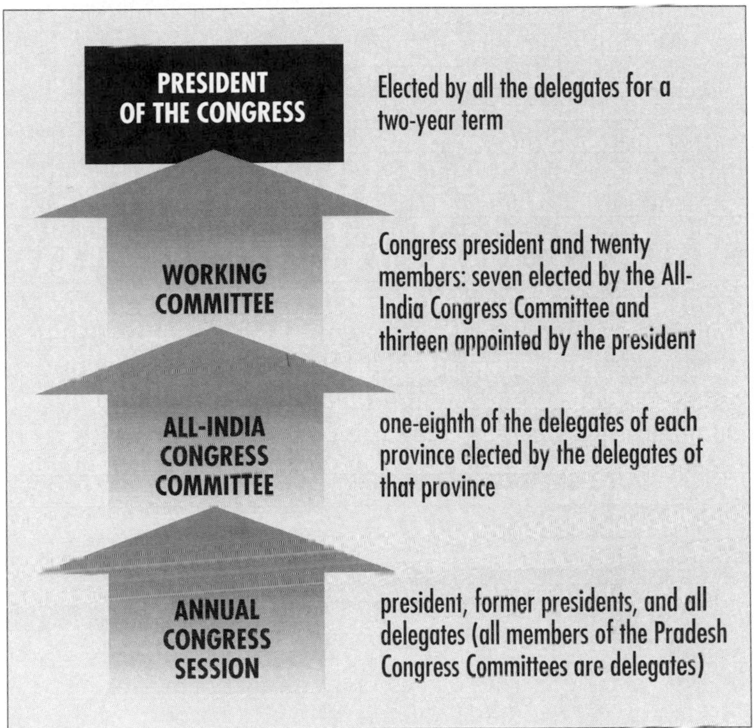

SOURCE: Stanley A. Kochanek, *The Congress Party of India* (Princeton, N.J.: Princeton University Press, 1968), p. xxii.

dominance of the parliamentary wing, the most powerful chief ministers and important Central Cabinet ministers forming the core of its membership. It

> came to play an important role in providing policy leadership to the party organization, in coordinating party–government relations, and in accommodating the conflicting demands of Congress leaders representing the broadening base of the party. The Working Committee became the sounding board by which the Prime Minister could test the acceptability of new policies as well as an important feedback mechanism by which to assess the reactions of party and state leaders.[19]

[19] Ibid., p. 307.

Nehru sought to use the Working Committee for the direction of state Congress ministries. The committee became the agent of arbitration, conciliation, and mediation in an effort to achieve a new national consensus on the Congress economic program. Divergent factions were drawn under the Congress umbrella through persuasion, reconciliation, and accommodation. In the process, however, as power devolved to leaders at the state level, the party confronted the dangers of bossism, entrenchment, and indiscipline.

While the Congress at the national level was made subordinate to the government, the lower levels of the party organization were gradually captured by a new generation of politicians. These men were brokers who, in understanding both traditional society and machine techniques, provided the channels of linkage between the villages and the modern political system. The party organization became the vehicle for their own advancement, the agent of upward mobility for an aspiring new leadership. For some, the movement into the party organization was from an established base of traditional influence within their village or district. For others, politics was a vocation. K. Kamaraj Nadar, for example, rose from the bottom of the party organization to secure control of the Tamilnad Congress Committee. In the states the new leadership gained control of the organization, challenged the old order, and took over the government, its power and patronage. These new "bosses" were all organization men who, with the party machinery in their hands, took control of their state governments as chief ministers and came to wield considerable power at the national level.

The changes evidenced in the states made their appearance at the national level in 1963 with the introduction of the Kamaraj Plan. Kamaraj proposed "that leading Congressmen who are in Government should voluntarily relinquish their ministerial posts and offer themselves for full-time organizational work."[20] All chief ministers and central Cabinet ministers submitted their resignations. The decision as to which resignations to accept was left to Nehru. Six chief ministers, including Kamaraj, and six Cabinet ministers were asked to take up organizational work. The Kamaraj Plan was generally regarded as a device to get rid of Finance Minister Morarji Desai, considered conservative and rigid, but its more significant consequence was the induction of state party bosses into positions of power at the national level, with Kamaraj at the helm of the organization as new Congress president. The plan "restored" the prestige

[20]Ibid., pp. 78–79.

and power of the central organization, which had been virtually eclipsed under the dominance of Nehru.[21]

The Congress and the Politics of Succession to the Prime Ministership Following the Kamaraj Plan in 1963, in an effort to deny Desai the Congress presidency and to isolate him further from power, a group of powerful state leaders, informally organized as "the Syndicate," united behind Kamaraj as the person most likely to provide stable, effective party leadership. In January 1964 Nehru suffered a stroke, and the question "After Nehru, who?" was now raised more poignantly than ever before. Nehru had long been described as a "banyan tree," under which nothing grows. He had groomed no heir apparent. Lal Bahadur Shastri, who had left the Cabinet under the Kamaraj Plan, was now brought back as Minister without Portfolio. With Nehru's blessing and the powerful support of the Syndicate, Shastri occupied a strategic position. Four months later, on May 27, 1964, Nehru was dead. The Home Minister was designated to act as Prime Minister until the Congress Parliamentary Party (CPP), composed of all Congress MPs, could elect a successor.

Although Shastri held majority support within the CPP, Morarji Desai sought to prevent Shastri's election. Maneuvering for a unanimous election, Kamaraj called a meeting of an enlarged Congress Working Committee. The 42-member body, which Michael Brecher has called "the Grand Council of the Republic," included the regular members of the Working Committee, the chief ministers, the leaders of the Congress party in Parliament, and senior Cabinet ministers. The Syndicate played a critical role in coalescing the diverse interests behind Shastri to assure his election. In response to overwhelming pressure, Desai agreed to second Shastri's nomination to secure his unanimous election.[22]

The succession served to reveal the shift in political gravity toward the states. The state party organizations occupied a pivotal position—both in the role of the chief ministers in the decisions of "the Grand Council of the Republic" and in their control over blocs of votes within the Congress Parliamentary Party.[23]

In January 1966, less than two years after he had taken office, Shas-

[21] Kothari, "Congress 'System,'" p. 16.

[22] For an analysis of the succession, see Michael Brecher, *Nehru's Mantle: The Politics of Succession in India* (New York: Praeger, 1966).

[23] Ibid., p. 72.

tri died, just hours after having signed a truce with Pakistan at Tashkent. Faced with the second succession, Kamaraj no longer commanded the position of strength from which he had directed the events following Nehru's death. The Syndicate had lost its cohesion: "The politics of unanimity" had given way "to the politics of overt conflict."[24] Kamaraj sought to weld a consensus behind Indira Gandhi by means of massive pressure conveyed indirectly through the chief ministers. The Syndicate had no choice but to go along. Kamaraj had again emerged as "king-maker," but the process had been more difficult. Morarji Desai, against the advice of his colleagues, pressed for an open contest. He would not step down in favor of another as he had done in 1964. In a vote, the first contested election for leadership, Mrs. Gandhi overwhelmed Desai, 355 to 169. The successions revealed the capacity of the Congress to absorb conflict, but at the same time exposed deep division within the party.

The struggle for succession revealed not merely the power of the party but, even more critically, the pivotal position of the state Congress organizations. The result was a polycentric system of decision making in which power was dispersed among several competing, but overlapping, groups: the Working Committee, the chief ministers, the Cabinet, and the Congress party in Parliament. With the national leadership split, the Working Committee could no longer effectively play its mediating role. Dominant factions in the states sought to consolidate their positions. Dissident state factions, "feeling isolated from power within the party because of the inability of the central leadership to intervene to protect them," defected from the party.[25] The dilemma confronting the Congress was basic: "To dominate, Congress must accommodate, yet accommodation encourages incoherence which destroys the capacity to dominate."[26] The more autonomous the Congress party in each state became, with its effectiveness derived from local resources, the more vulnerable it was to displacement by regional opposition parties from the same sources of strength.

The Breakdown of the Congress System, 1967–1977

Results of the 1967 elections revealed the breakdown of the Congress system of reconciliation and consensus. The elections radically

[24] Ibid., p. 205.

[25] Kochanek, *Congress Party*, p. 315.

[26] W. H. Morris-Jones, "Dominance and Dissent," *Government and Opposition*, 1 (July–September 1966): 460.

changed the political map of India, marking the end of one-party dominance and the emergence of a new political era. In the decade from 1967 to 1977, the Congress, at one time or another, lost control of nearly half the state governments. It was torn by schism and emerged, reincarnated, under Prime Minister Indira Gandhi's increasingly centralized and personalized authority. In 1975, in an atmosphere of crisis and unrest, Mrs. Gandhi assumed even greater power under emergency rule.

The 1967 campaign was conducted "in an atmosphere of frustration, despondency, uncertainty, and recurrent—almost continual—agitation."[27] Rising prices, food scarcities, near-famine in Bihar, strikes, and mass agitations contributed to a situation of such seeming gravity that some observers were exceedingly pessimistic about India's future as a democracy. The election results were dramatic: The Congress failed to secure majorities in eight states, and its majority at the Center was reduced to a narrow margin of 54 percent of the seats. Voters brought down from power not only the Congress party but also some of its prominent leaders. Congress president Kamaraj was defeated in his own hometown by a student leader. Nine Union ministers and four state chief ministers were also defeated.

The elections were interpreted variously as a swing to the right and as a swing to the left. In fact, the pattern of Congress defeats was highly idiosyncratic, related to the peculiarities of each state, with no consistency in the direction of opposition sentiments. The regional Dravida Munnetra Kazhagam (DMK) came to power in Tamil Nadu with an absolute majority. In Kerala a Communist-led United Front victory was decisive. Disparate coalitions of opposition parties formed shaky governments in the Punjab, Bihar, Orissa, and West Bengal. In order to retain power, Congress entered similar conditions in Haryana, Uttar Pradesh, Madhya Pradesh, and Rajasthan.

With "floor crossings"—defections from one group to another—endemic, the coalition governments in North India fell in rapid succession, punctuated by periods of President's Rule and midterm elections.[28] With half of North India under President's Rule, new elections were coordinated for what was to be a crucial test of the Congress's

[27] Norman D. Palmer, "India's Fourth General Elections," *Asian Survey*, 7 (May 1967): 277.

[28] See Paul R. Brass, "Coalition Politics in North India," *American Political Science Review*, 62 (December 1968): 1174–91. For a discussion of the phenomenon of defection, see Subhash C. Kashyap, "The Politics of Defection: The Changing Contours of Political Power Structure in State Politics in India," *Asian Survey*, 10 (March 1970): 195–208; and Kashyap, *The Politics of Defection* (Delhi: National Publishing House, 1969).

ability to recoup its strength. The assembly elections held in February 1969 in West Bengal, the Punjab, Uttar Pradesh, and Bihar seemed only to confirm the pattern of the earlier general election. The people's verdict of 1967 was renewed emphatically. The trend toward regional parties and bases of support had brought an end to the Congress system of one-party dominance.

Crisis and Split Defeats sustained by the Congress in the 1967 elections opened conflict over party leadership and control of the government. The Congress was in disarray, with dissension and defections on all sides. The electoral reverses, however, "had generated tremendous pressures for a consensus on the leadership issue in order to avoid a schism in the already weakened party."[29] Kamaraj, despite his defeat at the polls, achieved a bargain settlement by which Mrs. Gandhi was unanimously re-elected Prime Minister, while Morarji Desai was appointed Deputy Prime Minister.

From the time she came to power a year before, Indira Gandhi had been determined not to allow herself to become a puppet of the Syndicate, and her relations with Kamaraj quickly cooled. Now, freed of the pressures of the old state bosses by their election defeats, she emerged with new strength. Challenging the Syndicate, Mrs. Gandhi sought to re-establish securely the dominance of the Prime Minister within the party. To gain the initiative, she sent a note of "stray thoughts" to the Working Committee, urging a more aggressive and populist stance toward economic policy—nationalization of major commercial banks; effective implementation of land reforms; ceilings on urban income and property; and curbs on industrial monopolies.

In response to his notable lack of enthusiasm, the Prime Minister relieved Morarji Desai of his Finance portfolio, and to save his "self-respect," Desai resigned as Deputy Prime Minister. Mrs. Gandhi then announced the nationalization of the major banks, which involved the expenditure of little political capital and reaped widespread support for the Prime Minister. She called the action "only the beginning of a bitter struggle between the common people and the vested interests in the country."[30]

The 1969 presidential elections increased the tension between the government and the organizational wings of the party and initiated the four-month crisis that split the 84-year-old Indian National Con-

[29] Kochanek, *Congress Party*, p. 412.
[30] *Hindu* (Madras), 5 August 1969.

gress.[31] Now in alliance with its old nemesis Morarji Desai, the Syndicate was determined to retain its hold over the party. Toward that end the Syndicate secured the Congress presidential nomination for its own candidate, N. Sanjiva Reddy, Speaker of the Lok Sabha, in opposition to Mrs. Gandhi's preference for Acting President V. V. Giri.[32] Giri entered the presidential contest as an independent and, with the Prime Minister's unofficial support, won the election.

In November 1969 the Syndicate leadership of the party organization expelled the Prime Minister and instructed the Congress Parliamentary Party to elect a new leader. Instead, the Congress MPs reaffirmed their support for Mrs. Gandhi by a vote of 226 to 65, but her government no longer commanded an absolute majority in the Lok Sabha. The Congress had split. In the centenary year of Mahatma Gandhi's birth, two Congress parties fought for the tattered standard of the nationalist movement.

The "Indira Wave"—The Personalization of Power Without a Congress majority in the Lok Sabha, the government of Indira Gandhi was dependent on external support—notably from the Communist Party of India (CPI) and the Tamil nationalist DMK—and was thus vulnerable to political blackmail, for any one of the segments supporting her could threaten to withdraw and potentially defeat the government. Seeking a mandate from the people in the form of an absolute majority in her own right, the Prime Minister dissolved the Lok Sabha and called new elections for March 1971. Mrs. Gandhi commanded vast popular support; moreover, she was at a tactical advantage in holding parliamentary elections separately from the general elections, since distracting local issues in contests for state assemblies might have challenged her search for a stable Congress majority at the Center.

The Prime Minister sought to campaign on national issues, to turn the electorate away from the politics of patronage and manipulation. She sought, in direct appeal to the voters, to bypass the intermediary structures—the village notables and "vote banks"—that had been the

[31] For a detailed account of the events leading up to and surrounding the schism, see Robert L. Hardgrave, Jr., "The Congress in India: Crisis and Split," *Asian Survey*, 10 (March 1970):256–62; and Mahendra Prasad Singh, *Split in a Predominant Party: The Indian National Congress in 1969* (New Delhi: Abhinav Publications, 1981).

[32] By custom, the nomination is made by the eight-member Central Parliamentary Board elected by the AICC.

base of the old Congress machine.[33] Her efforts, however, were aimed particularly at certain disadvantaged groups—the Scheduled Castes and Tribes, Muslims, and the young. Her message was clear: *Garibi Hatao,* "Abolish Poverty." In opposition, Mrs. Gandhi confronted a Four-Party Alliance of the Jana Sangh, Swatantra, the Samyukta Socialists, and the Syndicate's Congress (Organization). The Alliance's campaign was based on the removal of Mrs. Gandhi ("*Indira Hatao*"), a tactic that only helped the Prime Minister "project a simple personal image throughout the country."[34]

The results were overwhelming. With 44 percent of the vote, Congress won 352 of the 518 seats in the Lok Sabha. Mrs. Gandhi's electoral allies, the CPI and the Tamil nationalist DMK, chalked up an additional 23 seats each. The parties of the opposition Alliance each suffered serious losses. The Congress (O), inundated by the "Indira wave," was reduced from 65 to 16 seats. The only opposition party to improve its position was the Communist Party of India (Marxist), with regional strength in West Bengal. With 25 seats, it became the second largest party in Parliament. (For a tabulation of the results of the 1971 elections, see Table 7–3, p. 320).

With a two-thirds majority in Parliament, Mrs. Gandhi had the mandate she sought, but she was not yet able to pursue a program of economic transformation. On March 25, 1971, the force of the Pakistani army came down upon the people of East Bengal, and in the next nine months, 10,000,000 refugees poured from East Pakistan into India, creating a situation that for India was economically, socially, and politically unacceptable. It was imperative that the refugees return to their homes in East Bengal. Although the Bengali guerrillas of the Mukti Bahini would in all likelihood have succeeded in their struggle for independence, only India's military intervention could have provided the leverage to ensure the return of these refugees, most of whom were Hindu and might well not have been welcomed back. Moreover, hundreds of thousands of Bengalis had already been killed, and in the Indian judgment a prolongation of Pakistani rule in Bengal could only bring a greater loss of life. With these considerations in mind, in December 1971 the Indian army crossed the border into East Bengal. With the fall of Dhaka (Dacca) two weeks later, the State of Bangladesh came into being.

India was euphoric over its victory. Humiliated militarily, broken

[33]See Myron Weiner, "The 1971 Elections and the Indian Party System," *Asian Survey,* 11 (December 1971): 1153–66.

[34]W. H. Morris-Jones, "India Elects for Change—and Stability," *Asian Survey,* 11 (August 1971): 727.

as a nation, Pakistan no longer challenged Indian hegemony in the subcontinent. A new opportunity for stability and development was seen on the horizon of Pax India. Ebullient with success, Prime Minister Indira Gandhi now sought to secure her strength in the Indian states, and in March 1972 elections were held for the legislative assemblies in all but four states. Almost across the board the results brought a landslide victory. The new Congress captured more than 70 percent of the assembly seats. Confirming the mandate of the 1971 parliamentary elections, Congress control in the states now gave Indira Gandhi unprecedented power. Freed from the interference of the old Syndicate bosses, freed from the vulnerability of reliance on allied parties, the Prime Minister now appeared to be in a position to implement her pledge to the people, to fulfill their demands for social justice, and to meet their expectations of economic betterment. The "Indira wave" had overcome the powers of reaction. In the eyes of the people, Mrs. Gandhi was no longer thwarted by an effective opposition to a program of radical economic and social transformation. Even the obstruction of the conservative Supreme Court could now be overridden by parliamentary majorities. The Congress could no longer offer excuses for inaction. "The country has taken her at her word," the *Hindustan Times* wrote, "and she will now have to deliver her promises."

Herein lay her Achilles' heel. The great electoral victories reflected more the weakness of the opposition than the secure power of the new Congress. Congress had won only 48 percent of the vote in the states, even though it had won 70 percent of the seats. Many of the new members of Congress were young, inexperienced, and lacking in political clout. Virtually appointed by the Center, they lacked any base of local power. The new chief ministers were particularly vulnerable to challenge from the power of entrenched local interests and the dominant factions of the state. Within 18 months of the 1972 elections, six chief ministers had been eased out of office and President's Rule imposed in four states. In relying heavily on personal charisma and populist politics, Indira Gandhi destroyed the boss-structure of the old Congress, but she did not replace it with an effective structure linking the Center with the local party units. "Moreover, the tendency to concentrate power at the centre," write Joshi and Desai, "reduced tolerance of factional competition and the decline in the autonomy of state party structures . . . led to a weak and attenuated party and lack of stable loyalty structures."[35]

[35] Ram Joshi and Kirtidev Desai, "The Opposition: Problems and Prospects," *Economic and Political Weekly*, 20 October 1973, pp. 1913–22.

Both within the party and the government, authority was centralized and personalized, with decision making concentrated in the hands of the Prime Minister. Cabinet members, party presidents, and chief ministers held tenure on the basis of personal loyalty to Mrs. Gandhi. Cabinet positions were regularly shuffled in order to keep any possible rival off-balance, and many key portfolios were under the Prime Minister's direct control.[36] A similar game—one of the distinctive marks of Mrs. Gandhi's political style—was played with party leadership. From 1969 to 1977 the Congress had five presidents, the turnover "apparently designed to prevent institutional consolidation of power by any potential political challenger."[37]

From the time of the party split in 1969, Mrs. Gandhi sought to centralize what was fundamentally a federal party. Through direct intervention in the state parties, she deposed entrenched chief ministers—the very leaders who had backed her against the Syndicate—and replaced them with her own nominees, personally loyal, but without established bases of power in their own states.[38] She also sought to transform the base of support of the Congress with an infusion from the "weaker sections" of society—youth, women, Muslims, Scheduled Castes and Tribes, and the poor. These newly mobilized sectors lost out, however, to the formerly dominant groups as state party factions vied for control of the organization.

Describing the dilemma that the Prime Minister confronted, the *Economic and Political Weekly* editorialized:

> In terms of rough and ready class alignments, Indira Gandhi's political infrastructure continues to be based on the support of the upper peasantry and the bulk of the urban bourgeoisie. These classes, in their turn, have made use of her populist image to swing in their favour a sizeable segment of the electorate. Her strategy of leaning on radical slogans succeeded in offering opiates to large groups of rural masses, industrial workers and the urban middle class; at the same time her pragmatism ensured that the gravy continued to flow to the kulaks and the urban industrialists.[39]

Despite the party split, the new Congress was still under an umbrella of highly disparate interests. The ideological polarization so

[36] Stanley A. Kochanek, "Mrs. Gandhi's Pyramid: The New Congress," in Henry C. Hart, ed., *Indira Gandhi's India: A Political System Reappraised* (Boulder, Colo.: Westview Press, 1976), p. 101.

[37] Ibid., pp. 96–97.

[38] Ibid., p. 110.

[39] *Economic and Political Weekly*, 16 June 1973, p. 1057.

many had foreseen never took place. In state after state, Mrs. Gandhi's nominees were challenged by dissident factions and forced to resign. As weak and ineffective governments struggled to survive, internal factionalism was joined by mounting popular discontent. Mrs. Gandhi, increasingly intolerant of dissent, came to rely more heavily on coercion. She viewed criticism from within Congress as traitorous and criticism from the opposition as antinational, fascist, or foreign-inspired. She took attacks on inept and often corrupt state governments as personal affronts—and so more and more they came to be.

The 1975–77 Emergency[40] The 1971 Parliamentary elections and the state assembly elections a year later had brought Mrs. Gandhi a commanding majority. As quickly as the "Indira wave" had swept across India, however, the trough followed. For all her political skill, the Prime Minister had no clear economic program. The burden of refugee relief that had been imposed upon India during the Bangladesh crisis and the cost of the war itself were compounded by the problems of severe drought in 1972 and 1973. A situation described by the President of India as "an unprecedented national crisis" was thus created. India's difficulties were exacerbated by the 1973 world energy crisis, with food shortages and spiraling prices.

India's deepening economic problems were accompanied by a rise in the tempo of political unrest. Processions and demonstrations voiced protest and opposition. Campuses were torn by "indiscipline," and disturbances closed universities for weeks at a time. Strikes threatened the economy with chaos. Each year recorded an increase in the number of riots and incidents of violence. The statistics, however, do not reflect the concomitant increase in the level of "official violence," as witnessed, for example, by the government's suppression of the 1974 railway strike. By the mid-1970s, hardly a day

[40]The indispensable source on the 1975–77 emergency is the three-volume *Interim Report* of the Shah Commission of Inquiry, 1978. Since the emergency was lifted, numerous books have been published. Among the most useful are Michael Henderson, *Experiment with Untruth: India under the Emergency* (Columbia, Mo.: South Asia Books, 1977); Kuldip Nayar, *The Judgement* (New Delhi: Vikas, 1977); Prashant Bhushan, *The Case that Shook India* (New Delhi: Vikas, 1978); and J. Thakur, *All the Prime Minister's Men* (New Delhi: Vikas, 1978). Also see Marcus F. Franda's series of reports from South Asia for the American University Field Staff, 1975. Distinguished Indian scholars contributed to a symposium, "Images of the Emergency," in the March 1977 issue of *Seminar*. An assessment of the sources of the emergency is provided by P. B. Mayer, "Congress (I), Emergency (I): Interpreting Indira Gandhi's India," *Journal of Commonwealth and Comparative Politics*, 22 (July 1984): 128–50. A special issue of *Sunday* (Calcutta), 30 June–8 July 1985, provides an excellent retrospective on the emergency.

passed when the newspapers did not carry an article relating a lathi charge or police firing somewhere in India.

Prelude to the Emergency The situation exploded in Gujarat in 1974, with widespread agitation against the Congress government of the state. Sarvodaya leader Jayaprakash Narayan, emerging from political retirement, called upon the students to lead a statewide *bandh*, or general strike. In confrontation with the police, demonstrations became riots in which 50 persons were killed. Under mounting pressure from without and torn by factionalism within, the government resigned, and President's Rule was imposed.[41]

In Bihar, as discontent erupted into mass agitation, Narayan assumed leadership of the movement against the corrupt Congress government. Beyond the specific aim of forcing the Bihar government to step down, Narayan sought "total revolution"—the fundamental transformation of Indian society. The movement was heavily urban and drew on a wide spectrum of the political opposition, from members of the Jana Sangh on the right to Socialists and Marxists on the left. The organizing force behind the movement was the paramilitary Rashtriya Swayamsevak Sangh (RSS), "parent" of the Jana Sangh. Their differences submerged in common opposition to the ruling Congress party, these disparate groups responded to J. P.'s call for satyagraha against the government of Bihar.

It was against this backdrop that, in the summer of 1975, Prime Minister Indira Gandhi suffered two major blows. On June 12, Mrs. Gandhi was found guilty by the High Court of Allahabad of election-code violations. The High Court decision was the result of charges brought four years before by Raj Narain, Mrs. Gandhi's Socialist opponent in the parliamentary constituency of Rae Bareli in Uttar Pradesh. The Court dismissed the more serious charges, including bribery and intimidation, but found the Prime Minister guilty of two relatively minor technical violations of the law. If the offenses were minor, the consequences were not. Under Indian law, Mrs. Gandhi had been convicted of "corrupt electoral practices." Her election in 1971 was declared invalid. In losing her seat in Parliament, she would have to resign as Prime Minister. The law furthermore barred her from elective office for a period of six years. In order to permit an appeal to the Supreme Court, the sentence was stayed for 20 days.

[41] See Dawn E. and Rodney W. Jones, "Urban Upheaval in India: The 1974 Nav Nirman Riots in Gujarat," *Asian Survey*, 16 (November 1976): 1012–23; and Ghanshayam Shah, *Protest Movements in Two Indian States: A Study of the Gujarat and Bihar Movements* (Delhi: Ajanta Publications, 1977).

The Court ruling was followed a day later by the results of the state assembly elections in Gujarat, which dealt the Congress—and Indira Gandhi—a severe blow. The state had been under President's Rule for more than a year when, in April 1975, Morarji Desai began a "fast unto death" in order to force the Prime Minister to call elections. Mrs. Gandhi yielded to the man who had once been her principal rival for Congress party leadership. With elections set for June, four opposition parties—the Congress (O), the Jana Sangh, the Bharatiya Lok Dal (BLD), and the Socialist Party—entered an uneasy alliance. With a common program, a single set of candidates, and the blessing of Jayaprakash Narayan, the Janata (People's) Front stood against the Congress in Gujarat. Mrs. Gandhi campaigned actively in the state and placed her prestige on a Congress victory. The Congress defeat was massive.[42]

Opposition parties called for the Prime Minister's resignation. Several national newspapers urged her to step down, as did a few members within her own party. The events of the two weeks following the Allahabad judgment remain unclear, but Mrs. Gandhi is believed, at least for a time, to have seriously considered temporarily stepping down in favor of a caretaker government while awaiting the result of her appeal to the Supreme Court. Those close to her counseled against such action, and her 29-year-old son, Sanjay, was adamant that she remain in office.

Demonstrations and rallies were staged on the Prime Minister's behalf. Government employees were pressed into service. Buses and trucks were, in effect, commandeered to bring demonstrators from all over Delhi and the neighboring states. On one occasion, all 983 buses of the Delhi Transport Corporation were taken off their routes and directed to converge on the Prime Minister's house in a show of support.

On June 24 Justice Krishna Iyer, the "vacation judge" of the Supreme Court, rejected the Prime Minister's request for a "complete and absolute" stay of the judgment against her. Instead, he granted a conditional stay until the Court could convene to consider her appeal. He ruled that Mrs. Gandhi could remain in office as Prime Minister, but she could neither vote nor participate in the proceedings of Parliament.

Imposition of Emergency Rule On the following evening, June 25, a

[42]See Marcus F. Franda, "The Gujarat Election, 1975," American University Field Staff Reports, South Asia Series, XIX (9), 1975; and Ghanshyam Shah, "The 1975 Gujarat Assembly Elections in India," *Asian Survey*, 16 (March 1976):270–82.

mass rally was held on the Ramlila festival grounds in New Delhi. Leaders of the opposition, including Jayaprakash Narayan and Morarji Desai, called for a nationwide movement to unseat the Prime Minister. Denouncing Indira Gandhi as "moving toward dictatorship and fascism," J. P. called upon the people of India to resist the corrupt and illegitimate government. As he had done before, he urged the police and the armed forces to refuse to obey "illegal and immoral" orders and to uphold the Constitution against those who would destroy it.

That night, across the city in the home of the Prime Minister, final plans were made for the declaration of emergency.[43] The list of political leaders to be arrested had already been drawn up, and during the day those state chief ministers counted as personally loyal were advised of the decision by Mrs. Gandhi. The decision itself was taken (probably as early as June 22) within the "household," Mrs. Gandhi's inner circle. No Cabinet member had been consulted, and it was not until late on the night of the 25th that the Home Minister was informed of what was to happen. He told the Prime Minister that an emergency already was in force, imposed in 1971 during the Bangladesh crisis and never rescinded, and that the government had sufficient powers to deal with the situation.[44] His argument was to no avail: The Proclamation was already in the hands of the President.

On the morning of June 26, the Government of India assumed extraordinary powers as the nation was placed under emergency rule. The Proclamation read:

> In exercise of the powers conferred by Clause (1), Article 352 of the Constitution, I, Fakhruddin Ali Ahmed, President of India, by this Proclamation declare that a grave emergency exists, whereby the security of India is threatened by internal disturbances.

Earlier that morning, before the Proclamation was issued, the principal leaders of the opposition were arrested under the Maintenance of Internal Security Act (MISA)—676 persons by the official tally. They included Jayaprakash Narayan; Morarji Desai; Charan Singh, leader of the BLD; and Raj Narain, who had successfully brought the case of election-code violations against the Prime Minister. On orders of the government, at 2:00 A.M., electricity to the major newspapers in New

[43] A detailed account of the events leading to the declaration of the emergency is presented in Chapter 5 of the *Shah Commission of Inquiry, Interim Report 1*, 11 March 1978, pp. 17–32.

[44] See the earlier discussion of emergency powers, pp. 73–75.

Delhi was cut off, imposing a news blackout on the city. At 8:00 A.M. Indira Gandhi addressed the nation on All-India Radio:

> The President has proclaimed an emergency. This is nothing to panic about. I am sure you are conscious of the deep and widespread conspiracy which has been brewing ever since I began to introduce certain progressive measures of benefit to the common man and woman of India. In the name of democracy it has been sought to negate the very functioning of democracy. . . . Certain persons have gone to the length of inciting our armed forces to mutiny and our police to rebel. . . . Now we learn of new programs challenging law and order throughout the country. . . .

The conspiracy, she asserted, threatened to disrupt the "normal functioning" of government. Moreover, it constituted a "threat to stability that would affect production and prospects of economic development."

Rigid press censorship was imposed from the first day of the emergency—more complete than at any time under the British. Initial precensorship was replaced by "Guidelines" and ultimately by legislation for the "prevention of publication of objectionable matter." The Indian news services were merged into a single, government-controlled agency, Samachar. Most of the press acquiesced, some resisted insofar as possible, and a few journals of opinion, like *Seminar* and *Mainstream,* chose to cease publication rather than accept censorship.[45]

Under the emergency regulations of the Defense of India Rules, 26 organizations were banned. The organizations were associated with four "extremist" groups: the Anand Marg, a Hindu religious sect; the Jamaat-i Islami, an orthodox Muslim group; the Naxalites, Maoist revolutionaries; and the RSS. Mass arrests followed the ban, with the largest number of all those jailed from the RSS.

During the 21 months of the emergency, a total of 110,000 people were arrested and detained without trial.[46] By presidential order, the right of any person to seek constitutional protection through the courts was suspended. India's bill of rights was, in effect, abrogated. Persons arrested were not advised of the charges against them, nor were the police required to inform judicial authorities of the reasons

[45] See the three-part series by Marcus F. Franda, "Curbing the Press," American University Field Staff Reports, South Asia Series, XX (12, 13, 14), 1976.

[46] According to figures now available, through the Government of India, the number of persons arrested under emergency regulations was 110,806 (34,988 under MISA and 75,818 under the Defense of India Rules).

for arrest. Newspapers were barred from publishing the names of those arrested. People simply disappeared. In addition to political arrests, those placed under detention included "bad characters" and such "antisocial" elements as smugglers, hoarders, and black marketeers. Arrests were often arbitrary, sometimes personal vendettas, and, as investigations later confirmed, incidents of torture and even murder occurred in the jails.

Under the emergency, the government made frequent use of presidential orders, but legislation and constitutional amendment gave permanence to what were first announced as temporary measures. Parliament was dominated by the Prime Minister. When the monsoon session opened in July, some 30 MPs, including Congress dissidents, were in jail. Others were absent or in hiding. As required by the Constitution, Parliament formally approved imposition of the emergency—by a vote of 336 to 59. Members of the opposition—except the Communist Party of India (CPI), which supported Mrs. Gandhi—walked out in protest.

Constitutional Change and the 20 Point Program Among its first acts, Parliament amended the electoral law under which Mrs. Gandhi had been convicted. The two offenses of which she had been found guilty were deleted retroactively so as to exonerate the Prime Minister and render her appeal to the Supreme Court unnecessary. The 38th Amendment, the first of three major structural assaults on the Constitution, denied the courts the power to review a presidential proclamation of emergency or the orders imposed under an emergency. The 39th Amendment barred the courts—again retroactively—from considering electoral disputes involving the Prime Minister, President, Vice President, or the Speaker of the Lok Sabha.

There was talk of a new constitution, but this was shelved in 1976 in favor of the 42nd Amendment.[47] The most sweeping of the constitutional changes brought during the emergency, it affected 59 clauses of the Constitution and was designed to further diminish the power of the courts and to secure parliamentary—that is, the Prime Minister's—supremacy. Among its most controversial provisions, the Supreme Court was denied the power of judicial review over amendments affecting the basic structure of the Constitution. The Directive Principles of State Policy were given primacy over the fundamental rights guaranteed by the Constitution, and no law enacted in pursuance of these principles could be challenged in the courts. A code of

[47]For an analysis of the constitutional changes during the emergency, see Rajiv Dhavan, *The Amendment: Conspiracy or Revolution?* (Allahabad: Wheeler, 1978).

Fundamental Duties was incorporated within the Constitution. Parliament was empowered to ban "antinational" associations and activities. Presidential discretion was circumscribed by the provision that the President's functions shall be exercised in accordance with the advice of the Prime Minister and the Cabinet. Finally, the length of the parliamentary and state assembly sessions was extended from five to six years (an action subsequently rescinded).

The actions taken under the emergency—arrests, censorship, and constitutional changes—were accompanied by continuing justification. Invoking the name of Joan of Arc, her childhood heroine, Indira Gandhi sought to cast herself as India's savior. She proclaimed her dedication to democracy and insisted that "what has been done is not an abrogation of democracy, but an effort to safeguard it." In her view, democracy in India had gotten "off the rails." In statements soon after the imposition of the emergency, she said, "There can be no return to the pre-emergency days of total license and political permissiveness." Borrowing Gunnar Myrdal's term, the Prime Minister described India as a "soft state." The emergency was necessary as a shock treatment. Order and discipline were to be the hallmarks of the new India. Industrial peace was imposed by a ban on all strikes; the campuses were quiet; bureaucrats arrived at their desks for a full day's work; and, as one enthusiast innocently observed, the trains ran on time.

"The Emergency," Mrs. Gandhi declared, "provides us with a new opportunity to go ahead with our economic tasks." Her 20 Point Program of economic and social reforms offered something for everyone: "To the poor it promised land reform, liquidation of rural indebtedness, new minimum agricultural wages and abolition of bonded labor. . . For the middle class there were promises of tax relief and price reductions. The rich were impressed by promises of liberalized investment procedures and a welcome absence of talk about further nationalization or higher taxes."[48]

Mrs. Gandhi's 20 Point Program was largely a rehash of long unimplemented Congress policies, but rhetoric was now accompanied by the benefits of two good monsoons. In the months following imposition of the emergency, inflation, which had reached a rate of 30 percent, was brought under control. Food and essential commodities were readily available. Industrial production rose significantly, exports expanded, and the nation's foreign exchange reserves reached

[48] Marcus F. Franda, "India's Double Emergency Democracy," Pt. 1: "Transformations," American University Field Staff Reports, South Asia Series, XIX (17), 1975, p. 16.

record levels. Mrs. Gandhi sought to credit the emergency, but the favorable economic situation was more the result of good harvests and policies already undertaken. Moreover, by mid-1976 the glow had begun to fade, and prices were again moving upward.

The Rise of Sanjay Gandhi The Prime Minister's program was augmented in 1976 by Sanjay Gandhi's 5 Point Program: "Limit families to only two children. Never accept dowries as a condition for marriage. Teach one illiterate person to read and write, and plant one tree every year." From the time of the Allahabad decision, Sanjay had assumed increasing influence within "the household." Tainted by the scandal surrounding the manufacture of the Maruti (a small car), Sanjay had an unsavory reputation, and his rise was viewed with apprehension in Congress party circles. Sanjay provided access to his mother, however, and was reputed to have considerable influence over her. As his bandwagon gained momentum, newspapers gave front-page space to his every word and movement. State chief ministers greeted him with garlands and accolades. Without political experience and holding no public office, Sanjay was touted as the hope of India. Clearly, he was being advanced as the heir-apparent.

The organizational vehicle for Sanjay's expanding power was the Youth Congress. Under his leadership, and richly financed, it grew in importance and reached a claimed membership of more than 10 million. Sanjay brought his friends into high places—like Bansi Lal, Chief Minister of Haryana, who became Minister of Defense and a member of the Prime Minister's inner circle. He sought to undermine those who opposed him, as seen in his successful ouster of Nandini Satpathy as Chief Minister of Orissa. Currying the favor of the right, Sanjay attacked the Communist party and, despite its support for Mrs. Gandhi, denounced its influence within the Congress.

Sanjay's favored cause was family planning, and in Delhi and the Hindi-speaking states of northern India, the government's vasectomy program was aggressively pursued by inducements and disincentives. Central government employees with more than three children, for example, were ineligible for government housing until they produced a sterilization certificate. Some states imposed vasectomy quotas on government officials. Their pay and promotion depended on producing evidence that they had induced the requisite number of persons to undergo sterilization. Quotas provided the impetus for compulsory sterilization. Widespread stories recounted raids on villages by government officials and roundups from the "weaker sections" of society—the poor and uneducated, untouchables, and Muslims. There were reports of resistance and police firings. The most notorious incident, later to symbolize emergency "excesses," occurred at Turkman Gate in Muslim old Delhi. In an antivasectomy riot, six persons were killed by the police. Rumor placed the figure at 400.

Often in concert with forced sterilization, slum clearance in Delhi was another of Sanjay's pet projects, and demolitions were often carried out under his personal supervision. The Muslim squatter settlements around the Jama Masjid mosque were razed, and their dwellers transported to new housing miles from the city and their place of work.[49]

In a climate of fear and repression, the police and paramilitary forces assumed increased importance. Intelligence and surveillance units were bolstered, especially the Research and Analysis Wing (RAW) of the Prime Minister's secretariat. The press, the opposition, and the normal articulation of demands within the Congress party had been silenced. With vital sources of information and "feedback" cut off, Indira Gandhi was now limited to her own intelligence sources and the trusted members of her political household.

The 1977 Elections and Congress Defeat On January 18, 1977, having twice postponed elections, Prime Minister Indira Gandhi announced that parliamentary elections would be held in March. The rules of the emergency would be "relaxed," press censorship lifted, and public meetings permitted. Thousands of members of the political opposition were released from jails.

A number of factors are believed to have entered into Mrs. Gandhi's decision to hold elections. Most important, she expected Congress to win. The economy was in good shape, and the benefits attributed to the emergency were believed to have wide support, especially in rural areas and among the poor. In addition, "it seemed unlikely that the splintered opposition parties could organize themselves into an effective political force with a common platform and a set of candidates on such short notice." Another factor may have been Mrs. Gandhi's desire to establish a base in Parliament for Sanjay to succeed her as Prime Minister. Finally, a Congress victory would legitimize the emergency and vindicate her actions before the world.[50]

Soon after the announcement, two decisive events upset Mrs. Gandhi's calculations. The first was the formation of the opposition Janata

[49]For a discussion of the sterilization and slum clearance issues, see Myron Weiner, *India at the Polls: The Parliamentary Elections of 1977* (Washington, D.C.: American Enterprise Institute, 1978), pp. 35–41.

[50]Ibid., pp. 7–12.

Party. Building on the alliance forged in the Bihar movement and the 1975 Gujarat elections, the new party, led by Morarji Desai, was composed of four constituent parties: the Congress (O), the Jana Sangh, the Socialist Party, and the Bharatiya Lok Dal (BLD).

Mrs. Gandhi was even less prepared for her second jolt—defection of Jagjivan Ram from the Congress fold—than she had been for the formation of the Janata Party. Ram, a senior member of the Cabinet and the most prominent untouchable in Indian public life, had long nursed ambition for the Prime Ministership. Having seen his power eroded during the emergency, he resigned from the government and denounced Indira Gandhi for the destruction of democracy in India and within the Congress party. In forming his own party, the Congress for Democracy (CDF), Ram was joined by two other Congress leaders, H. N. Bahuguna, former Chief Minister of Uttar Pradesh, and by Nandini Satpathy, who had been ousted as Chief Minister of Orissa by Sanjay Gandhi.

The CDF and the Janata Party agreed on a common slate of candidates and, in effect, waged the campaign as one party. They entered an electoral alliance with the Communist Party (Marxist) and with two regional parties, the Akali Dal in the Punjab and the DMK in Tamil Nadu. Congress was allied with the Communist Party of India (CPI) and with the All-India Anna DMK (AIADMK) in Tamil Nadu.

The Janata Election Manifesto defined the fundamental issue: "The choice before the electorate is clear. It is a choice between freedom and slavery; between democracy and dictatorship. . . ." The Janata Party committed itself to "revive democracy" and to "restore to the citizen his fundamental freedoms and to the judiciary its rightful role." It offered the voters "Both Bread and Liberty: A Gandhian Alternative."

The Congress offered a familiar litany of justification. Its message was simple: "For progress and stability—vote Congress." Chaos was the alternative. Congress pointed to the record of economic improvement under the emergency, but for whatever benefits claimed by the government, the emergency had adversely affected most Indians in some respect. The rigors of the emergency had been felt most deeply in the Hindi-speaking states of northern India, and its impact was most pronounced in urban areas. Industrial labor lost its guaranteed bonus and was denied the right to strike. Members of the salaried middle class saw a portion of their wages garnered in a compulsory savings scheme. Shopkeepers suffered police harassment, and business people and industrialists were selectively subjected to tax investigations and raids on their homes. Pressure to make political contributions was little more than extortion, and Youth Congress coffers were alleged to be filled by "black money" (income not reported for tax purposes) passed under the table in exchange for government contracts. The political intelligentsia—professors, lawyers, journalists—lived in an atmosphere of fear and suspicion. Of whatever class, Indians had experienced the exercise of arbitrary government.

The emergency had put the lid on discontent and had silenced opposition. With no political barometer other than her own intelligence sources, Mrs. Gandhi had called elections with the conviction that the Congress would win. The formation of the Janata Party and Jagjivan Ram's defection had surely cut into the expected margin of victory, but Congress remained confident. Most observers gave Congress the edge even as the polls opened on March 16.

The results were stunning. Janata and its allies won 330 of the 542 seats in Parliament, and the Janata/CFD combination alone won 298, a secure majority. Its leadership routed, Congress was reduced to 154. Mrs. Gandhi lost to Raj Narain by a wide margin, and Sanjay was overwhelmingly defeated. The overall shift in the vote was substantial. Janata increased its strength from 27.6 percent of the vote in 1971 (representing the combined strength of its constituent parties) to 43 percent in 1977. Congress fell from 43.6 to 34.5 percent of the vote. In the 1977 results, there were no significant differences between rural and urban voting—a surprise to many who discounted the impact of the emergency in rural India.

The pattern of support revealed a dramatic regional schism. Janata swept North India, but made virtually no inroads into the South. Of its 298 seats, 222 were from the Hindi-speaking region of northern India. Janata won only six seats in the four southern states. In contrast, 92 of the 154 Congress seats were in the South. Congress won only two seats in the Hindi North.

The pattern, in part, reflected the rigor with which the emergency had been imposed. North India had been much more deeply affected—especially in the "excesses" of arbitrary arrest and forced sterilization. The fear generated by the vasectomy campaign was probably the most important factor in accounting for the Congress's massive losses in the North. It is ironic that the principal victims of forced sterilization, as of Sanjay's slum-clearance demolitions, were untouchables and Muslims, who in 1971 had been among Mrs. Gandhi's most ardent supporters.[51]

[51]For an analysis of Muslim voting patterns, see Theodore P. Wright, Jr., "Muslims and the 1977 Indian Elections: A Watershed?" *Asian Survey*, 17 (December 1977): 1207–20.

Two other factors also contributed to the regional schism. First, the parties that had merged to form the Janata drew their support primarily from the North, and on the critical language issue, they were viewed in the South as strongly pro-Hindi. Second, in contrast to the North, where the emergency was the issue, southern voters were heavily influenced by local considerations. In Tamil Nadu the elections were fought out between two regional parties, the DMK and the splinter AIADMK. In Kerala, where the Congress was the dominant member of the popular United Front government, simultaneously held state assembly elections overshadowed national issues. In Karnataka and Andhra Pradesh, where Congress scored its most impressive victories, the vote was more an expression of confidence in effective Congress chief ministers than it was a rally of support for Indira Gandhi and the emergency.[52]

The Congress had been dramatically swept from office, but it had secured 34.5 percent of the vote—a decline of only 9 percentage points from its 1971 victory—and with 154 seats in Parliament, it was the major opposition party.

Indira and Sons

The Congress in Opposition Torn by recrimination over the emergency and by Indira Gandhi's re-entry into politics, the Congress split, and in January 1978 the breakaway Congress (I)—for Indira—was formed. The regular party, led by former ministers Swaran Singh and Y. B. Chavan, repudiated the emergency and condemned its "excesses." Mrs. Gandhi was unrepentent, although she did express "deep sorrow for any hardship caused." She justified the emergency in the name of the poor and appealed to the downtrodden—the landless, minorities, and especially untouchables—for their support.

Elections for five state assemblies in March 1978 tested their claims for popular allegiance—both against each other and against Janata. In the southern states of Karnataka and Andhra Pradesh, where popular chief ministers sided with Mrs. Gandhi, the Congress (I) won overwhelming majorities. Overall, the Indira Congress won 394 seats in the 5 states, compared to 271 for Janata and 147 for Congress. Defections from the regular Congress to Mrs. Gandhi accelerated, spurred by her own victory in November in the Chikmagalur parliamentary by-election. The election in Chikmagalur, a remote constituency in the Congress stronghold of Karnataka, was hardly a national

[52]James Manor, "Where Congress Survived: Five States in the Indian General Election of 1977," *Asian Survey*, 18 (August 1978): pp. 785–803; and Manor, "Structural Change in Karnataka Politics," *Economic and Political Weekly*, 29 October 1977, pp. 1865–69.

plebiscite, but the all-out effort by the Janata Party to defeat Mrs. Gandhi gave it special significance. She returned to New Delhi in triumph to take her seat in Parliament as leader of the opposition.

Indira Gandhi—as well as Sanjay and a number of her associates—faced pending criminal prosecution on charges of misconduct and abuse of authority. Among the charges, based on the findings of a judicial inquiry into the emergency, was that before the emergency was imposed, she had harassed officials engaged in an investigation of Maruti, Sanjay's automobile company. As the investigation had been undertaken at the request of Parliament, a parliamentary privileges committee made its own inquiry and found Mrs. Gandhi guilty of the charges. She was also held in contempt of Parliament for her refusal to testify. In December, six weeks after her election, Parliament voted to expel the former Prime Minister and had her jailed for the duration of the session—seven days.

A year before, Mrs. Gandhi had been taken briefly into custody, only to turn a bungled arrest to her own advantage. Again, she sought martyrdom. In widespread demonstrations protesting her imprisonment, 20 persons were killed in police firings and some 120,000 of her supporters were arrested. Upon her release, Mrs. Gandhi vowed to run again and return to Parliament.

Despite her political comeback, Mrs. Gandhi was beleaguered both by criminal charges against her and by rebellion within her own party. After the Janata Party came to power, various commissions were established to investigate criminal action and abuse of authority under the emergency. The Reddy Commission examined charges of corruption against Defense Minister Bansi Lal. The Gupta Commission looked into Sanjay's Maruti activities. The most far-reaching was the Shah Commission of Inquiry, which issued a three-volume report on emergency excesses. Mrs. Gandhi was involved in cases of harassment of government officials and the illegal detention of political opponents.

In 1979 Parliament enacted legislation to set up four Special Courts to try the political leaders and senior government officials responsible for emergency offenses. The first to stand trial would be Indira Gandhi herself. Sanjay had already been in and out of the courts and faced, awaiting appeal, a two-year jail sentence. The parliamentary vote on the Special Courts had come as a political jolt to Mrs. Gandhi. The Congress (I) was abandoned by the Communist Party of India, its long-time ally, and by the bulk of the regular Congress group.

In response to the passage of the Special Courts bill, Sanjay, with his mother's support, took the issue to the streets. Instead of a nationwide protest, however, his efforts ended as a series of Youth Congress brawls. Within the Congress (I), opposition mounted against Sanjay and the resurgent Youth Congress. Devraj Urs, Chief Minister of Karnataka, took the lead in the attack on Sanjay. Isolated and on the defensive, Mrs. Gandhi faced schism in her own party. When she tried to wrest control of the state party organization from him, Urs bolted the Congress (I) and took Karnataka into the Congress camp.

The 1980 Elections and the Return of Indira Gandhi If Indira Gandhi was beleaguered, the Janata Party was under siege. The Janata victory in 1977 had been greeted with euphoria and hailed as a democratic revolution. Twenty-eight months later, however, amidst drift, discontent, and defection, the Janata government collapsed. In its place, an uneasy coalition came to power under Charan Singh, leader of the breakaway Lok Dal faction. Less than one month later, facing a parliamentary vote of no confidence, Singh submitted his resignation as Prime Minister, and the President called new elections.

At the time of the dissolution of the Lok Sabha in August 1979, the parties were in disarray. Although the Janata Party was still the largest in Parliament, its majority of 302 seats had been reduced by defection to 203 of the total elected membership of 542.

With both the Janata and the Congress torn by schism, the prospect of any single party emerging with a parliamentary majority appeared dim. Negotiations among the various parties for alliances and electoral arrangements continued until the final lists of candidates were filed. Defections from one party to another further weakened any semblance of coherence. Two ministers from the caretaker government of Charan Singh resigned to join the Congress (I), and Finance Minister H. N. Bahaguna, with a substantial following among Muslims in the state of Uttar Pradesh, was made party secretary. Mrs. Gandhi, through her son Sanjay, even entered into negotiations with Jagjivan Ram, leader of the Janata Party, in an attempt to secure his defection.

The campaign was cast largely in terms of three contenders for the Prime Ministership: Charan Singh, Jagjivan Ram, and Indira Gandhi. Mrs. Gandhi alone commanded the status of an all-India leader. With political skill bolstered by the ineptitude of her opponents, Mrs. Gandhi made a spectacular comeback from the defeat she suffered in 1977. Poised for a return to power and without apology for the strong dose of discipline imposed during the emergency, she took the offensive, urging the electorate to vote against the sorry record of infighting and "nongovernance" in the Janata–Lok Dal phase. Mrs. Gandhi called on the nation to vote Congress (I) for "order, stability, purposeful governance and progress." With the promise of strong leadership, Mrs. Gandhi's appeal was direct: "Elect a Government that Works." The Congress (I) election symbol, the "hand," was well chosen, for within Hinduism it traditionally represents protection.

Campaign issues were specific: the deterioration of law and order and a faltering economy. Indira Gandhi applied each to the concrete experience of the individual voter. "Law and order" for the industrialist was the code word for strikes and labor indiscipline; for untouchables and the Muslim minority, it was an appeal to their sense of vulnerability; for women, it was a question of personal security. On the economic front, grocery prices had risen sharply over the previous six months, and widespread shortages made the situation more desperate. Energy, whether kerosene for the home or petroleum and coal for farm and factory, was critically deficient.

The Congress (I), though organizationally in disarray, was able to mobilize an impressive campaign—especially through the Youth Congress headed by Sanjay Gandhi. The party was richly financed—in substantial part by the business community with whom Sanjay's advocacy of free enterprise found favor. Sanjay too played a critical role in the selection of Congress (I) candidates, and approximately one-third of the tickets went to Sanjay's people. The Sanjay factor, as it came to be called, however, was a source of considerable apprehension for those who found little to admire in Mrs. Gandhi's controversial son.

Despite the money pumped into the campaign, the atmosphere was low key. The notable exception was provided by the personal dynamism of Indira Gandhi. With courage and determination, she waged a strenuous campaign. In 63 days on tour, Mrs. Gandhi covered a distance of some 40 thousand miles, visited 384 constituencies, and addressed more than 1500 meetings.

In January 1980, 33 months after a crushing electoral defeat forced her from office and ended 30 years of Congress rule, Indira Gandhi returned to power as Prime Minister of India. In the landslide victory, Mrs. Gandhi's Congress (I) won 351 seats, a two-thirds majority. The Lok Dal, with 41 seats, was reduced to little more than a regional party in the Jat strongholds of Uttar Pradesh. The Janata took only 31 seats, cut back to the core of its Jana Sangh support. The Congress, led by Devraj Urs, picked up a scattered collection of 13 seats, but failed to win a single constituency in Urs's own state of Karnataka. In humiliation, he submitted his resignation as Chief Minister. Alone among the opposition, the two Communist parties improved their positions in the Lok Sabha. The CPI won 11 seats, and the CPM, from its power base in West Bengal and Kerala, took 35.[53]

The Congress (I) victory was secured with 43 percent of the vote, as against 19 percent for the Janata and 9 percent for the Lok Dal. In at least 50 constituencies of North India, a united Janata–Lok Dal could have taken the seat from the Congress (I). Mrs. Gandhi's triumph, however, cannot be attributed simply to a divided opposition. A substantial number of Congress (I) victories were taken with absolute majorities, and many with wide margins. In Rae Bareli, Mrs. Gandhi, with 58 percent of the vote, defeated her closest rival by 140,000 votes, and she took the Medak seat in Andhra Pradesh by a margin of 219,000 votes. (Mrs. Gandhi ran in two constituencies—a form of insurance, as well as a demonstration of her support in both North and South India. Retaining the Medak seat, she relinquished Rae Bareli to a by-election.) In the Amethi constituency of Uttar Pradesh, adjacent to Rae Bareli, Sanjay won his successful bid for Parliament by more than a 100,000-vote lead.

Beyond the Marxist strongholds, one of the most striking features of the election was the genuinely *national* character of Mrs. Gandhi's victory. Even in Tamil Nadu, where regional factors were believed dominant, Mrs. Gandhi's sweep carried her DMK ally in a rout of the ruling AIADMK. Support for the Congress (I) cut across caste and drew under Mrs. Gandhi's umbrella rich and poor, high caste and untouchable, Hindu, Muslim, Sikh, and Christian. The untouchables—however sympathetic to Jagjivan Ram— were divided, but the larger number, even of Ram's own Chamar caste, followed Indira Gandhi. Women are believed to have voted overwhelmingly for Mrs. Gandhi—not so much in personal identification, but on the issues of law and order and rising prices. The voters responded in terms of immediate self-interest, symbolized by the price of onions, but their verdict was a plea for firm and effective government.

The Death of Sanjay, the Rise of Rajiv In taking office on January 14, 1980, Mrs. Gandhi confronted an international crisis in the Soviet invasion of Afghanistan, domestic unrest in Assam and the Northeast, and an economy under the strain of inflation and drought. Her

[53]For a detailed analysis of the elections, see Myron Weiner, *India at the Polls, 1980: A Study of the Parliamentary Elections* (Washington, D.C.: American Enterprise Institute, 1983). Also see James Manor, "The Electoral Process amid Awakening and Decay: Reflections on the Indian General Election of 1980," in Peter Lyon and James Manor, eds., *Transfer and Transformation: Political Institutions in the New Commonwealth* (Leicester: Leicester University Press, 1983), pp. 87–116.

selection of Cabinet ministers notably excluded those most closely associated with the emergency, but lesser lights among the Sanjay caucus were well represented within the new ministry.

Indira Gandhi's return to power brought back to the Congress fold many who had defected from the party during its time in the political wilderness. Most dramatic was the return of former Congress member Bhajan Lal, Chief Minister of Haryana, who simply changed the name of his government from Janata to Congress (I), bringing his legislative majority with him. While the welcome mat was out for all members of Congress to reunite, nonetheless personal loyalty was to remain the touchstone for advancement in the party and for entry into Mrs. Gandhi's inner circle.

In February 1980, so as to bring the states into alignment with the Congress parliamentary victory, the President, on instruction of the Prime Minister, dissolved the nine opposition-controlled state assemblies where Congress (I) had swept the polls and called for new elections. In so doing, Mrs. Gandhi cited the 1977 precedent set by the Janata Party in dismissing Congress state governments on the ground that they had lost their mandate. The state elections provided the opportunity for Sanjay Gandhi, who had been instrumental in engineering his mother's return to power, to establish his own independent base of political power. Sanjay was the chief election strategist, and his Youth Congress was the electoral machine through which the campaign was conducted. Securing 60 percent of the seats, the Congress (I) took power in eight of the nine states. Tamil Nadu alone, with the victory of the AIADMK, remained in the hands of the opposition. Through his control over the distribution of Congress tickets, Sanjay inducted his own people into the state assemblies and installed chief ministers whose power rested solely on the favor of his mother and himself. Both as a reward and as a recognition of the effective power he had assumed over the party organization, Mrs. Gandhi appointed Sanjay as Congress (I) General Secretary. Less than a week later, on June 23, Sanjay Gandhi, heir apparent to the prime ministership of India, was dead at the age of 33, killed in the crash of a single-engine stunt plane he piloted.

Deeply shaken by her son's death, Indira Gandhi seemed to lose interest in the affairs of both party and state. After some six months of drift, however, she gradually regained her bearings, this time with her elder son, Rajiv, at her side. As a youth, Rajiv Gandhi attended the prestigious English-medium Doon School, then went on to Cambridge University, where he studied engineering. It was in England that he met his wife, Sonia, the daughter of an Italian businessman. Upon his return to India, Rajiv became a pilot of Indian Airlines, the domestic carrier. With no experience in politics, it was only upon the death of Sanjay that Rajiv made his initially reluctant entry into public life. In contrast to his brash and aggressive younger brother, Rajiv—dubbed "Mr. Clean" by the press—had an open, subdued style. In 1981 Rajiv was elected to Parliament from Amethi, Sanjay's constituency in Uttar Pradesh. Six months later, he accepted leadership of the Youth Congress. It was as his mother's adviser and confidant, however, that Rajiv, now being groomed for dynastic succession, was drawn toward the center of political power. Party leaders and state chief ministers paid him court, a sycophancy he openly disdained. Without any official position, save that of Member of Parliament, Rajiv took an increasing hand in reorganizing the weakened Congress party.

The Congress in Disarray[54] Following the party split in 1969, Mrs. Gandhi made an attempt to rebuild the Congress organization, but from the early 1970s the party fell into increasing disarray. The "deinstitutionalization" of the Congress party was rooted in the leadership and style of Indira Gandhi.[55] She had sought to transform the party into an instrument of personal power and to assure that it nurtured no one who might challenge her position as Prime Minister or endanger the succession of her son—first Sanjay, then Rajiv. Organizational elections had not been held since 1972. The All-India Congress Committee and the Working Committee, once the crucial decision-making center of the party, were moribund. State party units had no autonomy, and provincial, district, and local Congress committees, insofar as they functioned at all, were creatures of the central party "high command"—a euphemism for Mrs. Gandhi. The grass roots had been cut, and the Congress, as it approached its centenary year, was an organization with no base. Inder Malhotra of *The Times of India* described the Congress as "no more than a rabble held together by one towering personality."[56]

While the state Congress party organization was torn by dissention, clearly identifiable and stable factions existed in only a few

[54] Portions of this section are adapted from Robert L. Hardgrave, Jr., *India under Pressure: Prospects for Political Stability* (Boulder, Colo.: Westview Press, 1984), pp. 85–89.

[55] James Manor examines the process of deinstitutionalization in two articles: "Party Decay and Political Crisis in India," *Washington Quarterly*, 4 (Summer 1981): 25–40; and "Anomie in Indian Politics: Origins and Potential Impact," *Economic and Political Weekly*, 18 (May 1983): 725–34. Rajni Kothari offers an even darker view in "Towards Intervention," *Seminar*, 269 (January 1982): 22–27; and "A Fragmented Nation," *Seminar*, 281 (January 1983): 24–29.

[56] Inder Malhotra, "State of the Ruling Party: A Cause for Serious Concern," *The Times of India*, 29 April 1982.

states. The bases of dissidence and factionalism varied from state to state: region, urban-rural, caste, personality, but in no state could factionalism be said to be ideologically based. Instead of factions, in most states there were free-floating, self-styled leaders in search of support. The Center played each off against the other, with no claimant for power permitted to establish an independent base of support. All professed personal loyalty to Mrs. Gandhi, and all were dependent on her. Indeed, one of the principal reasons that the party had not conducted organizational elections is that they would have provided local and state leaders not only the opportunity to test their strength against one another, but they would also provide the victors with bases of support independent of New Delhi. Mrs. Gandhi kept the pot boiling, and party dissention was the inevitable product of uncertainty.

In those states where the Congress was in power, chief ministers dangled like puppets on strings. Rather than rise up from their own base of political strength as leaders of the state legislative parties, they were imposed from above by Mrs. Gandhi. The Congress legislative parties, in fact, clamored for her to do so, unwilling to assume responsibility themselves. Personal loyalty, rather than competence, was the prime qualification for office. That Mrs. Gandhi largely limited her choices to those "faithful" who stood with her during her time out of power, rather than include more experienced politicians who came back to the Congress fold when they sensed a change in the political winds, is understandable, but it considerably narrowed the field. Moreover, it put a premium on "sycophancy," a term widely used in India to describe the relationship of chief ministers and Cabinet ministers alike with Mrs. Gandhi.

Continued manipulation from above encouraged dissidence in the party and increased the commuter traffic between the state capitals and New Delhi, as the various groups, trading allegations of disloyalty, corruption, and favoritism, vied for the ear of the Prime Minister. In an atmosphere of court politics, chief ministers were in frequent attendance—to defend themselves, to curry favor, and to bring matters of policy and politics before the party's high command. Just as state party candidates are screened by the Center, so chief ministers cleared any changes in their own state cabinets with New Delhi. In the process, holding out hope to party dissidents that their turn might come, the high command ensured the continued dependence of state Congress politicians on Mrs. Gandhi.

Following Sanjay's death, Mrs. Gandhi began to ease out of some of her more serious liabilities in the states and increasingly distanced members of the Sanjay brigade from power and influence. In March 1982 the most disgruntled among them linked arms with Maneka

Gandhi, Sanjay's young widow, and challenged the party leadership. This was, in effect, a personal challenge to Indira Gandhi and Rajiv, and it came from within the household. In a dramatic confrontation with her mother-in-law, Maneka was thrown out of the house.[57] In the following months, Maneka formed her own political party, the Rashtriya Sanjay Manch, and announced her intention to contest the Amethi constituency against Rajiv in the next election.

Against the backdrop of party disarray, Congress looked to the next parliamentary elections with increasing apprehension. In January 1983, elections for the state legislative assemblies were held in Andhra and Karnataka, the only two states in India to have been under continued Congress rule since independence. Politicians and the press viewed the elections as a referendum on the Congress (I)—not just on the discredited state governments, but on Prime Minister Indira Gandhi's leadership. In Andhra, Telugu film star T. N. Rama Rao, adored by his public as an avatar of the gods he portrayed on the screen, commanded center stage. In an appeal to regional sentiment, TNR's Telugu Desam crushed the Congress. With 46 percent of the votes, it won 69 percent of the assembly seats. In Karnataka the opposition parties united in a Janata-front to oust the unpopular Congress government. The Congress also lost in Tripura to the Communist Party (Marxist), a defeat for which it was prepared, but the overall result was to reduce the Congress to power in only 14 of India's 22 states. And although analysts sought too readily to read a national pattern into the elections, the results underscored the institutional weakness of the Congress organization and the costs of Indira Gandhi's imperial style.[58]

Assassination and Succession[59] On the morning of October 31, 1984, as she walked from her home to an adjacent office, Prime Minister Indira Gandhi was assassinated by two Sikh members of her se-

[57] After Sanjay's death, Maneka continued to live in the Prime Minister's residence, in accordance with Indian tradition, even as they were joined by Rajiv and family. For an account of these events, see *India Today*, 15 April 1982, pp. 14–21; 30 April 1982, pp. 22–32.

[58] For an analysis of the Andhra and Karnataka elections and their impact, see Robert L. Hardgrave, Jr., "India in 1983: New Challenges, Lost Opportunities," *Asian Survey*, 14 (February 1984): 212–13.

[59] Robert L. Hardgrave, Jr., "India in 1984: Confrontation, Assassination, and Succession," *Asian Survey*, 15 (February 1985): 139–44; and Hardgrave, "India after Indira," The Asia Society, New York, 16 April 1985.

curity guard. Within hours of Mrs. Gandhi's death, Rajiv Gandhi, at the age of 40, was sworn in as Prime Minister.[60] The choice of Rajiv, confirmed three days later by a unanimous Congress Parliamentary Party, was a foregone conclusion. Though criticized by elements of the press and opposition, haste was considered necessary to provide reassurance to the shaken nation. Rajiv's strength and calm demeanor in his statements that day were impressive, and in the wake of the assassination, the nation and the party of which he became president rallied to him. In a time of national crisis, he was the symbol of stability and continuity. Moreover, it was widely believed that only Rajiv, as bearer of the Gandhi name and the Nehru legacy, could lead the Congress to victory in the forthcoming elections.

While New Delhi was convulsed by anti-Sikh violence, thousands, including many world leaders, stood at the cremation ground, Shantivan, on the banks of the Jumna River and mourned the passing of the woman who had governed India for 15 years. At the end of the 12-day mourning period, Rajiv scattered his mother's ashes over the source of the Ganges high in the Himalayas, as she had desired. Adhering to the schedule believed to have been set before his mother's death, Rajiv announced that parliamentary elections would be held on December 24.

Rajiv in Power

Less than two months after taking office as the youngest Prime Minister to serve India, Rajiv Gandhi won a massive electoral victory, setting the course for both continuity and change. With 48.1 percent of the vote, the highest ever for Congress, the party won 77 percent of the seats contested, an unprecedented majority in the Lok Sabha. Rajiv's victory came against a background of fear, cynicism, and uncertainty. Jawaharlal Nehru had bequeathed to his daughter, Indira Gandhi, a unified nation; a highly institutionalized political order; a basic national consensus on the government's socioeconomic and foreign policies; and a reasonable climate of public morality. Indira Gandhi bequeathed to her son a divided nation; a highly centralized and personalized system of power; and a criminalized, weak, and corrupt party of sycophants.[61]

[60] Kuldip Nayar, "How the Succession Was Resolved," *India Abroad*, 16 November 1984, p. 6. New Delhi is a hothouse of rumor, and tales of court intrigue portray at least one of the principals close to Mrs. Gandhi as attempting to assume the role of interim Prime Minister.

[61] For a review of Rajiv Gandhi's tenure, see James Manor "India: State and Society Diverge," *Current History* (December 1985), pp. 429–432, 447; Myron Weiner, "Rajiv

Rajiv Gandhi had begun his political career under the tutelage of his mother and, at first, appeared to have adopted her style. Insecure and uncertain, he entered the 1984 electoral campaign as highly combative and divisive. During the campaign he played very heavily upon anti-Sikh sentiments, Hindu chauvinism, and confrontation with his opponents. This communalist and confrontational approach was initially developed by his mother in the early 1980s as Congress support in the South began to erode. It was also designed as a strategy to absorb and disarm the right just as the *Garibi Hatao* strategy of the late 1960s had been used to absorb and disarm the left. Unlike populism, however, a strategy of communalism can prove to be extremely dangerous in a heterogeneous country like India, where religious identities remain strong and just below the surface. The strategy, in fact, reflected both the very weakness of the Congress as an organization and a desperate effort to develop a mechanism to bind supporters and followers to the party.

Rajiv's massive victory at the polls in December 1984 appeared to have given him sufficient confidence so that he felt free to begin to retreat from the rhetoric of the campaign. Having received a clear mandate, Rajiv moved quickly to defuse the increasingly intense conflicts that threatened Indian unity. Settlement of the Punjab and Assam problems, which his mother had allowed to get out of control, became his highest policy priority. Moreover, as he gained confidence, he shifted from a style of confrontation to one of bargaining and consensus. Seduction rather than bullying became the guiding principle in dealing with both domestic and foreign policy problems.

The first major action by the new government was the enactment of an "anti-defection" bill, passed unanimously by both houses of Parliament in January 1985 as the 52nd Amendment to the Constitution. The legislation was designed to "clean up" public life and, in the words of Rajiv Gandhi, put an end to "politics without principles." Defections, or "floor-crossings," had long been the bane of Indian politics, with more than 2700 recorded cases since 1967, most within the state assemblies. Congress had been the principal beneficiary, with as many as 1900 defections to Congress. The typical pattern was to lure legislators away from a vulnerable ruling party in a

---

Gandhi: A Mid-Term Assessment," in Marshall M. Bouton, ed., *India Briefing, 1987* (Boulder, Colo.: Westview Press, 1987), pp. 1–23; and Lloyd I. Rudolph, "The Faltering Novitiate: Rajiv at Home and Abroad in 1988," in Marshall M. Bouton and Philip Oldenburg, eds., *India Briefing, 1989* (Boulder, Colo.: Westview Press, 1989), pp. 1–33.

state, sometimes with cash but usually with the promise of a ministry in a new government. Between March 1967 and June 1968, the high days of defection, 16 state governments were brought down by defections. Of the 438 legislators who changed parties during this period, 210 were rewarded with ministerships. Rajiv Gandhi's initiative in passing the long-promised antidefection law was hailed as ushering in a new era of politics. The act, however, which effectively ended party defection, gave to Rajiv Gandhi (as well as to the leaders of other parties) a powerful instrument of discipline against dissidents within the party. Under the amendment, which applied to both Parliament and the state assemblies, legislators lose their membership if they quit their party to join another; if, without prior permission or subsequent approval, they vote or abstain from voting in the house "contrary to any direction" issued by the political party to which they belong; or if they are expelled from their party "in accordance with the procedure established by the Constitution, rules, or regulations" of such party. Splits are permissible under the law, permitting possible defectors to retain their seats, provided that it involves at least one-third of the legislative party. Mergers would require two-thirds approval.

Like his mother in 1972, Rajiv's massive victory in the December 1984 Lok Sabha elections gave him much greater confidence and freedom of action in selecting Congress candidates for the March 1985 Assembly elections in 11 states and one of the Union Territories. Under Rajiv's direction, a set of guidelines was developed for removing sitting members for doubtful loyalty or integrity, casteism, poor performance, or for failure to carry the district during the December poll. In applying these guidelines, Rajiv conducted one of the most widespread purges of the Congress since the early 1970s. Some 40 percent of all sitting candidates were dropped and replaced by a new generation of young, educated professionals who fit the new management-oriented mold of Rajiv and his advisors. Ability to win was given less weight than the candidate's relationship to the competing personalities within Rajiv's new coterie, as Rajiv's kitchen cabinet members tried to strengthen their positions within the party.

Unfortunately for Rajiv, this attempted experiment at recasting the party, like the one attempted by his mother in 1972, was largely a failure. Many of Rajiv's new candidates simply lacked a local base of support and were defeated at the polls. In many cases, these candidates were defeated by the very people they were selected to replace. As in the past, disgruntled Congress members with a strong local base of support who were denied renomination by the party, bolted the Congress and successfully contested the elections on their own. Poor candidate selection, therefore, contributed at least in part to an overall decline in Congress support. The party succeeded in winning only 56 per cent of the seats in the assemblies in contrast to the 70 percent it had won during the December Lok Sabha poll. The Congress failed to secure a majority in Andhra, Karnataka, and Sikkim; and even in the western state of Maharashtra the Congress majority was substantially reduced. Overall, the assembly elections reflected the Congress party's dependence on the Hindi heartland and its continued weakness in the South and along almost the entire periphery of India.

Despite the electoral reverses of 1985, Rajiv continued his conciliatory approach in an attempt to solve ethnic and religious conflicts in Punjab and Assam. In July 1985, he signed the accord with Akali president Longowal on the Punjab, and a month later reached an accord with militants in Assam to end the anti-immigration agitation.[62]

Rajiv's reform agenda also included a program of economic liberalization that included liberalization of imports, industrial licensing, and foreign investment, as well as major tax reforms. The efforts to make the economy more dynamic were paralleled by attempts to rejuvenate the Congress (I) and prepare India for the 21st century. Rajiv was hailed as the messiah of a new, modern India, and as a man of courage, integrity, and vision. Popular euphoria in India over Rajiv's performance reached an all-time high.

As in the past, however, the euphoria did not last. By 1986 Rajiv's apparent solutions of India's seemingly intractable problems began to unravel. The scheduled transfer of Chandigarh to Punjab, which was to take place on January 26, 1986, was deferred. Communal violence erupted over the Babri Masjid in Ayodhya; Rajiv was accused of placating Muslims by supporting a bill that would reverse the 1985 Shah Bano case and limit the financial responsibility of Muslim men in divorce cases; and violence intensified in the Punjab as central government commandos raided the Golden Temple to seize it from Sikh militants. One of the few bright spots was the Mizoram accord of July 26, 1986, which ended a 20-year insurgency in the Northeast. This accomplishment, however, was offset by renewed trouble in Kashmir and a Gurkha agitation in West Bengal for the creation of a separate state of Gurkhaland. Euphoria turned to despair as India was once again plunged into a major political crisis that threatened the stability of the regime and the country.

[62] For a discussion of the two accords, see pp. 151–52 and 157–58.

Rajiv's Leadership Style By mid-term, Rajiv's post-election style of openness, compromise, and consensus was superseded by a return to the pattern of behavior reminiscent of his mother, but without her ruthlessness and decisiveness. He became increasingly arrogant, overcentralized power in the Prime Minister's Secretariat, and showed a lack of respect for institutional norms. This leadership style contributed to major failures in performance and an erosion of credibility. As Prime Minister, Rajiv Gandhi centralized power to an even greater extent than his mother. The Cabinet was subject to frequent changes, and power became concentrated in the hands of a very small, narrowly based group of inexperienced personal advisors in the Prime Minister's Secretariat. In less than three years, the Indian Cabinet was reshuffled at least a dozen times, and each change was accompanied by a promise that additional adjustments would follow. Every Cabinet minister was transferred at least once, and some ministers changed jobs four times. No one was in office long enough to learn the job or to take any meaningful action. During 1987, not only was the Cabinet reshuffled several times, but most of the effective and talented ministers simply resigned. The most prominent illustration of this phenomenon was the shifting of V. P. Singh from Finance Minister to Defense Minister in January 1987 and his resignation in April.

Rajiv's lack of respect for institutions extended to the President of the Republic. The Prime Minister's relationship with Zail Singh, the President of India, had been smoldering for over two years. During 1987 it erupted into a major constitutional crisis. The President, resentful over the Prime Minister's refusal to consult him on vital matters, began to fight back in late 1986. By the middle of 1987, as Rajiv's political position weakened, wild rumors swept India that the President might dismiss the Prime Minister in an effort to split the Congress (I) and topple the government. Rajiv was able to breathe a sigh of relief only after Singh decided not to seek re-election, and the Prime Minister's hand-picked successor, Vice President R. Venkataraman, won an easy victory and was sworn in on July 25, 1987.

Corruption Scandals While Rajiv's relations with the President created a credibility crisis, his handling of a series of corruption scandals substantially tarnished his image of incorruptibility. Prime Minister Rajiv Gandhi had given his new Finance Minister, V. P. Singh, a broad mandate to weed out corruption and reduce the size of the "black" underground economy. Singh cut tax rates and launched a major enforcement effort. Tax raids, court cases, and the arrest of leading industrialists became the hallmarks of his new regime.

V. P. Singh's rigorous enforcement policies generated enormous resentment against his "raid Raj" among India's top industrialists, and they pressed Rajiv to remove him. On January 24, 1987, Singh was suddenly removed as Finance Minister and made Minister of Defense. The enforcement machinery created by Singh in the Finance Ministry was quickly dismantled.

Shortly after he had left the Finance Ministry, however, a major furor erupted when it was learned that in October 1986 Singh had authorized his subordinates to hire the Fairfax Group, an American private detective agency, to investigate the overseas finances of wealthy Indians. Fairfax focused its investigation on three individuals known to be close to the Congress (I) and the Prime Minister. The three were Dhirubhai Ambani of Reliance Industries; Amitabh Bachchan, a film star, Congress (I) MP, and close friend of Rajiv; and Amitabh's brother Ajitabh. During the parliamentary debate that took place in early April on the Fairfax affair, members of his own party, including key Congress (I) ministers treated Singh as though he had committed a crime against the nation.

At the height of the affair, a second major scandal exploded involving the possible payment of kickbacks on a major defense contract. On April 9, 1987, Singh announced that he had ordered an inquiry into a commission paid for the purchase of two submarines from Howaldt Deutsche Werke (HDW) of Kiel, West Germany. Such payments were a violation of an agreement that defense contractors sign with the Government of India. Singh's decision was openly denounced by Congress MPs, and Rajiv's close aides saw Singh's actions as an attempt to discredit and topple the Prime Minister. On April 12, 1987, Singh resigned from the Cabinet and was later expelled from the Congress party.

The Fairfax affair, the HDW deal, and Singh's resignation combined to tarnish Rajiv's "Mr. Clean" image. Before the Prime Minister could even attempt to recover, his government was hit by yet another scandal. On April 15, 1987, a state-owned Swedish radio station broadcast a story alleging that a payment worth $4.92 million had been paid to an Indian as commission on a $1.3 billion defense contract to purchase Swedish Bofors 155-mm howitzers. Later reports confirmed the payment of an estimated $38 million in commissions. When Rajiv and his Cabinet denounced the report as part of a foreign conspiracy to destabilize India, the Swedish radio station not only repeated the charge, but added that it had documentary proof that four payments were made into a Swiss bank account code named "Lotus."

Rajiv's repeated denials and refusal to cooperate with any further investigation led to the resignation in July of Arun Singh, Minister of Defense Production and one of Rajiv's closest advisors. Later, in an effort to defuse the issue, Rajiv agreed to appoint a Congress-dominated parliamentary committee to investigate the charges. He also publicly declared before Parliament that neither he nor his family had been involved in any cases of corruption. This was the first time in Indian post-independence history that a Prime Minister felt compelled to make such a disclaimer.

Rajiv survived the political crisis of the summer of 1987 brought on by alleged corruption in defense procurement and his constitutional conflict with the President of India. These issues continued to haunt him, however, and new revelations blunted a successful counterattack. With his image tarnished and his credibility severely damaged, Rajiv was forced to turn to the Congress party for support and to embrace the very system he had pledged to transform. Rajiv made peace with the Congress old guard, and the power brokers of old were now characterized as proven workers and leaders. When Rajiv reshuffled his Cabinet in mid-1988, many of these proven leaders were given seats in the Council of Ministers.

Rajiv's political counterattack initially worked quite well in restoring his position. Yet, the past kept coming back to haunt him and threatened to undermine his political recovery. In late February 1988 Zail Singh, former President of India, conducted a series of public interviews in which he claimed he had been offered some $31 million to help him contest for re-election and had been offered support from dissident Congress members, including some of Rajiv's ministers. Rajiv's embarrassment became even more acute after revelations in June that the defense scandal involving the purchase of howitzers from Bofors did, in fact, involve the payment of some $50 million in commissions to Indian intermediaries. These new revelations came shortly after a joint commission of the Indian Parliament had found no record of such payments. These new disclosures blunted Rajiv's counterattack and gave new life to India's divided opposition.

In late January 1989 Indians went to the polls in three states—Tamil Nadu, Nagaland, and Mizoram. Although Rajiv's Congress (I) party was able to win victories in the small northeastern states of Nagaland and Mizoram, it was greeted by a crushing defeat in the key South Indian state of Tamil Nadu. The regionally based Dravida Munnetra Kazhagam (DMK), led by M. Karunanidhi, won 151 of 234 seats compared to a mere 26 for the Congress (I). The defeat was especially humiliating for Rajiv because of the highly visible and direct role that he played in the campaign. The defeat called into question not only his political judgment but also his vote-getting abilities. The defeat in Tamil Nadu meant that the Congress (I) had not won a single election in a major state since 1985.

Electoral defeat in the South was compounded by a simultaneous revolt of Congress (I) dissidents in the North. Revolts in Bihar, Madhya Pradesh, and Rajasthan reflected the growing indiscipline and chaos in the ruling Congress (I) brought on by Rajiv's ineffective style of political management. This style restored the centralized, manipulative system employed by his mother to maintain personalized control. Rajiv had changed chief minister in Congress (I)-ruled states 16 times since 1985 for an average of one every three months. As was the case under Indira Gandhi, this style prevented the emergence of competing power centers, but also resulted in party revolt; the rise of regionalism; and the loss of elections and popular support.

In a desperate effort to recapture the initiative, Rajiv took the dramatic step of reshuffling his advisors and recalling R. K. Dhawan, the former stenographer who had risen to become one of the most powerful advisors in his mother's household. As part of his initial attack against corruption, intriguers and power brokers in the Congress (I), Rajiv had sacked Dhawan shortly after becoming Prime Minister. Faced by crisis in the party and erosion of his authority, Rajiv came full circle and restored the very system he had condemned, symbolized by the return of Dhawan. Dhawan enjoyed the confidence of the Congress old guard, was a superb crisis manager, and was a loyalist without personal political ambitions. He had the remarkable ability of deflecting criticism away from Indira Gandhi, and it was hoped he could do the same for Rajiv.

The return of Dhawan gradually brought a halt to drift and paralysis. Rajiv began to counterattack and developed new political and policy initiatives. He announced a series of new populist programs designed to offset his pro-rich image. These initiatives included an antipoverty program designed to help the 35 percent of the Indian population below the poverty line, and a new system of democratic decentralization called *Lok Shakti*, or power to the people. The decentralization scheme would establish a third tier of panchayat (village) government in India's federal system by creating elected assemblies in each village to supplement state and federal levels of government. Control over development spending would be transferred to these new village assemblies and would create millions of new jobs. Similar schemes had already been introduced in the opposition-controlled states of Karnataka, Andhra, and West Bengal, and Rajiv was able to seize the political initiative by embracing one of the opposition's most popular reforms. Rajiv's initiative, however, was seen as a political ploy designed to bypass the state (with half under non-Congress rule) by establishing direct financial linkage from the Center to local government. Thus, while devolving power to local government, it enhanced central authority *vis-à-vis* the states. The Panchayat Bill died in Parliament.

By the summer of 1989, the defense kickback scandals that had plagued Rajiv since 1987 surfaced once again. In May the opposition in the Indian Parliament charged the Congress (I) with stalling the publication of a report by its Public Accounts Committee on the purchase of West German submarines by the Indian navy. An even greater hailstorm broke in July when the Controller and Auditor General issued a report highly critical of the government's handling of the defense contract to purchase Swedish Bofors howitzers. Charging that the report was a clear indictment of the Congress (I) and Rajiv, the opposition stalled the proceedings of Parliament for three days, demanded Rajiv's resignation, and shouted "Rajiv is a thief." Unable to vote Rajiv out of office because of the overwhelming majority of seats controlled by the Congress (I), almost the entire opposition dramatically handed in its resignation. While Rajiv dismissed the opposition's action as an election-year gimmick, the unity of the opposition represented a real threat. Even more frightening was the defection of several Congress (I) legislators who also decided to resign. Continued Congress dominance was once again threatened by opposition alliance and Congress defections.

Rajiv entered the November 1989 Lok Sabha elections in a weakened position. Congress factionalism, the absence of a major policy success, Rajiv's tarnished image, and kickback scandals, combined with a newly formed National Front of opposition parties, resulted in a stunning defeat for Rajiv and the Congress (I). Due to the high level of opposition unity, the Congress (I) was able to win only 197 seats despite the fact that it received 39.5 percent of the popular vote. Although the Congress (I) did very well in the South, a massive swing against the party in the North among Muslims, untouchables, and upper-caste voters brought an end to Congress (I) rule.[63]

[63] See Atul Kohli, "From Majority To Minority Rule: Making Sense of the 'New' Indian Politics," in Marshall M. Bouton and Philip Oldenburg, eds., *India Briefing, 1990* (Boulder, Colo.: Westview Press, 1990), pp. 1–23.

The defeat of the Congress (I), however, was accompanied by a hung Parliament. For the first time since independence, no single party was able to secure a majority in the Lok Sabha. The performance of the National Front of V. P. Singh in the elections fell far below expectations. The Front won only 17.8 percent of the vote and 143 seats. The poor showing of the National Front was accompanied by static support for the Communists, who received only 9.1 percent of the vote and 45 seats. The most unexpected development was the strong performance of the BJP, which received 11.4 percent of the vote and was able to win 85 seats. Although V. P. Singh was elected Prime Minister, he headed a minority government that depended on the support of the Communists and the BJP. As was the case in 1977 and 1979, the National Front, like the Janata Party, became embroiled in factional conflict among its leading personalities. Within less than a year in office, the Janata Dal split when Chandra Shekhar, one of the original contenders for the prime ministership, led a small faction out of the party and created the Samajvadi Janata Party. Like Charan Singh in 1979, he succeeded in forming a new government with the support of the Congress (I). The new minority government, however, lasted only four months. Chandra Shekhar resigned in April 1991, and India had to go to the polls for a second time in less than two years.[64]

No party was expected to secure a clear majority, but public opinion polls pointed to the Congress (I) as likely to win the largest number of seats and thus for Rajiv Gandhi to have the chance of forming a coalition government. On May 21, however, taking his campaign to Tamil Nadu after the first round of voting, Gandhi, together with 17 bystanders, was killed in a powerful explosion. Forensic experts determined the assassin to be a woman who had detonated the bomb strapped to her body when she bent forward to touch the feet of Gandhi, a traditional act of homage. Further clues identified her as part of a conspiracy by Sri Lankan Tamil guerrillas to assassinate Gandhi, probably in retribution for his role in sending Indian troops to Sri Lanka in 1987 and in pushing for a crackdown on their operations in Tamil Nadu.[65]

[64] See Robert L. Hardgrave, Jr., "South Asian Internal Politics and Policies" in Robert A. Scalapino et al., eds., *Asia in the 1990s: American and Soviet Perspectives* Berkeley: Institute of East Asian Studies, the University of California, 1991), pp. 194–210; and Robert L. Hardgrave, Jr., "After the Dynasty: Politics in India," *Current History, 91* (March 1992), pp. 106–112.

[65] On the assassination, see the special issue of *India Today*, June 15, 1991, and for the details of the conspiracy, "Rajiv Assassination: The Inside Story," *India Today*, July 15, 1991, pp. 82–89.

In the wake of Gandhi's assassination, and in fear of widespread violence, the Election Commission postponed the second and third rounds of voting until June 12 and 15. Hoping to draw a sympathy vote and to paper over deep factional divisions within the party, the Congress (I) high command invited Sonia Gandhi to succeed her slain husband as party president. She declined, and the party turned to P. V. Narasimha Rao, from Andhra Pradesh in the South. A former Foreign Minister, Narasimha Rao was 69 years old, and without a political base. He was perceived to be without ambition and thus an acceptable compromise.

The assassination had a dramatic effect on the election results. The first round, before the assassination, had reflected a shift away from the Congress (I). In the second and third rounds that followed the assassination, however, there was a swing of sympathy votes in favor of the Congress (I). In the final tally, although the popular vote for the Congress (I) declined from 39.5 percent in 1989 to 37.6 percent in 1991, a divided opposition enabled it to win 227 seats—just 29 seats short of a majority.

As the results came in, Sharad Pawar, the powerful Congress (I) Chief Minister of Maharashtra, made a bid for the party leadership, but contending factions within the party, each unwilling to yield to the other, again compromised on Narasimha Rao.[66] On June 21, he was sworn in as Prime Minister and given four weeks to prove in a vote of confidence that the Congress (I) could command the parliamentary support necessary to govern as a minority government. Rao's ministry accommodated the party's various factions and included the three strongest contenders for party leadership, each comparatively young and highly capable: Sharad Pawar; Arjun Singh, former Chief Minister of Madhya Pradesh and party trouble-shooter; and, less likely, Madhavrao Scindia, of the princely family of Gwalior. Some elements of Rajiv's "coterie" were brought into the ministry, but Rao remained wary of "the Sonia factor," even as she declined to contest the by-election for Rajiv's Amethi constituency.

The vote of confidence came on July 15. No party was prepared to face new elections, and none wanted to assume responsibility for bringing down the government. The Congress (I) and its allies voted 241 for the motion of confidence; the BJP, with 111 members present, voted against; and 112 of the National Front and Left Front MPs abstained. Each of the opposition parties indicated its willingness to

[66] Rao had not contested the elections, and he was thus named Prime Minister contingent on his election to the Lok Sabha within six months. In by-elections held in November, Rao was returned from a "safe" Congress (I) seat in Andhra Pradesh.

support the government selectively "issue to issue," and Rao, reaching out to the BJP for support on one set of issues and to the National Front and Left on another, began a balancing act over the minefield of issues that divided the parties: economic policy, reservations, Ayodhya, and regional separatism.

Rao acted decisively in announcing a series of major economic reforms designed to open the Indian economy, but he moved more carefully on the volatile ethnic and religious issues. On the Congress organization itself, in the fall, 1991, he announced that the process of party elections—not held since 1972—would begin. From the primary level through the block and district levels to the Provincial Congress Committee, party members elected delegates, each faction contending for advantage by enrolling bogus members. Members of the Provincial Congress Committees selected delegates to the All-India Congress Committee, composed of more than 600 members, and they, in turn, elected the Working Committee and the new Congress party president, P. V. Narasimha Rao. Rao, however impressively he moved into leadership, was nonetheless seen as a transitional figure, and the character of post-dynastic leadership in the Congress party was yet to be resolved.

The Non-Congress Parties: The Struggle for Opposition Unity

The decline of the Congress (I) has been accompanied by the rise of an increasingly fragmented and regionalized opposition. These combined forces in turn have made it more and more difficult to forge effective and stable coalitions. As seen in Table 6–1, the development of the non-Congress parties has been characterized by four distinct trends. The most significant trend has been the inability of opposition political leaders to forge a durable national, centrist alternative to the Congress. Neither the Janata Party of 1977 to 1979 nor the National Front of 1989 to 1991 was able to manage successfully their internal conflicts or overcome the personal ambitions of factional leaders. Party unity designed to achieve electoral victory could not be translated into stable and effective government. A second major trend has been the decline of the left and the inability of the Communists and their allies to extend their base of support. Communist electoral strength at the national level has remained static, and the movement remains confined to a narrow regional base. The third and most dramatic development has been the rise of the BJP and Hindu communal politics on the right of the Indian political spectrum. Unlike the old Jana Sangh, the BJP has been able to develop a wider support base and is attempting to move more toward the center. The final trend has been the growing regionalization of politics. Politics within each state has become increasingly bipolar, but the alternative to Congress rule tends to be a different party from state to state.

The Janata Party The Janata Party, created in 1977, was the first major effort in post-independence India to forge a centrist alternative to the Congress party. What came to be the Janata Party was composed of four parties: the Congress (O), the Jana Sangh, the Socialist Party, and the Bharatiya Lok Dal (BLD). In the elections that brought the party to power, they allied themselves with the Congress for Democracy (CFD), the Congress splinter led by Jagjivan Ram.[67]

The Congress (O) The largest of the four parties was the Congress (O), led by former Deputy Prime Minister Morarji Desai. The party was the product of the 1969 Congress split, when Indira Gandhi challenged the party bosses in her successful bid for control. Bound by personal association and only loosely ideological, the Congress (O) represented a blend of conservative and Gandhian perspectives. Its support (10.5 percent of the vote in 1971) was geographically dispersed and socially heterogeneous, but it brought to the Janata Party important links to the business community and an experienced leadership.

The Jana Sangh The Jana Sangh was the only party to join the Janata coalition that did not have roots in the Congress. Its origins were in the Hindu nationalism of the Mahasabha and the RSS. At the time of Gandhi's assassination, Dr. S. P. Mookerjee, President of the Hindu Mahasabha, was a member of Nehru's Cabinet. In December 1948 he resigned from the Mahasabha when his proposal to open membership to non-Hindus was rejected. In early 1950 he resigned from the Cabinet, a leader in search of a party. The *Organiser*, a semi-official publication of the RSS, called for a new political party, with

[67]For a lively, if biased, account of the alliance, see Brahm Dutt, *Five Headed Monster* (New Delhi: Surge Publications, 1978). The colorful personalities involved are portrayed in Janardan Thakur, *All the Janata Men* (New Delhi: Vikas, 1978).

Moorkerjee clearly in view, and in 1951 Moorkerjee announced the formation of the Bharatiya Jana Sangh, the people's party. The object of the party was the rebuilding of Bharat (India) as a modern, democratic society, while removing foreign cultural influences as much as possible. Four "fundamentals" guided the party: one country, one nation, one culture, and the rule of law.[68] Under the long leadership of Deendayal Upadhyaya (1954–1967), the Jana Sangh gradually shifted to the left in economic issues.

The program of the Jana Sangh in its formative stage was an eclectic mix of tradition and modernity. The party manifesto set forth a wide range of policy positions, but the Sangh carried a decidedly communal flavor despite its open membership. The ideology of the party was of *Bharatiya*, Indian culture, not of Hindu raj. Nevertheless, for all its "non-sectarian" claims, the Jana Sangh sought to promote national unity by "nationalizing all non-Hindus by inculcating in them the ideal of Bharatiya Culture."[69] Its Hindu nationalism was reflected in its refusal to recognize the partition of India and in its militantly anti-Pakistan stance. The Jana Sangh supported a foreign policy of "non-involvement," and actively lobbied for a powerful defense establishment with nuclear capability. It advocated a united India under a unitary state, with Hindi as the sole national language. Hindu dominance was symbolized by the party's stand for cow protection and the promotion of *Ayurvedic*, or traditional, medicine. Perhaps most controversial was the Jana Sangh's close association with the RSS. Indeed Nehru had once described the party as its "illegitimate child." However much a source for unease among the Jana Sangh's new colleagues, the RSS provided an indispensable network of organizational strength.

The Jana Sangh itself was well-organized and had a young and dynamic leadership, among whom the most notable was Atal Bihari Vajpayee. Regionally concentrated in the Hindi heartland of North India, the Jana Sangh had participated in coalition governments in five states between 1967 and 1971, and had intermittently controlled the Delhi Council. From its founding, the party had gradually in-

[68] Craig Baxter, "The Jana Sangh: A Brief Political History," in Donald E. Smith, ed., *South Asian Politics and Religion* (Princeton, N.J.: Princeton University Press, 1966), p. 81. See also Baxter, *The Jana Sangh: A Biography of an Indian Political Party* (Philadelphia: University of Pennsylvania Press, 1969); and Bruce Graham, *Hindu Nationalism and Indian Politics* (Cambridge: Cambridge University Press, 1990).

[69] *Manifesto and Program of the Bharatiya Jana Sangh*, 1958, quoted in Donald E. Smith, *India as a Secular State* (Princeton, N.J.: Princeton University Press, 1963), p. 471.

creased its strength to a peak of 9 percent in 1967, with a decline to 7 percent in 1971. The base of the party's support was the urban, educated Hindu middle class—professionals, small businessmen, and white-collar workers.

The Socialist Party The Socialist Party, founded in 1971, was heir to the faction-torn Indian socialist movement.[70] An amalgam of Marxist, Gandhian, and democratic socialist elements, the party had split and reunited a half-dozen times. With about 4 percent of the 1971 vote, its base of support, concentrated in North India and mainly Bihar, was predominantly rural, young, and poor. A major portion of its rural support was among untouchables and landless laborers. Through its trade union, the Hind Mazdoor Sabha, the Socialists had a scattered support among urban labor, notably in Bombay.

The patriarch of the Socialist Party, though not formally associated with any party, was Jayaprakash Narayan. The party's chairman was George Fernandes, leader of the railway workers union. When the 1975–77 emergency was imposed, Fernandes went underground and evaded police until his capture in June 1976. Charged with complicity in acts of violence during the emergency, he alone of the opposition leaders remained in jail during the election campaign.

The BLD The Bharatiya Lok Dal (BLD) was formed in 1974 in the merger of seven parties, some caste or personal parties, and each with essentially regional support. Its largest constituents were the Bharatiya Kranti Dal (BKD), led by Charan Singh, and the Swatantra Party. The BKD, a Congress splinter, was confined to Uttar Pradesh, India's most populous state, and was supported mainly by peasants from the middle castes. The Swatantra Party was India's party of free enterprise. Its support (concentrated in Gujarat, Rajasthan, and Orissa) derived principally from the business community, landowners, and former princely families. Among the smaller parties entering into the BLD was a socialist faction led by Raj Narain, Mrs. Gandhi's

[70]See Lewis P. Fickett, Jr., *The Major Socialist Parties of India: A Study in Leftist Fragmentation* (Syracuse, N.Y.: Maxwell School, Syracuse University, 1976) and Paul R. Brass, "Leadership Conflict and the Disintegration of the Indian Socialist Movement: Personal Ambition, Power, and Policy," in P. N. Pandey, ed., *Leadership in South Asia* (New Delhi: Vikas, 1977), pp. 341–71.

1971 electoral opponent. Under the leadership of Charan Singh, the BLD was committed to a "middle Gandhian path." The strength of the party was concentrated primarily among the prosperous agricultural classes of North India.

The 1977 Elections

The four parties merged into the new Janata Party, led by Morarji Desai. The bonds that united them had been forged in the jails during the emergency, and the urgency imposed by the impending elections left them little time to explore their differences. The announcement of the formation of the Janata Party was followed within a few days by the resignation of Jagjivan Ram from the Cabinet and his defection from the Congress fold.

The campaign released a surge of political activity. Loosely organized and poorly financed, the Janata Party, together with Ram's Congress for Democracy, took the offensives against the emergency and the personal rule of Mrs. Gandhi. Although the odds remained with Congress throughout the campaign, the predicted margin of victory narrowed, and some observers began to talk of a "Janata wave." Mass meetings—on the Ram Lila grounds in New Delhi, the Maidan in Calcutta, the Marina in Madras—drew hundreds of thousands of people, larger turnouts than in any previous election campaign. Throughout India, from New Delhi to the most isolated villages, campaign posters and graffiti covered every available space. In place of the stern emergency image of Mrs. Gandhi ("She Stood Between Order and Chaos. She Saved the Republic."), Congress campaign posters portrayed the Prime Minister as a benign, motherlike figure. The message was simple: "For Progress and Stability—Vote Congress." Janata relied more heavily on graffiti: "Our Pledge—Bread and Liberty—Vote Janata," "Save Democracy—Vote for Janata Party." The official poster of the national Election Commission proclaimed: "Vote Without Fear—Your Vote is Secret."[71]

The Janata victory was massive. With 43 percent of the vote, the Janata/CFD won 298 seats in the Lok Sabha (55 percent). Together with their allies, the CPM, DMK, and Akali Dal, they took 330 of the 542 seats. Congress, with 34.5 percent of the vote, was reduced to 154 seats. A 9-point drop in the percentage of votes from 1971 to 1977 had cost the Congress 198 seats and control of the government.

[71] Myron Weiner provides a firsthand account of the campaign and a systematic analysis of the election results in *India at the Polls, 1977*. Posters and graffiti are described on pp. 23–28.

The Janata Government

After the elections, Jagjivan Ram's CFD merged with the Janata, and the internal struggle to form a new government began. In many ways the Janata, as an umbrella party of disparate interests and conflicting personalities, looked remarkably like the old Congress. The task of maintaining party unity fell to Janata president Chandra Shekhar, a former Congress "Young Turk" and follower of Jayaprakash Narayan. J. P., 74 years of age and seriously ill, held back from active political involvement.

Within the Janata, the left favored Jagjivan Ram as Prime Minister, but for Charan Singh and many within the Jana Sangh, Ram was unacceptable. As infighting approached crisis, a vote was bypassed in favor of a decision by two elder statesmen, Archarya Kripalani and Jayaprakash Narayan. They gave the nod to Morarji Desai, 81 years of age, austere and puritanical.

The Cabinet selection reflected the relative strength of the Janata factions and gave a slightly right-of-center character to the government. In addition to the Prime Ministership, the Congress (O) was allocated the largest number of important portfolios in the 20-member Cabinet. The Home Ministry, the number-two position in the government, went to Charan Singh and the powerful Finance Ministry to a BLD colleague. Raj Narain, regarded by many as a buffoon and an embarrassment to the party despite his victory over Mrs. Gandhi, became Minister for Health and Family Welfare. Of the Jana Sangh's three portfolios, two were important, with Vajpayee appointed as Minister for External Affairs. Jagjivan Ram was given the Defense Ministry, number-three position in the government, but this was the only important portfolio going to the CFD group. The Socialists were allocated relatively unimportant ministries, with Industries ultimately going to George Fernandes.[72]

Before the new government took office, Mrs. Gandhi gave the order to lift the emergency imposed on June 26, 1975. This was followed, as one of the first acts of the Janata government, by withdrawal of the external emergency. In the "restoration of democracy," the Janata sought to roll back the more pernicious effects of emergency rule. The government ordered the release of political prisoners still held—save for those, like the Naxalite revolutionaries, who were perceived as a security threat to the nation. (Through the efforts of

[72]See the very perceptive article by Ram Joshi and Kirtidev Desai, "Toward a More Competitive Party System in India," *Asian Survey*, 18 (November 1978): 1091–116.

the Communist Party [Marxist], the Naxalite leaders were finally released in May 1979.) Press freedom was restored, and judicial authority taken from the courts was returned. But the Janata government was not prepared to rescind all structural changes enacted during the emergency, nor was it ready to repeal MISA or abandon preventive detention.

To consolidate its position, the Janata sought fresh elections for the assemblies in those states where Congress retained power but had suffered defeat in parliamentary polling. If Janata was to ensure the victory of its candidate in the presidential election due in August (six months after the death of President Fakhruddin Ali Ahmed), it was imperative that it control a majority in the state assemblies. Congress denounced the effort to dislodge "duly constituted" state governments. Amid controversy, but averting a confrontation with the Janata government that threatened to become a constitutional crisis, the Acting President dissolved the assemblies. Elections were held in June 1977 for the legislative assemblies in 11 states and 3 Union Territories. The election covered two-thirds of the Indian electorate. Factional battles over nominations threatened to tear the party apart, but despite internal conflict, Janata again swept the polls. Reflecting the pattern of its earlier victory, Janata strength was in the Hindi heartland of North India. The Marxists, with Janata backing, won in West Bengal, and regional parties came to power in the Punjab, Kashmir, and Tamil Nadu.

With a majority of seats in the state assemblies, the Janata was assured that its candidate would be elected President. Sanjiva Reddy, who had been the unsuccessful Congress candidate for President in 1969, was put forward as a consensus candidate. With the support of all parties, including the Congress, he was unanimously elected.

Ideological contradictions and a range of diverse interests reinforced personality and group conflict within the Janata Party. In foreign policy, the party reaffirmed India's commitment to nonalignment, seeking a more balanced relationship with the United States and the Soviet Union. It also stressed improved relations with India's South Asian neighbors. Domestic policy was less coherent. The Janata offered a "Gandhian alternative" to the Congress emphasis on heavy industry. Its economic program emphasized decentralization, rural development, and labor-intensive industry. In practice, Janata policy differed little from that of Congress.

Janata, like the Congress government before it, was fundamentally dependent on the middle sectors of society—the urban middle class and the prosperous agriculturalists. Each of the party's constituent elements contributed to a widely differentiated social base. The BLD brought the middle peasants. Ram's CFD brought support from untouchables, Muslims, and the landless. The Socialists contributed a following from the rural poor and from industrial labor. The Jana Sangh brought urban middle-class support, and through the Congress (O) and old Swatantra ties, the Janata Party gained support from the business community and industrialists. Though broadly-based, Janata support was geographically concentrated in the Hindi-speaking regions of northern India.

As the Congress party had done for 30 years, the Janata sought to balance the powerful interests to which it was beholden. Policy did not shift radically, and the new emphasis on rural development benefited the landed peasant more than the landless laborer. Redistribution of limited resources below the poverty line continued to meet resistance from the vested interests upon which power in India rests. Janata, like Congress, promised more than it could deliver, and for those at the bottom, the gap between achievement and aspiration continued to widen.

Crisis and Collapse The euphoria that greeted the Janata victory in March 1977 was soon displaced by frustration and uncertainty. Good monsoons and record harvests sustained the economy, but government policy lacked direction and was burdened by misplaced priorities—as symbolized by the Prime Minister's obsessive pursuit of total prohibition. Strikes increased, inflation surged, and student "indiscipline" again closed universities throughout North India. Caste tensions erupted in armed clashes and in attacks on untouchables. Communal violence erupted in a wave of Hindu–Muslim riots, with a death toll running into the hundreds. The tempo of political unrest was recorded in widespread agitation and violence, by rioting and police firings. Perhaps the most ominous unrest came in mid-1979, in a wave of police and paramilitary strikes that surged through the country. The government found it necessary to disband and disarm some paramilitary units, and at two camps battles between the military and the troopers resulted in several deaths.

Within the Janata Party conflict was endemic. In June 1978, with deepening enmity between Morarji Desai and Charan Singh, it reached a crisis point with the forced resignations of Charan Singh and Raj Narain. Singh's ouster from the Cabinet threatened the party with schism, but the BLD was itself split, and Singh could count on no more than 50 of the BLD's 81 MPs to leave the Janata. Instead, he suggested that the party be reconstituted as a federation of member parties, each retaining separate identities and organizations. It was, in fact, little more than that already, its cohesion maintained by the allure of office, the threat of Congress resurgence, and reluctance to face another general election.

Among the Janata constituents, alliances formed and disintegrated, and the struggle at the Center was acted out by proxy at the state level. In a fluid situation the Jana Sangh and the Congress (O) stood together against the BLD, while Ram's CFD and the Socialists, the weakest elements within the party, cast about for a strategy in the intraparty struggle. By July 1979, with the government virtually immobilized by factionalism, the tenuous solidarity of the Janata was finally broken.

The catalyst for the crisis within the Janata Party was the controversy over the role of the Jana Sangh and its continued ties with the RSS. Raj Narain took the initiative, denouncing the RSS as "fascist" and the source of communal violence. Acting clearly as a stalking horse for Charan Singh, Narain resigned from the Janata Party, taking with him 46 Lok Sabha members—most from the BLD faction—to form the Janata (Secular). The defections denied the Janata government its majority in Parliament, and on July 11, the leader of the opposition, Y. B. Chavan of the Congress, brought a motion of no confidence. He cited the dismal record of the Janata government, mounting inflation, the breakdown of law and order, and deepening communal tension.

Within the Janata the pace of defection increased, with resignations by Cabinet ministers H. N. Bahuguna and George Fernandes. Fernandes, with Madhu Limaye, formed a Socialist caucus within the Lok Sabha. At issue were the Jana Sangh connection and Desai's continued refusal to open inquiries into charges of corruption against his son Kanti. As the Janata disintegrated, Morarji Desai finally yielded to pressure from within the party to step down as Prime Minister. He submitted his resignation only a day before the parliamentary vote that almost surely would have toppled the Janata government. Following parliamentary practice, President Sanjiva Reddy asked Desai to remain in office as "caretaker" until a new government could be formed. Charan Singh, crossing the floor to the opposition, took the leadership of the Janata (Secular) and announced his intention to form a new government.[73]

[73]In 1982 Morarji Desai gave to Arun Gandhi, grandson of Mahatma Gandhi, some 200 files of papers and correspondence, Using these documents, Gandhi wrote a highly controversial account of the Janata government. See Arun Gandhi, *The Morarji Papers: Fall of the Janata Government* (New Delhi: Vision Books, 1983).

As the government crisis entered the second week. Desai and Charan Singh maneuvered for parliamentary support, each submitting to the President overlapping lists of those committed to their leadership. Sorting out conflicting claims in consultation with party leaders, President Reddy gave the nod to Charan Singh. Singh had marshalled a narrow majority of 280 seats—a number clearly open to challenge. The three-party coalition itself commanded only 182 seats: 92 from Charan Singh's Janata (Secular), 75 from the Congress, and 15 from the Socialists. The government's survival rested on outside support—the 7 members of the CPI and, most critically, the 73 members of the Congress (I). Charan Singh, jailed by Indira Gandhi during the 1975–77 emergency, was now dependent upon her support—much to his own discomfort as well as that of his coalition partners.

The Janata Party, now in opposition, retained 209 seats. The CPM, the Akali Dal, and the AIADMK adopted a neutral stance toward the new government, and in the fluid situation any one of them could potentially bring down the government on a vote of confidence. Without the test of a parliamentary vote, the figures for party strength varied among different sources and from day to day. Alignments were shifting, and disciplined party organization had broken down. Regional groupings, even within the parties, were taking on increased importance.

On July 28, 1979, Charan Singh, 77 years of age and suffering from a heart condition, became the fifth Prime Minister of India. His Cabinet was composed of 19 members: 10 Janata (S), 8 Congress, and 1 Socialist. Y. B. Chavan was named Deputy Prime Minister and Home Minister. Prime Minister Singh called for "a new atmosphere of hope in place of the present state of uncertainty, apprehension, and despair."

The day before the new government took power, Desai turned over the leadership of the Janata Party to Jagjivan Ram. Ram, who might have become Prime Minister had it not been for Desai's unyielding rigidity, vowed to bring down Charan Singh's "minority government" at the first opportunity. From outside the ministry, Indira Gandhi's Congress (I) held the balance. As the condition for her support, Mrs. Gandhi demanded that the Special Courts set up to prosecute cases arising from the emergency be scrapped. Singh was unable to accede to her demand without losing the support of other parties upon whom he was dependent. Facing inevitable defeat on a vote of confidence when Parliament reconvened in late August, Charan Singh, after 24 days in office, resigned.

In stepping down, the Prime Minister asked President Reddy to call new elections. Jagjivan Ram, as leader of the opposition, claimed the right to form a new government if he could secure the necessary majority. Resisting pressure on behalf of Ram, the President dissolved Parliament and called for elections.[74] The first effort to form a national, centrist alternative to the Congress ended in failure.

Renewed Opposition Fragmentation, 1980 to 1989

With the breakup of the Janata Party, the Congress (I) returned to power. Periodic unity efforts by the opposition parties ran aground on questions of leadership, allocation of seats in elections, and (more a smokescreen than a matter of substance) the allegedly communal character of the BJP. Initial efforts toward unity were frustrated by the continued bickering of Morarji Desai, Charan Singh, and Jagjivan Ram, in a replay of the dissention that brought the collapse of the Janata government. Increasingly, however, leaders of the next generation, the product of post-independence politics, began to take center stage—but to no greater effect in forging opposition unity.

There were a number of impediments to unity, with the issue of leadership, given the contentious personalities involved, among the most prominent. Regional parties, moreover, had no interest in submerging their separate identities in an all-India party, and those in power were not prepared to share the bounty of office. Furthermore, the BJP, while supporting party alliance and electoral adjustment, was opposed to merger in principle.

From 1980 to 1989 there were continuing efforts to merge the constituents of the once-united Janata Party. These parties and their progeny—principally the Janata, the Lok Dal, the Democratic Socialist Party, the Congress (S), and the Congress (J)—were divided heirs of the "Congress culture." In grappling for unity, elements of each have split, merged, and split again.

In August 1983 the Lok Dal and the BJP—together a major force in North India—formed the National Democratic Alliance. A month later four parties came together to form a United Front: the Congress (S), with strength in Maharashtra; the Democratic Socialist Party, with a Muslim following and a base in Uttar Pradesh; the Rashtriya Congress, the Gujarat splinter; and, at the helm, the Janata Party. Remaining outside, the Telugu Desam, the National Conference, and the two Communist parties indicated their support for the Front. United

[74]M. V. Pylee examines the role of the President in this "sordid drama" in *Crisis, Conscience and the Constitution* (Bombay: Asia Publishing House, 1982).

Figure 6–2
The Janata Party and BJP Since 1977

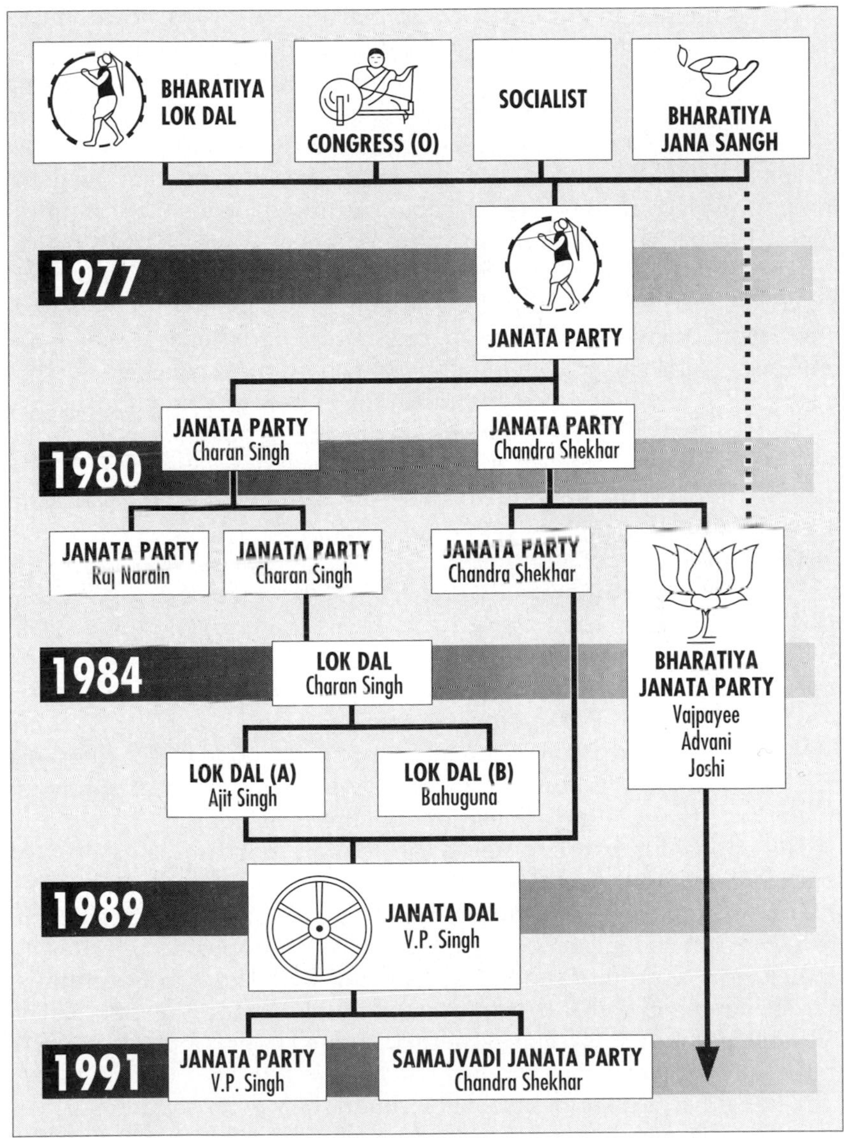

SOURCE: Adapted from David Butler, Ashok Lahari, Prannoy Roy, *India Decides: Elections 1952–1991* (New Delhi: Living Media, 1991), p. 26

Front leaders continued to court the Lok Dal, hoping to split the National Democratic Alliance and isolate the BJP. The Alliance was dissolved in October 1984 when the Lok Dal, the DSP, and the Rashtriya Congress merged to form the DMKP. But the new party, now the Lok Dal, split again following Charan Singh's death.

In May 1983, at the initiative of Andhra Chief Minister T. N. Rama Rao, 24 leaders of 14 opposition parties met at Vijayawada in Andhra to discuss their common interests. Although the Communists and the BJP used the occasion to take jabs at each other, the fact that the gathering took place at all was remarkable. Setting aside ideological differences, the parties unanimously adopted a statement sharply critical of Mrs. Gandhi and, in an expression favorable to regional sentiment, called for greater autonomy for the states. Pursuant to their agreement at the Vijayawada conclave, opposition party leaders met again in June at Delhi and in October at Srinagar. A fourth conclave, hosted by the CPM's Jyoti Basu, chief minister of West Bengal, met in January 1984 in Calcutta. The difficulties of achieving opposition unity, however, were underscored by the failure of the BJP to attend the Delhi meeting and by the absence of both the BJP and the Lok Dal from Srinagar and Calcutta.

The Center's "operation topple" directed against the governments of Kashmir and Andhra was the catalyst to unity that opposition leaders could only have prayed for. From the crest of solidarity in mid-August 1984 until the assassination of the Prime Minister at the end of October, they continued to explore arrangements, alliances, and mergers in the vain effort to achieve unity. Their efforts were frustrated time and again by the clash of egos—none larger than that of Charan Singh. With the death of Indira Gandhi, the focal point that might have brought the opposition together was gone.

The opposition parties entered the 1984 election campaign divided and in disarray, unable to reach even electoral adjustments in more than a few states. The results virtually wiped out the opposition in Parliament. The four national non-Communist opposition parties together won only 20 of the 541 seats contested. The two Communist parties fared somewhat better: the CPM took 22, and the CPI, 6. The Telugu Desam with 30 seats, emerged as the largest opposition party in the Lok Sabha.

Having discredited themselves through their petty squabbling, virtually all the opposition party leaders were defeated, including BJP president Atal Bihari Vajpayee and Janata leader Chandra Shekhar. H. N. Bahuguna fell to film star Amitabh Bachchan. An embittered Charan Singh was returned from his Jat stronghold in Uttar Pradesh, and Jagjivan Ram was narrowly returned from his reserved Scheduled Caste constituency in Bihar.

Reflecting on the devastating defeat of the opposition at the hands of the Congress (I), Chandra Shekhar said, "We lost the election the day Mrs. Gandhi was assassinated." It was surely a good deal more complicated than that, but had Indira Gandhi led the Congress party in the elections, the results would likely have been very different—a Congress victory, but by a narrow margin.

The Janata Dal and the National Front

From 1980 to 1988 the opposition to Congress (I) was fragmented, regionally disparate, and all parties were involved in continuous processes of fission and fusion. Efforts by the non-Communist national opposition parties to unite or even reach electoral understandings were frustrated again and again by the ambitions of their various leaders. Although single opposition parties emerged as credible alternatives to Congress rule in a number of states, no single party posed such a challenge at the Center. The strength of the opposition parties, however—regional parties and national parties that are all-India in name but regional in their concentrated bases of support—remained formidable at the state level and as a unified force had the potential to displace Congress at the Center.[75]

The Janata Dal Forms The approach of the 1989 parliamentary elections, defeat of the Congress (I) in several states from 1985 to 1989, and Rajiv's increased political vulnerability accelerated efforts by India's fragmented, centrist opposition to forge a new national alternative to the Congress (I). The process of opposition unity was triggered in the summer of 1988 by the massive electoral victory in the Allahabad by-election of V. P. Singh, a dissident Congress member and former Finance Minister. The size of Singh's victory demonstrated the strength of the corruption issue, Rajiv's vulnerability, and the importance of opposition unity. Within months of the Allahabad victory, a three-stage process was set in motion that led to the creation of the National Front. In the first phase a group of centrist parties, including the rump of the old Janata Party, two factions of the Lok Dal, and the newly created Jan Morcha (People's Movement)

[75]See Hardgrave, "South Asian Internal Politics and Policies," pp. 194–210, and "After the Dynasty: Politics in India," pp. 106–112.

came together to form the Janata Dal. In the second phase, the Janata Dal joined with three regional parties—the Telugu Desam of Andhra, the Dravida Munnetra Kazhagam (DMK) of Tamil Nadu, and the Asom Gana Parishad of Assam—and the Congress (S) to form the National Front. In the third and final phase, the National Front entered into electoral arrangements with the BJP on the right and the Communists on the left to raise the Index of Opposition Unity to its highest level since the Janata Party victory of 1977.

The Janata Party With the breakup of the Janata government, the party split and then reabsorbed elements from its breakaway parties. The Janata governed in Karnataka (with a repeat of its 1983 victory in the 1985 state elections), and it was a major opposition party in Orissa and Gujarat. The party's leadership included those with strong state bases, such as Ramakrishna Hedge (chief minister of Karnataka), Biju Patnaik (Orissa), Devi Lal (Haryana), and Kapoori Thakur (Bihar). It also contained socialist gadflies George Fernandes, Madhu Lamaye, and Raj Narain on the left and, though inactive politically, former Prime Minister Morarji Desai on the right.

Attempting to hold the party's various factions and feuding leaders together was Janata President Chandra Shekhar, a Gandhian socialist who was one of the few to emerge from the shambles of the Janata government relatively untarnished. In 1983 he walked the length of India, from Cape Camorin to New Delhi, 2700 miles in six months, to dramatize the Janata Party's concern for the rural poor and to call for a restoration of moral values to national life. Chandra Shekhar, however, fell with virtually all the other opposition leaders in the 1984 parliamentary elections. The party, contesting 207 seats, won 10 seats with 6.97 percent of the vote.

The Dalit Mazdoor Kizan Party/Lok Dal In October 1984 three parties—the Lok Dal, the Democratic Socialist Party, and the Rashtriya Congress—together with several disaffected Janata leaders, joined to form the Dalit Mazdoor Kizan Party (DMKP), with Charan Singh, the 83-year-old leader of the Lok Dal, as President. Of its constituent units, the Lok Dal was the most important, with support among the middle peasantry and "backward classes" of Uttar Pradesh, Haryana, Bihar, and parts of Rajasthan. Factional splits had reduced the party in strength and geographic reach, and it had become largely the personal party of Charan Singh. In his home base, however, Singh remained a powerful force.

The Democratic Socialist Party (DSP) had been formed in 1981 by H. N. Bahuguna, a former chief minister of Uttar Pradesh and itinerant politician who broke with Mrs. Gandhi in 1977, joined the Janata Party, went back to Congress, then came out again to organize his own party. The DSP projected itself as socialist, secular, and left-of-center; its support was limited largely to Uttar Pradesh, where Bahuguna (a Brahmin) had considerable following among Muslims.

The Rashtriya Congress formed in 1982 as a splinter from the Congress (I) in Gujarat, with support largely confined to the Saurashtra region of the state.

In the 1984 elections the DMKP contested 174 seats, and, with 5.6 percent of the vote, it won 3. The party, in fact, fared better than the results indicate, for in Bihar, Uttar Pradesh, Haryana, and Rajasthan, it ran a strong second in many constituencies, and in the 1985 state assembly elections, the party made a reasonably good showing in UP. Soon after the state elections, in April 1985, the party changed its name back to the Lok Dal, with Charan Singh as President and H. N. Bahuguna as Vice President. Following the death of Charan Singh, the party split into two factions—the Lok Dal (A) led by Ajit Singh, Charan Singh's son, and the Lok Dal (B) led by Bahuguna.

The Jan Morcha The Jan Morcha was founded by V. P. Singh in October 1987. Upon his resignation from the Congress (I) in April 1987, V. P. Singh appeared to drift. He was not quite sure whether he wanted to be a politician or a Gandhian style moral crusader. Initially he declared that he would devote his time to cleansing Indian politics of corruption and founded the Jan Morcha as a social reform movement open to members of all political parties. Like Mahatma Gandhi and Jayaprakash Narayan, Singh wanted to stand above party politics and seek to cleanse the system. In the summer of 1988, however, he decided to contest the parliamentary by-election in Allahabad in his home state of Uttar Pradesh. On June 16, he won a stunning victory that sent shock waves through the Congress and gave new life to an otherwise warring and divided opposition. In the summer of 1988, the Jan Morcha merged with the Janata Party and the two Lok Dal factions to become the new Janata Dal.

The Congress (S) Since 1980 the opposition Congress, identified as (S) for Socialist, had been weakened by attrition. There had been a steady movement of leaders back to the Congress (I); the Kerala and West Bengal units of the party formally merged with the Congress (I); and the Orissa unit joined the Janata Party in early 1983. The Congress (S) was reduced virtually to the status of a regional party in Maharashtra, where, under Sharad Pawar, it posed a powerful challenge to the ruling Congress (I). In 1984, contesting 31 seats and securing 1.46 percent of the vote, it won 4 seats. Later, however, even Pawar rejoined the Congress (I), leaving a small residue of Congress (S) fragments led by S. C. Sinha.

The National Front With the formation of the Janata Dal, the new party joined its regional party allies and the Congress (S) to form the National Front. The National Front was the second major effort since independence by India's disparate opposition to forge a national, centrist alternative to the Congress. It differed, however, from the Janata Party of 1977 to 1979 in several ways. In the first place, the National Front represented the first attempt by India's national opposition to accommodate the growing regionalization of Indian politics. Regional leaders played an important role in the formation of the National Front, and several regional parties became members of the new coalition. Second, the National Front did not include the BJP, the successor to the old Jana Sangh. The absence of the rightist BJP gave the National Front a more left-of-center orientation. Third, the Front accepted a centralized leadership structure under V. P. Singh, the only non-Congress leader with a strong national identity. Finally, the Janata Dal—the core of the Front—was built on a solid caste base of support that combined the Rajput leadership of V. P. Singh with an appeal to the "backward" peasant castes of North India. In an effort to attract the Other Backward Classes (OBCs), as they were designated officially, the new party committed itself to the implementation of the recommendations of the Mandal Commission Report, the government commission which had recommended that 27 percent of government jobs be reserved for OBCs as part of a program of affirmative action.

The 1989 Elections Although the National Front appeared to represent a formidable challenge to the Congress (I), the performance of the party in the 1989 parliamentary elections fell far short of expectations. The National Front won a total of 145 seats and only 21.7 percent of the popular vote. Most of the seats were won by the Janata Dal, as its regional allies performed poorly. Despite its less than stellar performance, the election was still seen as a mandate for V. P. Singh and a repudiation of Rajiv Gandhi. Singh was able to form a minority government with the help of its electoral allies, the BJP and the Communists.

The results of the parliamentary elections were reinforced by the February 1990 assembly elections in 8 states and 1 Union Territory. The Congress (I) was able to win only in Maharashtra and Arunachal Pradesh. The Janata Dal gained control of Orissa and Bihar. The big winner was the BJP, which repeated its unexpected success in the national elections by winning control of Himachal Pradesh, heading a coalition government in Rajasthan, and joining a Janata Dal-led coalition in Gujarat.

The National Front Government Although V. P. Singh was elected Prime Minister, he led a minority government that was dependent upon the support of a diverse group of opposition parties and a factionalized governing party composed of political prima donnas. Following the 1989 elections, the three most important leaders of the Janata Dal, the principal constituent of the National Front, were V. P. Singh, Chandra Shekhar, and Devi Lal. Each saw himself as a claimant to the prime ministership. Chandra Shekhar was outmaneuvered when V. P. Singh and Devi Lal struck a last-minute deal whereby V. P. Singh would become Prime Minister and Devi Lal would become Deputy Prime Minister and Minister of Agriculture. A defeated and embittered Chandra Shekhar was forced to wait on the sidelines for an opportunity to reclaim his perceived right to the prime ministership. Devi Lal, the boss of Haryana politics and leader of the Jats, saw himself as the behind-the-scenes kingmaker and senior advisor. Within months of its formation, however, the stability of the new government was threatened by the activities of Devi Lal and his family in Haryana politics. In March, Devi Lal resigned from the Cabinet to protest attacks against his son involving fraud and violence in the Haryana Assembly elections. V. P. Singh successfully defused the crisis only to have it reappear when leading members of his Cabinet resigned to protest Devi Lal's success in installing his son as Chief Minister of Haryana. In an effort to regain control, V. P. Singh submitted his resignation as president of the Janata Dal. When the party rallied behind him, he agreed to withdraw his resignation. Devi Lal was dismissed from the Cabinet and immediately began to conspire with Chandra Shekhar to topple V. P. Singh.

In an effort to gain popular support, strengthen his position, and undercut Devi Lal, V. P. Singh suddenly announced in August 1990 that he had decided to move on his party's pledge to implement the Mandal Commission Report and reserve 27 percent of all central government jobs for backward castes.[76] Singh's announcement let loose a firestorm of criticism from the press, the public, and the opposition parties. High-caste students engaged in numerous acts of self-immolation, and V. P. Singh was accused of having started a caste war. The BJP was especially incensed by Singh's announcement and accused him of failing to consult his coalition supporters. In November 1990 the BJP finally decided to withdraw its support of the V. P. Singh government when the government arrested L. K. Advani, the BJP President, in an effort to block his march on the Babri Masjid, the disputed religious shrine at Ayodhya in Uttar Pradesh.

On November 9, 1990, with only the backing of the Left Front and what was left of the National Front, V. P. Singh lost a vote of confidence in the Lok Sabha, 142 to 346, and submitted his resignation. Prior to the vote, Chandra Shekhar and Devi Lal had engineered a split in the Janata Dal and formed a new party, the Janata Dal (Socialist), subsequently renamed the Samajvadi Janata Party. The new party had sufficient support to avoid the sanctions of the antidefection law. Although the President of India asked the BJP and the Congress (I) to form a government, both refused. The President then turned to Chandra Shekhar when the Congress (I) indicated that it would support him for the prime ministership. As a result, Chandra Shekhar became the Charan Singh of the National Front. The Congress, however, used Chandra Shekhar in the same way it had used Charan Singh to topple the Janata Party. Chandra Shekhar's government was able to survive for only four months before it was forced to resign in March 1991. India's second major effort to build a centrist alternative to the Congress (I) party had ended in failure.

The Bharatiya Janata Party

The Bharatiya Janata Party (BJP) is the reincarnation of the old Jana Sangh, which had become incorporated into the Janata Party in 1977. The Jana Sangh had failed to become a major force in Indian politics because of its close ties to the Hindi-speaking North; its restrictive, Brahmanic interpretation of Hinduism; its isolated position in the party system; and its lack of a meaningful economic policy that would attract a broader base of support.[77]

The BJP sought to build a new, Hindu nationalist party that would

[76] For the Mandal controversy, see pp. 192–94.

[77] Graham, pp. 253–258.

be more moderate, more open, and more democratic than the old Jana Sangh. The basic dilemma for the BJP leadership, however, has been to retain its militant core support based on the RSS and its cadre, while at the same time developing a wider more centrist appeal. The party was founded in April 1980 and adopted a new program based on a moderate, Gandhian-oriented set of principles called *the five commitments*. These five commitments were (1) nationalism and national integration; (2) democracy; (3) positive secularism; (4) Gandhian socialism; and (5) value-based politics. By positive secularism the BJP meant a common set of moral values distilled from Indian civilization. The most important element in the new BJP program was its ideological commitment to Gandhian socialism as the basis of the BJP's economic policy.[78]

Although the new BJP program was designed to attract a broader, more centrist base of support, it generated intense conflict within the party between its more liberal leadership which wanted to take a more secular course and the more militant RSS cadre. Initially the strategy proved costly. It alienated the RSS cadre who formed the core of the party's organizational strength, and it deepened dissention within the party. In the 1983 assembly elections in Delhi and in Jammu and Kashmir, the RSS withheld support from the BJP, and in the 1984 parliamentary elections elements of the RSS actively worked for the Congress (I). The RSS organ, *The Organizer*, announced its support for Rajiv Gandhi. The 1984 elections dealt the BJP a stunning blow. Contesting 229 seats, it secured 7.4 percent of the vote (the most for any of the opposition parties) but only 2 seats. Parliament lost one of its most able members and its finest orator in the defeat of BJP president Atal Bihari Vajpayee. For all its losses, however, the BJP remained a major political force in North India—especially in Himachal Pradesh, Madhya Pradesh, Rajasthan, and Delhi. Although it had some rural support, mainly in Madhya Pradesh, its base of support remained concentrated among the urban Hindu, lower-middle class—small traders and civil servants. In 1984 the Congress made a deep cut into this base, but the BJP, more than the other non-Communist opposition parties, had a committed core of support that was unlikely to be permanently lost.

The BJP's electoral defeat in 1984 forced the party back to its roots. After considerable soul searching, the BJP in 1985 reincorporated many of the old ideological concerns of the Jana Sangh into its program and replaced the more liberal Atal Bihari Vajpayee as president

[78] See Geeta Puri, "A Question of Identity," *Seminar* 362 (October 1989), pp. 27–33.

by L. K. Advani, who was closer to the RSS. Although the party retained its original five commitments, it reincorporated the old Jana Sangh concept of integral humanism as the basic philosophy of the party and reiterated its commitment to build India as a strong nation that was modern, progressive, and enlightened, but inspired by India's age-old culture and values.

The BJP change in program and leadership was aided by the rise of communalism and Hindu fundamentalism in the mid-1980s sparked by conversion of Hindu untouchables to Islam; Sikh separatism in Punjab; the Babri Masjid issue at Ayodhya; and the movement for secession in Kashmir. These developments reinforced the sense of insecurity among Hindus and enhanced the appeal of the BJP's call to strengthen Hindu nationalism. In the words of Bruce Graham, "It would be wrong to conclude . . . that competing loyalties of caste, sect, dialect, locality and culture prevented Hindus from acting as a political community. . . . The fact is that many Hindus, and particularly those in the northern states, did indeed see themselves as a political community, but they also saw the Congress party rather than any one of the Hindu nationalist parties as their principal defender."[79] The BJP embarked upon a major effort to mobilize that sense of Hindu community identity.

Among the issues that has been most effectively used by the BJP in its mobilization of the Hindu community has been the Babri Masjid–Ramjanmabhumi issue at Ayodhya.[80] Heavily involved in the 1989 parliamentary elections and the assembly elections of 1990, this issue was used by Rajiv Gandhi to try to garner support for the Congress (I). Nonetheless, the BJP was able to convince many that the foundation stone–laying ceremony that had taken place two weeks before the elections had been achieved by them and not the Congress (I). Although the election was fought over the issues of corruption, inflation, and Rajiv's ineffective leadership, the BJP was also able to use the Ayodhya issue to its benefit. To the surprise of many, the BJP won 85 seats and 11.4 percent of the vote in 1989 compared to 2 seats and 7.4 percent of the vote in 1984. In the February 1990 assembly elections the party was able to win 556 of 1616 seats, more than any

[79] Graham, p. 255. Also see Yogendra K. Malik and V. B. Singh, "Bharatiya Janata Party: An Alternative to the Congress (I)?" *Asian Survey*, 32 (April 1992), pp. 318–36; and James Chiriyankandath, "Tricolour and Saffron: Congress and the Neo-Hindu Challenge," in Subrata Kumar Mitra and James Chiriyankandath, eds., *Electoral Politics in India: A Changing Landscape* (New Delhi: Segment Books, 1992), pp. 55–79.

[80] On the Ayodhya dispute, see pp. 182–83.

Table 6–2
The Growth of the BJP, 1984–1991 Lok Sabha Elections

	1984	*1989*	*1991*
Contested	229	225	461
Won	2	85	119
Percentage of vote	7.4	11.4	21

other party. As a result, it was able to form governments in Madhya Pradesh and Himachal Pradesh, and was a major coalition partner with the Janata Dal in Rajasthan and Gujarat.

By the time of the Tenth Lok Sabha elections in the summer of 1991, the Ayodhya issue had gained even greater prominence. In an effort to galvanize Hindu support and offset the potentially divisive impact of V. P. Singh's announcement that he would implement the recommendations of the Mandal Commission Report, Advani in late August 1990 launched a 10,000-kilometer *rath yatra* (chariot pilgrimage) across India to Ayodhya. As thousands of Hindu militants led by Advani converged on Ayodhya to witness the beginning of construction of the new Ram temple on October 30, 1990, the procession was halted, Advani arrested, and the militants were turned back after attempting to assault the Babri Masjid mosque, the proposed site of the temple.

The BJP became the chief beneficiary of the rise of Hindu fundamentalism and the Ayodhya issue in the 1991 elections. To the surprise of many, the BJP saw its popular vote almost double from 11.4 percent in 1989 to 21.0 percent in 1991 and its number of seats increase from 85 to 119. The BJP had gained a major foothold on the national scene, and in the accompanying state assembly elections, the party gained power in Uttar Pradesh, India's most populous state. Despite its success, however, the party remains divided between its militant RSS core, led by the BJP's president, Murli Manohar Joshi, and its more moderate leadership, associated with Vajpayee. Advani, with ties to each, bridges the two wings as a unifier. Like other parties, the BJP also faces the problems created by a party in power. Its governments in Uttar Pradesh, Rajasthan, and Madhya Pradesh have been characterized by administrative ineptitude, factionalism, and corruption. In addition, the party now faces the creation of an anti-communal front designed to stop the further growth of BJP support.

The rise of communal politics in India has begun to alter the entire party landscape as religion becomes an increasingly important force in India.

The Communist Parties

Since its inception in 1928 the Communist Party of India (CPI) has been divided in its social character, its base of support, and its ideological stance. These divisions reflect its origins in the regional organizations of the Workers' and Peasants' party. In its early years the CPI, closely tied to the Communist Party of Great Britain, was largely under Comintern control and followed Moscow directives with dutiful twists and turns. During the 1930s the party adopted a tactic of "the united front from above" in cooperation with the nationalist movement. Entering the Congress Socialist Party (CSP), Communists soon secured leadership in the Socialist organization, particularly in the South, where they gained effective control. Expelled in 1939, they took much of the CSP membership in the South with them. The final break with the Congress came with the Nazi invasion of the Soviet Union and the CPI's call for cooperation with the British in what was deemed an anti-imperialist war. The Congress chose noncooperation, and as Congress leaders languished in jail, the CPI infiltrated student, peasant, and labor organizations, expanding its membership from 5,000 in 1942 to 53,000 by 1946. Although the CPI effectively gained control of a number of mass organizations, its participation in the war effort, its continued attack on Gandhi, and its support of the Muslim League demand for Pakistan tainted the party as antinational and minimized its influence.

Closed out from above, the CPI adopted a tactic of "the united front from below" in alliance with workers and peasants against the Congress leadership. In 1948 P. C. Joshi was replaced as general secretary by B. T. Ranadive, with the advancement of a more militant "left" line. Under his leadership the CPI embarked on a course of revolution—with strikes, sabotage, and urban violence. Following the Russian model, Ranadive emphasized the working class as the instrument of revolution and discounted the peasant uprising in the Telengana region of Hyderabad. The Andhra Communists, however, pushed for the adoption of a Maoist line of revolution from the countryside and obtained a short-term victory for the tactic of rural insurrection with the election of Rajeshwar Rao as general secretary in

1950. The party became increasingly isolated, party membership declined, and in various states the CPI was outlawed.

During this period Nehru was denounced as a "running dog of imperialism" and the Congress, in both its foreign and its domestic policy, as the reactionary captive of capitalist and landlord elements. In the early 1950s, however, the official attitude of the Soviet Union toward the Nehru government began to change. The CPI was officially advised to abandon its "adventurist" tactics. The policy shift was welcomed by those within the party, notably P. C. Joshi, S. A. Dange, and Ajoy Ghosh, who favored participation in the forthcoming general elections. In 1951 the revisionist line won out, with the selection of Ajoy Ghosh as General Secretary of the party. Ghosh, from a centrist position, led the party toward "constitutional communism." The CPI sanctioned Indian foreign policy and extended its full support to all "progressive" policies and measures of the government.[81] Its willingness to engage in parliamentary politics and to seek alliances with parties of the left in a democratic front seemed vindicated by the success of the Kerala Communists in 1957, and the formation of the first democratically elected Communist government under E. M. S. Namboodiripad. The Amritsar thesis, drafted by the party conference in 1958, set forth the nationalist credentials of the CPI:

> The Communist Party of India strives to achieve full Democracy and Socialism by peaceful means. It considers that by developing a powerful mass movement, by winning a majority in Parliament and by backing it with mass sanctions, the working class and its allies can overcome the resistance of the forces of reaction and insure that Parliament becomes an instrument of people's will for effecting fundamental changes in the economic, social, and State structure.[82]

The Amritsar thesis only papered over fundamental tensions within the party between the right and left, between those favoring cooperation with the Congress and the "national bourgeoisie" and those advocating revolutionary struggle for the defeat of the Congress. Its relationship to the Congress in strategy and tactics posed a dilemma for the CPI. It was obliged, on the one hand, to fulfill its

[81] The evolution of this strategy is detailed in Victor M. Fic, *Peaceful Transition to Communism in India* (Bombay: Nachiketa Publications, 1969).

[82] Constitution of the Communist Party of India, adopted at the Extraordinary Party Congress, Amritsar, April 1958 (New Delhi: Communist Party of India, 1958), p. 4.

ideological commitment to the international Communist movement but, on the other, sought to retain a nationalist identity.[83]

The internal balance of the CPI was soon threatened. In Kerala, sparked by the Education Bill, widespread agitation was launched against the Communist government, bringing central intervention and the proclamation of President's Rule. The left saw it as patent that the Congress would never allow serious socialist reform, but the fate of the Kerala government only served to define more clearly the polarities emerging on the Sino-Indian question. The Tibet uprising in 1959 and the CPI's support for Chinese actions had already brought popular reaction against the party in India. The border clashes brought internal conflict into the open. Headed by S. A. Dange, a leading exponent of the right, or nationalist, faction, the national council of the CPI recognized Indian claims to all territories below the McMahon line, the border demarcation. The left regarded this as a betrayal of international proletarian unity. The positions, set in the context of increasing Sino-Soviet conflict, placed the left in what was regarded as the pro-Chinese camp.

In early 1962, as conflict deepened within the CPI, Ajoy Ghosh, the balancer, died. The factional settlement—election of Dange to the newly created post of Chairman, with Namboodiripad, the centrist, as General Secretary—proved fragile. In the wake of the Chinese invasion of Indian territory, as criticism of the CPI mounted, the national council resolved to condemn the Chinese action as "aggression" and to call upon the Indian people to "unite in defense of the motherland." In protest, the leftists resigned from the party secretariat, and as the situation deteriorated, Namboodiripad submitted his resignation as General Secretary of the party and as editor of *New Age*, the official party publication. In response to the widespread arrests of leftist Communist cadres, the CPI sought to reorganize state party units under rightist control. Their actions served only to stimulate the creation of parallel left structures outside the disciplinary organization of the CPI.

At the national council meeting in 1964 the left attempted, without success, to oust party Chairman Dange. They came armed with a letter, allegedly written by Dange in 1924, in which he had offered to cooperate with the British in exchange for his release from jail. Denouncing the letter as a forgery, the council refused to consider the

[83]Ralph Retzlaff, "Revisionism and Dogmatism in the Communist Party of India," in Robert A. Scalapino, ed., *The Communist Revolution in Asia* (Englewood Cliffs, N.J.: Prentice-Hall, 1965), p. 309.

charges. The left and center, led by Namboodiripad and Jyoti Basu, staged a walkout and appealed to the party to repudiate Dange and the "reformist" line. The split became final when all signatories to the appeal were suspended from the party. The left, organized as the Communist Party of India (Marxist) (CPM), claimed to be the legitimate Communist party of India. Although there was little real evidence to link the CPM with China, the Marxists were viewed as pro-Peking, and in 1965 leading CPM members were arrested throughout India and vaguely charged with promoting "an internal revolution to synchronize with a fresh Chinese attack."[84]

The CPM favored a tactic of united front from below, of alliance with peasants and workers to defeat the Congress, which it regarded as a party of the bourgeoisie and landlord classes, dominated by the big bourgeoisie. Elections were to be used as a means to mobilize the masses; the Constitution was to be used as "an instrument of struggle."[85] The Marxists sought to "break the Constitution from within."[86] The CPM's electoral strategy opened the party to internal conflict, however, as extremists, arguing from an avowedly Maoist position, opposed participation in elections and government in favor of armed struggle from the countryside.

In 1967 the Naxalbari uprising took place in northern Bengal. Those supporting the rebellion, the Naxalites, found general favor from the Marxist organization in Andhra Pradesh and from extremist factions within the CPM in various states. The various Naxalite factions came together in 1969 in the formation of a third Communist party, the Communist Party of India (Marxist-Leninist), Maoist and dedicated to revolution. Under the leadership of Charu Mazumdar, the CPI (M-L) took the lead in calling for immediate armed struggle, liberation of the countryside, and encirclement of the cities, following the Maoist formula. Naxalite solidarity soon foundered on Mazumdar's tactic of urban terrorism and annihilation of class enemies. Representing another "shade of Maoism," Nagi Reddy's Andhra Pradesh Revolutionary Communist Committee supported armed struggle, but one based on an agrarian program and mass peasant involvement.[87]

[84] Home Minister Nanda, quoted in the *Hindu Weekly Review*, 11 January 1965, p. 11.

[85] E. M. S. Namboodiripad, *The Republican Constitution in the Struggle for Socialism*, R. R. Kale Memorial Lecture (Poona: Gokhale Institute of Politics and Economics, 1968), p. 1.

[86] Joint statement of E. M. S. Namboodiripad and A. K. Gopalan, quoted in the *Hindu*, 8 July 1969.

[87] See Mohan Ram, *Maoism in India* (Delhi: Vikas, 1971), pp. 137–69. See also Mohan Ram, *Indian Communism: The Split within a Split* (Delhi: Vikas, 1969); and Marcus F. Franda, "India's Third Communist Party," *Asian Survey*, 9 (November 1969): 797–817.

In both Bengal and Andhra, police action crushed the uprisings, and the Naxalite leaders were jailed.

The regular CPI, closely associated with trade unions, retained control of the official party organs after the 1965 split and identified itself with Moscow. It sought to advance the cause of a "national democratic front" with progressive elements of the nationalist bourgeoisie in order to "complete the anti-imperialist, anti-feudal, democratic revolution."[88] Following the Congress split in 1969, the CPI gave strong, if cautious, support to Indira Gandhi. The party defended the imposition of the 1975–77 emergency and stood with Mrs. Gandhi—despite Sanjay's attacks on the CPI—through the 1977 elections. In the elections the central committee of the CPI announced qualified support for the Congress. At the same time, however, it permitted state party units to decide whether to side with the government or the Janata opposition. In West Bengal the CPI supported Congress; in Uttar Pradesh and Bihar it backed Janata.[89]

Although the Communist party has had an all-India organization, at least theoretically subject to the discipline of "democratic centralism," its structure has been essentially regional in orientation. Neither Communist party has been able to establish a firm base in the Hindi heartland. This may be related, in part, to the Communists' devotion to the Soviet treatment of the "nationalities problem," which in India stresses the development of regional identity. Tactics have been determined more by the local situation than by directive from the top.

The Communist movement in India is divided and regionally concentrated. Beyond the two major parties, the CPM and CPI, there is a pro-Congress CPI splinter, the All-India Communist Party (the Dange group), of no consequence, and 40 or more tiny Naxalite parties and factions once associated with the Communist Party of India (Marxist-Leninist). The Communists have been unable to break out of their regional bases of strength in West Bengal (and, by Bengali ethnic extension, Tripura) and Kerala; they have bogged down in Bihar; and they have lost support in Andhra and the Punjab. Communist trade unions in Bombay have also declined in influence. Overall, Communism in India is stagnant, and there is no state where support for either the CPM or CPI is growing.

In the parliamentary elections, the CPI gradually increased its support from 3.30 percent in 1952 to 9.96 percent in 1962. The 1964 split

[88] "Program of the Communist Party of India," *New Age*, 10 January 1965, p. 10.
[89] Weiner, *India at the Polls*, 1977, p. 53.

divided support almost evenly, but with time the CPM gained at the expense of the CPI. In 1971 the CPI and CPM secured 4.73 and 5.12 percent, respectively. Both parties declined in their share of the 1977 vote. The CPI, discredited by its support for the 1975–77 emergency, fell to 2.8 percent. The CPM, allied with the Janata Party, secured only 4.3. In 1980 the CPI slipped to 2.6 percent of the vote, but the CPM, largely on its strength in West Bengal, rebounded to 6.1. In subsequent elections, the two parties have held steady, and in 1991, the CPI got 2.54 percent and the CPM 6.68 percent of the vote.

The Communist Party (Marxist) has been the ruling party of West Bengal since 1977. With an absolute majority of seats in the state assembly, CPM Chief Minister Jyoti Basu commands great popularity, though his reputation for "clean" government has been tarnished in recent years. The CPM governs at the head of a Left Front coalition that includes the CPI and a variety of parties of the Bengali left, such as the Revolutionary Socialist Party and the Forward Bloc. In Kerala, the CPM—now in opposition after its 1991 defeat—has been in and out of office since 1957 (when the party was united), but it has stagnated, unable to expand its base of support. Beyond this concentration of strength, its overall weakness nationally has transformed the CPM into what is, in effect, a regional party—and, increasingly a Bengali party.[90]

Politics in India is not highly polarized in class terms, and even the two Communist parties draw support from a diverse social base. Although they favor more radical policies than those pursued by the Center, each has been restrained in its own policies by its participation in electoral politics and the responsibility of government. The parties have become more reformist than revolutionary, and it is for this reason that the more radical elements of the CPM advocate withdrawal from the electoral arena. Some attrition occurs from the CPM to Naxalite factions, but little prospect exists that the party will trade political power—even if regional—for the revolutionary underground.

The CPM leadership is aging, and its revolutionary fervor has been leavened by electoral politics and the responsibility of government.

[90]For analyses of the Communist movement in Kerala and West Bengal, see the chapters by Hardgrave and Franda in Paul R. Brass and Marcus F. Franda, eds., *Radical Politics in South Asia* (Cambridge, Mass.: M.I.T. Press, 1973); Franda, *Radical Politics in West Bengal* (Cambridge, Mass.: M.I.T. Press, 1971); and T. J. Nossiter, *Communism in Kerala: A Study in Political Adaptation* (Berkeley: University of California Press, 1982). For a yearly summary of Communist party activities in India, see Walter K. Andersen's annual contribution to Richard K. Staar, ed., *Yearbook on International Communist Affairs* (Stanford, Calif.: Hoover Institution Press).

Despite its pragmatic approach to governing West Bengal, however, the party has sought to retain an ideological purity that over the years placed it among the most ossified in the Communist world. Initially independent of Moscow, the CPM in the early 1980s moved closer to the Soviet Union, facilitating closer cooperation with the CPI, but with the advent of perestroika, the CPM assumed a sharply critical stance. The party attacked Gorbachev for the collapse of Communism in Eastern Europe; denounced Soviet support for the war against Iraq; and, in August 1991, celebrated the hardliners' putsch against Gorbachev, only to be further isolated with the coup's failure and the rise of Boris Yeltsin. At its 14th Congress in 1992, surrounded by portraits of Marx, Lenin, and Stalin, the CPM reaffirmed its faith in Marxism-Leninism, even as younger party members were beginning to question the leadership.

The Communist Party of India has a more evenly distributed national support than the CPM, but it is weak everywhere, save for pockets of Bihar. Before the collapse of world Communism, the CPI was officially recognized by Moscow, but while it gave formal support to glasnost and perestroika, the CPI looked with increasing unease on the events in the Soviet Union. With the apparent ouster of Gorbachev in the attempted coup, the CPI joined the CPM in celebration.

Isolated internationally, except for their fraternal ties to China, the CPM and CPI are still a vocal, if muted, force in Indian politics. At the national level, in the 1989 and 1991 elections, they allied with the National Front against the Congress (I), and, as the Left Front, they stand with the Janata Dal and scattered socialists in Parliament in opposition to the policies of economic liberalization pursued by the government of Narasimha Rao.

Regional Parties in India

The fortunes of India's numerous regional parties have fluctuated considerably over the past four decades. For the most part, regional parties remain important as a means of expressing local grievances. However, in the past, regional sentiments have not always been enduring, and the electoral performance of regional parties has been erratic. Most are single-issue parties that emerge as expressions of grievances due to some social or economic disparity or emerging new identity. They tend to disappear once their program is accomplished or their leader dies. Only a few have persisted and taken deep roots.

The most important have been the DMK and the AIADMK in Tamil Nadu; the Akali Dal in the Punjab; and the National Conference in Jammu and Kashmir. More recent arrivals on the scene are the Telugu Desam in Andhra Pradesh and the Asom Gana Parishad in Assam.[91]

The DMK and AIADMK

Rooted in Tamil nationalism going back to the turn of the century, the Dravida Munnetra Kazhagam (DMK) and its offshoot, the All-India Anna DMK (AIADMK), have dominated politics in Tamil Nadu since first taking power in 1967. The two parties are heirs of the Dravidian movement, in direct lineage from E. V. Ramaswamy Naicker's "self-respect movement," which aimed to purge South India of Brahmin tyranny, and of his Dravida Kazhagam (DK), or Dravidian Federation, founded in 1944, which called for the creation of a separate and independent state of Dravidasthan.

In reaction to the elitist character of the DK, C. N. Annadurai, a journalist and film writer, led a breakaway faction in 1949 to form the Dravida Munnetra Kazhagam, the Dravidian Progressive Federation. Whereas the DK, continuing as a reform movement, had never contested elections, the DMK combined the techniques of agitation with electoral activity. The party, although still waving the banner of Dravidasthan, became increasingly oriented to pragmatic economic issues. During the Chinese invasion, the DMK rallied to the national cause, and on adoption of the antisecessionist amendment to the Constitution in 1963, the party formally dropped its demand for an independent Tamil Nadu. Although the DMK failed to gain a foothold outside of Tamil Nadu, the party expanded its social base within the state, attracting non Brahmin and Brahmin alike with appeals to Tamil sentiment in the demands for greater state autonomy and less northern domination.[92]

With each election, the DMK extended its base of strength from the urban centers deeper into rural areas. The DMK and its army of student volunteers responded to the imposition of Hindi on an unwilling South with demonstrations against the state Congress govern-

[91] See S. Bhatnagar and Pradeep Kumar, eds., *Regional Political Parties in India* (New Delhi: Ess Ess, 1988).

[92] See Robert L. Hardgrave, Jr., *The Dravidian Movement* (Bombay: Popular Prakashan, 1965); and Hardgrave, "The Politics of Tamil Nationalism," *Pacific Affairs*, 37 (Winter 1964–65):396–411. For the DK, see Mohan Ram, "Ramaswami Naicker and the Dravidian Movement," *Economic and Political Weekly*, 9 Annual Number (February 1974): 217–24.

ment. A number of Tamil film writers, directors, and actors added their glamor to the rising party, and, in a symbiotic relationship with the party, the swashbuckling hero M. G. Ramachandran (M. G. R.), "idol of the masses," rose to become the most popular film star in South India.[93]

In 1967 the DMK crushed the Congress party in a landslide victory. As it gained increased support, the DMK transformed from a secessionist movement, nurtured by vague dreams of a glorious past and an impossible future, to a party of increasing political maturity and parliamentary discipline.[94] But in 1969 Annadurai, "Anna," founder and leader of the DMK, died. The leadership of the party and government was taken by M. Karunanidhi, who, like his predecessor, was a film writer and director. M. G. R. soon challenged Karunanidhi, and in 1972 the party split, with M. G. R. forming a new party, the All-India Anna DMK, which pledged to return the party to the principles of Annadurai.[95] The 1977 assembly elections brought the AIADMK to power in Tamil Nadu, with film star M. G. Ramachandran serving as chief minister until his death in 1987. On the death of M. G. R., his wife Janaki, a retired actress, succeeded to the leadership of the party and the state, but she was immediately challenged by Jayalalitha, AIADMK propaganda secretary and M. G. R.'s romantic heroine in scores of films.[96] The party split, and against a divided AIADMK, the DMK, under the leadership of film director M. Karunanidhi, returned to power in state assembly elections in January 1989. Little more than one year later, the government was dismissed and President's Rule imposed on Tamil Nadu—ostensibly for its failure to control the activities of Sri Lankan Tamil guerrillas operating within the state. The action, however, was probably taken by Prime Minister Chandra Shekhar at the behest of Rajiv Gandhi in a move against the National Front.

Both the DMK and the AIADMK have been, at one time or another, allied at the national level with the Congress party. M. G. R.

[93] Robert L. Hardgrave, Jr., "Politics and the Film in Tamil Nadu: The Stars and the DMK," *Asian Survey*, 13 (March 1973):288–305; and Hardgrave, "When Stars Displace the Gods: The Folk Culture of Cinema in Tamil Nadu," *Essays in the Political Sociology of South India* (New Delhi: Usha, 1979), 92–124.

[94] For an analysis of DMK ideology and the party's rise to power, see Marguerite Ross Barnett, *The Politics of Cultural Nationalism in South India* (Princeton, N.J.: Princeton University Press, 1976).

[95] K. Ramaswamy Sastry, "A Chronicle of the DMK Split," *Economic and Political Weekly*, 30 March 1974, pp. 527–31.

[96] These bizarre events are recounted in *India Today*, January 15, 1988, pp. 6–14, and February 15, 1988, pp. 20–22.

had secured an alliance with the Congress (I), and this was sustained by Jayalalitha as leader of a reunited AIADMK. The DMK was a part of the National Front. Elections for the Tamil Nadu assembly were held in conjunction with the 1991 parliamentary elections, and the AIADMK—supported by the Congress (I) and the sympathy wave generated by the assassination of Rajiv Gandhi—swept to a dramatic victory, with Jayalalitha as chief minister of the new AIADMK government.

The Akali Dal

The Akali Dal is both regional and communal. It is confined to the Punjab and is open only to Sikhs, of whom it claims to be the sole representative. The Akali Dal was first organized as a reform group to bring the gurdwaras (temples) under the control of the orthodox Sikh community. Following a policy of direct action, the Akalis succeeded, in 1925, in bringing the gurdwaras under the authority of a committee elected by universal adult franchise within the community. Control of the committee, with jurisdiction over hundreds of gurdwaras and their endowments and with great patronage powers, considerably strengthened the position of the Akali Dal in the Punjab. Master Tara Singh, leader of the dominant Akali faction until 1965, declared the necessity of a Sikh state to protect the gurdwaras and defend the Sikh religion. At the time of partition, the Akalis sought an independent Sikhistan, but in the agitation of the 1950s for linguistic states, the Akali demand was translated to that of a Punjabi-speaking state of Punjabi Suba. That goal, after prolonged agitation, was finally achieved in 1966.[97]

For all its influence, however, the Akali Dal has never had wide electoral appeal, even among the Sikhs. Having achieved its Punjabi Suba, the Akalis received only 25 percent of the vote in the 1967 elections, but in a united front with the Congress dissidents, the Jana Sangh, and the Communists, the Akali Dal led the formation of a coalition government. In 1971, as a result of Akali defections to Congress, however, the Punjab government fell, and President's Rule was imposed. It was not until 1977 that the Akalis again gained power, this time with the support of the CPM and the Janata Party. With Indira Gandhi's return to power in 1980, the Prime Minister called for dismissal of the governments in those states under opposition rule

[97]For the early history of the Akali Dal, see Baldev Raj Nayar, *Minority Politics in the Punjab* (Princeton, N.J.: Princeton University Press, 1966).

where Congress had won a majority of the parliamentary seats. Fresh elections brought the Congress party to power in the Punjab, and set the stage for the series of events that brought the state to crisis.

The Akalis sought to recoup their strength through the movement for greater Punjab autonomy, only to be overwhelmed by the rise of Sikh militancy. The 1985 Punjab accord provided the basis for elections and the formation of a new Akali Dal government, but its dismissal in 1987 returned the Punjab to President's Rule. The Akali Dal is today divided into five major factions and numerous splinters, and has lost all capacity to speak for the Sikhs with a united voice.[98]

The National Conference

The pre-eminent party in Jammu and Kashmir, India's only Muslim-majority state, was long the National Conference (NC). In 1982 the leadership of the party and the government passed from Sheikh Abdullah, "the Lion of Kashmir," who had dominated the affairs of the state for 50 years, to his son Farooq Abdullah. Virtually from the time Farooq took office, Indira Gandhi began machinations to oust the government, and she finally did so in 1984 by engineering a split in the National Conference that brought a pro-Congress NC faction to power. In assembly elections in 1987, Rajiv Gandhi sought to extend Congress (I) influence in the state through an alliance with Farooq, but the elections that returned the National Conference to power were marked by fraud, and Kashmiris viewed the new government as illegitimate, and Farooq as little more than a puppet of the Center. Deepened political alienation of Kashmir's Muslims soon erupted in violence and the movement for secession that has brought the state to civil war. In January 1990, the Center imposed President's Rule, dismissing the corrupt and inept Farooq government that by its conduct had relegated the National Conference to oblivion.[99]

The Telugu Desam

Formed in 1982 by film star T. N. Rama Rao, the party, in an assertion of "Telugu pride," defeated the Congress in the January 1983 Andhra elections.[100] The party is populist in orientation, but its *raison*

[98] See pp. 152–60 for a detailed account of the crisis that has engulfed the Punjab over the past decade.

[99] The Kashmir crisis is examined in pp. 160–63.

[100] See N. Innaiah, *Saffron Star over Andhra Pradash: Genesis, Growth and Critical Analysis of Telugu Desam Party* (Hyderabad: Book Links, 1984).

d'être is the issue of greater state autonomy. Within a few months after taking office, Rama Rao, grooming himself for a more national role, took center stage in hosting a conference of leaders of 14 opposition parties, a step toward opposition unity out of which came a call for the redress of the federal balance and devolution of power to the states.

Within the state Rama Rao's popularity began to wane, but in 1984 he gained a new lease on his political life when the Center made a clumsy attempt to depose him. The attempted "coup," staged by Indira Gandhi, brought a volley of opposition protest, and the national press, even those papers normally pro-Congress, were virtually unanimous in their condemnation of the "wholly illegal and unjustifiable" intervention by the Center in the affairs of a state. Restored to power with renewed strength, Rama Rao, clad in the saffron robes associated with his film roles as Hindu deities, led his Telugu Desam to victory with a two-thirds majority in the Andhra assembly elections in 1985.

Rama Rao continued his efforts to forge opposition unity and was instrumental in 1988 in forming the National Front, becoming its Chairman. At home, however, Rama Rao's autocratic style as chief minister was wearing thin. The 1989 elections brought the National Front to power at the Center, but in the Andhra assembly elections, the Telugu Desam fell to the Congress (I). In the 1991 parliamentary elections, the Telugu Desam won 13 of the state's 42 Lok Sabha seats, but in March 1992, in a test of support for the Congress (I) government of Narasimha Rao, a native of Andhra Pradesh, 9 members of the Telugu Desam broke ranks with the opposition, splitting the party. With only a rump of 4 in Parliament and his own charisma fading, T. N. Rama Rao oversees a party without a social base that is now little more than a projection of his own personality.

The Asom Gana Parishad

In Assam, the Asom Gana Parishad (AGP) was formed before the 1985 state assembly elections by various groups involved in the student-led anti-immigrant movement.[101] The party came to power on a program calling for the protection of Assamese language and culture, but its tenure in office was tarnished by corruption, misrule, and a breakdown of law and order, with the Bodo tribal agitation and the insurgency of the United Liberation Front of Asom. In 1990, dismiss-

[101] See pp. 150–52.

ing the AGP government, the Center imposed President's Rule. Just before the 1991 elections, the party split, and the AGP—a constituent of the National Front—suffered a steep decline in its statewide vote, from 33 to 18 percent, and the Congress (I) returned to power in Assam.

Perspective on Politics

The Indian party system since independence has been marked by a decline in the once-dominant Congress party; the inability of an increasingly fragmented opposition to forge a centrist alternative; and the growing regionalization of parties. Although the opposition was able to defeat the Congress in 1977 and 1989, neither the right-of-center Janata Party nor the left-of-center Janata Dal was able to hold its diverse coalition together for very long or provide effective government. Indian parties and the party system are entering a new era. The rise of Hindu fundamentalism; growing concern over Indian unity; the crisis of the Communist left brought on by the collapse of Communism in Eastern Europe and the former Soviet Union; and the end of the Nehru dynasty will shape new patterns of alliances, coalitions, and party development as the party system enters a new period of fluidity in the 1990s.

Recommended Reading

*Bouton, Marshall M., and/or Philip Oldenburg, eds., *India Briefing*. Boulder, Colo.: Westview Press, 1987– . Published in cooperation with the Asia Society, this annual collection of essays begins with an analysis of Indian politics in the previous year. Highly recommended.

Brass, Paul R., *Caste, Faction, and Party in Indian Politics*, Vol. 1, *Faction and Party*. Delhi: Chanakya, 1983. Collected articles.

———, *Factional Politics in an Indian State: The Congress Party in Uttar Pradesh*. Berkeley: University of California Press, 1966. An analysis of party organization at the local and district levels and of the impact of internal factionalism on party effectiveness.

*Available in a paperback edition.

———, and Marcus F. Franda, eds., *Radical Politics in South Asia*. Cambridge, Mass.: M.I.T. Press, 1973. A comparative study of regional radical movements, with an incisive introductory essay by Brass.

*Frankel, Francine R., *India's Political Economy, 1947–77: The Gradual Revolution*. Princeton, N.J.: Princeton University Press, 1978. A major work analyzing the contradiction between the practice of accommodative politics and the commitment to social change.

Graham, Bruce, *Hindu Nationalism and Indian Politics*. Cambridge: Cambridge University Press, 1990. An excellent study of the origins and development of the Bharatiya Jana Sangh.

*Hart, Henry C., ed., *Indira Gandhi's India: A Political System Reappraised*. Boulder, Colo.: Westview Press, 1976. A superb collection of papers which places the 1975–77 emergency in wide perspective.

Jayakar, Pupul, *Indira Gandhi: A Biography*, New Delhi: Viking/Penguin, 1992. An intimate portrait by a close friend.

Kochanek, Stanley A., *The Congress Party of India*. Princeton, N.J.: Princeton University Press, 1968. Focuses on the development of the party at the national level in the years since independence, the changing role of the Congress president and the Working Committee, and their relationship to the Prime Minister and the government.

*Kohli, Atul, *Democracy and Discontent: India's Growing Crisis of Governability*. Cambridge: Cambridge University Press, 1990. An astute analysis of an interventionist national government and weak political parties that have made governing India so difficult.

———, ed., *India's Democracy: An Analysis of Changing State–Society Relations*. Princeton: Princeton University Press, 1988. A fine collection of essays on leadership, parties, politics, and social conflict.

Kothari, Rajni, ed., *Party Systems and Election Studies*. Occasional Papers of the Center for Developing Societies, No. 1. Bombay: Allied Publishers, 1967. A collection of essays by some of India's most astute political scientists. Of particular importance are the essays on the system of one-party dominance.

———, *Politics and the People: In Search of a Humane India*. 2 vols. Delhi: Ajanta, 1989. Selected essays by one of India's most distinguished political scientists.

Malhotra, Inder, *Indira Gandhi: A Personal and Political Biography*. London: Hodder & Stoughton, 1989. A balanced portrayal by a leading Indian journalist.

Merchant, Minhaz, *Rajiv Gandhi: The End of a Dream*. New Delhi: Viking/Penguin, 1991. The first major biography.

Overstreet, Gene D., and Marshall Windmiller, *Communism in India*. Berkeley: University of California Press, 1959. Still the most complete study of the early Communist movement in India, its history, organization, and leadership.

Sen Gupta, Bhabani, *Rajiv Gandhi: A Political Study*. New Delhi: Konarak Publishers, 1989. An excellent critique of Rajiv Gandhi's performance.

Sirsikar, V. M., and L. Fernandes, *Indian Political Parties*. Meerut: Meenakshi Prakashan, 1984. A valuable survey of the background and environment of India's parties, their ideologies, organization, and performance.

Sisson, Richard, and Ramashraya Roy, eds., *Diversity and Dominance in Indian Politics*, Vol. I: *Changing Bases of Congress Support*. New Delhi: Sage, 1990. A perceptive collection of essays dealing with the adaptation, changing environment, electoral support base, and transformation of the Congress party.

*Vanaik, Achin, *The Painful Transition: Bourgeois Democracy in India*. New York: Verso, 1990. A Marxist class analysis of Indian politics.

*Weiner, Myron, *The Indian Paradox: Essays in Indian Politics*. New Delhi: Sage Publications, 1989. An excellent survey of the post-Nehru development of India.

Zaidi, A. M., *The Annual Register of Indian Political Parties*. New Delhi: S. Chand. A yearly compendium of information and documents pertaining to all the recognized national parties.

Chapter 7

Elections and Political Behavior

INDIA'S SUCCESSFUL COMPLETION OF 10 NATIONAL ELECTIONS since 1947 has confounded both the prophets of doom who see each Indian election as its last, and the theorists of political development who see elections as a luxury that the Third World cannot afford. Despite massive illiteracy and poverty, India has succeeded in developing both effective administrative machinery and popular enthusiasm that have enabled it to conduct the largest elections in the world based on mass franchise. In the past 45 years, elections have grown in size; the electorate has shown increased sophistication and awareness; and mass political mobilization has contributed to the integration of Indian diversities in the larger whole.

Changes in the party system, however, have begun to have dramatic effect on the stability of the Indian political system. The decline of the once-dominant Congress party, the persistence of opposition fragmentation, and the regionalization of parties have increased the importance of coalition and alliance politics.

The 1991 parliamentary elections that returned the Congress (I) to power were the second within two years, a span of time that embraced four prime ministers—Rajiv Gandhi, V. P. Singh, Chandra Shekhar, and P. V. Narasimha Rao—and the government of Narasimha Rao was India's third minority government since November 1989. While Congress allies among regional parties gave it majority support in the Lok Sabha, its ability to form a government was essentially the product of a divided opposition.

The 1989 Elections

In the 1980s, opposition parties struggled to forge a unity that would give them power. In 1988, seven opposition parties hammered out a coordinated strategy. Four centrist parties—the Janata Party, the two Lok Dal factions, and the Jan Morcha, led by V. P. Singh—merged into the new Janata Dal under Singh's leadership. The regional parties—the Telugu Desam (Andhra Pradesh), the Dravida Munnetra Kazhagam (Tamil Nadu), and the Asom Gana Parishad (Assam)—together with the tiny Congress (S)—allied to form the National Front. The National Front reflected the regional strengths of its constituent parties, and support for the Janata Dal, though "national" in name, was largely concentrated in North India. The National Front alone could not expect to secure a parliamentary majority. However, the Bharatiya Janata Party and the Left Front, while regarding each other as an unacceptable ally, were prepared separately to enter into electoral adjustments with the National Front on a constituency-by-constituency basis in order to field a united opposition to the Congress (I). This proved possible because BJP strength was mainly in the states of Madhya Pradesh, Himachal Pradesh, Delhi, Rajasthan, and Gujarat, while the Left was largely confined to its strongholds of Kerala and West Bengal, where the Communist Party of India (Marxist) (CPM) was the ruling party. Thus, with elections called for November 1989, the National Front, the BJP, and the Left were able in some 400 constituencies to select a single opposition candidate (usually from the locally strongest party) to give the Congress (I) candidate a straight fight.

The strategy worked, but for the first time, no party held a majority of Lok Sabha seats. The Congress (I), with 39.5 percent of the vote, emerged with the largest number (197), but the combined opposition parties against Rajiv Gandhi had enough seats to form a government. Prime Minister V. P. Singh headed a minority coalition government of the successful parties that had contested the elections as the National Front alliance: the Janata Dal (with 143 seats), the Telugu Desam (2 seats), and the Congress (S) (1 seat). Lacking a parliamentary majority, the National Front government depended on the outside support of the BJP on the right (85 seats) and the Left Front (52 seats). Each chose to remain outside the government to avoid being tainted by direct association with the other.

The 1989 elections had brought the National Front to power, but dissention within the Janata Dal doomed any chance for a stable and effective government. With the BJP's withdrawal of support on the

Ayodhya issue, the V. P. Singh government was poised to fall. In Parliament, as the vote of confidence approached, Chandra Shekhar engineered a split in the Janata Dal, denying Singh support from a substantial portion of his own party. With only the support of the Left Front and what was left of the National Front, Singh lost the vote, 142 to 346, and submitted his resignation. The President invited Rajiv Gandhi, as leader of the largest party in the Lok Sabha, to form a government, but he declined, as expected, preferring to build Congress (I) strength for an election at a time of his own choosing. Gandhi gave his support to Chandra Shekhar, who was sworn in as Prime Minister, with only 58 members in his splinter Samajvadi Janata Party. Chandra Shekhar and Gandhi were deeply distrustful of one another, and it was only a matter of time before Gandhi would withdraw support, forcing elections that he believed would return the Congress (I) to power. In March 1991, Chandra Shekhar, informing Parliament that he was no longer able to function as Prime Minister, resigned and asked the President to call elections.

The 1991 Elections

The May parliamentary elections, involving security concerns for anticipated violence, were scheduled for three rounds, with simultaneous assembly elections in Haryana, Kerala, Tamil Nadu, Uttar Pradesh, West Bengal, and the Union Territory of Pondicherry. The troubled states of Assam and Punjab were to conduct polling separately in June for both Parliament and state assemblies. Jammu and Kashmir, paralyzed by insurgency, would hold no elections. Facing an electorate of 514 million voters, some 9000 candidates filed for 537 seats in the Lok Sabha and 20,000 for 1456 state assembly seats.

The pattern of electoral confrontation varied from state to state, but overall, with Prime Minister Chandra Shekhar's Samajvadi Janata Party having only limited support, the contest for power was essentially triangular—the Janata Dal and its regional and Left allies; the Bharatiya Janata Party; and the Congress (I). Each campaigned on the issue it had made its own. The National Front, led by V. P. Singh (Janata Dal), and its allied Left Front emphasized social justice, with the Janata Dal's particular appeal directed to the backward castes (intended beneficiaries of the Mandal job reservations) and Muslims (for whom Singh's "secular" stand on Ayodhya had special appeal). The Bharatiya Janata Party, with the symbol of Ayodhya, appealed to Hindu sentiment and challenged what it portrayed as the "privileges" accorded Muslims and other minorities under India's secular state. The Congress (I), led by Gandhi, promised political stability and offered itself as the only party that could provide a government that works.

The assassination of Rajiv Gandhi on May 21, following the first round of the elections, shook the party and the nation. Stunned and in seeming admission of dependency on the Nehru–Gandhi dynasty, the party high command asked Rajiv's Italian-born wife Sonia to assume the Congress (I) presidency. Resisting pressure from the coterie that had surrounded Rajiv, Sonia refused, and the party turned, as recounted in Chapter 6, in compromise to Narasimha Rao. The Election Commission rescheduled the second and the third rounds of polling for June 12 and 15.

With the non-Congress parties divided, the Congress (I) was able to translate 37.6 percent of the vote into 227 seats, an increase from its 197 seats in 1989, but still short of a majority in the Lok Sabha. The results reflected what analysts thought to be a "sympathy vote" in the second and third rounds, following Gandhi's death, with an increase in voter turnout and in support for the Congress (I), accounting for as many as 30 to 40 seats. The shift was most notable in rural areas and among women and Muslims.Even then, its 37.6 percent of the vote was a decline from the 39.5 percent it secured in 1989, and the swings in support varied state by state, with Congress strength increasing in 1991 over 1989 in 11 states and 2 Union Territories, and declining in 12 states and 5 territories.

As in 1989, the party's greatest strength was in the South, but while it picked up seats in the North, the Congress (I) was virtually wiped out in the large states of Uttar Pradesh and Bihar. In UP, its share of the vote declined from 31.8 percent in 1989 to 19.9 percent in 1991: traditional support among the upper castes in the state was lost to the BJP on the Ayodhya issue; untouchables were weaned away by both the Janata Dal and the Bahujan Samaj Party (BSP), an untouchable party that garnered 9.5 percent of the vote in UP; and the Muslims went largely to the Janata Dal. In state assembly elections, the Congress (I) won in Haryana, Kerala, and Assam, and its All-India Anna Dravida Munnetra Kazhagam (AIADMK) ally took power in Tamil Nadu.

The Bharatiya Janata Party raised its strength in Parliament from 85 to 119 seats, and BJP candidates came in second in some 130 constituencies. Over all, the BJP increased its share of the vote to 21 percent from 11.4 percent in 1989. The party's gains were dramatic in Gujarat and in Uttar Pradesh, and in the latter, with support from upper-caste Hindus and, to some degree, from the backward castes, the BJP rode the Ayodhya issue to power in assembly elections, forming the first

BJP government in India's most populous state. Winning 221 of the 404 assembly seats for which polling was held, the BJP saw its share of the vote surge from 7.6 percent in 1989 to 35.3 percent. A cautionary note, however, is appropriate in assessing its success in UP. The BJP victory was essentially the product of the Janata Dal split, and a modest shift in a number of constituencies toward either the Janata Dal or Congress would have resulted in a BJP loss. Moreover, nationwide, impressive as its 21 percent of the vote may be, with the comparatively low voter turnout, it is less than 11 percent of the total electorate.

Notable in the BJP's advance were inroads into new areas, particularly in the South. In Andhra, it went from 2.0 percent of the vote in 1989 to 9.6 percent in 1990, and in Karnataka, its vote increased from 2.6 in 1989 to 28.1 in 1991. In West Bengal, though it did not win a single seat, the BJP took 11.7 percent of the vote. In the three states where the BJP took power in the 1990 assembly elections—Madhya Pradesh, Rajasthan, and Himachal Pradesh— the party lost parliamentary seats. Here, even as the BJP slightly increased its share of the vote, polarization against the BJP benefited the Congress (I).

The BJP was the only major party nationwide to increase its percentage of the vote over 1989, save for the CPM, which marginally increased its share. The Hindu paramilitary Rashtriya Swayamsevak Sangh (RSS) was at the core of the BJP campaign organization, and the party campaigned with a dual emphasis on Hindu identity (Hindutva) and nationalism—fused in the symbols of Ayodhya and Kashmir. The impact of Ayodhya varied considerably from state to state, however, and, as with the Janata Dal's Mandal reservation issue, it was shaped in the context of local issues. While national leaders like Advani stressed Ayodhya as a symbol of the Hindu majority's right to protect its own cultural heritage, at the lower levels, Hindu militants fully exploited Hindu religious sentiment and anti-Muslim feeling. Particularly disturbing in the analysis of the election results both in 1989 and 1991 is the apparent relation of communal tension to BJP success. An atmosphere of communal conflict mobilized Hindu support for the BJP, and BJP gains were most notable in those areas experiencing Hindu-Muslim rioting.

BJP support, as evidenced in exit polls, came heavily from higher-caste, urban, and younger voters, but, in 1991, the BJP extended its support more deeply into rural India, with inroads occurring among the backward caste and untouchables.

The National Front fared poorly, with the Janata Dal reduced from 141 to 56 seats, and from 17.8 percent in 1989 to 11.6 percent of the vote in 1991. Janata Dal strength was concentrated in Bihar, where

Table 7–1
1991 Lok Sabha Elections

Party	*Party Position before elections**	*Number of Candidates*	*Number of Seats Won***	*Percentage of Seats*	*Percentage of Votes*
Congress (I)	194	477	227	44.4	37.6
BJP	86	461	119	23.3	21.0
Janata Dal	76	297	56	11.0	11.6
SJP	54	353	5	1.0	3.5
CPM	33	59	35	6.8	6.7
CPI	12	38	14	2.7	2.5
Telugu Desam	2	34	13	2.5	3.0
AIADMK	11	11	11	2.0	2.3
Shiv Sena	3	21	4	0.8	0.8
Others	29	1556	26	5.1	6.3
Independents	10	5646	1	0.2	4.7
Nominated	2				
Speaker	1				
Vacancies	32		32		
TOTAL	545	8953	543		

*Party position as of March 13, 1991
**Elections were not conducted in Kashmir (6 seats) and Punjab (13 seats); other vacancies to be filled by by-election. Punjab elections were subsequently held in February 1992.
SOURCE Press Trust of India. Figures are unofficial and vary slightly among sources.

the Janata Dal Chief Minister, a backward-class leader, turned out the vote on the appeal of social justice symbolized by the Mandal reservations. The Left Front held its own, going from 44 to 49 seats, with about 9 percent of the vote. The CPM held its majority in the West Bengal assembly, but lost Kerala to the Congress (I). Chandra Shekhar's Samajvadi Janata Party (SJP) won only 5 seats in Parliament.

The electoral map reveals no national or, indeed, clearly discernible regional patterns in voting. There is considerable fluidity in the Indian electorate, as revealed in the swings in the percentage of support for the major parties from election to election. These swings, as underscored in 1991, vary from state to state, as seen in the pattern of voting for the Congress (I), and are shaped largely by local factors, such as caste, and the variable impact of "national" issues and leaders. In the state assembly elections, there was, to some degree, a swing against incumbent parties, and a willingness by the voters to

Table 7–2
1991 Lok Sabha Elections by State and Territory: Showing Number of Seats and Percentage of Votes

State	*Total Seats*	*Congress (I)*	*BJP*	*Janata Dal*	*SJP*	*CPM*	*CPI*	*Regional Party***	*Others*
Andhra Pradesh	42‡	24 45.8%	1 9.64%	0 0.58%	0 1.1%	1 2.6%	1 2.1%	Telugu Desam: 13 33.2%	1 10.0%
Arunachal Pradesh	2	2 69.5%	0 6.2%	0 24.1%					0 0.3%
Assam	14	8 39.3%	2 13.8%	0 7.7%	0 0.9%	1 7.0%	0 2.8%	AGP: 1 18.0%	2 10.5%
Bihar	54‡	1 22.5%	5 19.0%	28 32.4%	0 5.8%	1 1.7%	8 7.9%	JMM: 6 5.6%	0 4.5%
Goa	2	2 56.9%	0 15.4%	0 1.0%			0 1.5%		0 25.2%
Gujarat	26‡	4 28.8%	20 52.1%	0 3.48%	0 0.6%			JD (G): 1 13.7%	0 1.3%
Haryana	10	9 41.1%	0 11.2%	0 13.8%	0 28.2%				0 5.7%
Himachal Pradesh	4	2 45.9%	2 42.6%	0 6.9%	0 1.3%		0 0.7%		0 2.6%
Jammu and Kashmir	6				ELECTIONS NOT CONDUCTED				
Karnataka	28‡	22 43.7%	4 28.1%	0 18.5%	1 4.2%	0 0.2%	0 0.7%		0 4.6%
Kerala	20	13 38.1%	0 4.0%	0 4.5%	0 0.1%	3 22.3%	0 8.0%		4 23.1%
Madhya Pradesh	48	27 47.3%	12 43.7%	0 4.7%		0 .02%	0 0.4%		1 3.2%

(Continued)

Table 7–2 *(Continued)*

State	*Total Seats*	*Congress (I)*	*BJP*	*Janata Dal*	*SJP*	*CPM*	*CPI*	*Regional Party***	*Others*
Maharashtra	48‡	37 46.0%	5 19.5%	1 10.6%	0 0.7%	1 1.3%	0 1.0%	Shiv Sena: 4 7.8%	0 13.1%
Manipur	2	1 44.8%	0 9.4%	0 21.6%	0 0.8%			MPP: 1 23.37%	
Meghalaya	2	2 59.3%	0 9.9%				0 1.8%		0 29.0%
Mizoram	1	1 39.5%		0 24.6%				MNF: 0 35.6%	
Nagaland	1	0 44.3%	0 3.0%					NPC: 1 52.7%	
Orissa	21‡	12 44.4%	0 10.0%	6 34.7%	0 3.8%	1 2.1%	1 3.3%		0 1.8%
Punjab*	13	12 50.9%	0 16.6%	0 1.9%		0 3.5%	0 1.7%		1 25.4%
Rajasthan	25	13 45.0%	12 41.9%	0 5.9%	0 3.3%	0 0.7%	0 0.1%		0 2.7%
Sikkim	1					0 3.0%		SSP: 1 93.6%	0 3.4%
Tamil Nadu	39	28 43.5%	0 1.7%	0 3.0%	0 0.2%	0 2.5%	0 2.1%	AIADKM: 11 / DMK: 0 18.5% / 23.9%	0 4.77%
Tripura	2	2 86.0%	0 3.1%			0 6.8%			0 4.14%

Uttar Pradesh	85[‡]	5 19.9%	50 35.3%	22 23.0%	4 11.1%	0 0.8%	1 1.1%		0 8.8%
West Bengal	42	5 36.6%	0 11.7%	0 1.2%	0 0.2%	27 36.0%	3 3.8%		7 10.4%
Andaman and Nicobar Islands	1	1 50.4%	0 4.9%			0 44.1%			0 0.6%
Chandigarh	1	1 37.7%	0 30.2%	0 2.9%	0 24.3%				0 5.0%
Dadra and Nagar Haveli	1	1 62.4%	0 35.8%						0 1.8%
Daman and Div	1	0 30.7%	1 43.0%	0 3.7%					0 22.7%
Delhi	7	2 41.0%	5 41.7%	0 14.7%	0 1.3%		0 0.1%		0 1.3%
Lakshadweep	1	1 50.6%		0 49.4%					
Pondicherry	1	1 46.5%	0 1.7%		0 0.9%			DMK: 0 31.8%	0 19.6%

*Polling conducted Feb. 19, 1992.

**Regional parties:

AGP—Asom Gana Parishad
JMM—Jharkhand Mukti Morcha
JD (G)—Janata Dal (Gujarat)
MPP—Manipur People's Party
MNF—Mizo National Front
NPC—Nagaland People's Council
SSP—Sikkim Sangram Parishad

‡Countermanded seats: Andra Pradesh, 1; Bihar, 5; Gujarat, 1; Karnataka 1; Maharashtra, 1; Orissa, 1; and Uttar Pradesh, 3. The seats were subsequently filled in by elections.

SOURCE Press Trust of India

"throw the rascals out." Only in the CPM's West Bengal was the ruling party confirmed by the electorate. Within the variable pattern of electoral politics among India's 25 states and 7 Union Territories, the states individually reflect a relatively high degree of coherence in the swing from election to election, and in most states, two dominant parties have emerged. But the two parties vary from state to state, and, despite the dramatic expansion of BJP support, Congress remains the only genuine all-India party.

In November 1991, by-elections for 15 Lok Sabha seats and 57 assembly seats tended to reinforce the results of the general elections. Of the Lok Sabha seats, the Congress (I) won 8; the BJP, 2; and the Janata Dal, 3. The postponed elections for the Punjab assembly and parliamentary seats were conducted in February 1992. With an Akali boycott that reduced voter turnout to 21.6 percent, the Congress (I) took control of the state and won 12 of the 13 parliamentary seats. Although still short of a majority on its own, with its regional party allies, the Congress (I) government of Narasimha Rao now commanded the confidence of a majority in parliament.

Elections[1]

The Indian elections are a phenomenal undertaking. With some 272,000,000 people voting, the 1991 parliamentary elections were the largest ever conducted in world history. There were 9 officially recognized national parties, 38 state parties, and a total of 8953 candidates for the 537 contested seats.

Voting Procedure

The Indian Constitution provides for universal adult suffrage, and the 61st Amendment, passed in 1988, lowered the voting age from 21 to 18, adding 36,000,000 voters to the rolls. In 1991, some 521,000,000 people were eligible to vote, three times the number in 1952, when India first went to the polls. From the members of the Election Commission down to the polling officers, more than 3,500,000 civilian officials, along with some 2,000,000 police, paramilitary, and military forces, were involved in conducting the parliamentary elections. There were 2,400,000 ballot boxes in 600,000 polling stations, one each for

[1] On the mechanics of elections, see N. S. Gehlot, *Elections and Electoral Administration in India* (New Delhi: Deep & Deep, 1992).

Table 7–3
The Distribution of Candidates, Seats, and Votes in Lok Sabha Elections, 1952–1989

Parties	*Number of Candidates*	*Number of Seats Won*	*Percentage of Seats*	*Percentage of Votes*
1952				
Congress	472	364	74.4	45.00
CPI	49	16	3.3	3.30
Socialist Party	256	12	2.5	10.60
Kisan Mazdoor Praja Party	145	9	1.8	5.80
Hindu Mahasabha	31	4	0.8	0.95
Jana Sangh	93	3	0.6	3.10
Ram Rajya Parishad	55	3	0.6	2.03
Republican Party	27	2	0.4	2.36
Other parties	215	35	7.2	11.10
Independents	521	41	8.4	15.80
Total	1864	489		
1957				
Congress	490	371	75.1	47.78
CPI	108	27	5.4	8.92
Praja Socialist Party (SP and KMPP)	189	19	3.8	10.41
Jana Sangh	130	4	0.8	5.93
Republican Party	19	4	0.8	1.50
Hindu Mahasabha	19	1	0.2	0.86
Ram Rajya Parishad	15	—	—	0.38
Other parties	73	29	5.9	4.81
Independents	475	39	7.9	19.39
Total	1518	494		
1962				
Congress	488	361	73.1	46.02
CPI	137	29	5.9	9.96
Swatantra	172	18	3.6	6.80
Jana Sangh	198	14	2.8	6.44
Praja Socialist Party	166	12	2.4	6.84
DMK	18	7	1.4	2.02
Socialist Party	107	6	1.2	2.49
Republican Party	69	3	0.6	2.78
Ram Rajya Parishad	35	2	0.4	0.55
Hindu Mahasabha	32	1	0.2	0.44
Other parties	64	14	2.9	4.31
Independents	497	27	5.5	12.27
Total	1983	494		

(Continued)

Table 7–3 *(Continued)*

Parties	Number of Candidates	Number of Seats Won	Percentage of Seats	Percentage of Votes
1967				
Congress	516	283	54.42	40.73
Swatantra	179	44	8.46	8.68
Jana Sangh	250	35	6.73	9.41
DMK	25	25	4.80	3.90
CPI	109	23	4.42	5.19
Samyukta Socialist Party	122	23	4.42	4.92
CPM	59	19	3.65	4.21
Praja Socialist Party	109	13	2.50	3.06
Republican Party	70	1	0.19	2.48
Other parties	65	19	3.65	3.67
Independents	865	35	6.73	13.75
Total	2369	520		
1971				
Congress	441	352	67.95	43.68
CPM	85	25	4.82	5.12
CPI	87	23	4.44	4.73
DMK	24	23	4.44	3.83
Jana Sangh	157	22	4.24	7.35
Congress (O)	238	16	3.08	10.42
Swatantra	59	8	1.54	3.06
Samyukta Socialist Party	93	3	0.57	2.42
Praja Socialist Party	63	2	0.38	1.04
Other parties	403	30	5.84	9.99
Independents	1134	14	2.70	8.36
Total	2784	518		
1977				
Janata	424	298	55.0	43.0
Congress	492	154	28.4	34.5
CPM	53	22	4.1	4.3
AIADMK	21	19	3.5	3.0
CPI	91	7	1.3	2.8
DMK	19	1	0.2	1.7
Other parties	115	32	5.8	5.2
Independents	1224	9	1.7	5.5
Total	2439	542		
1980				
Congress (I)	492	353	66.7	42.7
Lok Dal (JPS)	294	41	7.8	9.4
CPM	63	36	6.8	6.1
Janata	432	31	5.9	19.0

(Continued)

Table 7–3 *(Continued)*

Parties	*Number of Candidates*	*Number of Seats Won*	*Percentage of Seats*	*Percentage of Votes*
DMK	16	16	3.0	2.1
Congress (Urs)	212	13	2.5	5.3
CPI	48	11	2.1	2.6
AIADMK	24	2	0.4	2.4
Other parties	222	17	3.2	4.0
Independents	2826	9	1.7	6.4
Total	4629	529*		
1984				
Congress (I)	517	415	76.7	48.1
Telugu Desam	34	30	5.5	4.1
CPM	64	22	4.1	5.7
AIADMK	12	12	2.2	1.6
Janata	219	10	1.8	6.7
AGP	10	7	1.3	1.0
CPI	66	6	1.1	2.7
Congress (S)	39	5	0.9	1.6
Lok Dal (DMKP)	174	3	0.6	5.6
BJP	229	2	0.4	7.4
Other parties	251	24	4.4	7.3
Independents	3878	5	0.9	8.1
Total	5493	541		
1989				
Congress (I)	510	197	37.3	39.5
Janata Dal	244	143	27.1	17.8
BJP	225	85	16.1	11.4
CPM	64	33	6.3	6.5
CPI	50	12	2.3	2.6
AIADMK	11	11	2.1	1.5
Telugu Desam	33	2	0.4	3.3
Other parties	1318	33	0.6	12.2
Independents	3703	12	2.3	5.2
Total	6158	528**		

*Elections were not held in 13 constituencies (12 in Assam, 1 in Meghalaya).
**Elections were not held in Assam (14 seats).
SOURCES Adapted from W. H. Morris-Jones, *Government and Politics in India* (London: Hutchinson, 1966), pp. 163–66, and Election Commission of India, *Report on the Fourth General Elections in India*, vol. 1 (New Delhi: Government Press, 1968), pp. 94–95; *Report of the Fifth General Election to the House of the People in India, 1971*, vol. 2, Statistical (New Delhi: Government Press, 1973); *Report on the Sixth General Election to the House of the People in India, 1977*, vol. 2, Statistical (New Delhi: Government Press, 1978); and the Ministry of Information and Broadcasting, Government of India. For 1980, 1984, and 1989 results, see David Butler, Ashok Lahari, and Prannoy Roy, *India Decides: Elections 1952–1991* (New Delhi: Living Media, 1991), pp. 70, 86–92.

some 800 to 1000 voters. The size of the electorate and convenience are major considerations in determining the number and location of the stations. They are spaced so that ordinarily no person should have to travel more than two kilometers (about $1\frac{1}{4}$ miles) to vote. The sheer magnitude of the elections has made extended voting periods necessary. The first general elections were held in the winter of 1951–52 over a four-month period. The time was reduced to a span of 19 days in 1957. With each election it has been further reduced, and in 1991 the balloting was scheduled for three rounds in May and June.

Voter registration is the responsibility of the Election Commission rather than the individual voter. Voter rolls are prepared on the basis of a house-to-house canvass. The lists are then made public so that each person may check whether his or her name has been included. Few, however, avail themselves of the opportunity, and inevitably on election day, a number of would-be voters find that their names are missing. By then it is too late, however.

In the first two general elections, each voter was given ballot papers for assembly and parliamentary seats. A ballot box existed for each candidate in each contest, and the voter placed the paper in the box marked by the symbol of the candidate he or she supported. (Some voters reportedly worshipped the ballot box after casting their votes.) The system was confusing and involved a vast number of ballot boxes. A new procedure that provides for marked ballots and a single box in public view was adopted in 1962 and has been used since then. Voters line up at the station, and a polling officer checks each voter's identity slip against his or her name on the electoral roll. The voter is then marked on the finger with indelible ink and receives a ballot. Marking the ballot secretly with a rubber stamp on the symbol of the chosen candidate, the voter folds the ballot, and drops it into the box. Although the procedure is involved, the number of invalid votes has been relatively small, averaging less than 3 percent of the total cast in recent elections. The whole procedure is scrutinized by polling agents representing each candidate. Their presence and assistance also serve to identify voters and prevent impersonations. Agents for each candidate are also entitled to be present at the ballot counting. This takes place under police protection at a central location to which the ballot boxes from the various polling stations have been brought.

Constituencies and Seats

The States Reorganization Act passed in 1956 provided for the establishment of the Delimitation Commission, consisting of the chief election commissioner and two active or retired judges of the Supreme Court or a state high court. Their responsibility is to delimit the constituencies for each election. These have varied somewhat with each election, but with the exception of the major changes caused by States Reorganization, sufficient continuity has existed to permit comparative analysis. The Lok Sabha constituencies have been drawn to contain an average of about 750,000, but their actual size varies widely from 30,713 in Lakshadweep to 1,744,592 in Thane, an urban constituency of greater Bombay that has grown enormously since the 1971 delimitation.[2] Of the 545 members of the Lok Sabha, 543 are directly elected, and 2 are nominated to represent the Anglo-Indian community. Within each parliamentary constituency are a number of state assembly constituencies, typically seven, varying in size from state to state, but having an overall average of some 216,000 people. There is a total of 3941 members of the state and Union Territory legislative assemblies.

Candidates

Over the course of India's 10 parliamentary elections, the number of candidates has grown enormously—from 1864 in 1952 to 8953 in 1991—with an increase in the number of candidates per constituency rising from 4 in 1952 to 17 in 1991. In one Haryana constituency in 1989, voters confronted a ballot listing 122 candidates by name and symbol. Most candidates are frivolous or are "dummy" candidates put up to draw support away from someone else, but such candidates win few votes from an increasingly discerning electorate. The numbers have grown because of the ease with which aspirants for office may place themselves on the ballot. To appear as a candidate, a nomination for a seat from a parliamentary constituency must be accompanied by a deposit of 500 rupees; for an assembly seat, a nomination must be accompanied by a deposit of 250 rupees. (Members of the Scheduled Castes and Tribes need deposit only half these amounts.) Unless the candidate receives at least one-sixth of the total vote, he or she forfeits the deposit. The Election Commission favors a substantial increase in the deposit in order to eliminate all but serious candidates, for the amount of money now required is so little that few are discouraged from running, even though most lose their deposits. In the last three elections some 80 percent of all candidates lost their deposits. Of independent candidates, 99 percent lost their deposits.

[2] As noted on p. 77, delimitation of constituencies has been "frozen" until 2001. Reflecting urbanization, this has resulted in a growing disparity in the size of constituencies.

These data are a measurement of the Indian electorate's increasing political sophistication—if not of the judgment of frivolous candidates. In 1952, 521 independent candidates were elected to the Lok Sabha, but with each election their number has declined. In 1991, only one of a record 5646 independent candidates was elected. Voters have increasingly voted for the candidates of major parties, and they have virtually ignored all but the two or three "serious" contenders for the seat.

The Selection of Candidates

Among the conflicts in Indian political life, perhaps none has been more intense or significant than the selection of candidates within the governing party. As conflicting interests become more vocal, parties are forced to reconcile their pledge to select the "best" candidates with the competing personal and parochial claims of those upon whom their support depends. Ramashray Roy, in analyzing this process in the states of Bihar and Rajasthan, argued that the selection process is "a crucial test of the party's flexibility and adaptability in coping with the pressures and counter-pressures that impinge upon it from both within and without."[3]

If a party is to be successful, it must be able to accommodate various group pressures, both state and local, in its selection of candidates. Five kinds of claims are advanced in the selection process: personal, regional, socioeconomic, institutional, and factional. Personal demands are those made by individuals who press for recognition and the reward of a ticket for their sacrifice, service, experience, and competence. Regional claims are those that derive from feelings of localism, such as the demand that the candidate belong to the constituency. Various socioeconomic groups may also seek to advance their interests by claiming the right to representation among the party's candidates. Institutional demands for representation are made by the various organs of the party, such as the student or youth organization and the trade union federation. Factional claims are advanced to ensure proportionate representation for the party's constituent elements. The failure of the party to respond to these conflicting demands might well mean that even before the election important social sectors are lost to the opposition. However, factional competition within the party may serve to articulate and aggregate diverse group

[3] Ramashray Roy, "Selection of Congress Candidates," Part I, *Economic and Political Weekly*, 31 December 1966, p. 835.

demands and to provide them with access to political power and a stake in the political process.[4] Thus, candidate selection is a vital recruitment and mobilization process.

The formal criteria established by the Congress for selecting candidates emphasizes (1) the applicant's record of party loyalty; (2) his or her commitment to the Congress program; (3) activity in "constructive work" as well as legislative experience; and, (4) in a reflection of the Congress's concern to broaden its base of support, his or her representation of groups the Congress may wish to attract.[5] Over the years, however, little agreement has been reached in the Congress on the mechanism of selection. Rather, a tug-of-war has occurred between the national leadership, which favors centralization of decision making, and the lower strata of the party organization, which push for more power. Consequently, different procedures have been adopted for each election. Those party members supporting centralization argue the importance of freeing the selection process from local and parochial considerations, whereas those at the bottom claim that they are in a better position to judge the merits of a winning candidate. In 1952 the district Congress committees played the key role in the selection of candidates, but in 1957 they were relegated to an advisory position and the pradesh (state) Congress committees were responsible for making recommendations to the party's Central Election Committee, which is responsible for the final approval of all Congress candidates. In 1962 the district organizations were given more importance, but the 1967 procedure placed the pradesh committees in decisive control again.[6] In 1971, in the wake of the Congress split, candidate selection was highly centralized, and many of the candidates were handpicked by the Prime Minister. Under both Indira Gandhi and son Rajiv, the selection of Congress candidates for both parliament and state assembly seats was highly centralized. Even when state party organizations again began to play a more significant role after 1984, the final decision remained with the Congress high command.

From the first parliamentary elections and, more dramatically, in state assembly elections, the distribution of Congress tickets has reflected the party's increasing congruence with society. Reflecting the

[4] See Ramashray Roy, "Selection of Congress Candidates," Part III, *Economic and Political Weekly*, 14 January 1967, pp. 61–62, 69.

[5] Roy, "Selection of Congress Candidates," Pt. I, p. 837.

[6] Ibid., pp. 838–39; and Stanley Kochanek, "Political Recruitment in the Indian National Congress: The Fourth General Elections," *Asian Survey*, 7 (May 1967): 298.

dependence of the party upon the rural sector, more and more candidates are drawn from the landowning agricultural classes. But the land was controlled primarily by the traditionally dominant castes and they remain dominant within the Congress party. The lower castes, increasingly politically conscious and well organized, are far better represented, however, than the Scheduled Castes or the Muslims.

Indira Gandhi sought to transform the social base of the Congress by selecting candidates from among the "weaker sections" of society—notably untouchables, Muslims, youth, women, and the poor. But,

> despite greater control and direction of the process of candidate selection, the overwhelming need to select candidates who were not just acceptable to Mrs. Gandhi, but who could also win at the polls, meant that even Mrs. Gandhi could not bypass local caste, regional, communal, and factional alignments. Although Mrs. Gandhi clearly attempted to manipulate state and local situations to her advantage, the Congress continued to remain a broadly aggregative electoral coalition, rather than a cohesive, ideologically coherent party.[7]

The Social Base of the Constituency In the selection of candidates each of the major parties, including the Communist parties, is sensitive to the social base of the constituency. When one community is dominant within a constituency—in the traditional terms of landed wealth, ritual status, and political power, or, increasingly, in terms of the modern calculus of numbers—each party is likely to draw its candidate from the community. It has been argued that this practice neutralizes caste as a political factor, but the fact remains that all castes do not have equal access to power.

Dominant castes are themselves arenas of political competition between factions, each of which may try to win the support of other castes. More frequently, a faction will seek vertical support, cutting through caste lines. Thus, the divisions within the dominant caste are mirrored in divisions within each of the other castes that follow traditional patterns of economic dependence and patron-client relationships. In such cases the candidates, while all from the same community, do not have equal claim to support from within their own caste. When the castes are self-conscious and cohesive in their political behavior, one candidate of the dominant caste may often be clearly identified as the "community man" and other castes will polarize in

[7]Stanley Kochanek, "Mrs. Gandhi's Pyramid: The New Congress," in Henry C. Hart, ed., *Indira Gandhi's India: A Political System Reappraised* (Boulder, Colo.: Westview Press, 1976), p. 106.

opposition around the other candidate, even though he is from that same community.

In constituencies in which two or more communities are in relative balance, candidates may be selected from numerically insignificant castes in order to depoliticize the caste factor. In constituencies in which there are a number of small castes, none of which commands disproportionate influence, the candidate may be selected without regard to caste. In any case, determination of the party candidacy must always take the caste complexion of the constituency into account, and there may be a conscious, statewide attempt to put together a balanced ticket, with each of the major communities represented. The political party that chooses its candidates from the dominant caste of a particular constituency does no more than the American city boss who seeks to aggregate the support of ethnic communities by offering candidacies to their leaders. Few politicians can afford to court a single caste, for in most constituencies no single caste predominates enough to command a majority. Although they may seek to gain the support of a caste by appealing to its particular interest in a given situation, they must do so without alienating the other communities and driving them into united opposition.

Frequently, "dummy candidates," running as independents, are put up to split votes and to draw support away from an opponent. Usually these are more a nuisance than a threat, but in a close election the loss of even a few votes may mean the difference between victory and defeat. An amusing example involved the 1962 parliamentary contest in Jaipur. The major contender was the Maharani Gayatri Devi on the Swatantra ticket. When the nominations were filed, it was discovered that another Gayatri Devi, an illiterate woman from a Scheduled Tribe, was also in the running—probably, it was suspected, at the instigation of others.[8] She polled only a few thousand votes.

Unification of the Opposition Whereas intraparty strife led to a decline in the Congress vote in some states in 1967, in others it was rather the ability of the opposition to unite that brought down the system of one-party dominance. In earlier elections Congress had been able to capitalize on the splintered opposition. Even in 1967, 184 Congress seats were won by less than 50 percent of the votes—and

[8] S. P. Verma and C. P. Bhambhri, *Elections and Political Consciousness in India* (Meerut: Meenakshi Prakashan, 1967), pp. 69–72.

80 of these by less than 40 percent.[9] The Congress was vulnerable and the opposition parties sought to advance their position. The Congress generally contested all seats, whereas the opposition parties, all-India as well as regional, followed a policy of selective confrontation until 1977. This contest policy of the opposition parties, the result of their limited organization and resources, was a critical element of their election strategy and influenced the election outcome. If a party's resources are limited, the more seats it contests, the more difficulty it may have in winning anywhere. Consequently, the opposition parties waited until the Congress announced its final lists of candidates, then took the Congress candidates and constituency strength as their reference points in choosing which seats to contest.

In single member–simple plurality constituencies the candidate with the largest vote wins. Such a system benefited the Congress, with its more extensive organization, but it also motivated the opposition to unite. In 1977 the Congress vote declined by only 9 percent against the Janata combine, but its share of seats in the Lok Sabha fell 40 points, from 68.1 to 28.5 percent.

In 1984 the failure of the opposition parties to form a united front both discredited their fractious leadership and ensured that Congress would be returned to power. No single opposition party even contested a majority of seats in the Lok Sabha. The Congress, with 48.1 percent of the vote won 76.7 percent of the seats. But even in those constituencies where, on a local basis, the opposition parties succeeded in reaching an agreement to support a common candidate, the "Rajiv wave" swept over all but a few. Of the 401 Congress victors, 289—a full 72 percent—won by an absolute majority. In 1989, the Congress faced a very different situation. Against a united opposition, it won 39.5 percent of the vote and 37.3 percent of the seats. Two years later, in 1991, the Congress vote declined to 37.6 percent. This time, however—against a divided opposition—it picked up 44.4 percent of the seats.

The relationship between percent of vote and percentage of seats reflects the Index of Opposition Unity (IOU), the generalized measure of vote-splitting, discussed in Chapter 6.[10] In the 1980s, Prannoy

[9] Gopal Krishna, "The Problem," in the special issue of *Seminar* on the Congress party, No. 121 (September 1969), p. 14.

[10] P. 217. See David Butler, Ashok Lahiri, and Prannoy Roy, *India Decides: Elections 1952–1991* (New Delhi: Living Media, 1991), pp. 30–41; and David Butler, "The Predictability of Indian Election Results," in Subrata Kumar Mitra and James Chiriyankandath, *Electoral Politics in India: A Changing Landscape* (New Delhi: Segment Books, 1992), pp. 261–66.

Roy and Ashok Lahari devised the Index of Opposition Unity to measure the extent of division among the parties fighting Congress.

$$\text{IOU} = \frac{\text{Vote of the largest opposition party}}{\text{Sum of the votes of all opposition parties}} \times 100$$

If the opposition to the Congress party is wholly united as one party, the IOU is 100. Only once has this even been approached—in 1977 when the non-Communist opposition united in the Janata Party against Indira Gandhi, yielding an IOU of 90. In 1989, opposition unity was only partially achieved—reflected in an IOU of 77, only 3 points higher than in 1984—but seat adjustments by the major opposition parties, while giving no single party a parliamentary majority, provided the basis for the National Front to come to power with the outside support of the BJP and the Left Front. The divided opposition in 1991 was measured in an IOU of 66 and translated for the Congress into an increase in the seats won.

Table 7–4
The Index of Opposition Unity (IOU) and Congress Vote and Seats

	Election Year							
	1962	*1967*	*1971*	*1977*	*1980*	*1984*	*1989*	*1991*
IOU	67	67	71	90	65	74	77	66
Percentage of vote	44.7	40.8	43.7	34.5	42.7	48.1	39.5	37.6
Percentage of seats	73.5	55.0	68.1	28.5	66.7	76.7	37.3	44.4

SOURCE Adapted from Butler et al., *India Decides: Elections 1952–1991*. Tables 4.1 (p. 31) and 4.6 (p. 35). Some figures vary slightly from other sources.

Polling and Prediction

Indian journalists have always had their hand at predicting election outcomes, but in the 1980s several magazines hired market research organizations to conduct nationwide surveys to forecast election results. The most successful was *India Today*, working with Prannoy Roy and the Marketing and Research Group (MARG). The strategy involved the use of the data on how constituencies voted in previous elections, the IOU, and exit polls of voters as they left the booths. In 1985, *India Today* came close to the mark in predicting the magnitude of the Congress victory.[11] In 1989, *India Today* predicted that the Congress (I) would win 195 seats. It got 197. In 1991, the magazine used a national sample of 90,005 in 72 constituencies—probably the largest exit poll ever conducted anywhere in the world. Polling followed each of the three rounds of voting, and combining the results for the pre- and post-assassination phases, *India Today* predicted 225—just 2 short of the Congress tally of 227.[12]

The Election Campaign

Party Funds and Campaign Financing Political parties in India derive their funds from a variety of sources: membership dues, contributions, public meetings, and so on. The Congress party—save for the 1977 elections—has been the best financed. Its paid membership[13] provides a portion of its financial backing, but additional contributions are secured from wealthy supporters and solicited in fund-raising campaigns. During the 1975–77 emergency, the business community was subjected to virtual extortion by the Congress and the auxiliary Youth Congress. Businesses, for example, were encouraged to take out exorbitantly expensive advertisements in the souvenir program of the party's annual session. A major portion of the donations that pour into the Congress coffers is from "black money"—unreported income. And it was the "black money" connection between business and politics that helped to perpetuate the system of controls that so long strangled the Indian economy, as politicians traded influence in return for business's contributions.[14] In the 1980s, the Congress party was alleged to have been the beneficiary of kickbacks on government contracts for major arms purchases from abroad, most notoriously the $1.3 billion Bofors contract.

The party in power has an obvious advantage in raising money for its campaign coffers, and the Congress's long control of the Center and most states gave it a tremendous advantage.

Dependent for licenses upon the "permit raj," businesses contributed richly to the Congress. Some, taking no chance with a volatile

[11] *India Today*, "The Rajiv Whirlwind," December 31, 1984, pp. 34–37.

[12] Butler, "The Predictability of Indian Election Results," pp. 261–62; Butler et al., *India Decides: Elections 1952–1991*, pp. 7–20; and *India Today*, July 15, 1991, pp. 34–35.

[13] Membership figures must be approached with some caution, as factional competition has inflated party rosters with bogus members. In 1992, in the first party organizational elections in 20 years, there was a claimed Congress membership of some 25,000,000, but "active members"—those who enroll at least 25 primary members and who alone vote in party elections—numbered less than 1,000,000.

[14] Stanley A. Kochanek, "Briefcase Politics in India: The Congress Party and the Business Elite," *Asian Survey*, 27 (December 1987), pp. 1278–1301.

electorate, have contributed to each of the major parties, right and left. The opposition, however, generally has had far less access to financial support than the Congress.

Each of the parties divides membership dues between the center and lower organizational units. The Congress party's constitution specifies that the central organization is to receive one-eighth of the income from dues; the rest is distributed among the state units. Other parties have similar arrangements, but ones involving considerably smaller amounts. Income from dues fluctuates considerably, since party membership is largest immediately before elections—often the result of mass recruitment or bogus membership arranged by factions to strengthen their bargaining position in the competition for party tickets. The candidates themselves may be expected to make sizeable contributions to the party election fund, and tickets are occasionally awarded for a major commitment of financial support. This practice varies considerably from party to party and from seat to seat, for there are clearly a number of candidates from the Congress as well as from other parties without any major source of private income. Levies are also made on the salaries of parliamentary and assembly members.

Each of the parties derives some income from publishing, and the most active have been the Communist parties. In addition to several newspapers, the Communist Party of India also operates a publishing house and a chain of bookstores once subsidized by the Soviet Union. Indeed, it is widely assumed that the Soviets financed the CPI, and the CPM is alleged to have at one time received support from China.

The costs of mounting a campaign are high and have increased with each election. In a closely competitive contest, each candidate spends far beyond the legal limit set by the Indian Election Commission. The laws governing campaign expenses allow, depending on the region, up to 150,000 rupees ($7500 in 1991) for a parliamentary seat and 50,000 rupees ($2500) for an assembly seat. Ceilings on campaign expenses are, in fact, openly flouted, in part because the ceilings are unrealistically low. Figures for campaign expenses are conjectural at best, given the lack of reporting requirements. In 1991, however, it is estimated that candidates from the major parties in seriously contested parliamentary constituencies spent from $50,000 to $250,000 aside from their own party's campaign budgets. For all parties, most expenses are paid by unreported "black money," the lubricant of the electoral machine.

Mobilizing Voters With each election Indian political campaigns have become more expensive and intense, a mixture of festival and struggle, penetrating even the most isolated villages. Each candidate, backed by party funds and contributions, builds a team of party volunteers and paid election workers for the campaign. Insofar as possible, local offices are set up throughout the constituency, and transportation, by jeep whenever possible, is arranged. Weeks before the election, posters, painted slogans, and party symbols appear everywhere, competing for available wall space. Great larger-than-life cutouts of party leaders are especially favored in Tamil Nadu. A flood of printed handouts ensues, and children parade through the streets with badges and party flags. Neighborhood party strongholds in villages and in cities prominently display flags, often vying with each other to raise the party flag highest. Vans, jeeps, scooters, and horse-drawn *tongas*, or carts, bedecked with party flags and the ubiquitous symbol, carry loudspeakers that saturate the air with a jumble of amplified slogans.

Each of the parties has an exclusive symbol by which it is identified. Because of widespread illiteracy and because the symbol, not the name of the party, appears on the ballot next to the name of the candidate, emphasis on symbols is a major part of the campaign.[15] The symbol is the critical link in the mind of the voter between the candidate and the party. Figure 7–1 shows the official symbols for the major recognized national parties as allotted by the Election Commission for the 1991 parliamentary elections. The symbols are supposed to be neutral, but each party strives to attach to them positive or negative connotations. The Congress (I) symbol, the hand, first used in the 1980 elections, was well chosen, for within Hinduism it traditionally represents reassurance and protection. In 1984 it was projected as "the healing hand" of Rajiv Gandhi. The BJP's lotus symbol carries rich religious symbolism and special association with the Lakshmi, the goddess of wealth; the Janata Dal's *chakra* (wheel) symbolizes the triumph of good over evil and evokes a Gandhian identity; and the SJPs chose the peasant within a wheel, the symbol of the old Janata Party.

News programs on Doordarshan, the government-run television monopoly, and All-India Radio (AIR) tend to focus on the Prime Minister—so much so that during the 1975–77 emergency, All-India Radio came to be called All-Indira Radio. With an expanding audience for television, Rajiv Gandhi became India's first "TV Prime Minis-

[15] B. D. Graham, "Electoral Symbols and Party Identification in Indian Politics," in Peter Lyon and James Manor, eds., *Transfer and Transformation: Political Institutions in the New Commonwealth* (Leicester: Leicester University Press, 1983), pp. 71–86.

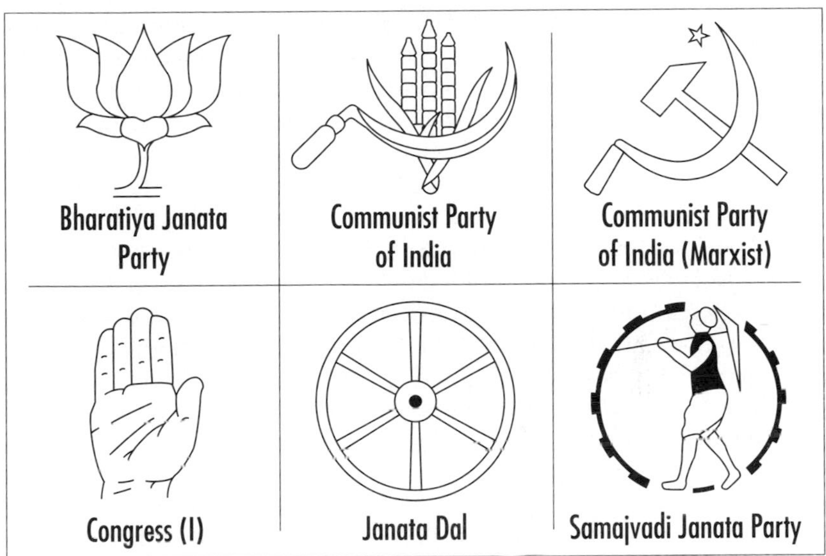

Figure 7–1
Symbols of the Major Political Parties, 1991 Elections

ter," but overexposure on what was mockingly called "Rajivdarshan" weakened him in popular standing.[16] Doordarshan and AIR carry no political advertising, but since 1977, the state-owned media have allotted time to the major political parties during elections. And from 1984, television has given increasing coverage to election campaigns.

In the early campaigns few political advertisements appeared in either the English-language or vernacular press, but from 1977 their number has increased dramatically. In 1984, reflecting the party's richly financed campaign and its first use of a professional advertising agency, the Congress (I) waged a newspaper blitz that was joined by private business advertising endorsements for the ruling party. Beyond the ads, the *Times of India*, the *Hindustan Times*, and the *Hindu* generally give their editorial support to the Congress, whereas the *Indian Express* has favored the opposition. Whatever their editorial preference, however, the major newspapers cover the elections objectively and with "op-ed" space for opposing views. Newspaper coverage of the elections is detailed and comprehensive, and *India Today*,

[16] Lloyd I. Rudolph, "The Media and Cultural Politics," in Mitra and Chiriyankandath, eds., *Electoral Politics in India*, pp. 86–87.

the nation's leading news magazine, surpasses any comparable magazine in the United States in the sophistication of its analysis.

Parties often organize mass processions, with decorated floats, elephants, and a throng of party cadres as a means of publicizing their campaign. Torchlight parades evoke memories of early American political campaigns. Parties also make use of traditional folk dramas, particularly for satirical purposes. Some parties, such as the DMK in Tamil Nadu and the Telugu Desam in Andhra, have successfully used motion pictures to advance their cause. In the 1989 elections, political parties used audio cassettes to bring voice messages and campaign songs to the voters, and in 1991 "video raths" ("video chariots") made their entry—vans equipped to set up large-screen video presentations, mainly for rural voters. Used most extensively by the BJP, videos were tailored to particular linguistic regions to project the party's message and the images of its leaders.

Mass public meetings bring a mixture of politics and entertainment, blending spellbinding orations with renditions of popular film songs. In 1984 three film stars contested the elections on Congress (I) tickets—Sunil Dutt, Vyjayanthimala, and Amitabh Bachchan, the leading hero of the Hindi screen and long-time friend of Rajiv Gandhi. Sixteen members of former princely families also contested for the Congress (I). In 1991, 7 of the 11 film stars running for Parliament won, and among the royal contenders, three winners were from one family, the Scindias of Gwalior—the Rajmata Vijaye Raje Scindia and daughter Vasundhara belong to the BJP, while son Madhavrao Scindia is in the Congress (I). In addition to the luster provided by film stars and royalty, national political figures make appearances with the local candidates, enhancing their "vote-catching" capacities. Depending on the drawing power of the main speaker and the galaxy of stars present, these meetings may attract several hundred thousand people. A major portion of the audience at any political rally, as in western societies, come simply to "see" the candidate. In India, however, this has a special meaning, for people come for *darshan*, that is, "to view the candidate as a sacred object from which they expect to derive spiritual benefit."[17]

The leaders of the major parties, aboard planes and helicopters, conduct whirlwind campaigns. In 1991, Rajiv Gandhi toured some 240 constituencies, with visits to as many as three states, addressing

[17]Paul R. Brass, "Political Parties and Electoral Politics," in Marshall M. Bouton and Phillip Oldenburg, eds., *India Briefing, 1989* (Boulder, Colo.: Westview Press, 1989), p. 78.

a dozen meetings, in a single day. He surged into the crowds and scolded his security guards for keeping the people back—an openness that was to cost him his life. The Nehru–Gandhi dynasty clearly had charisma, but Indian politics has always had a strong element of "the personal," whether in the factional leader or the great personality who becomes the embodiment of the party. Personalism tends to displace substance, just as slogans collapse the party manifesto into a catchy phrase.

Party Manifestoes Each of the parties prepares a manifesto, a formal electoral platform, which may be a statement of minimum ideological agreement or a pledge of aspirations. The manifesto can hardly be expected to have more importance in India, with its mass illiteracy, than the party platform does in the United States. In both nations few voters are aware of the formal party positions on most issues; fewer still ever read these documents. The fact that Indian parties devote such concern to the manifesto, however, may have policy significance, even if it is not a determinant of voting behavior.

The party manifestoes reflect the changing internal character of the party, the rise and fall of various factions, shifts in ideological stance, and efforts to secure new and broadened bases of support. In the first two elections the Congress manifesto, like the Congress campaign, emphasized the party as the embodiment of the freedom movement. The Congress stood before the people on the record of its struggle and achievement, and individual Congress members sought to establish their credentials of sacrifice by citing the time they had spent in British jails. By 1962, however, more than half of the electorate had come to political maturity after the struggle and sacrifice of the nationalist movement. These appeals were lost on them. To the young, the Congress was a party of privilege, wealth, and power, not of martyrdom. Responding to this change in the electorate, the Congress, no longer able to trade on history alone, tried to demonstrate that it could satisfy popular demands. The manifesto sought to do this, but it could do so only in terms of real issues.

Issues In India's first four general elections—1952, 1957, 1962, and 1967—parliamentary and state assembly elections were conducted together; local issues, varying from state to state, constituency to constituency, dominated the scene. It was only with "delinking" of parliamentary and assembly elections that national issues began to emerge. In 1971, the first parliamentary election delinked from state assembly contests, Indira Gandhi sought to raise national issues, summed up in the populist slogan *Garibi Hatao,* "Abolish Poverty." The major issue, however, was the Prime Minister herself. In 1977 the elections again took the form of a plebiscite on Indira Gandhi's rule—this time on the emergency and personalized power. In place of the stern emergency image of Mrs. Gandhi ("She Stood between Order and Chaos. She Saved the Republic"), Congress sought to portray the Prime Minister as a benign, motherlike figure. The message was simple: "For Progress and Stability—Vote Congress." For Janata the issue was liberty itself: "Save Democracy—Vote Janata."

In the 1980 elections the tables had turned. It was now a referendum on the Janata government and the capacity of the non-Congress parties to provide stability and coherent policy. The Janata Party sought a mandate to "finish the unfinished tasks: Giving the People Bread and Liberty; Giving the Country Stability and Freedom." With an emphasis on trust, party leaders pleaded for another chance. The Janata sought to revive fears of emergency excesses and dictatorship, but to little effect: The emergency was no longer an issue for a mass electorate whose concerns now lay with more immediate matters—rising prices and a breakdown of law and order. Mrs. Gandhi's appeal was simple and direct: "Elect a Government that Works."

In 1984 the opposition no longer had Mrs. Gandhi as an issue, and the petty squabbles among the opposition party leaders, frustrating their attempts at unity, made mockery of their promise to provide an "alternative" by forming a responsive and stable coalition government. For the Congress the traumatic events in the Punjab and the assassination of the Prime Minister gave force to what, even if Mrs. Gandhi had lived to lead the party, would have been the likely campaign issues: political stability and national integration. The Congress manifesto declared that: "Nothing less than the unity and integrity of the country are at stake." "The Congress (I) is the only political party which can and will keep the country together." "The Congress (I) alone stands between unity and disintegration, between stability and chaos and between self-reliance and economic dependence." Rajiv himself took up the unity theme but added to it the promise of efficient and clean government. He offered at once continuity and change.

By 1989 Rajiv had become the issue. The opposition depicted him as indecisive, autocratic, pro-rich, pro-urban, out of touch with the people, and—symbolized by Bofors—tainted by corruption. If the opposition personalized their attack, however, the Congress (I) reinforced its identity with Rajiv and the Nehru–Gandhi dynasty. Pictures of Rajiv were everywhere, providing a ready target for the National Front, with V. P. Singh projected, by contrast, as "Mr. Clean" and a platform that addressed issues of poverty, inequality, and rising prices. The Congress (I) theme was an unconvincing "Power to the People."

Two years later, India again went to the polls. As we saw in examining the 1991 elections, each of the three major political groups pursued a different issue. For the National Front and its Left Front allies, it was social justice, with particular appeals directed to the backward castes and to Muslims. The Bharatiya Janata Party took up the drum beat of Ayodhya, Hindutva, and national unity. After the assassination of Rajiv Gandhi, it sought as well to project itself as the party of order and stability. "Only the BJP Can Save India," its posters proclaimed. The Congress (I) began with emphasis on proven accomplishment and political stability, a promise it contrasted with the fractious and immobilized governments of V. P. Singh and Chandra Shekhar. Its campaign ended in evoking the memory of Rajiv: "Vote to fulfill Rajiv's dream. . . . Vote Congress." Ironically the most pressing issue—India's economic crisis—never came to the fore in the campaign, despite polling data that placed rising prices and the overall condition of the economy as the principal concern of Indian voters.

Since the delinking of parliamentary and state assembly elections, parliamentary elections have become essentially a plebiscite on the ruling party at the Center. Even illiterate rural voters have a sense of the power of their vote—that they are passing judgment on the performance of the government and that they have the capacity to "throw the rascals out"; they understand that they are voting for the next Prime Minister of India.

Whether in national or in state elections, however, to reach villagers or average urbanites, the campaign must not only be personalized, but also made immediate through translation into issues that affect them and that they feel they can to some extent control. They may know or care little for the problems of food distribution or for the economics of inflation, but they do know when commodities are scarce and that they can buy less and less with the rupees they earn. The issue of law and order is one of personal security. The most dramatic and starkly posed issue ever to come before Indian voters was the 1975–77 emergency, but it was the "excesses" of forced sterilization, slum clearance, and individual acts of highhandedness that aroused most intense opposition.

Although relatively uninformed, Indian voters are highly politicized. They have increasingly high expectations of government, and when frustrated, they will not hesitate to punish those in authority. Moreover, voters are becoming increasingly sensitive to a party's capacity to deliver results. Rajni Kothari argues that as "the voters are becoming aware of problems of policy and performance . . . , the appeals that parties make must increasingly be based on concrete items of social and economic change and less and less on either vague manifestoes or reliance on local party organizations and 'vote banks' to deliver the votes, no matter what the party appeal is."[18]

Appeals to Specific Groups Adept candidates have done their demographic homework. They have at their fingertips information on the patterns of social cleavage and the numbers and relative strength of each caste and religious group within their constituencies. Before they ever arrive in a village, they have attempted by whatever means possible to determine its caste and factional complexion, the degree of their support, and the specific felt needs of the villagers. Since voters may readily pledge to vote for every candidate, it may be necessary to get an independent assessment. Candidates therefore may enlist undercover workers in villages and neighborhoods to probe voter feelings. Some even infiltrate the organization of other parties.[19]

On village tours candidates may leave their jeeps some distance from the village and enter the village on foot, accompanied by an impressive group of party workers. Having previously ascertained what the villagers want most, they may well promise this alone if they are elected, emphasizing their credentials of integrity by *not* offering them everything but, conveniently, just what the villagers want. After a short public speech, they may make personal visits to villagers at all levels, particularly those in pivotal or decisive positions. The appearance may then be followed, perhaps some days later, with individual contacts by party workers.

Political candidates must make mass appeals, but much of their attention is directed toward specific groups. Candidates once sought to capture the support of traditional groups that could be guaranteed as a "vote bank" to deliver a bloc of votes on instruction by a leader. The framework of modern politics, however, structures new forms of behavior, and the traditional patron–client ties of the vote bank have

[18] Rajni Kothari, "The Political Change of 1967," *Economic and Political Weekly*, 6, annual number (January 1971): 250.

[19] A. C. Mayer, "Municipal Elections: A Central Indian Case Study," in C. H. Philips, ed., *Politics and Society in India* (London: George Allen & Unwin, 1963), p. 124.

weakened. In most cases, traditional sentiments are all that remain of the old structures of authority. Unless bloc leaders can reinforce these sentiments by securing for their groups the benefits they demand, traditional blocs are likely to disintegrate. In all but the most isolated villages, vote banks can no longer be relied on.

If blocs of votes can no longer be "delivered," caste and community are still powerful forces shaping political identity. Just as ethnic or racial groups do in the United States, such groups in India tend to vote together, and parties and candidates make their appeals accordingly. The Congress (I), for example, traditionally relied on support from Brahmins, Scheduled Castes, and Muslims in North India. From 1985 to 1989, the party saw the erosion of its social base over the course of state assembly elections—losses of support confirmed in the 1989 parliamentary elections. The message for the Congress (I), and for other parties as well, is that "vote banks" cannot be taken for granted, for even as such groups tend to vote as a bloc, they may shift their support from election to election, and the pattern may vary from state to state.

The Muslims form a critical electoral margin in a number of constituencies, mainly in North India. Some 100 constituencies exist in which Muslims number over 20 percent of the population, and another 100, where they form 10 to 20 percent of the population. While by no means united in their vote, they have traditionally supported the Congress party, with the notable exception of 1977.[20] In 1989 the Janata Dal bid for Muslim support met some success, as it did in 1991 in using "secularism" in its appeal. In 1991, however, Muslims voted strategically in support of the party most likely to defeat the BJP. In UP and Bihar, it was the Janata Dal; in Madhya Pradesh and other states, it was the Congress (I).

In 1989 and 1991, the Janata Dal, and even the BJP, made inroads into the Congress (I)'s base of support among the Scheduled Castes and Tribes, especially in Uttar Pradesh and Bihar. In addition, a substantial portion of the untouchables in UP voted for the Bahujan Samaj Party. The "backward" peasant castes were the principal target of the Janata Dal, but the Mandal reservation strategy by no means brought them into one political camp, and, in fact, it tended to pit rural or peasant castes against each other, with one caste supporting Chandra Shekhar's SJP, another going to the Congress (I), with the Janata Dal hanging onto others.

[20] See Violette Graf, "The Muslim Vote," in Mitra and Chiriyankandath, eds., *Electoral Politics in India*, pp. 213–40.

Table 7–5

How Indians Vote: Exit Polls, 1989 and 1991

Party	% of Votes (Actual)	*Gender*		*Age*				*Location*		*Caste and Community*			
		Men	*Women*	*18–20*	*21–30*	*31–50*	*50+*	*Rural*	*Urban*	*Upper Caste*	*Back-ward*	*SC/ST**	*Muslim*
Congress (I)													
1989	39.5	37.8	41.5	37.5	37.8	39.9	41.2	38.6	41.6			44.2	45.8
1991	37.6	36.6	37.9	32.2	35.8	38.0	40.1	37.3	36.1	32.2	30.6	44.1	46.3
Janata Dal													
1989	17.8	19.3	16.1	20.2	18.4	16.9	18.3	19.3	13.8			20.0	17.9
1991	11.6	12.1	9.0	11.1	10.7	11.8	9.3	11.3	9.8	5.7	15.9	9.8	24.9
BJP													
1989	11.4	11.9	10.9	13.2	12.1	11.6	9.8	8.0	20.5			9.5	3.9
1991	21.0	20.9	18.3	27.3	22.4	17.7	16.3	17.5	27.7	36.4	20.8	11.4	—

*Scheduled Castes/Scheduled Tribes

Exit poll percentages = + or − 5 percent.

SOURCE *India Today*, April 15, 1991, pp. 52–53; July 15, 1991, pp. 34–35.

The pattern and diversity of group support for the major political parties are revealed in the *India Today*–MARG exit polls taken during the 1989 and 1991 elections. The results, as seen in Table 7–5, do not show dramatic swings in bloc voting, and the average national percentage of votes for each party is reflected with remarkably little variation in votes registered for the various groups. Notable exceptions occur, as, not surprisingly, in the low percentage of Muslims voting for the BJP. Overall, however, the Indian electorate is more homogeneous than might be expected. The Indian voter as an individual responds to a range of issues and influences, and economic concerns may weigh more heavily than caste or community.[21]

"Money and Muscle" "Money politics" is an important lubricant of the Indian political machine. With every election, money has assumed increasing importance, but over the course of India's 10 parliamentary elections and the many state assembly elections, how that money is used has changed. In the first elections a candidate made a sizeable payment to a village or caste leader in return for a promise to deliver a bloc of votes. Such payment sometimes was used for the group's benefit, but more often it simply enriched the leader alone. As these traditional "vote banks" began to fragment, however, individual voter contacts and payments increasingly replaced group payments. The practice was more prevalent in rural than urban areas, and in many constituencies voters came to expect payment of money by all candidates. In the course of time, payment for votes made plain the importance of voting, and, as a result, payments had less and less effect on the way voters used their power. Widespread vote buying contributed to attitudes of cynicism, but ironically money politics impressed the people with the power of a single vote and served to draw new participants to the polls. In much the same way, the gifts of the American political machines early in this century politicized new immigrants to the United States and served to integrate them into the society and the political system. As individuals became increasingly involved politically and as voting practice thus became institutionalized, payment declined in importance.

Over the past two decades, direct payment to voters, with diminished payoffs for the candidates, has been increasingly displaced by the mass campaign. Money that might once have gone to the voters is now more likely to go to the myriad of campaign workers, to pos-

[21] *India Today*, "Psephology: Swings, Seats, Vote Banks," April 15, 1991, pp. 50–53.

ters and billboards, advertisements, video presentations, the fleets of cars and jeeps, and to the costs of air travel.

Campaign rallies draw both supporters and the curious, but in urban areas, and most visibly in New Delhi, they are frequently augmented by "volunteers" trucked in from surrounding slums and outlying villages. They are paid a few rupees and are often given a blanket and liquor for their day's work. It is from among these "lumpen elements," as they are typically described in India, and their rural counterparts that politicians have recruited the *goondas* who have come to assume an increasingly prominent role in public life, especially in North India. "Muscle" may be used to extort contributions, scare off opponents, or intimidate voters. This is by no means new to Indian politics, for in the past landlords often hired toughs to keep the landless and lower castes in political submission. Today, however, most notably in Bihar and Uttar Pradesh, the nexus among politicians, local police and bureaucrats, and criminals has in fact "criminalized" politics. Gangs of goondas associated with the various parties or their factions fight it out for control of the political turf, giving rise to widespread violence at the time of elections. In some constituencies, where once the politicians hired the goondas, the goondas have become the politicians. In the notorious Dhanbad constituency in Bihar, center of the mafia-dominated coal fields, the 1984 Janata Party candidate was mafia don Suryadeo Singh, a member of the Bihar legislative assembly. With 17 charges of murder against him, he was legally expelled from the district as a permanent threat to law and order, and contested the parliamentary election while on bail. His opponents, including the ultimate Congress (I) victor, bolstered by bodyguards, were prepared to match him with muscle power.[22] In Uttar Pradesh dacoit gangs entered the political arena in 1984 to "persuade" voters in the areas of their influence. The bandit queen Kusma Nain, sought by the police for mass murder, moved with apparent freedom throughout Jalaun District, mobilizing support among the Thakur caste for the Congress (I). Other dacoit gangs, largely on the basis of caste ties, got out the vote for the various opposition parties.[23] In 1989 at least 50 candidates for the Lok Sabha faced charges ranging from robbery to murder, and their numbers in 1991 were surely no fewer. Whether it is dacoits operating with ties to politicians, goondas hired by politicians, or criminals who have become politicians, their involvement in politics has raised the level of election violence.

[22] "The Battle for Booths," *Sunday Observer* (Bombay), 23–29 December 1984.

[23] "Bandits 'Persuading' Voters," *The Times of India*, 22 December, 1984.

Election Violence Elections sharpen social conflict and are the occasion for eruptions of violence. The campaigns are filled with charges and countercharges of assaults, kidnappings, and even murders, though few such allegations have been brought to court. Stories abound of candidates who stepped down because they were intimidated or "bought off." Posters and symbols are often defaced, and tensions, aggravated by rumor, often reach the breaking point. In recent elections, armed clashes between workers for the competing parties have become the norm in some constituencies. During the course of the 1980s, violence mounted with each election, and in 1991, some 350 persons were killed, including 5 Lok Sabha and 21 state assembly candidates. Aside from the Punjab, where election violence took a high toll, problems were most serious in Uttar Pradesh and Bihar, where, despite the presence of police and paramilitary forces in the most volatile constituencies, violence was widespread and numerous incidents of "booth capturing"—often with the complicity of polling officers—were reported.

In booth capturing, armed "muscle men" for one candidate either forcibly prevent voters from going to the polls or physically take over the polling station to stuff the ballot boxes. Often their presence alone around the polling station is sufficient to discourage would-be voters for the opposing candidates.[24] The Congress (I), the Janata Dal, and the BJP have each been implicated. Election law provides that where booth capturing has occurred, repolling is to be conducted as soon as possible—usually the following day—under police protection. In 1980, repolling was ordered in 39 polling stations. By 1984, it was 264, and in 1989, the Election Commission ordered repolling in 1139 stations, most in "problem areas" of North India. In 1991, booth capturing was again extensive, though primarily in Bihar and Uttar Pradesh, and, for the first time, election results were countermanded in five constituencies because of rigging.

The Indian Electorate

Expanding Participation and the Impact of Competitive Elections

Given the level of literacy in India, political consciousness is remarkably high. Since independence, political awareness and partici-

[24]For a description of booth capturing, see Myron Weiner, *India at the Polls, 1980: A Study of the Parliamentary Elections* (Washington, D.C.: Enterprise Institute, 1983), pp. 48–49.

pation have risen among all segments of the population, and there is evidence on any number of scales that political mobilization is taking place faster in rural areas than in urban areas. That village India has been politically penetrated is revealed in the minimal differences in the levels of partisanship and voter turnout between urban and rural areas. Dramatic increases have been noted among rural poor and illiterate populations. In the pattern of electoral behavior, "India's urban constituencies tend to resemble—both in voter turnout and in party preferences—the rural areas in which they are located more closely than they resemble each other."[25] The differences emerge, not between urban and rural sectors as such, but between regions and among the states.

Expansion of participation in rural areas is closely related to the impact of competitive elections. A critical determinant of the rural turnout is the degree to which local conflicts are identified with struggles at the constituency level. Factions become the vehicle of political mobilization and voting turnout. Almost every village is torn by factionalism, and almost inevitably village conflicts are drawn into the wider political arena. Party struggles thus become an opportunity for each village faction to further its interests and solidify its position within the village.

Factional struggle is by no means new. Land has traditionally been a source of intense conflict; various families in the dominant caste have fought among themselves to enlarge their holdings. Factional conflict has also served to divide castes as vertical relationships of dependence have cut through village society in the formation of client groups. Such factions, although not permanent, have often endured for several generations. Such linkages have been increasingly displaced, however, by the horizontal relationship of caste blocs, as witnessed most dramatically in the political rise of the middle agricultural castes.

Each village faction may try to associate itself with the winning assembly candidate both to command reward for support and to legitimize its local dominance. The Congress, with its own factional division, was often able to command the support of an entire village through the alignment of village factions with various Congress groups, often simply on the basis of polarization. That is to say, one

[25]Weiner, *India at the Polls*, p. 78. Also see Myron Weiner and John O. Field, "India's Urban Constituencies," in *The Impact of Modernization, Electoral Politics in the Indian States*, vol. 3 (Delhi: Manohar, 1977), pp. 1–121, and Samuel J. Eldersveld and Bashiruddin Ahmed, *Citizens and Politics: Mass Political Behavior in India* (Chicago: University of Chicago Press, 1978), pp. 45–60.

village faction sided with a particular faction within the Congress, so the opposing village faction aligned with the opposing Congress group. A village faction, however, might well extend its support to an opposition party candidate just because the dominant faction of the village supported the Congress. Voting may thus reflect issues and conflicts peculiar to a village alone and virtually unrelated to the issues of the larger constituency.[26]

Levels of Awareness and Political Participation

In early surveys the limited political horizon of most Indians was evidenced in a widespread inability to identify even such well-known national leaders as Nehru. Today there are few Indians in such isolation. Electoral campaigns, bureaucracy, and mass communications have penetrated the villages and expanded the average villager's threshold of political identity. Indians have become increasingly aware of the world beyond the village, increasingly conscious of their vote. Opinions are multiplying and are reflected in growing demands and heightened expectations. If surveys continue to register a large number of "don't knows," the statistics should not be taken to mean that Indians simply have no orientations or sentiments about the matters at issue. Although not articulate, they have real interests of which they are aware.

Parties and elections have been the fundamental catalyst to expanding participation and rising levels of support for the political system. The greatest increases in political participation have occurred among the middle castes and classes, and it is this middle sector of the electorate that has become the dominant force in Indian political life. And among the lower strata of society, increased electoral participation is registered, for example, in the mobilization of new voters among untouchables in Uttar Pradesh in 1989 and 1991 by the Bahujan Samaj Party, and in the sharpening of political consciousness by *dalit* and tribal protest movements. Social movements, as we saw in Chapter 5, "Arenas of Conflict," act to mobilize the otherwise politically uninvolved and to heighten participation. The movement for the construction of the Ram temple at Ayodhya brought young Hindus into the political arena, and in the 1991 elections, the BJP richly capitalized on an expanded base of active support.

In relative numbers of people politically active and in their range

[26]See Myron Weiner, "Village and Party Factionalism in Andhra: Ponnur Constituency," in Myron Weiner and Rajni Kothari, eds., *Indian Voting Behaviour* (Calcutta: Mukhopadhyay, 1963), pp. 177–202.

of participation—from voting to attending rallies, joining demonstrations or processions, and to campaign activities such as canvassing—India compares favorably with western democracies. Levels of participation are not matched by the citizen's sense of political efficacy, however.[27] Widespread frustration exists about politics and cynicism regarding politicians, a democratic malaise that India shares with many western countries, including the United States. Among the most alienated are those who join in violent protest or terrorism, but alienation is most frequently expressed in withdrawal from political life and, like apathy, is reflected in low voter turnout. Nevertheless, Eldersveld and Ahmed, in their study of *Citizens and Politics,* conclude that

> a large portion of the Indian public are cognitively aware of politics, support parties and the election system, and demonstrate considerable personal "psychological involvement" with that system. . . . This emergence of a "modern" set of political system orientations and attitudes . . . may be the most significant aspect of Indian political development.[28]

Voting Turnout and Trends

The Montagu-Chelmsford Reforms of 1919 provided for limited franchise based on property qualifications, the specific criteria varying among the provinces. The total electorate for the various provincial legislative councils was about 5,350,000. Easing the franchise qualifications, the Government of India Act of 1935 extended suffrage to include some 30,000,000 people. After independence the Constitution abolished all property qualifications and, in what Rajendra Prasad called "an act of faith," established universal adult suffrage. The electorate has grown from 173 million in 1952 to 521 million in 1991 (including Jammu and Kashmir, where elections were not held).

While the size of the electorate has expanded with population growth, a significant, though fluctuating increase has occurred in the percentage of voter turnout, from 45.7 percent in 1952 to a high of 64.1 in 1984. Turnout fell in 1989 and 1991—the latter, at 51.1 percent, the lowest turnout since 1957, suggesting both boredom and alienation and, in some areas, a degree of intimidation. (The United States

[27] For data on participation and efficacy from national surveys taken in connection with the 1967 and 1971 elections, see John O. Field, *Consolidating Democracy: Politicization and Partisanship in India* (New Delhi: Manohar, 1980), and Eldersfeld and Ahmed, *Citizens and Politics*.

[28] Eldersveld and Ahmed, *Citizens and Politics*, p. 44.

Table 7–6
Election Data, Indian Parliamentary Elections, 1952–1991

Year	Seats	Candi dates	Polling Stations	Electorate (in millions)	Votes Polled (in millions)	Turn-out
1952	489	1874	132,560	173.2	79.1	45.7
1957	494	1519	220,478	193.7	92.4	47.7
1962	494	1985	238,355	217.7	120.6	55.4
1967	520	2369	267,555	250.6	153.6	61.3
1971	518	2784	342,944	274.1	151.6	55.3
1977	542	2439	373,908	321.2	194.3	60.5
1980	542	4629	434,442	363.9	207.4	57.0
1984	542	5493	479,214	400.1	256.5	64.1
1989	543	6158	579,810	498.1	308.3	61.9
1991	537	8953	594,797	501.0	256.0	51.1

SOURCE Myron Weiner, *India at the Polls, 1980: A Study of Parliamentary Elections* (Washington, D.C.: American Enterprise Institute, 1983), p. 146; Butler et al., *India Decides*, p. 70; Press Trust of India, *The Tenth Round*; and Aggarwal and Chowdhry, *Elections in India*. Slight variations exist among sources for votes polled. The figures above represent percent turnout of electorate as listed.

turnout in 1988 was 51.8 percent.) Rates of participation vary considerably among the states, from highs in 1991 of 73 percent in Kerala and West Bengal, and 82 percent in tiny Lakshadweep, to lows of 41 and 42 percent in Gujarat, Madhya Pradesh, and Uttar Pradesh, and 36 percent in Meghalaya.

Urbanization is not a significant variable in differentiating voter turnout. Among the most salient variables affecting voter turnout is education, as reflected in aggregate terms at the state level, as well as in individual terms, as revealed in survey data. Perhaps more than anything else, however, it is heightened *political* literacy nurtured by competitive elections that has been the crucial determinant of expanded participation.

Participation by women has increased since 1952. During the first election many women refused to give their proper names and, therefore, were not registered. Voter turnout among women increased from 38.8 percent in 1957 to a high of 58.6 in 1984, as against an increase from 55.8 to 68.2 for men. Where once women followed the lead of male family members, impressionistic evidence, supported by survey data, suggests they are taking an increasingly independent role.[29]

[29] See Usha Thakhar, "The Women's Vote," in Mitra and Chiriyankandath, eds., *Electoral Politics in India*, pp. 199–211.

While women today vote in increasing numbers, their involvement in politics remains largely separate from men. Women may be enlisted in making banners and posters, and they are mobilized by the women's auxiliary organizations of the various parties to canvas votes—among women. They rarely attend the processions and rallies, and, when they do, it is in a special reserved section. Their role, as it has been since the 1930s, is primarily "behind the scenes"—separate, in what Wendy Singer has called "a kind of political purdah."[30]

Women, of course, played a prominent part in the nationalist movement, and the Congress encouraged them to enter politics by reserving a percentage of its tickets for them, but the numbers have remained small. In 1984 only 164 of the 5493 candidates for all parties were women. National parties promised more candidacies to women, but, in 1991, only 5.5 percent of all tickets went to women—for the Congress (I), 10 percent; BJP, 5 percent; and Janata Dal, 3 percent. Only 36 women were elected to the Lok Sabha in 1991. While their numbers are comparatively few, women have served as ministers in the states and at the Center, the most notable of whom is Prime Minister Indira Gandhi.

In 1991 a total of 8953 candidates stood for the Lok Sabha, an average of 17 candidates for every seat—the highest ever. Voters tend to ignore all but two or three "serious" candidates. In many constituencies in the 1989 elections, for example, it was effectively a two-way contest between the Congress and the most credible opposition party. Increasing sophistication of the electorate is registered in the defeats for independent candidates. Of 5230 independents in 1991, only one was elected and 99 percent forfeited their deposits.

Despite the dramatic swings in recent elections, the Congress's percentage of the vote has been remarkably stable. It has varied within 15 percentage points, from a high of 48.1 in 1984 to a low of 34.5 percent in 1977. Over ten parliamentary elections, it has averaged 42.4 percent of the vote, and although it has been able to win majorities in individual states, the Congress has never secured more than 50 percent of the vote in a national election. Even if the Congress can no longer take its traditional social base for granted, the party has a core of stable support. Indeed, "there seem to be," writes William Vanderbok,

[30] Wendy Singer, "Women's Politics and Land Control in an Indian Election: Lasting Influences of the Freedom Movement in North Bihar," in Harold A. Gould and Sumit Ganguly, eds., *India Votes: The Quest for Consensus, 1989 and 1991* (Boulder, Colo.: Westview Press, 1993).

> large, enduring and different groups that regularly mobilize in favour of the Congress or opposition banners in the various regions of the nation. The Congress is relatively consistent in its ability to mobilize and relatively unable to expand on its base. The opposition base, too, is stable, but opposition parties experience comparatively wider swings in their ability to bring new voters into the system and then keep them over time. The result is a situation of contained volatility.[31]

Within the framework of "contained volatility," swings in the vote between the party in power and the opposition, at both Center and state levels, express an electoral verdict on government performance. E. P. W. de Costa's observations, based on the 1967 results, have been prophetic:

> The Indian electorate, believed inert and incapable of dramatic choice, is showing signs of a revolutionary change. The young, the less educated, and particularly the illiterates, the minorities, and most unpredictable of all, the lowest income groups are all rewriting their basic loyalties. To the candidate this is, perhaps, a struggle for power. To a political scientist it is . . . the beginning of a break with the past.[32]

Political Mobilization and India's Future

Expanding participation provides the impetus for developing higher levels of institutionalization. The enhanced capacity of the party system to both generate and absorb change in expanding participation has held the critical balance in India's political development. The parties, in organizing and structuring participation, may provide access to demands, but they cannot wholly satisfy them. The viability of the political system depends on both the will and the capacity of the government to respond to these demands.

In their study of mass political behavior in India, Eldersveld and Ahmed argue that political development has occurred in four critical senses:

[31] William G. Vanderbok, "The Tiger Triumphant: The Mobilization and Alignment of the Indian Electorate," *British Journal of Political Science*, 20 (April 1990): 259. Also see his "Critical Elections, Contained Volatility and the Indian Electorate," *Modern Asian Studies*, 24 (1990): 173–94.

[32] E. P. W. da Costa, "The Indian General Elections, 1967" (New Delhi: Indian Institute of Public Opinion, 1967), p. 23.

> Citizens have become politically participant, party and electoral institutions have emerged, identification and commitment to national symbols and a national system have occurred, and the polity has expanded to the rural and social periphery. In an institutional and attitudinal sense, at the micro and macro levels, great political change has taken place since independence. And one senses that this political development has already had significant consequences for social and economic change, and will have an even greater impact in the future.[33]

India, however, confronts a crisis of governance. The institutions of government in India, notably the bureaucracy, were grounded in the structure of the British Raj. They were designed for administration and for the maintenance of stability; their purpose was to contain demands, not to respond to them. The fundamental problem of transition was to adapt these instruments of order to the needs of social change and democratic response. Rapidly expanding participation and escalating demands, however, quickly outran the capacity of the highly institutionalized structures that India's new leadership had inherited. Economic development, Nehru once said, is "for the growth of the individual, for greater opportunities to every individual, and for the greater freedom of the country." "Political democracy . . . will be justified if it succeeds in producing these results. If it does not, political democracy will yield to some other form of economic or social structure. . . . Ultimately, it is results that will decide the fate of what structure we may adopt in this country. . . ."[34]

Recommended Reading

Blair, Harry, W., *Voting, Caste, Community, Society*. New Delhi: Young Asia, 1979. Essays in aggregate data analysis, with special reference to Bihar.

Brass, Paul R., *Caste, Faction and Party in Indian Politics*, Vol. 2: *Election Studies*. Delhi: Chanakya, 1985. Election studies at their best.

Butler, David, Ashok Lahiri, and Prannoy Roy, *India Decides: Elections 1951–1991*. New Delhi: Living Media, 1991. An indispensable handbook to Indian elections, data, and methodological commentary.

[33] Eldersveld and Ahmed, *Citizens and Politics*, p. 6.

[34] *Parliamentary Debates—House of the People: Official Report*, vol. 6, no. 10, pt. II (15 December 1952), col. 2371.

Dasgupta, Biplab, and W. H. Morris-Jones, *Patterns and Trends in Indian Politics: An Ecological Analysis of Aggregate Data on Society and Elections*. Bombay: Allied Publishers, 1975. An analysis of political behavior on a district-wide basis in terms of a series of socio-economic variables.

Elkins, David J., *Electoral Participation in a South Indian Context*. Durham, N.C.: Carolina Academic Press, 1975. An ecological analysis of voting behavior, especially useful as a "handbook" of methodology on Indian electoral research.

Field, John O., *Consolidating Democracy: Politicization and Partisanship in India*. New Delhi: Manohar, 1980. Analysis of the sources, meaning, and impact of expanding political participation, based on survey data from the 1967 and 1971 elections.

*Gould, Harold A., and Sumit Ganguly, eds., *India Votes: The Quest for Consensus, 1989 and 1991*. Boulder, Colo.: Westview Press, 1993. Solid and provocative analyses.

Mitra, Subrata K., and James Chiriyankandath, eds., *Electoral Politics in India: A Changing Landscape*. New Delhi: Segment Books, 1992. A fine collection of papers focusing on the 1989 and 1991 elections.

Nuna, Sheel C., *Spacial Fragmentation of Political Behaviour in India: A Geographic Perspective on Parliamentary Elections*. New Delhi: Concept, 1989. Analysis of 1971, 1977, and 1980 elections; identifies geographic patterning of party domains.

Sheth, D. L., ed., *Citizens and Politics: Aspects of Competitive Politics in India*. Occasional Papers of the Centre for the Study of Developing Societies, No. 2. Bombay. Allied Publishers, 1975. Incisive political analysis.

Singh, V. B., and Shankar Bose, *Elections in India: Data Handbook on Lok Sabha Elections, 1952–85*. New Delhi: Sage, 1986. Contains in one volume electoral statistics for parliamentary elections and by-elections through 1984.

Singh, V. B., and Shankar Bose, *State Elections in India, 1952–85*, 5 vols. New Delhi: Sage, 1987, 1988. Basic data.

Weiner, Myron, and John O. Field, eds., *Electoral Politics in the Indian States*, 4 vols., Delhi: Manohar Book Service, for the Center for International Studies, M.I.T., 1974–77.
Vol. 1, *The Communist Parties of West Bengal*, 1974.
Vol. 2, *Three Disadvantaged Sectors*, 1975.

*Available in a paperback edition.

Vol. 3, *The Impact of Modernization*, 1977.
Vol. 4, *Party Systems and Cleavages*, 1975.
Detailed analyses of electoral data by 14 Indian and American scholars.

Studies of Specific Elections

1977:

Aiyar, S. P., and S. V. Raju, *When the Wind Blows: India's Ballot-Box Revolution*. Bombay: Himalaya Publishing Co., 1978.

Mirchandani, G. G., *320 Million Judges: Analysis of 1977 Lok Sabha and State Elections in India*. Columbia, Mo: South Asia Books, 1978.

*Weiner, Myron, *India at the Polls: The Parliamentary Elections of 1977*. Washington, D.C.: American Enterprise Institute, 1978.

1980:

Mirchandani, G. G., *Assembly Elections 1980*. New Delhi: Vikas, 1981.

———, *The People's Verdict*. New Delhi: Vikas, 1980. On the 1980 parliamentary elections.

*Weiner, Myron, *India at the Polls, 1980: A Study of the Parliamentary Elections*. Washington, D.C.: American Enterprise Institute, 1983.

1984:

Mirchandani, G. G., and K. S. R. Murthi, *1984 Lok Sabha Elections*. New Delhi: Sterling, 1985.

1989:

Andersen, Walter K., "Elections 1989 in India: The Dawn of Coalition Politics?" *Asian Survey*, 30 (June 1990), pp. 527–40.

*Kohli, Atul, "From the Majority to Minority Rule: Making Sense of the 'New' Indian Politics," in Marshall M. Bouton and Philip Oldenburg, eds., *India Briefing 1990*. Boulder, Colo.: Westview Press, 1990, pp. 1–23.

Suri, Surindar, *The Rise of V. P. Singh and the 1989 & 1990 Elections*. New Delhi: Konark, 1990.

1991:

Aggarwal, J. C., and N. K. Chowdhry, *Elections in India: Analysis and Overview*. New Delhi: Shipra, 1992.

Ahuja, M. L., and Sharda Paul, *1989–1991 General Elections in India.* New Delhi: Associated Publishing House, 1992.

Andersen, Walter K., "India's 1991 Elections: The Uncertain Verdict," *Asian Survey*, 31 (October 1991), pp. 976–89.

Press Trust of India, *The Tenth Round: Story of Indian Elections 1991.* Calcutta: Rupa, 1991.

Chapter 8

Policy and Performance: The Politics of Development

THE INDIAN MODEL OF DEVELOPMENT EMERGED FROM A series of strategic choices made during the early years after independence. These choices were based on a set of compromises that attempted to blend the experience of wartime planning and controls; domestic pressures for a policy of economic nationalism; and the liberal, Gandhian, and socialist ideological crosscurrents that existed within the nationalist movement. The model that grew out of these strategic choices evolved incrementally into a set of policies that became the basis of India's development consensus.[1] It called for a system of centralized planning and a mixed economy in which a government-owned public sector would dominate basic industry and the state would control, regulate, and protect the private sector from foreign competition. Foreign capital would be permitted, but only under highly controlled and restricted circumstances. Despite periodic shifts in emphasis, the basic outlines of the Indian development model remained unchanged until the 1990s, when a major financial crisis began to force some significant alterations.

The objectives of India's development model were to achieve rapid economic growth, self-reliance, full employment, and social justice. Four decades of planning, however, have produced mixed results. Although the Indian economy has achieved a considerable degree of

[1]Bruce Williams, "Strategic Choice, Justification and Institutionalization: A Model of the Public Policy Process," Paper prepared for delivery at the Midwest Political Science Association meeting, Chicago, 20–22 April 1978.

self-reliance, growth has been sluggish, unemployment intractable, and social justice has remained a distant goal.

Economic Policy

The Creation of a Development Model

Post-independence India engaged in a great debate over the future of the Indian economy and the economic content of freedom.[2] This debate took place in an environment of division, war, upheaval, and uncertainty. Attempts to develop a coherent and acceptable economic policy had to compete with other needs, such as how to cope with the social and strategic consequences of partition, communal riots, war with Pakistan over Kashmir, the integration of the princely states, and the framing of a new Constitution. This myriad of problems had to be managed by a divided and largely inexperienced political leadership confronted by a variety of domestic and external pressures.

Three distinct visions of India's economic future existed within the Indian leadership, the party, and the country at large: a Gandhian vision, a socialist vision, and a liberal capitalist vision. Mahatma Gandhi felt that a westernized pattern of industrialization for India would be dehumanizing and socially undesirable. He wanted an Indian economy and polity based on decentralized political and economic structures rooted in India's rural villages. Each village would be organized around agriculture, would be largely self sufficient, and would produce its own limited consumer needs, such as cloth, shoes, and soap, in village and cottage industries.

Nehru and Patel, on the other hand, were concerned about building a strong, centralized, industrialized state capable of defending India's freedom and meeting the needs of its poverty-stricken masses. They differed, however, over the role of government in achieving these objectives. Nehru was a socialist. He considered capitalism an outdated, exploitative, immoral system, and saw scientific planning and socialism as the inevitable wave of the future. He, therefore, wanted to create a system of not only centralized planning but also government ownership and control of the commanding heights of the

[2]For a discussion of this period, see Stanley A. Kochanek, *The Congress Party of India* (Princeton, N.J.: Princeton University Press, 1968), pp. 164–81; and Michael Brecher, *Nehru: A Political Biography* (New York: Oxford University Press, 1959), pp. 509–54.

economy. He distrusted India's private sector and felt that if it were allowed to continue at all, it should be tightly regulated and controlled to ensure that it served the public interest. Patel, on the other hand, distrusted planning, had little respect for vague socialist ideas, and favored private-sector development.

After Gandhi's assassination in January 1948, the debate focused primarily on the degree to which Nehru's vision of planning and socialism would prevail. The debate came to concentrate on several key issues, namely, the instruments government would use in guiding the economy; the size and scope of private-sector economic activity; the role of Gandhian village and cottage industries; the role of state enterprises; nationalization; economic controls; and the future of foreign capital. The strategic choices made in settling these issues were based on a series of major compromises that ultimately came to shape the entire economic system of independent India.

The great debate over the future of the Indian economy raged from 1947 to 1951 and was never fully set to rest until 1956. Initially the debate created enormous economic uncertainties and led to a serious domestic economic crisis. Foreign business began to divest its holdings, domestic investment came to a halt, and production declined sharply. Faced by this economic crisis, the government was forced to clarify its policy, and the result was the first of a series of key strategic choices outlined in the Industrial Policy Resolution of 1948.

The Industrial Policy Resolution of April 6, 1948, was essentially a compromise document that sought to clarify government economic objectives; placate each of the ideological tendencies in the Congress party and the government; and temper the growing fears of indigenous and foreign investors. The resolution called for a mixed economy in which public ownership would be confined to three industries—munitions, atomic energy, and railroads. In six other industries—coal, iron and steel, aircraft manufacturing, shipbuilding, telephone and telegraph, and minerals—government reserved the exclusive right to start new ventures. Most importantly of all, the resolution provided a preliminary blueprint for future industrial development. The resolution specified 18 key industries of national importance that would be developed under the control and regulation of the central government; indicated that foreign capital and enterprise would be welcome but subject to government control and regulation; and announced that the government would create a planning commission shortly. The resolution also promised that the government would encourage the development of village and cottage industries.

The Industrial Policy Resolution was a carefully crafted compromise document that contained a series of strategic choices and established the basic outlines of Indian development. First, it envisioned the creation of a mixed economy and recognized that the private sector had an important role to play in the future economy of the country. Second, it declared that the state would be expected to play a progressively larger role in the industrial development of India. Third, it accepted the principle that private foreign capital would be allowed to participate in Indian industrialization. This participation, however, was to be regulated by the state, with major interest in ownership and control normally in Indian hands. Finally, it held out the hope that a place would be found for the development of Gandhian village and cottage industries. In short, it contained elements intended to satisfy each of the ideological pressures in India.

Detailed implementation of the Industrial Policy Resolution came in the form of the Industries (Development and Regulation) Act, which became the legal framework not only for the control and regulation of the private sector, but also for Nehru's 1949 Statement of Policy on the future role of private foreign capital, for the creation of the Planning Commission in March 1950, and for the publication of the First Five-Year Plan in 1951.

Despite Patel's death in 1950 and Nehru's emergence as supreme leader of the Congress party, the government, and the country, the strategic choices made between 1947 and 1951 remained the basis of Indian planning and development. Instead of reversing these earlier decisions, Nehru attempted to build on these decisions to create a broad national consensus on development policy.

Although India entered the era of planned development in 1951, the First Five-Year Plan was hurriedly assembled by the newly created Planning Commission and consisted largely of projects already underway. The future shape of the Indian economy was left undetermined. Under the plan, the bulk of the development funds went to agriculture, power development, and irrigation. The pattern of industrial development remained uncertain, and the debate over the future of the private sector, nationalization, and the role of village and cottage industries continued. Although Nehru's socialist rhetoric initially frightened indigenous capital, business gradually moved toward a process of accommodation and cooperation.

The process of accommodation began with the formulation of the Second Five-Year Plan and became fully established with the proclamation of the Industrial Policy Resolution of 1956, another masterful consensus document that succeeded in satisfying all major constituencies and united the entire nation behind a series of Five-Year Plans that gradually transformed the economic base of India. The foundation for the golden decade of development from 1956 to 1966 was laid. Despite periodic shifts in emphasis, the Industrial Policy Resolution, issued on April 30, 1956, remains the basic strategy for the Indian model of development.

Although the resolution expanded the scope of public-sector development, it also allocated extensive areas to the private sector, guaranteed existing private-sector facilities from nationalization, and provided for their eventual expansion. Three categories or schedules of industries were created. Schedule A, consisting of 17 industries reserved for development by the public sector, included most basic and heavy industries. Schedule B contained a list of 12 industries in which public-sector investment would supplement private-sector development. All other industries were open to private-sector development.

The Second Five-Year Plan spelled out the details of the government's development strategy. A large, basic-industry sector would serve as the foundation for economic development. At the center of this scheme would be three giant public-sector steel mills as well as a variety of machine-building industries. In order to create employment and provide basic consumer goods, the development of village and cottage industries would be encouraged, with the government ensuring their protection from competition. Finally, the private-sector would have vast scope for expansion, free from the fear of nationalization, and would be controlled, regulated, and protected by the state from foreign competition.

In order to implement the new scheme, the government gave earlier controls a new orientation and supplemented them with additional regulatory measures. The result was the creation of one of the most comprehensive systems of control and regulation in the non-Communist world. The Planning Commission, assisted by numerous interdepartmental committees, commissions, and boards, attempted to direct the economy and the implementation of a series of Five-Year Plans.

The decade from 1956 to 1966, covering the Second and Third Five-Year Plans, produced a massive industrial boom. A growth strategy based on rapid industrialization through capital-intensive investment, import substitution, and emphasis on heavy industry provided opportunities for almost every industry to grow, and the lines between the public and private sectors became blurred. When an acute foreign-exchange shortage developed in 1958, India turned to outside private capital and foreign governments for support and aid. Both the public and private sectors grew rapidly, and India appeared headed for an economic takeoff into self-sustaining growth.

1963 to 1969: The Policy Debate Revived, the Shift Right

The first signs of uneasiness and doubt began to appear in the early 1960s as the economy began to falter; the development consensus came under attack; and the Nehru era began drawing to a close. The trouble started when achievements began to fall far short of plan targets; the economy began to stagnate; and rapid economic growth did not seem to be producing the desired results in relieving poverty. Moreover, despite the logic of planning, India was confronted by a slowdown in growth and a major recession. As a result, some began to question the entire utility of planning, regulation, and government controls, and the development consensus of the Nehru era itself began to erode.

Pressure for a major change in policy developed from a variety of sources. First, a potentially potent political challenge emerged with the creation of the Swatantra Party, a loose coalition of conservative elements that, for the first time, publicly challenged Nehru's socialist pattern of planning and regulation. The Swatantra characterized Congress rule as the "permit, license, quota Raj" and demanded an end to governmental control of the economy. It even went so far as to attack the very concept of planning, which had enjoyed an almost sanctified position in Indian political discourse. In its place the party advocated a policy of economic liberalism and championed private-sector development.[3]

A second major source of attack on the development consensus came from the World Bank and major foreign-aid donors. By the late 1950s India's development program had become heavily dependent on outside aid to pay its import bills and close its massive foreign-exchange gap. The World Bank began repeatedly to advise India to eliminate as many controls as possible in an effort to stimulate greater efficiency and accelerate economic growth.

A third source of pressure came from the Indian business community. A decade of planning and rapid growth had made the community a growing political force and an increasingly powerful segment of the economy. As business grew more self-confident, many sectors became willing to forego some controls in return for greater freedom of action, particularly the new, modern industrial sectors

[3]See Howard Erdman, *The Swatantra Party and Indian Conservatism* (Cambridge: Cambridge University Press, 1969), pp. 65–81.

that regarded price controls, distribution controls, and high taxation as barriers to faster private-sector growth.[4]

Fourth, there appeared a series of government-sponsored studies that were highly critical of the operations of the entire system of controls, which was increasingly equated with socialism and planning. These studies concluded that the system of controls as implemented and administered had failed to accomplish its stated objectives. In fact, the controls had resulted in monopoly, concentration, and unequal geographic development. The studies also revealed that the development strategy of heavy capital investment and growth had not significantly benefited the vast majority of the population. Unless the pattern of plan allocation was changed, the studies argued, the condition of the poor would continue to remain unchanged or might even grow worse.[5]

Finally, the confidence and certainty of the political leadership was itself shaken by a variety of events. Nehru, the architect of the system, died; his successor, Lal Bahadur Shastri, was much more receptive to pressures building up for modification of the system. Shastri set in motion a process of liberalization that lasted from his brief tenure in office (1964–66) to the early years of Indira Gandhi's rule. During this period, the concept of liberalization became so widespread that it was incorporated into the initial approach document of the Fourth Five-Year Plan. The document stated that "within the broad framework of control in strategic areas, there is an advantage in allowing the market much fuller play."[6]

From 1963 to 1969 the policy of liberalization took a variety of forms. First, the Government of India made major changes in its traditional policy of maintaining tight control over the pricing and distribution of major products. Sixteen items were decontrolled in 1963, cement was decontrolled in 1966, and cotton in 1967. Second, controls on investment were liberalized. Industrial units with fixed assets of less than 1,000,000 rupees (about $100,000) were exempt from the licensing systems; several key industries were decontrolled; and significant procedural reforms were introduced. In short, the Indian economy appeared to be moving in a new and different direction. These

[4]Stanley A. Kochanek, *Business and Politics in India* (Berkeley: University of California Press, 1974), pp. 214–25.

[5]For a summary of these studies see Rakesh Khurana, *Growth of Large Business: Impact of Monopolies Legislation* (New Delhi: Wiley Eastern, 1981), pp. 2–10.

[6]Charan D. Wadhua, *Some Problems of India's Economic Policy*, 2d ed. (New Delhi: Tata McGraw-Hill, 1977), p. 298.

changes in industrial policies were paralleled by equally significant changes in the government's attitude toward agriculture.

1969 to 1973: The Populist Counterattack

Nehru's death, the attack on planning and controls, and the tentative and halting steps toward deregulation frightened the left within the Congress party and its socialist and Communist allies in the opposition. These groups began a concentrated counterattack intended not only to stop the erosion of the development model that had emerged during the first three Five-Year Plans, but also to push the country even further to the left and along a more clearly socialist path. The key device they used was a concerted effort to transform the socialist rhetoric of the Congress party into public policy. In an effort to build and maintain a progressive image, the Congress party over the years had adopted a series of resolutions promising a fundamental transformation of the Indian economy. These resolutions had acquired an increasingly radical tone as Congress fortunes began to slip at the polls. Calls for nationalization of private-sector banks, insurance companies, and key industries entered the Congress program, in addition to demands to end the alleged concentration of economic power and provide a greater degree of social justice for every person.[7]

Demands for redistributive justice became embroiled in Congress factional politics when Indira Gandhi's power was challenged by her senior and more conservative colleagues in the Cabinet and the party. Mrs. Gandhi, on the advice of P. N. Haksar, decided to counter this challenge by transforming the factional dispute into an ideological crusade. This approach enabled her to build a new coalition of support among left-of-center Congress members, socialists, and Communists. The strategy was a resounding political success and resulted in reversing the process of economic liberalization. In its place, Mrs. Gandhi embarked on a massive populist program designed to restructure the Indian economy and provide redistributive justice. Public-sector development was to be accelerated; the private sector was to be brought under tighter control; and steps were to be taken to control the alleged concentration of economic power.

From 1969 to 1973 major structural, legal, and policy changes were made as part of a major effort to restructure the Indian economy. A series of sweeping constitutional amendments enhanced the govern-

[7]See Francine R. Frankel, *India's Political Economy, 1947–1977: The Gradual Revolution* (Princeton, N.J.: Princeton University Press, 1978), pp. 388–433.

ment's power to alter property rights and eliminate existing privileges. The power of Parliament to amend the Constitution, including the right to property contained in the provisions on fundamental rights, was affirmed, and parliamentary decisions relating to compensation in cases of nationalization were made independent of judicial review. In addition, the princes were deprived of their privy purses and other privileges. These changes were accompanied by a major assault on the independence of the judiciary in an effort to secure more liberal and responsive courts.

Along with the fundamental changes in the Constitution and the attacks on the judiciary came the first massive wave of nationalization since independence. Major private-sector banks were nationalized in 1969, followed by the coking coal industry in May 1972, insurance companies in September 1972, the remainder of the coal industry in 1973, as well as a series of small undertakings in shipping, gold, and copper. In addition, the government took over the management of 46 textile mills, the Indian Iron and Steel Company (IISCO), and a large railway wagon construction firm. Finally, the government took over the wholesale trade in wheat and rice.

The assault on the private sector was accompanied by the passage of a whole new array of regulatory measures and the initiation of a series of significant policy changes. The government pushed through the Monopolies Restrictive Trade Practices Act (MRTP); issued a new, highly restrictive licensing policy designed to curb the growth of large conglomerates (typically referred to in India as "business houses"); and amended the Foreign Exchange Regulation Act (FERA) as a new and comprehensive device to control foreign capital. These actions, along with revised patent legislation and a new drug policy, were all designed to control monopolies, dilute the concentration of economic power, and regulate foreign multinationals.

By the end of 1973, the populist wave of structural reform had run its course. Mrs. Gandhi's massive electoral victories of 1971 and 1972 had reduced her reliance on the left; India had begun to feel the full economic consequences of the Bangladesh war; the country was hit hard by the oil crisis of 1973; and the economy was confronted by a major drought. Spiraling inflation, loss of production, and economic stagnation brought structural reform to a halt and touched off a massive political and economic crisis.[8]

Although the populist wave lasted only four years, it had long-

[8]See Henry C. Hart, ed., *Indira Gandhi's India: A Political System Reappraised* (Boulder, Colo.: Westview Press, 1976).

lasting consequences. It superimposed a new series of laws and regulatory instruments on an already tightly controlled and regulated economy. The result was an increase in the degree of overlap and the complexity of laws, policies, and regulations; massive procedural delays; increased politicization of the regulatory process; shortages; and the rapid growth of the nonproductive sector. Manipulators, traders, and speculators and their political and bureaucratic allies prospered on shortages while production stagnated.

The System Restored: The Second Wave of Liberalization

The populist phase was followed by a second major effort to liberalize what had become the most controlled and regulated economy in the non-Communist world. Because of a quagmire of complex rules, regulations, and procedures, the Indian economy was plagued by excruciating delay, increasing project costs, rampant corruption and bribery, and one of the largest black-money systems in the world. Rigid price controls created massive shortages and black markets; industrial projects required 50 categories of approvals and took three years or more to pass through the Byzantine clearing process; technological development fell further and further behind; and India found itself increasingly unable to compete on world markets because of its high-cost economy.[9]

The liberalization process was begun in 1973 and was designed to keep the broad outlines of the system intact, while making just enough changes to prevent the system from collapsing. The changes were introduced in a slow and halting manner and passed through four phases: the initial steps from 1973 to 1975, the emergency from 1975 to 1977, the Janata phase from 1977 to 1979, and the Indira–Rajiv–coalition politics efforts of the 1980s. Although the liberalization process produced some results, incremental change and tinkering with the regulatory system proved to be insufficient, and the Indian economy began to slide deeper and deeper into economic crisis. By the early 1990s India was on the verge of bankruptcy and was forced to turn to the International Monetary Fund (IMF) for a bailout. This decision forced some fundamental changes in Indian economic policy that may mark the beginning of the end of the permit, license, quota Raj. The full implications of these changes, however, will not be clear for several years.

[9]V. P. Arya, *A Guide to Industrial Licensing in India* (Delhi: Iyengar Consultancy Services, 1981), pp. 32–33; and K. V. Iyer, *Clearances for Industrial Projects* (New Delhi: Indu Publications, 1983), pp. 5–18.

In its first steps toward liberalization, taken between 1973 and 1975, the government tried to regain the confidence of the private sector by reaffirming its commitment to the Industrial Policy Resolution of 1956, introducing a less restrictive industrial licensing policy, overhauling and revamping the industrial licensing procedures for the first time since their creation in 1951, and attempting to modify the rigidities that had developed in the regulatory system during the populist period.

The economic crisis of the early 1970s, however, fueled a major political crisis that threatened the very existence of the political system. Mrs. Gandhi proved unable to manage, and when her personal power was threatened by the Allahabad court judgment, she declared a national emergency. The emergency period, in turn, brought to the fore a new set of factors and a renewed effort at economic liberalization.

The most important new force to develop on the Indian scene during the 1975–77 emergency was Sanjay Gandhi, Indira Gandhi's younger son. Though he held no official position, Sanjay became his mother's closest and most trusted advisor. However, Sanjay not only failed to share his mother's commitment to some vague brand of socialism, but he also developed a strong antagonism toward the bureaucracy, the public sector, and government control and regulation of the economy.[10] As a result, the process of liberalization begun in 1973 was broadened and accelerated during the emergency from 1975 to 1977. At the same time, Sanjay also politicized the industrial regulatory system more than ever before. The system increasingly became a mechanism for extraction of resources and a reward to friends, allies, and supporters.

During the emergency, the government tried to further liberalize industrial licensing policies, relax price controls, and provide tax incentives for new industrial investment in an effort to accelerate the rate of economic growth. These policy changes, however, had only limited success. Although economic growth did increase, the new policies failed to bring about the production breakthrough expected. This failure was attributed to an inadequate revival of the construction industry, investment emphasis on expansion rather than on new projects, and weak consumer demand.[11]

The defeat of the Congress party at the polls in 1977 brought a new

[10] See Uma Vasudev, *Two Faces of Indira Gandhi* (New Delhi: Vikas, 1977).

[11] Frankel, *India's Political Economy*, p. 558.

government to power for the first time since independence. The Janata coalition was united on political issues and determined to restore the political system to its pre-emergency state. The party was sharply divided, however, on economic policy. Except for Communism, almost all of India's ideological tendencies were reflected in the Janata coalition. Of the three major tendencies—liberalism, socialism, and Gandhiism—the Gandhian sentiment appeared strongest. Initially unable to agree on an economic policy, the Janata proclaimed its basic commitment to the Industrial Policy Resolution of 1956. It became clear that the basic outline of the Indian economy would not be altered despite the change in government.

When it finally emerged, Janata economic policy took on a Gandhian tone. Major emphasis was placed on creating employment by concentrating investment in the development of agriculture and small-scale industry. Janata policy reflected a certain antagonism toward big business and heavy industry in favor of a dramatic expansion in the number of products to be reserved for production by the small-scale sector. The core of Janata industrial policy was: "What can be produced by cottage industry shall not be produced by the small-scale and large-scale sectors and what can be produced by the small-scale sector shall not be open for large-scale industry."[12]

Mrs. Gandhi's return to power in 1980 resulted in a restoration of the concept of economic growth through rapid industrialization. Once again, the basic consensus reflected in the Industrial Policy Resolution of 1956 was reaffirmed, and Mrs. Gandhi set about attempting to restore growth through a process of liberalization designed to maximize the utilization of resources, encourage investment, and move in the direction of a more open, market-oriented system. Among the major changes were a liberalization of licensing and procedures to stimulate investment and production; a relaxation of administered prices; a liberal import policy to reduce domestic shortages and supply raw material for industry; and increased efforts to encourage foreign private capital and technology. These steps, however, were taken in an atmosphere of caution. Control and regulation of the economy were to be loosened, not eliminated, and the government was prepared to reimpose tight controls if economic conditions worsened due to a poor monsoon, foreign-exchange crisis, or other unanticipated developments. Yet the changes marked a significant shift away

[12] Prem Shankar Jha, *India: A Political Economy of Stagnation* (Bombay: Oxford University Press, 1980), p. 191.

from the isolationist policies of the late 1960s and early 1970s, when self-reliance was a dominant theme. In fact, the very process of liberalization was to be financed by a massive drawing of $5.7 billion from the Extended Fund Facility of the International Monetary Fund.[13]

Rajiv's Policy of Liberalization

Following Mrs. Gandhi's assassination, the massive electoral victory of Rajiv Gandhi in the December 1984 parliamentary elections brought a new mood of optimism and a spirit of renewal to India. Rajiv's youth, his emphasis on economic liberalization, technology, and efficiency, and his new "Mr. Clean" image appeared to mark a new post-independence era for India. Indian business—protected by Indian government policy for three decades—was suddenly told that it must learn to compete or perish.[14] India was going to prepare itself for the year 2000, and Indian industry would have to learn to adjust to these changes. Initially Rajiv's actions seemed to confirm this new sense of direction to the horror of elements of the Congress (I) party, the bureaucracy, and those sections of the business community that enjoyed protected markets. During the first two years of his term as Prime Minister, Rajiv embarked upon a major process of economic reform. The first budget presented by V. P. Singh, Rajiv's Finance Minister, appeared to set the tone and was marked by several important breaks with the past. The government took a variety of steps selectively to decontrol and deregulate key industries in an effort to spur production, diversification, and modernization, enabling the private sector to bypass time-consuming licensing procedures. Liberalization of industrial policy and tax reform were accompanied by a major war on tax evaders and unreported "black money."

The permit, license, quota raj had generated huge stores of black money that were used to help pay party election costs, purchase government benefits, and support politicians and party leaders. The ruling Congress (I) was known to be a major recipient of such funds. In the words of a former minister in Mrs. Gandhi's government, "If a peon accepted money, it was called baksheesh; if a clerk took it, it was mamool (custom); if an officer took it, it became a bribe; and if a minister took it, it was called party funds." As Rajiv Gandhi told the 100th anniversary meeting of the Congress party in December 1985,

[13]Catherine Gwin and Lawrence A. Veit, "The Indian Miracle," *Foreign Policy*, 58 (Spring 1985): 79–98.

[14]Stanley A. Kochanek, "Politics of Regulation," *The Journal of Commonwealth and Comparative Politics*, 28 (November 1985), pp. 189, 209–10.

"Corruption is not only tolerated but even regarded as the hallmark of our leadership."[15]

Rajiv's initial onslaught against India's regulated economy proved to be short-lived. In early 1987 his government was rocked by a series of major scandals involving alleged favoritism toward Congress (I) business allies; illegal overseas bank accounts held by Rajiv's close Congress (I) friends; and huge kickbacks on government defense contracts involving the purchase of German submarines and Swedish Bofors artillery pieces. These scandals smashed Rajiv's "clean" image, and the young Prime Minister came under intense political attack. As a result, Rajiv was forced to fall back on the support of party regulars and reverted to the populist, socialist slogans of the past. Rajiv's policy of liberalization was quickly sacrificed to the demands of political survival, and the reform effort almost came to a halt.[16]

Faced by a hopelessly divided opposition, Rajiv was able to recover some initiative by early 1988 and went on a political counteroffensive. In the economic sphere, however, Rajiv moved very cautiously and was unable to stray very far from traditional Congress rhetoric. As a result, his economic policies became hesitant and uncertain, reflected in the limited changes made during his last years in office. Tinkering became the order of the day.

Rajiv's refusal to extend major concessions to the large MRTP and FERA companies led to frustrated demands from Associated Chambers of Commerce and Industry (Assocham), the Federation of Indian Chambers of Commerce and Industry (FICCI), and other business associations for an outright scrapping of these laws. They demanded a more open economy and an end to the long delays and discrimination against large houses and foreign multinationals.

The idea of scrapping FERA appeared to receive a major boost in April 1989 when Abid Hussain, a member of the Planning Commission, publicly called for a "total reappraisal" of the law. "India's present level of foreign equity investment of $150 million per year," he declared, "is laughable by international standards, socialist countries included."[17] Foreign investment, he insisted, could contribute to technological advancement; was cheaper to service than debt; and would encourage exports. Although this point of view had strong support from the World Bank, the donor community, and sectors of

[15] Stanley A. Kochanek, "Briefcase Politics in India: The Congress Party and the Business Elite," *Asian Survey*, 27 (December 1987), p. 1292.

[16] *Ibid.*, pp. 1294–99.

[17] Quoted in *The Financial Times* (Bombay), April 14, 1989.

India's business community, it became quite clear that Hussain's position reflected neither the majority of opinion in the Planning Commission nor the policy of the Government of India. Hussain came under intense attack of leftist economists, Congress (I) socialists, and the *swadeshi*, or protectionist, lobby.

Despite its cautious and tentative character, Rajiv's policy of liberalization did produce significant results. Under his leadership, the Indian economy seemed to break the cycle of stagnation that had been characterized by the 3.5 percent "Hindu rate of growth" of the previous three decades. During the 1980s, the Indian economy grew at an annual rate of 5 percent per year. In addition, the industrial sector grew at an impressive 8 percent a year, a rate that had not been achieved since the golden decade of industrial development from 1956 to 1966. For the first time since the early days of planning, the Seventh Five-Year Plan, which ended March 1990, exceeded several of its targets. The growth in GNP was 5.5 percent versus a target of 5 percent, and the growth for industry reached 8.5 percent. This growth, moreover, was accompanied by a booming stock exchange that saw the private sector raise $6 billion compared to a mere $550 million in 1981–82. The long-awaited takeoff of the Indian economy appeared to have arrived.

The apparent success of the Indian economy, however, was in part bought at the expense of bigger budget deficits and foreign borrowing. As a result, higher growth rates were accompanied by a major financial crisis brought on by a worsening balance of payments, raising internal and external deficits, and persistent inflation. This financial crisis, in turn, touched off a major debate over the wisdom and sustainability of the entire policy of liberalization. This debate became increasingly divisive and highly politicized, shattering the old consensus on which the Indian model of development rested. Three points of view emerged in this debate reflecting different lobbies, ideologies, and political perspectives.

Rajiv Gandhi and his supporters in the party, the bureaucracy, and sections of the business community defended the policy of liberalization and selective deregulation as a great success. The policy, they argued, was not just one of liberalization but one that involved structural change. Although it did not completely open up the economy, as some demanded, it did select priority areas and gradually removed controls on capacity, pricing, production, type of product, and protection. This selective liberalization, in turn, enhanced domestic competition and improved industrial growth and efficiency. The change also prepared the Indian economy to cope with greater international competition.

Rajiv's critics, composed of leftist, Gandhian, and anti-Congress (I) economists and intellectuals; small, medium, and regionally based businesses; and the *swadeshi* lobby, however, proclaimed the policy of liberalization to be "misconceived," "unworkable," and the "road to ruination." These critics questioned almost every aspect of the policy and charged that its supporters represented compradore (anti-national) political and business interests. First, they insisted that the policy had produced industrial stagnation not growth. Critics charged that the industrial growth claimed by the government was the result of a change in the measurement index. Both industry and employment from 1981 to 1988, they argued, had been stagnant. Second, they claimed that the policy was elitist. It had helped the rich at the expense of the poor. While the top 10 percent of the population had been provided with durable goods, items of mass consumption were in short supply. Third, the policy of liberalization had threatened the country's self-reliance and its political and economic sovereignty. It had created an internal and external debt trap; emasculated the public sector's indigenous capacity; and undermined the public sector with cheap imports. Fourth, by giving greater scope to the private sector and foreign capital, liberalization had sharply eroded the role of the Planning Commission, while, at the same time, aggravating unemployment, poverty, and external vulnerability. Fifth, the policy created false industrial growth based on a high import content and destroyed indigenous technological development and production. Finally, by cutting taxes for corporations and the rich, liberalization had not only aggravated social inequality but was also responsible for creating a massive budget deficit. In short, critics charged, Rajiv's policies had been a disaster and had produced a massive financial crisis that had made the Indian economy vulnerable to external pressure.

The most important step required to reverse Rajiv's policies, according to his critics, was a "restoration of faith in planning." The Planning Commission must then take steps to restrict imports, curb consumption, and restore the earlier model of development that had attempted to blend socialist demands for the development of heavy industry in the public sector with Gandhian demands for village-level self-sufficiency and employment-generating schemes. These demands for a restoration of the development consensus of the Nehru era were reflected in the non-Congress (I) coalition that defeated Rajiv Gandhi and the Congress (I) in the 1989 parliamentary elections.

While Rajiv's domestic critics attacked his policy of liberalization for going too far, the World Bank, the IMF, the donor community, and elements in the Indian business elite argued that India's financial crisis was the result of a policy of liberalization that had been too selective and had proceeded too slowly. The slow, partial, and half-hearted approach to liberalization had contributed to India's financial crisis in a variety of ways. First, the policy retained far too many restrictions and had an adverse effect on India's balance of payments. Second, India had allowed its fiscal situation to deteriorate by letting non-plan expenditures explode, especially the huge cost of subsidies and massive defense outlays. Third, India's hegemonic public sector had become a massive drain on the economy and would have to be either rehabilitated or closed down. Fourth, the Government of India would have to reduce tariffs and eliminate quota restrictions in order to make the Indian economy more competitive. Fifth, India would have to remove all barriers to direct foreign investment, such as FERA. In short, critics demanded a more comprehensive policy of structural reform designed to open up the Indian economy to foreign capital and greater foreign competition. Unless these policy reforms were enacted, the donors argued, India could not expect additional concessional assistance from the World Bank or the donor community. The donors wanted to see the old regulatory regimen scrapped and the Indian economy opened to global competition.

The New Coalition Politics

The defeat of the Congress (I) in the parliamentary elections of November 1989 intensified the economic policy debate as Rajiv's cautious, hesitant approach was replaced by near political paralysis. The National Front government of V. P. Singh was a weak coalition of socialist, Gandhian, and peasant based politicians supported by the Communists and the Bharatiya Janata Party. The unstable coalition reflected the entire gamut of economic thought in India, with a particularly strong socialist, Gandhian, and anti-foreign capital perspective. The new government came to power stressing the virtues of socialism, and during its first month or so in office was dominated by conflicting slogans pretending to be economic policy. The newly appointed nine-member Planning Commission talked of a revival of Gandhian-style, labor-intensive, small-scale, cottage industries. The socialists attacked Rajiv's concessions to foreign capital. The Prime Minister's economic advisors attacked the shortcomings of the liberalization policy. The peasant lobby pressed for massive debt relief for farmers, and V. P. Singh tried desperately to hold his unsteady coalition together.

By early 1990 pragmatism began to take hold, and the first budget appeared to stabilize the situation. It abolished the 30-year-old gold-control order, reduced the tax rates from 50 percent to 40 percent, and adopted a realistic credit policy. The budget was followed by the adoption of a three-year import–export policy that was oriented toward industrialization, export promotion, and continued liberalization. The most significant indication of the direction of the new government's economic policy came in May with the announcement of a new industrial policy that continued the trend toward liberalization and opening of the economy. The industrial policy of the National Front government, however, satisfied neither big business nor its socialist critics. While business was unhappy with the failure of the policy to apply to MRTP and FERA companies, the left charged that the policy would hurt the small-scale sector and encourage non-priority investment. Chandra Shekhar attacked the Prime Minister for failing to consult the party and for pandering to the multinationals. The result was continued confusion and uncertainty.

During the last months of the National Front government, the debate over economic policy was overwhelmed by political events as the coalition became divided over two events: V. P. Singh's decision to implement the Mandal Commission Report on job reservations for backward castes, and the threatened storming of the Babri Masjid in Ayodhya by Hindu militants. In early November 1990, V. P. Singh's government collapsed, and he was replaced by Chandra Shekhar.

Chandra Shekhar's government was totally dependent upon the support of Rajiv Gandhi and the Congress (I) to stay in power. It was, therefore, even less stable than its predecessor, and even the watered-down economic policies of V. P. Singh seemed threatened. Despite the increased economic difficulties brought on by the Gulf crisis, economic policy and implementation were totally set adrift; the Indian economy continued to deteriorate.

Despite almost two decades of spasmodic liberalization, the entire legal framework of private-sector control and regulation in India remained in place. In the words of the London *Economist*, India remained "one of the most regulated and distorted market economies in the world."[18] The very complexity and multiplicity of these instruments enabled political and bureaucratic decision makers to exercise enormous discretionary power by forcing private-sector entrepreneurs to submit to a Byzantine, case-by-case regulatory drill. The liberalization policies of the past simply lowered entry barriers; they did not remove them.

[18] *The Economist*, January 12–18, 1991, pp. 27–28.

The slow and uneven pace of liberalization from 1973 to 1991 represented efforts by key interests to make minor changes in India's regulatory policies in a desperate effort to prevent the system from collapsing. Incremental change and tinkering, however, produced only limited results—the system gradually slid into crisis. Increasing domestic deficits, inflation, and a foreign-exchange crisis brought the Indian economy to the brink of bankruptcy and collapse. The country was, therefore, forced to go to the IMF for a $5 to $7 billion bailout. Since IMF support required fundamental structural adjustments, the position of domestic reformers was substantially strengthened as India entered the 1990s.

The System Altered: The End of the License Raj?

Within weeks of taking office on June 21, 1991, the Congress (I) minority government led by P. V. Narasimha Rao introduced a set of monumental changes in Indian economic policy that promised to reduce domestic budget deficits, cut subsidies, curb defense spending, control inflation, build foreign-exchange reserves, increase private investment, strengthen revenue collection, close sick public-sector undertakings, and open the economy to foreign private investment. India then entered into an agreement with the IMF to provide massive long-term loans to help carry out the reforms. Although these steps alarmed many within the Congress (I) and the political opposition, criticism was muted by the fact that few of India's politician's were prepared to face the electorate for a third time in less than three years.

A key element in the reform package was the New Industrial Policy (NIP) announced in July 1991. The NIP abolished industrial licensing for all but a select list of 18 sensitive industries; removed asset limits for MRTP companies and dominant undertakings; eliminated phased manufacturing programs; eased location requirements for industries; promised "automatic" permissions for foreign direct investment up to 51 percent; increased foreign equity limits from a maximum of 40 percent to 51 percent; created a special board to negotiate with the top 40 to 50 international firms to invest in India; developed incentives for small-scale industry; and promised to begin disinvestment in the public sector.

While reformers saw the dismantling of controls as essential to Indian growth and survival, the Communist left and those committed to Nehruvian socialism condemned the government actions as "dangerous" and "reckless." In light of the political instability in the country and the tenacity of the Indian bureaucracy, most observers remained skeptical as to the permanence of the reform program. They pointed to the absence of support for the reforms within the Congress (I) and the political opposition; the inability of the government to adopt an exit policy to allow failed companies to close; the nit-picking character of the Indian bureaucracy and its ability to block implementation; and the usual exceptions, conditions, and hesitation reflected in the policy itself. Skeptics, moreover, argued that a change in policy was a necessary but not sufficient condition of reform. India would ultimately be judged on its track record and the degree to which its anti-business, anti-profit, and anti–foreign capital attitudes changed.

Within less than six months following the announcement of the reform package, reports indicated that the reform effort had slowed. The bureaucracy, the trade unions, and Congress (I) politicians supported by sectors of India's business elite, launched a major counterattack. The control apparatus remained in place and many of the old control functions were now performed by the Reserve Bank of India and the new Foreign Investment Proposal Board.

The new budget announced in February 1992, however, demonstrated that the Rao government was determined to press ahead with its economic reform package. Despite opposition charges that the government had sold out to the IMF, the budget introduced a variety of new initiatives. It made the rupee partly convertible; abolished nontariff barriers on imports; cut import duties; legalized gold imports; encouraged foreign participation in oil and gas; permitted foreign pension funds to invest in Indian shares; disbanded the Controller of Capital Issue; abolished the wealth tax on shares and slashed income-tax rates.

It will take a number of years before a full evaluation of economic and regulatory reform in India is possible. What is seen as a monumental change for India will be measured against opportunities elsewhere, as India must now compete for foreign capital in an increasingly scarce capital market. Some feel that India may have waited too long. In the past, India was stable and closed to the outside world. Today, it is attempting to open up to the outside world but faces domestic political instability and concern as to how long the change will last. Decontrol of the Indian economy will never be secure without also removing the controllers. In India, entire ministries and departments are involved in the control and regulation of the economy. Dismantling controls will ultimately require dismantling the system that operates these controls. This will not be an easy task. No one foresees a flood of foreign capital into India until India establishes a positive and consistent track record.

The Politics of Agriculture

The development of Indian agricultural policy, which roughly paralleled the fluctuations in Indian planning and industrial policy, also consisted of four distinct phases. The first phase covered the Nehru era from 1947 to 1964 and focused on attempts at structural reform. The second stage, from 1964 to 1971, concentrated on increasing production through the use of new agricultural technologies of the green revolution. The third phase, from 1971 to 1977, focused on basic needs and income redistribution. The fourth period, from 1977 onward, emphasized rural employment, asset creation, and income redistribution.[19]

The initial development consensus evolved by Nehru placed the major emphasis on industrialization rather than on agriculture. Government policy in agriculture focused primarily on structural reform. Over the years Congress land policy had come to concentrate on three key issues: abolition of intermediaries, ceilings on landholdings, and the development of cooperatives. The abolition of intermediaries concentrated especially on attempts to eliminate the zamindari system, which interposed a variety of rent-receiving intermediaries between the actual cultivator and the government. This process was long and complex due to numerous legal and constitutional challenges raised by powerful zamindars. The Congress and the government, however, were strongly united behind these reforms and succeeded in eliminating these zamindars and placing control of the land in the hand of the tiller. The reforms brought into being a powerful group of owner–cultivators who, in turn, have become a major political force in India.

The consensus that existed within the Congress on the issue of zamindari abolition did not exist on the issue of landholding ceilings. A major split developed between the central government and the Planning Commission, on the one hand, and the state governments, which were largely controlled by influential local landowners. As a result land-ceiling legislation was pursued with little seriousness and when enacted was so cleverly framed that little surplus land was ever created. Thus, although land-ceiling legislation ultimately appeared on the books in almost every state, its implementation was extremely uneven and mostly ineffective.

The Congress commitment to cooperatives had a strong Gandhian

[19]See Lloyd I. Rudolph and Susanne H. Rudolph, *In Pursuit of Laksmi: The Political Economy of the Indian State* (Chicago: University of Chicago Press, 1987).

content. As long as cooperative legislation centered around service cooperatives, the policy generated little real conflict. Congress's passage of the Nagpur resolution in 1959, however, proved to be a major turning point. The resolution, pressed by Nehru shortly after a trip to China, called for cooperative joint farming in which land would be pooled for joint cultivation, and those who worked the land would share in proportion to their work, not simply in proportion to ownership. The resolution touched off a massive wave of criticism and led to the formation of the Swatantra Party. Nehru quickly backed off from his commitment to the resolution and insisted that cooperative farming really meant only the development of service cooperatives.[20]

Nehru's death and the massive food crises of the mid-1960s resulted in a major shift in Indian agricultural policy. In 1964–65 the government adopted a production-oriented agricultural strategy based on new technologies of the green revolution. At best the new agricultural strategy affected only 30 percent of the total cultivated area of the country, but in these areas the use of high-yielding grain varieties, fertilizers and insecticides, irrigation, and tractors produced enormous increases in agricultural output. The strategy, however, accentuated regional disparities. In those areas experiencing the greatest increases in productivity, the green revolution, at least initially, widened the gap between the rich and the poor.[21]

The focus on increasing production and generating a process of sustained growth gave way, in the late 1960s and early 1970s, to a concern with the problems of poverty and distribution. Mrs. Gandhi's populism was an attempt to attack the alleged concentration of economic power and the growth in disparities and inequities that had developed. Beginning with the Fourth Five-Year Plan (1969–74), greater attention was paid to a variety of special programs to assist the poor. The Fifth Five-Year Plan (1974–79) attempted to attack poverty directly by accelerating the process of growth and redistribution of income. The objective was to curb the consumption of the top income levels in favor of the bottom levels. The effort to translate these objectives into specific policies, however, failed.

As a result the Sixth Five-Year Plan (1980–85) developed a series of special programs designed to assist specific target groups. These programs included the supply of inputs and credit to small and marginal farmers, employment-guarantee schemes, and transfer of some

[20] Kochanek, *Congress Party*.

[21] Francine R. Frankel, *India's Green Revolution: Economic Gains and Political Costs* (Princeton, N.J.: Princeton University Press, 1971).

income-yielding assets to agricultural labor. The Sixth Plan allocated 40 billion rupees (out of a public-sector outlay of 975 billion rupees) for poverty and welfare schemes. The Seventh Five-Year Plan (1985–90) under Rajiv attempted to further accelerate these poverty programs in order to assist the 35 to 40 percent of the Indian population that remains below the poverty line.[22] The approach to the Eighth Five-Year Plan (1990–95) accords primacy to the objectives of employment generation and poverty eradication through measures for guaranteeing the right to work, accelerating agricultural and social development, and promoting household and small-scale enterprise.

Despite its success in attaining basic self-sufficiency in food production, Indian agriculture continues to suffer from a variety of problems that will require the continued attention of planners and decision-makers. In the first place, long-term growth rates in agriculture have remained static and production continues to fluctuate widely. Despite the green revolution, the long-term growth rate for Indian agriculture has been 2.6 percent per year from 1949–50 to 1985–86.[23] Since only 30 percent of crop land is irrigated, most of India's agriculture continues to depend upon the monsoon rains, and, as a result, yearly production rates vary considerably. In 1986–87 India produced 144 metric tons of food, which dropped to 130 tons in 1987–88 due to drought, and then rose to 170 tons in 1988–89 and 1989–90. In addition, increases in food production have been confined to wheat and rice, while the production of pulses, a major source of protein in the Indian diet, has declined, as has the production of millet, the major source of cheap food eaten by the poor.

Second, increases in agricultural production have been very uneven across regions resulting in major economic disparities. The chief beneficiary of the green revolution has been a group of states located in northwestern India—Punjab, Haryana, and Uttar Pradesh—plus the state of Andhra in the South. At the other end of the spectrum, in the northeastern states of Assam, Bihar, West Bengal, and Orissa, increases in agricultural production have failed to keep up with population growth. In the west and most of the south, agricultural production has been largely stagnant. Five states—Karnataka, Maharashtra, Rajasthan, Gujarat, and Himachal Pradesh—are almost totally

[22] C. T. Kurien, "Paradoxes of Planned Development: The Indian Experience," in James R. Roach, ed., *India 2000: The Next Fifteen Years* (Riverdale, Md.: Riverdale, 1986), pp. 179–92.

[23] M. L. Dantwala "Emerging Challenges in Indian Agriculture" in M. V. Nadkarni, A. S. Seetharamu, and Abdul Aziz (eds.): *India: The Emerging Challenges* (New Delhi: Sage Publications India, 1991), p. 121.

dependent upon monsoon rains and have been designated as dry states.[24] The areas that have been left out of the green revolution suffer increased unemployment, underemployment, and poverty. Depending upon the region, Indian agriculture also suffers from waterlogging, increased salinity, floods, and spreading desertification. Flood control, soil conservation, and the development of new technology for dry land farming are critical to further increases in Indian food production.

Third, despite growth in food production, Indian agriculture has been plagued by increasing production costs that have especially threatened the survival of small and marginal farmers. Since this group is already threatened by declining size of holdings and fragmentation, their numbers are growing, and many are joining the already large group of landless laborers. The problem becomes further aggravated by India's 2.1 percent annual population growth and the inability of the nonagricultural sector to absorb additional employment.

Fourth, as a result of India's inability to further accelerate agricultural growth, rural poverty remains a major problem. The World Bank estimates that about 35 percent of the Indian population in 1990–91 remained below the poverty line. Over the years India has developed a whole series of rural poverty programs such as the National Rural Employment Programme (NREP), the Rural Landless Employment Guarantee Programme (RLEGP), and the Integrated Rural Development Programme (IRDP). The NREP and RLEGP are short-term income-generating schemes that offer 50 or so days of employment per year in some states. The long-term goal is to provide 100 workdays per year for one member of each of the 44.4 million poor households in the country or 4400 million workdays. At present it provides only 700,000,000 workdays per person. The IRDP is intended to provide the poor with assets that would allow them to develop long-term increases in their potential income. The IRDP was said to have reached 27,000,000 poor rural families between 1980 and 1988. At the same time, it is estimated that the program has enabled less than 10 percent of participating families to move out of poverty.[25] The program suffers from a variety of problems. Many who receive assets under the program sell them, often at a loss; the poorest groups tend

[24] *Ibid.*, pp. 123–124.

[25] Alan Heston, "Poverty in India: Some Recent Policies," in Marshall M. Bouton and Philip Oldenburg (eds.), *India Briefing* 1990 (Boulder, Colo.: Westview Press, 1990), pp. 115–116.

not to receive benefits; and the corrupt and inefficient delivery system tends to absorb the bulk of the resources. Rajiv Gandhi once remarked that only 20 percent of the funds ever reach the poor.

Finally, while poverty programs help the poor, the major political debates tend to center around agricultural policy toward the rich farmers who have become an increasingly powerful lobby. The farmers' lobby is much more vocal and powerful than the poor and has demanded high support prices and cheap subsidized inputs. Major debates center around the size of producer incentives, the method for calculating such incentives, and demands for higher subsidies on inputs.[26] The farm lobby has generally had a stronger voice among India's non-Communist opposition. These parties tend to advocate greater support for agriculture in Indian five-year plans and have accused the Congress (I) of placing too much emphasis on industry. The agricultural subsidy issue has already resulted in a major clash between the rich farmers and the new reform programs of the Congress (I) minority government.

India's recent agricultural strategy has attempted to expand agricultural research to include food grains other than wheat and rice as well as nonfood crops; has developed agricultural activities such as animal husbandry and forestry; has attempted to extend employment guarantee schemes; and has begun to focus greater attention on the environmental implications of agricultural development. Given India's population growth rate, however, increased agricultural production is essential to Indian stability and survival.

Planning Priorities and Contradictions

According to the First Five-Year Plan, "the central objective of planning in India is to raise the standard of living of the people and to open out to them opportunities for a richer and more varied life."[27] Poverty and inequality were to be fought by increasing production and redistributing wealth. As Baldev Raj Nayar argues, however, "the planners were torn between the compulsions of production and the necessity of distribution." In the first decades of planning, the

[26] Ashutosh Varshney, "Has Rural India Lost Out?" Paper presented at Center for South Asian Studies, University of Virginia, January 26, 1991.

[27] Planning Commission, *The First Five-Year Plan: A Summary* (New Delhi: Government Press, 1952), p. 1.

claims of production consistently took precedence over distribution.[28] The logic for the priority of growth, writes Lawrence A. Veit, rested on the assumption that "the achievement of growth would more or less automatically eliminate poverty. . . . In reality, India's development experience resembles that of many other developing countries in that targeted growth rates have not been achieved and increased production has not always 'trickled down' to the poor."[29]

The first three plans had emphasized industrial development, but a deepening crisis in Indian agriculture forced a shift in priorities. In 1969 the Fourth Five-Year Plan, far less elaborate and ambitious than those that preceded it, began to take shape under the direction of a considerably less powerful Planning Commission. The strategy emphasized agricultural development, with balanced industrial support, and concentration in those sectors and among those individuals with the brightest development prospects—the rich peasants, who were thus sustained in their traditional position of dominance. Hampered by limited investment resources, India's planners confronted an apparent dilemma: They were committed to growth, but also to equality and social justice. Distribution would make only a minimal difference in the lives of the poor, and it might well dissipate whatever opportunity existed to achieve a breakthrough in continuing economic growth. According to the Fourth Plan, "the concern for achieving the desired increase in production in the short run often necessitates the concentration of efforts in areas and on classes of people who already have the capacity to respond to growth opportunities."[30] Short-term growth and elite dominance, however, may have been purchased at the cost of economic polarization, increasing political dissent, and violence.

By emphasizing growth as growth per se rather than as a development plan of "growth with justice," India opted for production without social change, a policy that implicitly accepted the growing gap between the "haves" and the "have nots." As contradictions within the economy deepened, Prime Minister Indira Gandhi gave increasing rhetorical emphasis to the goals of social justice. With the slogan *Garibi Hatao*, "Abolish Poverty," she received a massive man-

[28] Baldev Raj Nayar, *The Modernization Imperative and Indian Planning* (New Delhi: Vikas, 1972), p. 32.

[29] Lawrence A. Veit, *India's Second Revolution: The Dimensions of Development* (New York: McGraw-Hill, 1976), p. 200.

[30] Planning Commission, *Fourth Five-Year Plan, 1969–74, Draft* (New Delhi: Government Press, 1969), p. 9.

date in 1971 parliamentary elections. When the Fifth Five-Year Plan appeared, distribution was emphasized once again, with the promise to mount an "attack on the low-end of poverty" in an effort to overcome income inequalities and regional disparities. The Prime Minister, however—confronted by rising inflation, deepening political unrest, and delegations of economists, industrialists, and bureaucrats—yielded to the pressures for growth.

Throughout the years since independence, debate over planning priorities has been constant, and each strategy has had its advocates: industry versus agriculture, growth versus distribution. Plan targets have been attacked as unrealistic, with rhetoric unmatched by achievement, but the record of India's accomplishments has been impressive, even if punctuated by drought, war, and recession.

Performance

Until the 1980s the performance of the Indian economy under the various Five-Year plans had been especially criticized due to poor growth performance, high capital-output ratios, and low industrial capacity-utilization rates. Overall growth averaged 3.0 to 3.5 percent annually, well below plan targets, but substantially above the 1 percent growth rate in the first half of the century. In the 1980s, however, the average annual growth rate increased to 5.4 percent, and the Eighth Five-Year Plan (1990–1995) has set a growth rate target of 5.6 percent. Although the growth in agricultural production was relatively stagnant in the 1980s, industrial growth accelerated. While most observers attributed the enhanced performance of the industrial sector to the liberalization policies of the 1980s, others insisted it was the result of improved efficiency, an increase in the application of technology, higher aggregate demand, and more effective performance of public infrastructure. Despite its higher growth rates, however, India still lagged well behind its Asian neighbors, and a 2.1 percent population growth rate has enabled it to increase its per-capita incline at a rather slow rate.

Figures 8–1, 8–2, and 8–3 outline India's industrial, agricultural, and real per-capita national income over the past four decades of planning. Each figure reflects widespread fluctuations as the effort to achieve a steady pattern of high growth continues to elude Indian planners. Industrial production was strong during the golden decade of development from 1956 to 1966 when industry grew at an annual

Figure 8–1
Index of Industrial Production: 1951–1990

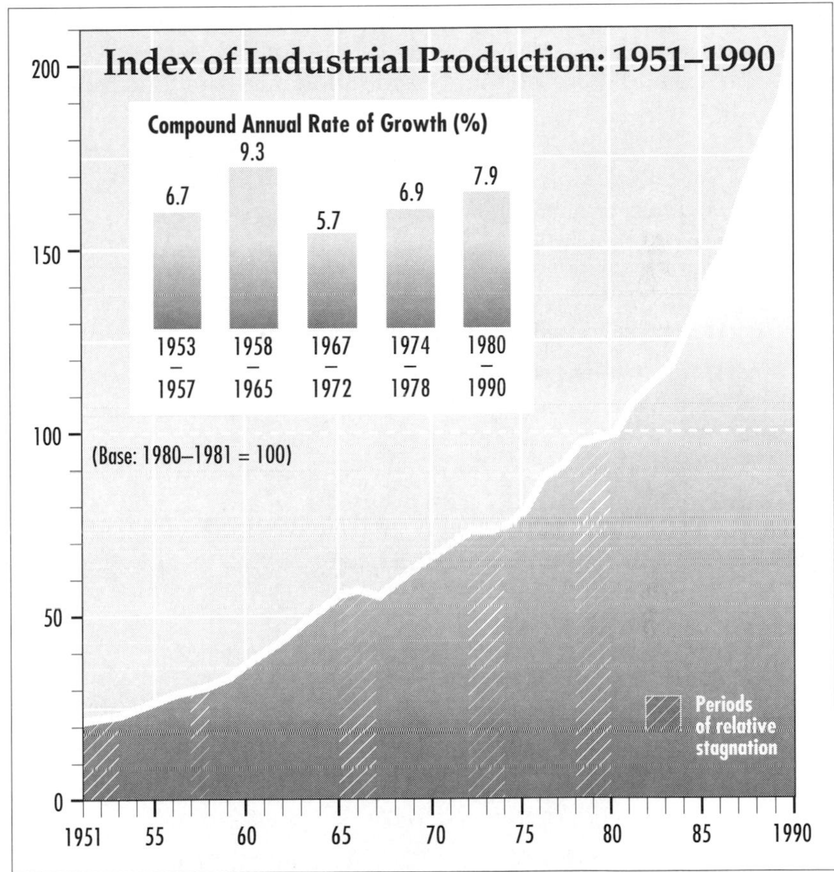

SOURCE: "Basic Statistics Relating to the Indian Economy, Vol. I: All India," *Economic Intelligence Service* (Bombay: Centre for Monitoring Indian Economy, August 1991), chart 14.1–2.

rate of 7.6 percent and reached an all-time high of 9.3 percent from 1958 to 1965. With the end of this import substitution phase of industrial development and the beginning of Indira Gandhi's populist onslaught, the rate of industrial growth fell to 5.7 percent from 1967 to 1972. During the early phase of liberalization from 1974 to 1978, the rate of industrial growth increased to 6.9 percent and then accelerated to 7.9 percent in the 1980s. Under Rajiv Gandhi's liberalization program, the rate of industrial growth from 1985 to 1990 reached 8.5 percent. Indian agricultural production has fluctuated even more erratically and in direct relationship to the vicissitudes of the monsoon. The underlying trends show a growth rate of 2.6 percent as India brought more and more land into production and extended the bene-

Figure 8–2
Trends in the Index of Agricultural Production

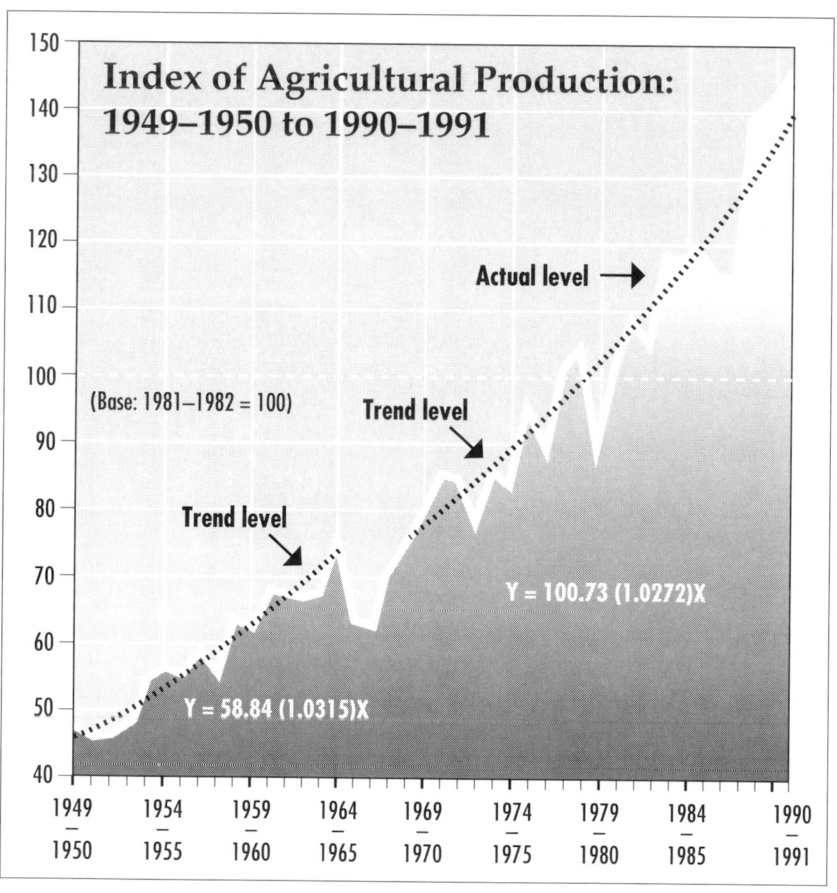

SOURCE: "Basic Statistics Relating to the Indian Economy, Vol. I: All India," *Economic Intelligence Service* (Bombay: Centre for Monitoring Indian Economy, August 1991), chart 13.1–1.

Figure 8–3
Real National Income at 1980–81 Prices

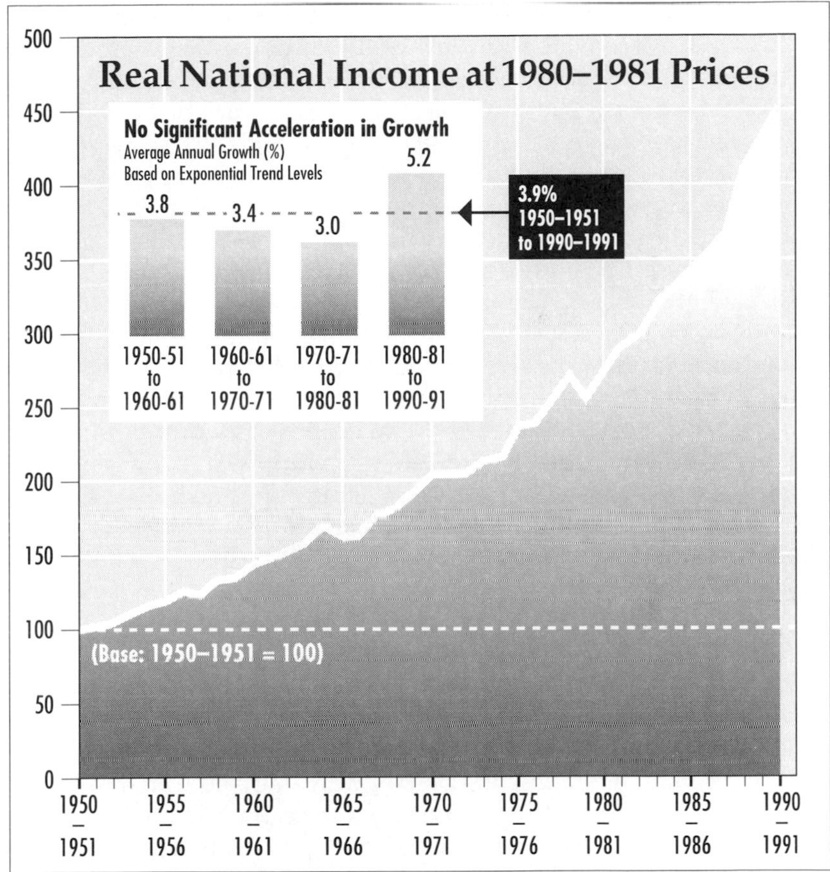

SOURCE: "Basic Statistics Relating to the Indian Economy, Vol. I: All India," *Economic Intelligence Service* (Bombay: Centre for Monitoring Indian Economy, August 1991), chart 8.1–2.

fits of the green revolution to selected areas in India, making agriculture less dependent on the monsoon.

Overall, Indian food production has more than tripled from 50 million tons in the 1950s to 170 million tons in 1989–90. Because of the fluctuation in rates of industrial and agricultural development and the overall slow rates of growth in the economy, only modest increases have occurred in the growth of India's real per-capita national income.

India's modest growth rate has, however, resulted in the creation of a large and extensive industrial infrastructure and a gradual improvement in the quality of life. Coal production has more than quadrupled; steel production reached 13.2 million tons in 1989–90 and is to increase to 19.8 million tons by 1994–95; domestic oil production has tripled since 1980. Consumer goods also made substantial, if less dramatic, progress. The availability of a rich variety of consumer goods, all made in India, contrasts sharply with the scarcities of a decade or two ago. Although the lot of most Indians improved in absolute terms in the years since independence, the gains have not been equally distributed. Despite the slogans of socialism, government policy itself has often served to subsidize the fundamental inequities of the society. Thus, India's achievements have not been secured without social costs, as evidenced in the wide regional and individual disparities in income. Moreover, with the enormous changes in education, transportation, and communication since 1950, even the most isolated villages have been penetrated, thus stimulating aspirations for a better life and frustration at the inability to achieve it. The breakthrough in communication has brought a new awareness of poverty to the Indian masses and a sensitivity to the widening gap that separates them from the rich.

Slow growth has also had other costs. One of India's most serious problems is unemployment. Unemployment increased from 3.5 million in 1961 to an estimated 20.6 million in 1978, and to 32 million in 1989.[31] The number of unemployed grows yearly at an accelerating rate, for each year a larger number of young people enters a labor market that is not expanding fast enough to absorb them. Among the unemployed are increasing numbers of university-educated men and women, often highly trained engineers and technicians, who are unable to find work in an industrial sector that continues to operate substantially below capacity. The urban unrest generated by deepening unemployment, especially among the young, is compounded by the deteriorating economic position of the lower middle classes, particularly salaried government employees, who have seen what little gains they have achieved swallowed by rapidly rising prices that have pushed them deeper into poverty.

In rural areas the largest estates have been reduced by a degree of land reform, but more to the benefit of the middle peasants than the landless. Reforms frequently have led to widespread eviction of ten-

[31] Planning Commission, *Draft Five-Year Plan, 1978–83* (New Delhi: Government Press, 1978), p. 81.

ants and to insecure seasonal employment for agricultural laborers. The poor, with no credit and little margin for risk, are often unable to take advantage of what new opportunities there are. The dominant agricultural classes, on the other hand, "have gained economically by access to credit, fertilizers, seeds, and implements, they have gained politically by control of a major source of influence and patronage, and they have gained socially by an improvement in their status as a result of their positions in the new institutions."[32]

The mixed results of India's development model have been attributed to a variety of factors. These include inadequate demand, poor economic management, a decline in public-sector investment, high capital–output ratios, an increasingly hostile global economic environment, overregulation, high-cost production, low productivity, and rapid population growth. Although many see India poised for a great leap forward in the 1990s, old dilemmas remain and may produce less than hoped for or expected results.[33]

The Politics of Economic Management

Initially, the Indian development model was centrally managed by Nehru and his newly created Planning Commission. The commission, an extraconstitutional advisory body under the chairmanship of the Prime Minister, is empowered to draw up plans for the effective and balanced use of the country's resources and to establish priorities within the development program. Under Nehru the Planning Commission assumed the power and centrality of a "super cabinet," but one removed from accountability to Parliament. Although still important, the commission today has a more strictly advisory, technocratic role. Key decisions are made within the Finance Ministry, and the final plan allocation is hammered out by the National Development Council (NDC). Composed of the Prime Minister, members of the Planning Commission, and the state chief ministers, the NDC was originally little more than a rubber stamp for central government policy. Today, however, government at the Center is confronted by chief ministers pushing for greater autonomy and leverage over planning policy and allocation. There are, therefore, calls to strengthen

[32] George Rosen, *Democracy and Economic Change in India* (Berkeley: University of California Press, 1967), p. 145.

[33] C. Rangarajan, et al., *Strategy for Industrial Development in the 80's* (New Delhi: Oxford and IBH Publishers, 1981).

the role of the NDC, which now meets about once every two years. In the 1950s the NDC met 16 times, in the 1960s it met 11 times, in the 1970s 7 times, and in the 1980s only 6 times.

The autonomy of the planning process in India's federal system has also become increasingly challenged by a variety of demand groups which have developed in the wake of an increasingly politicized society. Among the most organized demand groups in India has been the business community. Although India has committed itself to the development of a "socialist pattern of society," in practice the economy is overwhelmingly private. Harold Gould has characterized India as a "socialist state, capitalist society."[34] About 80 percent of India's national income is generated by the private sector, more even than in the United States.[35] Until fairly recently, however, the private sector was an object of suspicion and distrust. The public image of the business community, tainted by practices of usury, false weights, and quick profits, was further tarnished by rumors of undeclared "black money," the revelation of scandal, and the concentration of economic power in the hands of a few family-controlled industrial combines.

Most of the modern business and industrial conglomerates are owned by families from the traditional trading communities—Gujarati Vaisyas, Parsis, Chettiars, Jains, and Marwaris. The House of Birla (Marwari), headquartered in Calcutta, and the House of Tata (Parsi), headquartered in Bombay, each with assets of more than $1 billion, are the two largest, but such companies as Hindustan Lever, Reliance, United Breweries, and a host of newer houses have been growing at a very rapid pace and are now part of the top 20 industrial houses in India. These conglomerates, from Birla on down, are today largely in the hands of a new generation—young men in their 30s and 40s, many with MBAs from Harvard and MIT, who are applying modern, professional methods to management.[36] They have brought a new dynamism to the private sector that has not only spurred growth but has also brightened the image of Indian business. In con-

[34]Harold Gould, "India: Socialist State or Capitalist Society?" Paper presented at the annual meeting of the Association for Asian Studies, Washington, D.C., March 23, 1981.

[35]Wilfred Malenbaum, "Politics and Indian Business: The Economic Setting," *Asian Survey*, 11 (September 1971): 843; and D. H. Pai Panandikar, *Control and Over Control: A Critical Appraisal of India's Economic Policy* (New Delhi: Vidya Vahini, 1979), p. 2.

[36]"Big Business Families: The New Barons," *India Today*, March 16–31, 1981, pp. 66–72. Also see Thomas A. Timberg, *The Marwaris: From Traders to Industrialists* (New Delhi: Vikas, 1978).

trast, public-sector industry, sluggish and inefficient, is on the defensive. Since the late 1970s government policy has increasingly relaxed controls on the private sector, as reflected both in development planning and in the policy of economic liberalization. The government's 860 billion rupee investment in the public sector has yielded negative returns, sometimes with staggering losses.

The Indian business community is represented by a multiplicity of associations. These include trade and industrial associations, employer associations, and chambers of commerce. Some are regional; some, like the Marwari (now Bharat) Chamber of Commerce in Bengal, represent particular communities. Three major national federations coordinate the activities of the various associations, as well as individual firms: the All-India Manufacturers Organization (AIMO) represents medium sized industry, primarily in Bombay; the Associated Chambers of Commerce and Industry of India (Assocham) represents foreign capital and large managerially oriented, Indian-owned companies; and the Federation of Indian Chambers of Commerce and Industry (FICCI), "first in size, prestige, and influence among the apex organizations," is broadly representative of major industrial and trading interests.[37] With association constituents as well as individual firm members, the Federation represents some 100,000 firms employing over 5 million workers.[38] For all its size, however, FICCI involves less than 1 percent of all private business people in India,[39] and even among those it does represent, it is dominated by big business, to the neglect of small and medium trade and industrial interests. In the 1960s the six largest houses (all based in Calcutta, of which five are Marwari) provided a third of FICCI's total membership, with Birla House alone commanding 25 percent of the votes at the annual meeting.[40] In 1985 the FICCI underwent a major split when a large group of members withdrew and joined Assocham.

In its efforts to influence public policy, the major targets of FICCI have been the Prime Minister, the Cabinet, and the upper echelons of the bureaucracy. By custom most Prime Ministers in the past have addressed the Federation's annual meeting in what, in effect, is a dialog between government and business. The Federation has gained representation on nearly 100 government commissions, committees,

[37] Stanley A. Kochanek, "The Federation of Indian Chambers of Commerce and Industry and Indian Politics," *Asian Survey*, 11 (September 1971): 869.

[38] Kochanek, *Business and Politics*, p. 170.

[39] Malenbaum, "Politics and Indian Business," p. 847.

[40] Kochanek, *Business and Politics*, pp. 174–75.

and councils and, through its secretariat, maintains continuous contact with various ministers and the bureaucracy. The Federation has also established a parliamentary office for liaison with Members of Parliament.[41]

FICCI has stood back from direct involvement in politics, but it has sought aid from government and protection for industry, while protesting regulation, control, and the jungle of licensing procedures.

It is through informal personal contact that business people, as individuals and through chambers, have most frequently gained access to government and by which they have achieved what Dandekar has called the "private understanding between the ruling party and big business."[42] Under Congress, for example, the Birlas commanded a position of such power that they were given a strong voice in the selection of the Finance Minister. Contact between government and business is facilitated by traditional ties of community, family, and personal friendship, and often at the lower levels of the bureaucracy by the flow of *bakshish,* a bribe for the performance of an administrative duty, for example, expediting an application for a permit or a license. Contributions to the Congress party also served to facilitate political access, and the Congress, as the party in power, frequently extracted "contributions" from businesses dependent on government favor.

Although business pressure has sought to shape and modify policy formation, more often this pressure has been exerted by individuals in business than by organized lobbies, and most frequently it has been used to bend the administration and implementation of policy rather than to form it. Much of its activity has, for this reason, been focused at the state level—particularly in those states responsive to its interests. Business, however, has not been able to influence substantially the shape and direction of public policy in India, and it has never succeeded in blocking or even modifying a major redistributive policy. It may be able to delay an objectionable policy, but it has not been able to convert its considerable economic power into truly effective political power. As a result, the extent of business influence in India is exaggerated by its enemies and understated by its friends.[43]

> Business in India has considerable political capital and resources to draw upon, and because it has been able to mobilize at least a portion

[41] Kochanek, "Indian Chambers of Commerce," pp. 873–78.

[42] V. M. Dandekar, "Next Steps on the Socialist Path," *Economic and Political Weekly 7,* Special Number (August 1972): 1557.

[43] Kochanek, *Business and Politics,* pp. 321–33.

> of these resources, it has become the best organized interest group in the country. It is the only group in India capable of sustained action and continuous day-to-day contact with both the Parliament and ranking heads of government. Nevertheless, although business enjoys a high level of access to government decision-makers its ability to convert this capital into influence is substantially held in check by a variety of internal organizational and external systemic restraints.[44]

As India enters the last decade of the twentieth century, the country is faced by an increasingly disquieting social, political, and economic crisis. The polity has become sharply polarized, and political and social conflicts have come to overshadow a deepening economic crisis as the economic consensus of the Nehru era has given way to renewed debate over the future of the country and the economy.

While political uncertainty and conflict consume the energies of the entire government, the economy has been racked by a third oil shock, loss of remittances, a worsening balance of payments problem, chronic rising deficits, and escalating inflation. The Indian coffers are empty, its international credit rating has been downgraded, donors are becoming increasingly impatient, and the country has been forced to turn to the International Monetary Fund for a bailout. The growing economic crisis has triggered a renewed debate over the causes and remedies of the crisis. As in the past, however, the debate has not focused on the fundamental question of an Indian *perestroika*, but the tinkering process called liberalization, a gradual piecemeal process of deregulation and decontrol. This process has been going on since the early 1970s as India has attempted to gradually alter the pervasive system of controls that have come to represent the hallmark of the Indian model of planned development.

Recommended Readings

Ahluwalia, Isher J., *Industrial Growth in India*. Delhi: Oxford University Press, 1985. An excellent analysis of the impact of India's policy framework on industrial growth.

Bardhan, Pranab, *The Political Economy of Development in India*. Oxford: Basil Blackwell, 1984. An incisive analysis.

Chakravarty, Sukhamoy, *Development Planning: The Indian Experience*. Oxford: Oxford University Press, 1987. A useful review of Indian economic development.

[44] Ibid., p. 323.

*Frankel, Francine R., *India's Political Economy, 1947–1977: The Gradual Revolution*. Princeton, N.J.: Princeton University Press, 1978. A major work analyzing the contradiction between the practice of accommodative politics and the commitment to social change.

*Grindle, Merilee, ed., *Politics and Policy Implementation in the Third World*. Princeton, N.J.: Princeton University Press, 1980. A collection of essays dealing with the content and context of public policy. Many of the cases are drawn from the Indian experience.

Jalan, Bimal, ed., *The Indian Economy: Problems and Prospects*. New Delhi: Viking/Penguin, 1992. A valuable collection of essays examining the economic reforms of the Narasimha Rao government.

*Jannuzi, F. Tomasson, *India in Transition: Issues of Political Economy in a Plural Society*. Boulder, Colo.: Westview Press, 1989. Analysis of how growth-centered development has accentuated inequalities and social tension.

Khurana, Rakesh, *Growth of Large Business: Impact of Monopolies Legislation*. New Delhi: Wiley Eastern, 1981. An evaluation of India's monopoly legislation and its impact on the growth of large business houses.

Kochanek, Stanley A., *Business and Politics in India*. Berkeley: University of California Press, 1974. The major study on the role of business in Indian politics.

Kohli, Atul, *The State and Poverty in India: The Politics of Reform*. Cambridge: Cambridge University Press, 1985. A study of the role of public authorities in economic development and the success of the redistributive intervention, with case studies of West Bengal, Karnataka, and Uttar Pradesh.

Kurian, C. T., *Growth and Justice: Aspects of India's Development Experience*. Delhi: Oxford University Press, 1992. Critique of the "high-growth" strategy of the 1980s.

Madan, K. D., et al., eds., *Policy Making in Government*. New Delhi: Publications Division, Ministry of Information and Broadcasting, Government of India, 1982. A massive collection of papers on policy and policy making in a wide domestic sector.

Marathe, S. S., *Regulation and Development*. New Delhi: Sage, 1986 and 1989. A comprehensive review of the evolution of industrial and regulatory policies in India by a former civil servant.

Mongia, J. N., ed., *India's Economic Policies, 1947–1977*. New Delhi: Allied Publishers, 1980. A collection of papers outlining the de-

*Available in a paperback edition.

velopment of Indian policies in almost every government field and covering their development over the first 30 years of independence.

Nadkarni, M. V., Seetharamu, A. S., and Aziz, Abdul, eds., *India: The Emerging Challenges*. New Delhi: Sage, 1991. A useful critical overview of economic and political change in India.

Nayar, Baldev Raj, *The Modernization Imperative and Indian Planning*. New Delhi: Vikas, 1972. A compelling argument for a new perspective on India's economic planning.

———, *India's Quest for Technological Independence*, 2 vols. New Delhi: Lancers, 1983. A comprehensive study of India's science and technology policy and the results of that policy on Indian development.

———, *The Political Economy of India's Public Sector*. Bombay: Popular Prakashan, 1990. An excellent study of the consequences of the public sector for the Indian economy, society, and polity.

Papanek, George F., and Lucas, Robert E. B., eds., *The Indian Economy: Recent Development and Future Prospects*. Boulder, Colo.: Westview Press, 1988. An excellent collection of essays that review almost every dimension of the Indian economy.

Rao, V. K. R. V., *India's National Income, 1950–1980: An Analysis of Economic Growth and Change*. New Delhi: Sage, 1983. A comprehensive macrostudy of the Indian economy by a leading economist and a former Cabinet member.

Rudolph, Lloyd, I., and Susanne H. Rudolph, *In Pursuit of Lakshmi: The Political Economy of the Indian State*. Chicago: University of Chicago Press, 1987. An excellent analysis of India's political economy.

Chapter 9

Policy and Performance: The International Context

THE PROCESSES OF MODERNIZATION AND DEVELOPMENT IN any nation are fundamentally conditioned by the international context in which they occur. No nation is hermetically sealed in isolation or so strong militarily or economically that it is impervious to influence and challenge from outside. In a world of increasing interdependence, the policies and actions of one state may so impinge on others as to determine their domestic policies and developmental prospects. The international economic system has long been under the influence of a handful of nations—the United States, Japan, and those of Western Europe. American fiscal policy regarding interest rates, for example, has an impact on every nation in the world. The capacity for influence is not limited to the great powers, however, or to the affluent nations of the West. The energy crisis brought on by the 1973 Arab oil embargo and the subsequent rise in the cost of oil were felt throughout the world and significantly affected the character of international politics. Beyond the economic realm, a nation's defense policy is determined largely by the military strength and posture of other, potentially threatening nations. Unfortunately, in the quest for a margin of superiority that will ensure security, security itself may be undermined by an arms race.

The study of domestic politics in India cannot be separated from the larger consideration of the international context of development. Development involves the will and capacity to initiate, absorb, and sustain continuous transformation. This necessitates a response to changes within the international system. In that environment, India confronts both constraints and imperatives.

Indian foreign and domestic policies are fused in the concern for national security and economic independence. But India's autarkic socialist policies crippled economic growth, and instead of achieving self-reliance, India, with serious balance-of-payments problems and budget deficits exacerbated by arms purchases from abroad, finds itself today ever more vulnerable to the vagaries of the international economy and dependent on foreign succor.

Having experienced three wars with Pakistan and one with China; witnessing the erosion of "Afro-Asian solidarity"; and, with the end of the cold war, the disintegration of the Soviet Union, and the emergence of a unipolar world, India is less idealistic, moralistic, and doctrinaire than in the years in which Nehru dominated Indian foreign policy. Yet, the fundamental character of that policy—nonalignment—has not changed.[1] Indian foreign policy, even as it pragmatically opens toward the West, is only beginning to come to terms with the new realities of a world in which "non-alignment" has lost its meaning.

Indian Foreign Policy: Nonalignment

Indian foreign policy is rooted in two traditions. One is British India, with a concern for the territorial integrity and security of South Asia, especially on the Himalayan frontiers. The other is the Indian National Congress, which evolved from the 1920s almost wholly under the direction of Nehru and focused on the problems of world peace, anticolonialism, and antiracism. In a speech at Columbia University in 1949, Nehru succinctly stated the goals of Indian foreign policy:

> India is a very old country with a great past. But it is a new country also with new urges and desires. . . . Inevitably she had to consider her foreign policy in terms of enlightened self-interest, but at the same

[1]For an analysis of foreign policy decision making in India and an assessment of India's relations with its neighbors and the great powers, see Robert L. Hardgrave, Jr., "Continuity and Change in India's Foreign Policy," in *India Under Pressure: Prospects for Political Stability* (Boulder, Colo.: Westview Press, 1984), pp. 133–214. Also see Robert L. Hardgrave, Jr., "Linkage Politics in India: The Relationship of Domestic Politics to Foreign Policy," in Robert A. Scalapino et al., eds., *Asia and the Major Powers: Domestic Politics and Foreign Policy* (Berkeley: Institute of East Asian Studies, The University of California, 1988), pp. 306–40.

> time she brought to it a touch of her idealism. Thus she has tried to combine idealism with national interest. The main objectives of that policy are: the pursuit of peace, not through alignment with any major power or group of powers, but through an independent approach to each controversial or disputed issue; the liberation of subject peoples; the maintenance of freedom both national and individual; the elimination of want, disease, and ignorance, which afflict the greater part of the world's population.[2]

Central to Nehru's concept was nonalignment. Neither a policy of neutrality nor of isolation, nonalignment by no means precluded an activist stance in the Indian self-interest. In the Indian view nonalignment is a pragmatic policy of independent action. It is simply a refusal to make any advance commitments, political or military, to any nation or bloc. Policy positions are made on an *ad hoc* basis according to the merits and circumstances of each case.[3]

Indian foreign policy embodies three basic goals: First, India seeks to guarantee its national security against invasion from without and subversion from within, against external support for secessionist and insurgent movements and foreign interference in its internal affairs. Indian security is fundamentally regional in its scope of concern. For India, successor state to the Raj, the whole of South Asia constitutes a strategic entity and, therefore, also constitutes the proper perimeters of its defense concerns. As a nation of 850 million people, with the fourth largest standing army in the world, India is the pre-eminent power of the subcontinent. Viewed by its neighbors as having hegemonic ambitions, India seeks recognition of its status in the region it regards as its natural and rightful sphere of influence. India has opposed external intervention and great power presence in the region both as a threat to regional security and as a challenge to its own pre-eminent position.

Second, India seeks independence and self-reliance. Until the collapse of the Soviet Union in 1991, India pursued nonalignment as a tightrope act in balancing relations with the Soviet Union, with which it had a close relationship of friendship and cooperation, and the United States and the West, with which it sought improved relations. Heavily dependent on Moscow for arms, India from the late 1970s sought to diversify its arms sources and, at the same time, secure increased access to advanced Western military technologies. In eco-

[2]Quoted in William J. Barnds, *India, Pakistan and the Great Powers* (New York, Praeger, 1972), pp. 47–48.

[3]M. S. Rajan, "India in World Politics in the Post-Nehru Era." in K. P. Misra, ed., *Studies in Indian Foreign Policy* (New Delhi: Vikas, 1969), p. 249.

nomic development, India sought to secure its independence by balancing its dependence on the West for aid and loans with Soviet credits and technical assistance. In trade, India developed a barter arrangement with the Soviet Union, even as it sought to expand exports to the rest of the world to meet rising import costs. While Russia may re-emerge as an important military and economic partner for India, the "balance" in India's equation for nonalignment is gone, and it must address its quest for self-reliance and enhanced security in the context of a competitive international market economy and a security environment in which superpower rivalry has been displaced by the undisputed military power of the United States.

Third, India, already a "rising middle power," aspires to great power status, to be at least regarded as China's equal in world affairs. With its vast population and military strength, India seeks inclusion as a permanent member of an expanded United Nations Security Council, and in international economic forums, it wants both to be heard and taken seriously. With low GNP per capita, unimpressive growth, and a share of international trade that has declined to 0.5 percent, however, India plays a marginal role in the world economy.[4] And with the end of the cold war, the disintegration of the Soviet Union, and the virtual eclipse of the Non-Aligned Movement, India's international role is likely to diminish, save in the South Asia arena where it seeks to establish its dominance. Moreover, domestic concerns impose constraints on India's role in the world, and India today is reluctant, as Nehru was not, to venture outside South Asia as a world actor.

Foreign Relations

Although India did not come to independence until 1947, it was an international actor, albeit under British direction, as a charter member of the League of Nations and the United Nations. Nehru had long made pronouncements on international politics in the name of the Congress, and upon becoming Prime Minister he retained for himself the portfolio of foreign affairs.

Among the first problems confronting the new government was its relationship with Great Britain. Nehru overcame strong opposition

[4]Robert L. Hardgrave, Jr., "Projected U.S. and USSR Roles in South Asia," in Leo E. Rose and Eric Gonsalves, eds., *Toward a New World Order: Adjusting U.S.–India Relations* (Berkeley: Institute of East Asian Studies, The University of California, 1992), pp. 68–70.

from those who sought a complete break, and India secured Commonwealth status as a republic by a formula wherein the Crown became the "symbol of free association" among the independent member nations. It was within the Commonwealth, however, that India was to confront its most serious and persistent international conflict—that with Pakistan.

Pakistan

The 1947 partition presented a host of problems: the division of Indian financial assets; the split-up of the bureaucracy and the army; and, most critically, the conflict over use of the waters of the Indus basin, which was settled after 12 years of negotiation through World Bank mediation. Partition had been accomplished with staggering rapidity and at enormous human cost. The transfer of almost 12,000,000 people did not fulfill Jinnah's vision of "two nations," however. Some 40,000,000 Muslims remained in India and 10,000,000 Hindus in East Pakistan. Throughout the following years, several thousand Hindu Bengali refugees continued to flow each year into West Bengal and Assam, their numbers varying each month with the degree of communal tension. The focus of the "religious minority problem" as it affected Indo-Pakistani relations, however, was Kashmir.

In 1947 the population of Jammu and Kashmir was about three-quarters Muslim, but the maharajah, a Hindu, resisted the pressure to accede to either Pakistan or India. Pakistan sought to force the issue, first imposing an economic boycott against the state and then supporting Pakistani tribes in an invasion of Kashmir. The maharajah's appeal to India for protection was accepted on condition of Kashmir's accession, with the promise to consult the wishes of the Kashmiri people once law and order had been restored. Nehru reaffirmed this "pledge to the people of Kashmir" and agreed to Kashmiri self-determination through an internationally supervised plebiscite. It was by no means a foregone conclusion that the plebiscite would favor Pakistan, for Kashmir's most popular leader, Sheikh Abdullah of the National Conference, was strongly committed to a secular state and to accession to India. Making the conditions for such a plebiscite mutually acceptable to both India and Pakistan was another matter. Most important for India was a complete withdrawal of Pakistani forces from Kashmir.[5]

[5]For an analysis of the first Kashmir war and subsequent 1965 and 1971 wars, see Sumit Ganguly, *The Origins of War in South Asia: Indo–Pakistani Conflict Since 1947* (Boulder, Colo.: Westview Press, 1986.

In 1949 India and Pakistan accepted the United Nations cease-fire line, with one-third of the state under the control of the Pakistani Azad Kashmir government. There followed years of continuous negotiation under the auspices of the U.N., but with time Nehru, himself a Kashmiri Brahmin, increasingly came to regard Kashmir as the guarantee of India's secularism and as a denial of the "two-nation" theory upon which Pakistan was founded. The 1954 U.S.-Pakistan agreement brought another factor into the situation, as did Pakistan's strengthened hold on Azad Kashmir. Arguing that the circumstances in Kashmir had changed so completely that the original offer for a plebiscite was no longer valid, India accepted the Kashmir constituent assembly's vote of accession as equivalent to a plebiscite. Article 370 of the Indian Constitution had recognized, as a temporary provision, special status for Kashmir within the Indian Union. Kashmir's own constitution, adopted in 1956, specified that the "State of Jammu and Kashmir is and shall be an integral part of the Union of India," but Article 370 remains in force and the precise nature of Kashmir's position within India has yet to be defined.[6]

When communal unrest developed in Kashmir in 1963–64, Pakistan President Ayub Khan, a decade of American military assistance behind him, embarked on a policy of "leaning on India." In April 1965, following an increase in tension along the cease-fire line in Kashmir, an armed clash occurred in the Rann of Kutch in Gujarat over disputed boundaries in an area alternately marsh and desert but potentially rich in oil deposits. By the end of June, a cease-fire was reached, with a mutual withdrawal of forces and an agreement for arbitration. Kutch, however, was but a dress rehearsal. In August, Ayub sent Pakistani-trained guerrillas into Kashmir in hopes of triggering internal rebellion against Indian rule. India seized passes in Kashmir, Pakistani armored units moved into Jammu, and India launched an attack across the Punjab plain toward Lahore. In a reversal of their success in the Rann of Kutch, Pakistani tanks took a heavy beating. The U.S. was chagrined that American arms supplied to Pakistan should be used against another recipient of U.S. military assistance, and both the U.S. and Great Britain cut off further arms ship-

[6]A vast literature is available on the Kashmir dispute. For a succinct discussion, see Sumit Ganguly, "Avoiding War in Kashmir," *Foreign Affairs*, 69 (Winter 1990–91), pp. 57–73. For more detailed analyses, see Raju G. C. Thomas, ed., *Perspectives on Kashmir: The Roots of Conflict in South Asia* (Boulder, Colo.: Westview Press, 1992); Sisir Gupta, *Kashmir: A Study in India–Pakistan Relations* (Bombay: Asia Publishing House, 1966); and, for a view less sympathetic to India's case, Alastair Lamb, *Kashmir: A Disputed Legacy* (Hertingfordbury, UK: Roxford Books, 1991).

ments to India and Pakistan. China, on the other hand, sided with Pakistan and denounced India's "criminal aggression" with threatening ultimatums. The United Nations Security Council, with the support of the U.S., Great Britain, and the U.S.S.R., called for an immediate cease-fire, which India and Pakistan accepted in September. Soviet Premier Kosygin, seeking to strengthen ties with Pakistan, check Chinese influence, and at the same time maintain traditionally close ties with India, offered the good offices of the Soviet Union to negotiate a settlement. Ayub and Shastri proceeded to Tashkent in January 1966. The agreement, rather than solving the basic problems, represented a return to the status quo before the war. Given India's success in the war, the agreement to withdraw forces was not well received by many in Congress or the opposition. "Yet Shastri's untimely death at Tashkent made it certain that India would not repudiate his last official act."[7] In 1968 a three-member arbitration commission awarded Pakistan about one-tenth of the disputed Rann of Kutch. It was greeted with an angry Indian reaction, but it was accepted.

Indian performance in the 1965 war served to renew the confidence of the Army and to restore it to the prestige that had been lost in the 1962 Chinese conflict. Indian anxieties were heightened, however, by the supply of military aid to Pakistan by China. Moreover, despite assurances from the U.S.S.R., India felt uneasy about Pakistani–Soviet rapprochement and the limited shipment of Soviet arms to Pakistan.

Within Pakistan, political unrest had measurably increased. In 1969, under pressure to resign, President Ayub Khan stepped down in favor of General Yahya Khan, who pledged to restore democratic institutions. The two wings of Pakistan, created out of the Muslim majority areas within the subcontinent, were united by religion but divided by almost every other cultural factor and a thousand miles of Indian territory. West Pakistan from the time of independence held sway over the Bengali East. When the December 1970 elections yielded a victory for East Pakistan's Awami League, led by Sheikh Mujibur ("Mujib") Rahman, West Pakistan's leaders refused to accept the results. After talks between President Yahya and Mujib broke down, on March 25, 1971, Mujib was arrested, and in a wave of terror, the heel of the Pakistani army came down on the people of East Bengal.

During the nine months of repression that followed, thousands of

[7]Barnds, *India, Pakistan,* p. 212.

Bengalis were killed,[8] and some 10,000,000 refugees, most of whom were Hindu, crossed the borders into northeastern India. The refugee movement created a situation that was economically, socially, and politically unacceptable for India. India, however, was even more concerned about "the potentially destabilizing influence of the conflict in East Pakistan on strife-ridden West Bengal, as well as the tribal hill states and Assam in northeastern India."[9] Moreover, there was the danger that the events in East Bengal might set off communal rioting in India. Fortunately it did not happen.

Supplies already "in the pipeline" from the United States continued to flow into Pakistan, and while the U.S. government counseled Indian restraint, the Nixon Administration pursued a policy of "tilt toward Pakistan." Pakistan also found support not only from the Middle East, but from much of Asia and Africa as well—new nations, most of which had their own potential Bangladesh.

In August 1971 India and the Soviet Union signed a 20-year treaty of friendship and cooperation. Not a mutual security treaty but an agreement for consultation, it served to formalize the relations already existing between the two nations and involved specific commitments of neither.[10] While the USSR had condemned Pakistan's actions in Bangladesh, it sought a political settlement of the problem without war. The treaty was intended as a deterrent to Pakistan and China, but it also brought India into greater dependency on the Soviet Union. India, however, undoubtedly felt bolstered by the treaty, particularly in terms of deterring China's possible entry into the conflict.

As early as April, India decided to assist the Mukti Bahini, the Bengali resistance forces, as pressure on Pakistan to make basic concessions, but it soon became clear that this would not be sufficient. Beyond aid, training, and sanctuary, Indian military became indirectly involved in Mukti Bahini activities, and in a series of escalating moves, Pakistan, then India, ordered full mobilization of forces. Preceded by a series of Indian strikes across the border, described as "defensive" responses to Pakistani shelling, the Indian Army, on No-

[8]Figures vary widely, from tens of thousands to Mujib's claims that 3.5 million Bengalis were killed.

[9]Richard Sisson and Leo E. Rose, *War and Secession: Pakistan, India, and the Creation of Bangladesh* (Berkeley: University of California Press, 1990), p. 206. Of the many books on the Bangladesh crisis, this is surely the best analysis.

[10]See Ashok Kapur, "Indo-Soviet Treaty and the Emerging Asian Balance," *Asian Survey*, 12 (June 1972): 463–74; and Robert H. Donaldson, "India: The Soviet Stake in Stability," *Asian Survey*, 12 (June 1972): 475–92.

vember 21, established operational bases inside Pakistan "as part of the preliminary phase to the offensive directed at capturing and liberating Dhaka."[11] On December 3, Pakistan launched a series of air strikes from the west against Indian air bases. That night, India moved on all fronts against Pakistan.

On December 6, underscoring its lack of territorial ambition, India formally recognized the government of Bangladesh. In a blitzkrieg operation, the Indian army moved toward Dhaka, and on December 16 Indian troops entered the city and accepted Pakistan's surrender. India ordered a unilateral cease-fire on the western front. In disgrace, Yahya was forced to resign. Zulfikar Ali Bhutto, leader of the Pakistan People's Party, became president and, though refusing to recognize the dismemberment of Pakistan, ordered the release of Mujib.

By early autumn it probably had been clear to India that the liberation of Bangladesh was inevitable. The forces of the Bengali guerrilla Mukti Bahini had been growing, but on their own it would have been a protracted war with enormous loss of life. For India to sit on the sidelines could have proven politically costly. India had a vital interest in the character of the future government of Bangladesh and from the beginning had supported moderate Mujib. Within the Mukti Bahini, however, were Naxalite elements, and anarchy in Bangladesh might have invited Chinese involvement. For India, the stability of West Bengal and the Northeast was of fundamental concern, but most immediate was the question of the refugees. If Bangladesh had been liberated without Indian intervention, it is highly improbable that 10,000,000 largely Hindu refugees would have been welcomed back to the East. Only by direct military involvement could India ensure the return of the refugees to East Bengal.

Immediately upon Pakistan's defeat, the refugee return began, and by March 16, 1972, three months after the liberation of Bangladesh, the Indian Army was able to complete its final withdrawal. It was yet another month before the United States recognized the new nation of Bangladesh, the last major country to do so, save for China and Pakistan itself.

India was now the undisputed power on the subcontinent. A euphoric atmosphere permeated newspaper headlines proclaiming the liberation as the greatest day since Indian independence. Pakistan had been cut down to size, both figuratively and in real terms. The Simla Agreement, signed July 2, 1972, by Indira Gandhi and Bhutto, confirmed the new line of control in Kashmir and sought to provide

[11] Sisson and Rose, *War and Secession*, pp. 210–14.

the basis for a "durable peace" between the two countries. Both sides agreed to accept the principle that Indo–Pakistani problems would be settled through bilateral negotiations, without outside intervention and without recourse to force. The Simla Agreement remains the basis for official relations between India and Pakistan.[12]

In 1976 India and Pakistan renewed full diplomatic relations. After a 10-year interruption, railway links between the two countries were reopened, and air service was resumed. The improvement in Indo–Pakistani relations survived the 1977 military coup overthrowing Bhutto, as it did his execution nearly two years later. In the formation of the Janata government in March 1977, there was anxiety in Pakistan over the appointment of Jana Sangh leader A. B. Vajpayee as Minister of External Affairs. The Jana Sangh had long taken a vehemently anti-Pakistan stance and had pushed for Indian nuclear capability, but Vajpayee moved quickly to rest any fears of a breakdown in relations.

During the Janata period Indo–Pakistani relations improved markedly, but in December 1979, on the eve of Mrs. Gandhi's return to power, the Soviet invasion of Afghanistan fundamentally changed the strategic environment of South Asia. Even before taking office as Prime Minister, Indira Gandhi took command of Indian foreign policy. Under instructions from New Delhi, India's envoy to the United Nations delivered a speech (later, by most accounts, deeply regretted) in which the Soviet justification for the intervention was taken at face value. India abstained on the resolution calling for "the immediate withdrawal of the foreign troops from Afghanistan." In India's view, isolating the Soviet Union by condemning it would only strengthen Soviet resolve and make a political solution to the crisis more difficult. India also envisioned, however, a constructive role for itself in facilitating a solution that would enable the Soviet Union to withdraw its troops, confident that its security interests in the region were protected.[13] Soviet intransigence soon frustrated India's efforts to "defuse" the crisis. In meetings with Soviet Foreign Minister Andrei Gromyko, and later with President Leonid Brezhnev, Mrs. Gandhi made it clear that India wanted Soviet troops to withdraw from Afghanistan as soon as possible. In its public stand India pulled back

[12] Surjit Mansingh, *India's Search for Power: Indira Gandhi's Foreign Policy, 1966–1982* (New Delhi: Sage, 1984), pp. 226–30.

[13] India's position on Afghanistan is examined in Thomas P. Thornton, "India and Afghanistan," in Theodore L. Elliot, Jr., and Robert L. Pfaltzgraff, Jr., eds., *The Red Army on Pakistan's Borders: Policy Implications for the United States* (Washington: Pergamon-Brassey's, 1986), pp. 44–70.

from the earlier United Nations speech to assume a more critical position, but one that concomitantly decried American efforts to use the Afghan crisis as an excuse for rearming Pakistan and building a strategic consensus in Southwest Asia.

India's fundamental concern was to keep both the Soviet Union and the United States out of South Asia. India maintained that the Soviet action in Afghanistan was not the source but the consequence of deepening superpower rivalry in the region. Its reaction to the Afghan crisis was shaped by a regional perspective and by the fear that South Asia would become an arena of great-power confrontation and international conflict. In this context, India viewed American military support for Pakistan as destabilizing. With the American commitment of 3.2 billion dollars in arms and economic aid to Pakistan and the agreement to supply the sophisticated F-16 fighter to the Pakistani air force, India became increasingly alarmed, both at the level of U.S. involvement in the region and at what it viewed as the danger of an emboldened Pakistan attacking India in yet another adventure to seize Kashmir.

Pakistan harbored no such illusions, and with a military capability that could not begin to match Indian superiority, Pakistan President Zia ul-Haq proposed a "no-war pact" with India. Although Indira Gandhi initially dismissed the offer contemptuously as "a trap," India later responded with a counteroffer for a treaty of friendship and cooperation. The "war clouds" that some saw on the horizon in 1980 and 1981 receded as President Zia and Prime Minister Gandhi met for discussions. A joint commission was established to promote economic and cultural cooperation, but the no-war pact and the proposed treaty of friendship remained on the table, victims of the mutual distrust that divided the long-time adversaries.

In 1984 a new element of Indian concern brought a rapid deterioration in Indo–Pakistani relations. Indira Gandhi, and later Rajiv, together with a number of Indian officials, accused Pakistan of providing sanctuary, training, and assistance for Sikh extremists in the Punjab. Against a backdrop of rising tension between India and Pakistan, in late 1986, India began military exercises—Operation Brass Tacks—along the Pakistan border. It was an exercise of "unprecedented magnitude," designed to test the military's operational readiness, and Pakistan responded in alarm with parallel exercises, massing troops at the border in combat-ready formation.[14] The crisis was defused diplomatically, but Brass Tacks was yet another instance of

[14] *India Today*, 15 February 1987, pp. 8–14.

the mutual suspicion and misperceptions that have brought the two countries to the brink of war.

Armed conflict between India and Pakistan is almost a daily occurrence somewhere along the Kashmir line of control, and at its northern reaches, on the Siachen Glacier, they have engaged in a "miniwar" at altitudes above 17,000 feet. The 1972 Simla Agreement, in adjusting the line of control, did not delineate the border across the glacier, but indicated simply that it would run north. Beginning in 1984, India and Pakistan deployed troops on the glacier, each to prevent the other from securing claim to the icy waste. With periodic clashes, peaking in 1987, casualties have gone into the hundreds, though most result from terrain, altitude, and weather.

In 1989, the Siachen conflict was eclipsed by heightened tension over Kashmir itself. The separatist uprising in Kashmir stirred Pakistanis to expression of solidarity with those who would "liberate" Indian-held Kashmir. India denounced Pakistan for clandestine support in training and arming the rebels and warned Islamabad of reprisal. By the spring of 1990, with increasingly strident rhetoric on both sides of the border, Prime Minister Benazir Bhutto declared that the Pakistani people were prepared to struggle for a thousand years to free Kashmir, and Islamic fundamentalists in Pakistan called for *jihad* against India. Indian Prime Minister V. P. Singh called upon his compatriots to prepare for war and warned Pakistan that if it were to launch a "limited war," overt or covert, in Kashmir, "India's response would be total war" against Pakistan. Jolted by the imminence of war, leaders tempered their rhetoric, and the two countries entered into talks. Perhaps the special American envoy sent to Pakistan and India in April 1990, together with Soviet and Chinese efforts, had helped to ease the crisis. International concerns were heightened in the knowledge that both India and Pakistan have the capability to make and deploy nuclear weapons, if they have not already, as some believe, crossed the nuclear threshold. No external power, however, has sufficient leverage in South Asia to deter either India or Pakistan from a determined course of action. What has been critical through the course of the renewed conflict over Kashmir is that even as India and Pakistan exchange words and fire across the border, neither side wants war. Pakistan, facing a military force ratio with India of 3:1 and a cutoff in American military assistance,[15] would be crushed, and In-

[15]In October 1990, pursuant to the Pressler Amendment, the United States cut off economic and military aid to Pakistan when President Bush was unable to certify to Congress that Pakistan does not possess a nuclear explosive device.

dia, even with preponderant force, would bear a staggering economic burden in the conduct of war. Moreover, in "total war," each side could inflict terrible damage on the other, and with Pakistan's very survival at issue, the potential use of nuclear weapons dramatically raises the stakes. War between India and Pakistan is today unlikely, but misperception and miscalculation bring high risks in an atmosphere of mutual suspicion and unresolved grievances.

The "Nonaligned" World

From the time of Indian independence through the 1950s, India assumed a role of leadership in the Afro–Asian world. Special effort was given to ties with Islamic states, for India—concerned about its own Muslim population—sought to prevent Muslim unity in support of Pakistan. In the United Nations, India was ever ready to defend the interests of national liberation from the vestiges of imperialism throughout the world. India sought to exert a moral force for peace and to that effect became involved in mediation and "peace-keeping" operations in Korea, Indochina, the Congo, and Cyprus. India's stance often carried a moralizing tone, and when acting in pursuit of its own interests (as in the 1961 invasion of Goa after long efforts to dislodge the Portuguese from their enclaves in India), India was regarded in the west as inconsistent, if not hypocritical.

India was among the founders of the Non-Aligned Movement, and from its first conference in 1961, India assumed a position of leadership in what was projected as the voice for the newly independent states in a world divided by military blocs. For all India's efforts on behalf of the Third World nations, only a few countries offered even verbal support to India in its 1962 confrontation with China. India's military weakness had been exposed, and in military defeat it suffered a decline in international prestige. Nehru's foreign policy had been based "on global influence without military power."[16] That policy was shattered in 1962. India's position of influence was also affected by the increase in the number of new nonaligned nations and the conflicts between them.[17] Yet India's attachment to the Non-Alignment Movement has remained long after the movement lost coherence and ceased to speak with any moral authority. While the movement may

[16]Wayne Wilcox, "Nuclear Weapon Options and the Strategic Environment in South Asia: Arms Control Implications for India," Southern California Arms Control and Foreign Policy Seminar, 1972, p. 9.

[17]For a prescient review and analysis of the Non-aligned Movement, see Jagat Mehta, "Non-Alignment: A Spent Force?", *Seminar*, 287 (July 1983): 20–30.

have contributed to easing the tensions of the cold war, the end of the cold war has rendered it irrelevant. That irrelevance was evident in the movement's inability to respond to the Gulf crisis in 1990–91.

The Iraqi invasion of Kuwait presented India itself with a fundamental dilemma. India had long courted the Arabs as a foil against Pakistan, and in its close relations with Iraq had secured Iraqi support on the Kashmir issue. India was, moreover, dependent on Iraq and Kuwait for 40 percent of its oil imports, and some 185,000 Indians working in the two countries sent back much-needed hard currency. In the early stages of the Gulf crisis, India adopted an ambivalent stance and seemed more concerned about the buildup of U.S. forces in the area than any actions taken by Iraq. Its principal concern, however, was the safety and repatriation of Indian workers in the Gulf region.

India's initial stance left it isolated internationally, and by October, New Delhi began to shift its position behind United Nations sanctions against Iraq. But when, in January 1991, India permitted U.S. military aircraft to refuel en route from bases in the Philippines to the Gulf, the Chandra Shekhar government came under fire—most vocally from Rajiv Gandhi, who denounced the policy as a betrayal of India's nonalignment—and permission to refuel was withdrawn. India's response to the crisis reflected its attempts to come to terms with the end of the cold war, but it remained a captive of cold war mentality and, preoccupied with domestic concerns, found itself marginalized as an international actor.[18]

The Gulf war served as the catalyst for a reassessment of Indian foreign policy and a recognition of the realities of the post-cold war era. "The result," in the words of *India Today*, "has been a startling shift in its traditional stance on a crucial range of issues."[19] In December 1991, India voted to repeal the UN resolution equating Zionism with racism, a resolution it originally supported as a stalwart of the Palestinian cause. In January 1992, it voted with the United States on a UN resolution condemning Libyan support for terrorism. And in February, India established diplomatic relations with Israel.

If India today seeks a more active role in world affairs, however, its principal focus will remain, as it has since the death of Nehru in 1964, on the region of South Asia itself, where it seeks to establish and secure its own pre-eminence.

[18] J. Mohan Malik, "India's Response to the Gulf Crisis: Implications for Indian Foreign Policy," *Asian Survey*, 31 (September 1991): 847–61.

[19] *India Today*, "Foreign Policy: Groundbreaking Shift," 29 February 1992, p. 20.

South Asia

India's relations with its South Asian neighbors have, with the exceptions of Bhutan and the Maldives, been marked by strain. Pakistan, with whom India has fought three wars, is its principal foreign adversary, but in relations with the other states of the region, India has pursued friendship with a sometimes heavy hand.

India's relations with Sri Lanka have focused largely on the persistent problem of the status of the 3,000,000 Tamils who make up 18 percent of the island's population. In earlier years, the concern was for the "stateless" Indian Tamils, who had immigrated to the island as plantation workers in the nineteenth century, but in the 1980s, India's attention turned to the rising ethnic conflict between Sri Lanka's majority Sinhalese community and the Sri Lankan Tamils, whose dominance in the northern part of the island dates back more than 1000 years. In response to discrimination, in the late 1970s, young Tamil radicals voiced the demand for a separate Tamil nation ("Eelam") to be formed in the north and east. By 1983, Sri Lanka was in ethnic turmoil, as Tamil guerrilla raids on police stations and military patrols were met, in retribution, by Sinhalese attacks on Tamils. The escalating violence in the years since polarized the two communities in a civil war that has taken 20,000 lives.[20]

In the early 1980s, sensitive to reactions in Tamil Nadu to the ethnic conflict in Sri Lanka, the Indian government gave sanctuary to the Tamil guerrillas—the Liberation Tigers of Tamil Eelam (LTTE) and rival organizations—and supported training camps from which the guerrillas operated across the narrow Palk Strait to Sri Lanka. After Indira Gandhi's death, Rajiv sought to mediate a settlement, but with an unresponsive LTTE, Sri Lanka moved toward a military solution. In 1987, as the Sri Lankan military pushed into the northern Jaffna Peninsula, India, fearing a political backlash in Tamil Nadu, air-dropped relief supplies to the besieged Tamils and threatened Sri Lanka with armed intervention. Through secret negotiations, Rajiv Gandhi and Sri Lankan President J. R. Jayewardene reached agreement and, in July 1987, signed an accord that provided for the entry of an Indian Peace Keeping Force (IPKF) and a series of concessions by Sri Lanka that tacitly recognized Indian pre-eminence. Sinhalese nationalists denounced the accord as a violation of Sri Lankan sovereignty. The Tamil Tigers were not a party to the accord, however, and the IPKF, with a buildup to more than 50,000 troops, soon found itself fighting

[20] See especially S. J. Tambiah, *Sri Lanka: Ethnic Fratricide and the Dismantling of Democracy* (Chicago: University of Chicago Press, 1986).

the guerrillas. In 1989, the new Sri Lankan president, R. Premadasa, an opponent of the accord, ordered the removal of all Indian forces from Sri Lanka. The hold of the Tamil guerrillas had not been broken, and, in India's longest war, at least 1100 Indian soldiers had been killed, another 2800 wounded. In the wake of a political and military debacle, the last Indian troops pulled out in March 1990.[21]

India fared better in its adventure in the Maldives. India had long had good relations with the tiny republic of scattered islands off its southwest coast. In 1988, the president of the Maldives radioed New Delhi for help against a coup started by a disgruntled Maldivian businessman with a hired force of Sri Lankan Tamil militants. Within hours, India dispatched 1600 paratroopers and a naval force to aid its neighbor, crushing the rebellion. Other South Asian states viewed the operation with unease as India sought to establish itself as the guarantor of regional stability.[22]

India's relations with Nepal and Bhutan have involved matters of vital security concern. As had Great Britain, independent India has sought to maintain a buffer zone in the Himalayas against China. In 1950 India signed a treaty with Nepal, recognizing its "complete sovereignty." At the same time, however, India exerted enormous influence over the domestic affairs of Nepal. In an assertion of Nepali independence, the king sought to balance Indian influence by "regularizing" relations with China, and sought international recognition for Nepal as a "zone of peace"—a proposal that India viewed as an attempt by Nepal to opt out of India's security perimeter and to abrogate the special relationship with India under the 1950 treaty. In 1989, with particular concern over Nepal's secret acquisition of arms from China, India exerted its force by economic muscle. Facing renewal of the trade and transit treaties, India sought a renegotiated single treaty, and to pressure a recalcitrant Nepal, it imposed a blockade of all but two of the land transit routes between the two countries. The 15-month dispute imposed serious hardship on South Asia's poorest nation, but in 1990, with a new constitutional government in Kathmandu and a new government in New Delhi, agreement was reached to restore relations to that of the status quo before April, 1, 1987, when the trade and transit treaties lapsed, and to consult each other in all matters relating to their common security.

Bhutan, the most isolated of the Himalayan kingdoms, is an inde-

[21] For a succinct overview of these events, see Devin T. Hagerty, "India's Regional Security Doctrine," *Asian Survey*, 31 (April 1991), pp. 353–58.

[22] *Ibid*, pp. 358–60.

pendent state and a member of the United Nations. The British had exercised suzerainty over Bhutan, but in giving Britain control over its foreign relations, Bhutan had secured freedom from British intervention in internal affairs. In 1949, by a new treaty, Bhutan agreed "to be guided" by Indian advice on foreign relations, but although India provides an annual subsidy, it has chosen not to interfere in the domestic affairs of Bhutan. In recent years the two countries have differed on Bhutan's handling of illegal Nepali immigrants, and potentially the issue could become a serious problem.

Bangladesh, in its weakness and vulnerability, confronts India with potentially serious problems as a major source of political instability within the subcontinent. With more than 115,000,000 people, Bangladesh is one of the world's most densely populated nations—and one of the poorest. A victim of both nature and inhumanity, Bangladesh has been ravaged by cyclones, war, floods, and corruption. Its economic situation is desperate, and its political situation unstable. Although India had been midwife to the liberation of Bangladesh, resentment against India was widespread. Two months after the imposition of the 1975–77 emergency in India, Sheikh Mujibur Rahman was overthrown and killed during a military coup. Indian relations with Bangladesh rapidly deteriorated, with charges by Bangladesh that Indian agents were subverting the new government and fomenting rebellion. Resentment was especially deep over the issue of the Farakka barrage, a low dam that flushes out the heavily silted port of Calcutta by diverting a portion of Ganges water from its course into East Bengal. Tensions relaxed during the Janata phase, with the signing of an interim agreement in 1977 on the Ganges water problem, but the issue remains a subject of intermittent negotiations.

A territorial dispute also exists between India and Bangladesh over tiny islands in the Bay of Bengal. The islands themselves are of little consequence, but the boundary involves claims to potentially important offshore natural gas fields. Relations are also troubled periodically by Bangladeshi accusations of Indian interference in its internal affairs and of Indian attempts to destabilize the nation.

The most serious problem in Indo–Bangladeshi relations is the least susceptible to diplomatic effort—the illegal movement of people across the border from Bangladesh into India. The flow of migrants seeking work in India has been especially destabilizing in Assam, where, in the mid-1980s, it precipitated the violent anti-immigrant movement in defense of Assamese culture and political power. The violence, together with renewed efforts to control the border, stemmed the tide, but a deterioration of economic or political conditions in Bangladesh could again accelerate movement across the porous border. The movement of Bangladeshis into West Bengal is a matter of increasing concern as well, with a potential for fueling Hindu–Muslim communal conflict.

South Asian Regional Cooperation

Regional cooperation in the subcontinent has been undermined by the unequal distribution of power in South Asia and by the conflict between India and Pakistan. New Delhi has tended to view regionalism as a design enabling the other states to "gang up" against India. Thus India has sought to deal with each country bilaterally and to discourage communication and contact among the nations on its periphery. For their part the smaller countries have been reluctant to enter into regional cooperation for fear that India would inevitably dominate any association, and that such an association would, in effect, institutionalize Indian hegemony.

This situation has begun to change. In 1980 President Ziaur Rahman of Bangladesh proposed that there be a greater degree of regional cooperation among the seven South Asian nations—India, Pakistan, Bangladesh, Nepal, Bhutan, Sri Lanka, and the Maldives—in facing their common problems. India and Pakistan were initially reluctant, but through discussion at the foreign secretary level, the groundwork was laid for limited multilateral cooperation in what became the South Asian Association for Regional Cooperation (SAARC). In 1983 the foreign ministers of the seven nations met in New Delhi to give their formal assent to the promotion of "collective self-reliance" in nine fields: agriculture, rural development, planning, health, education, transport, telecommunications, sports, and culture. To emphasize the equality of each member, the association charges each nation with responsibility for at least one field of cooperation. The declaration proclaims the goal as one of mutual assistance "to accelerate economic growth, social progress and cultural development in the region." All decisions are to be unanimous, and "bilateral and contentious issues shall be excluded from the deliberations."

SAARC has provided an important framework for an annual meeting of the South Asian leaders. From the first summit in Dhaka in 1985, the meeting rotates among the seven members, with the leader of the host nation assuming the SAARC chairmanship for the ensuing year. The process has not been without problems, as in the postponement of the 1991 Colombo summit, forced when India, as a rebu

Sri Lanka's President Premadasa, refused at the last minute to attend. India's action, however, drew sharp criticism within India due to the role SAARC plays as a forum for conflict management in the region. Its significance here is not in the formal sessions of the summit, but in the opportunity it affords for South Asian leaders (as, for example, the prime ministers of India and Pakistan) to meet privately to address their bilateral problems.[23]

China

India's first encounters with the new government of the People's Republic of China were clouded by the reassertion of Chinese suzerainty over Tibet. India had inherited the British concern for a Himalayan buffer zone and sought to maintain Tibetan autonomy. Despite Peking's denunciation of India as an imperialist lackey, Nehru worked for improved relations. In 1954, recognizing Tibet as a "region of China," India negotiated an agreement with China, setting forth the five principles—*Panchsheel*—that were to be the basis of their friendship and, as reaffirmed at the Afro–Asian Conference at Bandung in 1955, a cornerstone of Indian foreign policy: (1) mutual respect for each other's territorial integrity and sovereignty; (2) nonaggression; (3) noninterference in each other's internal affairs; (4) equality and mutual benefit; and (5) peaceful coexistence.

From 1954 until 1959 India continuously declared its friendship for China. In 1959, however, revolt in Tibet and the Dalai Lama's flight into India served to expose serious tensions between India and China. India had long been aware that Chinese maps showed large areas claimed by India (some 40,000 square miles) as parts of China, regions that had at one time been under Chinese imperial suzerainty. The areas claimed by China included nearly all of the North East Frontier Province (now Arunachal Pradesh), small pockets along the India–China border between Nepal and Kashmir, and the Aksai Chin plain of eastern Ladakh in Kashmir. In the east the dispute focused on the legitimacy of the McMahon Line, defining the border between the North East Frontier Agency (NEFA) and Tibet, which was drawn in 1914 by the Simla convention. Even in its position of weakness at that time, China had refused to sign the convention. In Ladakh, China's claim to the vast and desolate Aksai Chin, again historical,

[23]See J. D. Muni, "Prospects for SAARC," *Mainstream*, 20 August 1988, pp. 7–13; Partha S. Ghosh, *Cooperation and Conflict in South Asia* (New Delhi: Manohar, 1989); and Bhabani Sen Gupta, ed., *Regional Cooperation and Development in South Asia*, 2 vols. (New Delhi: South Asia Publishers), 1986.

disputed the imperial frontier imposed by Great Britain upon China. Far more important for China, however, was the strategic position of the Aksai Chin, for along the old caravan route was China's most secure access between Xinjiang (Sinkiang) and Lhasa. The Aksai Chin occupied a position of strategic importance to China in terms of both internal security within Tibet and the perceived threat posed by the Soviet Union, particularly as directed against Xinjiang. Chinese concern deepened with Tibetan unrest and the intensification of the Sino–Soviet controversy. In 1957 China completed an all-weather road across the Aksai Chin, linking Xinjiang with Tibet. A year later Indian patrols discovered the road, but it was not until the Tibetan revolt and border clashes along the Tibet–NEFA border in 1959 forced the issue that Nehru revealed to Parliament the full extent of the dispute with China.[24]

In 1960 Nehru and Chou En-lai entered into "talks" on the border problem. The Chinese proposed to abandon their claims in NEFA in exchange for the Aksai Chin, already under Chinese control. By this time the dispute had become a matter of emotional intensity in India. India was unwilling, and politically unable, to accept the proposal. Despite its comparative military weakness, India embarked on a "forward policy" on the frontier "intended to check Chinese advances everywhere and, if possible, force Chinese withdrawals in Ladakh."[25] In the fall of 1962, in an effort to force India to negotiate and give up claims to the Aksai Chin, China began a push along the NEFA frontier. On October 20 the invasion of NEFA began. The move in the Northeast was clearly designed to secure a quid pro quo in Ladakh, and on October 24 Chou En-lai proposed a cease-fire and a mutual withdrawal of forces from the current line of contact, to be followed by negotiations. In a position of weakness, negotiation for India could only mean capitulation. In preparation for continued war with China, the Government of India proclaimed a state of emergency.

Within a month Indian defenses collapsed: China had penetrated 150 miles below the McMahon Line. India's lack of military preapredness and the debacle in NEFA became a national scandal, and Defense Minister V. K. Krishna Menon, Nehru's closest friend, was forced to

[24]Of the many books on the border question, see especially Steven A. Hoffman, *India and the China Crisis* (Berkeley: University of California Press, 1990); Allen S. Whiting, *The Chinese Calculus of Deterrence: India and Indochina* (Ann Arbor, Mich.: University of Michigan Press, 1975); and, for a fascinating account, though highly critical of India's position, see Neville Maxwell, *India's China War* (New York: Pantheon, 1970).

[25]Charles H. Heimsath and Surjit Mansingh, *A Diplomatic History of Modern India* (Bombay: Allied Publishers, 1971), p. 467.

resign. The United States and Great Britain rallied to India's aid with emergency airlifts of arms and supplies. The USSR, as well, reaffirmed its commitment of military assistance to India. On November 20, as Chinese troops stood on the foothills above the Assam valley, China announced a unilateral cease-fire and withdrawal of forces to the 1959 "line of actual control." And there the matter has remained, with China's *de facto* occupation of the Aksai Chin.

In the mid-1970s—much to Soviet concern—India moved toward an improvement in relations with China, and in 1976, after a hiatus of 15 years, the two countries exchanged ambassadors. In 1981, India and China held the first of a series of talks on the border dispute and other outstanding issues. The annual rounds, however—held alternately in Beijing and New Delhi—failed to yield a breakthrough. Calling for "mutual accommodation and mutual understanding," China renewed its package proposal—a quid pro quo involving essentially formal recognition of the status quo: Chinese control of the Aksai Chin in the west and, in the east, Indian control of the area claimed by China south of the McMahon Line, Arunachal Pradesh. In 1986, China toughened its position, asserting that no settlement could be reached unless India made concessions in the east. Each accused the other of border incursions, and tensions were exacerbated in December 1986 when India granted statehood to Arunachal Pradesh, drawing sharp Chinese protest. In the spring 1987, with troop reinforcements on both sides of the border, Indian and Chinese leaders moved to cool tempers and avert war. The talks that fall provided the avenue to a diplomatic breakthrough—Prime Minister Rajiv Gandhi's visit to Beijing in December 1988.[26]

Only weeks before Rajiv's departure for China, Soviet President Gorbachev visited India, and with improved Sino–Soviet relations, it was assumed that he urged India to find its own rapprochement with China. In India, Rajiv's China visit was hailed as a great success, and in the joint communique, the two sides agreed to seek "a fair and reasonable settlement" of the border question "while seeking a mutually acceptable solution." Supplanting the annual rounds, a higher-level Joint Working Group was established to deal with the border dispute. Two years later, in December 1991, China responded with Prime Minister Li Peng's visit to New Delhi, but for all the expressions

[26]For analyses of Sino–Indian relations in the 1980s, see Sumit Ganguly, "The Sino–Indian Border Talks, 1991–1898," *Asian Survey*, 29 (December 1989): 1123–35; and Surjit Mansingh and Steven I. Levine, "China and India: Moving beyond Confrontation." *Problems of Communism* (March–June 1989), pp. 30–49.

of goodwill—the accord reopening consular offices in Bombay and Shanghai, a resumption of trade across the Indo–Tibetan border, and a commitment to expanded bilateral ties—India and China remain deeply suspicious of each other. The border dispute remains unsettled—a victim, to use the words of former Indian foreign secretary A. P. Venkateshwaran, of "lost opportunities." Even as India seeks to normalize relations with China, many Indians regard China, armed with nuclear weapons, as a continuing threat, with the power, motives, and opportunities to challenge Indian security.

The United States

Relations between India and the United States have been broadly characterized by strain, punctuated by periods of friendships and cooperation. The point of contention, most frequently, has related to Pakistan. During the period of the cold war, the U.S. had sought to forge a chain of alliances from Europe to the Far East for the containment of Communist expansion. India, committed to a policy of nonalignment, was unresponsive. Pakistan, seeing the opportunity to escape Indian hegemony within the subcontinent, was very interested. In 1954 the United States and Pakistan signed a mutual defense treaty, and in the next year Pakistan was linked to the Southeast Asia defense system through SEATO and to that of the Middle East through CENTO. The United States regarded Pakistan as the eastern flank of the "northern tier," an indispensable link in the containment of Soviet aggression against the Middle East.

Although Eisenhower assured Nehru that the arms supplied to Pakistan would never be used in aggression against India, India regarded U.S. military aid to Pakistan not only as a threat to the peace and stability of South Asia, opening the subcontinent to foreign penetration, but also as a challenge to its own security, for Pakistan commanded easy access to Kashmir and occupied part of the plain upon which New Delhi itself was situated. Even in the improved relations of the late 1950s and the Kennedy years of the 1960s, which witnessed a substantial economic assistance program and the inauguration of military aid to India, India deeply resented the parity accorded India and Pakistan by the United States. India was, after all, a nation with four times Pakistan's population, and in the military sphere Pakistan's effort to secure U.S. arms to match Indian capabilities could only be a source of instability and potential armed conflict. That conflict came in 1965, when Patton tanks were used by Pakistan against India in the Rann of Kutch and later in Kashmir. Even though the United States cut off arms to both Pakistan and India during the 1965 war, the shipment of spare parts and nonlethal military equipment to Pakistan was subsequently resumed. In October 1970 an agreement was reached between the United States and Pakistan under which a limited quantity of weapons (largely armed-personnel carriers and some aircraft) was to be shipped to Pakistan.

Bangladesh brought Indo–American relations to an all-time low. The United States appealed to India for restraint and, with Pakistan, counseled for a political settlement. Although the American press denounced Pakistani atrocities in Bengal, and members of Congress and many State Department officials urged the White House to exert all its leverage on Pakistan to release Bengal, the administration remained publicly silent. Privately, President Nixon ordered the "tilt toward Pakistan," even when Pakistan's defeat was inevitable. In a final act of futility the U.S. aircraft carrier *Enterprise* was ordered into the Bay of Bengal, with the ostensible purpose of evacuating American and foreign nationals at the port of Chittagong.

U.S. action during the Bangladesh crisis has been explained variously as the product of concern that American access to China through Pakistan not be jeopardized; as an attempt to show an old friend and ally gratitude for the American air base at Peshawar; and as the result of "personality"—Nixon's personal regard for Yahya Khan and his distaste for Indira Gandhi. Whatever reasoning was involved, American interests were ill served. India was forced into increasing reliance upon the Soviet Union, and American prestige and influence in South Asia reached rock bottom.[27]

As the ferment of Bangladesh receded, India and the United States sought to explore the terms of a new relationship. It had already been in the making when so rudely interrupted. The United States was assuming a "low profile" in India, a position of less visibility, reflected, for example, in the cutbacks in bilateral aid and in the reduction of American personnel in India. This lower profile rested fundamentally on the understanding that the United States had no vital strategic interests in South Asia. The United States recognized "legitimate" Soviet and Chinese geopolitical interests in the region, and American concerns were directed toward countering the dominance of any one major power in the area. While Indo–American relations

[27]For two differing perspectives on U.S. policy in the Bangladesh crisis, see Henry Kissinger, "The Tilt: The India–Pakistan Crisis of 1971" in *White House Years* (Boston: Little, Brown, 1979), pp. 842–918; and Christopher Van Hollen, "The Tilt Policy Revisited: Nixon-Kissinger Geopolitics and South Asia," *Asian Survey*, 20 (April 1980): 339–61. On the U.S. role, also see Sisson and Rose, *War and Secession*.

improved, points of tension remained—for example, the establishment of the United States naval and air facility on the island of Diego Garcia in the Indian Ocean, and the increasing U.S. naval presence in the Indian Ocean. The Indian government viewed the base not as a response to Soviet naval buildup in the Indian Ocean, but as an invitation to Soviet–American confrontation. This position, embodied in a United Nations resolution, reflected the concern of India and other littoral states that the Indian Ocean be preserved as a "zone of peace," free from big-power rivalries that might affect the political stability of the region.[28]

When the emergency was proclaimed in 1975, the American press denounced Mrs. Gandhi, but the United States government had no official reaction and remained noncommital. President Carter, who had a personal interest in India, sought to reorder American priorities in South Asia, and the Janata victory afforded the opportunity for improved relations. Carter initiated an extensive correspondence with Prime Minister Desai, but the issue of nuclear proliferation soon dampened the relationship. Desai underscored India's commitment to the "peaceful" uses of nuclear energy and its continued rejection of the nuclear weapons option. The United States, however, continued to express concern over India's refusal to sign the nuclear Non-Proliferation Treaty. As a result of the 1978 Nuclear Non-Proliferation Act, the United States threatened to terminate sales of enriched uranium for the Indian nuclear power plant at Tarapur, near Bombay—for which a 30-year contract had been negotiated in 1963—unless India opened all of its nuclear facilities to international inspection. This the Indian government declined to do, while charging the United States with breach of contract. Neither President Carter's visit to India in January 1978 nor Desai's visit to Washington later that year could overcome the differences between the two governments, but the issue became moot in 1982 when the U.S. and India reached agreement to permit a third party (France) to supply the enriched uranium.

With the Soviet invasion of Afghanistan in 1979 and the United States' response of military assistance to Pakistan, U.S. support for Pakistan again became the major source of tension between New Delhi and Washington. India viewed the multibillion-dollar arms

[28] U.S. interest in the Indian Ocean is essentially an extension of strategic concern for the Middle East and specifically for the oil sheikhdoms of the Persian Gulf. See Selig Harrison and K. Subramanyam, eds., *Superpower Rivalry in the Indian Ocean: Indian and American Perspectives* (New York: Oxford University Press, 1989).

packages, with F-16 fighter aircraft, as threatening its own security and destabilizing to the region. In expressing its concern, however, India was careful not to overplay its hand, and after a low in Indo–American relations in 1980–81, both India and the United States sought to improve relations, to downplay differences of strategic perception, and to accentuate the positive. Indira Gandhi's visit to Washington in 1982 was an important atmospheric breakthrough that was extended three years later with Prime Minister Rajiv Gandhi's 1985 visit to inaugurate the Festival of India in the United States. The Soviet withdrawal from Afghanistan and the cutoff of American aid to Pakistan in 1990 removed the major obstacle to closer relations, and by the early 1990s, India and the United States looked to significantly improved relations.

The United States has no vital strategic interests in South Asia, but it does have an interest in the stability, democracy, and economic progress of the region. India, as the most powerful nation in South Asia, has a special role to play as the keystone of stability within the subcontinent. The United States has come to recognize and, insofar as it is exercised responsibly, support this role.[29] Thus, the United States endorsed the India–Sri Lanka accord and India's assistance to the Maldives, but it quietly expressed concern over India's heavy-handedness in dealing with Nepal. On the Kashmir dispute, the United States urged restraint on both sides and called for "political dialogue" under the terms of the Simla Agreement—a position India viewed as both constructive and satisfactory.

American economic involvement with India is low, with total U.S. investment in India less than $600 million (less than one-quarter of American investment in tiny Singapore), and India accounts for less than one percent of all U.S. trade. The United States looms large on India's economic horizon, however, as its major investor and number-one trading partner, accounting for about 14 percent of India's trade. India seeks an expanded trade relationship and, under liberalized economic policies, a substantial increase in American investment through joint ventures with Indian companies. India's restrictive trade and investment policies, however, remain a major issue between the two countries. The United States has taken a hard line against India on intellectual property protection—patents and copyrights—and targeted India for potential trade retaliation if it does not bring its patent laws into line with international standards. Both sides

[29] American and Indian strategic concerns are explored in Jasjit Singh, ed., *Indo–US Relations in a Changing World: Proceedings of the Indo–US Strategic Symposium* (New Delhi: Lancer, 1992).

have sought to resolve the issue, and India, with a powerful incentive to secure closer economic ties with the United States, has begun to modify its position.

More difficult to reconcile will be the American commitment to halt nuclear proliferation in South Asia and India's resolve to retain a nuclear weapons option, but even in the realm of security, the United States and India are drawing closer together. High-level military contacts have occurred, and, with the disintegration of the Soviet Union, upon which India was heavily dependent for arms, the United States may emerge as an important source of advanced military technologies for India. Indeed, with Russia struggling to survive economic collapse, the United States, and the western industrial nations and Japan more generally, assume greater importance for India as the source of technology, investment, and aid. From the vantage point of Washington, American strategic and economic interests in India are likely to remain at a comparatively low level, but the now 800,000 Indians in the United States will act as an increasingly strong and positive force for good relations with India.[30]

The Soviet Union and Successor States

During the course of the cold war, Soviet interests in South Asia, and India in particular, were driven principally by security concerns directed to the denial of preponderant influence within the region by any external power—that is, the United States or China—and by competition with the United States for "the hearts and minds" of the people of the Third World, with South Asia as its central arena. Even before the final collapse of the Soviet Union, these interests had ceased to be compelling. Rapprochement with China and, with the end of the cold war, a closer relationship with the United States were the products of "new thinking" in Soviet foreign policy under Gorbachev, but it was primarily the internal pressures released by *perestroika* that fundamentally altered Soviet involvement with the Third World.

India's relationship with the Soviet Union had long been cultivated to what each regarded as mutual advantage. The Soviet Union regarded India as an important political asset, as seen in India's positions on Afghanistan and Cambodia, and India looked to the USSR for support in the United Nations and elsewhere on such issues as Kashmir. Indo–Soviet friendship had been sustained through 29 summits, from Kruschev's visit to New Delhi in 1955 to V. P. Singh's

[30] Hardgrave, "Projected U.S. and USSR Roles in South Asia," pp. 66–70.

1990 meeting in Moscow with Gorbachev. By the late 1980s, however, India became increasingly apprehensive as to its place in Soviet priorities, and today, in a very different world, India seeks to redefine and rebuild its relationship with Russia and the successor states of what was once the Soviet Union.[31]

Although Nehru had long expressed his admiration for the Soviet Union, especially in its industrial development, the Soviets were initially suspicious of India, regarding it as a tool of "Anglo–American imperialism." By 1952 Soviet policy began to change, and with its support for India on Kashmir (and subsequently on the Goa issue), the foundation of Indo–Soviet friendship was laid. The exchange of various delegations was soon followed, in 1953, by the Indo–Soviet trade agreement and, two years later, by the exchange of visits by Nehru and Krushchev and Bulganin, and by the Soviet commitment to construct the Bhilai steel works, the first of a number of highly visible projects in India. (By contrast, U.S. aid was aimed principally at increasing food production in rural areas.) In the domestic context Indo–Soviet relations served to undercut the CPI and to "domesticate" the Communist movement in India. Nehru's eagerness to secure Soviet friendship came, at points, under sharp criticism from within India as well as from abroad—most notably, in India's defense of Soviet repression in Hungary in 1956.

In 1960, as the Sino–Soviet controversy began to deepen, the USSR began to supply arms to India. As India's own conflict with China approached war, the Soviets agreed to supply MiG fighters to India and to set up a plant within India for their production. (The first Indian MiGs were completed in 1968.) Although Soviet aid to Pakistan, which was designed to counter increasing Chinese influence, was a source of anxiety to India, the Russian position of neutrality in the 1965 war eased the way for the Tashkent Declaration, a triumph of Soviet diplomacy. In 1971, in the Bangladesh crisis, a 20-year Indo–Soviet Treaty of Peace, Friendship, and Cooperation gave formal character to the developing "special relationship" between the two nations.[32] The importance of the relationship was underscored by the continuity of Indian policy in the transition from Congress to Janata rule in 1977. In its earliest foreign policy pronouncements, the Janata government reaffirmed India's nonalignment and gave a clear

[31] *Ibid.*, pp. 70–77.

[32] For an analysis of the Indo–Soviet relations from its inception through the treaty, see Robert H. Donaldson, *Soviet Policy toward India: Ideology and Strategy* (Cambridge: Harvard University Press, 1974).

signal that it sought a more balanced relationship vis-à-vis the Soviet Union and the United States. At the same time, however, India moved quickly to allay Soviet fears that improved relations with the United States and China would come at the cost of Indo–Soviet friendship.[33]

In the immediate wake of the Soviet invasion of Afghanistan, Moscow welcomed Indira Gandhi's return to power. Although India was not prepared to condemn the Soviets' action in Afghanistan, New Delhi was uneasy at the realization that the Soviets were at the gates of the Khyber Pass. Soviet withdrawal from Afghanistan in 1989 eased Indian concern, but it also marked a significant change in Soviet involvement in South Asia more generally. Since Gorbachev's 1986 Vladivostok speech, projecting closer Soviet ties to China and East Asia, India had been apprehensive about a relative decline in its importance for the USSR. Sino–Soviet detente deepened that anxiety, especially given India's heavy reliance on Soviet arms. In fact, however, from the late 1970s, beginning in the Janata interregnum and sustained under Indira Gandhi and Rajiv Gandhi, India moved to balance its relationship with the superpowers and reduce dependence on the Soviet Union. However, Soviet diplomatic support for India; Soviet aid and technical assistance for India's public-sector heavy industry; the Indo–Soviet barter trade; and the favorable terms the USSR extended for arms purchases continued to be important factors underlying Indo–Soviet friendship that were not to be lightly abandoned.[34] Even as it sought to diversify its sources of arms and widen its options, India's relationship with the Soviet Union remained "special"—symbolized by the renewal of the Indo–Soviet treaty of friendship and cooperation on August 8, 1991, less than two weeks before the aborted Soviet coup.

That India had not come to terms with the dramatic events in the Soviet Union, however, was made all too painfully clear in the August 1991 putsch against Gorbachev, when India refused to condemn the plotters and dismissed Gorbachev's captivity, in the words of a junior minister, as an "internal affair of the Soviet Union."[35] Gorbachev's return left India deeply embarrassed and the "special relationship" a

[33]See Robert C. Horn, *Soviet–Indian Relations: Issues and Influence* (New York: Praeger, 1982).

[34]See Ramesh Thakur, "India and the Soviet Union: Conjunctions and Disjunctions of Interest," *Asian Survey*, 31 (September 1991): 826–46.

[35]The Indian government's response came in for a beating in the Indian press and from leading Indian intellectuals, while the two Indian Communist parties, on news of the coup, celebrated the apparent triumph of the hardliners.

relic of the cold war. India now confronts the task of establishing new relationships with Russia and the republics of the former Soviet Union as they rebuild their shattered economies and shape their own foreign policies. The Central Asian republics will be a target of Indian diplomacy to prevent their alliance with Pakistan, but the greatest challenge and need will be in rebuilding political, economic, and military ties to Russia.

The Quest for Security

India occupies a position of international vulnerability to external leverage within both the areas of defense and the economy. Although India's dependency in the weapons field is dispersed widely among a number of nations, the Soviet Union was, until 1990, its major outside source of armaments. Whatever dependencies may now exist, however, India is committed to strategic as well as political independence. In India's perspective, nonalignment is a policy of self-interest. India seeks self-reliance, knowing that ultimately it cannot rely on any outside protection, nor would such reliance be consistent with its self-image of national integrity. India's "peaceful nuclear explosion" in 1974 and its commitment to keeping a nuclear weapons option must be seen in this light.

In May 1974, in the desert of western Rajasthan, India detonated an underground nuclear device, thereby becoming the sixth member of the exclusive "nuclear club" previously consisting of the United States, the Soviet Union, Great Britain, France, and China. Against a specter of nuclear proliferation, many within the international community condemned India's action. India demonstrated its nuclear capability, but resisting pressure from within the Congress party as well as the opposition, the Indian government announced that it would not build a bomb. India, however, reserved the option to "go nuclear" should India's security be threatened and refused to sign the nuclear Non-Proliferation Treaty (NPT). India viewed the NPT as discriminatory and argued that nuclear proliferation had to be addressed comprehensively so as to include those nations already possessing nuclear weapons. India's position reflected security concerns, particularly vis-à-vis China, but there was a prestige factor as well: In a world in which "great power" status seems dependent on having nuclear capability—as reflected in the deference accorded China by the United States—India was unwilling to relegate itself to an inferior international position. Perhaps the main factor in India's decision to develop a nuclear potential was its isolation in the 1971 Indo–Pakistan war and its increasing dependency on the Soviet Union.

The 1974 nuclear explosion served to underscore India's pre-eminence in South Asia, but it also gave impetus to Pakistan to develop its own nuclear capability. By the late 1980s, both India and Pakistan were on the nuclear weapons threshold, if they did not already have, as some believed, "a bomb in the basement." In the judgment of such specialists as Leonard S. Spector of the Carnegie Endowment for International Peace, neither India nor Pakistan has deployed nuclear weapons, but each could do so in a matter of weeks, if not sooner.[36] Over the years, Pakistan has put forward various proposals to limit nuclear proliferation in South Asia—that both India and Pakistan simultaneously sign the NPT, that India and Pakistan open their nuclear facilities to mutual inspection, and, in 1991, that a five-nation conference (India, Pakistan, China, Russia, and the United States) be convened to work for a "nuclear free" South Asia. India has rejected each proposal, citing Pakistan's clandestine nuclear weapons program, China's nuclear capabilities (an Indian security concern now magnified with the collapse of the Soviet Union), and the inherent inequality of the NPT in according the five nuclear weapons powers privileged status.

For the United States, nuclear proliferation in South Asia is a matter of serious concern and is the major issue in bilateral relations with both Pakistan and India. The United States and other nations have put increasing pressure on India to enter into discussions with Pakistan to prevent the spread of nuclear weapons to South Asia, but many analysts are convinced that proliferation is inevitable. For them, the challenge is to devise a means by which nuclear weapons in South Asia can provide greater security through mutual deterrence rather than heighten the risk of nuclear war. Given the history of mutual suspicion and misperception in Indo–Pakistani relations and the danger of miscalculation, that is a daunting prospect. But perhaps the likeliest scenario is for continued nuclear ambiguity, with emphasis

[36]See Spector's annual survey on the status of nuclear proliferation around the world. On India and Pakistan specifically, see the Report of the Carnegie Task Force on Non-Proliferation and South Asian Security, *Nuclear Weapons and South Asian Security* (Washington, D.C.: Carnegie Endowment for International Peace, 1988). There is a considerable literature on nuclear proliferation in South Asia. Especially valuable is Stephen P. Cohen, ed., *Nuclear Proliferation in South Asia: The Prospects for Arms Control* (Boulder, Colo.: Westview Press, 1991), and Bhabani Sen Gupta for the Centre of Policy Research, *Nuclear Weapons: Policy Options for India* (New Delhi: Sage, 1983).

on enhanced conventional weapons capabilities and the development of intermediate-range delivery systems.[37]

Indian defense expenditures grew rapidly over the course of the 1980s, accounting for roughly 4 percent of GNP and at least 17 percent of the budget. In part in response to Pakistan's buildup of U.S.-supplied, sophisticated arms, India became one of the world's leading arms importers, but its force capabilities far outstripped any challenge Pakistan might pose. Seventy percent of India's weapons came from the Soviet Union, a dependence that was a source of increasing unease for New Delhi, as it faced unreliable supplies of spare parts and essential components for its own production of Soviet-designed weapons like the MiG fighter. Both to diversify its weapons sources and to secure the most advanced technologies available, India looked to Western Europe and, cautiously, to the United States. During the 1980s, the Indian military acquired greater high-performance capabilities: In 1988 it tested the Indian-designed Prithvi short-range missile, and in 1989 the Agni intermediate-range ballistic missile, capable of carrying a nuclear warhead.[38] India's military expenditures impose a heavy burden, however, fueling budget deficits and coming, inevitably, at the cost of social and economic development.

Since independence, India has received billions of dollars in foreign aid—in grants, commodity assistance, and, primarily, loans. Long a recipient of low-interest development loans from the International Monetary Fund, International Bank for Reconstruction and Development (the World Bank), and the Indian aid consortium of western industrial nations and Japan, India in the 1980s turned as well to commercial loans at higher interest. By 1990, India carried an international debt of more than $70 billion and interest payments that placed its balance of payments under increasing pressure.

The United States has been India's principal donor. In the 1960s, under Public Law 480, the United States provided India some $5 billion worth of food and agricultural commodites. This involved more than 50,000,000 tons of wheat, and at the program's height in

[37]See Brahma Chellaney, "South Asia's Passage to Nuclear Power," *International Security*, 16 (Summer 1991): 43–72.

[38]For a range of perspectives on Indian defense policy, see Raju G. C. Thomas, *Indian Security Policy* (Princeton: Princeton University Press, 1986); Stephen P. Cohen, ed., *The Security of South Asia* (Urbana: University of Illinois Press, 1987); Rodney W. Jones, "Old Quarrels and New Realities: Security in Southern Asia after the Cold War," *Washington Quarterly*, 15 (Winter 1992): 105–28; Akhtar Majeed, "Indian Security Perspectives in the 1990s," *Asian Survey*, 30 (November 1990): 1084–98; and, for a Soviet view, M. V. Bratersky and S. I. Lunyov, "India at the End of the Century: Transformation into an Asian Regional Power," *Asian Survey*, 30 (October 1990): 927–42.

the mid-1960s, one-fourth of the American wheat crop went to India. In the 1970s, through the green revolution, India achieved basic self-sufficiency in agriculture, and direct U.S. economic and technical assistance to India declined substantially. Today, American assistance to India is principally through multilateral international lending agencies like the World Bank and the IMF. The United States is India's leading trading partner and the major source of foreign investment, and trade and protectionism are issues at the center of Indo–American relations.

Economic concerns have become increasingly important in India's foreign relations. In the 1970s, India took a leading role in the "North–South" dialogue to make the international economic system more responsive to the needs of developing nations, and through the United Nations Conference on Trade and Development (UNCTAD) and the developing nations' "Group of 77," India spoke for the interests of the Third World more generally in international trade and monetary negotiations. Today, the "South" no longer represents a distinct economic interest, if ever it did; the Non-Aligned Movement has lost coherence, and nations of the Third World are competitors for markets and investment in an increasingly interdependent global economy. India, as most developing nations, has liberalized its foreign investment policies and pursues access for its exports in markets around the world. With the end of the cold war and the collapse of the Soviet Union, India has begun to look more to the west and to closer ties with the United States.

"Nonalignment" will remain the hallmark of Indian foreign policy, even as it is redefined to accommodate new realities, and the fundamental goals in India's quest for security will be sustained: the struggle for self-reliance, the assertion of its pre-eminence in South Asia, and aspiration for recognition as a major world power. The greatest challenge to India's security is internal. India is under enormous political pressure: It faces secessionist movements in Kashmir, the Punjab, and the Northeast; a communal divide between Hindus and Muslims; and, more generally, the rising demands of competing groups in an economy of scarcity, where the challenge is greater economic growth, with equity and social justice.

Recommended Reading

Babbage, Ross, and Sandy Gordon, eds., *India's Strategic Future: Regional State or Global Power?* New York: St. Martin's, 1992.

Bajpai, U. S., *India's Security: The Politico-Strategic Environment*. New Delhi: Lancers, 1983. The product of a conference, an important perspective on Indian security doctrine and its implications for the region.

Bandyopadhyaya, J., *The Making of India's Foreign Policy*, 2d ed., New Delhi: Allied, 1980. A study of the policy process, focusing on the Ministry of External Affairs and the personal role of the Foreign Minister.

Barnds, William J., *India, Pakistan and the Great Powers*. New York: Praeger, 1972. An examination of the international politics of the subcontinent, with particular concern for America's role in South Asia.

*Bradnock, Robert, *India's Foreign Policy Since 1971*. New York: Council on Foreign Relations Press, 1990. A brief examination of the factors influencing Indian foreign policy and its relations with neighbors and the superpowers.

Cohen, Stephen P., ed., *The Security of South Asia: American and Asian Perspectives*. Urbana: University of Illinois Press, 1987. An important contribution to the dialogue on security in South Asia.

Damodaran, A. K., and U. S. Bajpai, eds., *Indian Foreign Policy: The Indira Gandhi Years*. New Delhi: Radiant, 1990.

*Ganguly, Shivaji, *U.S. Policy toward South Asia*. Boulder, Colo.: Westview Press, 1990. An examination of U.S. policy and policy making with focus on four case studies.

*Ganguly, Sumit, *The Origins of War in South Asia: Indo–Pakistani Conflicts Since 1947*. Boulder, Colo.: Westview Press, 1986. A study of the three wars: 1947–48, 1965, 1971.

Glazer, Sulochana Raghavana, and Nathan Glazer, eds., *Conflicting Images: India and the United States*. Glenn Dale, Md.: Riverdale, 1990. Studies in mutual perceptions and misperceptions.

Gould, Harold A., and Sumit Ganguly, eds., *The Hope and the Reality: U.S.- India Relations from Roosevelt to Reagan*. Boulder, Colo.: Westview Press, 1992. In depth analyses of motivations, constraints, and agendas in the evolving relationship.

Heimsath, Charles H., and Surjit Mansingh, *A Diplomatic History of Modern India*. Bombay: Allied Publishers, 1971. A comprehensive account of Indian foreign relations, with emphasis on the Nehru era.

*Available in a paperback edition.

Mansingh, Surjit, *India's Search for Power: Indira Gandhi's Foreign Policy, 1966–1982*. New Delhi: Sage, 1984. An assessment of pragmatism in policy and practice.

Mellor, John W., ed., *India: A Rising Middle Power*. Boulder, Colo.: Westview Press, 1979. A collection of essays on a range of issues relating to India's global role.

Nanda, B. R., ed., *Indian Foreign Policy: The Nehru Years*. New Delhi: Vikas, 1976. An appraisal of India's relations with the world during the two formative decades after independence.

Palmer, Norman, *The United States and India: The Dimensions of Influence*. New York: Praeger, 1984. With chapters on economic, security, and nuclear issues, the volume provides a comprehensive perspective on Indo–American relations by a distinguished observer of Indian politics.

*Rose, Leo E., and Eric Gonsalves, eds., *Toward a New World Order: Adjusting U.S.–India Relations*. Berkeley, CA: Institute of East Asian Studies, The University of California, 1992. Common concerns from different perspectives.

*Sisson, Richard, and Leo E. Rose, *War and Secession: Pakistan, India, and the Creation of Bangladesh*. Berkeley: University of California Press, 1990. A masterly reconstruction of the decisions leading to the 1971 Bangladesh war.

Tharoor, Shashi, *Reasons of State: Political Development and India's Foreign Policy under Indira Gandhi, 1966–1977*. New Delhi: Vikas, 1982. A brilliant study of the institutions, practices, personalities, personnel, and processes in the creation of Indian foreign policy.

Thomas, Raju G. C., *Indian Security Policy*. Princeton: Princeton University Press, 1986. A comprehensive study of Indian defense and security policy.

*Ziring, Lawrence, ed., *The Subcontinent in World Politics: India, Its Neighbors, and the Great Powers*, rev. ed. New York: Praeger, 1982. A valuable collection, with contributions by leading specialists on South Asia.

*Available in a paperback edition.

*Research Guide**

General Bibliographies

Guide to Indian Periodical Literature
A major reference source in the social sciences for India. Published quarterly since 1964.

Index India
This periodical index, published quarterly by the University of Rajasthan, is an extremely valuable source for research in contemporary politics.

Indian Books in Print
A selected bibliography of English-language books printed in India.

Indian National Bibliography
Quarterly and annual. Two sections—"Books and Articles" and "Government Publications"—each with an index. Exhaustive listings of all items published in India in all languages. Useful for students who are engaged in fairly specialized research or who read an Indian language.

Journal of Asian Studies
Since 1956 this scholarly quarterly has published a fifth bibliographical number. A most useful guide to the literature.

*Adapted from a research guide originally prepared by Loyd I. Rudolph and Susanne H. Rudolph, the University of Chicago. Their permission is gratefully acknowledged. Special thanks to Merry Burlingham, South Asia Librarian at the University of Texas at Austin for assistance in updating materials. Some listings may no longer be published, but are of continued value for research.

Patterson, Maureen L. P., *South Asian Civilizations: A Bibliographic Synthesis*. Chicago: University of Chicago Press, 1981.
The bibliographic bible for India. The first place to turn for sources on India, prior to 1980.

Public Affairs Information Service, *Bulletin*
An invaluable guide to the literature of public policy around the world. Lists books, articles of a scholarly and a more popular nature, and publications of the United States and other governments, international agencies, and private research groups. Indexing and cross-indexing are particularly valuable. Also available as a computer database and as CD-Rom.

Reference Sources on South Asia
Compiled by Kanta Bhatia, South Asia bibliographer, University of Pennsylvania. Very useful.

Sharma, H. D., *Indian Reference Sources: An Annotated Guide to Indian Reference Material*, 2d ed. Varanasi: Indian Bibliographical Centre, 1988–

Social Sciences Index
Important guide to scholarly articles. Useful for book reviews. Also formatted on CD-Rom.

Special Bibliographies

Case, Margaret H., *South Asian History, 1750–1950*. Princeton, N.J.: Princeton University Press, 1967.

Cohn, Bernard S., *The Development and Impact of British Administration in India: A Bibliographic Essay*. New Delhi: Indian Institute of Public Administration, 1961, 88 pages.

Ghosh, Arun, and Ranjit Ghosh, *Indian Political Movement, 1919–1971: A Systematic Bibliography*. Calcutta: Indian Book Exchange, 1976.
Useful bibliography of party documents.

Gokhale Institute of Politics and Economics, *Annotated Bibliography on Economic History of India (1500–1947)*, 4 vols. Poona: 1977.

Gopal, Krishna, and Dhanpat Rai, eds., *Theses on Indian Subcontinent, 1877–1971: An Annotated Bibliography in Social Sciences and Humanities.* Delhi: Hindustan Publishing Corporation.
Doctoral dissertations.

Matthews, William, *British Autobiographies: An Annotated Bibliography of British Autobiographies Published or Written before 1951*. Berkeley: University of California Press, 1955, 376 pages.
Indexed by subject; thus, works that deal with India can be located readily.

Mukherjee, D. K., *Elections and Electorate in India Since 1977: A Select Bibliography*. New Delhi: Select Books, 1988.

Nehru Memorial Museum and Library, *Jawaharlal Nehru: A Bibliography*. New Delhi: 1989.

Rana, M. S., *Indian Government and Politics: A Bibliographical Study (1885–1980)*. New Delhi: Wiley Eastern, 1981.

Sharma, Jagdish S., *Indian National Congress: A Descriptive Bibliography of India's Struggle for Freedom*, 2d ed. Delhi: S. Chand, 1971.

———, *Indian Socialism: A Descriptive Bibliography*. Delhi: Vikas, 1975.

———, *Mahatma Gandhi: A Descriptive Bibliography*, 2d ed. Delhi: S. Chand, 1968.

Sukhwal, B. L., *South Asia: A Systematic Geographic Bibliography*. Metuchen, N.J.: Scarecrow Press, 1974.

References and Sources

All-India Reporter
The official reports of High Court and Supreme Court cases.

Asiun Almanac
Weekly abstract of Asian affairs. (Singapore)

Asian Bulletin
A monthly news digest of political and international affairs. (Taipei, Taiwan)

Asian Recorder
A very useful archive of public events based on a collation and reproduction of the English press in Asia. Published in India, its

coverage of India is extensive and detailed. The index is well done.

Census of India
1891, 1901, 1911, 1921, 1931, 1941, 1951, 1961, 1971, 1981, 1991.

Chanakya Defence Annual

Conparlist
Monthly survey of major constitutional and parliamentary developments. Published by the Institute of Constitutional and Parliamentary Studies. (New Delhi)

Data India
Press Institute of India.

Dictionary of National Biography
A major reference in four volumes.

Economic Intelligence Service
Published by the Centre for Monitoring Indian Economy, Bombay. Provides ongoing statistical analyses and assorted special studies. The best and most immediate source of reliable economic data.

Encyclopedia of Asian History
In four volumes, edited by Ainslie T. Embree for the Asia Society. A valuable source.

Encyclopaedia of India
Thirty volumes, with separate volumes for each state. Edited by P. N. Chopra. New Delhi: Rima, 1991.

Encyclopaedia of the Indian National Congress
Annual volumes. Record of the sessions of the Congress proceedings—now 26 volumes. Edited by A. M. Zaidi. (New Delhi)

Foreign Affairs Report
Monthly of the Indian Institute of World Affairs. (New Delhi)

Hindustan Yearbook and Who's Who

Historical Atlas of South Asia
A major reference work edited by Joseph E. Schwartzberg et al., 2d ed., Oxford University Press, 1992.

ICSSR Journal of Abstracts and Review

An important source on current research in Indian anthropology and sociology, and on political science. Published by the Indian Council of Social Science Research. (New Delhi)

ICSSR Newsletter

India: A Country Study

Edited by Richard F. Nyrop for Foreign Area Studies, American University, 4th ed. Washington, D.C.: U.S. Government Printing Office, 1986.

India, A Reference Annual

Convenient summaries of all aspects of government. Published by the Ministry of Information and Broadcasting. For research purposes, the bibliographies of each chapter are collected at the end of each annual volume. They contain an excellent inventory of major government reports. (New Delhi)

Indian Annual Register: An Annual Digest of Public Affairs of India, 1919–1947

The major source for political events in the interwar years. A contemporary archive.

Indian Armed Forces Yearbook

Indian Behavioural Science Abstracts

Indian Council of Social Science Research, *Survey of Research in Political Science*, 5 vols. New Delhi: Allied Publishing, 1979–

The volumes include: 1. *Political System* (1979); 2. *Political Process* (1981); 3. *Political Dynamics* (1981); 4. *Political Thought* (1986); and 5. *International Studies* (1988).

Indian Dissertation Abstracts

Published quarterly by ICSSR.

Indian Economic Diary

A digest of economic events. (New Delhi)

Indian Foreign Policy, Annual Survey

Edited by Ram Sharma and published 1971–82. Succeeded by *Yearbook on India's Foreign Policy*.

Indian Information

A fortnightly record of the activities and official announcements of the Government of India. (New Delhi)

Indian Institute of Public Opinion, New Delhi
Publishes three excellent periodicals: *Monthly Public Opinion Surveys*, *Monthly Commentary on Indian Economic Conditions* (including political analysis), and *Quarterly Economic Report*.

Indian Press Index
Index of Indian newspapers.

Kessing's Contemporary Archives
An extremely useful, objective, and detailed record of national and international events, including extensive selections from speeches and public documents. Its Indian coverage, both domestic and international, is quite good. Excellently indexed. Published in Bristol, England.

Lok Sabha Secretariat, *Abstracts and Index of Reports and Articles*
Quarterly. (New Delhi)

Reports of the Election Commission
Published since 1952.

Research Abstracts Quarterly
Reports on findings of projects sponsored by the Indian Council of Social Science Research.

Yearbook on India's Foreign Policy
Edited by Satish Kumar, 1982–present. New Delhi: Sage.

Microfilm and Microfiche Collections

Confidential U.S. State Department Central Files, India, 1945–1949
Internal and foreign affairs. University Publications of America, microfilm.

Confidential U.S. State Department Central Files, India, 1950–1954
Internal and foreign affairs. University Publications of America, microfilm.

Political Pamphlets from the Indian Subcontinent
Over 2000 English-language pamphlets from 1915 to the 1980s. University Publications of America, microfiche.

Scholarly Journals

The journals listed below regularly publish articles on India.

Asian Economic Review
Quarterly journal of the Indian Institute of Economics. (Hyderabad)

Asian Survey
Published by the University of California, it is one of the best sources of current developments.

Contemporary South Asia
Excellent new journal devoted to the subcontinent as a region.

Contributions to Indian Sociology
A major international journal of Indian social science, published by the Institute of Economic Growth, University of Delhi.

Demography India
Journal of the Indian Association for the Study of Population. (Delhi)

Eastern Anthropologist
A scholarly journal of high standards that often contains articles of first-rate interest and importance. (Lucknow)

Economic and Political Weekly
A leading periodical in the social sciences. (Bombay)

India International Centre Journal
Quarterly devoted to special-issue topics. (New Delhi)

India Quarterly
Published by the Indian Council of World Affairs, one of the best Indian journals in the field of international politics.

Indian Anthropologist

Indian Economic and Social History Review
Edited at the Delhi School of Economics, one of the best journals in India. Regularly carries contributions from western scholars.

Indian Economic Journal
Published by the University of Bombay.

Indian Economic Review
The biannual journal of the Delhi School of Economics.

Indian Historical Quarterly
(Calcutta)

Indian Historical Review
Published twice yearly by the Indian Council of Historical Research. Excellent book reviews.

Indian Journal of Asian Studies
Published twice yearly by the Indian Council of Social Science Research.

Indian Journal of Defence Studies
Published by the Department of Defence Studies, University of Allahabad.

Indian Journal of Political Science
Journal of the Indian Political Science Association.

Indian Journal of Politics
Published by Aligarh Muslim University.

Indian Journal of Public Administration
Published by the Indian Institute of Public Administration in New Delhi, the journal maintains good standards and carries articles on a broad variety of topics on public policy.

Indian Journal of Social Research
Published three times a year. (Meerut)

Indian Journal of Social Work
A quarterly devoted to the promotion of professional social work, scientific interpretation of social problems, and advancement of social research. (Bombay)

Indian Political Science Review
Quarterly, published by Delhi University.

Indian Sociological Bulletin

Indian Studies: Past and Present

Institute for Defence Studies and Analyses Journal
Quarterly. (New Delhi)

International Journal of Asian Studies
(New Delhi)

International Studies
Quarterly publication of the Indian School of International Studies, Jawaharlal Nehru University. Good standard journal. Extensive bibliographies in the manner of *Foreign Affairs*. (New Delhi)

Journal of Asian and African Studies
An international quarterly of sociology and anthropology.

Journal of Asian Studies
Publication of the Association for Asian Studies. Sound and scholarly. Excellent book review section and very useful annual bibliographic number.

Journal of Commonwealth and Comparative Politics
Published by the Institute of Commonwealth Studies. (London)

Journal of Constitutional and Parliamentary Studies
Quarterly of the Institute of Constitutional and Parliamentary Studies. (New Delhi)

Journal of the Indian Anthropological Society

Journal of Indian History
Published three times a year by the University of Kerala. (Trivandrum)

Journal of the Maharaja Sayajirao University of Baroda
A social-science journal.

Journal of Rural Development
Bimonthly journal of the National Institute of Rural Development. (Hyderabad)

Journal of South Asian and Middle Eastern Studies
Quarterly from Villanova University.

Man in India: A Quarterly Record of Anthropological Science with Special Reference to India

Modern Asian Studies
A leading quarterly, published by Cambridge University.

Modern Review
Monthly. (Calcutta)

Pacific Affairs
An established and lively scholarly journal from the University of British Columbia. (Vancouver)

Parliamentary Studies
Published by the Indian Bureau of Parliamentary Studies.

Political Science Review
Biannual journal of the University of Rajasthan. (Jaipur)

Quarterly Journal of Indian Studies in Social Sciences

Quarterly Journal of the Local Self-Government Institute
(Bombay)

Quarterly Review of Historical Studies
Published by the Institute for Historical Studies. (Calcutta)

Regional Studies
Quarterly journal of the Institute of Regional Studies, Islamabad. Excellent source for Pakistani views on India.

Social Scientist
Monthly journal of the Indian School of Social Sciences. Marxist.

South Asia
Australian journal of the South Asian Studies Association.

South Asia Journal
Quarterly of the Indian Council for South Asian Cooperation. (New Delhi)

South Asian Studies
Published by the Department of Political Science, University of Rajasthan. (Jaipur)

Strategic Analysis
Monthly of the Institute of Defence Studies and Analyses. (New Delhi)

Strategic Digest
Published by the Institute for Defence Studies and Analyses. (New Delhi)

Journals of News and Opinion

Asian Bulletin
Monthly news digest for all Asia. Excellent chronology of events. (Taipei)

Asiaweek
(Hong Kong)

Blitz
Sensational and exposé-oriented, with a strong leftist (pro-Moscow) perspective. (Bombay)

Business India
Well-edited financial weekly. (Bombay)

Business Today
Fortnightly by the publishers of *India Today*. (New Delhi)

Business World
(Bombay)

Capital
By its own admission, India's leading financial newspaper devoted to the development of industry and commerce. Weekly.

Commerce
Weekly magazine of news, business, and industry. (Bombay)

Economic and Political Weekly
A leading periodical of analysis and opinion.

Economic Trends
Published by the Federation of Indian Chambers of Commerce (FICCI) (New Delhi). Formerly *Fortnightly Review*.

Far Eastern Economic Review
An important weekly of political and economic events for the whole of Asia. (Hong Kong)

Fortune India
Business magazine. (Bombay)

Frontier
Weekly magazine reflecting a quasi-Maoist position somewhere to the left of the CPM. (Calcutta)

Frontline
High-quality news weekly by the publishers of *The Hindu*. (Madras)

Illustrated Weekly of India
India's *Life* magazine, published by the *Times of India*. (Bombay)

India Today

Bimonthly newsmagazine in the *Time* format. Superbly done and a valuable source for current events. Indian and North American editions.

Indian and Foreign Review

An independent government publication. Semimonthly. (New Delhi)

Indian Worker

Journal of the Indian National Trade Union Congress (INTUC), affiliated with the Congress party. Weekly. (New Delhi)

Link

Published since 1959, weekly companion to the daily *Patriot*, *Link* models itself on *Time*, but with a CPI orientation. (New Delhi)

Mainstream

Independent leftist. Ably edited by Nikhil Chakravarthi. (New Delhi)

New Quest

An Indian version of *Encounter* by the Indian Committee for Cultural Freedom

PUCL Bulletin

Publications of the People's Union for Civil Liberties. (New Delhi)

Radical Humanist

Weekly, founded by M. N. Roy. (New Delhi)

Sarvodaya

Monthly of Vinoba Bhave's movement. (Thanjavur)

Seminar

Examines one topic per issue, with a wide range of opinion and a good bibliography. Monthly. (New Delhi)

Sunday

Lively newsweekly from Calcutta.

Surya India

Monthly, founded by Maneka Gandhi, and now, under new ownership, associated with the RSS.

The Week
Publication of the Malayali Manorama from Kerala.

Yojana
Publication of the Indian Planning Commission.

Newspapers

Amrita Bazar Patrika
Reflects the views of the Congress Bengali middle class. (Calcutta)

Economic Times
India's *Wall Street Journal*, published by the *Times of India* group.

Hindu
A conservative paper, with thoughtful editorials and extensive coverage. (Madras)

Hindustan Times
Birla-owned and pro-Congress. Good coverage and features. (New Delhi)

India Abroad
Published weekly from New York, with regional editions, for the Indian community in the United States. Contains news of major events in India. Excellent source for current events.

India West
News weekly from Oakland, California.

Indian Express
With editions published throughout India, India's largest English-language newspaper. Generally reflects an opposition perspective.

National Herald
Founded by Nehru, generally reflects the Gandhi family's views. (New Delhi)

Overseas Hindustan Times
Weekly airmail edition provides good, independent coverage. (New Delhi)

Patriot
Daily companion to *Link* and generally pro-CPI. (New Delhi)

Statesman

Somewhat elitist, but with good, reliable coverage. Before independence, it was the voice of the British community. (Calcutta)

Statesman

Airmail edition, extensive coverage, good features. Weekly. (Calcutta)

Sunday Observer

Weekly. (Bombay)

Telegraph

India's newest English-language daily, published by *Ananda Bazar*. (Calcutta)

Times of India

Perhaps the best coverage of any paper, with an independent, but generally pro-government viewpoint. Excellent features. (Bombay and New Delhi)

Party Periodicals

(AICC) Economic Review

Published by the All-India Congress Committee of the National Congress.

Call

Published on behalf of the Central Committee of the Revolutionary Socialist Party. (Delhi)

Congress Bulletin

Issued by the Indian National Congress.

Janata

Weekly journal of the Janata Party.

Liberation

The official publication of the Naxalite CPI (ML) Monthly. Proscribed. (Calcutta)

Mankind

Socialist quarterly founded by Lohia.

New Age

Weekly journal of the Communist Party of India. Primarily news.

Organiser
Weekly journal of the RSS.

People's Democracy
The official publication of the CPM. Weekly. (Calcutta)

Index

A

Abdullah, Farooq, 161, 304
Abdullah, Sheikh, 304, 396
Advani, L. K., 121, 182–183, 193, 290, 292, 293
Afghanistan, Soviet invasion of, 256, 400–401, 415–416, 418
Afro-Asian world, 404–405
AGP. *See* Asom Gana Parishad (AGP)
Agriculture
  green revolution, 20, 197–198, 375, 376, 383
  growth of, 382, 383–384
  modern technology for, 20
  percent of population dependent on, 21
  policy of, 374–378
  resources for, 20
  subsistence agriculture, 19
Ahmed, Bashiruddin, 345, 349–350
Ahmed, Fakhruddin Ali, 65–66, 73, 278
AIADMK. *See* All-India Anna DMK (AIADMK)
AIMO. *See* All-India Manufacturers Organization (AIMO)
AIR. *See* All-India Radio (AIR)
AITUC. *See* All-India Trade Union Congress (AITUC)
Akali Dal
  defeat of, in Punjab, 152–153
  demands for Sikh state by, 139, 140, 145
  and desecration of Golden Temple, 156
  divisions within, 153–154, 157
  and government accord with Sikhs, 158
  and Janata government's collapse, 281
  language and, 11
  political activity at Sikh shrines, 186
  as regional party, 148, 223, 303–304
Akbar, 27
Akhil Bharatiya Vidyarthi Parished, 179, 199
Aksai Chin, 410–411
Algeria, 22
Aligarh Muslim University, 199
All-Assam Students' Union, 151, 199
All-Bodo Student Union, 150
All-India Anna DMK (AIADMK)
  demands for state autonomy by, 145
  and Janata government's collapse, 281
  in 1977 election, 250
  in 1991 elections, 312
  as regional party, 11, 133, 148, 223, 301–303
All-India Communist Party, 298
All-India Congress Committee, 258, 272
All-India Kisan Sabha, 194
All-India Kisan Sammelan, 194–195
All-India Manufacturers Organization (AIMO), 387
All-India Radio (AIR), 332–333
All-India Railwaymen's Federation, 201
All-India Sikh Students Federation, 155

All-India Trade Union Congress (AITUC), 200
All-India Women's Conference, 204
All-Jharkhand Students Union, 164
Ahmed, Bashiruddin, 346, 349–350
Ambani, Dhirubhai, 266
Ambedkar, B. R., 47, 60, 70, 113, 119, 191
Amendments, constitutional
  allocation of seats in Lok Sabha, 77
  anti-defection bill, 262–263
  antisecessionist amendment, 301
  declaration of emergency and suspension of due process clause, 211–212
  denial of Supreme Court's judicial review over constitutional amendments, 102, 246
  during emergency of 1975–77, 246–247
  emergency provisions, 74
  land reform, 102
  number of, 59–60
  Parliament's right to amend Constitution, 102
  President's relationship with Council of Ministers, 71
  process for amending Constitution, 80
  Sikkim statehood, 144
  Supreme Court, 101–102
  village government proposed amendment of, 114–115
Anand Marg, 245
Anandolan, 174
Anandpur Sahib Resolution, 153
Andhra Pradesh
  commercialization and urbanization in, 20
  demands for state autonomy in, 145
  landless laborers in, 13
  linguistic basis for reorganization of, 136, 138
  President's Rule and, 107
  rural unrest in, 196, 197
  statehood movement in, 164
  student political unrest in, 199
  Telegu Desam in, 11, 148, 223
Annadurai, C. N., 133, 301, 302
Anti-defection bill, 262–263
Antipoverty programs, 268, 376–377
Appleby, Paul, 96–97, 131
Armed Forces Special Powers Act (1956), 210
Army. *See* Military
Arunachal Pradesh, 10, 141
Arya Samaj, 34, 178, 181
Asoka, 27
Asom Gana Parishad (AGP), 152, 223, 286, 305–306
Assam
  agriculture in, 376
  Asom Gana Parishad in, 223
  desire for redistribution of income among states, 148
  Naga National Council and, 141
  political unrest in, 150–152
  President's Rule in, 152, 306
  purposeful neglect by government, 149
  student political unrest in, 199
  violence in, 149
Assam Rifles, 208
Associated Chambers of Commerce and Industry (Assocham), 367, 387
Attlee, Clement, Prime Minister, 51
Attorney General, appointment of, 72
Austin, Granville, 63, 64
Awami League, 398
Ayodhya, v–vi, 182–183, 264, 290, 292, 310, 311–313, 345, 371
Ayub Khan, 397, 398
Azad, Maulana Abul Kalam, 52, 60–61

B

Babri Masjid. *See* Ramjanmabhumi-Babri Masjid conflict
Babri Masjid Action Committee, 182, 186
Bachchan, Ajitabh, 266
Bachchan, Amitabh, 266, 284, 334
Backward Classes Commission, 192
Bahuguna, H. N., 250, 254, 280, 284
Bahujan Samaj Party (BSP), 191, 312, 345
Bailey, F. G., 109
Bajrang Dal, vi, 180

Bandh, 173
Banerjea, Surendranath, 35, 36, 37, 39
Bangalore, 165
Bangladesh
creation of, 238
immigration from, 150, 151, 408–409
and Indo-American relations, 414
Islamic fundamentalism in, 181
liberation of, 73, 74, 88, 117, 400, 418
previously East Bengal, 39
Bano, Shah, 184–185
Barnala, Surjit Singh, 158–159
Basu, Jyoti, 284, 297, 299
Beals, Alan, 8
Balgaum District, 144
Bengal. *See also* East Bengal; West Bengal
desire for redistribution of income among states, 148
Extremist support in, 38, 39
partition of, 39
and partition of India, 52
statehood movement in, 164
Bentinck, Governor General, 32
Besant, Annie, 41
Bhagavad Gita, 5
Bhagwati, P. N., 104, 205
Bharat (Hindu nation), 62–63
Bharatiya Jana Sangh. *See* Jana Sangh
Bharatiya Janata Party (BJP)
alliance with Shiv Sena, 180
appeals to specific groups, 339–341
communalism and, 180–181
development of, 223, 290–294
elections of 1987, 69
elections of 1989, 270, 289, 310
elections of 1991, 311–318, 337
electoral support for, 224
and fragmentation of opposition parties, 283, 284
in Punjab, 159
Kashmir and, 163
labor unions and, 200
and Mandal recommendations, 193
and Singh as Prime Minister, 159
student movement in, 200
symbol of, 332, 333
Bharatiya Kisan Union (BKU), 197
Bharatiya Kranti Dal (BKD), 275
Bharatiya Lok Dal (BLD), 222, 223, 275–276, 278–279
Bharatiya Mazdoor Sangh (BMS), 179, 200
Bhatt, Ela, 204
Bhave, Vinoba, 168, 202
Bhindranwale, Sant Jarnail Singh, 153–156
Bhoodan movement, 168
Bhopal industrial accident, 205
Bhutan, 407–408
Bhutto, Benazir, 403
Bhutto, Zulfikar Ali, 400
Bicameralism, 42
Bihar
agriculture in, 19, 376
communalism in, 177
gang rule in, 206
Janata Dal government election in 1989, 108
legislative assembly in, 110
political interference in administration of, 98
political unrest in, 177, 196–197, 242
poverty of, 20
reorganization of, 140
statehood movement in, 164
BJP. *See* Bharatiya Janata Party (BJP)
BKD. *See* Bharatiya Kranti Dal (BKD)
BKU. *See* Bharatiya Kisan Union (BKU)
BLD. *See* Bharatiya Lok Dal (BLD)
BMS. *See* Bharatiya Mazdoor Sangh (BMS)
Bodoland, 150
Bofors contract, 68–69, 266–267, 269, 330, 336
Bombay
Arya Samaj in, 34
bifurcation of, 140
British commercial enclaves in, 27
population of, 115
reorganization of, 139
Shiv Sena in, 165
Border Security Force (BSF), 118, 208
Bose, Subhas Chandra, 45, 49
Brahmins, 9, 30, 32, 190
Brahmo Samaj (Divine Society), 33–34
Brass, Paul, 228, 229
Brecher, Michael, 55, 86, 87, 233

Brezhnev, Leonid, 400
British East India Company, 27–28, 31
British India
  awakening nationalism in, 31–50
  beginning of British commercial foothold in, 27–28
  British colonial policy in, 28, 30, 31–35
  call for dominion status of, 45–46
  civil disobedience campaign in, 46–47, 49–50
  creation of Indian National Conference in, 36–37
  as dominion in British Commonwealth of Nations, 62
  education in, 32–33
  foreign policy and, 393
  Gandhian era of, 43–50
  governance of, 39–42, 47–49, 126–127
  growing political consciousness of, 35–36
  Indian Civil Service in, 35–36
  language of, 146
  map of, 29
  Moderates in, 39–40
  Montagu-Chelmsford Reforms in, 42, 45
  Morley-Minto Reforms in, 39–41
  period of Extremists in, 38–43
  period of Moderates in, 37–38
  reform and revivalism in, 38
  Sepoy Mutiny in, 30–31
  village government in, 112
  westernization during British rule, 28–30
BSF. *See* Border Security Force (BSF)
BSP. *See* Bahujan Samaj Party (BSP)
Buddhism, 26, 191
Bureaucracy
  corruption in, 94, 98, 99–100
  under Indira Gandhi, 98
  mistrust of, 95–96
  political interference in, 98
  power of, 98
  under Rajiv Gandhi, 98–99
  red tape in, 96–97
  relationship between politician and bureaucrat, 97–98
Burma, 149
Business community, 367, 386–389

C

Cabinet
  Cabinet Secretariat of, 87–88
  under Desai, 88–89
  Emergency Committee of, 86–87
  functions of, 85
  under Indira Gandhi, 87–88
  of Janata government, 277
  membership in, 85–86
  under Nehru, 86–87
  Political Affairs Committee of, 87
  under Rajiv Gandhi, 89–90, 265
  ranking of members of, 86
  relationship to Lok Sabha, 78
  under Shastri, 87
Cabinet Secretariat, 87–88
Calcutta, 18, 27, 36, 52, 115
Campaigns. *See* Elections
Candidates. *See* Elections; and names of specific candidates
Carter, Jimmy, 415
Caste system, 8–9, 186–188
CBI. *See* Central Bureau of Investigation (CBI)
Censorship, during emergency of 1975–77, 245–246
CENTO, 413
Central Bureau of Investigation (CBI), 68
Central Industries Security Force (CISF), 208
Central Reserve Police Force (CRPF), 118, 208
Central Secretariat Service, 92
Centre of Indian Trade Unions (CITV), 200
CFD. *See* Congress for Democracy (CFD)
Chandigarh, 140, 153, 157–158, 264
Chandra Shekhar
  creation of Samajvadi Janata Party, 270
  defeat of, in election of 1984, 284, 285
  dismissal of Asom Gana Parishad government, 152

elections of 1989, 311
foreign policy of, 405
and Janata Party, 223, 277, 286
and National Front government, 289, 290
as Prime Minister, 72, 76, 90, 91, 302, 309, 310, 371
resignation as Prime Minister, 71, 310
Sikhs and, 159
Chandrachud, Y. V., 103
Charter Act (1833), 36
Chatterjee, A. K., 97
Chavan, Y. B., 252, 280, 281
Children, 22, 23
China
foreign relations with India, 410–413
growth-rate of, 22
protest over statehood of Arunachal Pradesh, 141
support for Pakistan, 397–399
war with India, 73, 85, 117, 134, 393, 404, 411–412
Chipko Movement, 204
Chogyal of Sikkim, 141, 143
Chota-Nagpur region, 140
Chou En-lai, 411
Christianity, 26, 140, 186
CISF. *See* Central Industries Security Force (CISF)
Citizens for Democracy, 205
City government. *See* Urban areas
Civil disobedience, 46–47, 49–50, 172
Civil Service. *See* Indian Civil Service
Civil-liberties groups, 205
Class. *See* Social class
Coal production, 384
Cohen, Stephen P., 118, 211
Commonwealth of Nations, 62
Communalism
description of, 176–178
electorates and, 46
Hindu communalism, 178–183
Muslim communalism, 183–186
violence based on, 177–178
Communist governments, 3, 12, 75, 114, 134
Communist Party (Marxist)
and collapse of Janata government, 281
development of, 297–300
elections of 1977, 250
elections of 1980, 255–256
elections of 1983, 260
elections of 1984, 284
elections of 1989, 310
labor unions and, 200
and Naxalites, 278
student movement in, 200
symbol of, 333
Communist Party of India (CPI)
demands for state autonomy by, 145
development of, 294–300
elections of 1980, 255–256
elections of 1984, 284
elections of 1987, 69
and imposition of emergency in 1975, 246
labor unions and, 200
and Mandal recommendations, 193
political strategy of, 221
publishing of, 331
and rural unrest, 195
support for Indira Gandhi, 287
symbol of, 333
and Telengana uprising, 195
Communist Party of India (Marxist-Leninist), 297, 298
Comptroller and Auditor General, appointment of, 72–73
Conference of Chief Ministers, 133
Congress for Democracy (CFD), 222, 250, 273, 276, 277, 279
Congress (I)
appeals to specific groups, 339–340
elections of 1978, 252–253
elections of 1980, 254–256
elections of 1983, 260
elections of 1989, 223, 267–271, 289, 310
elections of 1991, 309, 311–318, 337
formation of, 252
labor unions and, 200
leadership of Parliament in 1991, 220, 224
legislative majority in Parliament, 217
opposition of Sanjay Gandhi, 254
Rao and, 91
return to power in 1979, 283
support for presidential system, 121
support of Shekhar by, 72, 91

Congress (J), 283
Congress (O), 78, 222, 223, 273, 277, 279
Congress party
  breakdown of, from 1967–1977, 234–252
  bureaucracy and transition from Congress to Janata and back again, 98
  and Center-state relations, 133
  centralization and, 148
  Christians' support for, 186
  crisis in, 135, 236–237
  criteria for candidate selection, 325–326
  death of Sanjay and rise of Rajiv, 256–258
  defeat of, in 1977, 220, 249–252
  disarray in state organizations, 258–260
  dominant role of, 220
  election of 1980, 254–256
  and emergency of 1975–77, 241–252
  factional character of, 226–230
  federalizing the Congress system, 132, 230–233
  before independence, 216, 225–226
  Indira Gandhi and, 237–241
  and Indira Gandhi's assassination, 260–261
  and language as basis of political divisions, 10, 136
  manifestos of, 64, 335
  Muslim support for, 184
  and Nehru's foreign policy, 393
  one-party dominance of, 225–226
  as opposition party in late 1970s, 252–254
  party elections in 1991, 272
  party funds and campaign financing, 330–331
  periods of, 225
  and Rajiv Gandhi as Prime Minister, 261–272
  regionalism as opposition to, 148
  split of, 77, 134, 222, 237, 252
  student movement in, 199–200
  and succession to Presidency, 66
  and succession to Prime Ministership, 233–234
  symbol of, 332, 333
  Working Committee of, 230–232, 234, 236, 258, 272
Congress (S), 223, 283, 286, 287–288, 310
Congress Socialist Party (CSP), 221, 294
Constituent Assembly, 60–63, 136
Constitution. *See also* Amendments, constitutional
  abolition of untouchability in, 188
  amendment process in, 80
  central tenets of, 60
  date when in effect, 61
  Directive Principles of State Policy section of, 64, 246
  distribution of powers among central government and states, 128–130
  drafted by Constituent Assembly, 60–63
  due process clause of, 211
  Emergency Provisions of, 73–75, 129
  financial provisions on distribution of revenues, 128, 130–131
  Fundamental Rights section of, 63–64, 101–102, 102
  governance described in, 61–63, 126
  Hindi as official language in, 146
  length of, 59–60
  Parliament in, 76–91
  preamble of, 61
  President and Vice President in, 64–76
  Prime Minister and Council of Ministers, 83–85
  public services in, 92–93
  settlement of interstate disputes, 144
  significance of, 55–56
  state government in, 105–110
  universal adult suffrage in, 61, 125, 169, 318, 345
Corruption
  in antipoverty programs, 378
  in bureaucracy, 94, 98, 99–100
  in elections, 341–342
  Indira Gandhi and, 242–243, 253
  in local government, 112
  Rajiv Gandhi and, 68–69, 265–272, 367

Council of Ministers
- membership of, 84–85
- President's relationship with, 65, 70, 71, 72
- relationship with Lok Sabha, 79

Courts. *See* Judicial system; Supreme Court
CPI (M-L). Communist Party of India (Marxist-Leninist)
CPM. *See* Communist Party (Marxist)
Crime and criminals, 110, 207, 342. *See also* Corruption
Cripps, Sir Stafford, 49
CRPF. *See* Central Reserve Police Force (CRPF)
CSP. *See* Congress Socialist Party (CSP)

D

Dacoity (gang robbery), 28, 206, 342
Dal Khalsa, 153, 210
Dalit Mazdoor Kizan Party (DMKP), 223, 284, 286–287
Dalit Panthers, 192
Daman, 141
Dange, S. A., 295, 296
Dar Commission, 136, 138
Darjeeling Gurkha Hill Council, 164
Das, C. R., 45
Dayananda, Swami, 34
De Costa, E. P. W., 349
Defence of India Act, 74
Defence of India Rules (DIR), 74, 245
Defense Security Corps (DSC), 208
Delhi, population of, 115
Delhi University, 200
Delimitation Commission, 322–323
Democracy. *See also* Governance
- in Great Britain, 2–3
- in India, 15, 119

Democratic Socialist Party, 283, 286, 287
Dependency theory, and India's political development, 14–15
Desai, Kirtidev, 239
Desai, Morarji
- Cabinet under, 88–89
- in Congress (O), 273
- as contender for Prime Minister with Indira Gandhi, 234
- as Deputy Prime Minister, 236
- fasting by, 173, 243
- as Finance Minister, 232
- on Indira Gandhi, 244
- in Janata Party, 250, 276, 286
- on lawlessness, 74
- as Prime Minister, 277, 415
- Ram and, 283
- resignation as Prime Minister, 71, 72, 280–281
- Shastri and, 233
- Singh and, 279, 283
- and Syndicate leadership, 237

Desam, Telugu, 260
Deshmukh, C. D., 65
Devanagari, 139
Development. *See also* Political development
- agriculture, 374–378
- economic policy, 355–373
- model of, 354–355
- performance of Indian economy, 380–385
- planning priorities and contradictions, 378–380
- politics of economic management, 385–389

Devi, Maharani Gayatri, 327
Dharma (duty), 5–6, 167
Dharna, 173
Dhawan, R. K., 268
DIR. *See* Defence of India Rules (DIR)
Diu, statehood of, 141
Divine Society, 33–34
DMK. *See* Dravida Munnetra Kazhagam (DMK)
DMKP. *See* Dalit Mazdoor Kizan Party (DMKP)
Dogras, 161
Doordarshan, 182, 333
"Drain theory" of British exploitation of India, 37
Dravida Kazhagam (DK), 301
Dravida Munnetra Kazhagam (DMK)
- demands for state autonomy by, 145
- dismissal as government of Tamil Nadu, 76
- elections of 1989, 267–268
- in National Front, 286
- on official languages, 147

Dravida Munnetra Kazhagam (DMK) (*continued*)
  as regional party, 11, 148, 223, 301–303
  support for Indira Gandhi, 237
  in Tamil Nadu, 76, 133, 223, 235
Dravidian Federation, 301
DSC. *See* Defense Security Corps (DSC)
Due process, 211
Dushkin, Lelah, 190
Dutt, Sunil, 334
Duumvirate, 55
Dyarchy, 42, 47, 62
Dyer, General, 42–43

E

East Bengal, 39, 238
East India Company. *See* British East India Company
Eastern Europe, 3, 299
Economic policy
  creation of development model for, 355–359
  during early 1970s, 361–363
  Eighth Five-Year Plan, 376, 380
  Fifth Five-year Plan, 375, 380
  First Five-Year Plan, 357, 378, 379
  Fourth Five-Year Plan, 359, 375, 379
  Indira Gandhi's approach to, 361–366
  Janata economic policy, 365
  Mohandas Gandhi's vision of, 355
  Nehru's vision of, 355–356
  during 1960s, 359–361
  from 1973–1984, 363–366
  during 1990s, 370–373
  Patel's vision of, 355–356
  and performance of Indian economy, 380–385
  planning priorities and contradictions, 378–380
  politics of economic management, 385–389
  Rajiv Gandhi's policy of, 366–370
  Second Five-Year Plan, 357–358
  Seventh Five-Year Plan, 368, 376
  Sixth Five-Year Plan, 375–376
  Third Five-Year Plan, 358
Economy
  agriculture's contribution to, 21
  "drain theory" of British exploitation of India, 37
  foreign aid and, 422–423
  growth-rate of, 21–22
  income, 21–22, 383
  industry's contribution to, 21
  during 1980s, 368
  performance of, 380–385
  20 Point Program, 247–248
Education, 23, 32–33
Eisenhower, Dwight D., 413
Ekta Yatra, 163
Eldersveld, Samuel J., 346, 349–350
Election Commission, 322, 343
Elections
  appeals to specific groups, 338–341
  candidate selection for, 324–329
  candidates in, 323–324
  constituencies and seats, 322–323
  election campaign, 330–343
  expanding participation and impact of competitive elections, 343–345
  issues in, 335–338
  levels of awareness and political participation, 345–346
  "money politics" in, 341–342
  party funds and campaign financing, 330–335
  and party manifestos, 335
  political mobilization and India's future, 349–350
  polling and prediction, 329–330
  of President, 65
  in Punjab, 159–160
  size of, 318
  and social base of constituency, 326–327
  and unification of opposition, 327–330
  violence and, 343
  voting procedures for, 318, 322
  voting turnout and trends, 346–349
Elections of 1952, 319, 335, 347
Elections of 1957, 319, 335, 347
Elections of 1962, 319, 335, 347
Elections of 1967, 65, 75, 106–107, 108, 234–235, 236, 320, 327–328, 335, 347
Elections of 1969, 65, 236–237

Elections of 1971, 87, 102, 237–238, 320, 336, 347, 380
Elections of 1972, 239
Elections of 1974, 65–66
Elections of 1977, 66, 76, 81, 249–252, 276, 320, 328, 347, 348
Elections of 1978, 252
Elections of 1980, 254–256, 320–321, 336, 347
Elections of 1981, 329–330
Elections of 1982, 66
Elections of 1983, 260
Elections of 1984, 261–262, 284–285, 286, 287, 291, 321, 328, 336, 347, 348
Elections of 1985, 263–264
Elections of 1987, 69
Elections of 1989, 108, 117, 223, 267–271, 288–289, 310–311, 321, 336–337, 347
Elections of 1990, 292–293
Elections of 1991, 83, 84, 91, 159–160, 193, 220, 224, 293, 305, 309, 311–318, 330, 347, 348, 337
Elections of 1992, 69
Electorate
  expanding participation and impact of competitive elections, 343–345
  levels of awareness and political participation, 345–346
  voting turnout and trends, 346–349
Embree, Ainslie, 185
Emergency
  conditions in which central government can intervene in states, 129
  and extension of term of Lok Sabha, 77
  powers of President in, 210
Emergency Committee, of Cabinet, 86–87
Emergency of 1962, 73–74
Emergency of 1971, 73, 74
Emergency of 1975–77
  censorship during, 245–246
  centralization of government during, 120
  compulsory sterilizations during, 17, 248–249
  constitutional amendments during, 102, 246–247
  election of 1977 and defeat of Congress Party, 249–252
  imposition of, 73, 74, 81, 88, 243–246
  Indira Gandhi and, 241–252
  labor unions during, 201
  lifting of, 277
  military's role in, 119
  oppressive measures during, 135, 212
  prelude to, 242–243
  Research and Analysis Wing during, 88
  RSS banned during, 179
  Sanjay Gandhi and, 248–249
  Supreme Court during, 103
  20 Point Program during, 246–248
Employment. *See* Labor
Environmental groups, 204–205
ESMA. *See* Essential Services Maintenance Act (ESMA)
Essential Services Maintenance Act (ESMA), 201–202, 210
Europe. *See* Great Britain; Eastern Europe; and names of other countries
Evangelicals, 28, 30, 32, 33
Executive branch of government. *See* Presidents; Prime Minister; Vice Presidents
Extremists, in Indian National Congress, 38–43

F

Fairfax Group, 266
Family planning, 17, 248–249
Federalism. *See also* Governance
  Center-state relations, 128–136
  origins and nature of, 126–136
  and politics of language, 145–147
  and regionalism in Indian politics, 147–165
  and States Reorganization, 136–145
Federation of Indian Chambers of Commerce and Industry (FICCI), 367, 387–388
Feminism, 203–204
FERA. *See* Foreign Exchange Regulation Act (FERA)

Fernandes, George, 275, 280, 286
FICCI. *See* Federation of Indian Chambers of Commerce and Industry (FICCI)
Finance Commission, 130
5 Point Program, 248
Five-Year Plans
  First, 357, 378, 379
  Second, 357–358
  Third, 358
  Fourth, 359, 375, 379
  Fifth, 375, 380
  Sixth, 375–376
  Seventh, 368, 376
  Eighth, 376, 380
  and development funds to states, 130–131
Foreign aid, 422–423
Foreign Exchange Regulation Act (FERA), 362, 367, 370, 371
Foreign Investment Proposal Board, 373
Foreign relations
  with China, 410–413
  with Great Britain after independence, 395–396
  with "nonaligned" world, 404–405
  nonalignment as foreign policy, 393–395
  with Pakistan, 396–404
  and quest for security, 420–423
  with South Asia, 406
  South Asian regional cooperation, 409–410
  with Soviet Union, 417–420
  with United States, 413–417
Forster, E. M., 63
Forum Against Oppression of Women, 204
Forward Bloc, 49
Fundamental Rights section, of Constitution, 101–102, 102

G

Gahuguna, H. N., 287
Galanter, Marc, 105
Gandhi, Indira
  appointment of Chief Justice of Supreme Court, 103
  assassination of, 7, 66, 118, 156, 212, 225, 260–261
  and candidate selection, 325, 326
  and centralization of government, 120, 125, 134–135, 148, 209, 237–241
  compulsory sterilization and, 17
  and Congress Party in disarray in 1980s, 258–260
  criminal charges against, 242–243, 253, 281
  criticism of appointment as Prime Minister, 84
  death of Sanjay and rise of Rajiv, 256–258
  defeat of, 81, 135
  economic policy of, 102, 236, 361–366, 375, 379
  election as Prime Minister, 87, 88, 234
  election of 1971, 336
  election of 1977, 249–252, 276
  election of 1978, 252–253
  election of 1980, 254–256, 336
  electoral victories of, 237–239
  and emergency of 1975–77, 73, 74, 88, 222, 241–252
  and fall of Andhra government, 107
  foreign relations and, 400–402, 416
  Hindu appeal in Jammu and Kishmir by, 181
  judicial system and, 104
  military and, 119
  and National Conference, 304
  Nixon's view of, 414
  and power for bureaucracy, 98
  Presidential Order abolishing privy purse and privileges of princes, 102
  and President's Rule, 75
  and Punjab, 156
  and radio, 332
  Rao and, 91
  re-election in 1967, 236
  Reddy and, 66
  relationship to Parliament, 81
  response to Desai's hunger fast, 173
  Singh and, 66
  succession after death of, 174
  support from Communist Party of India, 298

and Telugu Desam, 305
20 Point Program of, 247–248
Gandhi, Maneka, 259–260
Gandhi, Mohandas
arrests of, 44
assassination of, 53, 59, 179
civil disobedience campaign of, 46–47, 49–50
contributions of, 53
early life of, 43
early work with *satyaqraha* (nonviolent resistance), 43–44
on economic policy, 355
entrance into Congress politics, 44
fasting by, 44, 47, 52–53, 173
final writing of, 202
on Hindi language, 146
imprisonment of, 44, 46, 50
and Indian National Congress, 228
Muslims and, 52–53
on partition of India, 51, 52–53
and political parties, 168
release from prison in 1944, 50
response to massacre in Amritsar, 42
response to violence, 44
revitalization of village life, 113
in South Africa, 43
support for Nehru Report, 45
swadeshi campaign of, 45
untouchables and, 45
vision of society of, 45
Gandhi, Rajiv
agreement with Assam, 151–152
and anti-defection bill, 262–263
assassination of, 83, 91, 212, 224, 225, 270, 312
bureaucracy under, 98–99
Cabinet under, 89–90
Chandra Shekar, and, 72, 91
on corruption in antipoverty programs, 378
corruption scandals and, 265–272, 367
defeat in 1989, 117
economic policy of, 366–370
education and early career of, 258–259
elections of 1984, 261–262
elections of 1989, 267–270, 310–311, 336–337
entry into politics, 258
foreign relations and, 402, 406, 412, 416
leadership style of, 120, 265
and Muslim Women (Protection of Rights on Divorce) Bill, 185
political campaigns of, 334–335
political crisis under, 120–121
as Prime Minister, 67–69, 76, 89–90, 261–272, 309
Punjab and, 157–159
relationship with President, 265
and television, 332–333
Tripura accord and, 150
village government proposed amendment of, 114–115
and violence after Indira Gandhi's assassination, 157
Gandhi, Sanjay
criminal charges against, 253
death of, 257
defeat of, 251
election of 1980, 255
opposition to, 254
political power of, 88, 243, 248–250, 257, 364
Singh and, 67
Gandhi, Sonia, 91, 257, 271, 312
Gandhi-Irwin pact, 46
Gandhians, 202–203
Ghana, 22
Gherao, 173
Ghose, Aurobindo, 38
Ghosh, Ajoy, 295, 296
Giri, V. V., 65, 66, 237
GNLF. *See* Gurkha National Liberation Front (GNLF)
Goa, 141, 418
Goenka, Ram Nath, 68
Gokhale, G. K., 38, 39, 40, 41, 43
Golaknath case, 102
Golden Temple, in Punjab, 154–156, 159, 210, 264
Golwalkar, M. S., 179
Goondas (criminal element), 207, 342
Gorbachev, Mikhail, 299, 412, 418
Gorwala, A. D., 99
Gough, Kathleen, 8
Gould, Harold, 386
Governance. *See also* Federalism
bureaucracy in, 95–100

Governance (*continued*)
Cabinet, 85–91
Center-state relations, 128–136
and Fundamental Rights and Directive Principles in Constitution, 63–64
local government, 110–116
military, 116–119
Parliament, 76–91
political stability and, 212–213
President and Vice President, 64–76
Presidential powers in, 70–76
Prime Minister and Council of Ministers, 83–85
responsive capacity of, 119–122
state govenment, 105–110
structure of public services, 92–93
Supreme Court and judicial system, 100–105
type of, as decided on by Constituent Assembly, 61–63
union territories, 110
Vice Presidential powers in, 70
village government, 268
Government of India Act (1935), 47–49, 60, 127, 345
Governmental Regulatory Acts (1773), 126
Governors of states
appointment of, 72
powers of, 106–108
and President's declaration of constitutional emergency in, 75
Graham, Bruce, 292
Grass-roots organizations, 203–205
Great Britain
and awakening nationalism in India, 31–50
beginning of commercial foothold in India, 27–28
British rule during 18th and 19th centuries, 28–30
and civil disobedience campaign in India, 46–47, 49–50
colonial policy of, 28, 30, 31–35
Communist Party of, 294
crisis in political development of, 2–3
and Gandhian era of India, 43–50
governance of, 70, 77, 84, 70, 101
Government of India Act of 1935, 47–49, 60, 127, 345
as ideal model of political development, 2
and independence of India, 4, 50–52
India as colony of, 27–50
and Indian Civil Service, 35–36
India's relations with after independence, 395–396
Montagu-Chelmsford Reforms in India, 42, 45, 345
Morley-Minto Reforms in India, 39–41
and period of Extremists in Indian National Congress, 38–43
and period of Moderates in Indian National Congress, 37–38
Sepoy Mutiny and, 30–31
war with Turkey, 41
Green revolution, 20, 197–198, 375, 376, 383
Gromyko, Andrei, 400
Gujarat
agriculture in, 376–377
commercialization and urbanization in, 20
demands for elections in, 173
landless laborers in, 13
President's Rule in, 242, 243
reorganization of, 139
statehood movement in, 164
student political unrest in, 199
Gujarati, 139
Gulf war, 405
Gupta Commission, 253
Gurdwaras (Sikh shrines), 186
Gurkha National Liberation Front (GNLF), 164
Gurkhaland, 164, 264
Gurmukhi, 139
Gurumurthy, S., 68

H

Haksar, P. N., 361
Harijans. *See* untouchables
Hartal, 43, 173
Haryana
agriculture in, 376

commercialization and urbanization in, 20
creation of, 140, 153
interstate disputes of, 158, 159
river water allocation in, 144
statehood movement in, 164
HDW. *See* Howaldt Deutsche Werke (HDW)
Health, 22
Hedge, R. K., 121, 286
Hedgwar, Keshav, 179
Hezb-ul-Mujahideen (HUM), 162
Himachal Pradesh, 140, 376–377
Hind Mazdoor Sabha (HMS), 200, 275
Hindi language, 10–11, 23, 140, 146
Hindu Mahasabha, 178, 179, 221
Hindu Manch, 180
Hinduism
beliefs of, 5–7
British reforms aimed at, 30
caste system of, 8–10
communalism and, 178–183
conflicts between Hindus and Muslims, v–vi, 34–35, 44, 48, 52–53, 181–183, 184
interest in creation of Hindu nation, *Bharat*, 62–63
reform movement in, 34
Sepoy Mutiny and, 30
statistics on number of, 186
unifying nature of, 26–27
view of Sikhism, 153
Hindutva, 181–182, 313
HMS. *See* Hind Mazdoor Sabha (HMS)
Home Ministry, reorganization in 1986, 89
Home Rule League, 41
Hong Kong, 22
Howaldt Deutsche Werke (HDW), 266
HUM. *See* Hezb-ul-Mujahideen (HUM)
Hume, A. O., 36–37
Hussain, Abid, 367–368
Hussain, Zakir, 65, 66
Hyderabad, 53, 54, 127, 195

I

IAS. *See* Indian Administrative Service (IAS)
IISCO. *See* Indian Iron and Steel Company (IISCO)
Ilbert bill, 36
IMF. *See* International Monetary Fund (IMF)
Income, 21–22, 383
Independence
achievement of, 4, 26, 50–56
and awakening Indian nationalism, 31–50
demands for in 1930s–1940s, 49–50
Extremists and, 38–43
Gandhi's civil disobedience campaign for, 43–50
Moderates and, 37–38
and partition of India, 51, 52–53
Index of Opposition Unity (IOU), 217, 328–329
Indian Administrative Service (IAS), 92, 92, 93–95, 111, 189
Indian Association of Calcutta, 35
Indian Civil Service Act (1861), 36
Indian Civil Service (ICS), 35–36, 91–92, 93, 111
Indian Councils Act (1861), 39–40
Indian Foreign Service, 92
Indian Forest Service, 92
Indian Iron and Steel Company (IISCO), 362
Indian Liberal Federation, 41, 45
Indian National Army, 49
Indian National Congress. *See* Congress party
Indian National Trade Union Congress (INTUC), 200
Indian Police Service, 92
Indian Post Office (Amend) Bill, 67
Indian Revenue Service, 92
Indo-Pakistani War. *See* Pakistan
Indo-Tibetan Border Police (ITBP), 208
Industrial Policy Resolution, 356–358, 365
Industrialization
growth of, 358–359, 380–383
Industrial Policy Resolution, 356–358, 365
industry's contribution of GNP, 21
New Industrial Poilcy, 371–372
resources for, 20–21
workforce for, 12
Industries (Development and Regulation) Act, 357

Infant mortality, 22
Integrated Rural Development Programme (IRDP), 377
Interest groups. *See also* specific groups
  areas of conflict of, 174–176
  in political development, 170–174
  protest techniques used by, 172–174
  public interest groups, 202–205
International Bank for Reconstruction and Development. *See* World Bank
International Monetary Fund (IMF), 363, 366, 369, 372, 373, 422, 423
INTUC. *See* Indian National Trade Union Congress (INTUC)
IOU. *See* Index of Opposition Unity (IOU)
Iran, 22, 181
Iraqi invasion of Kuwait, 405
IRDP. *See* Integrated Rural Development Programme (IRDP)
Irwin, Lord, 45–46
Islam. *See* Muslims
ITBP. *See* Indo-Tibetan Border Police (ITBP)
Iyer, V. R. Krishna. *See* Krishna Iyer, V. R.

J

J. P. Movement, 203
Jail boro, 173
Jamiat-i-Islami, vi, 151, 162, 185, 245
Jamiat-ul-Ulema, 185
Jammu and Kashmir, 53, 54, 107, 160–163, 180–181, 396. *See also* Kashmir
Jammu and Kashmir Liberation Front (JKLF), 161, 162
Jammu and Kashmir People's League, 162
Jan Morcha (People's Movement), 173, 223, 285–286, 287, 310
Jana Sangh, 180, 221, 273–275, 277, 279, 280
Janata Dal, 69, 194, 223–224, 285–286, 290, 310–318, 332, 333, 339–340
Janata government
  actions of, 277–279
  crisis and collapse of, 254, 279–283
  economic policy of, 365
  foreign relations of, 400
  leadership of, 277
Janata Party
  bureaucracy and transition from Congress to Janata and back again, 98
  Cabinet members in, 89
  compared with National Front, 288
  composition of, 273
  compulsory sterilization as issue of, 17
  creation of, 203, 220, 222, 273
  defeat of Congress Party by, 220
  elections of 1977, 249–252, 276
  elections of 1980, 254–256, 336
  elections of 1989, 310
  Jana Sangh's merger with, 180
  since 1977, 282
  and President's Rule in states, 76
  Reddy and, 66
  in United Front, 283
Japan, 22
Jati (casters, 8
Jawaharlal Nehru University, 200
Jayalalitha, 302, 303
Jayewardene, J. R., 406
Jharkhand, 139, 140
Jharkhand Mukti Morcha (JMM), 164
Jharkhand Party, 140
Jinnah, Mohammed Ali, 48, 50–51
JKLF. *See* Jammu and Kashmir Liberation Front (JKLF)
JMM. *See* Jharkhand Mukti Morcha (JMM)
Jones, Sir William, 33
Joshi, Murli Manohar, vi, 163
Joshi, P. C., 294, 295
Joshi, Ram, 239
Joshi, Sharad, 197, 198
Judicial system. *See also* Supreme Court
  case load of, 104, 105
  jurisdiction of high courts, 105
  politicization of, 104–105
  state courts, 104–105
  Supreme Court, 100–104

Junagadh, 53–54
"JVP" Committee, 138

K

Kali, 39
Kamaraj Nadar, K., 232–236
Kamaraj Plan, 232–233
Kannada Chaluvaligars, 165
Karnataka
  agriculture in, 376–377
  border dispute of, 144
  commercialization and urbanization in, 20
  interstate dispute of, 144
  Other Backward Classes in, 192
  "sons of the soil" in, 165
  village government in, 114
Karunanidhi, M., 267, 302
Kashmir
  Army involvement in control of violence in, 209
  autonomy of, 160
  civil-liberties groups and, 205
  domestic unrest in, 149, 264
  Indian-Pakistani conflict over, 54, 161, 396–398, 403–404
  Muslims in, 127
  National Conference in, 223
  President's Rule in, 161, 304
  state autonomy and secessionist movements in, 125
    violence in, 149
  Kashmiri Muslims, National Conference of, 11
  Keith, A. B., 48
  Kenya, 22
  Kerala, 13, 75, 136, 148, 186, 235
  Kesavananda decision, 102
  Khadi (homespun cloth), 45
  Khalistan, 149, 153, 156, 158, 160
  Khan, Sayyid Ahmed, 34–35
  Khilafat issue, 44, 186
  Kipling, Rudyard, 33
  Kosygin, Premier, 398
  Kothari, Rajni, 96, 122, 206, 221, 226, 338
  Kripalani, Archarya, 277
  Krishna, Gopal, 228
  Krishna Iyer, V. R., 69, 104, 205, 243
  Krishnamachari, T. T., 64
  Krushchev, Nikita, 418
  Kshatriyas, 9
  "Kulaks," 12
  Kuwait, Iraqui invasion of, 405

L

Labor
  industrial workforce, 12
  unionization of, 200–202
  wages of, 201
Labor unemployment and, 384
Labor unions, 200–202
Ladakh Scouts, 208
Lahari, Ashok, 329
Lal, Bansi, 248, 253
Lal, Bhajan, 257
Lal, Devi, 223, 286, 289, 290
Laldenga, 141, 150
Lalung tribals, 150
Lamaye, Madhu, 286
Land ownership, 12–13, 19, 197–198
Land reform, 12, 19, 102, 195, 227, 384–385
Languages
  as basis for reorganization of states, 136–145
  major language groups, 10–11
  number of languages and dialects, 5, 26
  official languages, 10–11, 26, 32, 146–147
  for Parliamentary transactions, 77
  politics of, 145–147
  problem of, 10–12
  of states and territories, 143
  three-language formula, 146
Law and order
  Army involvement in, 209
  breakdown in, 205–206
  instruments of law for control of, 209–212
  levels of force for, 208
  parliamentary forces and, 208–209
  police and internal security, 206–209

LDC. *See* Less-developed countries (LDC)
Le Corbusier, 140
League of Nations, 395
Left Front, 193, 310–318
Legislative Assembly, state, 108–110
Legislative branch of government. *See* Parliament
Legislative Council, state, 108–110
Less-developed countries (LDC), characteristics of, 15. *See also* specific countries
Li Peng, 412
Liberation Tigers of Tamil Eelam (LTTE), 406
Life expectancy, 22
Limaye, Madhu, 280
Literacy rate, 23
Local government
  under British, 111
  Collector's role in, 111–112
  local administrative hierarchy, 110–112
  urban government, 115–116
  village government, 112–115
Lok Dal, 223, 254–256, 283, 284, 286–287, 310
Lok Dal (A), 287
Lok Dal (B), 287
Lok Sabha. *See also* Parliament
  legislative process of, 79–82
  members of, 77, 82–83
  powers of, 76, 77–78
  Prime Minister as leader of majority party in, 72
  relationship with Prime Minister, 83, 84
  Speaker of, 77–78
  term of, 77
Lok Shakti, 268
Longowal, Harchand Singh, 155, 157–158, 264
LTTE. *See* Liberation Tigers of Tamil Eelam (LTTE)
Lucknow Congress, 41
Lucknow Pact (1916), 41, 178

M

Macaulay, Lord, 32
Madhya Pradesh
  agriculture in, 19
  gang rule in, 206
  landless laborers in, 13
  political interference in administration of, 98
  rural unrest in, 196
  statehood movement in, 164
  student political unrest in, 199
Madras, 27–28, 115, 138
Mahabharat, 182
Maharashtra
  agriculture in, 376–377
  border dispute of, 144
  commercialization and urbanization in, 20
  Extremist support in, 38
  linguistic basis for reorganization of, 136
  reorganization of, 139
  rural unrest in, 197
  "sons of the soil" in, 165
  statehood movement in, 164
Mahasabha Party, 53
Maheshwari, S. R., 100
Maintenance of Internal Security Act (MISA), 74, 210, 244, 278
Maldives, 117, 407, 416
Malhotra, Inder, 258
Mandal, B. P., 192
Mandal Commission report, 192–194, 199, 288, 290, 293, 311, 313, 371
Manipur, 141, 149, 150
Manohar, Murli, 293
Maratha kingdom, 38
Marathi, 139
Marxists. *See* Community Party (Marxist)
Mazumdar, Charu, 297
Meghalaya, 10, 150
Menon, V. K. Krishna, 85, 411–412
Middle class, 30–35
Military
  assistance from Soviet Union, 118
  and control of police or paramilitary unrest, 207–208
  expenditures for, 117–118, 422
  Indian National Army, 49
  and insurgents of Mizo National Army, 150
  intervention in civil disturbances, 118, 208, 209
  nonpolitical nature of, 116–117

in Punjab, 155–156
scandals involving, 117
Sikhs in, 7
strength of, 117
and violence in reorganization of states, 141
Minerva Mills case, 102
Ministry of Home Affairs, 94
MISA. *See* Maintenance of Internal Security Act (MISA)
Mizo, 141, 149–150
Mizo National Army, 150
Mizo National Front, 141
Mizoram, 118, 150
Mizoram accord, 264
Moderates, in Indian National Congress, 37–40
Monopolies Restrictive Trade Practices Act (MRTP), 362, 367, 371
Montagu, Edwin, 41
Montagu-Chelmsford Reforms (1919), 42, 45, 345
Mookerjee, S. P., 179, 273–274
Morcha, 173
Morley-Minto Reforms, 39–40, 41
Morris, Morris D., 22
Morris-Jones, W. H., 39, 79, 135, 167
Mountbatten, Lord, 51–52, 54, 62
MRTP. *See* Monopolies Restrictive Trade Practices Act (MRTP)
Mughals, 27, 30, 34
Mukti Bahini, 399, 400
Müller, Max, 33
Municipal government. *See* Urban areas
Muslim League, 40–41, 44, 45, 48–51, 60, 62–63, 184, 294
Muslim Women (Protection of Rights on Divorce) Bill, 185
Muslims
alienation of, 34
communalism of, 183–186
conflicts between Hindus and Muslims, 34–35, 44, 48, 52–53, 181–183, 184
as constituency of political parties, 339, 341
demands for greater autonomy, 126
demands for separate electorates, 40–41
geographic distribution of, 127
as heterogeneous group, 183
as Jammu and Kashmir, 160–161
National Conference of Kashmiri Muslims, 11
reaction to British rule, 34–35
rise of Islamic fundamentalism, 181
Sepoy Mutiny and, 30
statistics on, 6, 7, 126–127, 183
support for Gandhi, 44
Myrdal, Gunnar, 6–7, 247
Mysore, 54

N

Nadar, K. Kamaraj. *See* Kamaraj, Nadar
Naga National Council, 141
Naga People's Convention, 141
Nagaland, 10, 118, 139, 140–141, 149–150
Nagpur resolution, 375
Naicker, E. V. Ramaswamy, 301
Namboodiripad, E. M. S., 187, 295–297
Naoroji, Dadbhai, 37
Narain, Raj, 242, 251, 275, 277, 279, 280, 286
Narasimha Rao, P. V., 83, 84, 91, 160, 183, 194, 272, 309, 371–373
Narayan, Jayaprakash, 168, 202–203, 242–244, 275, 277
Narayanan, K. R., 70
Narmada Valley Project, 205
National Conference, 223, 304
National Conference of Kashmiri Muslims, 11
National Council of Khalistan, 210
National Democratic Alliance, 283–284
National Development Council (NDC), 133, 385–386
National Front, 223–224, 270, 285–294, 310–318, 337
National Integration Council, 146
National Police Commission, 206–207
National Rural Employment Programme (NREP), 377
National Security Act (1980), 210
National Security Guards (NSG), 208
National Security (Second Amendment) Ordinance, 210
National Socialist Council of Nagaland, 149

Nationalism
awakening of, in British India, 31–50
and creation of Indian National Congress, 36–37
Extremists and, 38–43
and Gandhi's civil disobedience campaign, 43–50
Moderates and, 37–38
obstacles to, 35
Nativism. *See* "Sons of the soil"
Natural resources, 20–21
Naxalites, 196–197, 199, 245, 277–278, 297–298, 299
Nayar, Baldev Raj, 13–14, 378
NDC. *See* National Development Council (NDC)
NEFA. *See* North East Frontier Agency (NEFA)
Nehru, Arun, 90
Nehru, Jawaharlal
agricultural policy of, 12, 375
appointment of States Reorganization Commission, 138
Cabinet under, 86–87
civil disobedience during Gandhian era, 44
as Congress president, 46
in Constituent Assembly, 60–61
death of, 174, 233
economic policy of, 350, 355–356, 385
on "essential unity" of India, 4
foreign policy of, 393–396, 404, 411, 413
on Gandhi's assassination, 53
on Government of India Act of 1935, 48
on independence of India, 52
on Indian Civil Service, 92
Indian secularism and, 62
linguistic states and, 138
on official languages, 146, 147
opposition to dominion status for India, 45
Parliament and, 80
and partition of India, 52
as party president, 230–232
personality of, 55
and President's Rule, 75
as Prime Minister of interim government, 51
on Sepoy Mutiny, 31
shared power with Patel, 55
Soviet Union's attitude toward, 295
stroke suffered by, 233
support for Gandhi's leadership, 49
Supreme Court and, 101
on village life, 113
Nehru, Motilal, 44, 45, 46, 45
Nehru Report, 45
Nepal, 150, 164, 407, 416
New Industrial Policy (NIP), 371–372
NIP. *See* New Industrial Policy (NIP)
Nixon, Richard, 398, 414
Non-Aligned Movement, 404–405, 423
Nonalignment, as foreign policy, 393–395
Nongovernmental organizations, 203–205
North East Frontier Agency (NEFA), 141
Northeast, 125, 148–152
NREP. *See* National Rural Employment Programme (NREP)
NSG. *See* National Security Guards (NSG)
Nuclear energy, 20–21, 415
Nuclear Non-Proliferation Treaty, 415, 420–421
Nuclear weapons, 415, 417, 420–421
Nutrition, 22

O

OBCs. *See* Other Backward Classes (OBCs)
Official Languages Act, 147
Oil industry, 20, 384
Operation Bluestar, 155–156, 159
Operation Brass Tacks, 402–403
Ordinances, of President, 73
Orientalists, 33
Orissa
agriculture in, 19, 376
and creation of Jharkhand, 140
legislative assembly in, 109
rural unrest in, 196
statehood movement in, 164
student political unrest in, 199

Other Backward Classes (OBCs), 192–194
Ottoman Empire, 44
Outcastes. *See* Untouchables

P

Pakistan
  creation of, 7, 51–53, 127, 184
  dispute over Kashmir, 160, 161
  foreign relations with United States, 413–416
  Hindus' view of creation of, 178
  India's foreign relations with, 396–404
  Islamic fundamentalism in, 181
  Muslims' in, 48, 62–63
  nuclear weapons and, 421
  per-capita income of, 22
  support for Kashmir, 162
  support for Sikh terrorists, 159
  wars with India, 63, 73, 117, 134, 140, 161, 238–239, 393, 396–400
Panchayat Bill, 269
Panchayat (council of elders), 8, 112–113
Panchayati Raj, 112–115
Panchayati Samiti, 113
Paramilitary forces, 208–209, 279
Parliament
  approval of imposition of emergency in 1975, 246
  creation of all-India services by, 92
  decline of, in 1980s, 81–82, 83
  legislative process of, 79–82
  Lok Sabha, 76, 77–78
  members of, 82–83
  money bills in, 80
  plurality of popular vote producing legislative majorities in, 217
  policy process in, 80–81
  President's power to dissolve, 71
  and President's veto power, 73
  Rajya Sabha, 76, 78–79
  relationship with Supreme Court, 80, 101–102
  reserved seats for Scheduled Castes in, 190–191
  special legislative powers over state legislatures, 130
Parties, political. *See* Political parties
Partition of India, 51, 52–53, 127, 184, 396
Patel, Sardar Vallabhbhai, 49, 51–55, 60–61, 63, 92, 138, 355–356
Patiala and East Punjab States Union (PEPSU), 139
Patnaik, Biju, 286
Pawar, Sharad, 271
Peasants, and rural unrest, 194–198
People's Movement (Jan Morcha), 173, 223, 285–286, 287, 310
People's Union for Civil Liberties, 205, 211
People's Union for Democratic Rights, 205
People's War Group, 197
PEPSU (Patiala and East Punjab States Union), 139
Petroleum industry. *See* Oil Industry
Phizo, A. Z., 141
Physical Quality of Life Index (PQLI), 22
Places of Worship Act, 183
Planning, priorities and contradictions in, 378–380. *See also* Five-Year Plans
Planning Commission, 130, 357, 358, 367, 369, 370, 379, 385
Police
  Central Reserve Police, 118
  demands for improvements in working conditions, 207–208
  and election violence, 343
  image of, 206–207
  Indian Police Service, 92
  military involvement with, 118
  number of, 208
  strikes by, 279
Political advertising, 332–334
Political Affairs Committee, of Cabinet, 87
Political culture, 3–4, 168–170
Political development
  challenge in India, 14–23
  context of, in India, 4–14
  crisis of, 1–4
  India's experience of, 15–16
  India's lack of conformity to existing models of, 15
  interest groups in, 170–174
  "revolution of rising frustrations" in India, 23–24

Political parties. *See also* Elections
appeals to specific groups, 338–341
candidate selection by, 324–329
candidates of, 323–324
Communist parties, 294–300
developmental periods of, 220–221
factors influencing, 216–217
issues and, 335–338
manifestos of, 335
non-Congress parties, 272–276
and political tendencies, 217–225
regional parties, 223, 300–306
social base of constituency of, 326–327
status as "official" party, 77
symbols of, 332, 333
unification of opposition, 327–329
Political system, definition of, 3
Politics, distrust of, 167–168
Polling and prediction, of elections, 329–330
Population
age structure in, 18
caste system, 8–10
growth of, 16–18
family planning, 17, 248–249
number of untouchables in, 9
eligious divisions, 5–8
in rural areas, 12, 19, 115
social class, 12–14
social structure of, 5
statistics on, 4, 16–17
tribals, 10
in urban areas, 12, 18, 115
Postal Service, 92
Poverty, 18, 22, 377–378
PQLI. *See* Physical Quality of Life Index (PQLI)
Praja Socialist Party (PSP), 221, 227
Prarthana Samaj, 34
Prasad, Rajendra, 49, 52, 60–62, 65, 66, 70–71, 345
Premadasa, R., 407, 409
Presidents. *See also* names of specific Presidents
chronology of, 65–70
election of, 65
emergency powers of, 210
and legislative process, 80
ordinances of, 73
powers of, 64–65, 70–76, 106, 110
term of office, 65
veto power of, 73
President's Rule, 75–76, 107, 152, 159, 161, 235, 239, 242, 243, 302, 303, 304, 306
Preventive Detention Act, 101, 172
Prime Ministers. *See also* specific Prime Ministers
appointment of, 71, 72, 83
appointment of Cabinet by, 86
chronology of, 84
politics of succession of, 233–234
powers of, 65, 83–84
Prime Minister's Secretariat, 88, 89, 265
relationship to Cabinet, 86–91
relationship to Lok Sabha, 78, 83, 84
relationship to President, 71
succession after Indira Gandhi's assassination, 66–67
Prime Minister's Secretariat, 88, 89, 265
Prisoners, rights of, 205
Protest movements
communalism, 176–178
environmental groups, 204–205
Hindu communalism, 178–183
Muslim communalism, 183–186
rural unrest, 194–198
students, 198–200
techniques associated with, 172–174
urban unrest, 198
Provisional Parliament, 60
PSP. *See* Praja Socialist Party (PSP)
Public administration
in British India, 35–36
bureaucracy of, 95–100
Indian Administrative Service, 92, 93–95
Indian Civil Service, 91–92, 93, 111
positions for Other Backward Classes in, 192–194
positions reserved for Scheduled Castes, 189–190
under Rajiv Gandhi, 90
structure of, 92–93
Public interest groups, 202–205
Punjab
agriculture in, 20, 376
Akali Dal in, 148, 223, 303
Army involvement in control of violence in, 209

Arya Samaj in, 34
civil-liberties groups and, 205
commercialization and urbanization in, 20
demand for Sikh state within, 139
demands for state autonomy in, 125, 135, 145
disturbances in, 149
Extremist support in, 38
landless laborers in, 13
and partition of India, 52
President's Rule in, 159, 303, 304
purposeful neglect by government, 149
reorganization of, 139, 139–140
resistance of redistribution of income among states, 148
riot against Rowlatt Bills in, 42
rioting in, before India's independence, 51
river water allocation in, 144
Sikhs in, 7, 11, 152–160
terrorism and violence in in, 118, 149, 157–159, 211, 264
Punjabi language, 139–140, 153, 158
Punjabi Suba, 140, 153, 303
Pylee, M. V., 71

Q

Queen's Proclamation, 36
Quit India movement, 50

R

Radhakrishnan, Sarvapalli, 65, 66
Radio Beijing, 196
Rahman, Sheikh Mujibur, 398
Rahman, Ziaur, 409
Rail roko, 173
Railway Protection Force (RPF), 208
Rajagopalachari, C., 50, 62
Rajasthan
agriculture in, 19, 376–377
commercialization and urbanization in, 20
consolidation of, 54
gang rule in, 206
Haryana's interest in, 164
landless laborers in, 13
river water allocation in, 144, 153
Rajpramukh, 54
Rajya Sabha
creation of all-India services by, 92
legislative process of, 79–82
membership of, 78–79
powers of, 76, 78–79
special legislative powers over state legislatures, 130
term of, 79
Ram, Jagjivan, 71, 89, 250, 254, 273, 276, 277, 281, 283, 285
Ram, Kanshi, 191
Ramjanmabhumi-Babri Masjid conflict, v–vi, 182–183, 264, 290, 292, 311–313, 345, 371
Ram-rajya, 181
Rama Rao, P. N., 11, 107, 260, 284, 304–305
Ramachandran, Janaki, 302
Ramachandran, M. G., 302
Ramaswami, V., 103
Ramayana, 182
Ranade, M. G., 34, 38
Ranadive, B. T., 294
Rao, P. V. Narasimha. *See* Narasimha Rao, P. V.
Rao Rjeshwar, 294–295
Rao, T. N. Rama. *See* Rama Rao, T. N.
Rashtriya Congress, 283, 284, 286, 287
Rashtriya (National) Rifles, 209
Rashtriya Sanjay Manch, 260
Rashtriya Swayamsevak Sangh (RSS), v–vi, 53, 151, 154, 178–181, 199, 245, 221, 242, 280, 291, 292, 313
Rasta roko, 173
Rath yatra (chariot pilgrimage), 182–183, 293
RAW. *See* Research and Analysis Wing
Ray, A. N., 103
Reddy Commission, 253
Reddy, Nagi, 297
Reddy, Neelam Sanjiva, 65, 66, 71, 135, 237, 278, 280, 281, 283
Reform movement, 28, 30, 32, 33–34, 38
Regionalism
continuing challenge of, 163–165
Jammu and Kashmir, 160–163
Northeast, 149–152
origins and nature of, 147–149
Punjab, 152–160

Religion, 5–6, 26–27, 34, 126–127, 178–186. *See also* names of specific religions
Republican Party, 191
Research and Analysis Wing (RAW), 88, 249
Reserve Bank of India, 373
Resolution of 1882, 112
Revivalism, 33, 38
Rights
  grass-roots organizations for, 203–205
  in Constitution, 63–64, 101–102
Ripon, Lord, 112
RLEGP. See Rural Landless Employment Guarantee Programme (RLEGP)
Round Table Conference, 46
Rowlatt Bills, 42, 43
Roy, Prannoy, 328–329
Roy, Ram Mohan, 30, 33
Roy, Ramashray, 324
RPF. *See* Railway Protection Force (RPF)
RSS. *See* Rashtriya Swayamsevak Sangh (RSS)
Rudolph, Lloyd I., 187
Rudolph, Susanne H., 187
Rural areas
  and agricultural policy, 374–378
  farmers' movement in, 197–198
  health centers in, 22
  land ownership in, 12–13, 19, 197–198
  land reform and, 12, 19, 102, 195, 227, 384–385
  Other Backward Classes in, 192–194
  political unrest in, 194–198
  poverty in, 377–378
  social class in, 12–13
  statistics on population of, 19
  village government in, 112–115
Rural Landless Employment Guarantee Programme (RLEGP), 377
Russia. *See* Soviet Union
Ryotwari system, 28

S

SAARC. *See* South Asian Association for Regional Cooperation (SAARC)
Samajvadi Janata Party (SJP), 270, 290, 311, 314, 332, 333
Samant, Dr. Datta, 201
Samyukta Vidhayak Dals, 222
Sanata Dal (Socialist), 290
Sanitation, 22
Sarkaria, R. S., 135
Sarkaria Commission on Centre-State Relations, 107–108, 135–136
Sarvodaya (the welfare of all), 202, 242
Sati, 30, 204
Satpathy, Nandini, 248, 250
Satyagraha (nonviolent resistance), 43–44, 173, 202, 242
Satyagraha Society, 43
Saurashtra, consolidation of, 54
Savarkar, V. D., 178
Scheduled Caste Federation, 191
Scheduled Castes. *See* Untouchables
Scindia, Madhavrao, 271, 334
Scindia, Rajmata Vijaye Raje, 334
Scindia, Vasundhara, 334
SEATO, 413
Self-Employed Women's Association (SEWA), 204
Senas (gangs), 180
Sepoy Mutiny, 30–31
Servants of India Society, 38
SEWA. *See* Self-Employed Women's Association (SEWA)
Shah Bano case, 184–185
Shah Commission of Inquiry, 253
Sharma, Shankar Dayal, 66, 69, 70
Shastri, Lal Bahadur, 75, 87–88, 174, 233–234, 359, 398
Shekhar, Chandra. *See* Chandra Shekar
Shetkari Sanghatana, 197
Shiv Sena, 145, 165, 180
Shiv Shakti Dal, 180
Shivaji, 38
Siachin Glacier, 403
Sikh Students Federation, 155
Sikhs
  anti-Sikh violence after Indira Gandhi's assassination, 156–157, 261
  demand for Sikh state by, 139
  Hindus' view of, 153
  landuage and, 11
  partition of India and, 52
  in Punjab, 152–160
  religion of, 7, 26

Sepoy Mutiny and, 30
terrorism of, in Kashmir, 163
terrorism of, in Punjab, 155–160
Sikkim, 107, 141, 143–144
Silent Valley Project, 205
Simla Agreement, 400–401, 403, 416
Simon Commission, 45, 46
Singapore, 22
Singer, Wendy, 348
Singh, Ajit, 223, 287
Singh, Arjun, vi, 271
Singh, Arun, 90, 267
Singh, Charan
death of, 284, 287
as Deputy Prime Minister, 89
Desai and, 279
dissension with other political leaders, 283
election of 1984, 284
as Finance Minister, 89
in Janata government, 277
as leader of Bharatiya Kranti Dal, 275
as leader of Bharatiya Lok Dal, 275
as president of Dalit Mazdoor Kizan Party, 286–287
as Prime Minister, 71, 72, 98, 254, 280–281
resignation as Prime Minister, 254, 281
and rural unrest, 194
Singh, Jaipal, 140
Singh, L. P., 106
Singh, Master Tara, 303
Singh, Suryadeo, 342
Singh, Swaran, 252
Singh, V. P.
election of 1989, 337
electoral victory in 1988, 285
as Finance Minister, 265–266, 366
foreign policy of, 403, 417–418
and Jan Morcha, 173, 223, 287
and Janata Dal, 223
and Mandal recommendations, 192–193
Singh, Zail, 66–69, 265, 267
Singhal, Ashok, 179
Sinha, S. C., 223, 288
Sitaramayya, Pattabhi, 138
Slum clearance, 249, 251
Social class
industrial workforce, 12
middle class support for British, 30–31
rise of middle class in British India, 32–34
in rural sector, 12–13
system of, 12–14
Socialist Party, 275, 279
"Sons of the soil," 149, 151, 164, 165
South Asian Association for Regional Cooperation (SAARC), 409–410
South Korea, 22
Soviet Union
Afghanistan invasion by, 256, 400–401, 415–416, 418
collapse of, 394
and Communist Party (Marxist), 299
foreign relations with India, 118, 399, 395, 412, 417–420
move toward democracy by, 3
Speaker, of Lok Sabha, 77–78
Spear, Percival, 33
Spector, Leonard S., 421
Sri Lanka, 117, 270, 302, 406–407, 416
Srikakulam, 196
State Civil Service, 111
State List, 129, 130, 131
States, Indian. *See also* names of specific states
Center-state relations, 128–136
Chief Minister of, 108
conditions in which central government can intervene in, 75–76, 107, 129
court systems of, 104–105
financial grants to, 130–131
government of, 105–110
Governor of, 106–108
integration of, 53–56, 136, 137
interstate disputes of, 144
languages of, 143
Legislative Assembly and Legislative Council in, 108–110
maps of, 137, 142
number of, 141, 143
opposition to creation of additional all-India services, 92–93
patronage networks and jobbery in, 110

States, Indian (*continued*)
powers of, 131–132
princely states, 53, 54–55, 59, 62, 126, 127, 136
reorganization based on language, 136–145, 145–157
representation in Parliament, 77, 78–79
and States Reorganization, 136–145
struggle among states for resources, 148
States Reorganization, 138–145
States Reorganization Act (1956), 138–139, 144, 322–323
States Reorganization Commission, 139–140
Steel industry, 20, 384
Stevenson, Adlai, 1
Strikes
Bombay textile strike, 201
after emergency of 1975–1977, 201
during Gandhian era, 44
by police and paramilitary forces, 279
railway strike, 201, 241
Students, and political unrest, 198–200
Sudras, 9
Supreme Court
appointment of judges to, 72, 103
case load of, 103
constitutional amendment to deny judicial review over constitutional amendments, 246
impeachment of justice of, 103
judges of, 72, 102–103
and Mandal recommendations, 193–194
on National Security Act, 210
powers of, 100–101
relationship with Parliament, 80, 101–102
Shah Bano case, 184–185
social action and citizens' rights cases of, 103–104
Swadeshi, 39, 45, 368
Swaraj (self-rule), 38, 50–56. *See also* Independence
Swaraja party, 45
Swatantra Party, 222, 227, 275, 327, 359
Swell, George G., 69

T

Tabligh Jamaat, 151
Tagore, Radindranath, 39
Taiwan, 22
Tamil Nadu
commercialization and urbanization in, 20
and conflict in Sri Lanka, 406
conversions to Islam in, 181
demands for state autonomy in, 145
interstate dispute of, 144
landless laborers in, 13
legislative assembly in, 109
opposition to Hindi as official language in, 146
political parties in, 235
regional political parties in, 148, 223, 235, 301–302
river water allocation to, 144
"sons of the soil" in, 165
student political unrest in, 199
support for states' rights from, 133–134
violence in, 146–147, 270
Tamiland Congress Committee, 138
Tamils, 144, 406–407
Tashkent Declaration, 418
Taxation, 80, 130
Telengana movement, 195, 199
Television, 67–68, 182, 332–333
Telugu Desam, 11, 145, 148, 138, 223, 283, 286, 304–305, 310
Territories. *See* Union Territories
Terrorism. *See* Violence
Terrorist Affected Areas (Special Courts) Ordinance, 210–211
Terrorist and Disruptive Activities (Prevention) Act, 211
Thackeray, Bal, 180
Thakur, Kapoori, 286
Thapar, Romesh, 121
Tikait, Mahendra Singh, 197, 198
Tilak, Bal Gangadhar, 38–39, 41, 42, 178
Travancore-Cochin, consolidation of, 54
Tribals, 10, 150
Tripura, 141, 150
Trishul, 180
Turkey, 41
20 Point Program, 247–248

U

ULFA. *See* United Liberation Front of Asom (ULFA)
UNCTAD. *See* United Nations Conference on Trade and Development (UNCTAD)
Union Executive powers, 129–130
Union List, 128–129
Union Public Service Commission (UPSC), 93–94
Union Territories, 110, 141, 143
United Front, 283–284
United Liberation Front of Asom (ULFA), 152, 305
United Nations, 140–141, 395, 398, 400–401, 404, 405, 415
United Nations Conference on Trade and Development (UNCTAD), 423
United Provinces, 34
United States
 establishment of naval and air facility on Diego Garcia, 415
 foreign aid to India, 422–423
 foreign relations with India, 413–417
 foreign relations with Pakistan, 397, 399, 413–416
 nuclear nonproliferation and, 415, 420–421
Universities, student political unrest at, 198–200
Unlawful Activities Prevention Act (1967), 210
Untouchability (Offenses) Act, 189
Untouchables
 as arena of conflict, 188–182
 British proposal of separate electorates for, 46–47
 in caste system, 9
 constitutional abolition of untouchability, 188
 Gandhi's work with, 45
 number of, 9, 188
 political participation of, 345
 violence against, 191
Upadhyaya, Deendayal, 274
UPSC. *See* Union Public Service Commission (UPSC)
Urban areas
 conditions in, 18–19
 government in, 115–116
 political unrest in, 116, 198
 statistics on, 18, 115
 statistics on population in, 18
Urdu, 139
Urs, Devraj, 254
USSR. *See* Soviet Union
Utilitarians, 28, 30, 32
Uttar Pradesh
 agriculture in, 19, 376
 commercialization and urbanization in, 20
 gang rule in, 206
 Haryana's interest in, 164
 landless laborers in, 13
 legislative assembly in, 110
 rural unrest in, 197
 statehood movement in, 164
 violence due to communalism in, 177

V

Vaisyas, 9
Vajpayee, Atal Bihari, 274, 284, 291, 400
Vanderbok, William, 348–349
Varna system, 9
Vasectomy program, 17, 248–249
Vedas, 34
Veit, Lawrence A., 378
Venkataraman, R., 66, 69, 71, 265
Venkateswaran, A. P., 99, 413
VHP. *See* Vishwa Hindu Parishad (VHP)
Vice Presidents
 election procedures for, 69–70
 powers of, 70
 term of office, 69
Vidhan Parishad, 108
Vidhan Sibha, 108
Villages
 cultural world of, 27
 government of, 112–115, 268
 life of, 18, 19
 political participation in, 344–345
Violence
 in Amritsar after Rowlatt Bills, 42–43
 and civil disobedience campaign, 43–44, 46, 50
 of communalism, 177–178

Violence (*continued*)
elections and, 343
Gandhi's response to, 44
gangs and, 206
after Indira Gandhi's assassination, 156, 261
in Kashmir, 163
military's role of control of, 118
on official language in Tamil Nadu, 146–147
at partition of India, 52–53
in Punjab, 154–156, 158–159
Ramjanmabhumi-Babri Masjid dispute, v–vi, 182–183
in reorganization of states, 141
rising level of, 1
of "sons of the soil" in Assam, 149
over state autonomy issue, 135
and student political unrest, 198–200
terrorism, 157, 158, 159, 163, 210–211
against untouchables, 191
in West Bengal, 164
against women, 204
Vishal Haryana, 164
Vishwa Hindu Parishad (VHP), 178–183, 185–186
Voting. *See* Elections; Electorate
Vyjayanthimala, 334

W

Weiner, Myron, 172
West Bengal
agriculture in, 376
autonomy of Darjeeling in, 164
Communist Party of India in, 145
domestic unrest in, 196, 264
landless laborers in, 13
"sons of the soil" in, 165
student political unrest in, 199
support for states' rights from, 134
village government in, 114
violence in, 164
Wilson, Woodrow, 41
Wolpert, Stanley, 38–39
Women
advocacy groups of, 203–204
literacy rate for, 23
Muslim women and divorce, 184–185
voting and political participation of, 347–348
Workforce. *See* Labor
World Bank, 359, 367, 369, 370, 377, 396, 422, 423
World War I, 41
World War II, 49

Y

Yahya Khan, 398–400, 414
Yeltsin, Boris, 299
Young Muhammadans, 41
Youth Congress, 248, 253–254, 257, 258, 330

Z

Zamindars, 28
Zelliott, Eleanor, 189–190
Zia ul-Haq, 402
Zila Parashad, 113, 114
Zoroastrianism, 26